CW01246339

EARLY SOCIETY IN CYPRUS

Early Society in Cyprus

edited by
EDGAR PELTENBURG

EDINBURGH UNIVERSITY PRESS
in association with
THE NATIONAL MUSEUMS OF SCOTLAND
and
THE A.G. LEVENTIS FOUNDATION

© Edinburgh University Press 1989
22 George Square, Edinburgh

Set in Lasercomp Plantin
and printed in Great Britain by
Redwood Burn Limited,
Trowbridge, Wilts

British Library Cataloguing
  in Publication Data
Early society in Cyprus.
1. Cypriot civilisation. Archaeological sources
I. Peltenburg, E. J. (Edgar J.)
939'.37
ISBN 0 85224 633 1 (cased)
     0 85224 659 5 (pbk)

Contents

Foreword *V. Karageorghis*	ix
Introduction *Edgar Peltenburg*	xii
Acknowledgments	xiv
Abbreviations	xv
Chronological Table	xvi

Part One. Settlement Evidence

1 Early prehistoric society: a view from the Vasilikos Valley
  Ian A. Todd — 2

2 From round house to duplex: a re-assessment of prehistoric Cypriot Bronze Age society
  Stuart Swiny — 14

3 A Late Cypriot community at Alassa
  S. Hadjisavvas — 32

4 Maroni and the monuments
  Gerald Cadogan — 43

5 Society and settlements in Late Cypriot III
  Maria Iacovou — 52

POSTER SUMMARIES

6 Prehistoric food plants
  S. Colledge — 60

7 Prehistoric Cypriot building traditions and methods
  Gordon D. Thomas — 62

8 Topological analysis of an architectural element
  Kenneth W. Schaar — 63

9 Correlation model for analysing prehistoric Cypriot culture
  Kathryn M. Schaffer — 64

Part Two. Funerary Evidence

10 Whence the first Cypriots?
   Melodie Domurad — 66

11 Le traitement des morts et les représentations des vivants à Khirokitia
    A. Le Brun — 71

12 The Chalcolithic Cemetery 1 at Souskiou-Vathyrkakas
    D. Christou — 82

13 Death in everyday life: aspects of burial practice in the Late Bronze Age
    Elizabeth Goring — 95

    POSTER SUMMARY

14 Early Iron Age—Dead and living
    Henryk Meyza — 106

Part Three. Religion

15 The beginnings of religion in Cyprus
    Edgar Peltenburg — 108

16 The identification of Cypriot cult figures through cross-cultural comparison: some problems
    Linda Carless Hulin — 127

    POSTER SUMMARY

17 Identification of Cypriot votive statues. A preliminary case study
    Cecilia Beer — 140

Part Four. Artefact Evidence

18 Regionalism, cultural variation and the culture-area concept in Later Prehistoric Cypriot studies
    Diane L. Bolger — 142

19 The glyptics of Bronze Age Cyprus: 'through a glass darkly'
    R. S. Merrillees (with P. H. Merrillees) — 153

20 Local Cypriot features in the ceramics of the Late Cypriot IIIA period
    Barbara Kling — 160

21 Hunting scenes on Cypriot vases of the Geometric Period
    M. C. Loulloupis — 171

22 Témoignage des documents figurés sur la société chypriote d'époque classique
    Antoine Hermary — 180

    POSTER SUMMARIES

23 Selective use of clays within Red Polished ware
    Jane A. Barlow — 197

24 Cypriot bronzework in the Levantine world
    Graham Philip   199
25 On the origin of Black-on-Red ware
    F. De Cree   200

Part Five. Trade and External Influence

26 Trade in the Late Cypriot Bronze Age
    P. Åström   202
27 Trade and local production in Late Cypriot faience
    A. Caubet & A. Kaczmarczyk   209
28 Late Bronze Age long distance trade in the Mediterranean:
    the role of the Cypriots
    Lucia Vagnetti & Fulvia Lo Schiavo   217
29 Cypern und Sardinien im frühen 1. Jahrtausend v. Chr.
    Hartmut Matthäus   244
30 Le rayonnement des terres cuites chypriotes au Levant aux
    premiers siécles de l'âge du Fer
    Anna Maria Bisi   256
31 Has Phoenician influence modified Cypriot terracotta
    production?
    Freida Vandenabeele   266
32 Cypriot mosaics: local traditions and external influences
    D. Michaelides   272

POSTER SUMMARIES

33 A comparative analysis of the Late Cypriot pottery from
    North Sinai and Egypt in the Late Bronze Age
    Celia Bergoffen   293
34 Cypriot finds in Greece and Greek finds in Cyprus *ca* 950–
    500 BC
    Lone Wriedt Sørensen & John Lund   294

Part Six. The Emergence of Social Complexity

35 The organisation of the copper industry in Late Bronze Age
    Cyprus
    J. Muhly   298
36 From copper to kingship: aspects of Bronze Age society
    viewed from the Vasilikos valley
    A. South   315
37 Status symbols in Cyprus in the eleventh century BC
    J. N. Coldstream   325

38	Puttin' on the Ritz: manifestations of high status in Iron Age Cyprus *David W. Rupp*	336
39	Sur l'administration de Kition à l'époque classique *M. Yon*	363
40	Priest Kings in Cyprus *Franz Georg Maier*	376
Envoi *David Ridgway*		392
Subject Index		396

Foreword

In 1985 the Cyprus Department of Antiquities celebrated its 50th anniversary since its creation by the enactment of the Antiquities Law of 1935, and its 25th Anniversary within the Government of the Republic of Cyprus. Having had the fortune and privilege to serve as its Director since 1963, I have been able to witness its growth both in size and scope. During most of the colonial period archaeological activity in Cyprus was a local affair with the exception of a few isolated cases of foreign involvement (the Swedish Cyprus Expedition, the French excavations at Enkomi, and Australian excavations at Vounous). In 1963–4 when it was decided to open up the island to international co-operation in archaeological research, few believed in the soundness of this policy. Now, after a quarter of a century, we feel that this move has been justified. Despite the tragic problems caused by the Turkish invasion of the island in 1974 for scholarly work and archaeological activity in general, we have experienced during these twenty-five years an ever-growing interest in Cypriot archaeology and an increasing appreciation of the role which ancient Cyprus played in the development of 'world affairs' from the Bronze Age to the end of antiquity. Through prompt publication of the results of excavations, the bibliography on ancient Cyprus from the Neolithic to Mediaeval periods has increased in a way which can only be described as phenomenal.

Particular encouragement has been given to research by younger scholars with the aim of creating a new generation of Cypriot specialists in all continents. This policy is now bearing fruit: dozens of young men and women, even in remote places in Europe, America, Australia and the Near East, have written doctoral dissertations on topics related to Cypriot archaeology and many of them have made Cyprus the main subject of their research. It is not surprising, therefore, that the events of 1974 have not diminished the vigour of Cypriot archaeology.

The early periods of Cypriot prehistory have been the focal points of research, and rightly so. In several instances scholars have been encouraged to deal with these periods in order to clarify obscure points and fill chronological lacunae. Research in the Cypriot Bronze Age, especially the Late Bronze Age, has fascinated two generations of archaeologists and continues increasingly to do so. Cyprus now takes a leading role in our understanding of the Late Bronze Age as a whole. The excavators of Ekron in Palestine, of Ras Shamra and Ras Ibn Hani in Syria, of Kommos in Crete and of Sardinia, cannot afford to ignore contemporary events at the relevant sites in Cyprus.

Research in the first millennium BC has revealed many new chapters of the island's past and opened new horizons for study. Without the prejudice of the past we may now appreciate more fully the role of the Phoenicians and the part played by Cyprus in the relations between the Orient and Occident. Excavations at Hellenistic and Roman sites have created possibilities for the encouragement of cultural tourism through archaeology.

The organization of a Conference in Edinburgh in April 1988 on *Early Society in Cyprus* was the result of a long-standing collaboration between the Cyprus Department of Antiquities and the University of Edinburgh and latterly also with the National Museums of Scotland. Excavations and research on prehistoric Cyprus carried out by members of these two institutions have greatly enriched our knowledge of the early society of the island, particularly as regards the Neolithic and Chalcolithic periods. The Conference, inevitably limited to a relatively small number of speakers but with ample opportunities for discussion, proved of considerable scientific value. It was a real pleasure to see old and new faces engaged in lively discussions, questioning all the ideas and 'taboos' of the past and proposing new solutions. It was necessary, however, occasionally to remind the younger generation that there are limits to their enthusiasm for 'destruction' and innovation and that the solution of intricate problems related to cultural changes should not be based on one or two isolated phenomena or the examination of limited categories of objects, but on a global survey of everything that is known about the period under discussion in order to achieve convincing interpretations. The close of the Late Bronze Age is an example; 'events' in the Aegean, at Enkomi, Maa-Palaeokastro, Kalavassos-Ayios Dhimitrios, Ras Shamra and elsewhere should all be taken into consideration if we wish to penetrate this critical period which witnessed serious cultural changes in the Eastern Mediterranean.

A word of appreciation should be expressed for the introduction of multi-disciplinary studies in the field of Cypriot archaeology which was very much felt at the Edinburgh Conference. New methods for the interpretation of archaeological data are now gaining ground and help to elucidate problems relating to social structure and 'society'. The title of the Conference thus responded perfectly to these new trends.

The Edinburgh Conference has demonstrated the 'universality' of Cypriot Archaeology. Scholars from a variety of geographical areas, Sardinia, the Aegean, Syro-Palestine and Egypt, found themselves on common ground with specialists on Cyprus with a broad spectrum of interest: settlement and artefact evidence, religion, funerary evidence, physical anthropology, industries, trade and external influence, social complexity. It is regrettable that the serious and lively discussions which followed each communication are not included in this published volume, but the Conference participants will no doubt remember and consider them in their research.

In an after-dinner speech at the University of Edinburgh I described this Conference as 'the best which has been organized outside Cyprus'. It follows a series of very successful specialized Symposia organized on specific topics in Cyprus during the last fifteen years or so. An equally successful Colloquium was organized by the British Museum on 'Cyprus and the East Mediterranean in the Iron Age' immediately after the Edinburgh Conference. It is only in fairly small gatherings with a specific theme to examine that we make real progress in the understanding of our research topic.

On the occasion of the Edinburgh Conference, the National Museums of Scotland organized a very important exhibition of art in Cyprus covering the whole of the island's past including folk art. Participants at the Conference had the opportunity to see some rare objects 'dug out' from private collections and Scottish Museums' storerooms.

Participants at the Colloquium in London could visit the newly created A. G. Leventis Gallery of Cypriot antiquities, where some of the many treasures of Cypriot art which have been in the British Museum since the end of the 19th century are now exhibited.

Behind the success of the Edinburgh Conference lies a group of people who laboured enthusiastically to make the meetings both profitable and enjoyable in every respect. Even lifelong 'opponents' could be seen walking briskly in the streets of Edinburgh and discussing problems of ancient Alasia in a spirit of real friendship; so 'humane' was the atmosphere. It is impossible to thank everybody by name for their contribution to this success. In thanking one man, Eddie Peltenburg, who has done so much for Cypriot archaeology and has almost become an 'honorary Cypriot', I wish to express on behalf of all participants our gratitude to the individuals and institutions for the organization of a very successful Conference and for the prompt publication of its proceedings.

Vassos Karageorghis
Director, Department of Antiquities of Cyprus

Introduction

In describing the ancient Cypriots, Herodotus (VII.90) noted that
> 'their dress was, for their kings, mitres on their heads; the rest wore tunics and otherwise wore clothes like the Greeks. The natives of Cyprus', he continued, 'are these: some are from Athens and Salamis, some from Arcadia, ... some from Phoenicia, some from Aethiopia, all according to the accounts of the Cypriots themselves.'

He and the Cypriots thus recognised the diversity of Cypriot society and what Aeschylus in *The Suppliants* specified as the special 'Cypriot character'. Archaeologists likewise have recognised the distinctive material expressions of the islanders, but unlike historians such as Isocrates, it is only rarely that they have grappled with the organization of the social structure that fostered such unique qualities.

One reason for this reluctance lies in the constant interaction between foreigner and native on an island whose geo-political destiny meant recurrent population mixture. This has led to a scholarly focus on discontinuities and the identification of what is judged to be foreign, but as Merrillees recently observed at an earlier conference, 'there is a danger that in attempting to define what is Cypriote by defining what apparently is not Cypriote, we approach the island's civilisation from the wrong perspective' (*Acts 1986,* xxvi). Another prevalent reason for this reluctance on the part of archaeologists is the entirely appropriate caution regarding the limits of legitimate inference from material culture. Many would argue, as did Christopher Hawkes in *American Anthropologist 61,* 1954, 155–68, that the second most difficult level of inference in archaeology is social reconstruction (the first, he believed, concerns religion). Yet many would also agree that any solidly based effort to elucidate early social systems must contribute to a clearer understanding of the associated cultures that is a basic objective of our researches.

In April 1988 some 130 archaeologists and other specialists directly and indirectly involved in the early history of Cyprus gathered in Edinburgh to address these issues. Such was the encouraging response to the initial announcement that the programme of lectures was extended from the planned two days to two and a half and a number of poster presentations were added to allow graphic display of recent research. Of the total of 29 papers and 12 poster presentations given at Edinburgh, all but one poster summary are published here. The former are presented as papers revised in the light of the lively and fruitful discussions which followed the lectures, the latter as summaries that take into account the feedback gained not just from the all-too-short officially scheduled time allotment for the Poster Session, but also from more informal conversations in the coffee room where delegates assembled amongst the poster stands.

The aim of these participants then was to attempt, however inadequately, to decipher information about early Cyprus in its own terms, and not primarily from external vantage points, in order to see what progress can be made in reconstructing something of its social organisation. Archaeology is a much divided subject today but no apology is made for the incorporation of allegedly opposed nomothetic and idiographic treatments here. That conclusions are often but tentative and questioning is perhaps to be expected in the present state of the art. In practical terms (since the majority of contribtors carry out survey and excavations on Cyprus) many papers infer the growing need for the application of new kinds of fieldwork strategies, including retrieval and recording designs, if progress is to be made in resolving some of these posed questions.

From fieldwork design to conference design. In order to emphasize that entire populations were not replaced on Cyprus as a result of changes in prehistory, in order to discern persistent elements of continuity on the island and in more general terms to explore Braudel's concept of *le long durée* in Mediterranean history, we organised our Sessions by theme, and not in the normal (Cypriot) fashion, by period. Thus we witnessed the (almost) unheard of (in Cypriot archaeology), when a neolithic specialist expounded alongside a Classical colleague about potentials from similar sets of evidence. It follows that a second, but no less important, motive for the unorthodox programme arrangement is to allow us to juxtapose and assess the different interpretative methodologies used by period specialists who after all fashion their deductions from similar archaeological data, be it funerary, settlement, artefactual, religious, industrial or exotic evidence. This design is retained as far as possible in the present publication.

Naturally, to attempt this extended perspective we foresake a tidy chronological approach and we risk confusion between the richly distinctive societies of Cyprus. An outline chronological table has been included therefore to try to overcome some of the difficulties which the non-specialist may possibly experience. On the other hand it is hoped that we may eventually gain clearer insights into these societies as a result of the comparative approach which has been adopted here.

Acknowledgments

As so often happens in Cypriot archaeology, the genesis of a rewarding idea, in this case for a gathering of scholars in Edinburgh to discuss innovatory approaches to the island's early history, came from the Director of the Department of Antiquities of Cyprus, Dr Vassos Karageorghis. It is a pleasure therefore to record here my sincere thanks to him for planting that seed, for continued support before, during and after the event and for his good offices in contacting the Leventis Cultural Foundation. I am deeply grateful to that Foundation for a most helpful grant towards the publication of these papers.

I should also like to thank Sir David Smith, Principal of the University of Edinburgh, for welcoming speakers at a memorable dinner in the University's Old Senate Room and to Professor Dennis Harding, Abercromby Professor of Archaeology, for his warm encouragement and advice throughout.

To Dr Robert Anderson and his staff at the National Museums of Scotland I am deeply obliged for their very enthusiastic co-operation from the outset and for the use of their most attractive Royal Museum of Scotland as our conference centre.

The British Council and the British Academy enabled the organisers to fulfil their aim of involving as many members of the Cyprus Department of Antiquities as possible in the conference deliberations by their valuable support.

Sir Reo Stakis most magnanimously provided accommodation for several speakers in Edinburgh at the Stakis Grosvenor Hotel.

I am also grateful to the Munro Lectureship Committee and to the Department for Advanced Studies in Humanities for their support and to Mr Peter Freshwater for opening the University Library especially in order to enable delegates to visit the Department of Archaeology's 60th Anniversary Exhibition, 'Piecing together the Past'.

That the conference took place at all and that its publication saw the light of day is in no small way due to the very professional efforts of many, staff and students alike. My particular thanks are due to members of a small Organising Committee, Jenny Bradbury, Louise Maguire, Gordon Thomas and, above all, to Elizabeth Goring who also organized the successful exhibition 'Aphrodite's Island' which proved so much more rewarding than simply a complement to the conference. David Ridgway assisted in various ways in his engagingly inimitable fashion and Louise Maguire tailored the diverse papers into suitable text files for transmission for publication with efficiency and good humour.

EDGAR PELTENBURG
Department of Archaeology
University of Edinburgh

Abbreviations

In addition to standard abbreviations to journals (see *Archäologische Bibliographie* 1987, X-XXXIX) the following special abbreviations are used:

EC Early Cypriot Period
MC Middle Cypriot Period
LC Late Cypriot Period
CG Cypro-Geometric Period
CA Cypro-Archaic Period
PPNA/B Pre-Pottery Neolithic A/B

Acts 1973 Department of Antiquities, Cyprus, (1973) *Acts of the international archaeological symposium 'The Mycenaeans in the Eastern Mediterranean'*. Nicosia.
Acts 1979 Department of Antiquities, Cyprus, (1979) *Acts of the international archaeological symposium 'The relations between Cyprus and Crete, ca. 2000–500 B.C.'* Nicosia.
Acts 1985 Papadopoulos, T. Editor (1985) *Acta of the Second International Congress of Cypriot Studies. A, Ancient Section*. Nicosia.
Acts 1986 Karageorghis, V. Editor (1986) *Acts of the international archaeological symposium 'Cyprus between the Orient and Occident'*. Nicosia.
Chronique 1959– Karageorghis, V. (1959–) Chronique des fouilles et découvertes archéologiques à Chypre en 1958–   annually in *BCH* from vol 83, 336–61.
EMC Muhly, J. D., Maddin, R. & Karageorghis, V. eds. (1982) *Acta of the International Archaeological Symposium 'Early Metallurgy in Cyprus, 4000–500 B.C.'* Larnaca, Cyprus 1–6 June 1981. Nicosia.
Enkomi Dikaios, P. (1969–71) *Enkomi excavations 1948–1958*. Mainz am Rhein.
HST 1–8 Åström, P. et al. (1976–83) *Hala Sultan Tekke (SIMA XLV.1–8)*. Göteborg.
ICS Masson, O. (1983) *Les inscriptions chypriotes Syllabiques*. Paris.
Kition I-V Karageorghis, V. et al. (1974–85) *Excavations at Kition I-V*. Nicosia.
SCE I-IV Gjerstad, E. et al. (1934–72) *The Swedish Cyprus Expedition I-IV*. Lund and Stockholm.

Chronological Table

(This table is only a general guide; contributors may have varied its details).

Period		Date
Epi-palaeolithic		8000 bc*
Early (Aceramic) Neolithic		> 6000–5200 bc*
Late Neolithic		4500–3800 BC
Early Chalcolithic		3800–3500 BC
Middle Chalcolithic		3500–2800 BC
Late Chalcolithic		2800–2300 BC
Early Cypriot Bronze Age	I	2300–2075 BC
	II	2075–2000 BC
	III	2000–1900 BC
Middle Cypriot Bronze Age	I	1900–1800 BC
	II	1800–1725 BC
	III	1725–1600 BC
Late Cypriot Bronze Age	I	1600–1450 BC
	II	1450–1200 BC
	III	1200–1050 BC
Cypro-Geometric	I	1050–950 BC
	II	950–850 BC
	III	850–750 BC
Cypro-Archaic	I	750–600 BC
	II	600–475 BC
Classical	I	475–400 BC
	II	400–325 BC

Note: All dates are approximate. * dates are based on uncalibrated radiocarbon determinations; calendrical dates are likely to be higher. For the epi-palaeolithic see A. H. Simmons, *Nature* 333, 1988, 554–7. For the divisions of the Chalcolithic see E J Peltenburg, The Chalcolithic Period, in *History of Cyprus* (Makarios Foundation) forthcoming. For the remainder see V. A. Tatton-Brown, *Cyprus BC*, 15 (London), a table which is moderated here at the MC/LC transition to account for the effects of finds in Egypt (P. Åström, *High, Middle or Low (SIMA Pocket-book 56)* Part I, 57–66) and at the LCII/III transition to correlate the appearance of Myc IIIC:1 style pottery in Cyprus with its occurrence on more closely dated mainland Levantine sites.

PART ONE
Settlement Evidence

1
Early prehistoric society: a view from the Vasilikos valley

Ian A. Todd
Brandeis University, Waltham

INTRODUCTION

The Vasilikos Valley Project, based on the village of Kalavasos in the Larnaca District, entails excavation at selected prehistoric sites in the valley together with an archaeological field survey and various environmental studies. The overall aim of the project is the reconstruction of past ways of life in the valley from the earliest period of occupation (*ca* 7000 BC or earlier?) to the end of the Late Bronze Age; the chronological scope of the field survey has, however, been extended until modern times. Excavations have so far been undertaken at four Kalavasos area sites (Fig 1.1): the Aceramic Neolithic and Ceramic Neolithic/Early Chalcolithic site of Tenta, the Early Chalcolithic site of Ayious, the predominantly Middle Bronze Age cemetery in Kalavasos village and the Late Bronze Age town-sized site of Ayios Dhimitrios. All activities of the project pertaining to the earlier prehistoric phases have been summarised in five preliminary reports (Todd 1977; 1978; 1979; 1982; 1986a; two final reports have been published in the series *Studies in Mediterranean Archaeology* (Todd ed 1986; Todd 1987), and others are now in press (Todd 1988a; b). This paper concerns itself solely with the Neolithic and Early Chalcolithic periods, and the Bronze Age is treated (with full references) in a subsequent paper by Alison South.

THE ACERAMIC NEOLITHIC PERIOD

Information concerning Cypriot society in the Vasilikos valley during this phase has been derived from the excavations at Kalavasos-Tenta. The village at Tenta constitutes one of at least two settlements of the Aceramic period in the valley, the other being located further south at Mari-Mesovouni (Todd 1979, 285); at least two other small sites in the valley may have

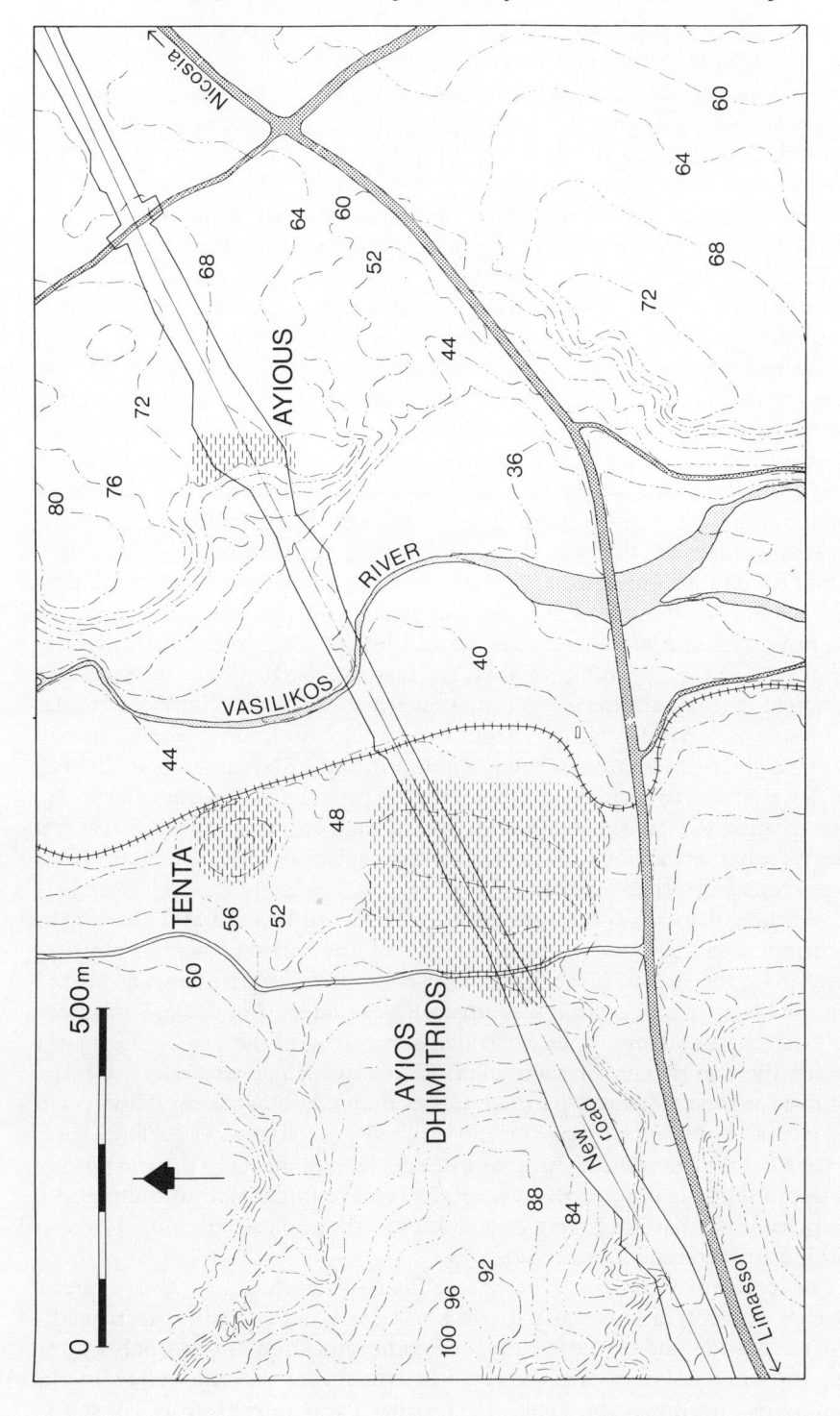

Figure 1.1 Map of the Vasilikos valley showing the location of the excavated sites of Tenta, Ayious and Ayios Dhimitrios.

seen limited or specialized use in this phase, and these will be published in the first volume of the field survey report.

Even a cursory comparison of the settlement at Tenta (and the other best known Cypriot settlements of this period at Cape Andreas-Kastros and Khirokitia-Vounoi) with those on the adjacent mainland reveals that the Cypriot Aceramic sites represent a distinctively Cypriot culture and society, although some evidence of mainland contact is apparent (Todd 1986b; Le Brun 1986). Architecture, religion, burial customs and artefacts may be examined in turn, in conjunction with chronology, to determine the extent to which the society of the island differed from those on the mainland.

The architecture of the Tenta village consists of circular/curvilinear domestic dwellings of mud-brick and/or stone surrounded by an encircling wall of solid proportions. Access to the village was rendered more difficult by a ditch cut into the natural deposits, at least on the south side of the site (see Todd 1987 for a full description of the architecture). The use of circular architecture is in marked contrast with the mainland where rectilinear structures are the norm at approximately contemporary sites such as Çatal Hüyük East (Anatolia), PPNB Jericho and other sites in Syria-Palestine (see Moore 1982 for a summary of the evidence in this latter area; the Cypriot Aceramic Neolithic sites should be contemporary with the later part of his Stage 2 and probably at least the earlier part of Stage 3). Although it may ultimately be demonstrated that the Cypriot circular architecture derived originally from the circular architectural tradition of the Syro-Palestinian area of the mainland in the PPNA phase (or earlier), the fact that such a form of architecture was retained in Cyprus after it had been abandoned on the mainland itself bears on the nature of Cypriot society, whether or not it indicates insular isolation, lack of receptiveness to new ideas or other factors.

Evidence of social differentiation is probably to be seen at Tenta in the occurrence on the west side of the top of the hill(the most prominent position on the site) of three superimposed buildings (Structures 36 and 17 and the Structure 14 complex, from earliest to latest; Fig 1.2), all of which are differentiated from other excavated structures on the site by their large size or the complexity of their plan. The two former structures are also notable for their thick red-painted plaster floors. While plaster floors occur in some of the other buildings on the site, red-painted plaster surfaces seem to have been reserved for buildings of special significance. the purpose of these buildings is unknown. Few artefacts were found within them and it is unclear whether they served a domestic or public function. There is nothing to recommend a religious use.

The location of the site of Tenta itself is also significant for the nature of Cypriot society in this early period. A small natural hill, strategically situated astride one or more routes of communication and probably at an easy crossing point of the river, with a fine view up the valley to the mountains and down the valley to the coast, was purposefully chosen in

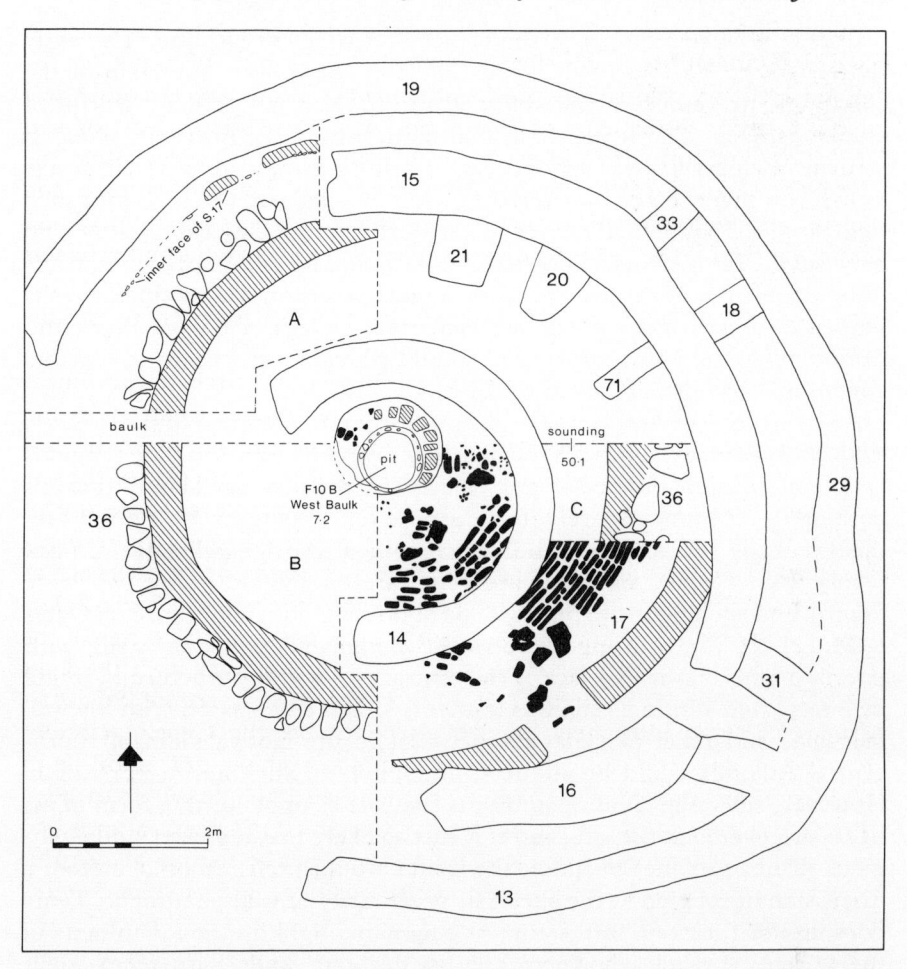

Figure 1.2 Kalavasos-Tenta: plan of Structures 17 and 36 in relation to the overlying (unshaded) walls of the Structure 14 complex. The plaster floor associated with Structure 36 was found in Areas A, B and C. Mud-brick walls and *in situ* mud-bricks are diagonally shaded; fallen mud-bricks are shown in solid black.

preference to the flat-topped plateaux which border the valley on its eastern side or the gentle slopes on the west side of the valley. The position of the settlement was made more secure by a wall around it and a ditch outside at least part of the wall. Whatever the reasons for the choice of such a location, it is clear that the majority of Cypriot Aceramic settlements were situated in strategic locations, unlike their mainland counterparts which were usually located with reference to water supply and good agricultural land rather than strategic considerations. The initial settlers of sites such as Tenta and Khirokitia clearly perceived the need for security; the choice of Mari-Mesovouni, an isolated very steep-sided hill the top of which stands *ca* 36 m above the level of the Vasilikos river, for an Aceramic settlement further demonstrates that security took precedence over immediate proximity to water supply in the choice of settlement location. The early settlers of the Vasilikos valley must, at best, have been uncertain of the conditions prevailing in the valley at the time, if not actually fearful of known dangers. The sequence at Khirokitia within the Aceramic phase of settlement enlargement, each settlement being surrounded by a wall, seems to indicate that the need for security was not considered to be diminished following the initial settlement. The exact chronological relationship between the settlements of Tenta, Khirokitia and Mari-Mesovouni remains to be established, but greater chronological precision would elucidate the sequence of settlement in the adjacent river valleys of the Vasilikos and Maroniou/Ayiou Mina rivers, and should provide insight into the factors governing early settlement in this area.

Apart from the information derived from the human burials, little evidence was recovered from the Tenta excavations regarding the religious beliefs of the inhabitants of the village. As pointed out above, there is nothing to recommend a religious purpose for Structures 36, 17 or 14 on the top of the site, and no buildings contained features indicative of non-secular use. Human figurines are very rare on the site (only two were found), and such figurines may well be of no religious significance (*cf* Oates 1978, 121–2). The painting of probably two human figures side by side with upraised arms on the east face of the central pier within Structure 11 might be interpreted within a religious framework, and comparison with the wall paintings and relief of Çatal Hüyük East in the Konya Plain of south-central Anatolia could be adduced in support of such an interpretation. However, since the Tenta painting is the sole example of this form of art so far discovered at the site, and it is just as likely that it served a non-religious (if not profane) purpose, the writer would prefer to omit it from a discussion of religion at the site. The great rarity of wall painting at Tenta does, in itself, cast an interesting, if enigmatic, light on the inhabitants of the village; they clearly knew how to decorate walls with paint, their buildings provided ample scope for such paintings and the state of preservation is such that if wall painting had been widely practised the evidence would have been retrieved during the excavations. The villagers clearly did not avail themselves to any extent of the opportunity provided by large expanses of wall covered with whitish plaster, but whether for practical or less tangible reasons is unknown.

Burial customs are comparatively well attested at Tenta. Bodies were deposited in pits below the floors of domestic structures, occasionally in a pit outside a building but adjacent to it, or they were placed in rubbish deposits between buildings with no signs of a pit having been dug. In the latter case they were clearly not exposed for any length of time since they were found generally intact and had not been disturbed by animal or other agencies. Primary inhumation was clearly the norm, but the partial remains of two skeletons in a pit/ditch outside the main settlement area attest to the existence of secondary burials. The pit burials within the buildings, if not all of the burials, indicate a degree of respect for the dead, but this apparently did not extend to supplying the dead with grave gifts (with the exception of one lump of red ochre which seems to have been intentionally deposited with the skeleton of a child). Disposal of the body appears to have been the primary concern rather than equipping the dead with accoutrements necessary for the afterlife. The reason for the varied choice in location for burial is unclear; adult burials were found both underneath and outside structures while children were predominantly found in pits below house floors, with one exception in a pit adjacent to the exterior face of the wall of a building. Stones were found in several burials in positions suggesting that they were purposefully placed on top of the body at the time of burial. In the case of one burial deposited in rubbish layers between structures, the posterior portion of the cranial vault displayed evidence of burning, but this could have resulted either from ritual activities or from the incidental burning of rubbish adjacent to the skull.

Comparison of the burial customs evident at Tenta with those at nearby Khirokitia reveals some significant differences as well as similarities. While half of the Tenta burials occur in contexts outside buildings, none of the Khirokitia burials was definitely interred in such a context (pers comm Dr A. Le Brun). A further important fact is that grave goods were deposited with a number of the Khirokitia burials, whereas at Tenta, with the exception noted above, gifts are not found with the dead. Such differences at sites separated only by a straight-line distance of *ca* 6 km are surprising, and they highlight an important general point: in studying Cypriot society, it may be erroneous and positively misleading to try to identify a single set of distinctively Cypriot societal traits. Rather than being homogeneous as might be desired, even in this early period (and perhaps especially at this early period) the Cypriot population may have been a heterogeneous mixture reflecting the varied origins of the different groups.

Comparison of the Cypriot Aceramic Neolithic burial customs with those on the mainland reveals certain basic similarities as well as some significant differences. Burial in pits below house floors is a well attested custom at Çatal Hüyük East (Mellaart 1967, 204–9) and elsewhere in the Levant, and burial in a variety of contexts on the same site under buildings and outside them is attested at various sites in Syria-Palestine (Moore 1982, 11). On the other hand, the practice of decorating the skeleton with ochre which is widely attested on the mainland is unknown in Cyprus, as is the custom of applying plaster or other forms of elaboration to the skull. Conversely *in vivo* cranial deformation appears to have been a comparatively common practice in the Cypriot Aceramic Neolithic whereas it is absent at Çatal Hüyük East and rare at Jericho (see Todd 1987, 184–5 for further comparisons and references). These comparisons allow at least the burial customs of Cyprus to be placed within the general Anatolia-Levant interaction sphere (Stanley Price 1977, 82), but they also indicate significant divergence in basic customs governing both life and death. Such divergence emphasizes the distinctively Cypriot character of the Aceramic Neolithic on the island.

The various categories of artefacts found on the Cypriot Aceramic sites also add weight to the insular nature of the period as a whole. Stone vessels occur widely in early mainland contexts, but nowhere is there found a group with all the characteristic Cypriot features. The chipped stone industry of the island sites is markedly different from those on the mainland from Anatolia to southern Jordan, and the only real point of contact is provided by the occurrence of a steady scatter of obsidian blades of Anatolian origin on the Cypriot sites. The characteristic finely retouched projectile points of the mainland are absent on Cyprus, with the exception of a few dubious examples and a probably imported point of PPNB (or earlier) type found in the Akrotiri peninsula reported by Stuart Swiny (forthcoming in *RDAC* 1988). Considering the typological similarity of the chipped stone tools (whether in flint or obsidian) throughout the adjacent mainland area, the lack of parallels on Cyprus is very striking, especially in view of the fact that some contact, although very limited, with the mainland is clearly attested by the occurrence of imported obsidian. Such a difference may reflect a divergent development in the two different areas, different concepts or that different conditions in Cyprus necessitated different tool types.

The chronology of the Cypriot Aceramic Neolithic settlements may not be considered to be of direct relevance to the nature of Cypriot society at the time, but it does affect views concerning the degree of insularity exhibited in this phase. The problems posed by the chronometric position of Tenta have been discussed by the writer elsewhere (Todd 1987, 173–8), and only the societal implications of chronology need be mentioned here. If the Cypriot Aceramic settlements are dated to the sixth millennium BC, the contrast with those on the mainland is glaring in terms of architectural and artefactual differentiation. If, however, the date of at least the earlier part of the Aceramic phase in Cyprus is raised in accordance with the earlier radiocarbon dates from Tenta, then the apparent divergence of the Cypriot sites is not as striking. The problem of a certain degree of divergence, whether due to retention of archaic cultural traits or different settlement organization adopted by colonists on arrival in Cyprus (Stanley Price 1977, 85), still remains, but it is not necessary to posit as prolonged a period of divergence as is required by the dating of the Cypriot Aceramic Neolithic in its entirety to the sixth millennium BC. Only greater chronological precision, together with more data concerning the processes governing the development of the early settlements in Cyprus, will allow a more accurate definition of the extent and longevity of the differences between the early inhabitants of Cyprus and their mainland neighbours.

THE CERAMIC NEOLITHIC PERIOD

Following the end of the occupation of the Aceramic Neolithic settlement at Tenta, there appears to have been a lengthy gap during which no evidence whatsoever has been found for settlement in the valley. Unfortunately, little can be said about Cypriot society in the ensuing Ceramic Neolithic phase. The excavations at Tenta did not reveal any architectural remains contemporary with the sites of Sotira-Teppes (Dikaios 1961) and Ayios Epiktitos-Vrysi (Peltenburg 1982a), to name but two of the best known examples. While it was originally assumed by the writer that at least most of the deposits at Tenta which contained ceramics should be dated to this phase, recent ceramic analysis by Douglas Baird has indicated that the majority of these deposits actually date to the Early Chalcolithic. Thus the pits found on the east side of Tenta adjacent to the eroded east section (in area K/L 6/7; Todd 1987, 169–71) are of this later date, and only the lowest deposits in the large and ill-understood pit in O 16 B (Todd 1987, 171–2) may be ascribed to the Ceramic Neolithic. Only further excavation will reveal whether standing architectural remains of the period are to be found in the valley, or whether the change apparent at the Early Chalcolithic site of Ayious had already taken place by the Ceramic Neolithic period.

THE EARLY CHALCOLITHIC PERIOD

The best excavated evidence for the nature of Cypriot society in this period in the Vasilikos valley was derived from the site of Kalavasos-Ayious (Todd 1988b), dated to the middle of the fourth millennium BC. No standing architectural remains were found on the site, only pits of varying shape and size (see Fig 1.3 for plan of part of the NW Area). The interpretation of the site is problematic, but the view is taken in the final report that Ayious represents a settlement of lightly built huts, most traces of which have been lost through erosion and ploughing. Some of the pits may originally have been dug for extraction of raw material (possibly for building), but in their excavated form they are interpreted as hearths, storage facilities and possibly as occasional domestic work areas. Although it cannot be conclusively demonstrated, there is little to recommend the deeper pits as the lower parts of long-term pit-dwellings, and there is similarly little evidence that the deeper pits served a specialized industrial or manufacturing purpose. The reasons for the cutting of the tunnels in the NW Area remain unknown; while the tunnels do provide a means of communication safe from the elements, movement along them would have been difficult. It seems unlikely that they served as places of refuge, being themselves inherently dangerous and liable to collapse. The fill of the tunnels contained comparatively few artefacts, and was not indicative of any special purpose.

Scattered parallels exist within Cyprus for the various types of subterranean or semi-subterranean features at Ayious. The closest parallels are not surprisingly to be found at Kalavasos-Kokkinoyia/Pamboules (which may represent a southward continuation of the Ayious site; Dikaios 1962, 106–112, 133–40), although no tunnels were found at the latter site. The

10   IAN A. TODD

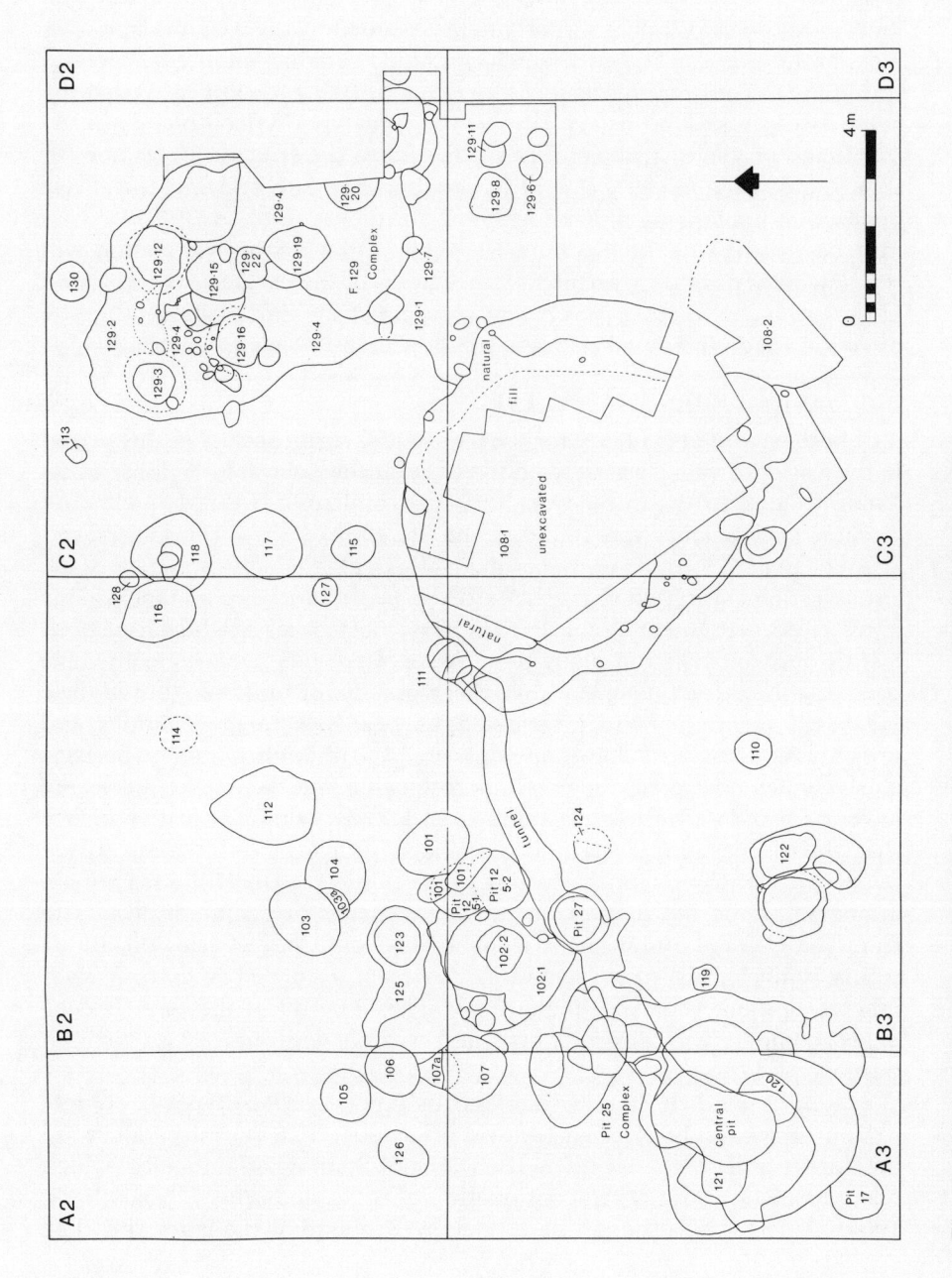

Figure 1.3 Kalavasos-Ayious: general plan of the pits in the northern part of the NW Area.

tunnels at Ayious are, however, very similar to features found (in a probably earlier context) at Philia-Drakos A to the west of Nicosia, in association with the above ground settlement architecture (Watkins 1969). The lack of extant evidence of standing structures, in conjunction with a large area honeycombed by pits, is parallelled at contemporary Kissonerga-Mylouthkia (Peltenburg 1982b, 56–66), and it is clearly significant that no solid architectural remains were found at either site. However, the pit typology at the two sites varies considerably, and some at least of the Mylouthkia pits seem to have served as dumps, lacking the evidence of activity surfaces found in the larger pits at Ayious. Artefactual parallels (ceramics, human figurines and other categories) are also indicative of connections between the Kalavasos and Kissonerga sites, but the two sites are by no means identical.

The excavations at Ayious support the picture presented by Peltenburg of a transitional phase after the end of the Ceramic Neolithic settlements such as Sotira-Teppes and Ayios Epiktitis-Vrysi and prior to the Chalcolithic settlements such as Lemba-Lakkous (Peltenburg 1985) and the main occupation at Erimi-Pamboules (Dikaios 1936), the phase being marked by settlements at which only lightly built huts were erected (Peltenburg 1982b, 51–66). They support the suggestion of a serious disruption at the end of the Ceramic Neolithic (Peltenburg 1982a, 109–10) (or possibly earlier in the Vasilikos valley). The Ayious excavations have not provided any new definitive information on the reasons for this radical change, although there is the possibility that environmental deterioration may have been a factor in the Vasilikos valley. If the picture presented by the excavations at Ayious and Kissonerga-Mylouthkia is an accurate reflection of Cypriot settlement in the earliest part of the Chalcolithic period, Cypriot society must have undergone a major change at the end of the Ceramic Neolithic.

The Ayious excavations again raise the problem posed by the clear divergence of Cypriot society during the fourth millennium BC from the complex societies that were appearing (with all their ramifications) on the mainland at (or before) this time. Whatever date may be assigned to the appearance of complex society in Cyprus, it is clear that there is no evidence of such during the Chalcolithic phase, at least in the fourth millennium BC. The contrast between the pits at Ayious and the developments in Mesopotamia in the Late Ubaid/Early Uruk periods, to take an extreme example, amply demonstrates the degree of divergence within the Near East as a whole. Although it is almost certainly erroneous to look for one single factor to explain this divergence, discontinuities in the sequence of settlement in Cyprus may have been responsible to a large extent for the delay in the appearance of complex society on the island.

CONCLUSIONS

The excavations at Kalavasos-Tenta have reinforced the view that the culture of Cyprus in the Aceramic Neolithic period was distinctively Cypriot with little evidence of contact with the mainland, despite the geographical position of the island. The distinctive nature of the Aceramic sites may be taken to indicate that Cypriot society developed in isolation on the island for a lengthy period of time, although there is currently little evidence to support this; in the opinion of the writer the degree of originality of the Aceramic settlements and their inhabitants cannot be explained purely by the loss of cultural traits in transmission. The site at Akrotiri-Aetokremnos (reported recently by S. Swiny at a public meeting in Boston, and forthcoming in *RDAC* 1988) may be taken as a pointer to antecedent development, but much more needs to be known about the site before it can be placed in its proper context and its implications fully realized.

Following what appears to have been a lengthy break in the settlement of the valley at the end of the Aceramic Neolithic, the scanty Ceramic Neolithic phase remains provide little evidence for the nature of Cypriot society at this time. Peltenburg has suggested that there was an island-wide discontinuity in settlement at the end of the Sotira phase, and this may be true for the Vasilikos valley although the excavated data are too few to support such an idea. However, it is clear that by the time of the utilization of Kalavasos-Ayious in the Early Chalcolithic, society in the valley had again undergone a radical transformation; lightly built huts replaced the sturdy stone (and mud-brick) structures of previous phases, and numerous pits were dug for various purposes. The way of life had no doubt changed, for whatever reasons, in many aspects (Peltenburg 1982a, 110), and this picture mirrors that found at Kissonerga-Mylouthkia in the Paphos area. In the latter region more substantial dwellings were built at sites such as Lemba-Lakkous (Peltenburg 1985) and Kissonerga-Mosphilia (Peltenburg 1987) following the Mylouthkia phase, and settlements seem to have acquired a certain degree of complexity which was not apparent at the beginning of the Chalcolithic period (see Peltenburg, below 108–26). The nature of the post-Ayious Chalcolithic settlement in the Vasilikos valley remains to be established by excavation, and the extent to which the overall Chalcolithic sequence of the Vasilikos valley mirrors that of the Lemba/Kissonerga area is presently unknown.

One of the most important implications of the Vasilikos valley excavations with regard to the nature and development of Cypriot society is the apparent confirmation of the lack of solidly constructed dwellings at the beginning of the Chalcolithic period. This adds weight to the suggestion of a major disaster at the end of the Ceramic Neolithic, probably accompanied by a considerable reduction in population on the island. If this is correct, it would be the second significant disruption of settlement in at least many regions of the island (the first disruption following the end of the Aceramic Neolithic). In view of these disruptions it is not surprising that Cypriot society did not evolve at the same rate with ever increasing complexity as did that of their neighbours on the mainland. By the middle of the fourth millennium BC the islanders were not ready to construct large urban centres for which they probably saw no need, and complex society only arose on the island at a much later date.

LIST OF REFERENCES

Dikaios, P. (1936) The excavations at Erimi, 1933–1935. *RDAC*, 1–81.
Dikaios, P. (1961)*Sotira*. Philadelphia.
Dikaios, P. (1962) The Stone Age, in *SCE* IV.1A 1–204. Lund.
Le Brun, A. (1986) Khirokitia une civilisation originale? *Acts 1986*, 1–11.
Mellaart, J. (1967) *Çatal Hüyük, a Neolithic Town in Anatolia*. London.
Moore, A. (1982) A four stage sequence for the Levantine Neolithic, ca. 8500–3750 B.C. *BASOR 246*, 1–34.
Oates, J. (1979) Religion and Ritual in Sixth-Millennium B.C. Mesopotamia. *World A 10*, 117–24.
Peltenburg, E.J. (1982a) *Vrysi. A Subterranean Settlement in Cyprus*. Warminster.
Peltenburg, E.J. (1982b) *Recent Developments in the Later Prehistory of Cyprus. (SIMA Pocket-book 16)* Göteborg.
Peltenburg, E.J. (1985) *Lemba Archaeological Project I: Excavations at Lemba Lakkous, 1976–1983. (SIMA 70.1)* Göteborg.
Peltenburg, E.J. (1987) Lemba archaeological project, Cyprus, 1985. *Levant 19*, 221–4.
Stanley Price, N.P. (1977) Khirokitia and the initial settlement of Cyprus. *Levant 9*, 66–89.
Todd, I.A. (1977) Vasilikos valley project: first preliminary report, 1976. *RDAC*, 5–32.
Todd, I.A. (1978) Vasilikos valley project: second preliminary report, 1977. *J Field A 5*, 161–95.
Todd, I.A. (1979) Vasilikos valley project: third preliminary report, 1978. *J Field A 6*, 256–300.
Todd, I.A. (1982) Vasilikos valley project: fourth preliminary report, 1979–80. *J Field A 9*, 35–77.
Todd, I.A. (1986a) Vasilikos valley project: fifth preliminary report, 1980–1984. *RDAC*, 12–27.
Todd, I.A. (1986b) The foreign relations of Cyprus in the Neolithic/Chalcolithic periods: new evidence from the Vasilikos valley. *Acts 1986*, 12–24.
Todd, I.A. (1987) *Vasilikos Valley Project 6: Excavations at Kalavasos-Tenta I. (SIMA 71.6)*. Göteborg.
Todd, I.A. (1988a) *Vasilikos Valley Project 7: Excavations at Kalavasos-Tenta II. (SIMA 71.7)*. Göteborg, forthcoming.
Todd, I.A. (1988b) *Vasilikos Valley Project 8: Excavations at Kalavasos-Ayious. (SIMA 71.8)*. Göteborg, forthcoming.
Todd, I.A. ed (1986) *Vasilikos Valley Project 1: The Bronze Age Cemetery in Kalavasos Village. (SIMA 71.1)*. Göteborg.
Watkins, T. (1969) The first village settlements. *Archaeologia Viva 3*, 29–38.
Watkins, T. (1981) The Chalcolithic period in Cyprus, in *Chalcolithic Cyprus and Western Asia (BMOP 26,)* (ed. J. Reade) 9–20. London.

2
From round house to duplex: a re-assessment of prehistoric Cypriot Bronze Age society

Stuart Swiny
Cyprus American Archaeological Research Institute, Nicosia

It is a painstaking and hazardous task to derive societal conclusions from the archaeological remains of pre-literate cultures. The interpretation of the evidence is mainly subjective and is in danger of being manipulated according to the thesis of the investigator. Every statement should be qualified. Of all this I am fully aware, but if the comments that follow provide the basis for further discussion, we will at least have taken a step in the right direction.

The picture of Early, and by extension, Middle Cypriot society painted by James Stewart over thirty years ago, has proved, despite its many generalisations frowned upon today, remarkably accurate in the light of recent investigations. This view, deduced almost solely from the evidence provided by funerary material (*SCE* IV.1A, 286–95) was of an island inhabited by scattered rural communities with a dual polarisation: copper production coupled with trade on the one hand, agriculture and pastoralism on the other. Since then, the excavation or detailed survey of five settlement sites, usually with their associated burial grounds, has provided a far more detailed picture. Listed in chronological order they are: Sotira-Kaminoudhia (Swiny 1986a; 1986; 1985a; 1985), first settled at a time when small quantities of Chalcolithic pottery and diagnostic Philia Culture wares were in use side by side with a whole range of early Red Polished fabrics, and abandoned in the EC III period.

Alambra-Mouttes (Coleman 1985) which has been satisfactorily dated by its assemblage of White Painted II ware to an early phase of the MC, contemporary with Ambelikou-Aletri (Merrillees 1984), but preceding Episkopi-Phaneromeni, Area C (Carpenter 1981), Kalokhorio-Khalandrikas (Swiny 1986a, 15 n 119) and Dhali-Kafkallia (Swiny 1972). The latest settlement is Episkopi-Phaneromeni, Area A (Carpenter 1981; Swiny 1986a) belonging to the transitional MC-LC phase.

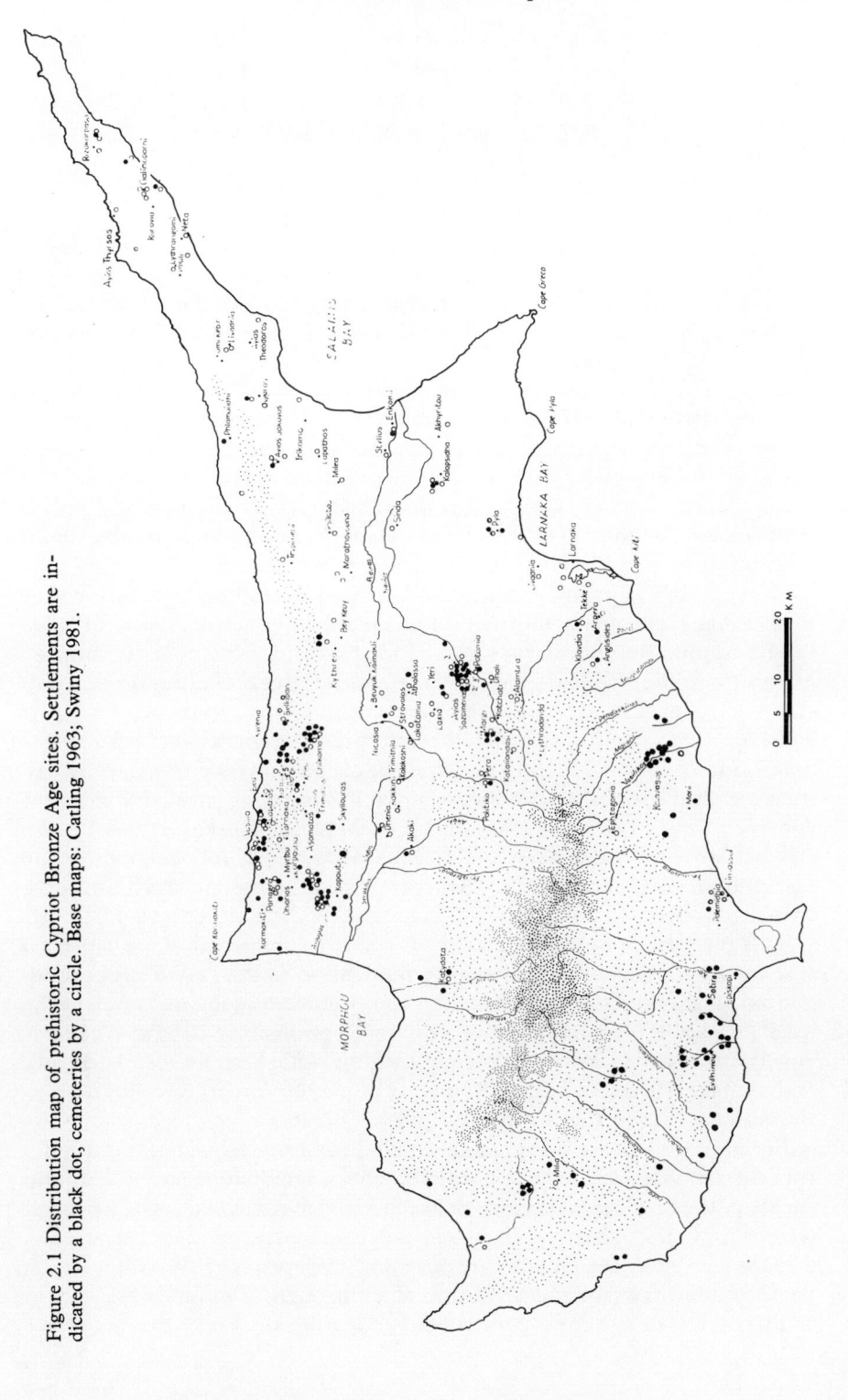

Figure 2.1 Distribution map of prehistoric Cypriot Bronze Age sites. Settlements are indicated by a black dot, cemeteries by a circle. Base maps: Catling 1963; Swiny 1981.

In view of the problems of differentiating between EC and MC artefact assemblages, which implicitly suggest a high degree of cultural unity, sites belonging to both periods, as well as those with Philia Culture traits, are treated as a whole and are described as the 'prehistoric Cypriot Bronze Age' a term suggested by D. Frankel (1988). Such a decision is supported by the material evidence in any case, as our division between EC and MC is purely arbitrary.

The settlement pattern during the Cypriot Chalcolithic is well distributed, though clustered. Diagnostic Erimi Culture material has been recorded at approximately 80 different localities, but not as yet in the Karpass Peninsula (Stanley Price 1979; Held, in preparation, see his map D for site distribution).

Some settlements such as Kissonerga-Mosphilia (Peltenburg 1986, 29) or Erimi-Pamboula (Heywood *et al* 1981, 28) have artefact scatters of between 12 and 15 hectares, but in size and numbers they do not compare with EC and especially MC sites, some of which cover 35 hectares.

Fig 2.1 emphasizes the island-wide distribution of prehistoric Cypriot Bronze Age sites, not all of which would have been occupied simultaneously during this period which lasted almost a millennium.

In 1963 H.W. Catling published a list of about 135 prehistoric Cypriot Bronze Age settlements, mostly located outside the southwestern quadrant of the island. Recent surveys have added considerably to this number, especially in the Vasilikos Valley, the Episkopi area and around Margi, so that well over 185 are known for the entire island. Evidence from the Episkopi area suggests, logically, that every major cemetery served a settlement (Swiny 1981), therefore, most of the cemeteries listed by Catling and others should have habitation sites nearby. Taking all the available data into consideration, a conservative estimate of 270 prehistoric Cypriot Bronze Age settlements seems reasonable. Such a wealth of information on the distribution and function of settlements provides material which can serve to analyse social organization (for Palestine see Esse, in press).

This increase in numbers and size is certainly the result of a substantial and sustained increase in the island's population as the period progressed. Indeed, as the Ayios Sozomenos, Episkopi and Margi regions as well as the Vasilikos Valley, exhibit a concentration of prehistoric Bronze Age sites superior to those of any other period (Catling 1963; Swiny 1981; Todd nd). Individual Hellenistic to Late Roman sites may be larger, but the cumulative surface area of the Bronze Age sites is greater.

Locational analysis demonstrates that proximity to water is the only constant factor governing the establishment of a habitation site and around Episkopi the maximum distance between a major settlement and its nearest water supply is 250 metres. In some valleys the settlements are clustered in areas where today the streams are perennial, a dependence on water which does not hold true for the scattering of farmsteads (Swiny 1981).

The choice of site for a permanent occupation does not appear to have been affected by the quality of the local soils as long as sufficient arable land existed to support the community. So far, no settlements have been located in gorges or extensively escarped areas lacking easy access to cultivatable land and the local biota.

An interesting and as yet unexplained aspect of the settlement pattern is the continued tendency towards clustering which can no longer be attributed to inconsistent survey strategies. The Vasilia, Lapithos, Karmi, Dhikomo, Ayios Sozomenos (for these sites see Catling 1963), Margi (Swiny 1986), Vasilikos Valley (Todd 1988), Episkopi Area (Swiny 1981) and Stavros tis Psokas (Peltenburg 1987) conglomerations were indeed discovered as the result of systematic surveys, but other surveys have shown that equally viable areas from an agricultural point of view seem to have been ignored. This is especially true of the major river valleys investigated by the Canadian Palaepaphos Survey Project (Rupp 1984; Rupp nd) and the Ayia Napa region (Hadjisavvas 1983).

Around Episkopi, settlements have sherd and artefact scatters up to 17.5 hectares, and components of 14 to 15 hectares are quite common, but none reach the 35 hectares recorded for Alambra-Mouttes (Coleman *et al* 1981, 98). Excavation, land improvement and irrigation schemes have proved that at any given time during the life of a settlement, there would have been large open spaces between the discrete clusters of habitations.

After the basic requirements of water and arable land had been satisfied, there was little consistency in the choice of a geophysical location. A slight preference for plateaus with a commanding view is noted, but in most instances strong natural positions were shunned in favour of well-drained slopes above a perennial water supply.

With the exception of the northern fortified sites at Dhikomo (Catling 1963, 140; Fortin 1981), Krini (*Chronique 1960*, 298; Fortin 1981), Nitovikla (*SCE* I) and Dhali-Kafkallia (Swiny 1972), all belonging to a late phase of the period, not a single settlement has any evidence of a perimeter wall, which proves that defence can hardly have been a concern for the prehistoric Bronze Age settlement founders. Unlike contemporary EB III Palestine, peaceful conditions must have existed on an island-wide basis with no fear of an external threat. The lack of seaborne aggression, however, does highlight the Cypriots' curious avoidance of coastal locations. In the Episkopi region and the Vasilikos Valley no settlement is less than 2.5 km from the sea, although two cemeteries are slightly closer. Lapithos-Vrysi tou Barba is the only known coastal site of this time period on the island.

The clearest evidence for the nature of inter-site relationships during the prehistoric Bronze Age is provided by Frankel's (1974; 1974a; 1978) studies of White Painted Ware. In addition to demonstrating, as might be expected, that the greatest contact was between neighbouring communities, with a gradual fall-off as the distance increased, his research also indicated strong links between the Margi/Kotchati area and north coast Lapithos on the one hand and between eastern sites on the other. Frankel postulated, as did Stewart (*SCE* IV.1A) before him, that the metals trade was the prime motivating factor in long-distance inter-island communication during the MC.

Settlements which were unaffected by the metals trade make it more difficult to use pottery as a means of diagnosing inter-site contacts. Frankel (1988) has convincingly argued that almost all vessels were used and deposited as funerary offerings close to the household-based production centres.

South and southwest of the Troodos Massif where White Painted wares are replaced by monochrome traditions, this kind of detailed comparative study requires intimate knowledge of the Red Polished assemblages before they can be objectively classified in discrete regional styles. Here, more than in the north, one gains the impression of self-contained communities that exhibited limited and sporadic contact with other parts of the island. One wheel-made Bichrome sherd, Red-on-Black from the distant Karpass, some White Painted vessels and a number of diagnostic Lapithos style bottles found their way to southern settlements and cemeteries, but in such limited quantities that their presence can hardly be the result of formal trading contacts.

Whatever the nature of these island-wide links, they were sufficient to have enabled and promoted at the beginning of the prehistoric Bronze Age period the establishment of a remarkably durable cultural *koiné* in which ceramics showed more stylistic variation than other classes of artefacts, a prime example being the metal assemblage. For example, the characteristic spiral earrings favoured by the Philia Culture had an island-wide distribution (Swiny 1986, 38), which was also true for most other metal types and the so-called gaming stones (Swiny 1986a, 34, 50). Such a lack of pronounced regionalism would suggest a degree of craft specialization and standardization caused by the presence of a central authority (Esse, in press).

With the exception of three sites in the Kyrenia area, the evidence suggests that as the distance between sites and the ore bodies north and east of the Troodos increased, so did their isolation. Following this argument, the paucity of prehistoric Bronze Age sites in the vicinity of the copper belt on the south flank of the range, stretching from Trimiklini to Asproyia, let alone those with demonstrable external contacts, suggests that little to no copper was being mined and distributed from this area.

It is unfortunate that none of the settlements relevant to our discussion has provided the wealth of undisturbed archaeological data such as Sotira-Teppes, Lemba-Lakkous or Kissonerga-Mosphilia. All prehistoric Bronze Age settlements appear either to have been rather sparsely furnished or else stripped of most movable items post-abandonment. This phenomenon could be due to the increased population density and apparent lack of inter-site strife. At Sotira-Kaminoudhia certain areas were sealed by tumble that looks suspiciously like earthquake debris, yet few finds lay sealed on the undisturbed floors.

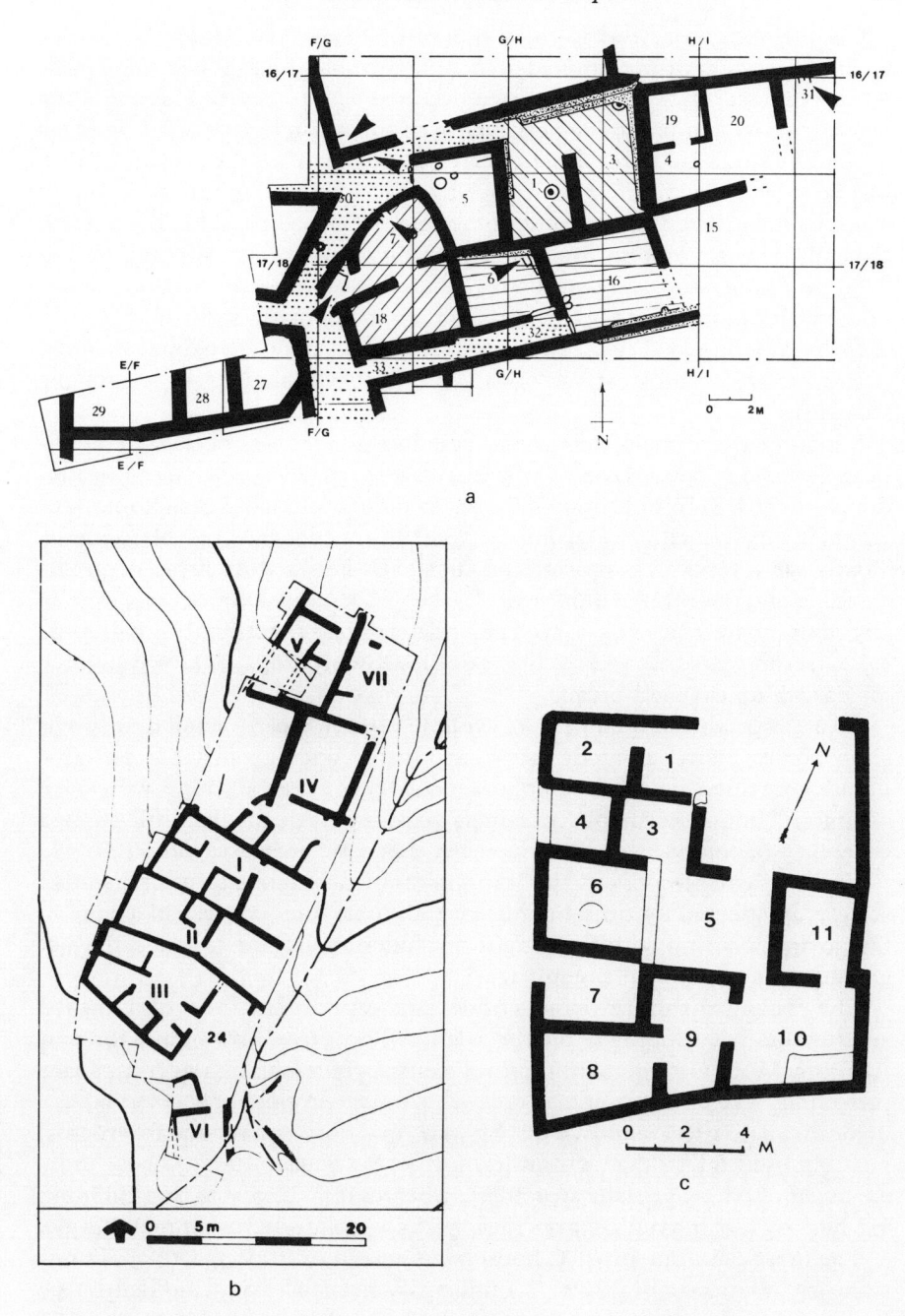

Figure 2.2(a) Plan of Sotira-Kaminoudhia Area A. Access corridor and benches stippled. Discrete units hatched. Hearths indicated by arrows. (b) Plan of Alambra-Mouttes Area A (*from* Coleman 1985, Fig 4). (c) Plan of Kalopsidha House (*from* Gjerstad, E. (1929) *Studies on Prehistoric Cyprus*, Fig 3. Uppsala.

Despite the characteristic clustering of buildings at Chalcolithic settlements, discrete units are immediately recognizable (Peltenburg 1985, 322–9) in contrast to the agglutinative architecture at Sotira-Kaminoudhia where it proved impossible to excavate a complete unit. The building plans at Kaminoudhia fail to reveal a preferred house form but they can nevertheless be broken down into a series of theoretical habitation units varying in shape, but consistent in size and in the number of rooms. This house form typically consists of a narrow corridor of different length (stippled on Fig 2.2a) providing access to two rooms. There is no preference in the orientation and location of either the approach or the doorways.

In Area A at least (Fig 2.2a), the common space between habitation units is so restricted that most activities can only have taken place within the structures.

Functional analysis of each room failed to isolate any specialized activities restricted to certain rooms or areas: all seem to have served a multifunctional purpose (Humphreys 1987). Most units included freestanding rectangular clay hearths set against a wall, low benches, lime plaster bins alternatively serving as mortars or jar stands and a wide array of grain-grinding and pounding equipment. Large, thick, coarse ware trays, especially common near hearths, served an undetermined function. Ethnographic evidence suggests that the circular griddles (Swiny 1986, 37) were suitable for baking unleavened bread.

All areas produced quantities of ceramic vessels, mostly small to medium sized bowls, many spouted, and coarse ware cooking pots; but portable liquid containers such as amphorae and two types of jugs were also common. Unless perishable containers were used, Area A had little storage capability in comparison with the other domestic area excavated (B).

This settlement conveys the impression of belonging to an innovative society, unaffected by time-honoured traditions, one that was in a state of flux, experimenting with building form, funerary architecture and the full gamut of its artefactual assemblage.

The evidence from settlements does not support the view of a unified architectural development on the island. The early MC house form at Alambra-Mouttes (Fig 2.2b) typically consists of a rectangular front space providing access to an inner area of similar proportions reserved for domestic activities, subdivided by one or more small square rooms, possibly used for storage and utility purposes (Schaar 1985). These units are interpreted as domestic structures, whereas it is suggested that Building III housed manufacturing activities, perhaps connected with metallurgy.

The most elaborate pre-LC house plan known, was excavated at Kalopsidha by Gjerstad (Fig 2.2c). Confidently, perhaps over confidently, he ascribed functions to most rooms on the basis of their contents.

Clustered around a central court where food preparation and cooking were located, there were sleeping quarters, store and work rooms as well as a possible shrine (No. 6). Here, the walls surrounding the central raised

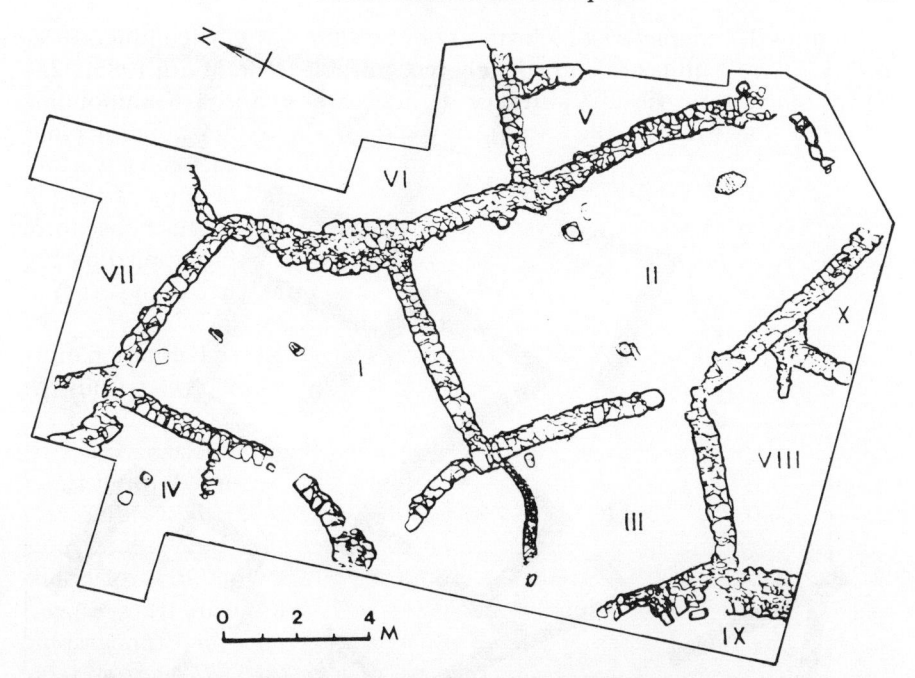

Figure 2.3 Plan of Ambelikou-Aletri Area 1 (*from* Dikaios 1960, Pl 29c).

circular hearth were lined with coarse and fine ware vessels, perhaps stored on shelves. These arrangements, which make the room the obvious focal point of the entire structure, are without parallel. Room 6 has, however, also been interpreted as a 'kitchen with hearth' (Åström 1969, 75).

More typical is the apparently haphazard development at Dhali-Kafkallia (Swiny 1972) and especially Ambelikou-Aletri (Dikaios 1960) and Episkopi-Phaneromeni (Carpenter 1981). The last two sites (Figs 2.3, 4), with their irregular rooms, meandering walls and apparent lack of architectural cohesion, continue the tradition first noted at Sotira-Kaminoudhia.

A functional analysis of the Area A settlement at Phaneromeni concluded that most areas, small or large, showed evidence of domestic activities and the preparation of foodstuffs, with emphasis on spinning and weaving in Rooms 7a, 14 and 15, and storage in Room 7. The smaller Rooms, 8 and 17, suggest a concentration of flint knapping in the former and the preparation of foodstuffs, specifically meat, in the latter.

The accretive nature of prehistoric Bronze Age architecture in which free-standing structures were shunned for multi-roomed complexes is a decision which certainly has a bearing on the social organization of the culture. The sizes and arrangements of the individual units, typically consisting of two rooms, one for habitation and the other for storage, which might also be subdivided, suggest that these discrete units correspond to the space requirements of a nuclear family. But the scarcity of *in situ* finds and diagnostic features makes it difficult to elaborate on this hypothesis.

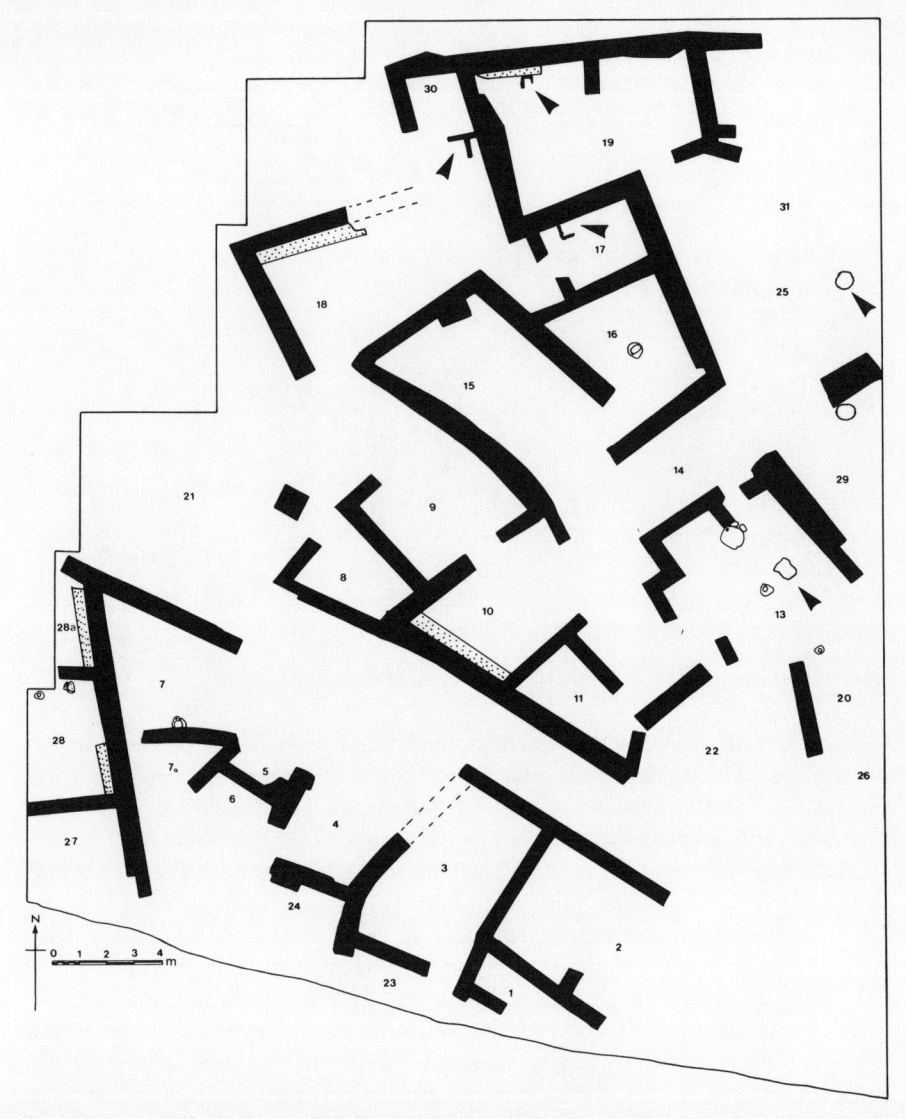

Figure 2.4 Plan of Episkopi-Phaneromeni Area A. Benches stippled. Hearths indicated by arrows.

The evidence at hand suggests that the subsistence system was primarily agrarian (Åström 1969), supplemented by hunting Persian fallow deer (and at Kaminoudhia the occasional fox), some fishing and a limited collection of marine molluscs and crustacians. Little primary information on agriculture has been recorded. South coast sites do provide evidence for the cultivation of wheat, barley, lentils and the olive. Grape pips and a small apple or pear seed have also been recovered, but the samples were too poorly preserved to determine whether they were domesticated or not.

Table 2.1. Distributional analysis of the faunal remains from Sotira-Kaminoudhia and Episkopi-Phaneromeni.

	Cattle	Deer	Pig	Caprines
Sotira-Kaminoudhia	33%	20%	12%	36%
Episkopi-Phaneromeni	31%	11%	26%	32%

Since most of these species have been found at earlier sites, their existence is only to be expected. The large number of saddle querns, rubbing stones, pounders and grinders at excavated and surveyed sites is ample testimony to the importance of cereals in this period (Swiny 1986a, 65, Table 1).

More informative are the results obtained from the study of the faunal remains (Table 2.1) at Sotira-Kaminoudhia and Episkopi-Phaneromeni, separated by a straight line distance of only six kilometres, but at either end of the time period which concerns us here.

During the main phase of occupation at Kaminoudhia cattle represent 33 per cent of the assemblage and if the size ratio between this taxon and caprines is taken into consideration, they were certainly the main meat source. It appears that cattle bones belonged to mature animals, in contrast with the larger number of young female caprines, which suggests a population geared to the production of milk. This possibility is supported by the number of spouted containers, traditionally labelled 'milk bowls' by analogy with the contemporary *galeftiri* (de Sike 1982, 21, 50).

The decline in the importance of Fallow deer as a meat source, already noted at Chalcolithic sites in the west, continued throughout the Bronze Age, as shown by the figures in Table 2.1. Nevertheless, at Kaminoudhia deer might have produced as much as 22 per cent of the meat consumed, followed by 14 per cent pig and 9 per cent caprines. Their importance to the culture is emphasized by the numerous representations on E and MC vessels, whereas caprines only appear rarely. At Kaminoudhia the demand for antler as a raw material ideal for the manufacture of flint knapping hammers continued, whereas Phaneromeni Settlement A, failed to yield a single specimen (pers obs).

By comparison with deer, pigs show an increase from 12 per cent at Kaminoudhia to 26 per cent at Phaneromeni, though the small size of the samples calls for caution.

A few edible molluscs were recovered from both sites as well as a dozen crustacian claws. Despite their proximity to the sea the inhabitants of Phaneromeni were apparently not keen fisherman as no fish remains were recovered.

This factual but sketchy view of the prehistoric Cypriot Bronze Age economy and lifestyle can fortunately be supplemented by the numerous scenic compositions, either free-standing or applied to ceramic vessels, that began to appear around the turn of the third millennium BC. Many are enigmatic and open to widely differing interpretations, none more so than the Oxford and Vounous Bowls (Morris 1985, 269, 281), but others are quite explicit (Dikaios 1940, Pl 35a). D. Morris (1985) has recently assembled this material and interpreted it in his typically spirited manner!

With the exception of four models of obvious religious nature, all appear to represent scenes of daily life, unlike so many ancient Near Eastern compositions concerned with warfare, political dominance or the chase. In Cyprus the subject matter is women, perhaps kneading dough, pounding (?) grain, baking bread in square ovens, giving birth, nursing children or tending their livestock. In most instances the gender of the naked figures remains undetermined, but where the choroplast deemed it necessary to specify the sex, they conveyed the impression of clearly segregated activities. Nowhere is this more obvious than on the Oxford Bowl which depicts on one side a series of females apparently involved in bread making and on the other three men sitting beside two circular ridges provided with runnels, containing a series of carefully formed conical lumps. In between stands a fallow deer and a smaller unidentified quadruped. This scene has been variously connected with baking and copper leaching. The latter interpretation is considered most unlikely since the evidence from Cyprus, the Near East and Europe suggests that Bronze Age copper was smelted. Another vessel has similar rings encircling cones (Morris 1985, 276) so the association with animals is probably significant and these two scenes are perhaps agricultural or pastoral in nature rather than industrial.

Much less enigmatic and more significant for our understanding of prehistoric Bronze Age society are the well known ploughing scenes (Dikaios 1940, Pls 9,18). The Cypriots had obviously realised that a castrated bull (ie a bullock) produced a superior draft animal and the introduction of the elbow plough early in the period would have enabled larger areas to be put under cultivation with less expenditure of effort. The estimated six acres of land necessary to provide the requirements in cereals for a family of five (Swiny 1981, 80) could be tilled quite rapidly, thereby providing the opportunity for other activities.

With the exception of a MC II pit (*SCE* I, 356) all the evidence for prehistoric Cypriot Bronze Age religious beliefs is secondary. Most informative are the genre scenes from Bellapais-Vounous (Dikaios 1940) and Kotchati (Karageorghis 1982), which have been interpreted so often and in so many different manners (for a non-ritualistic interpretation see Morris 1985) that in the absence of new primary evidence yet another view seems superfluous.

Burial customs show minor variations between regions, mainly in the position of the corpse which may be sitting, or supine, or again lying flexed on the right-hand side, facing east. The frequence of funerary offerings deposited with the deceased suggests a strong belief in afterlife, in which the models and figurines probably had a role to play (Orphanides 1987).

Despite the information provided by the genre scenes on certain aspects of society, they are silent on others which concern us here, namely copper production, trade and inter-community relations.

However viable, the self-contained agrarian economy just described is unlikely to have instigated the changes leading to the establishment of wealth accumulating centres that laid the foundations for the spectacular development of the LC urban centres. No single prehistoric Bronze Age settlement, either excavated or surveyed, stands out by its size, complexity and lavishness of architectural fixtures or number of foreign imports. None shows signs of extensive trading connections.

All the settlement data suggests that Cypriot society was unstratified. The Kalopsidha house is certainly more elaborate and better organised, but fails to stand out by its size or quality of appointments.

What then can be added to this picture by a study of the extensive body of funeral evidence, our only other source of information? Thousands of

Table 2.2. Distributional analysis of metal objects from four prehistoric Cypriot Bronze Age cemeteries.

	No. of chambers excavated	No. of chambers with Cu objects	Total no. of Cu objects	Av. no. of Cu objects per chamber
Bellapais-Vounous Cemetery A	43	23	42	1.2
Bellapais-Vounous Cemetery B	65	41	175	2.7
Lapithos-Vrysi tou Barba	97	63	701	7.2
Lapithos-Vrysi tou Barba: 9 chambers*	with > 20 Cu objects	9	446	49.5
Lapithos-Vrysi tou Barba	86 with > 20 Cu objects	54	255	2.9
Kalavassos	30	16	79	2.6
	Tombs** excavated	No. of tombs with > 42 objects	Total no. of Cu objects	Av. no. of Cu objects per tomb
Lapithos-Vrysi tou Barba	59	7***	493	70.4

*T313A, 313B, 315A 315B-c, 316, 320, 322, 804, 805
**According to the Swedish excavators a *tomb* represents a *dromos* and all its associated chambers. Nine tombs have from 5 to 17 Cu objects, but none falls within the 17 to 41 range.
Sources: SCE I 33–162; Herscher 1978; Todd 1986; Todd unpublished ms.
***T313, 315, 316, 320, 322, 804, 805

prehistoric Bronze Age burials have been excavated and robbed over the past century or so. At fifteen cemeteries in the Episkopi area alone 1095 *dromoi* were recorded (Swiny 1981), providing access to at least 2500 chambers. A conservative estimate of over 200 known prehistoric cemeteries for the island as a whole provides some idea of the sheer quantity of grave goods recovered by one means or another. When burials from any cemetery illicitly excavated in the past 60 years yielded unusual grave goods or substantially greater quantities of certain categories of grave goods, metal especially, this was rapidly reflected by the antiquities market. Despite the regrettable means by which these artefacts were recovered, this has at least resulted in an accurate and comprehensive island-wide picture of funerary architecture and offerings.

Although a steady increase in size of burial chamber and quantity of grave goods—mostly ceramic—is detectable as the period progresses, only three north coast cemeteries stand out by their wealth of metal or elaborate architecture.

The monumental and sophisticated, but disturbed tombs at Vasilia-Evriman (Stewart 1957), hastily excavated and incompletely documented, remain to this day an enigma and are omitted from the present discussion (Swiny 1985a, 23).

Over the years much has been made of the wealth of metal mortuary offerings deposited in the tombs of Lapithos-Vrysi tou Barba and Bellapais-Vounous. It has generally been suggested that this opulence is the result of the metals trade. But does this impression withstand close scrutiny?

The EC burial ground at Vounous Area A (Stewart & Stewart 1950), yielded 43 chambers, 23 of which contained the 42 copper-base objects recorded, which makes an average of 1.2 object per tomb (Table 2.2).

At Cemetery B (Dikaios 1940) in use from EC II but most active in EC III and MC I, 65 chambers were excavated, 41 containing 175 pieces of metal, providing an average of 2.7 objects per chamber.

The Vounous Cemetery B interments are notable for the numerous genre scenes rather than a wealth in metal. But genre scenes are not a prerogative of this site alone and many have recently been recovered from the centre of the island around Margi and Kotchati (Morris 1985). *If* those cemeteries had been scientifically excavated in the manner of Vounous, where the often fragmentary and scattered elements of the scenic compositions required skill both to excavate and to reconstruct, Vounous would certainly fall into line with cemeteries elsewhere on the island.

Despite protracted survey work, no major contemporary habitation site is known in the vicinity of Vounous, although saddle querns, handstones and a game have been noted in the vicinity of Cemetery B (Swiny 1986, 35). The site is almost two and a half kilometres from the coast which fails to offer a natural harbour or anchorage nearby, thus trade can hardly be the obvious reason for the relative wealth of this cemetery. Trade, however, did have some role to play, and over a considerable period of time, for Syro-Palestinian vessels and Minoan bronzes (*SCE* IV.1A, 276, 280; Merrillees 1974, 76) were discovered in EC I and MC I tombs.

The 97 MC chambers excavated at Vrysi tou Barba (*SCE* I; Herscher 1978) yielded 701 copper-base objects, or an average of 7.2 objects per chamber (Table 2.2). Of the 97 chambers, 34 were devoid of metal offerings and the most significant aspect of this cemetery is that a mere nine chambers, or less than 10 per cent, contained 64 per cent of the metal finds. It is clearly no coincidence that certain *dromoi* only provided access to metal-rich chambers and the burials related to seven of the 59 *dromoi* yielded 493 out of the 701 metal finds. No other cemetery on the island rivals Lapithos in terms of metal, but when the nine tombs are isolated from the rest, the figures for the remaining chambers are comparable to those obtained, for example, from Vounous Cemetery B of the Kalavassos Village tombs for example (Table 2.2). A mere nine chambers, then, exhibit a remarkable wealth of metal and the presence of unusual articles, such as a 'fetish stone' and gypsum idol, but no substantial increase in ceramics. Indeed, there is a hint that the quantities of both categories of grave goods are inversely proportional. These same chambers are noticeably larger than most, but conversely, they saw extended use as they contained multiple burials, so the quantity of gifts per burial need not have been out of the ordinary.

Our knowledge of Bronze Age Cypriot burial customs is not sufficient to determine whether chambers were reserved for individuals or next of kin, therefore it is impossible to state whether the metal-rich Lapithos tombs contained unrelated individuals of high status and wealth or kinship groups of common high status.

At this site the human bones were poorly preserved, so the age, sex and frequently the number of individuals per chamber, remains undetermined.

None of the copper-base objects from Vrysi tou Barba is typologically different from other contemporary Cypriot assemblages. The only prestige items that we are able to isolate are the intrinsically valueless fetish stone and gypsum idol, as well as the foreign imports. The LC and Iron Age ornamental maces and the Kourion sceptre (Snodgrass 1988, 16–17; Karageorghis 1982, 85) are a far cry from anything of earlier date, except perhaps the 18th century BC shaft-hole axes from central Cyprus (Buchholz 1979).

Ethnographic research has amply demonstrated that mortuary distinctions only 'communicate a very limited sub-set of the social differentiation known to exist in the living society' (O'Shea 1981, 43). The variables that have been noted within and between prehistoric Cypriot Bronze Age cemeteries do tend to cluster, but not in a manner which enables the isolation of features denoting social stratification (*contra* Goldstein 1981).

In Cyprus the variables are less qualitative and more regional and temporal. Whatever status did exist was probably inherited, because abundant grave goods are also found with children (see Brown 1981, 34 in this connection).

Neither the settlement nor the mortuary evidence suggests that the Cypriots went through a 'Chiefdom Stage' before developing urban society (for the Palestinian model see Esse, in press), yet as previously noted an unusual degree of cultural uniformity is exhibited for a primitive society. In this respect Cyprus does not follow the usual development towards social complexity.

It is our misfortune that the settlement at Vrysi tou Barba was never located and excavated. It is probably close by the burial ground, as saddle querns were used on occasion to secure the slabs sealing the tomb chambers. The site's unique location and proximity to a natural harbour, the wealth of certain tombs and presence of imports is no coincidence. These factors combine to set Lapithos-Vrysi tou Barba apart from contemporary sites and suggest that trade is the reason for this conspicuous wealth.

The most likely article of exchange, naturally, is copper, and Lapithos is in an ideal location to export the metal obtained from the ore deposits surrounding the Northwest flank of the Troodos, the closest of which is Mitsero at a straight line distance of 33 km. Although there is little agreement on whether oxide or sulphide ores were smelted at the beginning of the period, the early MC miners were certainly capable of driving deep adits into the ore bodies in order to exploit the more plentiful sulphides at Ambelikou-Aletri, a site which also provided evidence for smelting (Merrillees 1984). In what form copper was transported from the production centres to a redistribution centre like Vrysi tou Barba we do not know, but contemporary bun-shaped ingots existed in Anatolia, and for practical and technical reasons a similar shape would be expected in Cyprus. It is puzzling, nevertheless, that none has ever been discovered on the island. If, however, the metal was transported from the mines to the coastal sites in a semi-refined form—such as matte—and then smelted and cast into (bun) ingots for export, the likelihood of a chance of discovery of a matte shipment lost in transit is greatly reduced. This scenario does not explain how the scattered Cypriot settlements received their copper: was it too in the form of matte, or was it cast into some kind of ingot?

Copper mining and primary smelting would have required a technical expertise beyond that found in rural communities where the domestic and village mode of production was the norm, so the copper industry and its organization would have promoted the development of elitist groups. The archaeological evidence suggests that prior to the late prehistoric Bronze Age period, in the 17th century BC, production was on a small enough scale not to significantly affect Cypriot society by the importation through exchange of numerous foreign trade items and ideas, by the accumulation of wealth and by the creation of status conscious elites. As Knapp (1986) has succinctly argued, these developments only start at the close of the MC period, so this writer will leave it up to him to complete that section of the picture!

ACKNOWLEDGMENTS

I would like to thank Dr E.J. Peltenburg for the invitation to take part in a conference which, I hope, will be considered as a turning point in ancient Cypriot studies. It was certainly an excellent reason for many of us to take a long, hard, look at the people behind the remains. After all, archaeology is only the study of the 'material expression of human thought and action' (A. Glock). Discussion of the faunal and floral remains from Sotira-Kaminoudhia and Episkopi-Phaneromeni is based on studies undertaken by G. Nobis, J.P.N. Watson, P. Croft and J.M. Hansen, to be published in the final excavation reports. S.O. Held kindly permitted me to make use of unpublished material in his Ph.D dissertation.

LIST OF REFERENCES

Åström, P. (1969) The economy of Cyprus and its development in the IInd millennium. *Arch Viva II.3*, 73–80.
Brown, J.A. (1981) The search for rank in prehistoric burials, in *The Archaeology of Death* (eds. R.Chapman et al) 25–37. Cambridge.
Buchholz, H-G. (1979) Bronzene Schaftrohräxte aus Tamassos und Umgebung, in *Studies Presented in Memory of Porphyrios Dikaios* (eds. V. Karageorghis et al) 76–88. Nicosia.
Carpenter, J.R. (1981) Excavations at Phaneromeni, in *Studies in Cypriote Archaeology. (Institute of Archaeology, University of California, Los Angeles. Monograph 18)*, (eds. Biers, J.C. & Soren, D.) 59–78.
Catling, H.W. (1963) Patterns of settlement in Bronze Age Cyprus. *Op Ath 4*, 129–69.
Coleman, J.E. (1985) Investigations at Alambra, 1974–1984, in *Archaeology in Cyprus 1960–1985* (ed. V. Karageorghis) 125–41. Nicosia.
Coleman, J.E. et al (1981) Cornell excavations at Alambra, 1980. *RDAC*, 81–98.
de Sike, Y. (1982) *Chypre les travaux et les jours. (Association Française d'Action Artistique)* Paris.
Dikaios, P. (1940) The excavations at Vounous-Bellapais in Cyprus, 1931–1932. *Archaeologia 88*, 1–14.
Dikaios, P. (1960) A conspectus of architecture in Ancient Cyprus. *Kypriakai Spudai Vol D*, 3–30.
Esse, D.L. (in press) Secondary state formation and collapse in Early Bronze Age Palestine, in *L'Urbanisation de la Palestine à l'Age du Bronze Ancien. CNRS* (ed. P. de Miroschedji). Jerusalem.
Fortin, M. (1981) *Military Architecture in Cyprus during the Second Millennium BC.* Unpublished Ph D dissertation, Institute of Archaeology, University of London.
Frankel, D. (1974) *Middle Cypriot White Painted Pottery: an Analytical Study of the Decoration (SIMA 42)*. Göteborg.
Frankel, D. (1974a) Inter-site relationships in the Middle Bronze Age of Cyprus. *World A 6*, 190–201.
Frankel, D. (1978) Pottery decoration as an indicator of social relationships: a prehistoric Cypriot example, in *Arts and Society* (eds M. Greenhalgh & J.V.S. Megaw) 147–60. London.
Frankel, D. (1988) (in press) Pottery production in prehistoric Cyprus. Assessing the problem. *J Med Arch.*
Goldstein, L. (1981) One-dimensional archaeology and multi-dimensional

people: spatial organisation and mortuary analysis, in *The Archaeology of Death* (eds. R. Chapman *et al*) 53–69. Cambridge.

Hadjisavvas, S. (1983) New light on the history of the Ayia Napa region. *RDAC*, 315–18.

Held, S.O. nd *Early Prehistoric Island Archaeology in Cyprus: Configurations of Formative Culture Growth from the Pleistocene/Holocene Boundary to the Mid-3rd Millennium B.C.* Ph D dissertation, Institute of Archaeology, University of London, in progress.

Herscher, E. (1978) *The Bronze Age Cemetery at Lapithos, Vrysi tou Barba, Cyprus. Results of the University of Pennsylvania Museum Excavation, 1931.* Unpublished Ph D dissertation, University of Pennsylvania. University Microfilms International. Ann Arbor.

Heywood, H. Swiny, S. & Whittingham, D. (1981) Erimi revisited. *RDAC*, 24–42.

Humphreys, I.K. (1987) *A Functional Analysis of the Structures at Sotira-Kaminoudhia in Cyprus.* Unpublished M.A. thesis, Drew University.

Karageorghis, V. (1982) *Cyprus. From the Stone Age to the Romans.* London.

Knapp, A.B. (1986) Production, exchange, and socio-political complexity on Bronze Age Cyprus. *Ox J A 5*, 35–60.

Merrillees, R.S. (1974) *Trade and Transcendence in the Bronze Age Levant. (SIMA 39).* Göteborg.

Merrillees, R.S. (1984) Ambelikou-Aletri: a preliminary report. *RDAC*, 1–13.

Morris, D. (1985) *The Art of Ancient Cyprus.* Oxford.

Orphanides, A.G. (1986) *Towards a Theory for the Interpretation of Material Remains in Archaeology: the Bronze Age Anthropomorphic Figurines from Cyprus.* Unpublished Ph D dissertation, State University of New York at Albany.

O'Shea, J. (1981) Social configurations and the archaeological study of mortuary practices: a case study, in *The Archaeology of Death* (eds. R. Chapman *et al*) 39–52. Cambridge.

Peltenburg, E.J. (1985) *Lemba Archaeological Project I: Excavations at Lemba Lakkous, 1976–1983. (SIMA 70.1).* Göteborg.

Peltenburg, E.J. (1986) Excavations at Kissonerga-Mosphilia 1985. *RDAC*, 28–39.

Peltenburg, E.J. & Project Members (1987) Excavations at Kissonerga-Mosphilia 1986. *RDAC*, 1–18.

Rupp, D.W. *et al* (1984) Canadian Palaipaphos (Cyprus) Survey Project: second preliminary report, 1980–1982. *J Field A 11*, 133–54.

Rupp, D.W. nd *The Canadian Palaipaphos (Cyprus) Survey Project: An Overview of the 1986 Season.*

Schaar, K.W. (1985) House form at Tarsus, Alambra and Lemba. *RDAC*, 37–44.

Snodgrass, A.M. (1988) *Cyprus and Early Greek History. 4th Annual Lecture. Cultural Foundation of the Bank of Cyprus.* Nicosia.

Stanley Price, N.P. (1979) *Early Prehistoric Settlement in Cyprus, 6500–3000 BC. (BAR InterSer, 65).* Oxford.

Stewart, J. & Stewart, E. (1950) *Vounous 1937–38. (Skrifter Utgivna av Svenska Instituet I Rom 14).* Lund.

Stewart, J.R. (1957) The Melbourne Expedition, 1955. *University of Melbourne Gazette 13.1-April.*

Swiny, S. (1972) *in* Overbeck, J.C. and Swiny, S. *Two Cypriot Bronze Age Sites at Kafkallia (Dhali). (SIMA 33).* Lund.

Swiny, S. (1981) Bronze Age settlement patterns in southwest Cyprus. *Levant 13*, 51–87.

Swiny, S. (1985) Sotira-Kaminoudhia and the Chalcolithic/Early Bronze Age transition in Cyprus, in *Archaeology in Cyprus, 1960–1965* (ed. V. Karageorghis) 115–24. Nicosia.

Swiny, S. (1985a) The Cyprus American Archaeological Research Institute excavations at Sotira-Kaminoudhia and the origins of the Philia culture. *Acts 1985*, 13–26.

Swiny, S. (1986) The Philia culture and its foreign relations, in *Acts 1986*, 29–44.

Swiny, S. (1986a) *The Kent State University Expedition to Episkopi Phaneromeni. Part 2. (SIMA 74.2)*. Nicosia.

Todd, I.A. (1986) *Vasilikos Valley Project 1: The Bronze Age Cemetery in Kalavasos Village. (SIMA 71.1)*. Göteborg.

Todd, I.A. (1988) The Middle Bronze Age in the Kalavasos area. *RDAC*, in press.

3
A Late Cypriot community at Alassa

S. Hadjisavvas
Department of Antiquities, Cyprus

A note on the original topography of this site was published in 1986 in the first preliminary report on the results of the excavations at Alassa (Hadjisavvas 1986, 62 Fig 1). However, the radical changes which have occurred since then as a result of the construction of the Kouris dam require another topographical description to accord with the present key locations. The excavated remains at the locality Pano Mandilaris are situated some 500 m south of the recently erected village of Alassa and north of the artificial lake of the Kouris dam. The site now has a commanding position over the two bays of the lake formed by the Kouris and Limnatis river valleys where these two rivers meet (Fig 3.2).

The only archaeological site known in the area of Alassa prior to our 1983 survey was that at the locality of Paliotaverna situated in the northern outskirts of the old village. This site, although not excavated is of particular importance for this presentation and a more detailed description of the surface remains is essential. A large number of huge blocks of finely worked stone, some measuring two metres in length, were brought to the surface by bulldozers engaged in deep ploughing in 1963 (Hadjisavvas 1986, Pl 17.2). Along with the stones which are decorated with drafted margins many sherds of large storage *pithoi* with characteristic relief wavy bands came to light. Both the ashlars and the pottery are attributed to the Late Bronze Age. Among the stones there is one cross-shaped resembling another from the sanctuary at Myrtou-Pighades; it most probably belongs to an altar. According to witnesses the stones which are now at the surface formed long parallel walls, the lower courses of which are still *in situ*.

Among the elderly villagers there is a tradition that during the nights a strange light came from a bush situated close to the north of the remains. Today under a lentisk bush there is a heap of ashlars forming a shelter for a candle lit occasionally by local people. Further uphill the remains of an

A community at Alassa

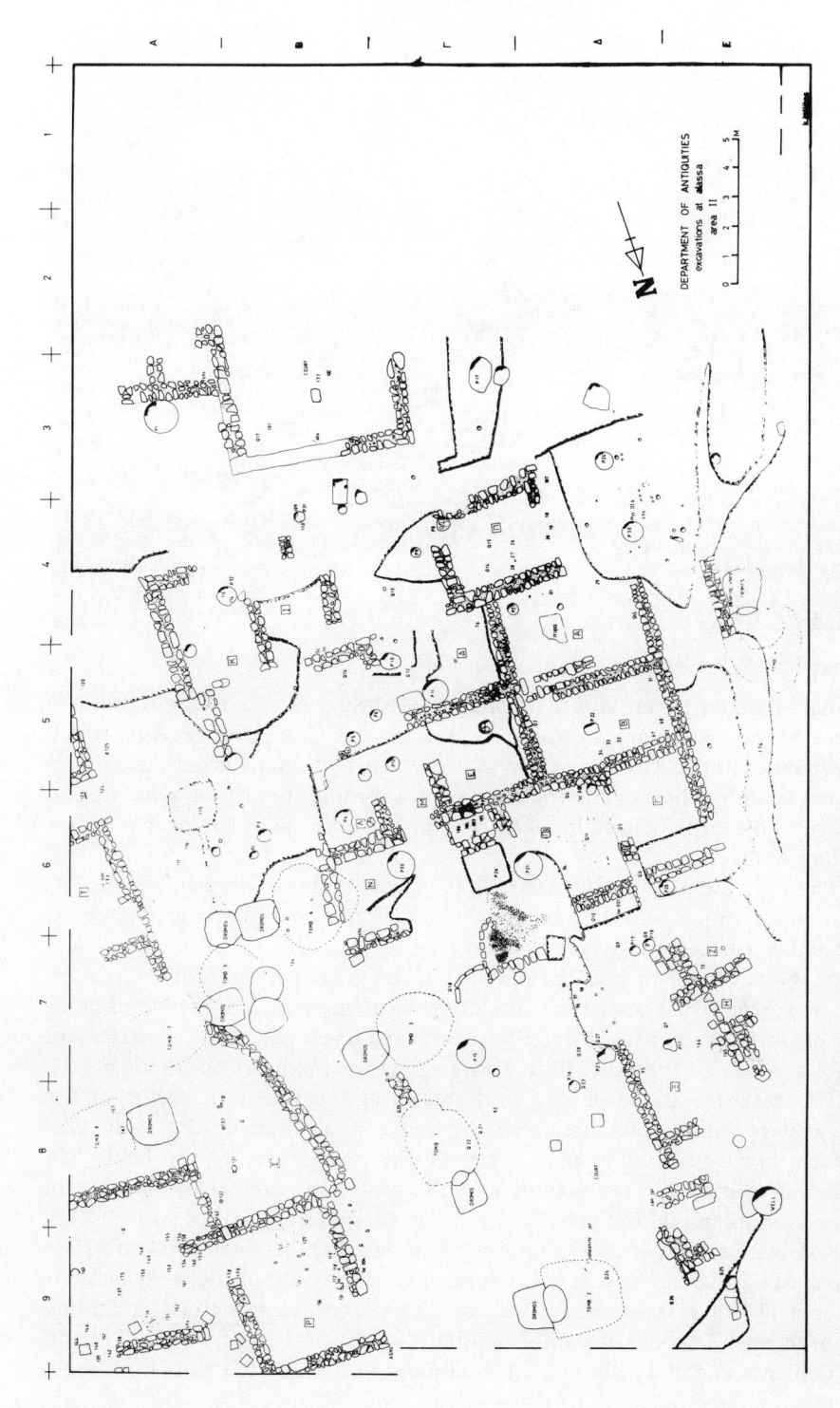

Figure 3.1 Plan of the excavated remains at Alassa-Pano Mandilaris.

Figure 3.2 The site overlooking the artifical lake.

archaic sanctuary were found during the 1983 survey. No doubt in this area there was a sanctuary established during the Late Bronze Age which survived until the Archaic period as is the case with many other sanctuaries on the island. Whether the tradition comes through to our days, as suggested by the candle or was invoked by another episode in the near past, we do not know.

The 1983 survey (Hadjisavvas 1986, 63) defined the extension of the LC settlement which occupies the localities of Pano Mandilaris and Kampos located southeast and east of Paliotaverna respectively. The surface indications, however, show that the remains of the great buildings at Paliotaverna, whatever its use was, were outside the settlement on a higher commanding position at an altitude of 260 m above sea level, whereas the settlement itself is at an altitude of 240 m above sea level (Hadjisavvas 1986, Fig 1).

The recent excavation was undertaken in the southern sector of the settlement which was threatened by the construction of the dam. Our choice, however, was restricted by the fact that many of the fields had suffered from bulldozer activities in the past. One plot at the locality of Pano Mandilaris which promised well-preserved architecture was selected for excavation. The investigations were undertaken between 1984 and 1986 and a total of 18 weeks was spent at the site. As a result of these excavations an area of 1000 m^2 was uncovered revealing part of the settlement including eight tombs. The site of Pano Mandilaris is one of the very few LC inland settlements and the only one on the mountains excavated thus far (Negbi

Figure 3.3 Aerial view of the excavations. Tombs are numbered 1–8.

1986). Its proximity to an area rich in sulphide ores and other copper alloys adds to the importance of its investigation.

What we have actually uncovered at Alassa-Pano Mandilaris is a small part of a LC IIC to LC IIIA settlement with a small square and a street (Fig 3.1). The open spaces were used as burial grounds and seven out of eight excavated tombs were found sealed under the hard surface of the square and the street. The architecture is well preserved at the northern part of the excavation while the southern part had been affected by deep ploughing in the past (Fig 3.3).

THE EVIDENCE FROM THE BUILDINGS

The houses are provided with several rooms usually built around an inner court. The rooms are more or less rectangular having an interior space from 9 to 15 m². The walls are well constructed with chosen stones; especially noteworthy are the ones placed in doorways. The thickness of the walls range from 50 to 60 cm and they are orientated south/north and east/west with slight variations. The walls were built directly on the rock surface usually on a shelf at a higher level than the floors, a well known practice observed in many other sites of the same period (Karageorghis & Demas 1984, 6; Weinberg 1983, 54). Entrances were always placed at one end of the partition walls. It was common practice to level the natural rock in order to construct floors. In cases where some natural depressions occurred they were filled in with reddish *havara*. In one case sherds from large storage *pithoi* were used as flooring while in another slabs were used. Both methods of paving are known from Episkopi-Bamboula (Weinberg 1983, Pls 12b, 14c) the nearest LC site to Alassa and a sherd pavement is also known at Maa-Palaeokastro. Some of the houses have indications of enlargement and much material such as *pithos* sherds and querns has been reused for the construction of walls.

A large number of pits were found mainly in the courtyards. Some of them were used as receptacles for storage *pithoi*, others are basins constructed for various uses (Fig 3.3). One bottle-shaped pit was probably used for the storage of grain or other commodities. A well was also found but this is not yet completely excavated.

The evidence for the habitation zone of the settlement shows that in a comparatively small area there existed two sanctuaries and a household cult place. Although I have reservations concerning the identification of sanctuaries, I am inclined to acknowledge the presence of these three cult places based on generally accepted criteria (Renfrew 1985, 14–21). A short description of the architecture and associated finds will, I think, better clarify this question. In the NE corner of the excavation there is a screen wall within an enclosure not entirely excavated. Two terracotta bull figurines were found on the eastern part of the wall while other similar figurines were resting on the floor near the screen wall. Six finely-worked square stones were also found around the screen wall while a large fragmentary *pithos* lay on its side, on the southern part of the wall (Fig 3.4). The

Figure 3.4 The screen wall with some finds *in situ*.

collection of finds south of the screen wall includes a small finely worked bowl of steatite decorated with vertical grooves, two jugs of Plain White Wheel-Made II ware, a fine steatite spindle whorl, two circular loom weights, seven pounders, two platters of diabase, a whetstone, a pumice and the neck of a storage *pithos*. The whole arrangement reminds us of the sanctuary at Ayios Iakovos-Melia where instead of a *pithos* there was a bath-shaped terracotta basin (*SCE* IV.1C, 1 Fig 1). Since the excavation of the described complex at Alassa is not complete it is difficult to say whether this cult place forms part of a house, or is an independent structure and should be considered as a communal shrine (Renfrew 1985, 21–2).

The second case represents a curious complex of constructions and is one of the few instances where two building periods were apparent. The upper level consists of a sherd floor (Fig 3.5) enclosed by a single course of stones accidentally placed and it is adjoined by another semi-apsidal structure in which a large concentration of pottery was found including two strainer jugs and Plain White ware. North of the sherd floor the finds include a bronze axe, slag pieces and natural copper alloys. On the sherd floor itself we found the best preserved bull figurine (Fig 3.6) lying alongside a Plain White juglet and a diabase pounder. South of the sherd floor there is a rectangular pit which belongs to the earlier phase. This is flanked by a wall which encloses a rectangular space measuring 150 × 75 cm. In this space, which also belongs to the earliest phase, two Base Ring II bull figurines were found. West of the sherd floor there was a slab-floor on which we

Figure 3.5 The sherd floor with adjoining structures and two finds *in situ*.

Figure 3.6 Bull figurine found on the sherd floor.

found a haematite cylinder seal and a bronze handle. The architecture north of this complex is not well-preserved but the finds indicate that some kind of metallurgical activity was taking place. As we have no indication that the sherd floor and the adjoining structures might have belonged to a house we may presume that they were used as a popular shrine.

The third cult place was found in Room Π which most probably formed part of a multiroomed house built around a courtyard (Fig 3.7). In this room a group of five terracotta bull figurines were found along with a miniature bronze oxhide ingot (Hadjisavvas 1986, Pl 18.6), an incense burner, White Painted Wheelmade III and Plain White Wheelmade II

Figure 3.7 Room Π

pottery. It is worth noting here that the well-known bellows from Alassa were found in the adjoining Room Δ (Hadjisavvas 1986, Pl 16.3). In this case I could suggest the presence of a domestic cult place (Renfrew 1985, 402 Table 10.1).

Traces of metallurgical activity have been found at four different parts of the site. The bellows were found in a room adjacent to Room Π where the miniature bronze ingot was found. Slag and copper alloys such as sulphide ore were found elsewhere indicating that some primary smelting in small quantities was taking place within the settlement. The majority of finds consists of *pithoi*, large plain vessels and querns which attest to the agricultural occupation of the inhabitants.

THE EVIDENCE FROM THE BURIAL GROUNDS

As I have already mentioned, eight tombs situated within the settlement area have been excavated. Seven of them have common architectural features such as an irregular pit-shaped *dromos*, a more or less circular *stomion*, a bilobed chamber and, usually, an oblong rectangular basin sunk into the middle of the chamber. The tombs were used for a number of burials and the normal practice was to place the dead on the benches on both sides of the basin. The *stomia* were closed by a slab supported with river stones and in one case by a large sherd from a *pithos*. One of the tombs was provided with a rectangular pillar situated at the far side of the chamber opposite the entrance (Hadjisavvas 1986, Pl 18.1). So far this is a unique feature in a LC tomb. The remaining tomb which seems to be the earliest in date consists of a similar pit-shaped *dromos* and a plain beehive chamber. The *dromoi* of Tombs 5 and 6 adjoined each other but on a different level.

Only three of the tombs were found intact and any comparisons as far as their furniture is concerned should be limited to those. The richest of all was Tomb 3 (Fig 3.1) with 93 burial gifts including five of gold, three of bronze and a haematite cylinder seal. Tomb 1 contained 28 items, while the most elaborate in construction, Tomb 2, produced 18 items including one of gold. Mycenaean pottery was found only in Tombs 3 and 6 while Tombs 4 and 5 produced Syrian pottery, namely Red Lustrous ware. The sole evidence of literacy derives from two bone styli in Tombs 1 and 3 respectively (Hadjisavvas 1986, Pl 18.5).

CONCLUSIONS

This, in short, is all the evidence we have from both the excavated remains at the locality Pano Mandilaris and the surveyed area of Paliotaverna. Now to what extent we can reconstruct the everyday life, the socio-economic and religious aspects of the inhabitants, is, I believe, a matter of interpretation. No doubt the economy of the village was based on agriculture. The settlement is situated on a triangular plateau surrounded by a large territory of arable land and two rivers. This fact in association with the large number of querns and pounders found in the area of the settlement is convincing evidence for one of the main activities of the inhabitants. Animal breeding would be an inseparable occupation of the farmers and, when identified, the large number of animal bones discovered during the excavations will show which animals were there.

The second main occupation of the inhabitants was metallurgy and related activities such as mining and transportation. Although the locality Pano Mandilaris is not too far from the copper producing areas of Ayios Mamas and Yerasa, recent investigations undertaken by the University of Erlangen (Zwicker 1988) have shown that three stratified slag pieces found at Alassa contained a high proportion of arsenic bronze. This could probably be produced by the addition of an iron arsenide ore which can be mined at the locality Pefkos northeast of Limassol town and comparatively far away from Alassa. It seems that copper alloys were transported to Alassa from different areas. Most probably primary smelting took place at the area of the mines which also supplied the fuel. The produced metal-cake was then taken to the settlement for resmelting into suitable shapes and weight for trade. One possible further destination of the metal was the settlement at Episkopi-Bamboula which is the nearest LC II settlement and within easy access via the Kouris river route. Our suggestion made some years ago that the two settlements were part of a chain connecting the metal producing area of the lower hills of Troodos with the southern coast was supported in 1986 by the discovery of a LC II tomb half way between Alassa and Episkopi in the Kouris valley.

The production and trade in copper with all these complex operations could only be effective with division and specialization of labour. The different production units would be administered by a supreme authority or an organization consisting of the elite of this community. Class differentiation is obvious in LC communities and this is manifested in the form of very rich tombs such as those at Enkomi (*SCE* II, 569–73), Kalavassos-Ayios Dhimitrios (South & Todd 1985), Hala Sultan Tekke (*HST* 8, 169–213), Palaepaphos and elsewhere. Literacy along with the introduction of weights and the appearance of monumental buildings in the same period attests to this differentiation (Knapp 1986, 75–6). Some evidence for the division of labour at Alassa-Pano Mandilaris derives from the grave goods which hint at the occupation of the deceased: daggers for warriors, styli for the scribes and so on. Class differentiation is apparent in the case of the monumental building at the locality of Paliotaverna. There is little doubt about its use as a sanctuary and it is widely accepted that either the priest-king or the priesthood was in charge of the production and trade in copper and of any other important commodity in the region. No doubt this king or the upper class elite was exercising administrative authority over a prosperous community living at the lower settlement. The official cult was located in the monumental building which most probably served as the king's residence. It housed the treasury which contained the surplus of the accumulated production.

We may conclude from this evidence that the inhabitants of the settlement were involved in agriculture and metallurgy. They worshipped their deities both in popular shrines and in their spacious houses. The prevailing ritual artefact was the symbolic image of a bull modelled in terracotta figurines, inscribed on seals or impressed on pottery. Another symbolic artefact offered along with bull figurines was the ingot in miniature form which no doubt is related to a deity, protector of metal-working.

The material culture of the people is purely Cypriot and represents a development of the previous periods. The insignificant presence of foreign imports is an indication that the occupants experienced only interregional and not international trade.

The dead were buried in family chamber tombs with grave goods which sometimes included food offerings in bowls.

At the close of the Bronze Age and more precisely during the LC IIIA the settlement was abandoned. There is no evidence of violent destruction or fire and most of the household utensils were left behind to be rediscovered at the close of the 20th century.

LIST OF REFERENCES

Hadjisavvas, S. (1986) Alassa. A new Late Cypriote site. *RDAC*, 62–7.
Karageorghis, V. & M. Demas (1984) *Pyla-Kokkinokremmos. A Late 13th century B.C. Fortified Settlement in Cyprus*. Nicosia.
Knapp, B. (1986) *Copper Production and Divine Protection: Archaeology,*

Ideology and Social Complexity on Bronze Age Cyprus. (SIMA Pocket-book 42). Göteborg.
Negbi, O. (1986) The climax of urban development in Bronze Age Cyprus. *RDAC*, 97–122.
Renfrew, C. (1985) *The archaeology of cult: the sanctuary at Phylakopi, (BSA Supp. Vol 18)*. London.
South, A.K., & I.A. Todd (1985) In quest of the Cypriote copper traders: excavations at Ayios Dhimitrios. *Archaeology 38*, 40–7.
Weinberg, S.S. (1983) *Bamboula at Kourion: The Architecture*. Philadelphia.
Zwicker, U. (1988) Investigations on material from the excavations at Alassa. pers comm.

4
Maroni and the monuments

Gerald Cadogan
Culworth

The excavation at Maroni-Vournes (Fig 4.1) is not yet complete (Cadogan 1983; 1984; 1985; 1986; 1986a; 1987; 1988; Herscher 1984), but enough has been found to show that the site is of great interest for the history of Late Bronze Age society in Cyprus. Vournes and Kalavassos-Ayios Dhimitrios, barely two hours walk apart in adjacent valleys (Cadogan 1986a, 105 Fig 1), seem to have the two earliest monumental buildings in Cyprus, the Ashlar Building of Vournes and Building X of Ayios Dhimitrios (South, see below 315–24). On present evidence, they were both built, used and abandoned in the 13th century BC.

From a Maronite point of view, but constantly keeping Ayios Dhimitrios in mind, I shall discuss the following questions.

(1) What happened in and around the Ashlar Building?
(2) Why was it built at Vournes, when it was, and not somewhere else?
(3) What changes—or revolution—in the society, politics and economy of Cyprus does the appearance of this grand and expensive edifice suggest?
(4) Why was it abandoned at the end of LC II?
(5) How do these matters affect the history of the Late Bronze Age of Cyprus?

I am not sure that the answers will be satisfactory, except perhaps to show how much we are still trying to find out. Any explanations must make sense as much for Ayios Dhimitrios as for Vournes.

Finally, I shall discuss briefly the problem of why, if these are the earliest monumental buildings, they did not appear until LC II, when there had been similar buildings in Egypt and the Near East, and even on the island of Crete, for many centuries.

1. WHAT HAPPENED IN AND AROUND THE ASHLAR BUILDING?

Our present evidence continues to suggest that the Ashlar Building was built early in the 13th century (and possibly a little earlier than Building X,

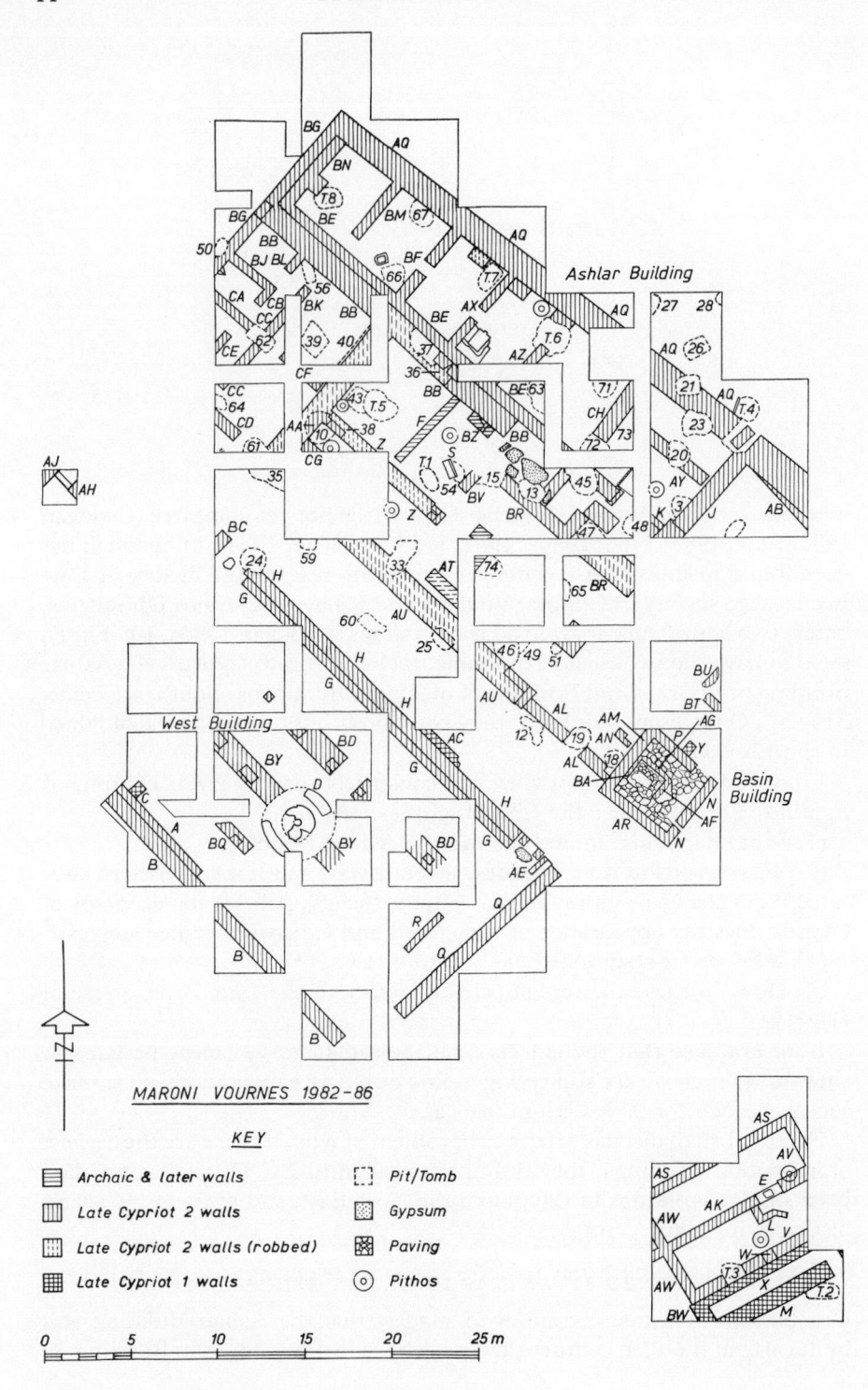

Figure 4.1 Maroni-Vournes general plan.

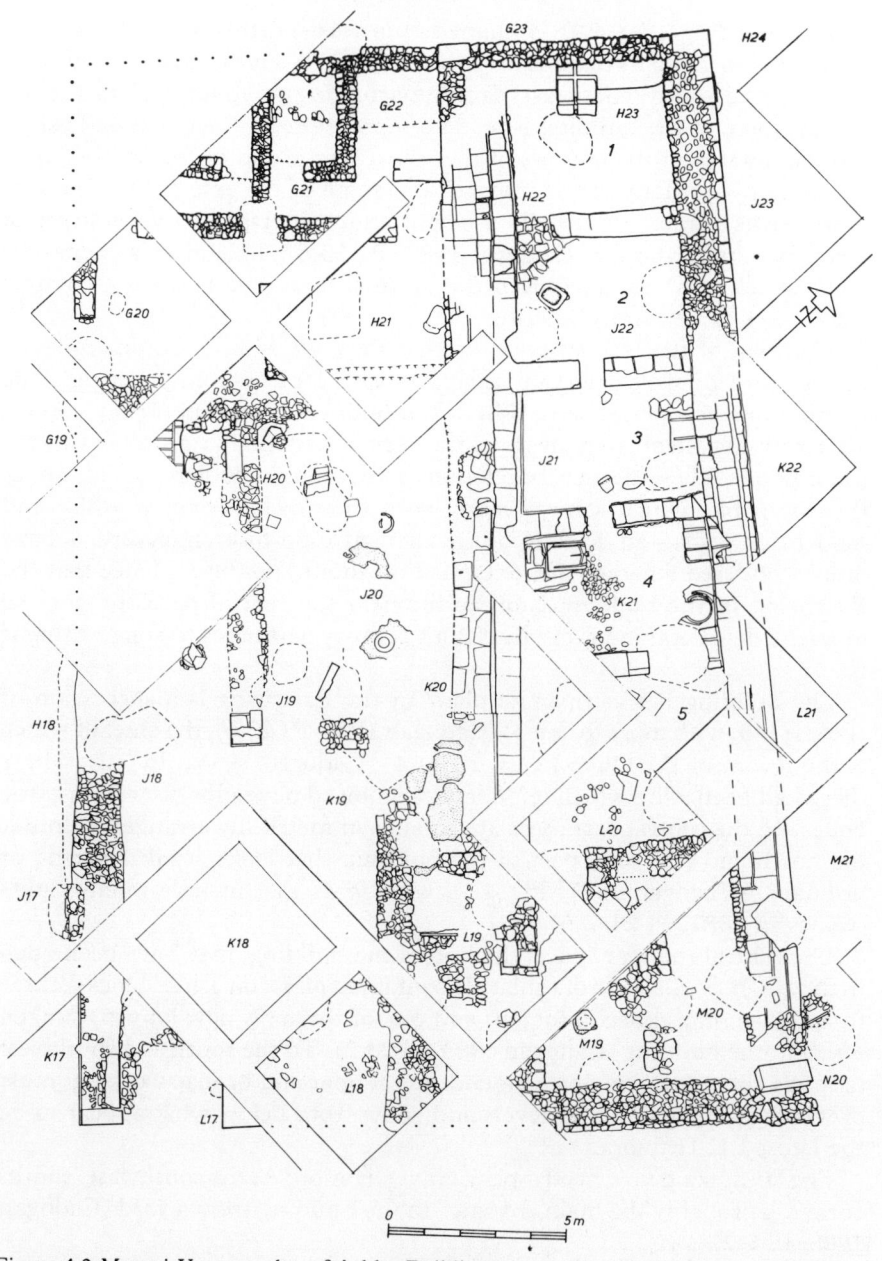

Figure 4.2 Maroni-Vournes plan of Ashlar Building.

though that issue needs more study (Cadogan 1988)). Its walls have been badly robbed, but some may have been standing above ground until as late as the last century. Enough of the building survived for an Archaic, Classical and Hellenistic shrine to be fitted inside it, and for robbing in early Roman times (Cadogan 1988).

The building (Fig 4.2) is aligned southeast-northwest, and measures about 30.5 m along its main (conventionally north-south) axis by about 20.5 m along the south (southeast) facade narrowing to about 18.5 m further north. Some of the building is made of exceptionally finely dressed ashlar blocks, notably at the corners of the south facade and in the central room or open space. Many of the internal and some of the external walls are of mud bricks, which are usually a bright white interspersed with layers of terra rossa mud mortar (Cadogan 1987, Pl 23.6). This gives a Siena-like look, which may not have been the original intention as there are ample traces of a white mud plastering.

The plan of the building was carried through with determination as a major—and doubtless labour-intensive—piece of civil engineering. The foundations show this best. Where the builders came upon deep tombs, after robbing them, they made extra deep foundations right down to the tomb floors. These deeper foundations sometimes include pieces of ashlar, then invisible, which shows—along with the juxtaposition of ashlar and mud brick walls—an eclectic or cavalier attitude to architecture. I have often wondered whether the juxtaposition should not be evidence that the East wing of the building is an addition to the central part but, for the moment, I see nothing more than 20th century aesthetics to suggest that it is.

The building has a tripartite plan. In the East wing is a succession of rooms (1–5, with more to come) (Cadogan 1987, Pl 23.6), the chief of which is the Room of the Olive Press (room 4) (Cadogan 1986a, Pl 7.2), where there had been a fire which left many carbonised olive pips, as well as cattle bones. In the central part there are small, symmetrically arranged rooms at the north end (the only part of the building that looks at all domestic or ordinary) (Cadogan 1987, Pl 24.3), with finds that include loomweights (Cadogan 1987, Pl 24.5, 6).

The central room or space, the hub of the building, may have been open to the air. Its walls were of ashlar. It contained *pithoi* on ashlar blocks (three to date; we may expect a fourth) and one of three (as now known) sunken *pithoi* in the building (Cadogan 1983, Pl 23.2). To the south and southwest of it has come the principal evidence for copper and bronze working, most of which is in clear LC II levels and some from below what appear to be the latest LC II floors.

The West wing now needs special investigation. At the southwest (south) corner is probably the main entrance to the building from a yard (Cadogan 1986, Pl 7.2).

Many of the walls are loadbearing. Some are even 2 m wide. So it is easy to imagine a building of two or more storeys. It would have been an imposing building that glared in the sun, standing out against the skyline on the low knoll of Vournes, particularly if we may imagine away the present carobs and olives that obstruct the view. But even if the trees were there in the 13th century BC, the Ashlar Building would have dominated its surroundings since soundings around Vournes suggest that it was in open ground that may have stretched as far as the presumed main settlement at Tsaroukas 500 m away.

The remains to the west of the Ashlar Building are taking shape as the West Building (Fig 4.1). It seems of similar size and alignment to the Ashlar Building. What gap in time, if any, there was between the construction of the two, we do not know and may never be able to tell. The West Building is not of ashlar, but of rough field stones, as is a wall, AL, tacked on to the southwest (south) corner of the Ashlar Building (Cadogan 1986, Pl 7.2). Ashlar blocks were used, however, in the internal walls of what seems to have been a four-aisled building (Cadogan 1987, Pl 24.8).

There is no evidence from the exiguous remains of floor deposits in the West Building to support the idea that it continued in use after the Ashlar Building. (One of the two fragmentary LC III deep bowls from Vournes is from an upper level in the West Building; the other was in a robbing trench in the Ashlar Building.) We may imagine then one or two buildings set apart on the low rise of Vournes that were in use for up to a century.

Nothing in the West Building yet indicates its use. Its manner of building could suggest it was subsidiary to the Ashlar Building, and its aisled plan that it might have been a storehouse but *pithos* sherds are rare—unlike in the Ashlar Building; the mill (Cadogan 1986, Pl 8.3), I am almost certain, was mediaeval or later.

As for the Ashlar Building its grandeur points to its having been the chief building of the region. The olive press and the *pithoi* suggest that it was involved in, and presumably in charge of, food production while if we had more loomweights we could argue that, in the ten months of the year not spent in making oil, textiles were made in the building (Cadogan 1987, 84). A stylus and pot- and loomweight-marks in Cypro-Minoan are some evidence of literacy.

The metal finds include debris from both smelting and melting, as Professors Muhly and Maddin kindly point out (pers comm). Their analyses of pieces, including some oxhide ingot fragments, show that it was Cypriot copper that was used, of the same group as at Ayios Dhimitrios, Maa and Pyla-Kokkinokremmos; but, Professor Muhly remarks, we have yet to find the Kalavassos mine's fingerprint. There are fragments of Canaanite jars, of Cypriot or Palestinian origin, but no positive evidence to show that Vournes was exporting copper or bronze.

Was the Ashlar Building a shrine, as it was in Archaic times? I find it tempting to think so, especially for its metal, and for general resemblances to Myrtou-Pigadhes in architecture, *pithoi* and the olive press, presses being known from shrines (*cf* Cadogan 1987, 83 and n 10). But it is not certain. (And if the Ashlar Building is a shrine, what are we to think then of Building X ?).

2. WHY WERE THE ASHLAR BUILDING AND THE WEST BUILDING BUILT AT VOURNES?

Part of the answer must lie in the connections with Kalavassos (on the assumption that there was the source of Maroni's copper). Part lies in the earlier history of Maroni.

Vournes and Tsaroukas by the sea and, probably, Kapsaloudhia 500 m inland from Vournes seem all to have been first used in LC IA (Johnson 1980; Herscher 1984; Cadogan 1984; 1988). They may be considered part of the expansion then on the South and East coasts (which is one of the few parts of the old gospels of Late Cypriot history not to have been demythologized). Tsaroukas and Kapsaloudhia have tombs, and Vournes was a settlement. (The pottery suggests links throughout the Mesaoria and as far as Morphou Bay, but noticeably with the South West (Herscher 1984)).

Tombs provide, at present, the principal evidence of the transition to LC II and for LC IIA; for LC IIB we have the Basin Building at Vournes (Cadogan 1986a, Pl 6.1) which had collapsed and gone out of use (being sealed by a LC II floor) before the Ashlar Building was built. More study of that building and its sequence is needed, and of the LC I—IIA—IIB progression at Vournes (by trials below the Ashlar Building's floors) and at Tsaroukas, where we want to know what settlement there was, or how much has survived erosion by the sea. Despite these gaps, we see that there was (a) a building unique in the whole East Mediterranean, of purpose still unknown (industrial? hygienic? religious?) but with metalworking debris on the floor of its basin to suggest that metalworking had been practised at Maroni for some time before the Ashlar Building. And (b) there is considerable evidence of wealth, in terms of imported Aegean pottery, Syro-Palestinian finds, gold jewellery, glass and faience, mostly coming from the tombs cleared by the British Museum at Tsaroukas and Vournes (Johnson 1980; Crouwel & Morris 1987).

So the sites were rich, and metal was already being worked, by the time the Ashlar Building was built. That seems sufficient explanation for putting it at Maroni. The choice of Vournes may have been governed by its being a low eminence, or by the former presence of the Basin Building, or because it was the place for metal working, or for other reasons to be discovered.

3. WHAT WERE THE NEEDS AROUND THE BEGINNING OF THE 13TH CENTURY BC THAT LED TO CHANGING THE FACE OF CYPRUS IN SUCH AN OSTENTATIOUS WAY?

The answer is not clear, but it is likely that Vournes and Ayios Dhimitrios were not alone. Other new monumental buildings of the time probably include places such as Myrtou-Pigadhes (du Plat Taylor & others 1957) and Toumba tou Skourou (Vermeule 1974) which, like Maroni and Ayios Dhimitrios are both near the copper supplies, while the evidence becomes stronger that this was the time of the burst of true urbanism (as against the proto-urbanism of LC I) (Negbi 1986), not least in Ayios Dhimitrios town.

If the power and demands, trade-led presumably, of the cities and settlements further away from the copper sources were great, that could well explain the need to control the country near the sources, for both food and metal. Hence the *pithoi* and olive press; hence the metal-working.

The relations between Vournes and Ayios Dhimitrios will be clearer when the excavator of Ayios Dhimitrios has spoken. The two big buildings are sufficiently similar in building techniques, size, plan and contents that they probably had similar functions. Whether they were in the charge of officials, or local dynasts, possibly related, and how they ranked against each other, who knows. Although Ayios Dhimitrios is close to the copper source and has a large town which presumably owed its existence to copper, some ore was brought still to Maroni for smelting. Finally, there is no necessity that Maroni was the principal port for Ayios Dhimitrios; nor can it be proved that it was not. The ancients did not always choose the most economical ways of doing things.

4. WHY WAS IT ABANDONED AT THE END OF THE LC II PERIOD?

We do not know why the Ashlar Building lay abandoned in LC III, as did Building X, but we may be sure that the particular needs they filled had ceased. If their main activity was the supervision of food and metal, that must have moved elsewhere. This suggests, if we assume that the Kalavassos mine continued to produce (which may not have been the case, the mining industry being famously prone to slumps and booms), that control, now at a distance, passed to Larnaca Bay cities that still flourished such as Hala Sultan Tekke and Kition, and possibly even to Enkomi. That means greater centralisation in LC III, for which there may have been political or military reasons. The LC IIC decentralisation to Maroni and Ayios Dhimitrios should reflect prosperity and security. Even if prosperity continued into LC III, security probably did not.

5. HOW DOES THIS ELUCIDATE THE HISTORY OF LATE BRONZE AGE CYPRUS?

Although we do not know nearly enough of the patterns of society and settlement in LC II and LC III to put the changes in their true context, the rise and fall of the Ashlar Building and of Building X are firm facts. Their appearance does suggest an explosive growth in the 13th century, a time of rising prosperity when the official control (and I do not think we may be more precise than that) of copper and of food near their sources became essential. The growth probably came from the development, even a boom, of the copper industry which we may be able to fix more precisely in place and time in a few years when metal analysis gives a clearer and synoptic view of the fluctuations in copper supply in the whole East Mediterranean. The hints to the effect that Cyprus became the major source only from the 14th century—the time of the first metalworking at Vournes—provide the sort of background we are seeking.

The *pithoi* in the two buildings and at the two sites in North West Cyprus emphasize what is so often forgotten in giving socio-economic explanations, the ever-present need for food (not for export). Their large number is a counterweight to the copper, since as much—if not more—of the power of these grand buildings must have rested on the land that supplied the food, as on copper trading. Their appearance, and any growth of the towns around them, shows the consolidation of rural power (tithe-based perhaps) that has to be now a major feature of the economic growth of the 13th century BC.

Similar phenomena may be seen in Minoan Crete. Around 1900 BC (but probably after some smaller precursors) the buildings had appeared that we know as 'palaces' (Cadogan 1986b) but functioning more like monasteries. Their power was based in land and farming, Crete being poor in metal. The importance of the land is still more obvious with the arrival of dominant country houses, about a score by now, in Late Minoan I which became immediately the local centres of the administration, society and the economy—and had plenty of *pithoi*. In Cyprus we are still talking of a few buildings only, whose relations with their settlements is not yet clear. But the general analogy is helpful, especially in the primacy of *pithoi*.

Those working in Cyprus and Crete often ponder why Cyprus did not develop anything like these grand buildings until 600 years or so after the first Minoan palaces. While the islands are similar in size and structure, Cyprus has copper and is closer to, and therefore could have been more easily influenced by, Egypt and the Near East, with their rich menu of palaces, temples and palace-temples. It is easy enough to see the growth of Cypriot trade in the later Middle Bronze Age as contributing to the LC I beginnings of urbanism along the South and East coasts. But why did the equivalents of the palaces or country houses take so long to appear?

Part of our difficulty in explaining this is that we know so little of EC and MC settlements. Almost all the evidence for the periods is from tombs. Their contents show a slow progress of technology and sophistication: the first cylinder seal belongs to the 16th century (Merrillees 1986; see below 153–9) and the first clay tablet only after 1500; faience is restricted to a few imports in EC and MC; metal-working and pottery were conservative, in contrast to the rapidly changing dynamic of Crete; and we cannot identify places of pilgrimage. The picture is of a slow and self-sufficient rural society, which started to move in LC I when new settlements were founded —the stage Crete passed in Early Minoan II.

The new LC I settlements brought war and forts (Åström 1972); but the major events of planting new towns and big buildings in the countryside —the real change to Mediterranean urbanism—did not come for two or three centuries. The leap to monumental buildings was doubtless influenced by politics (which we can only guess at) and was probably the decision of one person—since it is hard to see this great move as the result of a committee. Once work began, the schemes had their own momentum, in the marshalling of labour and ordering of plans and rations and creating a group of master masons expert in ashlar. Whoever was in charge would have been a person of strength, even magic, whether that came from the sword, or lineage, or religion, or happening to own the Kalavassos mine. He or she had the tough test of dealing with builders, and could even have sent them to Syria to see how ashlar was made there, or brought one from Syria to teach them. Above all, the *pithoi* had to be kept full.

ACKNOWLEDGMENTS

The excavation at Maroni-Vournes is authorised and helped constantly by Dr Vassos Karageorghis and the Department of Antiquities, sponsored by the Department of Classics of the University of Cincinnati and the British School at Athens, and supported principally by the British Academy, the Institute for Aegean Prehistory, the A.G. Leventis Foundation and the Trustees of the Semple Classics Fund.

The account appears with the permission of the Managing Committee of the British School at Athens; I first discussed the differences between Cyprus and Crete at the Prehistoric Society's conference on 'Across the Wine-Dark Sea' in London in April 1987.

LIST OF REFERENCES

Åström, P. (1972) Some aspects of the Late Cypriot I period. *RDAC*, 46–57.
Cadogan, G. (1983) Maroni I. *RDAC*, 153–62.
Cadogan, G. (1984) Maroni and the Late Bronze Age of Cyprus, in *Cyprus at the Close of the Late Bronze Age* (eds. V. Karageorghis & J.D. Muhly) 1–10. Nicosia.
Cadogan, G. (1985) Maroni, in *Archaeology in Cyprus 1960–1985* (ed. V. Karageorghis) 195–7. Nicosia.
Cadogan, G. (1986) Maroni II. *RDAC*, 40–4.
Cadogan, G. (1986a) Maroni in Cyprus, between West and East. *Acts 1986*, 23–8.
Cadogan, G. (1986b) Why was Crete different?, in *The End of the Early Bronze Age in the Aegean (Cincinnati Classical Studies n.s. 6)* (ed. G. Cadogan) 153–71. Leiden.
Cadogan, G. (1987) Maroni III. *RDAC*, 81–4.
Cadogan, G. (1988) Maroni IV. *RDAC*, in press.
Crouwel, J.H. & Morris, C.E. (1987) An early Mycenaean fish krater from Maroni, Cyprus, *BSA 82*, 37–46.
Herscher, E. (1984) The pottery of Maroni and regionalism in Late Bronze Age Cyprus, in *Cyprus at the Close of the Late Bronze Age* (eds. V. Karageorghis & J.D. Muhly) 23–8, Nicosia.
Johnson, J. (1980) *Maroni de Chypre (SIMA 59)*. Göteborg.
Merrillees, R.S. (1986) A 16th century BC tomb group from central Cyprus with links both East and West. *Acts 1986*, 114–48.
Negbi, O. (1986) The climax of urban development in Bronze Age Cyprus. *RDAC*, 97–121.
Taylor, du Plat J. *et al* (1957) *Myrtou-Pigadhes*. Oxford.
Vermeule, E.T. (1974) *Toumba tou Skourou*. Boston.

5
Society and settlements in Late Cypriot III

Maria Iacovou
Bank of Cyprus Cultural Foundation, Nicosia

As long as the establishment of periods in archaeology stems from a need to define major socio-cultural changes, and if these periods along with their respective subdivisions are still the artificial turning points they were meant to be, then I hope that this paper will be received as a contribution towards a meaningful subdivision of LC III and more so, towards a definition of LC IIIB, the final phase of the Cypriot Bronze Age (Sjöqvist 1940, 125). And, since I am convinced that the late Einar Gjerstad maintained a thoroughly correct viewpoint regarding LC IIIB and its characteristic pottery—which *he* christened Proto-White Painted ware (Gjerstad 1944, 75)—this paper is humbly dedicated to the memory of the father of Cypriot Archaeology.

When does LC III begin and when should it be subdivided, if need be? Following a horizon of apparently contemporary catastrophies that left both coastal and inland sites in ruins at the end of the 13th century BC (Karageorghis 1982, 82), we have, I would think, good reason to consider this point in time as the end of LC IIC, the phase that is identified with —and here I quote the title of a recent article—"The Climax of Urban Development in Bronze Age Cyprus" (Negbi 1986, 97). The new era is one in which no new sites were founded, while some of the thriving LC II settlements, like Kalavassos-Aghios Dhimitrios (South 1984) and Maroni-Vournes (Cadogan 1984), were abandoned.

Thus, the first significant characteristic of the opening phase of LC III is that settlements drop in number (Negbi 1986, 99, Table 1), but they do *not* shift. Nor have we observed, in association with sites rehabilitated in LC IIIA, a shift to new burial grounds. On the contrary, there are numerous instances of LC I and LC II traditional type tombs being re-used for LC IIIA interments (eg *SCE* IV.1D, 695–6; Maier & Wartburg 1985, 146).

This indicates that the society in the rebuilt towns was not compelled to disassociate itself from the burial grounds, or burial practices of old, and felt no qualms against re-using earlier tombs.

The architecture in the reconstructed settlements may be less grand at times, but since the introduction of ashlar masonry is now safely dated back to LC IIC (Negbi 1986, 108), LC IIIA does not present us with striking architectural innovations: certainly, no Mycenaean-type 'megara' have been located.

The major innovations of LC IIIA seem confined to the field of metallurgy and ceramics: "the explosive outburst" (Snodgrass 1981, 133) of the former—in a copper producing island where the history of its earlier bronze industry has been described as 'conservative and rather uninspiring' (Snodgrass 1980, 341)—is as striking a change as the appearance of locally produced Myc IIIC pottery (Maier 1973, 74; Jones *et al* 1986, 595, 609). For both, however, the impetus and the prototypes have a common origin :the Aegean.

Thus, while Base Ring and White Slip wares, the 400-year old ceramic trade-marks of Bronze Age Cyprus, dropped quickly out of circulation, a select group of local Myc IIIC shapes (for which I also use the term Cypro-Mycenaean IIIC) developed alongside a loosely defined entity, called Decorated Late Cypriot III (Jones *et al* 1986, 595). Cypro-Mycenaean IIIC pottery represents the tableware of the newcomers credited with the Achaean Colonization of Cyprus in the 12th century BC.

The remarkable consistency observed in the development of this local Myc IIIC pottery along the lines of its Aegean counterpart (French & Åström 1980, 268), suggests that sea routes were kept open and that there was a steady flow of settlers arriving in the island in the course of LC IIIA.

Let us stress, however, the following two points:

(1) local Myc IIIC has never been found in separate clusters in either settlements or graves (with the sole exception of a tomb at Palaepaphos-Kaminia: Maier 1973, 72);

(2) ceramic analysis has shown that Decorated Late Cypriot III and Cypro-Mycenaean IIIC could be made from the same clay (Jones *et al* 1986, 605). It is, therefore, not an inconceivable hypothesis that they were also produced in the same workshops.

So the Achaeans had come, and they had come to stay, but they did not uproot the indigenous society and apparently they did not exercise political control in LC IIIA. Maybe they were not strong enough to do so; maybe this was not a conscious goal, yet.

But the coexistence of dissimilar ethnic elements in LC IIIA must have been a fragile affair and the destruction levels observed at LC IIIA sites (eg Furumark 1965, 114–16; *Enkomi* 494–5) reflect a turbulent phase and an unstable political and economic substratum.

Thus, one after the other, nearly all settlements rebuilt in LC IIIA—with the exception of Kition (*Kition V* 277–80) and Palaepaphos (Maier &

Wartburg 1985, 152)—were destroyed or abandoned: Sinda and Hala Sultan Tekke, Athienou and Apliki, Maa-Palaeokastro and Bamboula at Kourion; they all ceased to be inhabited (eg Karageorghis 1982, 112–13).

Because they were deserted after destruction, or simply deserted, these sites remained stratigraphically intact. They avoided the inevitable obliteration that continuity of habitation causes, especially when extensive remodellings take place, or cleaning of grounds for new buildings.

This is the one fundamental difference between LC IIIA settlements as we know them today, and the new settlements founded immediately after, which we know hardly at all. From this stems the lack of balance between settlement and cemetery evidence that characterizes, not only LC IIIB —the final phase of the Cypriot Bronze Age—but the ensuing Early Iron Age as well (eg *SCE* I 264, 276; *SCE* II 138–41, 455–9).

The fact that settlements dating to LC IIIB are not readily visible, has rendered LC IIIB a disputed and much misunderstood phase; to the extent that this apparent absence of settlements has led some scholars (eg Kling 1986, 767, n 1808) to compress the material culture of LC IIIB to LC IIIA and to explain it as tomb and sanctuary objects. By the same reasoning, however, one will have to treat accordingly the massive evidence of the 300-year long Cypro-Geometric period, known almost exclusively through cemetery evidence (eg *SCE* IV.2 1–3, 428–48).

The new sites to which the population shifted after the gradual abandonment of LC IIIA settlements, and along with them the two that survived the transition (ie Kition and Palaepaphos), were destined to become the major urban centres of Iron Age Cyprus; indeed, in Assyrian records of the early 7th century BC (Snodgrass 1988, 9–10) they were already acknowledged as the island's established city-kingdoms (Tatton-Brown 1984, 73).

One, therefore, can hardly over-estimate the implications of the changes that characterize LC IIIB, for it is defined as a time when the habitation pattern of the island changed drastically; a time when all earlier burial grounds—most of which had been continuously used from LC I to LC IIIA—were altogether abandoned in favour of new cemetery sites; a time when people refused to use any of the pre-existing graves, and known burial practices changed, so that the traditional Cypriot tomb was abandoned in favour of the chamber-tomb with a *dromos*; a time when the burial assemblages of the newly dug graves no longer combined Decorated Late Cypriot III and local Myc IIIC pottery, but are instead distinguished by the sheer predominance of a new, uniform ware: Proto-White Painted (hereafter PWP).

Before a brief survey of the most significant LC IIIB sites, it is necessary to stress that the final stage of LC IIIA is often assigned to LC IIIB (eg Kling 1986, 765–73). This late stage in LC IIIA was not reached by many sites other than Kition, Enkomi and Palaepaphos; Sinda for instance had certainly been abandoned early in LC IIIA (Iacovou 1988, *Introduction*). With respect to pottery, the final stage of LC IIIA is characterized by the *floruit* of local Myc IIIC open shapes (skyphoi and cups) decorated with wavy lines (Karageorghis 1982, 110). The style is not particular to Cyprus. In the Aegean it occurs in LH IIIC Middle as the 'Granary Style' and it is also well attested in LH IIIC Late and Submycenaean deposits (Mountjoy 1986, 156, Figs 254, 286).

It is, therefore, erroneous, in my opinion, to take Cypro-*Myceanaean* IIIC "wavy line" pottery out of context, to rename it, as Furumark did, "early PWP" or "PWP I" (Furumark 1965, 115; *Enkomi* 495) and, to confuse it with PWP shapes of a distinct profile and fabric—such as the deep bowl and the cup—because the latter may also employ the wavy line in their decoration (*cf* Benson 1973, Pl 16). As a matter of fact, while PWP cups are almost always decorated with wavy lines, PWP deep bowls seldom, if ever, are (*cf* Pieridou 1973, Pls 4, 6). Enkomi Areas I and III were abandoned when wavy line style pottery was in use but before the appearance of PWP pottery (*Enkomi* 492, 534, 855). Thus, following the destruction of Enkomi level IIIC, the population shifted down to the plain of Salamis.

SETTLEMENTS AND CEMETERIES OF THE LC IIIB PERIOD

We owe our knowledge of the LC IIIB settlement of Salamis to the careful recordings of the French team. They found PWP in association with a hearth during deep soundings in the 1960s (Yon 1980, 75). Other soundings to the north-west of the basilica of Campanopetra (Calvet 1980, 116, Fig 2) and below the Temple of Zeus (Yon 1980, 77 Figs 2-3) also produced PWP and, as it is distinctly reported, the construction of Hellenistic and Roman buildings obliterated the earlier strata and also destroyed LC IIIB and CG I tombs. In the summer of 1974 the excavation of a sanctuary, which was established in LC IIIB, was under way (Yon 1980, 76, Pl 4), and directly south of it, a section of the city wall was also found to have originated in the 11th century BC (Jehasse 1980, 150, 152).

I will go a step further into probability and suggest that the new sanctuary at Salamis was meant to replace the Sanctuary of the Ingot God, the only building at Enkomi to have been rehabilitated for a short while after the rest of the town lay deserted (Iacovou 1988, *Introduction*). Floors I-III in the Sanctuary (Courtois 1971) contain PWP pottery in a rare association with LC IIIA wares, a fact that indicates a transitional or early LC IIIB phase.

Certainly, it was not the inhabitants of Salamis who rode up to Gastria to bury their dead in the necropolis of Alaas. Alaas remains the most extensive and exclusively LC IIIB necropolis (Karageorghis 1975, 1-4, Figs 1,3). It ceased to be used before the transition to early CG I and it is, therefore, a single-phase burial site, a fact that allows me to hope that it served a single-phase settlement: one, that if located someday will supply tangible evidence for a LC IIIB township.

Still, from Alaas we learn that the construction of the chamber-tomb with a *dromos* was not learnt overnight; it rather underwent gradual development. We also learn the full range of the rich and imaginative PWP repertoire (Karageorghis 1975, 47–56). Lapithos to the north (Ohnefalsch-Richter 1893, Pl. 48), Idalion inland (Karageorghis 1965, 185–99), Soloi to the west (*Chronique 1973*, 662 Fig 92) and even the Komissariato sanctuary in Limassol (Karageorghis 1977, 65) have also provided evidence for LC IIIB occupation, while at Kition (Area II) the transition to LC IIIB occurs after the destruction of Floor III (*Kition V*, 266).

At Palaepaphos, as at Kition, one assumes that the settlement did not shift to a new location. But the shift of the town's cemeteries from Kaminia, Mantissa and Evreti to Xerolimni, Xylino and Lakkos tou Skarnou, and from there to the major CG cemeteries at Skales and Hassan Agha has been admirably illustrated (Maier & Karageorghis 1984, 120–9).

Furthermore, at Palaepaphos we get a glimpse of the archaeologically elusive transition from LC IIIA to LC IIIB. Carefully collected data shows that before the final abandonment of LC IIIA burial sites, like Kaminia, some PWP stirrup-jars and juglets, together with one or two decorated LC III vases were the only gifts deposited in earth burials or pit graves (Maier 1973, 76). This unusual evidence indicates that impoverished and strained conditions must have prevailed at the end of LC IIIA and the inception of LC IIIB.

I will finally stop at Kourion where, I believe, the Enkomi-Salamis model is repeated. The settlement at Bamboula behind the hills of Episkopi was abandoned towards the end of LC IIIA. What J.L. Benson once described as the pottery of a LC IIIB stratum (1972, 45, 54) has since been correctly identified as White Painted Wheelmade III or White Painted ware (Adelman 1976, 283–5).

Kaloriziki, the burial site below the bluff of Kourion (Benson 1973) was in use from the very beginning of CG I; only the famous Tomb 40 belongs to LC IIIB (Iacovou 1988, *Introduction*). There is, however, much more PWP material in the area which is unfortunately the product of illicit excavations (eg *Chronique 1975*, 825, Figs 39, 44).

I maintain, therefore, that the settlement shifted in LC IIIB from Bamboula to the Kourion bluff where it continued to expand and prosper down to the Early Christian Era. Just as at Salamis, the construction of monumental edifices of the Hellenistic and Roman city, which have indeed justifiably preoccupied all excavators, must be responsible for the obliteration of earlier strata. However, there remain several unexcavated areas on the acropolis of Kourion.

CONCLUSIONS

LC IIIB shows that the destruction and abandonment of LC IIIA settlements is synonymous with the end of the political and economic structure of Bronze Age Cyprus. LC IIIB is on the one hand, a smooth transition to the Early Iron Age culture of Cyprus (Coldstream 1985, 48); but, on the other, it is the product of an intense amalgamation process that occurred in LC IIIA. With respect to pottery, the end result of this amalgamation was PWP, a ware that healed the existing ceramic dichotomy (or, even better, polymorphy). It was, in fact, the only local decorated ware produced in LC IIIB.

On the socio-political level, the end result was a new society, the material culture of which—in particular the almost exclusively Mycenaean ancestry of PWP shapes (eg Benson 1973, 23; Pieridou 1973, 108)—suggests that the Aegean element had far from been absorbed into the indigenous population.

This situation is classified by comparison with a contemporary phenomenon on the nearby Levantine coast: the Philistine culture. The same basic factor generated the process which caused the production of Philistine pottery in the Levant and of PWP pottery in Cyprus: it was the arrival of people of Aegean origin who managed to organize a local manufacture of their pottery (Gitin & Dothan 1987, 201–20).

Philistine pottery was the result of an amalgamation which took place early in the 12th century BC, following the production of local Myc IIIC pottery in the midst of indigenous Canaanite fabrics (Mazar 1985, 102–7). By the 10th century BC, however, Philistine culture became assimilated with the surrounding Canaanite cultures (Dothan 1982, 296) and nothing survived of the heritage of the Aegean settlers who had reached the Syro-Palestinian coast in the 12th century BC.

Not so in Cyprus, where the Greek-speaking successors of the "Mycenaeans" appear to be closely associated with the dissolution of the old political system and the foundation of new seats of power in the 11th century BC. Their supremacy over the indigenous population may have led some of the latter to withdraw to separate enclaves, like Amathus, and eventually to become known to classical authors as "Eteo-Cypriotes". Nevertheless, the Early Iron Age material culture and burial customs of these "Eteo-Cypriotes", in particular that of CG I-II (1050–850 BC), does not distinguish them from the rest of the island's population.

Thus, by the mid 11th century BC, at the dawn of its Iron Age, Cyprus emerged with a solid, homogeneous culture and a society which, as it grew literate, adopted the Cypro-Syllabic script to write the Greek language (Tatton-Brown 1984, 73–4). By the mid 9th century BC when the Phoenicians first and the Assyrians, Egyptians and Persians afterwards began exercising political control over part, or the whole of Cyprus, *Hellenization* was no longer a reversable process.

Elusive though the townships of the first Greek-Cypriots may be today, their establishment in the course of the 11th century BC provided the natural cradles where Herodotus' Κύπριος Χαρακτήρ came to be.

LIST OF REFERENCES

Adelman, C.M. (1976) Review of Benson (1972) *JNES 35*, 283–5.
Benson, J.L. (1972) *Bamboula at Kourion: The Necropolis and the Finds*. Philadelphia.
Benson, J.L. (1973) *The Necropolis of Kaloriziki (SIMA 36)*. Göteborg.
Cadogan, G. (1984) Maroni and the Late Bronze Age of Cyprus, in *Cyprus at the Close of the Late Bronze Age* (eds. V. Karageorghis & J.D. Muhly) 1–10. Nicosia.
Calvet, Y. (1980) Sur certains rites funeraires á Salamine de Chypre, in *Colloques Internationaux du CNRS. Salamine de Chypre: Histoire et Archéologie*, 115–21. Paris.
Coldstream, N. (1985) Archaeology in Cyprus 1960–1985: the Geometric and Archaic periods, in *Archaeology in Cyprus 1960–1985* (ed. V. Karageorghis) 45–59. Nicosia.
Courtois, J-C. (1971) Le sanctuaire du Dieu au l'Ingot d'Enkomi-Alasia, *Alasia I*, (C.F.A. Schaeffer) 151–325. Paris.
Dothan, T. (1982) *The Philistines and their Material Culture*. New Haven.
French, E. & Åström, P. (1980) A colloquium on Late Cypriote III Sites. *RDAC* 267–9.
Furumark, A. (1965) The excavations at Sinda. Some historical results. *Op Ath 6*, 99–116.
Gitin, S. & Dothan, T. (1987) The excavation at Tel Miqne-Ekron. *Bibl A* 197–222.
Gjerstad, E. (1944) The initial date of the Cypriote Iron Age. *Op Arch 3*, 73–106.
Iacovou, M. (1988) *The Pictorial Pottery of Eleventh Century B.C. Cyprus (SIMA 78)*. Göteborg.
Jehasse, J. (1980) Le rampart méridional de Salamine, in *Colloques Internationaux du CRNS. Salamine de Chypre: Histoire et Archéologie*, 147–52. Paris.
Jones, R.E. et al (1986) *Greek and Cypriot Pottery: A Review of Scientific Studies (BSA Fitch Laboratory Occasional Paper 1)* Athens.
Karageorghis, V. (1965) Idalion—"Ayios Georghios", Tombe 2, in *Nouveaux Documents pour l'Etude du Bronze Récent á Chypre* 185–99. Paris.
Karageorghis, V. (1975) *Alaas. A Protogeometric Necropolis in Cyprus*. Nicosia.
Karageorghis, V, (1977) *Two Cypriote Sanctuaries at the End of the Cypro-Archaic Period*. Rome.
Karageorghis, V. (1982) *Cyprus from the Stone Age to the Romans*. London.
Kling, B. (1986) *Mycenaean III C:1b and Related Pottery in Cyprus*. Ann Arbor.
Maier, F-G. (1973) Evidence for Mycenaean settlement at Old Paphos. *Acts 1973*, 68–78.
Maier, F-G. & Karageorghis, V. (1984) *Paphos. History and Archaeology*. Nicosia.
Maier, F-G. & Wartburg, M-L von (1985) Reconstructing history from the earth, c. 2800 B.C.-1600 A.D. Archaeology at Palaepaphos, 1960–1985, in *Archaeology in Cyprus 1960–1985* (ed. V. Karageorghis) 142–72. Nicosia.
Mazar, A. (1985) The emergence of the Philistine material culture. *Isr Expl J 35*, 95–107.
Mountjoy, P. (1986) *Mycenaean Decorated Pottery: A Guide to Identification (SIMA 73)*. Göteborg.
Negbi, O. (1986) The climax of urban development in Bronze Age Cyprus. *RDAC,* 97–121.

Ohnefalsch-Richter, M. (1893) *Kypros, die Bibel und Homer*. Berlin.
Pieridou, A. (1973) *Ο Πρωτογεωμετρικοσ ρψθμοσ εη κψπρω*. Athens.
Sjöqvist, E. (1940) *Problems of the Late Cypriote Bronze Age*. Stockholm.
South, A. (1984) Kalavasos—*Ayios Dhimitrios* and the Late Bronze Age of Cyprus, in *Cyprus at the Close of the Late Bronze Age* (eds. V. Karageorghis & J.D. Muhly) 11–18. Nicosia.
Snodgrass, A. (1980) Iron and early metallurgy in the Late Bronze Age, in *The Coming of the Age of Iron* (eds. A. Wertime & J.D. Muhly) 335–74. New Haven.
Snodgrass, A. (1981) Early iron swords in Cyprus. *RDAC*, 129–34.
Snodgrass, A. (1988) *Cyprus and early Greek history. (The Bank of Cyprus Cultural Foundation Fourth Annual Lecture)*. Nicosia.
Tatton-Brown, V. (1984) Archaic Cyprus 750–475 B.C., in *Footprints in Cyprus* (ed. D. Hunt) 73-91. London.
Yon, M. (1980) La fondation de Salamine, in *Colloques Internationaux du CNRS. Salamine de Chypre: Histoire et Archéologie*. 71–80. Paris.

POSTER SUMMARY

6
Prehistoric food plants

S. Colledge
London

For many of the excavated sites in Cyprus there are lists of plant species which have been identified in prehistoric contexts. The plant record for the island begins in the Neolithic. Ancient charred plant remains recovered from the earliest sites include the primitive wheat species, hulled barley, and several of the legume crops. The archaeobotanical reports for the prehistoric sites vary in the amount of information they detail with regards recovery methods, sampling techniques and seed identification criteria. It is apparent, however, that for all the sites there are great differences in procedures undertaken to investigate environmental evidence. The prime aims of archaeobotanical research are: to document chronological changes in the plant based economy; to assess the relative importance of certain crop plants; and to describe the crop husbandry practices for particular periods. Any quantitative intersite comparison designed to investigate these aspects of the prehistoric plant record requires a standardisation of the archaeobotanical results. For Cyprus such a study has not been possible beyond a very general level because of the inadequacies outlined above. One method which allowed comparison of the diversified results and thereby a limited assessment of the economic importance of crop species was that of 'presence analysis'. It is suggested that a standardisation of methodology is required so as to produce results which will allow for more rigorous statistical analyses. Work which is currently being undertaken in Greece provides examples of procedures which could be followed in Cyprus (Jones 1981; 1983; 1987).

Three sites in the south western part of the island have been investigated by the author; Lemba-Lakkous, Kissonerga-Mosphilia and Kissonerga-Mylouthkia. The first two sites produced charred plant material which was poorly preserved. These assemblages highlighted the problems of differential preservation and subsequent biases in the prehistoric plant record. The quantities of remains retrieved from the site of Kissonerga-Mylouthkia were far greater and they were in an excellent state of preservation. The crop plants present at Mylouthkia include; *Triticum dicoccum* (emmer wheat), *Triticum monococcum* (einkorn wheat), *Hordeum sativum* (barley), *Secale cereale* (rye), *Avena* sp. (oats), *Lens culinaris* (lentil), *Pisum* sp. (pea), *Cicer arietinum* (chick pea), *Linum* sp. (flax), *Olea* sp. (olive), *Ficus carica* (fig), *Vitis vinifera* (grape) and *Pistacia* sp. (pistachio).

At Kissonerga-Mosphilia the flotation process is fully integrated within the excavation programme. The flotation machine permits large scale recovery of charred remains. There is a greater control over the retrieval of adequate plant material and the residues from the flotation process can be sorted for small items such as bones, metal objects and chipped stone tools which may otherwise have been overlooked during excavation.

LIST OF REFERENCES

Jones, G.E.M. (1981) Crop processing at Assiros Toumba: a taphonomic study. *ZfA 15*, 105–11.

Jones, G.E.M. (1983) *The Use of Ethnographic and Ecological Models in the Interpretation of Archaeological Plant Remains: Case Studies from Greece.* Unpublished Ph.D dissertation. University of Cambridge.

Jones, G.E.M. (1987) A statistical approach to the archaeological identification of crop processing. *JA Scien 14*, 311–23.

POSTER SUMMARY

7
Prehistoric Cypriot building traditions and methods

Gordon D. Thomas
University of Edinburgh

The architectural or building traditions of a society reflect many aspects of that society's history, socio-economic structure and environment. The form that these buildings took can be established with some degree of certainty through a study of the archaeological evidence that is available. In particular, excavations on the Chalcolithic sites of Kissonerga-Mosphilia and Lemba-Lakkous have provided a wealth of information on buildings of that period. A consideration of past environmental conditions combined with the experimental reconstruction of one of these buildings is under way and will help establish the architectural forms that existed then as well as helping with our interpretation of site formation. A consideration of these different architectural forms within their cultural setting is also possible.

The development of differentiated contemporary buildings on the same site during the Middle Chalcolithic period must reflect great social change. Earlier periods are characterised by small replicated building units, for example Area 1 at Lemba, with little or no differentiation and repeated similarity of function. The Middle Chalcolithic, as exemplified by periods 2 and 3 at Lemba and period 3 at Mosphilia saw the development of more specialised building complexes with larger elaborate structures and smaller subsidiary special function buildings. It is suggested that this reflects a major reorientation within society with structures like Building Unit 3 at Mosphilia pointing to the emergence, possibly, of more complex social and economic systems involving redistribution or specialisation for example. The artefactual evidence also suggests major changes within society with a concentration and *floruit* of the figurative industry, the elaboration and skill demonstrated in the ground stone tool manufacture, and the craftmanship and quality reflected in the pottery industry. Similar changes are also recorded at other sites of the period, for example at Souskiou. All this speaks of a society in which the formalisation of the social order and the development of hierarchical structures are reflected in the artistic elaboration of artefactual symbols and in the physical structure of the village.

As far as the developed building types are concerned, the emergence of a unique and distinctive type which is represented at both Lemba and Mosphilia is interesting. The size of these structures which is often in excess of 10 m (diam), the quality and regularity of the constructional details, for example the walls and floor, and the regularity of their plan suggests that we may be looking at formal structures which serve a specific role within the community. Whatever that role may be is problematic and can only be hinted at through further research; however, it is not unrealistic to suggest that we can see here the emergence of a true architectural form.

POSTER SUMMARY

8
Topological analysis of an architectural element

Kenneth W. Schaar
Louisiana Tech University, Ruston

Principles of mathematical topology (Norberg-Schulz 1965, 43–44, 133–56; Piaget & Inhelder 1963, xi, 6–9) can help to discern the history of a distinctive architectural element that was found at Sotira-Kaminoudhia, Alambra-Mouttes, and Kalopsidha.

Characteristic features which comprise the architectural element at these sites include a single-cell enclosure; rectilinear form; an entrance along a side wall; and a front porch. As is evident from the architecture of Lemba-Lakkous, the single-cell enclosure was indigenous to Cyprus. The other features appear first in Anatolia. The side-wall entrance prevailed at Early Bronze Age (EB) Tarsus (Schaar 1985) while both the rectilinear form and the porch were features at EB Tarsus and Troy (Schaar forthcoming).

At Sotira-Kaminoudhia, the architectural element functions as a complete dwelling. Forming this element at Sotira was a tentative act, essentially a testing of alternative possibilities (Swiny 1985, 119; Kubler 1962, 62–82; Gilfillan 1970, 6). At Alambra-Mouttes the element occurs in a rudimentary cluster as well as in a row-house arrangement. The element is used at Alambra both as a complete dwelling and as a partition to sub-divide a dwelling. At Kalopsidha, the element is part of a larger complex that was formed according to other organizing principles. The element is auspiciously located at the entrance to the complex as a vestige or symbol of a previous tradition.

The features that comprise the architectural element originated as separate phenomena in either Cyprus or Anatolia. These features were amalgamated to create the element which in time evolved from Sotira-Kaminoudhia, through Alambra-Mouttes, to Kalopsidha. The element embodies a distinctly Cypriot tradition, at first functional and ultimately symbolic.

LIST OF REFERENCES

Gilfillan, S.C. (1970) *The Sociology of Invention*. Cambridge, (Mass.)
Kubler, G. (1962) *The Shape of Time*. New Haven.
Norberg-Schulz, C. (1965) *Intentions in Architecture*. Cambridge, (Mass).
Piaget, J. & Inhelder B. (1963) *The Child's Concept of Space*. London.
Schaar, K.W. (1985) House form at Tarsus, Alambra and Lemba. *RDAC*, 37–44.
Schaar, K.W. (forthcoming) Generation of the architectural form at Poliochni V and Troy IIg. *Proceedings, 6th International Colloquium on Aegean Prehistory, 1987*.
Swiny, S. (1985) Sotira-*Kaminoudhia* and the Chalcolithic/Early Bronze Age transition in Cyprus, in *Archaeology in Cyprus, 1960–1985* (ed. V. Karageorghis) 115–24. Nicosia.

POSTER SUMMARY

9
Correlation model for analyzing prehistoric Cypriot culture

Kathryn M. Shaffer
Louisiana Tech University, Ruston

A method for correlating cultural trends and built forms can, from a given dwelling form, provide valuable insight into an unknown culture, such as on Prehistoric Cyprus.

This method uses an 'interactional' model where two factors, culture and form, are interdependent on each other. The culture side of the model includes information on the society, the place, and external influences. These three categories can be subdivided into subsystems (subsistence, technology, social structure, etc) to define all of the components which make up a culture. The built form side of the model includes corresponding changes in the size, shape, partitioning and structure of the form.

A theory of natural evolution (such as the theory of entropy) must be considered when interpreting the effects of change. A cultural change may not directly cause a change in built form, but a particular combination of cultural changes, at a particular point in a culture's history (a point of high degradation/high energy) may be combined to cause a morphological change.

The model indicates that as cultural events change, built form will change, and conversely that if built form changes it will cause cultural modifications.

PART TWO
Funerary Evidence

10
Whence the first Cypriots?

Melodie Domurad
Center for Nutritional Research, Boston

The question of where the first emigrants to Cyprus came from has persisted since the first human remains on the island were discovered. Previous attempts to locate similar populations and to determine the place of origin of these settlers have yielded little result. This study offers new hope for an old problem by combining evidence from archaeological artifacts and social practices, as well as standard skeletal information, to find a probable parent population for the earliest human remains we have, from aceramic burials at Khirokitia.

Traditionally, the relative proximity of two or more populations has been determined by the degree of similarity of a complex of genetic traits. These include many skull measurements and their proportions to each other, dental features, and presence or extent of non-metric inherited features such as browbridges. Although it is thorough and objective, this method has its drawbacks when used alone. Poor preservation due to repeated winter flooding in tombs, lime in the soil and disturbances from subsequent burials seriously limit the amount of material available for study. Currently the only published Neolithic skeletal material we have from Cyprus other than that from Khirokitia comes from Sotira. Comparative samples from the surrounding mainland are equally few, and often have been published in preliminary form only. In addition, most of the human remains from the sites involved in this discussion were studied a generation or more ago when it was commonly accepted that there were determinable 'racial types', and the contribution to skull shape from environmental and other non-genetic factors was still unknown. Therefore, as useful as the comparison of physical features is, it is insufficient for the purpose of finding a probable origin for the earliest Cypriot inhabitants.

A synthetic approach which takes account of cultural evidence is less affected by this deficit. The traditions and customs which immigrants bring with them from their homeland are as much a trademark and identifying characteristic as their appearance and inherited traits. Social customs also have the advantage of being long-lived, while physical features can change quickly. Burial methods, for instance, are frequently retained for many generations, but the same does not hold true for appearances. It is a major problem in the discussion of the earliest populations in Cyprus that we do not know if the skeletal remains from Khirokitia represent the first inhabitants on the island, or whether there were previous arrivals. If the original settlers did not completely represent the traits and appearance of the founding population, within only a few generations differential fertility and microevolution could have combined to produce a population which only generally reflected its origins. The degree to which the settlers represented the genetic pool in the home population is a less critical factor, however, when we have corroborative evidence from other media.

Cypriot art and pottery are extraordinary in the frequency of their portrayals of daily life, and it is partly from these artifacts that we know of a tradition which came with the Khirokitians and continued among the inhabitants of various towns at least through Roman times—the use of cradleboards. Although there are no Neolithic representations of these devices, we have a very good idea of what they looked like from Early Cypriot terracotta figurines, and we can infer their use at Khirokitia from their effect on the skulls. Children were laid on a board or other firm backing, then wrapped approximately to chest level to keep them secure. Arms are usually not visible in the models, and, therefore, were probably under the bands. There appear to have been two slight variations, although this may be the result of more or less detailed representations.

Some models (Karageorghis 1981, Pl 24) have an additional band over the forehead to hold the child's head in place, or as a guard against bruising if the board should fall. Others (Karageorghis 1981, Pl 25) lack this feature. This equipment was useful for propping babies upright, keeping them out of harm and for transporting them easily. Modern Armenians in Syria use similarly constructed cradleboards in the hope of improving the child's posture (Hasluck 1947).

Whatever the intended use of these carriers, they also produced what was perhaps initially an unintended result—flattened backs of heads. The pressure of the skull against the firmness of the board produced a slanted, flattened area (Angel 1953). By the LC this effect was purposely enhanced by additional boards and pads for 'beautification'. When Angel first studied the bones from Khirokitia he noted that flattening was present to a 'striking' degree in over half of the sample, and probably to a lesser degree in others (Angel 1953, 416; 1961, 229). The length of time a child remained in one, as well as the tightness of the bindings would have an effect on degree of change. Angel hypothesized that cradleboards were the cause, but this was not widely accepted. Other physical anthropologists believed that the modification of the skulls which resulted from this practice reflected the natural shape of Cypriot crania, and they began to search for a 'short-headed race' (Buxton 1931; Fürst 1933; Hjortsjö 1947), confusing inherited traits with enviromental effects. This artificial deformation which was once part of the problem in finding a mainland origin for the population at Khirokitia is now part of the solution.

Deformation did not occur in mainland Greece, but it was not unknown there in later times. A passage in the Hippocratic corpus from the 5th century BC describes the people from the Caucasus as follows:

> 'The people believe that long-headedness is a mark of distinction, and the local custom in question is as follows. As soon as a child is born, they begin while the bone is still soft, to refashion the skull with their hands, and they lengthen it by pressure, using bandages and other suitable appliances (Jones 1959).

Anatolia and the Levantine mainland seem the most likely points of origin for emigrants to Cyprus due to the island's proximity. There is no evidence that there was ever a landbridge or stepping-stone islands between Cyprus and the mainland. This means that whenever the first settlers came they had to do so by boat, indicating that they could see the area they were setting out to explore. Mersin, Tarsus, Ras Shamra and Byblos on the adjacent mainland, all seemed possible points of departure. These origins, of course, depend on a sixth millennium BC date for the earliest settlement of Khirokitia. If that date should be pushed back, we would perhaps need to look elsewhere.

Mersin and Tarsus are physically closest to Cyprus, but there is no evidence of deformation among the skulls found there (Senyürek 1954, 1–9; Ehrich 1940, 87–91), and burial traditions in Anatolia tend toward defleshing and decapitation, as occurred to some degree at Hacilar (Mellaart 1970) and Çatal Hüyük (Mellaart 1976). There is no sign of these practices at Khirokitia. In addition to this lack of cultural similarity, there was no close correlation of inherited traits at either site to those found in Neolithic Cyprus.

While it is not possible to compare every inherited trait due to incomplete information in some publications, two feature are almost always noted: metopism and wormian bones. The first is the retention of the suture between the left and right halves of the forehead. It is present in everyone at birth, but closes in most individuals by the second year of age. Average occurrence in modern American Whites is 11 per cent (Angel 1953, 418), but was present in 18 per cent of the Khirokitians and ranged as high as 75 per cent in Roman Cypriots (Domurad 1986, 134). Wormian bones are small islands of bone which can occur in any cranial suture, but are most common in the lambdoid, at the back of the head. Average occurrence in modern Europeans is 15 per cent (Zivanovič 1982, 93–5), but ranges as high as 87 per cent at Khirokitia (Angel 1953, 424). These two characteristics are especially useful because they are visible without special equipment, can often be detected in photographs even if they are not described in the text, and they vary widely even between small populations and short geographical distances. No two groups, however similar, will be exactly alike, but in general, the more similar the rate of occurrence of genetic features, the closer the relationship between samples.

Byblos seemed a strong possibility, given its location on a direct diagonal across the water, and while most of the Neolithic skulls from this site were unmodified, a few were startlingly deformed (Vallois 1937). Unfortunately, the style adopted at this site is the opposite of that found at Khirokitia. At Byblos heads were extraordinarily elongated from binding, perhaps to imitate the naturally long shape of Egyptian populations (Harris & Wente 1980). In addition, burials at Byblos in this early period were largely in *pithoi*, while those at Khirokitia were simple inhumations below floors or near houses.

Ras Shamra, finally, produced the most promising material. While there were no portrayals of cradleboards in art, several of the skulls dated before the Late Bronze Age showed some skull flattening (Charles 1962, Figs 14–18). Rates of occurrence of metopism and wormian bones, 40 and 30 percent respectively (Charles 1962, 521–55; Vallois & Ferembach 1962, 565–620), were close to those in the Khirokitia sample at 18 per cent metopism and 87 per cent wormian bones (Angel 1953, 424). Despite the relatively close match, this parallel is not without problems. The Ras Shamra skulls are considerably later than those from Khirokitia, so there is the possibility that they not only resembled Cypriots, but that they were Cypriots. If this were so, however, we would expect the similarity to increase in the Late Bronze Age when contact with Cyprus was frequent, but the later the skeletal remains, the less the similarity.

The N.Syrian evidence, however, suggests an origin for only part of the Neolithic population. What of the later inhabitants at Sotira? Their homeland has been as uncertain as that of the Khirokitians, but one thing which is definite is that the two groups did not originate from the same population. The people of Sotira did not practice cradleboarding, and displayed neither wormian bones nor metopism. It is possible that the preserved skeletal sample is not representative of the settlement's population due to the small sample size, but lack of continuity is discernible also in the material cultures of aceramic phase Khirokitia and Sotira (Peltenburg 1982, 16–18).

Thus, this approach does not solve all questions about ancestors of the Cypriots, but it is a beginning. Larger skeletal samples are needed from more sites, both in Cyprus and on the mainland. Fortunately, the prospects for further study are improving steadily. The importance of human bones as archaeological material has been recognized, and archaeologists have begun to consolidate bones before excavating them, resulting in more representative samples in a better state of preservation. New skeletons are being found at current excavations in the Kalavassos Valley, Khirokitia and Lemba which add to the sample available for comparison. With better material and more data, computers are able to compare up to forty inherited traits simultaneously using multivariate analyses, allowing us to make more accurate deductions and correlations than were possible before.

LIST OF REFERENCES

Angel, J.L. (1953) The human remains from Khirokitia, in *Khirokitia* (P. Dikaios) Appendix II. Oxford.
Angel, J.L. (1961) Neolithic crania from Sotira, in *Sotira* (P. Dikaios) 223-9. Philadelphia.
Buxton, L.H.D. (1931) Künstlich deformierte Schädel von Cypern. *Anthropologischer Anzeiger 7*, 236–40.
Charles, R-P. (1962) Contribution à l'étude anthropologique du site de Ras Shamra, in *Ugaritica IV* (C.F.A. Schaeffer) 522–66. Paris.
Domurad, M.R. (1986) *The Populations of Ancient Cyprus*. University Microfilms, Ann Arbor.
Ehrich, R. (1940) Preliminary notes on the Tarsus crania. *AJA 44*, 87–92.
Fürst, C. M. (1933) *Zur Kenntnis der Anthropologie der Prähistorischen Bevölkerung der Insel Cypern*. Lund.
Harris, J.E. & Wente, E.F. (1980) *An X-Ray Atlas of the Royal Mummies*. Chicago.
Hasluck, M. (1947) Head deformation in the Near East. *Man 47*, 130–1.
Hjortsjö, C-H. (1947) *To the knowledge of the prehistoric craniology of Cyprus*. (Sartryck ur Kungl. Humanistika Vetenskapssamfundet, Arsberattelse). Lund.
Jones, W.H.S., ed. (1959) περὶ Ἀέρων Ὑδάτων τόπων Cambridge, MA.
Karageorghis, V. (1981) *Ancient Cyprus*. Baton Rouge.
Mellaart, J. (1967) *Çatal Hüyük: A Neolithic Town in Anatolia*. New York.
Peltenburg, E.J. (1982) *Recent Developments in the Later Prehistory of Cyprus (SIMA Pocket-book 16)*. Göteborg.
Senyürek, M.S. (1954) Skulls of the Chalcolithic age. *Belleten 18*, 1–23.
Vallois, H.V. (1937) Note sur les ossements humains de la nécropole énéolithique de Byblos. *B Mus Beyr 1*, 23–33.
Vallois, H.V. & Ferembach, D. (1962) Les restes humains de Ras Shamra et de Minet el-Beida: étude anthropologique, in *Ugaritica IV* (C.F.A. Schaeffer), 567–631. Paris.
Zivanovič, S. (1982) *Ancient Diseases*. New York.

11
Le traitement des morts et les représentations des vivants à Khirokitia.

A. Le Brun
Centre National de la Recherche Scientifique, Paris

L'étude du monde mental des hommes du Néolithique précéramique de Chypre est un sujet qui, jusqu'à present, n'a été qu'effleuré au hasard des découvertes dont la plus éloquente à cet égard est, sans conteste, celle des restes d'un décor mural peint faite à Kalavassos-Tenta (Todd 1987, Fig 39). Aussi la tenue de ce colloque consacré aux sociétés anciennes de Chypre m'a-t-elle paru être l'occasion pour tenter, en utilisant les informations fournies par les fouilles, anciennes et récentes, du site de Khirokitia (Dikaios 1953; Le Brun 1984), de combler cette lacune. Une telle tentative semble possible car nous disposons d'une documentation, importante pour ce qui concerne les sépultures, au nombre de deux-cent trois, plus restreinte pour ce qui concerne les figurations humaines et animales, matériel sur lequel je vais m'appuyer. Pour importante qu'elle soit numériquement, cette documentation n'en est toutefois pas moins limitée: le contexte dans lequel les figurines ont été découvertes n'est pas toujours bien connu, l'étude anthropologique des restes humains n'est pas achevée et le sexe des individus exhumés n'a été déterminé en partie que pour la série des sépultures dégagées par P. Dikaios. Aussi les conclusions qu'il sera possible de tirer seront-elles plus l'indication de directions de recherches que des affirmations définitives. Ce sont ces pistes que, malgré ces manques, je vais tenter maintenant d'ouvrir en examinant les données de Khirokitia.

A Khirokitia, les sépultures sont des inhumations individuelles, primaires, dans des fosses creusées à l'intérieur des habitations. Les rares sépultures qui, ne pouvant pas être associées à une habitation, paraissent contredire cette règle, sont situées à proximité de la surface si bien qu'il n'est pas possible de déterminer si elles représentent réellement une exception ou bien si l'habitation à l'intérieur de laquelle elles auraient été creusées n'a pas été emportée par une érosion active sur un site accroché aux flancs d'un éperon rocheux. Aussi peut-on considérer cette pratique, qui inscrit dans le sol la continuité entre les générations, comme caractéristique des coutumes funéraires observées par les habitants de Khirokitia.

Si la présence des ancêtres est matériellement moins visible qu'elle ne l'est, par exemple, sur le continent au PPNB avec le 'culte des crânes', elle n'en reste pas moins vive dans la mémoire: malgré l'exiguïté de la surface qu'offre un élément d'habitation de 2 m à 2,50 m de diamètre pour le creusement de fosses, les cas de recoupement ou de chevauchement,—pour des fosses creusées à partir du même sol s'entend—sont extrêmement rares, tout se passant donc comme si la mémoire des vivants avait gardé inscrit l'emplacement ou les emplacements déjà utilisés pour des sépultures. L'élément d'habitation S.97 fournit un bon exemple de cette mémoire (Le Brun *et al* 1987, Fig 12).

Souci d'affirmer la filiation entre les générations en la marquant dans le sol, mais aussi souci de marquer la valeur attachée à un territoire en y enracinant en quelque sorte le groupe humain, souci qui s'exprime, par ailleurs et sur un autre registre, par la construction d'ouvrages collectifs dessinant la limite entre le monde habité par la communauté et le monde extérieur.

Mais qu'entendre exactement par territoire? Faut-il garder à ce terme une valeur restrictive et n'entendre par là que le fragment d'espace où la communauté vit ou bien faut-il en étendre le sens et le comprendre comme le territoire ou une partie du territoire dont le groupe humain tire sa subsistance? Car, rappelons-le, nous avons à faire à une communauté d'agriculteurs,—les restes abondants des plantes cultivées recueillies au cours de la fouille (Hansen 1987), les aménagements architecturaux comme les installations à broyer les grains (Le Brun 1984, 57–8) en témoignent —communauté dont la relation à l'espace est modelée par la pratique même de l'agriculture, ainsi que l'a suggéré K.V. Flannery (1972, 28–9). Ce dernier voit précisément dans l'affirmation d'un 'concept of descent' s'exprimant, entre autres, par le fait d'enterrer les morts à l'intérieur des habitations, l'un des moyens utilisés pour marquer et maintenir cette appropriation nouvelle de l'espace au sens large.

Le mort, qu'il soit un adulte, un enfant ou un jeune enfant de moins d'un an, c'est-à-dire d'âge périnatal, repose en position contractée. Il ressort toutefois des observations faites sur le terrain par F, Le Mort (1987), sur un échantillon limité, il est vrai, de sept individus, observations qui demandent donc à être confirmées, qu'une différence existerait quant au degré de contraction entre les modalités d'inhumation des adultes dont le corps est en position hypercontractée et celles des enfants d'âge périnatal dont le corps est en position contractée ou partiellement contractée.

Cette différence de traitement entre les adultes et les très jeunes enfants n'apparaît cependant pas si l'on considère la façon dont le corps est couché. Il peut, en effet, reposer sur le côté droit, sur le côté gauche, sur le ventre ou sur le dos, avec, toutefois, une nette préférence pour le côté droit

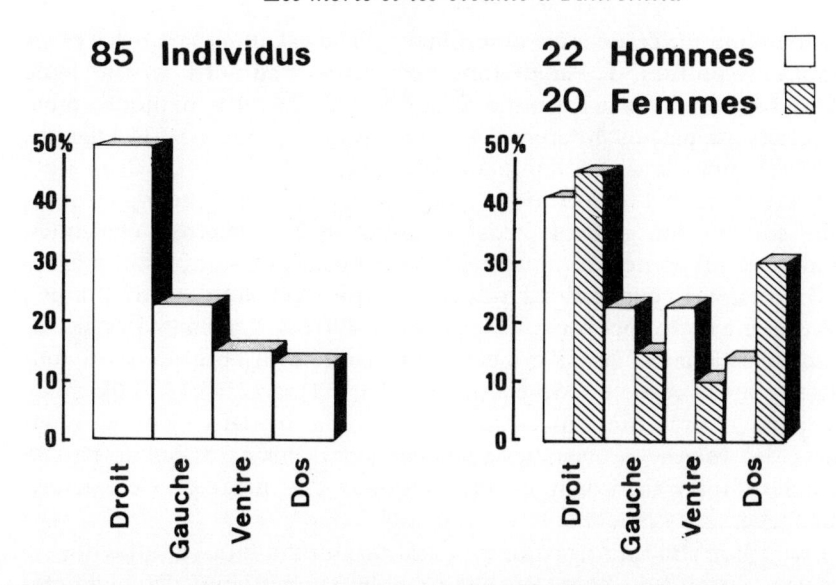

Figure 11.1 Khirokitia. Position du corps dans les sépultures.

indépendamment du niveau auquel la sépulture appartient, indépendamment de sa situation dans le secteur est ou dans le secteur ouest: ainsi, sur un lot de quatre-vingt cinq individus, regroupant des adultes, des enfants et des jeunes enfants, quarante-deux, soit près de la moitié, reposent sur le côté droit, dix-neuf sur le côté gauche, treize sur le ventre et onze sur le dos (Fig 11.1). L'âge du défunt ne paraît jouer aucun rôle particulier dans cette disposition: sur les soixante-trois adultes dont la position est connue, vingt-sept, soit près de 43 pour cent, sont sur le côté droit, quatorze sur le côté gauche, douze sur le ventre et dix sur le dos. Pour un échantillon, certes moins élevé, d'enfants d'âge périnatal portant sur douze individus, les proportions sont comparables: sept, soit 58,3 pour cent, reposent sur le côté droit, quatre sur le côté gauche et un sur le dos. La même prédominance du côté droit apparaît si l'on introduit un nouveau paramètre: le sexe (Fig 11.1). Sur vingt-deux individus reconnus comme étant de sexe masculin sûr ou probable, neuf, soit 40,9 pour cent, sont sur le côté droit, cinq sur le côté gauche, cinq également sur le ventre et trois sur le dos. Les vingt individus de sexe féminin, sûr ou probable, se répartissent de façon à peu près analogue: neuf d'entre eux, soit 45 pour cent, étant sur le côté droit, trois sur le côté gauche, deux sur le ventre et six sur le dos. Si la préférence pour le côté droit caractérise aussi bien les sépultures d'hommes que celles de femmes, la similarité entre ces deux groupes n'est toutefois pas totale. En effet, les squelettes reposant sur le ventre sont majoritairement masculins, à l'inverse, ceux reposant sur le dos sont majoritairement féminins. Peut-être exagérée dans ce cas par la petitesse de l'échantillon étudié, une telle divergence dans le traitement des hommes et des femmes ressort plus nettement de l'étude de l'orientation des sépultures.

L'orientation du crâne a été déterminée par le calcul, à partir des plans de sépultures publiés, de l'angle formé par rapport au nord par une ligne reliant le bassin à la base du crâne. L'application de cette méthode donne des résultats qui parfois diffèrent des orientations indiquées par P. Dikaios, mais si les conclusions que l'on peut tirer de ces dernières (Le Brun 1987 *et al*, 294) se trouvent, dans le détail, modifiées, elles n'en restent pas moins valables sur un plan général, dans la mesure où elles mettent également en lumière la différence de traitement des sépultures féminines et masculines. Les valeurs, exprimées en degrés et qui s'échelonnent de 0 à 360 degrés, ont été regroupées en huit secteurs de 45° chacun, matérialisant les points cardinaux. Ainsi est considéré comme orienté au nord tout squelette dont le crâne est situé entre 327°30' et 22°30'. Ce mode de découpage présente l'inconvénient de répartir dans deux groupes distincts des valeurs proches les unes des autres mais situées de part et d'autre des limites ainsi définies, mais il donne une image plus condensée et plus facilement maniable.

L'échantillon ainsi étudié compte quarante-huit individus adultes dont le sexe a été déterminé de façon sûre ou probable, à savoir vingt-deux hommes et vingt-six femmes. La comparaison entre les deux schémas (Fig 11.2) montre une différence nette entre ces deux groupes. La presque totalité des sépultures masculines,—vingt et une sur vingt-deux—s'échelonnent de 270° à 140°, c'est-à-dire du nord-ouest au sud-est, en passant par une pointe au nord-est, alors que la majorité des sépultures féminines se répartissent en deux groupes opposés, l'un allant de 30° à 120°, c'est-à-dire du nord-est au sud-est et qui coïncide donc avec l'orientation préférée pour les sépultures masculines, l'autre allant de 220 à 330°, c'est-à-dire du sud-ouest au nord-ouest qui apparaît en revanche être plus proprement féminin. Et, sur l'axe nord-est—sud-ouest qui rassemble la nombre le plus élevé de sépultures des deux sexes, tous les squelettes masculins ont le crâne placé au nord-est alors que pour les squelettes féminins, le crâne est placé soit au nord-est, soit au sud-ouest, orientation, semble-t-il, évitée pour les hommes.

Cette indication de l'existence d'une différenciation sexuelle dans le traitement des morts est certes discrète. Mais on peut se demander si elle ne prolonge pas, au-delà de la mort, l'observation faite par J. Angel (1953, 416) suivant laquelle les déformations artificielles du crâne sont environ deux fois plus fréquentes sur les sujets féminins que sur les sujets masculins, la proportion étant de 50 pour cent pour les femmes et de 29 pour cent pour les hommes.

En outre, quoique du matériel d'accompagnement soit déposé indifféremment dans les tombes d'hommes et de femmes, la nature de ce matériel paraît, dans certains cas, être liée au sexe du défunt. Ainsi sur les six sépultures où un collier avait été déposé avec le mort, quatre sont des sépultures féminines, une celle d'un adulte de sexe indéterminé, la dernière étant celle d'un enfant. Inversement, la pratique qui consiste à placer sur

26 Femmes   **22 Hommes**

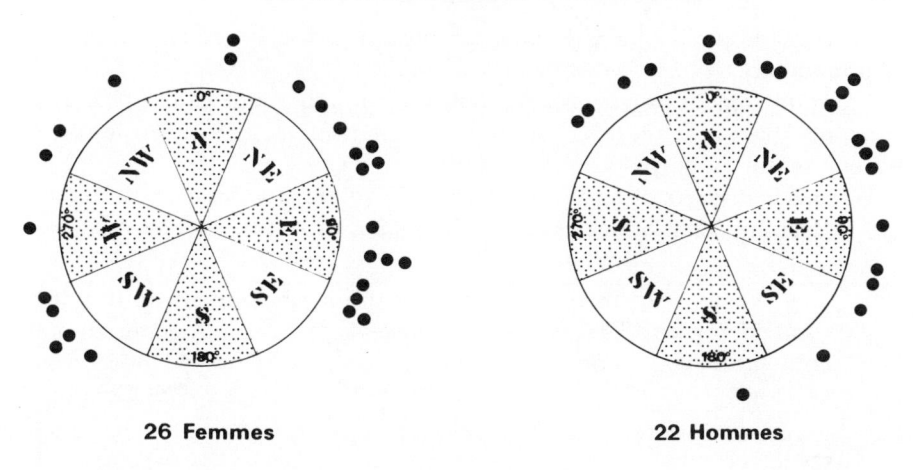

Figure 11.2 Khirokitia. Orientation des sépultures.

le corps une pierre est deux fois plus fréquente pour les sépultures masculines (neuf cas) que dans les sépultures féminines où elle ne se rencontre que quatre fois.

Aussi, pour discret qu'il soit, un clivage déterminé par le sexe du défunt est-il néanmoins sensible. Et, bien que la sépulture la plus riche en mobilier funéraire soit celle d'une femme (Dikaios 1953, tholos X (II), sépulture 5), ce clivage ne recoupe pas toutefois un autre clivage qui divise, indépendamment d'ailleurs de l'âge du défunt, les sépultures de Khirokitia en deux groupes suivant qu'elles contiennent ou non du matériel d'accompagnement: colliers dont il a déjà été fait mention mais aussi outils en silex ou en os, ou bien vaisselle en pierre, dont il est difficile de dire, dans l'état actuel de nos connaissances, s'ils symbolisent le statut social du défunt. Mais l'examen de ce matériel amène à constater que certaines catégories d'objets, certaines formes particulières paraissent être plus intimement liées à un contexte funéraire que d'autres.

C'est le cas, notamment, pour les bols ou bassins à bec verseur (par exemple, Dikaios 1953, Fig 52). Sur la vingtaine de sépultures où de la vaisselle en pierre a été retrouvée, le plus souvent brisée intentionnellement comme l'a noté P. Dikaios (1953, 219, 230), seize contiennent un ou plusieurs vases de ce type et sur les trente et un récipients en pierre trouvés dans les tombes, vingt-deux sont munis d'un bec verseur.

Serait-il alors possible de considérer les bols ou bassins de ce type comme des objets rituels? On ne peut que déplorer sur ce point que pour près des deux tiers des récipients à bec verseur publiés par P. Dikaios nous manquions de renseignement sur leur provenance, mais si l'on s'en tient aux exemplaires dont le contexte où ils furent découverts est connu, vingt-deux ont été recueillis dans une sépulture, quatre proviennent du sol d'une tholos, deux, enfin, sont des réemplois. Aussi, quelles que soient les distortions introduites par la méthode d'enregistrement qui a été suivie, il semble donc bien qu'un lien existe entre ce type de vaisselle et les pratiques d'inhumation.

C'est un lien de même nature qui apparaît dans une autre pratique funéraire, bien illustrée à Khirokitia: celle qui consiste à recouvrir le corps ou une partie du corps par une ou plusieurs pierres.

Hormis la discrète différenciation sexuelle qui transparaît dans ce rite, et qui a déjà été mentionnée, rien ne distingue les tombes de ce type, au

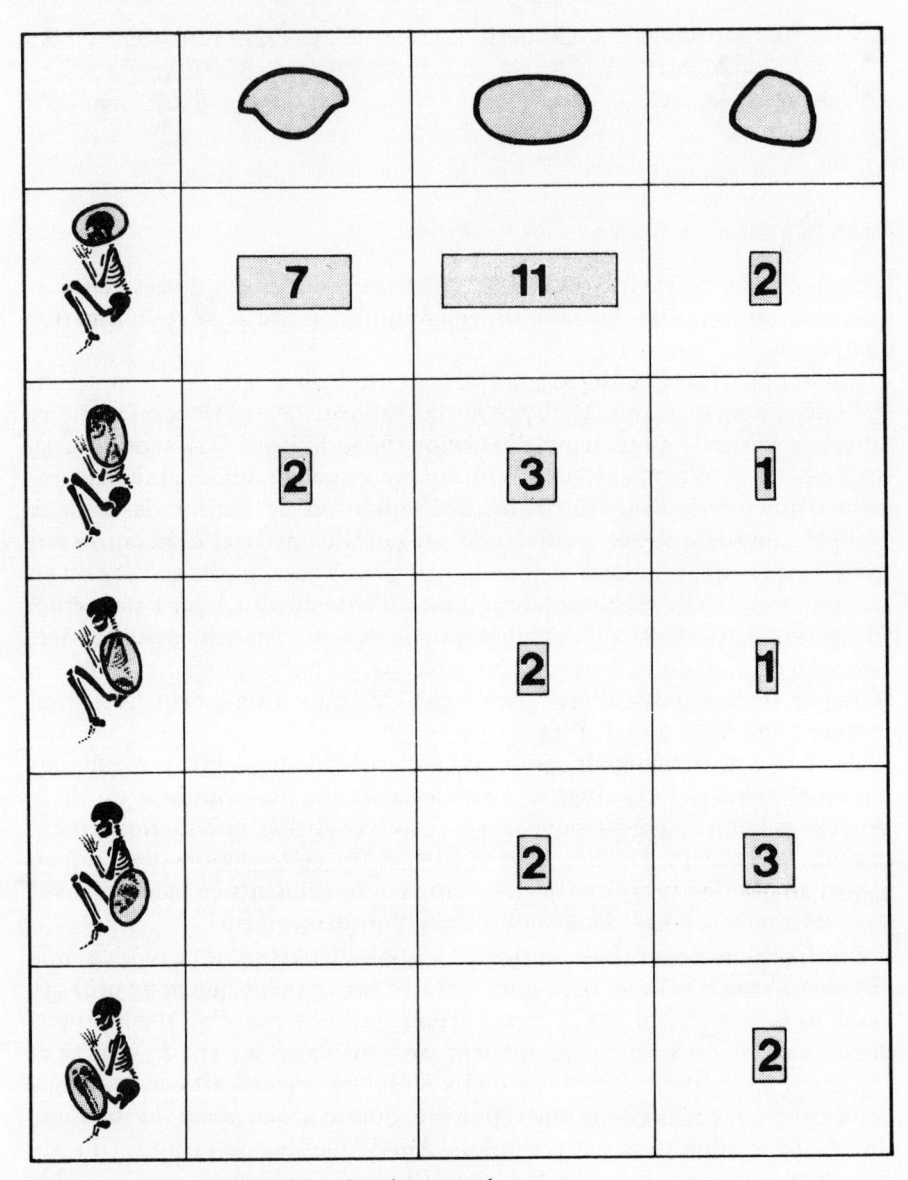

	◐	⬭	◯
🦴	7	11	2
🦴	2	3	1
🦴		2	1
🦴		2	3
🦴			2

Figure 11.3 Khirokitia. Position des pierres sur les corps.

nombre de trente-neuf, des autres tombes: le matériel d'accompagnement n'y est pas plus fréquent qu'ailleurs, elles se rencontrent, comme les autre tombes, également à tous les niveaux, aussi bien dans le secteur ouest que dans le secteur est, et ne montrent pas d'orientation particulière.

Le corps, dans la majorité des cas celui d'un adulte, mais ce peut être aussi celui d'un enfant ou d'un très jeune enfant, y est recouvert par une pierre brute ou par plusieurs pierres entassées, par une meule ou bien par ce que j'appelle une 'pierre à tenons' (Le Brun 1984, Fig 43, Pls XVI-XVII). Il s'agit de galets d'andésite, de forme ovale, mesurant entre 30 et 40 cm de long, entre 20 et 33 cm de large et épais de 8 à 11 cm, dont une face est plane ou concave et montre des trace de piquetage, l'autre face étant bombée et laissée brute. Sur les petits côtés, des excroissances ou tenons ont été dégages par piquetage. Or dix de ces onze pierres à tenons trouvées en stratigraphie proviennent de sépultures, la onzième ayant été recueillie sur l'un des sols de la tholos XVI. Le lien paraît donc évident entre ce type d'objet et les rites d'inhumation.

Qu'on ait à faire à un objet auquel était attachée une signification particulière est aussi montré par sa position sur le corps (Fig 11.3). C'est en effet sur le crâne du défunt, qu'elles recouvrent totalement ou partiellement, que les pierres à tenons sont placées, jamais sur le thorax, le bassin ou les jambes, contrairement aux meules qui, préférentiellement placées aussi sur le crâne, se trouvent aussi sur le thorax et le bassin, contrairement aux pierres brutes qui sont, elles, déposées plus fréquemment sur le thorax et les jambes que sur le crâne.

Ce souci de maintenir le défunt dans le monde des morts en le recouvrant ainsi d'une ou de plusieurs pierres paraît aussi trouver une illustration dans la découverte faite au cours de la dernière campagne menée à Khirokitia d'une sépulture (538) où le crâne du mort, un enfant âgé de six mois environ, était recouvert non pas par une pierre, mais par une omoplate de daim. Une telle substitution n'est toutefois pas sans poser de questions.

A-t-on réellement à faire là à une variante de cette pratique où l'omoplate, en raison peut-être simplement de sa forme plate, a été utilisée comme une pierre? Ce serait alors le geste de recouvrir le mort qui serait plus important que l'objet même avec lequel on le recouvre. Mais comment, dans ces conditions, alors que n'importe quelle pierre aurait pu faire l'affaire, expliquer l'utilisation des pierres à tenons, c'est-à-dire de pierres mises en forme selon un modèle précis et dont la seule fonction paraît être d'accompagner le mort.

La présence d'un ossement animal dans une sépulture ne serait-elle pas plutôt à comprendre comme l'expression sans ambiguïté de l'existence d'une relation de type non utilitaire entre l'homme et le monde animal? Dans cette relation le daim ne paraît pas d'ailleurs occuper une place privilégiée. Les rares exemples de la présence de restes animaux dans une sépulture font en effet état aussi bien d'ossements de daim: un fragment de bois de daim trouvé sur la face interne de la partie droite du bassin d'un adulte (Le Brun 1984, 75, sépulture 380), que de mouton/chèvre: un fragment de corne sur lequel reposait le squelette d'un très jeune enfant et une corne marquant le bord de la sépulture d'un jeune enfant (Le Brun 1984, 76–7, sépultures 207 et 382). L'absence du porc dans cet inventaire ne saurait être considérée comme significative en raison du petit nombre des exemples connus.

C'est toutefois un écho très assourdi d'une telle relation que renvoient par leur rareté les productions de l'art mobilier. Mais, avant de procéder à leur discussion, une remarque préliminaire s'impose touchant le support matériel utilisé aussi bien pour les représentations zoomorphes que pour les représentations anthropomorphes. Les propriétés plastiques de l'argile, connues et largement utilisées dans le domaine de l'architecture, ainsi qu'en témoignent briques crues et enduits posés sur les sols et sur les faces des murs, sont, en effet, pour ainsi dire totalement ignorées pour ce qui concerne l'art mobilier: à l'exception d'une représentation humaine modelée en argile (Dikaios 1953, Pls XCVIII, CXLIV.1063), toutes les autres figurines sont en pierre. Et par les contraintes techniques qu'il implique, le choix de ce support contribue à donner aux figurines trouvées à Khirokitia et sur les autres sites précéramiques de Chypre une allure solennelle, un peu compassée, contrastant vivement avec l'allure des figurines trouvées sur le continent qui donnent l'impression, particulièrement les figurines animales, d'être le résultat d'un jeu où la distance entre le 'sculpteur' et son oeuvre est comme abolie ou presque.

L'inventaire des représentations animales du Néolithique précéramique chypriote est rapidement dressé: ce sont une figurine trouvée en surface à Mari-Mesovouni (Todd 1979, 285, Fig 14) et deux exemplaires recueillis par P. Dikaios à Khirokitia (1953, 299. 561, 1252, Pls XCVIII, CXLIII). S'il peut être téméraire de commenter un si petit nombre de documents, un point toutefois mérite d'être souligné. Seule la pièce recueillie à Mari-Mesovouni est à proprement parler une figurine, de relativement grande taille d'ailleurs, les deux têtes d'animaux de Khirokitia, aux cous démesurément longs, sont, en revanche, des fragments d'un objet composite. Qu'elles aient été un élément décoratif, une sorte de 'protomé' comme le propose P. Dikaios, est possible, toujours est-il que leur fonction est là complètement différente de celle d'une simple figurine. L'ignorance où nous sommes de la nature de cet objet et, plus encore, de son utilisation interdit tout autre développement, mais ce traitement des représentations animales laisse pressentir l'existence d'un système de pensée complexe dont les moyens d'expression intègrent naturellement le monde animal, mais un monde animal en quelque sorte repensé.

Les représentations anthropomorphes constituent un autre de ces moyens d'expression. Il a déjà été fait allusion au décor mural peint de Kalavassos-Tenta qui représente deux figures humaines, les bras levés, dont la posture n'est pas sans rappeler le décor d'un bol en andésite trouvé à Khirokitia (Fig 11.4). Ce sont aussi des figurines qui ne sont qu'excep-

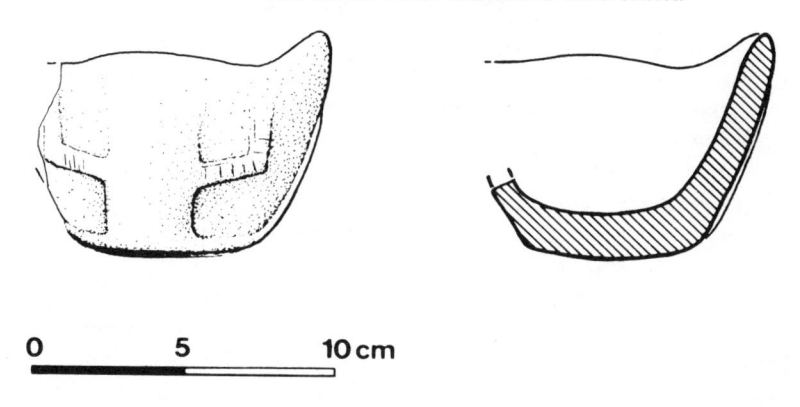

Figure 11.4 Khirokitia. Bol en andésite (Kh 86/2).

tionnellement associées à des sépultures (Dikaios 1953, 106, tholos XVII, sépulture 3, Fig 52.822, et encore s'agit-il vraiment d'un fragment de figurine?). Trois observations concernant leur variété, le contexte dans lequel elles ont été trouvées, enfin leur sexe méritent d'être faites à leur sujet.

Ces figurines présentent, en effet, une grande variété de formes. Certaines sont des silhouettes découpées sur un petit galet par deux ou quatre encoches latérales que complète parfois une encoche marquant la séparation des jambes (Dikaios 1953, Pl CXLIII.938, 1092). D'autres sont aménagées sur de grands galets dont le pourtour a été abattu, le corps étant alors figuré par un long appendice surmonté par une tête en forme de disque (Le Brun 1985, Fig 74.) Sur d'autres encore, le travail de mise en forme, plus poussé, s'attache à rendre les volumes du corps humain par des volumes géometriques simples (Dikaios 1953, Pl CXLIII.967). Enfin, l'existence d'un quatrième type est suggérée par des fragments de têtes où de nombreux détails sont indiqués (Dikaios 1953, Pls CXLIII-CXLIV.1, 1068, 1093, 1404).

Qu'on suppose à ces figurines un même sens ou une variété de sens en accord avec une telle variété de formes, il paraît évident, ne serait-ce que par leur différence de taille, qu'elles ne pouvaient pas être utilisées de la même manière. Dans ces conditions, on serait donc en présence de témoignages de rites divers impliquant chacun l'utilisation d'un type particulier de figurine.

Rien, il est vrai, dans le contexte dans lequel les différentes représentations humaines ont été découvertes ne permet de préciser ce point, toutefois, le caractère peu exceptionnel de ce contexte, quand il est connu—le plus fréquemment des couches de remplissage à l'intérieur comme à l'extérieur des habitations—amène à s'interroger, sous un nouvel angle, sur les modalités de leur utilisation. En effet, une telle négligence, un tel désintérêt montré à l'égard des représentations anthropomorphes inclinerait à penser que leur utilisation devait être limitée dans le temps; après quoi, vidées du sens dont elles avaient été investies, elles étaient abandonnées, au point même que les exemplaires de grande taille pouvaient être réemployés comme matériau de construction au même titre qu'un simple galet ramassé dans le lit du Maroni.

Une troisième observation, enfin, doit être faite concernant le sexe de ces figurines, ou plus exactement, l'extrême discrétion de l'indication du sexe. Même si certaines d'entre elles ont une allure phallique qui ne saurait échapper, on reste toujours dans l'ordre de l'allusion, à l'exception d'une figurine sur laquelle la représentation d'un sexe féminin est gravée (Dikaios 1953, Pls XCV, CXLIII.680). Cette discrétion et surtout cette absence de la femme dans l'imagerie du Néolithique précéramique chypriote est d'autant plus à remarquer que le Proche-Orient voit, à partir du 8e millénaire la 'montée de la figure humaine dans l'art, d'abord et par prédilection sous une forme féminine' (Cauvin 1987, 1476). Faut-il ainsi rappeler que c'est dès 8000 avant notre ère, c'est-à-dire juste avant les premières expériences agricoles, que les figurines féminines apparaissent à Mureybet, dans la vallée du Moyen Euphrate (Cauvin 1973, Figs 2, 3), qu'elles apparaissent avant le 8e millénaire, avant les débuts de l'agriculture aussi, dans la vallée du Jourdain (Bar-Yosef 1980, Fig 3)? Faut-il rappeler également leur fortune au 7e millénaire au sein de la civilisation du Levant dite PPNB?

Cette particularité du Néolithique précéramique chypriote est à prendre en compte dans l'étude des relations entre l'île et le continent voisin. De même que le seraient les ressemblances, mais aussi les différences, montrées par les pratiques funéraires que, pour Khirokitia, l'étude anthropologique et palethnologique actuellement en cours et que les résultats des analyses polliniques préciseront. Les inhumations en fosse à l'intérieur des habitations sont pratiquées sur le continent au PPNA et au PPNB, mais les inhumations secondaires sont inconnues à Khirokitia, comme le sont les crânes surmodelés. La pratique de recouvrir le mort de pierres est connue au Natoufien (Perrot 1966, 461), celle de déposer du matériel d'accompagnement, en particulier des récipients, se rencontre à Byblos au Néolithique Ancien (Dunand 1973, 30–2). Et le laps de temps qui sépare sur le continent les manifestations de ces deux pratiques, qui, rappelons-le, sont respectées simultanément à Khirokitia dans la même sépulture, donne la dimension de l'originalité du Néolithique précéramique de Chypre, tout en rendant plus urgente la solution du problème de son ancrage chronologique dans la séquence du Proche-Orient.

RÉFÉRENCES

Angel, J.L. (1953) The human remains from Khirokitia, in Dikaios 1953, 416–30.

Bar-Yosef, O. (1980) A human figurine from a Khiamian site in the lower Jordan Valley. *Paléorient 6,* 193-9.

Cauvin, J. (1973) Les origines de la vie sédentaire: le village de Mureybet. *La Recherche 4, no 39,* 1008–9.

Cauvin, J. (1987) L'apparition des premières divinités. *La Recherche 18, no 194*, 1472–80.

Dikaios, P. (1953) *Khirokitia*. Oxford.

Dunand, M. (1973) *Fouilles de Byblos V: l'architecture, les tombes, le matériel domestique des origines néolithiques à l'avènement urbain*. Paris.

Flannery, K.V. (1972) The origins of the village as a settlement type in Mesoamerica and the Near East: A comparative study, in *Man, Settlement and Urbanism* (Ucko, P.J., Tringham, R. & G.W Dimbleby ed.), 23–53 London.

Hansen, J. (1987) Les restes végétaux, *in* Le Brun, A. *et al* 1987, 309–11.

Le Brun, A. (1984) *Fouilles récentes à Khirokitia (Chypre): 1977–1981*. Paris.

Le Brun, A. (1985) Fouilles de Khirokitia, *Chronique 1985*, 922–4.

Le Brun, A. *et al* (1987) Le Néolithique précéramique de Chypre. *L'Anthropologie 91*, 283–36.

Le Mort, F. (1987) Les restes humains de Khirokitia. Programme d'étude et premiers résultats. Non publié.

Perrot, J. (1966) Le gisement natoufien de Mallaha (Eynan), Israël. *L'Anthropologie 70*, 437–84.

Todd, I.A. (1979) Vasilikos Valley Project: Third preliminary Report, 1978. *J Field A 6*, 265–300.

Todd, I.A. (1987) *Excavations at Kalavassos-Tenta, I. Excavations at Kalovasos-Tenta I (SIMA 71.6)*. Göteborg.

12
The Chalcolithic Cemetery 1 at Souskiou-Vathyrkakas

D. Christou
Department of Antiquities, Cyprus

The presentation of the discoveries of the Cyprus Department of Antiquities in the Chalcolithic Cemetery 1 at Souskiou-Vathyrkakas and their deeper meaning and significance in connection with other finds from regular and illicit excavations at the same cemetery are the main objectives of the present paper. Most of these discoveries have already appeared in various publications[1] but several details concerning certain important aspects of the material and the overall picture of the site remain for further discussion.

The Vathyrkakas Cemetery 1 lies in one of the most picturesque and impressive landscapes of the Paphos Region in southwestern Cyprus. It is *ca* 1.5 km southwest of the ex-Turkish village of Souskiou and 2 km northeast of Kouklia-Palaepaphos (Fig 12.1). It occupies a commanding position near the edge of a rocky plateau overlooking the step ravine of the homonymous Vathyrkakas stream and the nearby fertile valley of the Dhiarizos river. Two other Chalcolithic cemeteries have been located in the same area: Cemetery 3 on a prominent hillock at the Laona locality and *ca* 700 m northeast of Cemetery 1, and Cemetery 2 which is closer to the village of Kouklia and *ca* 400 m southwest of Cemetery 1. Opposite Cemeteries 1 and 2 a large settlement of the same Chalcolithic period has been traced, which is so far the only one known in the vicinity (*cf* Hadjisavvas 1977, Fig 2). The proximity of the three cemeteries at Vathyrkakas and Laona in combination with the architectural similarity of their contemporary tombs, lead to the plausible suggestion that they constitute a common cultural unity belonging to this settlement.

Cemetery 1 was discovered in 1951 by the British Kouklia Expedition after the excavation of three tombs of the Chalcolithic period which produced some exceptional specimens of Red-on-White pottery, two necklaces of dentalium embellished with cruciform pendants of picrolite, several

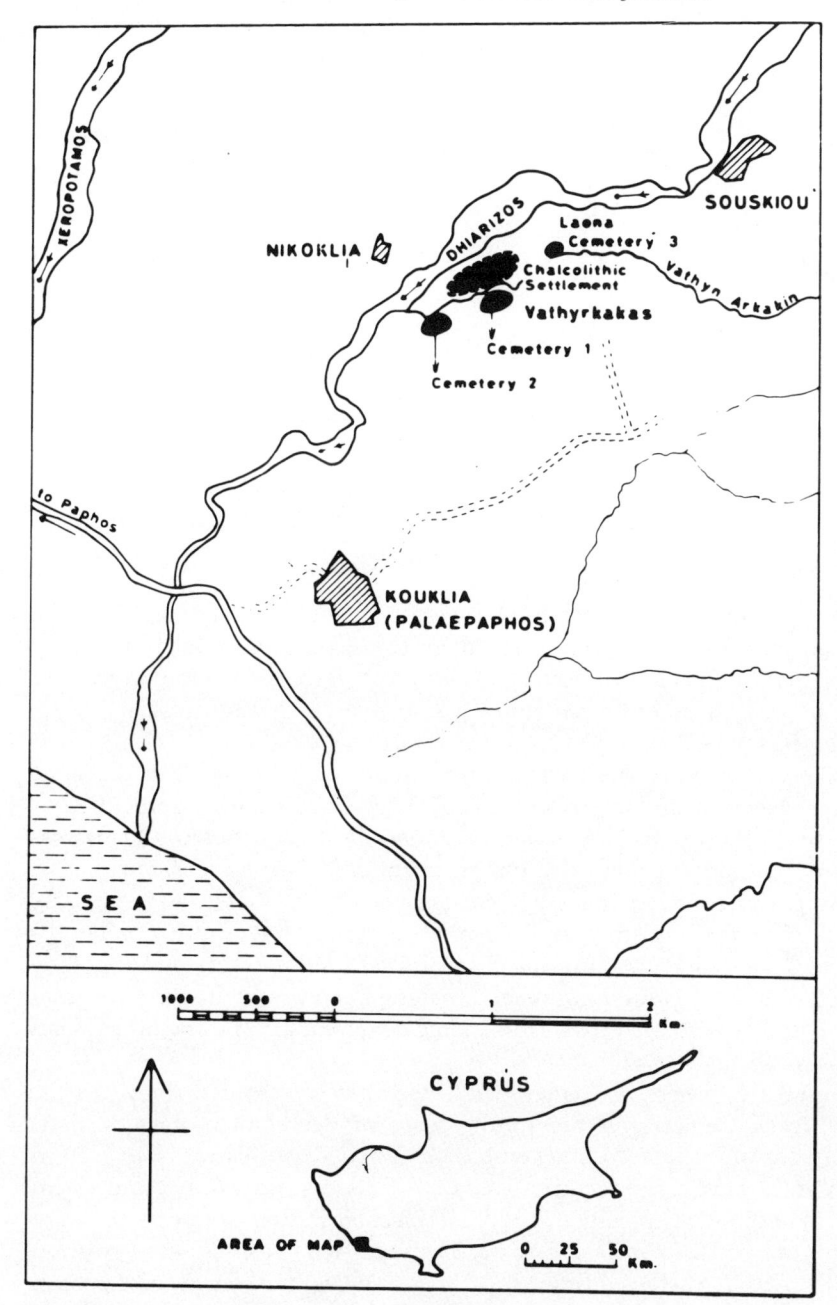

Figure 12.1 Plan of the Souskiou-Vathykarkas area.

stone axes and a pestle (Iliffe & Mitford 1951; Mitford 1951; Iliffe 1952, 50–1).

In August 1972 seventeen rock-cut tombs, similar to those excavated by the British Kouklia Expedition, were looted in Cemetery 1. In the middle

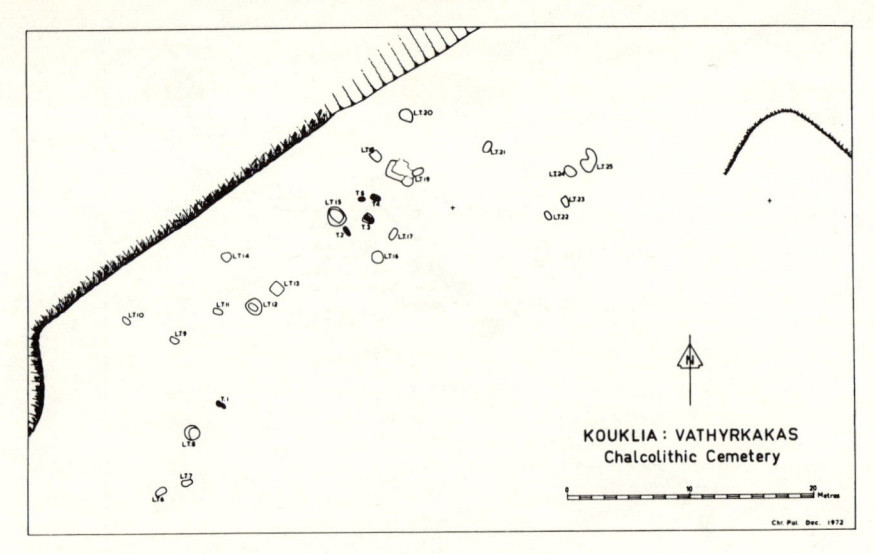

Figure 12.2 Site plan of the uncovered tombs in Cemetery 1.

of the same month all these tombs were thoroughly investigated by the German Mission at Kouklia, headed by Professor F.G. Maier, and they yielded various sherds of Red-on-White and Red Lustrous pottery and seven cruciform picrolite pendants (*Chronique 1973*, 680–1; Maier 1973, 193–4; 1974, 41–3).

The excavations of the Cyprus Department of Antiquities in the same cemetery lasted from December 4 to 10, 1972. They resulted in the discovery of five other tombs (*Chronique 1973*, 680–1). In addition to the excavation and planning of these five tombs, numbered 1–5, a separate site plan was prepared showing the exact position of all the looted and regularly excavated tombs in Cemetery 1, numbering 25 in total (Fig 12.2). Tombs 1, 2 and 3 were intact and produced several selected funerary offerings (Fig 12.3). Tomb 4 was found unfinished, having been abandoned at a depth of 50 cm and Tomb 3, apart from some fragmentary bones of a child, produced no finds at all.

Like all the others in Cemeteries 2 and 3 the excavated tombs in the Vathyrkakas Cemetery 1 are in the form of deep bottle-shaped shafts entirely cut into the hard limestone rock. Their depth varies from 1.50 m to 2.20 m and the diameter from 1.20 m to 1.50 m at the bottom and 75 cm to 90 cm at the *stomion*, which is ovoid or circular in shape. The tombs were used for one or more burials. The dead were buried in a contracted position accompanied by various offerings. After each burial the *stomion* of the tomb was sealed with a large limestone slab and small rough stones. In the fill of the intact Tombs 1, 2, and 3 thick layers of ash mixed with animal and bird bones were found, indicating the existence of certain sacrifices before burial in honour of the dead. The architectural type of the Vathyrkakas shaft tombs is so far unique in the whole of Chalcolithic Cyprus. It differs

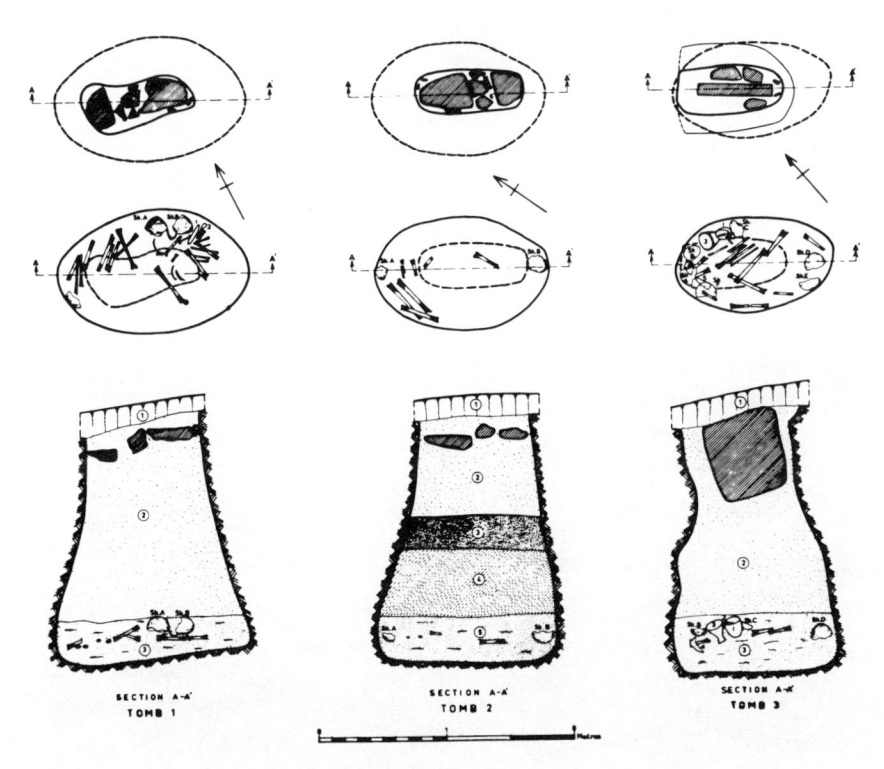

Figure 12.3 Plans and sections of Tombs 1, 2 and 3.

considerably from the type of pit-shaped tombs at Erimi in the Limassol District and is closer to one of the tombs at Lemba-Lakkous in the Paphos District, which however, like the tombs at Erimi, is much smaller and lies within the settlement area (Peltenburg 1977; 1980; *Chronique 1977*, 740–6). This type of tomb, together with evidence of sacrifices before burial in honour of the dead and the distinct separation of cemetery from settlement, recorded only at Souskiou-Vathyrkakas and not elsewhere in Cyprus, constitute important new evidence for the study of Chalcolithic settlements and burial evidence in Cyprus.

The funerary offerings from the three intact tombs excavated by the Cyprus Department of Antiquities in Cemetery 1 comprise several specimens of pottery, necklaces of dentalium shells decorated with small pendants of various types and several other objects of extreme importance and particular interest. The pottery types include small deep handleless bowls of Red-on-White ware, the decoration of which is strictly geometric in orange to red paint applied on a whitish or buff-pinkish slip. One of these bowls with curved sides and flattened base is decorated with an encircling thick line below the outer part of the rim and dotted triangles all over the surface. Another similar but smaller bowl of Red-on-White ware, bearing the same characteristic encircling line below the outer part of the rim and

Figure 12.4 Red-on-White handleless bowl resembling bowls from Erimi.

oblique zig-zag lines on the body resembles the style of the Chalcolithic I bowls found in the pit-shaped tombs at Erimi (Fig 12.4). A third bowl of medium size with slightly curved sides and low splaying foot with flat base is definitely not of Red-on-White ware but its ware is difficult to determine since no traces of paint exist on the worn surface of the vase. It may be classed either as Plain White ware or Coarse Ware. The same problem of ware determination appears on a fragmentary small bottle with globular body, flattened base and wide neck tapering upwards, the upper part of which is missing. The gritty clay and rough surface of this vase suggest a Coarse Ware, but some traces of obliterated reddish paint all over its worn surface may justify a Red Lustrous Ware designation. In fact a few sherds

Figure 12.5 Neck of Red-on-White bottle.

a Red Lustrous Ware, similar to those collected by the German Mission and mentioned earlier, were found in Tomb 3. Another restored bottle with slightly curved sides, conical lower body, pointed base, irregular depressed shoulder and short concave neck is an unusual type and a unique example of Red-on-White ware. A composite decoration of alternate dotted and plain triangle framed by thick reddish lines covers the lower part of its body. The rest of the surface, excluding the neck of the vase, is decorated with groups of vertical double lines in the same reddish paint. The peculiar shape, the fairly fine, soft, buff clay, the elaborate white creamy slip and the composite decoration of this bottle indicate an advanced form of Chalcolithic Red-on-White pottery, obviously later than the usual types of vessels from the same cemetery which correspond to the pottery types of the Erimi first phase. A wide concave neck from Tomb 3, the decoration of which is strictly geometric and symmetrically arranged in chequered compositions is an additional specimen of developed Red-on-White ware in the cemetery. It most probably belonged to a third bottle (Fig 12.5). This same neck shape appears on a bottle with globular body and pointed base. It is decorated with broad wavy bands all over the surface and was found in one of the three tombs in Cemetery 1 excavated by the British Kouklia Expedition in 1951 (Karageorghis 1985, 45.6).

The advanced Red-on-White ware from the Vathyrkakas Cemetery 1 is mainly illustrated by a rich variety of pottery revealed in clandestine excavations. The types represented include an unusual vase in the form of a quadruped with a human face, now in the Pierides Foundation Museum in Larnaca (Karageorghis 1981, 25.11). It has been identified with a kind of prehistoric 'centaur' which may have parallels in the Balkan region. They also include vase specimens of stemmed and mastoid bowls, askoi and several other forms which have not yet been found at other Cypriot Chalcolithic sites. Among these forms worthy of presentation is a composite bottle, now in the Hadjiprodromou Collection, consisting of one main bottle with a long cylindrical neck and two other small bottles communicating with it (Karageorghis 1981, 23.8). No doubt this Red-on-White vase heralds the appearance of the homogeneous composite Red Polished vases in the Early Bronze Age and indicates a late date in the Chalcolithic I period. This indication, in connection with the fact that neither Combed nor Red Polished wares exist among the pottery known from the Vathyrkakas Cemetery I, suggests that the relative chronology of the vessels presented could be assigned to the last phase of the Chalcolithic I period which Dikaios, using C-14 dates, placed between *ca* 2700 and 2500 BC (*SCE* IV.1A, 184–7; *cf* also Catling in CAH³ 551–5).

Apart from pottery, Tomb 3 produced various other objects of minor art including numerous dentalia and 28 miniature picrolite and bone pendants of different shapes some in the form of anthropomorphic figurines. Eight of the pendants are made of bone and the other twenty of picrolite. The picrolite pendants comprise sixteen similar types with cruciform body, two types with triangular body, one type with bottle-shaped body. Ten groups of dentalia, eight cruciform pendants and the unique animal-shaped pendant have been selected to create one of the restored necklaces (Fig 12.6, left). The animal-shaped pendant is made of grey-green picrolite and measures 1.85 cm in height and 3.4 cm in width. The miniature cruciform pendants are made of green picrolite and they are less than 2cm in height.

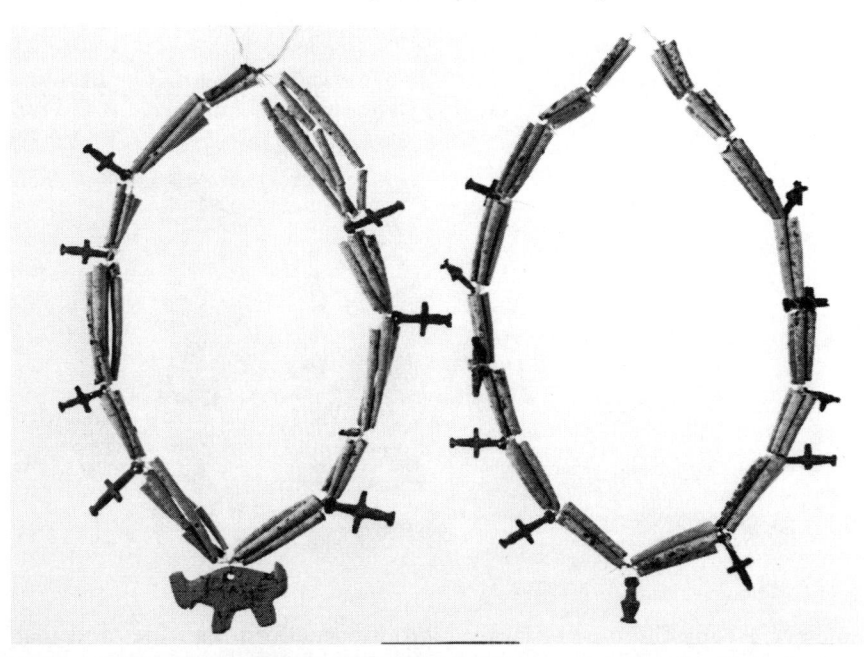

Figure 12.6 Restored necklaces with dentala, cruciform and animal-shaped pendants and pendants with triangular and bottle-shaped bodies.

Both these pendant types have a perforated head for threading. The cruciform pendants are characterized by an oval or square head, long neck, out-stretched arms and triangular or crescent-shaped feet. The second necklace consists of similar cruciform pendants and pendants with triangular and bottle-shaped bodies (Fig 12.6, right). The feet of the triangular pendants are denoted by two small diverging appendages and the bottle-shaped pendants have a conical lower part ending in a disc-shaped base instead of feet. The bone pendants have more or less the same shape consisting of a long shaft ending in a flat quadrangular perforated appendage. Their lower part is usually conical (Fig 12.7).

Miniature pendants of the cruciform type have also been found in the looted tombs of the Vathyrkakas Cemetery 1 by the German Mission. The largest of these pendants, 3.4 cm in height and 2.35 cm in width, presents some technical details not observed on the contemporary pendants yielded by Tomb 3. It has a perforated quadrangular head with rounded angles, surrounded by a square incision, out-stretched arms and hands represented in the swastika position, fingers indicated by incised lines, drawn up knees, legs divided by a deep incised line and feet with a schematic indication of toes (Fig 12.8). Excluding the hands the other general characteristics of this pendant appear on the well known picrolite figurine from Yialia, in the Paphos northern region, and on the small cruciform pendant hanging on the necklace round the neck of the figurine (Karageorghis 1976, 52 Fig 25). Therefore, it is obvious that the small pendants from the Vathyrkakas

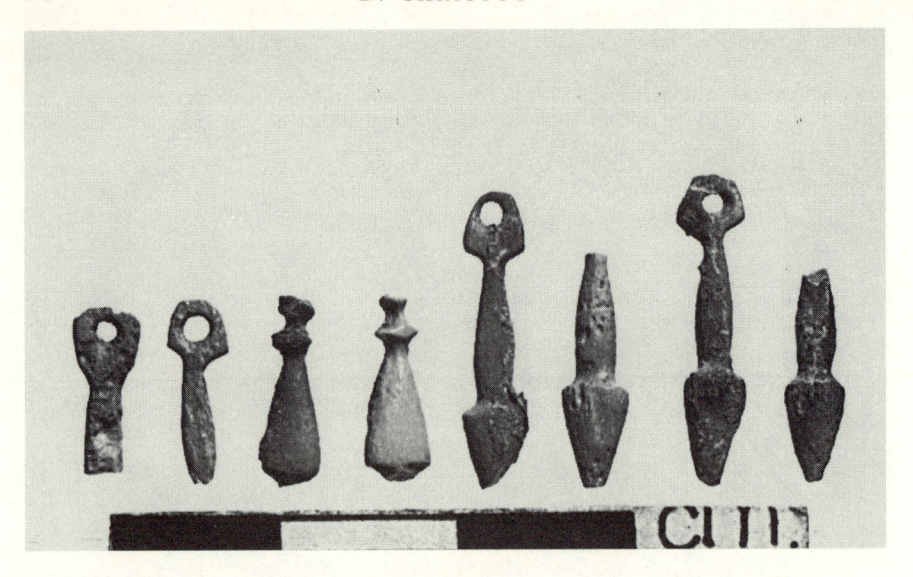

Figure 12.7 Bone pendants.

Cemetery 1 copy the type of larger picrolite cruciform figurines and that they were also worn as amulets (Budge 1961; J.Karageorghis 1977, 26–8). Since all the Paphian picrolite cruciform figurines have been correctly interpreted as cult images of a female or a mixed female and male divinity connected with fertility (J. Karageorghis 1977, 25–32; Reitler 1960–3), no doubt the contemporary pendants constitute miniature reproductions imitating the same cult images and religious beliefs.

The dating of the Vathyrkakas picrolite cruciform figurines and pendants could be assigned to the same period as the pottery produced in Cemetery 1. This conclusion is entirely based on some parallels with similar stratified examples from Erimi and Kythrea (Dikaios 1936, Pl 29; *SCE* I, Pl 13.1) which fall into the second phase of Erimi, i.e. around 2600 BC. Moreover, it is apparent that there are certain similarities with pendants from the Amuq valley in North Syria (Braidwood & Braidwood 1960, 513-9, n. 52) and that there are also a few affinities with Cycladic marble idols (Renfrew 1969, 8,9,30) which are dated approximately to the middle of the 3rd millennium BC.

A phallic representation from Tomb 3 is another notable discovery (Fig 12.9). Measuring 13.6 cm in length and made of limestone, this phallic-shaped object is elongated and rounded and has a rough and irregular surface. Its presence among picrolite cruciform pendants and especially bone pendants in the same tomb, (the conical body of which is in fact reminiscent of the phallic shape), could be interpreted as having the same symbolic character possibly connected with the divinity of fertility. No other phallic representations of the Chalcolithic period are so far known in Cyprus, but a similar symbol, originally identified with an idol's head, has

Figure 12.8 Cruciform pendant found by the German mission.

been found at the Khirokitia Neolithic settlement and two others at Ayios Epiktitos-Vrysi (*Chronique 1969*, 452–3 Fig 33a-b; Peltenburg 1975, 29 Fig 5, Pl 5 lower). The famous clay statuette of a nude male figure seated on a low four-legged stool with hands holding the head and elbows on the knees, purchased in Switzerland by the Pierides Foundation Museum, was labelled as coming from Souskiou (Karageorghis 1981, 29.15; 1985, 47.7; Karageorghis & Vagnetti 1981). At the top of the statuette's head there is a perforation through which a liquid could be introduced. It could then exit from the erected penis. If its Souskiou provenance were to be confirmed, the statuette could be considered not only as the first and unique specimen of its kind in the whole of Chalcolithic Cyprus but also as having possibly immediate connections with certain ritual ceremonies taking place in south-western Cyprus in honour of the fertility female or male deity. However, similar figures dated to the end of the Neolithic period were found in Thessaly (Wace & Thomson 1912, 163 Fig 110) and Romania (Gimbutas 1982, 232 Figs 247–52) and therefore these regions may have a more just claim on the origins of this important statuette.

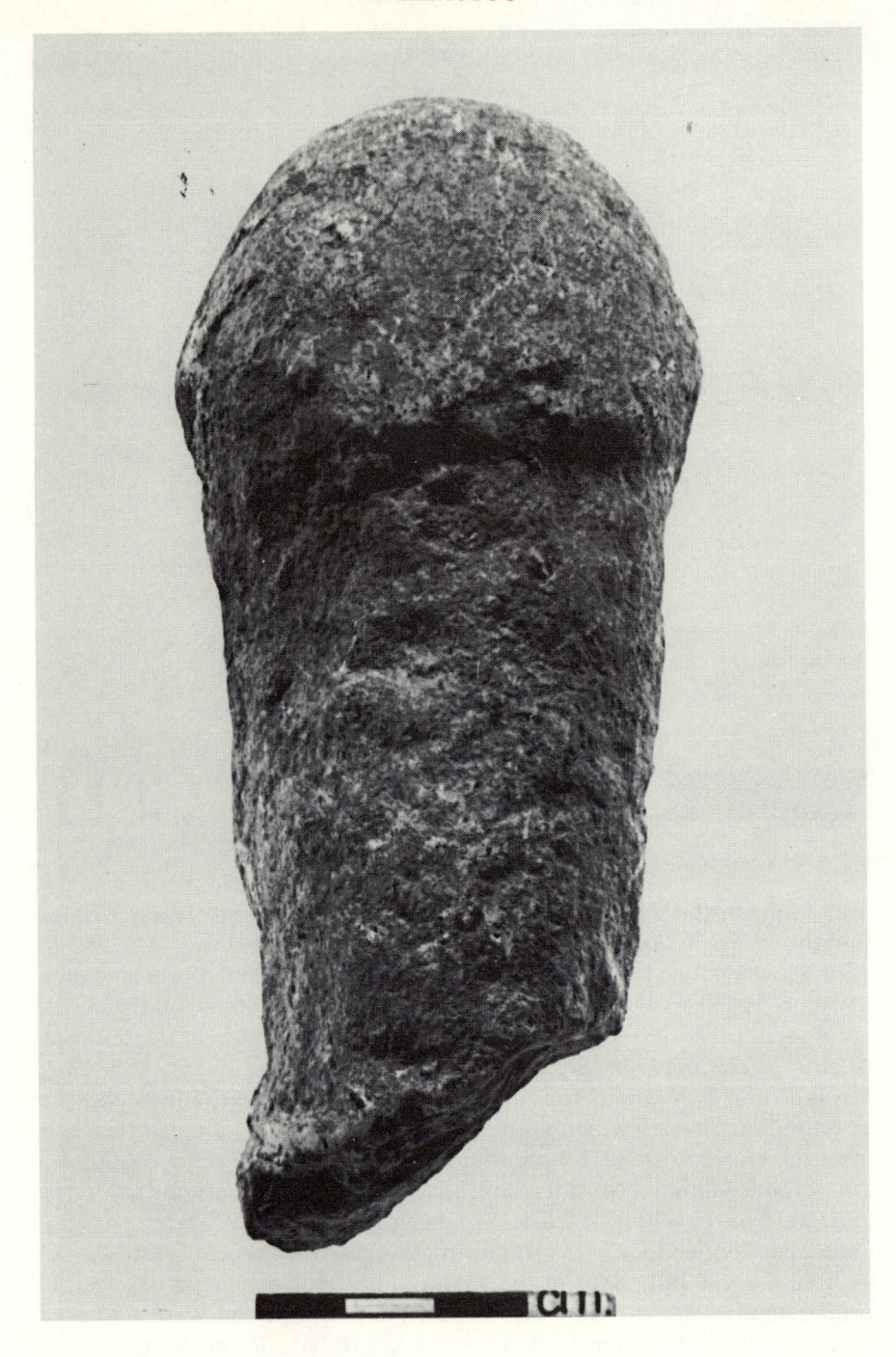

Figure 12.9 Phallic representation from Tomb 3.

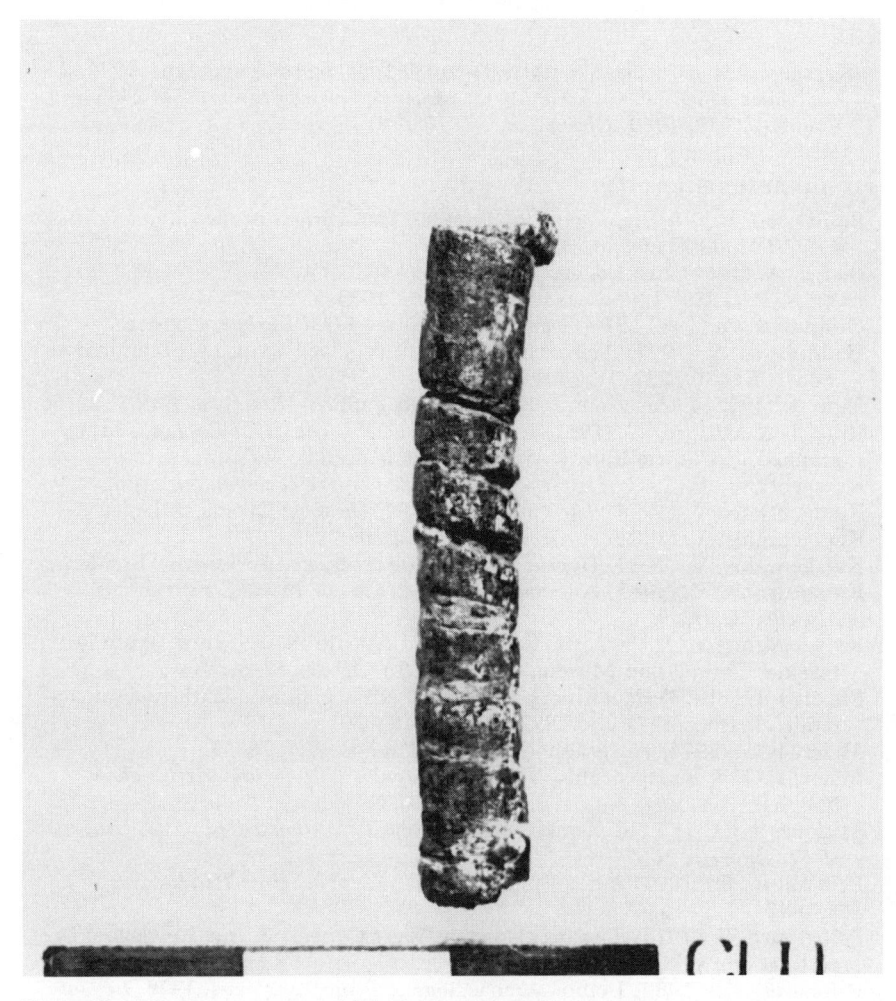

Figure 12.10 Copper ornament with incised spiral pattern.

An elongated and rounded ornament made of pure copper and decorated with spiral incised patterns (Fig 12.10) is the last, but not the least discovery, made in the Vathyrkakas Cemetery 1. This is the second copper object to be found in the whole of Chalcolithic Cyprus. The first one is a chisel found by Dikaios at Erimi in 1935 (1936, 50 Figs 13, 14). After the Souskiou copper ornament three other copper objects, a chisel, a fish-hook and an awl were found respectively by E. Peltenburg at Lemba-Lakkous, Kissonerga-Mylouthkia and Kissonerga-Mosphilia (1985a, Pl 48.11; 1981, 27 Fig 6; 1985b, 62 Fig 4).

In summary, these are some of the results of the Cyprus Department of Antiquities excavations in Souskiou-Vathyrkakas Cemetery 1 and other activities on the site. Hopefully, much more light will be shed on tomb architecture, burial customs, religious beliefs and the cultural substance of Paphos in particular and Cyprus in general by future excavations.

NOTE

[1] Karageorghis 1976, 32–57; 1981, 23-9; 1982, 35–6; J.Karageorghis 1977, 22–30; Maier 1973, 193–4; 1974, 41–3; Maier & Karageorghis 1984, 24–30; Vagnetti 1975; 1980; *Chronique 1973,* 680–1.

LIST OF REFERENCES

Braidwood, R.J. & Braidwood, L.S. (1960) *Excavations in the Plain of Antioch I (OIP* 61) Chicago.
Budge, A. (1961) *Amulets and Talismans.* New York.
Dikaios, P. (1936) The excavations at Erimi 1933–5. *RDAC,* 1–81.
Gimbutas, M. (1982) *The Goddesses and Gods of Old Europe.* London.
Hadjisavvas, S. (1977) The archaeological survey of Paphos. A preliminary report. *RDAC,* 222–31.
Iliffe, J. (1952) Excavations at Kouklia (Old Paphos). *Liverpool Bull 2,* 29–66.
Iliffe, J. & Mitford, T. (1951) *Excavations at Kouklia (Old Paphos).* Mineographed text in the library of the Cyprus Museum, Nicosia.
Karageorghis, J. (1977) *La Grande Déesse de Chypre et son culte.* Lyon.
Karageorghis, V. (1976) *The Civilization of Prehistoric Cyprus.* Athens.
Karageorghis, V. (1981) *Ancient Cyprus.* Athens.
Karageorghis, V. (1982) *Cyprus from the Stone Age to the Romans.* London.
Karageorghis, V. (1985) *Ancient Cypriote Art in the Pierides Foundation Museum.* Larnaca.
Karageorghis, V. & Vagnetti, L. (1981) A Chalcolithic terracotta figure in the Pierides Foundation Museum, Cyprus. *BMOP 26,* 53–6.
Maier, F.G. (1973) Excavations at Kouklia (Palaepaphos). Sixth preliminary report; seasons 1971 and 1972. *RDAC,* 186–201.
Maier, F.G. (1974) Ausgrabungen in Alt-Paphos. *AA,* 28–51.
Maier, F.G. & Karageorghis, V. (1984) *Paphos, History and Archaeology.* Nicosia.
Mitford, T. (1951) The Kouklia Expedition. *The Alumni Chronicle. University of St. Andrews 36,* 7.
Peltenburg, E. (1975) Ayios Epiktitos Vrysi, Cyprus. *Proc Pr Hist Soc 41,* 217–45.
Peltenburg, E. (1979) The prehistory of West Cyprus. Ktima Lowlands. Investigations 1976–1978. *RDAC,* 69–9.
Peltenburg, E. (1980) Lemba Archaeological Project, Cyprus, 1978. *Levant 12,* 1–21.
Peltenburg, E. (1981) Some implications of recent Lemba Project radiocarbon dates for the later prehistory of Cyprus. *BMOP 26,* 23–40.
Peltenburg, E. (1985a) *Lemba Archaeological Project I, Excavations at Lemba-Lakkous, 1976–1983. (SIMA 70.1).* Göteborg.
Peltenburg, E. (1985b) Lemba Archaeological Project, Cyprus, 1983. *Levant 17,* 53–64.
Renfrew, C. (1969) The development and chronology of the Early Cycladic figurines. *AJA 73,* 1–32.
Reitler, R. (1960–3) Neolithische Statuetten aus Cypern. *IPEK 20,* 22–7.
Vagnetti, L. (1975) Some unpublished chalcolithic figurines. *RDAC,* 1–4.
Vagnetti, L. (1980) Figurines and minor objects from a Chalcolithic Cemetery at Souskiou-Vathyrkakas. *SMEA 21,* 17–72.
Wace, A. & Thomson, M. (1912) *Prehistoric Thessaly.* Cambridge.

13
Death in everyday life: aspects of burial practice in the Late Bronze Age

Elizabeth Goring
National Museums of Scotland, Edinburgh

'All discussion of prehistoric material, where it goes beyond the mere descriptive, ventures into the unknown and the unverifiable. Our interpretations can be no more than the product of contemporary experience broadened by some awareness of ethnographic data so that the sole test of our conclusions, assuming no basic distortion of what passes for archaeological fact, must be their plausibility for the reader' (Clarke, Cowie & Foxon 1985, 229).

Studies of prehistoric burial practice must venture firmly into the realm of the unknown and the unverifiable once they depart from the purely factual evidence and embark upon interpretation. Notwithstanding the problems involved, in recent years there has been a great development of interest in the analysis of funerary remains as one means of establishing the nature of ancient social systems. This interest has stemmed largely from New Archaeology, with extensive research emanating principally from the United States and from Cambridge.[1] A positive outcome of this research has been the feeling that, with appropriate methodology, an awareness of the potential problems and conceptual pitfalls, and with a degree of circumspection, it is indeed possible to use burial evidence in the interpretation of ancient social systems. One reason for this optimism seems to be the general acceptance of the principle that burials do at least represent deliberate rather than accidental depositions. O'Shea, for instance, writes

'Mortuary evidence is an extremely valuable archaeological resource, since it represents the direct and purposeful culmination of conscious behaviour, rather than its incidental residue' (*in* Chapman, Kinnes & Randsborg 1981, 39–40);

and again, in a later work,

'Since the time of Worsaae, archaeologists have recognized the uniqueness of the funerary context because of its conscious and purposive elements. The artefact is not in the grave as a result of accident or stochastic processes, in most cases, but rather as a result of conscious and intentional action' (O'Shea 1984, 24; see also, for instance, Pader 1982, 42).

Another reason for optimism, perhaps linked with the first, is the immediacy of contact with prehistoric peoples when dealing with actual human burials. Thus O'Shea writes

'The ready acceptance [of the study of mortuary practice to infer social organization] may also have been due to a common intuitive feeling among all archaeologists that they are somehow very close to the essence of a past culture when working with burial remains' (O'Shea 1984, 1–2).

There has been little attempt to apply to Cypriot burials the kinds of approaches adopted for British and New World evidence by studies of the type referred to above. Rather, as Pader writes in a different but comparable context,

'The emphasis has been on 'what', not 'how' or 'why', on description, not explanation . . . I feel that many misinterpretations . . . have resulted from underestimating the information value of artifact use by concentrating on the relative quantity and quality' (1982, 50).

Therefore, it might be useful to begin with a brief review of the limitations of archaeological methodology in reconstructing aspects of prehistoric society from the evidence of burials. The last part of this paper focuses on the evidence provided by one particular tomb, Kalavasos-Ayios Dhimitrios Tomb 11.

The interpretation of prehistoric burial practice, at least in the Cypriot Late Bronze Age, is affected by several crucial factors. One of the most critical is the scarcity of burials undisturbed by natural or human action. Studies of the kind mentioned above have emphasized the importance of examining the variability or consistency of mortuary practice throughout complete or at least substantial cemeteries. This level of information is hard to achieve in Cyprus, where so many tombs have been looted or otherwise disturbed. As a result of the lack of good comparative data, we have no firm basis for statistical analysis and the establishment of norms. A second factor is the prevalent custom of re-using tombs.[2] This confuses the evidence and often renders it unreliable due to the risk of interference with the introduction of each new burial. However, the most overwhelming problem may be the general difficulty for the modern archaeologist of interpreting thought, belief and intention in a prehistoric period. What may seem perfectly rational deductions are rational only in terms of our own experience since our interpretation is inevitably seen from a modern perspective. Pader, whilst acknowledging the problem, is optimistic that it can be at least partially overcome:

'All aspects of our world view, all our structuring principles and values, in seeming to be natural, timeless and universal, have an effect on our interpretations of other societies' (1982, 31); '. . . with considerable conscious effort we can, to some extent, see into and through our own ideological constraints—even if we are unable to live outside them' (1982, 35).

Perhaps the main task is to be aware of the bias imposed by the 'logic' of our contemporary perspective.

It would be unreasonable to expect to understand prehistoric burial practice on the evidence of tomb finds alone. The actual interment of a body or bones within a tomb usually represents only one part of the total funerary activity. Yet archaeology is incapable of supplying information about those aspects that leave no trace in the material record of the tomb itself. Such aspects might include the laying-out and display of the corpse, funeral processions, the dedication of flowers and food, ritual meals, wakes and the formal and informal processes of mourning.[3] All these events might occur outside the tomb (indeed most of them must have done) and in the absence of pictorial evidence we have no way of visualizing the form they may have taken in a prehistoric period.

There are many pitfalls when dealing with the general interpretation of burial goods. One example of this is the practice of equipping the dead with personal possessions. Are we right in assuming that these are personal possessions at all? Pader notes

'A common assumption (is) that the grave inclusions...represent the deceased's personal possessions . . . It is suggested here that we cannot assume *a priori* that grave goods necessarily represent the deceased's personal possessions and that it is thereby the individual's wealth or "true" status that is being recognized' (1982, 57).

She makes the point

'To start with the presumption that cemeteries/graves with fewer artefacts necessarily represent poorer and/or lower rank communities/ individuals than more elaborately furnished cemeteries/graves, rather than possibly representing distinctive burial rites related to cultural factors is to make an unjustifiable jump from the empirical data to the social organization' (1982, 195).

She advocates a careful application of the concept of space-use, combined with analysis of other types of data, to obtain a more accurate picture.

'This multi-dimensional framework puts to question the commonly applied presupposition that if a grave has no artefacts it is of a poor person or if there are many artefacts the deceased was wealthy' (1982, 79).

Are we necessarily right in assuming that the deposition of grave gifts implies a belief in an after-life? We know this to be the case in ancient Egypt since the Egyptians told us this themselves, but can we presume that this applies in the Cypriot Bronze Age as well? And if the presence of tomb gifts implies a belief in an after-life, does their absence necessarily imply a *lack* of belief? An absence of tomb gifts might simply be a manifestation of a funerary belief that did not call for such depositions. Many explanations for the deposition of objects might be suggested, other than their use in an after-life. For instance, perhaps the building and servicing of tombs played an important part in the activities of the living, and the deposition of objects fulfilled a specific need on the part of the surviving community. Perhaps the collection and display of grave goods provided an opportunity for the family to show off its wealth and to reap the prestige that could be gained from being able to abandon luxurious objects. Perhaps there was a simple economic explanation: the deliberate removal of objects from circulation amongst the living might help to stimulate local craft production. Perhaps superstition demanded the burial of all objects intimately associated with the dead person.

The discovery of Kalavasos-Ayios Dhimitrios Tomb 11 in 1984 gave rise to great excitement (Fig 13.1). Intact and unplundered, it offered a rare opportunity to retrieve burial evidence in a systematic way. It was hoped that this tomb would shed light on Late Bronze Age funerary practice, at least in the Vasilikos Valley area, and help to understand something of the social organization of its occupants. It did indeed offer a unique opportunity to go beyond an analysis of the chronology, style and development of artefacts to apply techniques of interpretation based on space use, comparative data within a closed group, orientation and the position of the objects (*cf* Pader 1982, 79), but other problems soon emerged. The post-excavation study of Tomb 11 illustrated the difficulties of dealing with a single tomb, rather than a cemetery with its potential for comparative data. It was clear that the evidence would in fact produce more questions than answers. Nevertheless, it is worthwhile formulating these questions, as they point the way to some basic interpretation. The discovery of more intact tombs at Ayios Dhimitrios would help answer many of these questions and confirm or deny the conclusions drawn from Tomb 11 alone.

Tomb 11 at Kalavasos-Ayios Dhimitrios is an exceptionally rich and undisturbed tomb dated to the LC IIA period on the evidence of the finds recovered from it. Excavations at the site of Ayios Dhimitrios form part of the Vasilikos Valley Project based at Brandeis University and headed by Professor Ian Todd (Todd 1986, 17–18). I am most grateful to Alison South, who directed the work, for allowing me to discuss the tomb in advance of the final publication. (South *et al* forthcoming).

The nature of much of the material, and the context in which it was found, provide further evidence for the complexity of Late Bronze Age burial practice which is suggested at many other more disturbed sites. Although the material recovered from the tomb *seems* remarkable, it may only seem so because we simply do not know what was the norm.

There is nothing remarkable about the tomb itself, whose features can be paralleled individually, although not all together, in other Late Bronze Age tombs.[4] Its most obvious feature consists of the substantial benches cut

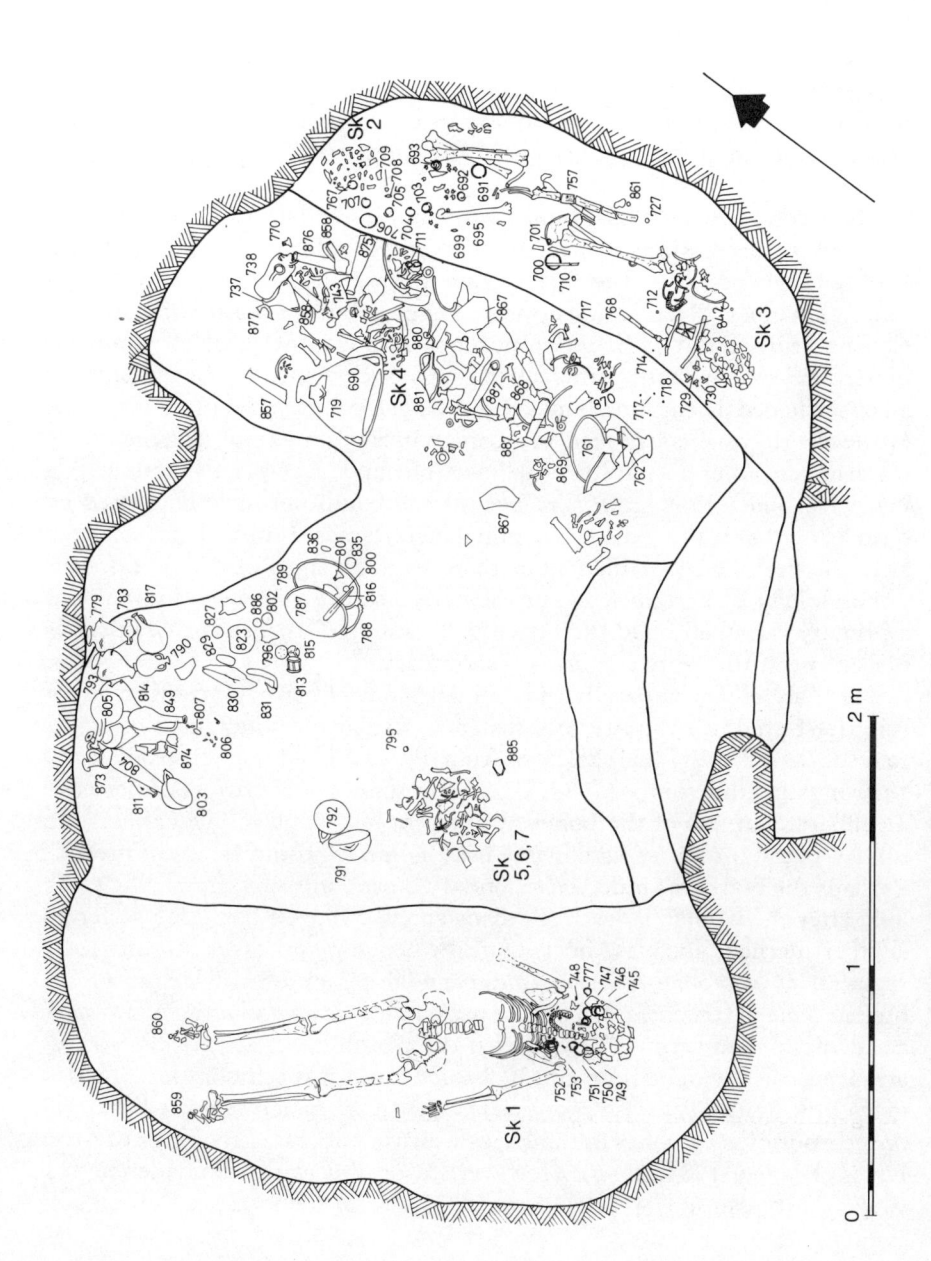

Figure 13.1 Plan of Tomb 11 at Kalavasos-Ayios Dhimitrios.

into the rock of the east and west walls. Both benches are approximately the same height, but the west bench is noticeably longer and wider than the east bench. Could this difference in size be accounted for by a distinction in their use or status? This question might best be tackled by a brief summary of the occupants of the tomb and their relative positions.

The remains of two adult females were found on top of the east bench. One of them was a woman aged between 21 and 24 at the time of her death. Her bones were found scattered over the top of the bench and on the floor beside it, with only the cranium and a few vertebrae left undisturbed at the north end of the bench. By no means were all the skeletal elements represented, and therefore some bones must have disintegrated or else they had never been present. This raises the question of whether this was a secondary interment.

The second female, whose bones were mingled with those of the first, was a slightly younger woman, aged about seventeen. Her skull lay at the south end of the bench, but the rest of her skeleton was disposed in a most unusual manner. What at first appeared to be a random scatter of disturbed elements turned out to be far from random, but rather a deliberate post-mortem re-arrangement. Whereas the smaller elements had been scattered all over the bench, the long bones had been gathered up and placed in pairs. However, they were arranged in an anatomically impossible manner with, for instance, an upper limb with a lower one and an upper leg bone with a lower leg bone. This kind of re-positioning could not have happened by chance, neither was it caused by animal disturbance. It must have occurred after the flesh had mortified since there were no signs of dissection. It is impossible to be certain whether the body had been deposited initially as a primary burial and had then been deliberately disturbed, or whether its placement in the tomb was in fact secondary.

There are plenty of parallels for similar kinds of bone re-arrangement or selective burial in antiquity. For instance, Richard Bradley notes attempts to reconstitute individual skeletons from disarticulated bones introduced to British megalithic tombs (1984, 19–20). In these cases, however, there was a deliberate mixing of the bones of different individuals. The explanation for the post-mortem re-arrangement in Tomb 11 could be quite prosaic. Perhaps the body was indeed a secondary burial, introduced into the tomb long after the woman's death. Perhaps she was moved from one bench to another. Perhaps she was knocked off the bench by mistake, and hurriedly replaced by someone with an understandable lack of knowledge of the human skeletal structure. All these explanations assume that the bones were accidentally misplaced. There is also the possibility that this kind of re-arrangement was deliberate and had some kind of specific import. British megalithic tombs have also produced evidence of specially selected removal or incorporation of bones in tombs, as well as deliberate groupings of these bones (Bradley 1984, 22–3). However, in dealing with the evidence of a single tomb, caution is wise (compare Buikstra, for instance, 'A conservative and critical stance is essential when investigating skeletal samples of small size' (*in* Chapman, Kinnes & Randsborg 1981, 123). In Ayios Dhimitrios Tomb 11 we cannot be certain whether all elements of the first skeleton were ever incorporated within the chamber, and we have no comparative data from other tombs to support the evidence or otherwise.

In contrast with the burials on the east bench, the burial on the west bench was undisturbed and fully articulated. The body was that of a woman aged around 19 or 20. She lay on her back in an extended position with her skull towards the entrance. The upper part of her body was at a strangely high angle. This could not be explained by wrapping in a shroud, since the arms were held away from the body. It is more likely that the body was pulled into position along the bench and not adjusted into a more relaxed attitude. This implies that the body was unlikely to have been placed in the tomb in a state of rigor mortis.

Only one body lay on the west bench, although it was the larger of the two. Why was this articulated body placed on a different bench from the disarticulated bodies? There are several possible explanations. Firstly, the west bench might have been intended for the initial laying-out of the body, with individuals later being moved to the east bench. This might explain the lack of articulation evidenced on the east bench. Perhaps the east bench was considered to be full, and so the west bench came into use. Perhaps the larger of the benches was reserved for individuals of a particular status. (This status was evidently not related to age, since the woman on the west bench was neither the oldest nor the youngest in the tomb). Whatever the explanation, it is important to note the different treatment of the adult skeletons. Was it eventually intended to move the west bench skeleton, so that its condition would ultimately correspond with that of the east bench women?

While the adults all lay on the benches, the remains of four children were found on the floor. Was this a reflection of their relative status? There is very slight evidence that this might not have been the case. The body of a child aged about 3 was found on the floor. However, three milk teeth were found on the east bench. It is clear from their lack of wear that these were not retained deciduous teeth belonging to either of the two adult females. Therefore, the child may have been originally laid out on the bench, and moved to the floor after mortification of the flesh. Alternatively, someone had gathered up the three teeth from the floor and placed them on the bench. A third possibility is that they belonged to an otherwise unrepresented child.

Three tiny infants were found on the floor beside the west bench. Their bones were mixed with disarticulated fish and bird bones, and all were densely concentrated within a defined, roughly circular area on the floor. This deposit apparently represents a multiple secondary deposition, probably within a single container which has not survived. There is no evidence that the infants were allowed access to a bench.

The following general conclusions might be drawn about the disposition of the bodies in the tomb. Firstly, this appears to be an example of communal burial. There was little emphasis on maintaining the integrity of the individual, and one might conclude that some importance lay in the collectiveness of the group. Secondly, this appears to be a selected group since the tomb contained only young adult females and children. Thirdly, the adult burials may have been treated in a different way to the infants. The adults could all have been introduced to the tomb as primary articulated burials, although this is only provable for the body on the west bench. If all the adult burials were originally articulated, then two of the three were treated in a specific manner once the flesh had mortified. Although a certain amount of respect was accorded to the bodies on the east bench, in that they were not simply swept to the floor or cleared out of the tomb altogether, yet they were pushed to one side or deliberately moved as if the integrity of the body was no longer important at a certain stage. Fourthly, the interment of the infants within the tomb was a secondary activity, and interment might have taken place long after death. The infants were presumably involved in some kind of primary funerary event outside the tomb itself.

At present we have no way of relating the individuals buried in the tomb to each other. However, a closed group like this might offer an ideal opportunity for palaeoserology, and other forms of genetic or osteological examination.

A large number of artefacts was found on the benches and on the floor. In some instances, it was possible to relate these artefacts to specific individuals. For, example, the intact skeleton on the west bench was buried with a complete set of jewellery, whilst the three infants on the floor could be stratigraphically associated with three White Slip milk bowls. Space allows the consideration of only two particular aspects of the artefacts: the nature of the burial gifts and some intriguing evidence provided by the jewellery.

One of the most noticeable aspects of the grave goods is that they are almost all of a luxurious nature, such as gold, ivory, glass and rather special pottery including an exceptional number of Red Lustrous Ware vessels. Particular factors may have governed selection. Another noticeable feature was the presence of sets. There were, for instance, two kraters, each containing a cup, two bull rhyta, two core-formed glass vessels, two ivory cosmetic palettes in the form of ducks, three identical piriform jars, three pedestalled dishes and three milk bowls. Because of the difficulties of associating the finds on the floor with the bodies on the benches, other than spatially, it is hard to interpret the existence of these sets. The groups of two or three identical items might reflect the way they were used. Alternatively, they might reflect the number of burials introduced into the tomb during particular episodes.

Besides artefacts, food was also deposited in the tomb. Evidence for this includes eggshells, as well as the bones of sheep, goat, rock doves and fish.

What was the purpose of the grave goods? Selection does not seem to have been based on domestic necessity since there were few items which could be associated with the more mundane requirements of daily life (although such items could have been made of organic materials). Although the food might have been intended as provision for an after-life, or a journey to an after-life, it might equally have demonstrated the family's ability to dispose of it. The burial of high-quality artefacts could have been intended to ensure a high standard of living in the next world, or it could have underlined the wealth and status of the dead and their family. The discovery of a series of intact tombs similar to Tomb 11 might provide a basis for a statistical determination of the type of objects considered suitable for burial. It might be possible to relate particular types of objects with particular types of individuals, and to compare their positions in the tomb. This in turn might give some indication of their purpose.

Unless all the grave goods belonged to the final burials in the tomb, it seems that the possessions of the earlier burials were respected. This might imply that the group was closely linked, perhaps as members of a single family, and perhaps all buried within a short time in terms of human memory.

A study of the jewellery found in the tomb revealed some unexpected facts. The woman on the west bench was buried with an impressive set found *in situ* on her body. She wore six gold earrings, four gold spirals for her hair or ears, at least one necklace, two gold signet rings and two silver toe rings. All the jewellery, as well as that found on the east bench, showed sufficient signs of wear to indicate that it had been worn in life.

Three simple gold hoops were worn to each side of the head. The plainness of these earrings seemed surprising at first sight. Why was such a wealthy woman not wearing some of the more decorative types of earrings available at the period?[5] Was there a cultural explanation, perhaps peculiar to Ayios Dhimitrios? An examination of their weights produced interesting results and a possible answer.

Courtois has argued for the existence of a number of weight standards in use during the Late Cypriot period, based on several different units (1984, 114–34). Amongst these, there is a standard based on 10.8 gms. The weight of each earring correlated very closely to this amount, suggesting that each could represent a single unit of such a standard. Six more earrings were found on the east bench. Their weights were such that, in practical terms, the group could have been produced from four units of gold of the same standard.

If the earrings do indeed represent specific units of weight, this raises interesting questions about their function. They are undecorated solid gold objects. It is possible that they were intended to be worn *en masse* as conspicuous signs of wealth, representing not only items of adornment but also units of convertible currency. Part of their value may have lain in their existence as a group of six. A comparable group of six found in Enkomi Swedish Tomb 18 may lend support to this theory (*SCE* I, 551, 549 Fig 209/7 (plan)).

Similar weight patterns can be distinguished amongst the gold spirals found in the tomb. Our sample is very small, but it does result from a closed group, and it raises the possibility of similar patterns within other assemblages of undecorated gold earrings and spirals. It would be interesting to find that the dead were equipped not only with items of adornment but also units of exchangeable currency. It may be going too far to suggest that these women were buried with their dowries, but if this were the case, there might be interesting implications regarding their requirement in death.

The social organization of the group to which the occupants of this tomb belonged evidently required, or at least enabled, the deposition of substantial amounts of artefacts. However, we cannot begin to explain the choice of objects. Were they personal possessions or simply typical accompaniments at death? Despite all the data the tomb has produced, what do we actually know about the three women and four children who were buried in it? The evidence of this single tomb can reveal little about the way they lived. We can tell nothing about their beliefs or experiences. We do not know exactly why they died. We do not even know if this was a typical example of how Bronze Age people dealt with death in their everyday lives. When considering burials, especially isolated tombs, it is clearly prudent to be aware of the limitations of our methods of collecting and assessing evidence. In our approaches to understanding prehistoric society generally, we must also try to be aware of those aspects which are archaeologically undetectable and keep sight of the facets of humanity which we cannot hope to recreate.

NOTES

[1] For a useful survey of development in approach and interpretation, see Chapman & Randsborg *in* Chapman, Kinnes & Randsborg 1981, 1–24. O'Shea 1984, 2–3 offers a survey of the literature concerning the direct application of funerary analysis to social reconstruction, and studies that use funerary evidence as a constant for analysing other aspects of social systems such as economics, demography, pathology etc.

[2] This problem is briefly discussed for instance by Chapman & Randsborg, *in* Chapman, Kinnes & Randsborg 1981, 13.

[3] See Chapman, Kinnes & Randsborg 1981, 12–13.

[4] No comprehensive and up-to-date study of tomb types exists at present, although a useful survey can be found in *SCE IV*. 1C, 44–51. A study of tombs from MC III-LCI is currently being undertaken by Priscilla Schuster Keswani (University of Michigan).

[5] For example, earrings made of two twisted strips (*cf SCE* 1, Pl 80.2, Enkomi Sw.T. 8 no 7) from around LC IB; bull's head earrings (*cf SCE IV*. 1D, 509, Fig 65.12), probably from LC IB/IIA.

LIST OF REFERENCES

Bradley, R. (1984) *The Social Foundations of Prehistoric Britain*. London.
Chapman, R., Kinnes, I. & K. Randsborg (1981) *The Archaeology of Death*. Cambridge.
Clarke, D.V., Cowie, T. & A. Foxon (1985) *Symbols of Power at the Time of Stonehenge*. Edinburgh.
Courtois, J-C. (1984) *Alasia III. Les objets des niveax stratifiés d'Enkomi: Fouilles C.F-A. Schaeffer (1947–1970)* Paris.
O'Shea, J.M. (1984) *Mortuary Variability: An Archaeological Investigation*. London.
Pader, E-J. (1982) *Symbolism, Social Relations and the Interpretation of Mortuary Remains (BAR Int Ser 130)*. Oxford.
South, A. et al (forthcoming) *Vasilikos Valley Project: Kalavasos-Ayios Dhimitrios III, Tomb 11 (SIMA 71.4)*. Göteborg.
Todd, I. (1986) *Vasilikos Valley Project I: The Bronze Age Cemetery in Kalavasos Village (SIMA 71.1)*. Göteborg.

POSTER SUMMARY

14
Early Iron Age—dead and living

Henryk Meyza
Research Centre for Mediterranean Archaeology, Warsaw

An attempt to interpret tomb assemblages of the Cypro-Geometric Period had to start from establishing a concordance between chronological and typological systems used for different sites. These vary in most cases in spite of their common origin in *SCE* IV.2. Apart from tomb description, the database used (in fact multiple databases) contains data on two different levels of detail relating to every recovered object. The more general identifies the function of the object, its stylistic variant and its position in the tomb. The more detailed contains a full description of the object and therefore was used in few types only—eg amphorae. The typological concordance used well-defined stylistic variants to control the classification of each object and particularly pottery type discrimination in all cases.

This was followed by an analysis of published tomb groups aimed at separating the equipment of single burials. Here, along with stratigraphy, a concept of spatio-functional groups of objects was used and, with all due reservations, typological grouping. Burial assemblages discriminated in this manner permitted a revision of chronology (particularly necessary for *SCE* tombs, where only stratigraphy was used as a separating factor), a study of the burial rites involved and the determination of attitudes to previous interments. Further on a study of regional and temporal variation of these is being made in ascending order—from a single site in one period to the area of the whole island in the Early Iron Age. Burials and cemeteries are compared first in pairs. An attempt to explain the observed differences is made using the suggested meaningful discriminations in order to present a coherent picture in the wider setting of data from sanctuaries and settlements as well as burial practices of Greece and the Levant. A case study of these initial steps was presented on the basis of the site of Alaas.

PART THREE
Religion

15
The beginnings of religion in Cyprus

Edgar Peltenburg
University of Edinburgh

Discussion of possible evidence for religion in pre-Bronze Age Cyprus has been hampered by a variety of reasons. For Rutkowski (1979, 224–5) it is the absence of cult places prior to the Early Bronze Age Vounous 'Sacred Enclosure' model (Fig 15.4). For Masson, as for many others, the major indicators for religious beliefs are rather uninformative stone and other 'idols' which, he avers, recall fertility figurines of the Near East. The smallest figurines however, he classes as amulets (1969, 53–4). It is this distinction which has recently become a central issue with Morris' contention that they are all no more than birth charms (1985, 115–22).

To propose that the mainly female figures were used as charms rather than simply as play or pedagogic dolls for example (*cf* Ucko 1968, 421–6) is nonetheless to admit the existence of archaeological correlates for the use of magic in society. Charms may be regarded as attracting supernatural guardians, amulets as warding off evil. The debate, therefore, is about the level of sophistication of religious beliefs if we accept Durkheim's definition of religion as a system of beliefs and practices relating to the sacred. He described the sacred as a realm apart from the profane (1964, 38–9), a distinction which is not always easily drawn. The thrust of Morris' interpretation is that because there are 'no temples to the Great Goddess, no remains of huge effigies and no models of the faithful' in prehistoric Cyprus (1985, 114–15), religious beliefs excluded the notion of deities. He visualizes nothing more complex in prehistoric times than ghosts or spirits and he ascribes the growth of religious cults to the development of urbanization. Thus, the Vounous and Kotchati models, and, following Merrillees (1980), the Early and Middle Bronze figurines, are dismissed from the corpus of representations of deities (Morris 1985, 281–4).

Many have criticised Morris' interpretations, especially of the Vounous bowl as simply another *genre* scene (eg Catling 1986, 158). Here the general implication is resisted mainly for two reasons. First, it reverts to the evolutionary positions of rationalists such as Tylor (1958) in which religion was thought to develop in orderly stages from animism to polytheism and eventually monotheism. It was a theory which Evans applied in his influential study of early religion in the Aegean (1901, 123–6) when he argued that aniconic images preceded anthropomorphic representations, but while he allowed of transitional stages, Warren (1973) has shown that developments were much more complex. Unilineal schemes have long since been abandoned in response to Lang's arguments (1898, 160) and repeated observations of primitive religions in which the concept of deity is certainly attested (eg Schmidt 1912–54). Second, in formulating the above archaeological criteria for the recognition of deities, criteria extracted from urban and Classical evidence, Morris is culpable of the very 'retrospective error' he levels at those who uncritically interpret fertility figurines as Mother Goddesses. The absence of later types of archaeological evidence for deities does not necessarily prove the absence of the divine in prehistoric societies.

Apart from funerary practices, there has been little contextual information for pre-Bronze Age religion in Cyprus hitherto. What existed has been passed over in favour of the study of objects. J Karageorghis in her comprehensive treatment of the iconography of the Great Goddess notes that most chalcolithic picrolite figurines were used as pendants in life and as grave offerings (1977, 28), a conclusion with which Vagnetti (1980, 53–6) concurs. Vagnetti also agrees that the small figures may be copies of larger cult statues such as the single *in situ* example from Lemba (Peltenburg 1977). This then is an important context which we shall return to below. Meanwhile, it is instructive to note how starkly the Cypriot situation contrasts with that pertaining in the Aegean. There, a spate of discoveries has led to vigorous debate concerning the interpretation of material evidence for religion (eg Hägg & Marinatos 1981). A growing concensus exists for the primacy of context and associations and this is taken as fundamental here. Particularly useful is Renfrew's study of Phylakopi in which he attempts a general interpretative framework for the archaeology of cult (1985). Valuable though this is, it should be noted that while for Renfrew sacred ritual is indicative of the worship of divinity, here it is understood to be a bridging mechanism between humans and the supernatural, without prejudice as to whether the latter was conceived of as deities or as impersonal supernatural powers.

In what follows, I shall briefly assess some non-mortuary contexts of pre-Bronze Age date with possible evidence for religious activity. These will be dealt with in chronological order.

KALAVASSOS-TENTA

This aceramic neolithic settlement demonstrates a link with Asiatic traditions in the deployment of figurative artwork on its walls. Only one decorated panel survives. On the internal pier of Structure 11 are two schematized anthropomorphic figures with uplifted arms and with legs probably spread apart, their upper parts horizontal, lower vertical (Todd 1981, 50). Despite the fact that this posture is duplicated in 'Mistress of the Animals' relief paintings at Çatal Hüyük (Mellaart 1963, 77 Pl VII; 1967 109–55, Figs 23, 27–8, 37–8, 40, 45) Todd is reluctant to admit of religious, or any other, significance (1982, 48). In the Near East such wall paintings are usually interpreted in ritualistic terms (eg Redman 1978, 184–6). Lorenz's general statement, quoted by Marinatos, that "all human art was primarily developed in the service of rituals and that the autonomy of 'art for art's sake" was achieved only by another, secondary step of cultural progress' (1984, 31) supports this position, but we are still far from having compelling specific evidence. Unfortunately, the lack of associated remains and the unexceptional character of the building hinders meaningful contextual analysis.

KHIROKITIA

The contemporary, prolific settlement of Khirokitia has yielded many schematic figurines, mostly from general habitation levels or erosion deposits (see Le Brun, above, 79–80). Only four are from inside buildings. Nos 1175B, 1063 and 1089 come from two *tholoi*, XXXV and XLVII, which are unremarkable save for the presence of large numbers of burials (Dikaios 1953, 155, 181, 183). J. Karageorghis' hypothesis that the figures are linked to an ancestor cult (1977, 17) is plausible in the light of these associations, but clearly more pristine contextual evidence is needed.

In the later neolithic period, the paucity of figurines is offset by sound contextual information. Two possible sacred places lack the spatial autonomy typical of public shrines. They were not devoted exclusively to worship and so might be regarded as domestic cult places (*cf* Renfrew 1985, 22). As we shall see however, there are other factors which mark these out as unconventional and atypically rich centres.

AYIOS EPIKTITOS-VRYSI

Floor 4a of House 1 at Ayios Epiktitos-Vrysi had a discrete arrangement of fixtures and artefacts (Peltenburg 1982, 24–6). Against its east wall and adjacent to an off-centre platform hearth were unique stone seats with back and armrests. On the opposite side of the floor were two concentrations of artefacts: domestic equipment in the SW and a unique group of three small pillar-figures, a pestle and a grinder in a small enclosure in the NW (Fig 15.1a). The figures are elongated stones, *ca* 60 cms high and unlike any other artefacts or building stones (Fig 15.2). All are self-supporting and they retain traces of grass or reeds as if they had been wrapped in organic material. The most elaborate is phallus-shaped with a roughly domed terminal demarcated by a deep groove (Peltenburg 1982, 316–17, Fig 60.353, Pl 33A). The grass silicates on its flattened sides were plaited and in one case they formed a large oval.

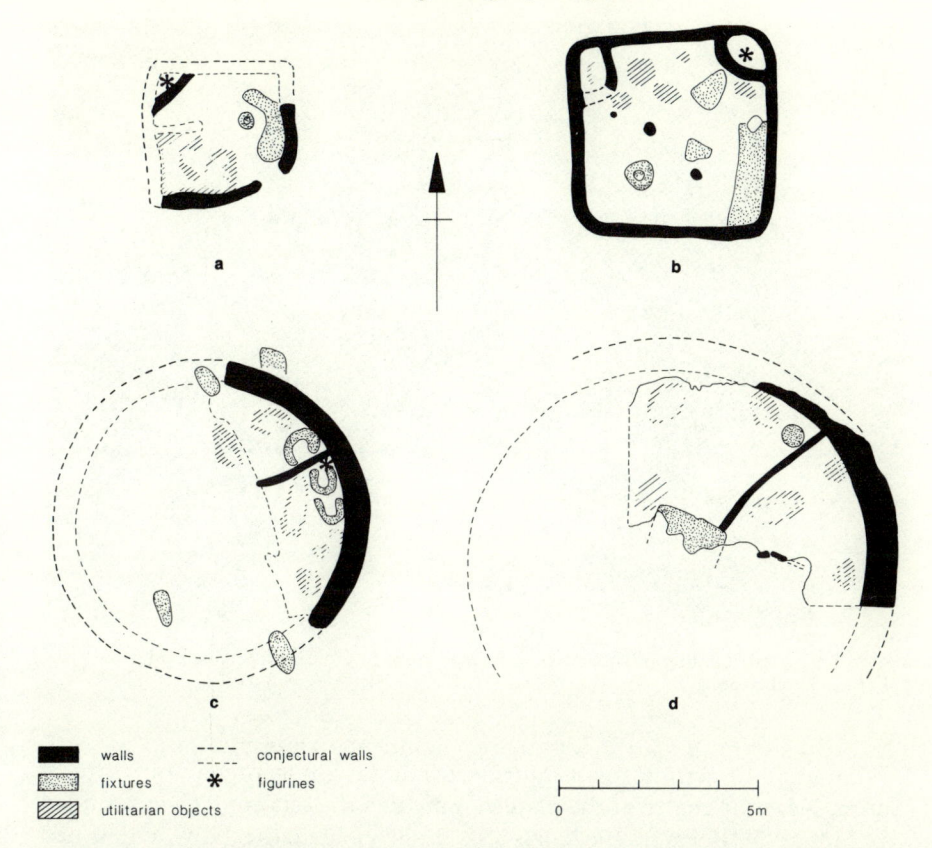

Figure 15.1 Possible cultic places in pre-Bronze Age Cyprus: (a) Ayios Epiktitos-Vrysi House 1; (b) Sotira House 5; (c) Lemba-Lakkous Building 1; (d) Kissonerga-Mosphilia Building 855.

These figures have no known parallels in Cyprus. The importance of this lies in the fact that some Vrysi buildings were destroyed and most were abandoned with abundant portable equipment left behind (Peltenburg 1985, 48). If domestic cult had been a regular institution one would have expected similar items and fixtures in the other buildings. The fixture in this case is the low walled enclosure which served to separate these objects from the rest of the room. Other enclosures only recur in two buildings, H2A and H2B, where they are much larger and only contain cobbled floors (Peltenburg 1982, 42, 44). Thus, in H1 two conditions for domestic cult are evident: 'a specific place [and] well defined forms not commonly used in secular contexts' (Renfrew 1985, 22). The virtual absence of the former and complete absence of the latter in the remaining Vrysi buildings emphasize the unconventional character of H1. Its importance is further supported by the fact that it is located in the 'wealthier' North Sector of the settlement and that it has the longest and earliest history of all the excavated buildings. H1 therefore, probably had more than domestic status and/or the presence of the pillar figures may have conferred on the occupants an elite status.

Figure 15.2 Free-standing pillar figures in an enclosure in House 1 at Ayios Epiktitos-Vrysi (Photo E J Peltenburg).

SOTIRA

A similar focal setting for a figurine occurs at the contemporary site of Sotira. Near the centre of the plateau on which the settlement was founded lies House 5 (Dikaios 1962, 41–50). This yielded the only undoubted figurine from the site, a modelled and incised limestone phallus (Ht 16.5 cm). Like the Vrysi baetyls, it too was located in an unusual corner enclosure in a monocellular structure (Fig 15.1b). Distinguishing features of this enclosure are: small size, associated low platform in front and boundary wall that did not extend up to the rafters. Its distinctiveness is further corroborated by the fact that H5 is the only square building with any enclosure and the only one of all the Sotira buildings to have two enclosures. The second one is like the others. In his study of Sotira, Stanley Price commented on two further special aspects of H5 (1979, 78–9). First, the enclosure containing the figurine was the only one with pottery vessels: at least eight bowls and well over eleven jugs. Some are of the finest Sotira quality (Watkins 1969, Pl III). Second, he argued that H5 played a central role in the distribution of ceramics amongst the complexes on the plateau. It may also be noted that both Vrysi H1 and Sotira H5 have nearly square plans. These are rare and although it is not the intention here to argue that such plans indicate a religious function, they do constitute evidence for the employment of the best constructional techniques. There are, therefore, several reason why H5 is to be regarded as a pre-eminent structure at Sotira and its enclosure with figurine as a sacred ritual focus.

The settlements of Ayios Epiktitos-Vrysi and Sotira provide clear evidence that late neolithic ritual foci were associated with important buildings. They demonstrate religious associations with inequalities in neolithic society. They also suggest that distinctions between exclusively 'public' and 'domestic' buildings may be misleading in emergent religious organisations.

UNDERGROUND FEATURES

Elaborate tunnels incorporating chambers, portholes and other features are recorded at two pre-Bronze Age sites. Philia-Drakos A yielded a complex series of these subterranean features which are contemporary with or postdate the buildings of the Late Neolithic settlement (*Chronique 1968*, 297–302; Watkins 1969, 34–5). Considerable labour was involved in the construction of these 'hypogea' with their multiple entrances, sills between shafts and tunnels, benches, and heavy stone blockings. They are reported to contain the finest objects from the site, including large numbers of unused stone axes, as well as animal bone. Watkins concluded that they were without utilitarian purpose and that they had a ritual significance.

Another set of tunnels some 10 m in length occurs at the Early Chalcolithic site of Kalavassos-Ayious (Todd 1982, 54–7). In addition to many of the Philia features it has steps leading into it, gypsum blocking slabs and a posthole. Again, use of the tunnel, as distinct from the many pits found at the site, is uncertain. Todd did not rule out 'metaphysical beliefs about chthonic forces' and he noted the concentration of figurines in the area of the complex. It appears that of a total of nineteen from the site as a whole, some nine figurines were recovered from its area along with several chisels, bone points, bead and other objects (South 1985, 67).

These tunnels have no later parallels in Cyprus whereas in W. Asia networks of tunnels occurred beneath temples at Hazor (Yadin 1975, 70–7) and Tell Brak (Mallowan 1947, 32–3, Pl 58) for example. The affinities are not very helpful and it is therefore on the basis of the contexts and associations that the use of these features should be assessed. The association of so many figurines at the one site and high quality finds at the other suggests that they were important constructions. There are no picrolites amongst the figurines and hence a funerary aspect seems unlikely. Since they are all so badly broken it may be of course that they are simply derived and part of the fill. More explicit evidence therefore is required to establish the purpose(s) of these intriguing features.

KISSONERGA-MOSPHILIA

During the 1987 excavations at this major western site a unique deposit was recovered from a building belonging to its Middle Chalcolithic Period 3. This consists of a pit which contained burnt material, a stack of pottery bowls with, in and around the lowest, nineteen figurines, a pottery stool (?), a triton shell, pestles and other ground stone tools, a total of 54 recorded

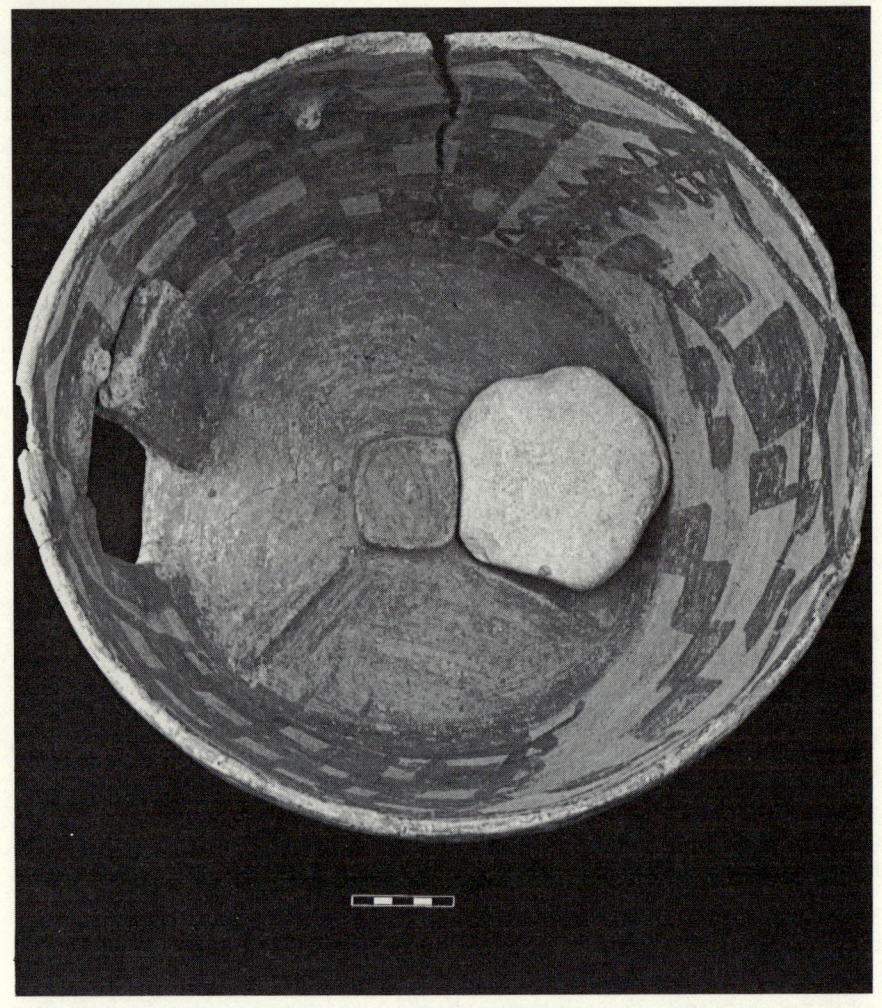

Figure 15.3 Building model from a ritual deposit at Kissonerga-Mosphilia (Photo Lemba Archaeological Project).

objects. The basal bowl is shaped like a roofless building with entrance, detachable door that swung in a pivot and such internal fixtures as a hearth and partitions (Fig 15.3). The figurines are varied and include schematic stone examples and elaborate pottery ones. Of the latter, those which are seated on stools deserve special attention since one, more detailed than the rest, is shown in the act of childbirth, with the painted head and arms of the child clearly emerging between her legs (Figs 15.5–6). Silhouetted on her neck is an anthropomorphic pendant reminiscent of the one on the Yialia picrolite figurine (J. Karageorghis 1977, Pl 8a), but in this case the legs are spread in a birth-giving posture. These objects are described in detail elsewhere (Peltenburg *et al* 1988). Here we will concentrate on those aspects which could signify ritual activity.

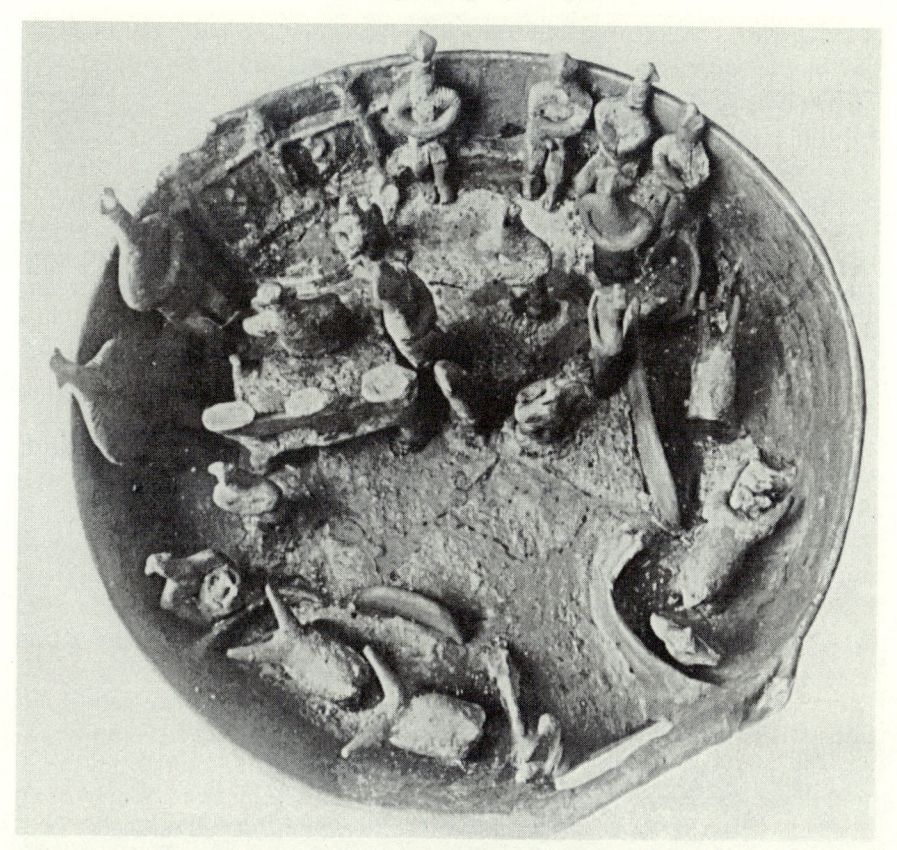

Figure 15.4 Enclosure model from Vounous Tomb 22 (*from* Dikaios 1940).

1) *Defacement* The relief decoration, door tenons and loop for the upper tenon of the building model were all deliberately snapped off and some were gouged away before it was inserted in the pit. Its painted door frame was damaged in the process. On the interior, the fantastic wall decoration and the monochrome red floor were smeared with a thin, opaque coating of yellowish clay. This was an obvious attempt to conceal the internal features before the objects just mentioned were crammed into it.

The figurines were also broken before insertion. All the pottery ones are incomplete and half the more robust stone ones are in a fragmentary state. It could be argued that this was due to prolonged use but several features suggest that damage was intentional. Breaks occur on figures that show little sign of wear and on figures and stool (?) at junctures where the clay is thick and unlikely to break in the normal course of events. In the case of one anthropomorphic vessel the flat breasts of a standing female have been partially chipped away. Breaks are not necessarily fresh, so we cannot be certain if damage was sustained at the time of the deposition.

Parts of two other large bowls were placed over the model. In destroyed buildings where other Red-on-White bowls are found they survive in smaller pieces hence the large size of these fragments indicates special selection and perhaps careful breakage.

2) *Burning* The outside of the building model where it rested against the contents of the pit was discoloured and effaced. It was precisely at this contact point that the ash of the pit was densest. Since the model and its contents show no other signs of secondary burning it would appear that hot or corrosive material was thrown against it as pit-fill. That the remaining fill consisted of the residues of a fire or that it had at least been affected by intense heat is indicated by the presence of many small heat-cracked and shattered stones, some with red ochre adhering. Fire, therefore, accompanied the actions preserved for us here.

3) *Burial* All this material was accommodated in a pit whose contents remained partially visible during occupation associated with the last floor of the ultimate building of Period 3. The pit was then sealed by the collapse of the pise wall of the structure. In other words, the construction of the pit and the insertion of this assemblage took place near the very end of Period 3. Since pottery styles of the next level are quite different from those of Period 3, it is very likely that there was an interruption in the occupation of at least this part of the settlement after Period 3.

These features of the extraordinary deposit signify ritual behaviour. Thus, to deliberately deface and conceal the model is most readily explained as an attempt to nullify or desanctify its role. To render powerless by 'killing' an object is well known in later times and the same may hold true here of both it and the figures. 'Killed' weapons for example are found in tombs (*cf* Åström 1987), but this pit does not conform to grave shapes (*cf LAP* I, Figs 18–21, 38–43) and the figurine repertory excludes picrolites typical of mortuary contexts (Vagnetti 1980). Burnt deposits occur for a variety of reasons on prehistoric sites, but in Cyprus they have not been found in association with such a concentration of modified objects. The exceptional nature of the deposit therefore is assured, and the many distinctive features described here indicate ceremony in which several rare objects were deliberately 'killed' and taken out of circulation. Since figurines normally occur singly in non-funerary contexts we can assume that this was a public ceremony and not a domestic one.

Concentrations of so many prehistoric figurines in the East Mediterranean are rare. At Çatal Hüyük Mellaart found them in groups of up to 13 in 'shrines' (1963, 82), but his interpretation of them as deities is disputed (eg Spycket 1981, 12–13). Further groups occur at Nea Nikomedeia (Rutkowski 1986, 155–6) and other sites in Greece (Ucko 1968, 442–3) where contexts are so varied that no single explanation carries conviction. The caches of figures at Ain Ghazel in Jordan on the other hand may have to do with ancestor cults because of associations with skulls (Rollefson 1986).

Analogies from later times in Cyprus and the Near East suggest that, leaving aside their role in Egyptian mortuary contexts, there were four main occasions for the deliberate deposition of figures (*cf* Moorey & Fleming 1984, 76). The first is as so-called foundation offerings. A close analogy from prehistoric Thessaly (Gallis 1985), in terms of the association of figurines and model, belongs to this class. Second is in an effort to conceal them from danger. The third is at the time of the renewal of sanctuaries. Older cultic equipment is then sometimes formally discarded into *bothroi* as in Shrine II of the Abu Temple at Tell Asmar (Frankfort 1939, 3) and the Archaic Precinct at Kourion (Young & Young 1955, 6, Pl 2). Fourth usually consists of single figures, either representing divinities such as the Ingot God, or kings such as Idri-Mi of Alalakh. Their 'burial' would seem to mark a crisis in society in which ideological and perhaps even political systems suffered upheaval (Ussishkin 1970; Knapp 1986, 109–10). The circumstantial similarity between the first and third types of burial and the Mosphilia deposit is noteworthy. While we may rule out the depiction of royalty here, it still remains to resolve if this ritual equipment constitutes a plausible case for the existence of divinities in Cyprus *ca* 3000 BC. To examine this question further we need to turn to more specific aspects of the deposit.

It is clear from contemporary excavated structures that the building model is a realistic portrayal of a specific type. The distinguishing features are the rectilinear hearth and radial floor partitions. These have only been located in one of seven explored contemporary structures (Fig 15.1d), and only two of dozens if we extend comparisons to the Early and Late Chalcolithic periods (Peltenburg 1988). These partitions should not be confused with weight-bearing radial walls of the kind employed in aceramic period structures (*cf* LeBrun 1984, Figs 14.1, 15.3). Preliminary analysis of artefacts from the relevant exception, Building 855 at Mosphilia, disclosed the presence of many fine wares but little else of note. This is partly excavated so at present we can only state that some of its essential architectural features are unconventional.

Assuming that the figurines are connected with, or symbolize activities in, such a special structure, then that structure was at times devoted to non-secular matters of fertility. Given the explicit scene of Fig 15.5 then it may be linked to parturition itself. Birth huts are well known in the ethnographic record, but Near Eastern textual sources suggest that similar structures were rare in early urban contexts. Thus Mesopotamian references to birth huts involve deities and especially Ninhursaga who in her role as mother and birthgiver is referred to as.'Lady Birthhut' (Jacobsen 1976, 107). In Hittite Anatolia a seclusion hut (*kallishtarwana*-house) may be attested, but Beckman states that the more usual practice was for the woman to deliver at home (1983, 154–6). It may be noted that our structure (both the model and Building 855) is a fine affair, unlike the mean huts which typify ethnographic instances. However, it has to be conceded that there are great difficulties in extrapolating from urban and ethnographic

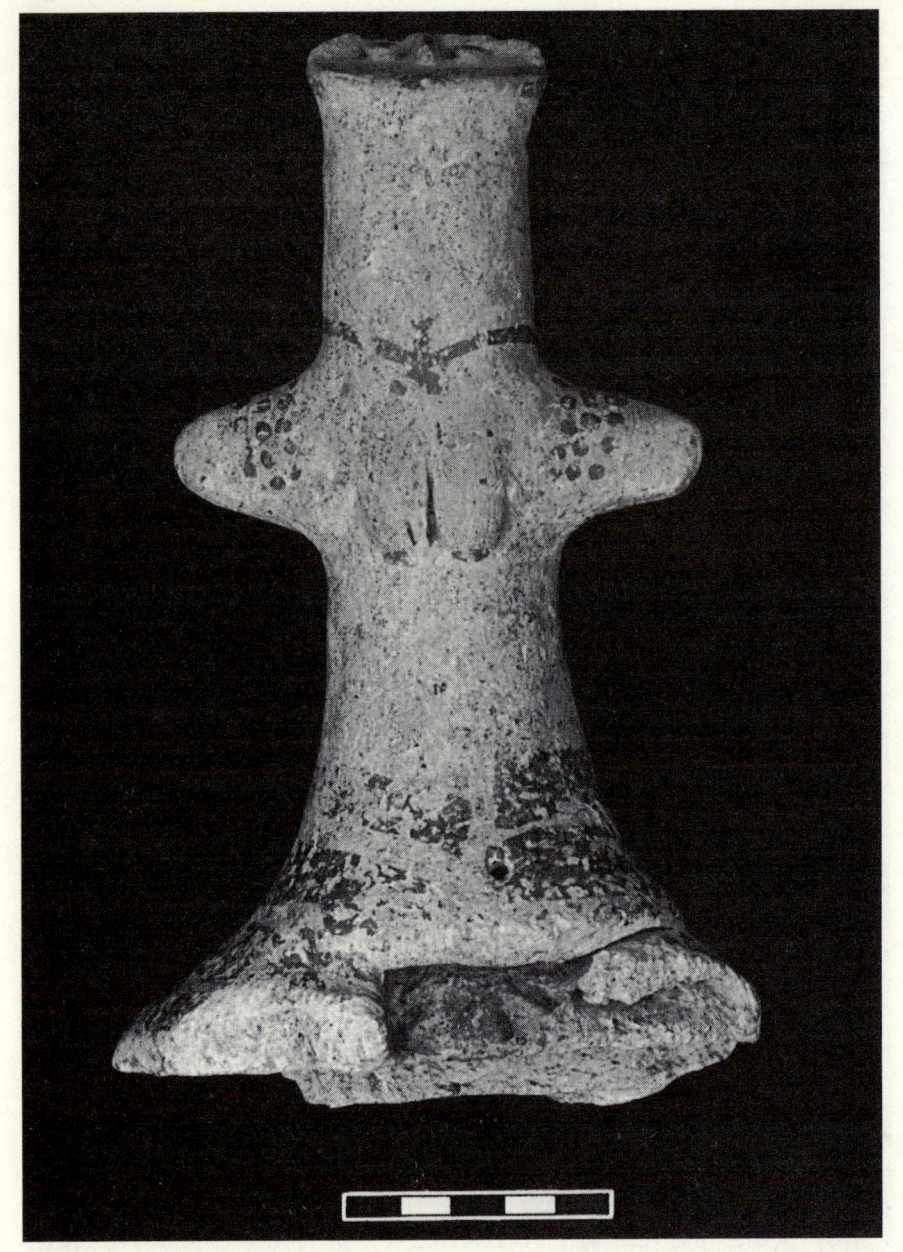

Figure 15.5 Birth-giving figurine from a ritual deposit at Kissonerga-Mosphilia (Photo Lemba Archaeological Project).

settings to pre-urban Cyprus and hence the role of the figures and other equipment associated with the building is more revealing for the question of religion.

Quite a variety of figurines were gathered here: animal, anthropoid

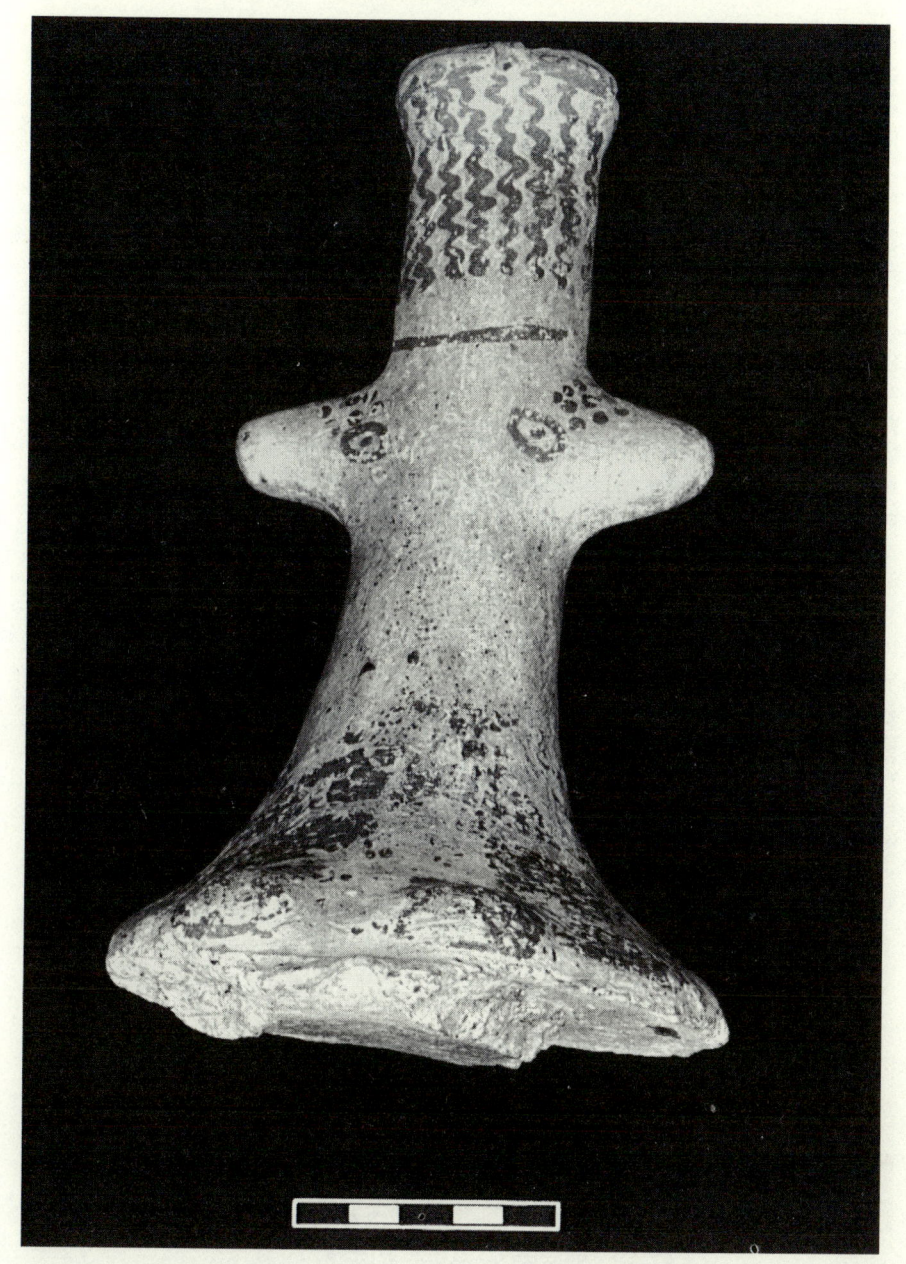

Figure 15.6 Backview of Fig 15.5 (Photo Lenba Archaeological Project)

concretions, a male, slender and matronly females in different postures and schematic representations. While normally any number of interpretations might be possible, the very unusual circumstances of the deposit help to narrow options. Since they are so closely associated and some are giving birth presumably all symbolize aspects of fertility. And since they were ritually buried and defaced they have more significance than toys intended for play or 'dolls' for pedagogic purposes. One possibility is that they were charms used in sympathetic magic. Malinowski's influential study on magic is pertinent here since he shows that that magic is particularly common in rituals during pregnancy (1954, 37–8). However, Evans-Pritchard's observation that

> 'magic . . . may be made at public feasts . . . but generally magical actions concern only the welfare of an individual who performs them in the privacy of his hut or alone in the bush' (1937, 424)

is equally relevant. Our deposit consists of an extraordinary variety of associated paraphernalia, ritually interred and likely to have involved public ceremony. Bearing in mind Evans-Pritchard's descriptions, such ceremonies of corporate affirmation are characteristic of religious rituals rather than essentially private magical rites. While this does not necessarily bring us closer to the identity of the figures, it should of course also be noted that there are many instances in antiquity of pregnant women worshipping mother goddesses (eg Beckman 1983, 241–3).

A triton shell was carefully placed in the model. During the Bronze Age in the East Mediterranean tritons are a constant feature of sanctuaries, sacred caves and votive deposits (Reese 1985, 353–31). The Idaean Cave seal with an altar shows how it may have been used as a libation vessel or trumpet in sacred rites (Fig 15.7). Yet, even if the Mosphilia triton is one of the earliest explicit associations of the triton with ritual (*cf* Vagnetti 1975, 95 for contemporary Cretan examples) it does not necessarily follow that the figurines must represent divinities. The shell could simply have been used as a charm for protection against disease spirits for example (Sigeret 1951, Pl XVI.34 top left).

Figure 15.7 Idaean Cave (Crete) seal showing ritual use of triton shell (*from* Evans 1901).

A square-topped four-legged object was also included in the deposit. It is unlike the circular birthing stools attached to the figures and clearly served a different purpose. Similar ones from the eneolithic Ovcharevo hoard in Bulgaria which also contains many figurines have been classed as model altars (Todorova 1978, 80). There is no proof of such an interpretation, but it remains a possibility. Its cross-hatched decoration is appropriate to a stool.

Slotted between the hearth and the wall of the model was a large flat stone (Fig 15.3). Its top surface was the highest element on the floor of the model and it seems to have served as a dais or stand. The only items inside the model which could be placed comfortably on it are the stool, a whorl, a bone point, a flint, pebbles or any of the pottery figurines. Of these, it is most likely to have provided an elevated focus for one or more of the self-supporting pottery figurines.

It is primarily on this reconstruction that the argument for the existence of a shrine with deities must turn. In attempting to isolate archaeological correlates for elements of religious worship Renfrew recently stressed attention focusing devices and the presence of the transcendent with its symbolic focus (1985, 18). This usually means a platform for the cult statue in the Levantine Bronze Age (cf Kuschke 1977). If, as suggested here, the recovered assemblage imitates a real structure with its facilities and equipment then these two recurrent components of later shrines may be present. Thus the flat stone opposite the entrance may have served as a platform for the proportionately immense pottery figurines, the equivalents of platforms for cult statues in later shrines. That it was unlikley to have been a bed, an explanation favoured for similarly positioned platforms in Tell Mureybit structures (Beazley 1985, 168 bottom left), is evident from the awkwardness of the figurines when laid horizontally on it, the association of objects like the triton and the treatment meted to the whole. Unusual care was taken to hide the contents by the provision of a swivel door and this may have been required at certain times to protect an image from profane view. Associated items for the practice of sacred ritual such as a special hearth and triton shell could be readily interpreted as suitable elements of a sanctuary. They recur in East Mediterranean Bronze Age examples, as at Tell Qasile, Kition and Phylakopi (Mazar 1980; Renfrew 1985). Since equipment characteristic of later shrines is extant in the Mosphilia assemblage, it is likely that numinous powers are also represented, and the most obvious candidates for these are the anthropomorphic pottery figures.

It should be noted that not all the Mosphilia figures need be regarded as cult images. There are significant differences in scale and wear; and the stone ones cannot stand unaided. Some, therefore, served other functions. The vessels in the shape of females represent older women and so it is interesting to note that Brunner-Traut (1970), in her study of later parallels from Egypt and the Levant, suggested they contained items for midwifery. Detailed iconographic analysis may reveal further differences, but the above are so obvious that it could be argued that a hierarchy is present with smaller figurines depicting votaries, largest birthgiving ones cult figures.

We have seen that many of the widely accepted archaeological criteria for a public shrine are present in modular form here. Yet it occurs in a non-urban context, without immediate successors. Thus, we have evidence for a communal cult place with physical characteristics that foreshadow later temples but not the complex temple organisations that properly functioned in urban centres.

In sum therefore, the Mosphilia ritual deposit provides evidence for non periodic sacred ritual, for its public character of local or perhaps even regional significance given the large size of the assemblage, for a rich and complex religious imagery and support for the case for special cult places and representations of birth goddesses in 4th millennium BC Cyprus. It also casts some light on a contemporary structure at Lemba.

LEMBA-LAKKOUS

One of the distinguishing features of the Kissonerga model is the radial floor ridge. A modified version of this occurs in partly preserved Building 1 at Lemba (Fig 15.1c). Here a row of stake holes succeeded by a bedding trench for something like a low partition screen equates with the ridge. At its terminal against the wall was found a stone female figurine some 40 cm in height with arms outstretched, elongated neck and swollen head with facial markings typical of small anthropomorphic pendants. In a preliminary note the building was tentatively described as a 'sacred place', primarily on the basis of this exceptionally large representation (Peltenburg 1977, 141). In the light of the Kissonerga model, its clear radial division provides further support for such an interpretation.

Other exceptional features of Building 1 indicate that it is not the ordinary 'dwelling' described by Morris (1985, 119). It is the only structure in prehistoric Cyprus to be so completely isolated from other buildings in the nucleated settlements. The nearest known contemporary structure is *ca*100 m away (*LAP I*, 316, Fig 6.2). It is situated prominently on the lip of a terrace, unlike other buildings at Lemba which are set inconspicuously. Rutkowski postulates that one of the characteristics of what he calls 'temples' in earlier prehistory is a place set apart from other buildings and one where a divinity dwells in anthropomorphic or aniconic form (1986, 154). Lemba Building 1 meets at least the first criterion and there is some positive evidence for the second. That it was also founded in the area of a pre-existing cemetery may be relevant given the recurrence of cruciform pendants in burials (Vagnetti 1980). The building lacks an altar and other ritual equipment, but these could have existed in the missing half.

The figurine could simply have been in storage since it lay between large vessels. These are significant, not only because the types help to assign the building to the Middle Chalcolithic, contemporary with the Kissonerga evidence mentioned above, but also because they are amongst the earliest instances of large pottery containers in Cyprus. Building 1, therefore, was also remarkable in terms of the concentration of internally stored goods. We have already seen that prestige was attached to Late Neolithic buildings with evidence for ritual foci. Those buildings were inside the settlements, so Lemba Building 1 provides some evidence for the evolution of separateness during the Chalcolithic. The other physical features of the building are not so distinctive and hence, as argued above, these are but emerging institutions in society.

The question of a religious legacy

With the appearance of bucrania on the subsequent Vounous and Kotchati models, there begins a long history in Cyprus of links between bulls and sacred rituals (Loulloupis 1979). Earlier iconography connected with religion all but disapppears. That preceding beliefs may have continued in some form is suggested by a cruciform figurine in Red Polished pottery (Flourentzos 1982, Pl 11.3–5) and by the morphological links between the Mosphilia and Vounous building models (Figs 15.3–4). Yet the many important differences in the contents of those two models point to significant shifts in belief systems. It would seem, therefore, that there is a profound discontinuity in the development of religion in Cyprus at the beginning of the Bronze Age.

Such a rupture corresponds to several other breaks in material culture at that time. For many centuries afterwards the centre and north of the island are pre-eminent and the west is such a backwater that Catling suggested a withdrawal of population from that part of the island (1963, 138). Other discoveries rather indicate that a conservative society persisted there (Herscher 1980) and so we might expect greater cultural continuity in the west. It was inferred above that sacred rituals and perhaps buildings or sanctuaries with divinities were connected especially with female fertility in Chalcolithic times. This was particularly true of western Cyprus. Nothing like the variety and sophistication of western pottery figurines have been found elsewhere on the island. The distribution of the picrolite cruciforms is also essentially a western phenomenon. This is evident from their absence at Kalavassos-Ayious, their poor quality at Erimi which is located beside one of the most prolific picrolite sources on the island and the large numbers recovered from the west, even excluding those from excavations. Their concentration in the Paphos District has been attributed to the existence of local sources of picrolite, but preliminary work on the characteristics of those sources suggests that virtually all are small and unsuitable. Their recurrence here was thus due to compelling religious reasons rather than ease of access to favoured materials.

It is precisely in this area, near Souskiou which has yielded so many of these female representations, that the famous cult of Aphrodite was established. A temple already existed at Kouklia in the Late Bronze Age and Chalcolithic cruciform figurines come from its area (Maier & Karageorghis

1982, 91–102). Although there is a chronological gap between the last female figurines and the temple at Kouklia, the strength of this western tradition of fertility figures, coupled with evidence for conservatism and weak participation in developments in the north of the island provide an explanation for the growth of her cult in the west. The location of the cult of the *Paphaia* may prove to be not so much an historical accident as the resurgence of flourishing earlier traditions.

LIST OF REFERENCES

Åström, P. (1987) Intentional destruction of grave goods. *Aegaeum 1*, 213–18.
Beazley, M. ed (1985) *The World Atlas of Archaeology*. London.
Beckman, G. (1983) *Hittite Birth Rituals (Studien zu den Bogazköy-Texten 29)*. Wiesbaden.
Brunner-Traut, E. (1970) *Gravidenflasche: das Salben des Mutterliebes*, in *Archaeologie und Altes Testament (Festschrift für K. Galling)* 35–48. Tübingen.
Catling, H. (1963) Patterns of settlement in Bronze Age Cyprus. *Op Ath 4*, 129–69.
Catling, H. (1986) *Review* of Morris 1985, *Antiquity 229*, 157–8.
Dikaios, P. (1953) *Khipokitca*. London.
Dikaios, P. (1962) *Sotira*. Philadelphia.
Durkheim, E. (1964) *The Elementary Forms of the Religious Life*. London.
Evans, A. (1901) Mycenaean tree and pillar cult and its Mediterranean relations. *JHS 21*, 99–204.
Evans-Pritchard, E. (1937) *Witchcraft, oracles and magic among the Azande*. Oxford.
Flourentzos, P. (1982) Selected antiquities of Red Polished Ware from Cypriote private collections. *Op Ath 14*, 21–6.
Frankfort, H. (1939) *Sculpture of the Third Millennium B.C. from Tell Asmar and Khafajeh (Oriental Institute Publications 44)*. Chicago.
Gallis, K. (1985) A late neolithic foundation offering from Thessaly. *Antiquity 59*, 20–1.
Hägg, R. & Marinatos, N. eds (1981) *Sanctuaries and Cults in the Aegean Bronze Age* (Skrifter utgivna av Svenska institutet i Athen 28) Stockholm.
Herscher, E. (1980) Southern Cyprus and the disappearing Early Bronze Age. *RDAC*, 17–21.
Jacobsen, T. (1976) *The Treasures of Darkness*. London.
Karageorghis, J. (1977) *La Grande Déesse de Chypre et son culte*. Lyon.
Knapp, A. (1986) *Copper production and divine protection: archaeology, ideology and social complexity on Bronze Age Cyprus (SIMA Pocket-book 42)*. Göteborg.
Kuschke, A. (1977) s.v. *Tempel* in K. Galling, *Biblisches Reallexikon*^{2} 333–42. Tübingen.
Lang, A. (1898) *The Making of Religion*. London.
LAP I. E. Peltenburg et al (1985) *Lemba Archaeological Project I. Excavations at Lemba Lakkous, 1976–1983 (SIMA 70.1)*. Göteborg.
LeBrun, A. (1984) *Fouilles recentes à Khirokitia, 1977–1981*. Paris.
Loulloupis, M. (1979) The position of the bull in prehistoric religions in Crete and Cyprus. *Acts 1979*, 215–22.
Maier, F. & Karageorghis, V. (1984) *Paphos, history and archaeology*. Nicosia.
Malinowski, B. (1954) *Magic, science and religion and other essays*. Garden City.
Mallowan, M. (1947) Excavations at Brak and Chagar Bazar. *Iraq 9*, 1–266.

Marinatos, N. (1984) *Art and religion in Thera. Reconstructing a Bronze Age society*. Athens.
Masson, O. (1969) Religious beliefs and sanctuaries in prehistoric times. *Arch Viva II.3*, 53–6.
Mazar, A. (1980) *Excavations at Tell Qasile I. The Philistine sanctuary: architecture and cult objects (Qedem 12)*. Jerusalem.
Mellaart, J. (1963) Excavations at Chatal Hüyük, 1962, Second Preliminary Report. *Anat St 13*, 43–104.
Mellaart, J. (1967) *Çatal Hüyük: a neolithic town in Anatolia*. London.
Merrillees, R. (1980) Representation of the human form in prehistoric Cyprus. *Op Ath 13*, 171–84.
Moorey, P. & Fleming, S. (1984) Problems in the study of anthropomorphic metal statuary from Syro-Palestine before 330 BC. *Levant 16*, 67–90.
Morris, D. (1985) *The Art of Ancient Cyprus*. Oxford.
Peltenburg, E.J. (1977) Chalcolithic figurine from Lemba, Cyprus. *Antiquity 51*, 140–3.
Peltenburg, E.J. (1982) *Vrysi. A Subterranean Settlement in Cyprus. Excavations at Prehistoric Ayios Epiktitos Vrysi 1969–73*. Warminster.
Peltenburg, E.J. (1985) Pattern and purpose in the prehistoric Cypriot village of Ayios Epiktitos Vrysi, in *Chypre. La vie quotidienne de l'antiquité à nos jours*. Actes du Colloque. Musée de l'Homme. 46–64. Paris.
Peltenburg, E. (1988) A Cypriot model for prehistoric ritual. *Antiquity 235*, 289–93.
Peltenburg, E. *et al* (1988) Kissonerga Mosphilia 1987: ritual deposit, unit 1015. *RDAC*, forthcoming.
Redman, C. (1978) *The Rise of Civilization*. San Francisco.
Reese, D. (1985) Shells, ostrich eggshells and other exotic faunal remains from Kition, *Kition V.II*, 340–415.
Renfrew, C. (1985) *The Archaeology of Cult. The Sanctuary at Phylakopi (BSA Supp Vol 18)* Oxford.
Rollefson, G. (1986) Neolithic 'Ain Ghazel (Jordan): ritual and ceremony II. *Paléorient 12*, 45–5.
Rutkowski, B. (1979) Religious architecture in Cyprus and Crete in the Late Bronze Age. *Acts 1979*, 223–7.
Rutkowski, B. (1986) *The Cult Places of the Aegean*. London.
Schmidt, P. (1912–54) *Der Ursprung der Gottesidee*. Munster.
Sigeret, H. (1951) *A History of Medicine I*. New York.
South, A. (1985) Figurines and other objects from Kalavasos-Ayious. *Levant 17*, 65–79.
Spycket, A. (1981) *La Statuaire du Proche Orient Ancien*. Leiden.
Stanley Price, N. (1979) The structure of settlement at Sotira in Cyprus. *Levant 9*, 46–83.
Todd, I. (1981) A Cypriote neolithic wall-painting. *Antiquity 213*, 47–51.
Todd, I. (1982) Vasilikos Valley project: fourth preliminary report, 1979–1980. *J Field A 9*, 35–78.
Todorova, H. (1978) *The eneolithic period in Bulgaria in the fifth millennium B.C. (BAR Int Ser 49)*. Oxford.
Tylor, E.B. (1958) *Religion in Primitive Culture*. New York.
Ucko, P. (1968) *Anthropomorphic figurines of predynastic Egypt and neolithic Crete with comparative material from the prehistoric Near East and mainland Greece*. London.
Ussishkin, D. (1970) The Syro-Hittite ritual burial of monuments. *JNES 29*, 124–8.
Vagnetti, L. (1975) L'insediamento neolitico di Festos. *ASAtene 50–1 (1972–3)*, 1–138.

Vagnetti, L. (1980) Figurines and minor objects from a chalcolithic cemetery at Souskiou-Vathyrkakas (Cyprus). *SMEA 21*, 17–72.
Warren, P. (1973) The beginnings of Minoan religion, in *Antichita Cretesi. Studi in onore di Doro Levi*. 137–47. Catania.
Watkins, T. (1969) The first village settlements. *ArchViva II.3*, 29–38.
Yadin, Y. (1975) *Hazor*. London.
Young, J. & Young, S. (1955) *Terracotta figurines from Kourion in Cyprus*. Philadelphia.

16
The identification of Cypriot cult figures through cross-cultural comparison: some problems

Linda Carless Hulin
University of London

The Ingot god, a Late Bronze Age smiting figure armed with spear and shield (Schaeffer 1971, 506–10) and the Bomford figurine (Catling 1971, 15–32) have been the subject of much debate since their discovery; debate which serves to highlight inconsistencies in the way in which cultic phenomena are interpreted by archaeologists.[1]

The Bomford figurine (Fig 16.1) lies within the native Cypriot stylistic traditions, and has been identified as a local goddess by Catling (1971) and J. Karageorghis (1977, 104–5). However, the goddess is assumed to have been the consort of the Ingot god (since both figures stand upon an ingot), and is therefore also seen as a Near Eastern goddess: 'Astarte-on-the-Ingot' (Catling 1971, who suggests a schizophrenia of personalities) or, most recently, Mamma/Mammitum (Dalley 1987). Consequently, the identification of this figurine must be assessed in the light of the arguments put forward for the Ingot god; this paper will concentrate upon the debate surrounding this figure.

The diversity of opinions offered regarding the Ingot god (Fig 16.2) is remarkable. While most see him as a representation of the Babylonian god Nergal, or his Levantine equivalent Resheph (Schaeffer 1971, 506–10; Dalley 1987; Collon 1972, 131–2), some regard him as Hephaistos (Catling 1971, 29–30). Others have been content to note his generally oriental (Seeden 1981, 130–1), Syro-Palestinian (Negbi 1976, 39) and Achaean (Karageorghis 1973, 108) aspects.

INFLUENCES UPON PREVIOUS INTERPRETATIONS

Although each identification of the Ingot god has been reinforced by the relevant textual and material comparanda, these conclusions have been coloured by other, more general considerations. The most obvious of these is the undeniably eclectic appearance of the figure, the implications of

Figure 16.1 The 'Bomford figurine', unprovenanced.

Figure 16.2 The 'Ingot god' from Enkomi.

which will be dealt with more fully below. Equally influential is the perceived nature of the LC IIIA period to which the Ingot god and, by extension, the Bomford figurine are customarily dated (Courtois 1971; 1973; Schaeffer 1965; 1971; but see also Knapp 1986a; 1986b; 1988 and Muhly 1980).[2] The LC III period need not be described in any detail here; it is sufficient to note that Cyprus did not escape the social disruption experienced by the eastern Mediterranean in the late 13th and early 12th centuries BC, and that during this period of localized destructions and population shifts, Levantine and Aegean populations settled upon Cyprus. What is relevant here is that the socially fractured nature of the period permits a wider range of interpretations than would have been acceptable for earlier, more stable times, such as for LC II. Indeed, when the figurines were first discovered, it was assumed that Cypriot culture subsumed itself into that of the incoming populations, and consequently an indigenous identity for the Ingot god was scarcely considered.

It is now clear, and was perhaps inevitable, that the identification put forward by each scholar reflected the source and relative breadth of his or her training. From a review of the literature, it is plain that those trained in Near Eastern archaeology favoured a Levantine identity for the figurines, while classically trained scholars were more familiar with parallels in the Aegean world.

Obviously, it is neither possible nor wise to divorce one's perceptions of a culture from the study of the objects which belong to it. However, scholars have moved from the general (cultural change) to the particular (the meaning of specific objects) with insufficient consideration of the intervening process. Religious organizations react to general social trends in specific ways, and the assumption of a non-Cypriot identification for the Ingot god has far-reaching consequences for the way in which society should be interpreted.

INTERPRETATION OF THE FIGURINES THROUGH STYLISTIC AND CROSS-CULTURAL COMPARISON

In the absence of accompanying descriptions, the Ingot god and the Bomford figurine have been identified on the basis of their appearance. However, an assessment of the role and meaning of style in the production and meaning of ritual objects indicates that such an approach is not necessarily a reliable guide to the meaning of the piece. I would argue that three considerations are brought to bear during the manufacture of cultic paraphernalia—the technological, the 'informational' and the 'stylistic'.

The first of these is not immediately relevant to the argument here; it is sufficient to note that the level of technology available to the craftsman governs his capacity to express detail, and by extension, the degree of artistic merit attainable by him. The information contained within a piece is conveyed by its fundamental attributes: in the case of the Ingot figurines, these are their age, sex, the presence or absence of clothing, the *type* of clothing (including weaponry and armour), and non-realistic phenomena, in this case, the ingot upon which each of the figures stand. I would argue that the style of an object represents that which is left to the craftsman after the technological and informational requirements have been met. Therefore, the manner in which the hair of the Bomford figurine is dressed constitutes style, as does the cut of the Ingot god's clothes.[3]

THE INTERPRETATION OF STYLE

While the previous identifications of the Ingot god were based upon 'Informational' considerations, the deciding factor was the *style* in which they were executed; in other words, whether the figure 'looked' Aegean, or Levantine. However, if identification is determined by style, how is *eclecticism* of style to be interpreted? As evidence for a syncretised deity—for if one aspect is significant, are not they all? Syncretism has not been favoured by scholars, who have consequently failed to address the logical implications of the eclectic style of the Ingot god. For example, Negbi (1982) and Catling (1971) recognized a mixture of stylistic elements on the Ingot god derived from the Near East and the Aegean; both selected what was most germane to their argument (Negbi the Near Eastern, Catling the Aegean) and consigned the rest to the periphery of interest. A syncretic identity for the Ingot god will be opposed below on theoretical grounds, but while scholars were indeed correct in rejecting such a solution, the means by which the significant elements were distinguished from the insignificant were not well formulated.

The identification of significant elements in style has proved to be a persistent problem for archaeologists. Significance is generally seen in terms of the links between individual motifs and the wider symbolic repertoire (Goff 1963; Goodenough 1954; Hodder 1982; a point elaborated upon in art history by semioticists, eg Eco 1976). However, while a theoretical distinction between 'live' and 'dead' symbols (meaningful versus decorative) has been recognized, (eg Ortner 1973), separation of the two for analytical purposes remains a difficult procedure. Archaeologists have tended to concentrate upon the relationships of individual motifs and design arrangements with the aim of delineating interaction spheres either within or between groups (eg Friedrich 1970; Plog 1978; Wobst 1977). In the case of the Ingot god, the fact of interaction between cultural spheres is not in doubt: it is the *operation* of that interaction that needs to be explored, and unfortunately the wider symbolic background is not yet clear.

Studies of style in a specifically religious setting have been few: for the most comprehensive in a Near Eastern context see Goodenough 1954, Goff 1963 and below. Moreover, the definition of 'style' in religious paraphernalia, especially cult figures, has been of interest to both archaeologists and art historians. The art historical definition of style, as the fingerprint of the individual or a group of artists is not helpful here: the subjective viewpoint in art, or pictorial realism, first appeared in Greece in the 6th century BC (Gombrich 1960, 100–20). Prior to that, Near Eastern art employed *schema*, ie non-realistic conceptual modes, that resulted in a relatively standardized image (eg Schäfer 1930). Individual expression seems to have been generally unimportant in the pre-Greek world. Consequently, craftsmen performed primarily in the tradition within which they had been trained (see Wright in an architectural context: 1985, 259; a point that was noted, but not followed through, by Catling 1964, 255).

If, then, the nationality of a craftsmen could affect the appearance of an object, what would have been the result if foreign craftsmen were employed upon a project? A well-documented example is that of the first Jewish Temple in Jerusalem, built by King Solomon not only for the greater glory of God, but also for the self-aggrandizement of the Davidic line (1 Kings 6–7; 2 Chron.2:1–5:5; Ahlström 1982). Craftsmen were brought in from Tyre and directed by one Hiram, who was of mixed Naphtalite and Tyrian parentage (1 Kings 7:13–14) and presumably conversant with the modes of both cultures. The resulting building was fundamentally Canaanite in appearance, with some Yahwist modification (Wright 1985, 254–67, and refs, 267–8), an unsurprising result in that Israel, as a young nation, had not yet had time to develop its own material culture. However, the temple was decorated with *Phoenician* cosmological iconography which was quite definitely alien to the official cult, and which, it is more important to note here, did not arouse the hostility of the notoriously truculent Yahwist priesthood (1 Kings 7:19–27; Albright 1942, 148–50).

It would seem then, from this example at least, that a distinction could be drawn in the ancient world between the basic information to be conveyed, and elements additional to, or extraneous to those basic informational requirements which are decorative, and carry less information, and are the repositories of style.

To sum up, while the implicit assumption made by previous scholars that only some stylistic elements found upon the Ingot god are of significance is essentially correct, as yet we have no procedure by which to isolate paramount groups of stylistic elements. However, it is clear that while style may be linked with social or ethnic groups, it clearly cannot be regarded as a guide to identification where an ethnically mixed social milieu (or at least the presence of foreign craftsmen) may be envisaged, as in Cyprus. Thus the eclectic style of the Ingot god may well indicate that the piece was manufactured by non-Cypriot, Levantine craftsmen, as has been suggested (eg Negbi 1982, 180), but this in no way implies a Canaanite (or Aegean) identity for the piece. However, the eclecticism of the Ingot god, which has so exercised scholars, may be now explained as merely the result of craftsmen employing a number of stylistic conventions, which did not jeopardize the integrity of meaning of the piece as a whole.

It is certain that the identification of the Ingot god and the Bomford figurine is best explored through a study of the 'informational' elements.

For the Ingot god, these are maleness, youth/not age, body armour, weaponry, an aggressive stance, and the ingot. For the Bomford figurine and her parallels, it is femaleness, youth/not age, nudity, and the ingot. Given that their only explicitly symbolic element—the ingot—is known to be part of the religious repertoire of LC II (Knapp 1986a; 1986b; 1988), there is no reason to assume that the deities are not Cypriot. Indeed, the arguments for a foreign identification are shown to have been made on faulty grounds.

SOCIAL IMPLICATIONS OF THE WORSHIP OF A FOREIGN DEITY IN CYPRUS

It was noted above that the presence of a foreign deity on Cyprus would have wider social implications. What, despite the non-Cypriot appearance of the Ingot god, is the *likelihood* and implications of a non-Cypriot (Aegean or Levantine) identification for the piece (and, by extension, for the Bomford figurine)?

Religion explains the visible and invisible world, ordering and validating community experience in terms of its own explanation (Geertz 1965; Durkheim 1957; Radcliffe-Brown 1939). In the Bronze Age Near East, theological and sociopolitical realities were contiguous: political territories were regarded as the property of the gods, and monarchs ruled either on behalf of the gods or as divine or semi-divine beings themselves (Ahlström 1982, 3–4 and n 4; Frankfort 1948). Thus the religious system upheld existing social configurations. Knapp has clearly demonstrated the relationship between religion and society during the Late Bronze Age in Cyprus (1986a; 1986b; 1988): the economic basis of the country, the copper industry, was incorporated into the religious system, and reflected in ritual, to the reciprocal advantage of the cultic organization and the economic elites. The religious iconography came to be dominated by symbols of the copper trade, especially ingots; to incorporate ingots into the cult was to sanctify them, to make them holy, and to encourage the continuity and well-being of the industry. It is significant to this argument to note that Knapp, after a study of the information-carrying attributes of the Ingot god and the Bomford figurine, dated these pieces to the 14th century BC, on the basis of their fit with the religious system as a whole. Muhly also supports a pre-12th century date (in fact the 13th century BC), and also pointed out that buried objects do not date to the time of their deposition, but to the preceding period (1980, 159).[4]

The question of whether the Ingot god was buried at the end of a long LC I-II life or a short LC IIIA life is not to be solved by stratigraphic considerations, and the question revolves around the perceived relationship of the figurines to the religious system as a whole. It has been established that the religious system ratifies existing social norms: Knapp would argue that those norms were those of the copper-based LC I-II economy; what, however, is the likelihood that the figures represent incoming Aegean or Canaanite deities in LC IIIA?

The central question is the relative importance of the Ingot god in Cypriot religion. In order to address this question, it is necessary to examine the find-spot of the piece. The plan of the city of Enkomi is reasonably clear (*Enkomi*; Schaeffer 1952). The town was surrounded by a wall, and had a planned overall layout. The northern half of the city was laid out on a grid: seven streets each 3 metres wide, ran east-west at intervals of exactly 31.5 m, and were crossed by a single north-south street (Schaeffer 1953). The industrial quarter lay in the northern sector, while the central area was dominated by ashlar buildings of a public, official and religious character. Thus the Sanctuary of the Ingot God occupied a prominent position within the city. Given the prime location of the public buildings at Enkomi, it is reasonable to assume that they were utilized by the dominant social, political and religious organizations at the time. Thus, to assume an Aegean or Levantine identity for the Ingot god is to imply a dominant religious *and* socio-political role for the incoming populations.

Although the fact of the arrival of an Achaean population during the LC III period is not in doubt, the extent and impact of that colonization is by no means clear. Over the past decade the criteria by which the impact of the Achaeans upon Cypriot culture is assessed has begun to be re-examined (eg Maier 1986; Muhly 1980). What is certain is that, given the informaion now available, one cannot posit a dominant role for the Aegean or Levantine populations in LC IIIA (Karageorghis 1982, 89; Catling 1973, 38–9). Thus the Ingot god is unlikely to have been non-Cypriot in character.

SOCIAL IMPLICATIONS OF THE WORSHIP OF A SYNCRETIC DEITY IN CYPRUS

On the other hand, what is the likelihood that the eclecticism of style of the Ingot god reflects a syncretic character? As religion serves to legitimate existing social structures, it is naturally resistant to change; for a religious system to alter theological perceptions of reality is to undermine its own power base. Sjöberg (1960) suggested that religion reinterprets itself only when society changes slowly; for example, it may be argued that Cypriot relgion incorporated industrial symbolism into what had previously been an agricultural, and probably at least partially a fertility religion, over the few hundred years in which Cypriot society expanded its economic base. It would have had to: for the official cult to have continued to extol the virtues of agriculturalism in an urban society would have been to lose credibility. On the other hand, rapid social development is more likely to lead to religious collapse (*cf* Drennan 1976).

In order to address the problem of the likelihood of syncretism, it is necessary to envision the process of Aegean and Levantine settlement on Cyprus. It is not yet certain that they came in large numbers, at least not to Enkomi. Culture is not monolithic, it is segmented, and it is necessary to the argument to consider the point of entry of minority foreign groups into Cypriot culture, and its effects therein.

For the purposes of this discussion, two broad social classes are defined: the Large Group, those with large, national or inter-city powers and concerns—the king, his court, economic and social elites, the high-ranking priesthood and army commanders; and the Small Group, those with small concerns—village-based agriculturists, the urban work-force, low-ranking priesthood, and ordinary soldiers.

As in the secular sphere, the potential for diffusion within the religious system depends upon the relationship between the Small Group and Large Group spheres (Carless Hulin 1988). Social stratification is expressed in the religious system by the presence of practices either peculiar to or more commonly found in one social level than another. In the ancient Near East, most of the rituals involving royalty, the senior priesthood and other members of the Large Group were predominantly concerned with Large Group issues: the fertility of the land and the livestock, the continuation of the economy and national security. Small Group rites localized these issues, reducing concerns to such matters as the fertility of the immediate district, local markets or personal health (see Pritchard 1950). This stratification of roles and concerns reduces the likelihood of diffusion from the Large Group levels, since there is less unity of interest and concern. Indeed, the Small Group may be considerably ignorant of all but the practical application of its own religious duties (Berger and Luckmann 1967; Sjöberg 1960; Sperber 1977; Ladurie 1978); the more highly educated members of the elite group enter the clergy at high levels, while the lower positions tend to be filled by poorly educated individuals from the same low-status group as the congregations which they serve (Sjöberg 1960). As a result, there is often a considerable difference between the folk-rites of the Small Group and the more formal observances of the Large Group, which adheres more closely to the ideal norms of society.

However, Large Group interest may indicate the limited acceptance of an innovation. For example, Ahaz introduced a 'foreign' altar into the temple in Jerusalem as an expression of his symbolic subjugation to the Assyrians, an act demanded by the victorious Assyrians as a matter of course (II Kings 16:10–16). As such it had no discernible effect upon the Yahwist cult as a whole, despite the outrage of the prophets, since access to the temple was a Large Group privilege. Innovation at a Large Group level may spread to those sections of the community that share or aspire to Large Group aims. For example, in New Kingdom Egypt, as a consequence of royal patronage (which was itself a political expression of Egyptian military superiority), certain Asiatic gods were adopted by the court and thereafter by royal tomb builders. The army embraced the worship of the warlike goddess Anat. By contrast, however, the mass of Egyptian society seems not to have come into contact with the Asiatic gods at all (Carless Hulin 1982).

Conversely, innovation promoted by the Small Group represents a threat to the realities imposed by the ruling elites, and the potential for diffusion from this level depends on the relationships between different social strata, and particularly the way in which the Large Group seeks to control Small Group activity by restricting individual action. Thus, Douglas (1970) has noted that the relationship between public obligation and individual negotiation (group and grid) governs the willingness of society to accept 'alien' symbols, in that the more forcibly the socio-religious norms are imposed, the less room there is for Small Group expression. Powerful religious institutions develop 'theories of deviance' designed to prevent challenge to the existing system. Aberrant individuals may be accused of demon-possession, or madness; they are killed or 'cured'. Alternatively, 'rising' deities may be defeated in theological battles, or denied theological reality (Berger & Luckmann 1967). Thus, Neoplatonist attempts to systematize and unify all known significant world religions on the basis of resemblances between their various deities may be seen as an effort to 'tame' the non-Greek world. Should diffusion at a Small Group level become significant, it may be (explicitly or implicitly) designated proper only for those of low status to worship, thus confining the spread of an innovation to those strata. Niebuhr (1969) argued that denominations and sects represent the accomodation of religion to the caste system. Alternatively, deities may amalgamate, thereby checking the ascendancy of a potential rival; the legends of the Near East record numerous modifications of this type.

Where some measure of Small Group autonomy is favoured, innovation is encouraged in its spread through the system. For example, in Samoa, the Congregational Mission conversion programme proved successful because the strongly individual church structure was compatible with patterns of village authority. The more hierarchical Catholic mission had less impact (Brown 1957). Alternatively, where Large Group authority is strong but remote, deviant or alien theories may take root. It was noted above that a large proportion of Small Group communities are relatively ignorant about fundamental religious tenets. It is clear that in the 14th century AD, the inhabitants of Montaillou (France) confused the tenets of Catholicism and Albigensianism, and saw no difficulties in this; indeed, the local Catholic priest was a leading heretic (Ladurie 1978).

Talmon (1969), in a study of millinarism, noted that such cults, while finding their support in all levels of society, particularly attract those who suffer from a radically different relation between social aspirations and the realities of life. Obviously this is more likely to occur within the Small Group, especially in times of social or economic uncertainty or deprivation. At such times, the Small Group will tend to be receptive to alien phenomena simply because such elements do not belong to the system which has proved unsatisfactory to Small Group members.

Thus to sum up, there are three possible scenarios which may be imagined before syncretism can have occurred between the Cypriot cult and the religions of the incoming peoples: (1) the Aegean or Levantine colonists were so numerically abundant as to have radically altered Cypriot society, thus triggering an adaptive change in the Cypriot system; (2) the colonists entered society at a Large Group level, just as the Indo-Europeans did in 15th century BC Syria (Drower 1973, 419–20); (3) they occupied Small Group status, but, as newcomers outside existing class systems, offered a way of life congenial to the Cypriot Small Group, leading to an alteration in Cypriot society, again triggering an adaptive change within the indigenous system. Unfortunately, as noted above, there is not yet enough material evidence to suggest a substantial Mycenaean or Levantine presence in Cyprus sufficiently radical to alter society in Cyprus. Consequently, it is unlikely, for the reasons stated above, that the Ingot god expresses a syncretism with a deity from a non-prominent social group.

CONCLUSION

The purpose of this paper has not been to offer yet another interpretation of the Ingot god and Bomford figurines; indeed Masson has pointed out the futility of such an exercise (1973). With the current state of our knowledge, it is unlikely that the Ingot god and Bomford figurine represent non-Cypriot deities. Therefore, this discussion has provided incidental support for the arguments of Muhly and Knapp, and especially the latter, who would see figures as a part of the LC II culture. It may be that evidence may yet be revealed which proves otherwise. However, the central concern of this argument has been to plead that religion should not be divorced from the wider social context when religious phenomena are examined by archaeologists.

NOTES

[1] Two more figurines, similar to the latter, are known: one from Kouklia-Palaepaphos and an unprovenanced piece now in the Cyprus Museum in Nicosia (Dalley 1987, 61).
[2] See note[4] below.
[3] Dunnell (1978) defined style as those traits which have no adaptive or selective function. While Hodder opposed this view on the grounds that it consigns style to the periphery (1982, 205), this view accords well with the problem as stated here.
[4] Muhly argued that the usual date of the figures was based not only 'on the stratigraphy of Enkomi, but also on the general historical nature of the metal industry' (1980, 156).

LIST OF REFERENCES

Ahlström, G.W. (1982) *Royal Administration and Religion in Ancient Palestine.* Leiden.
Albright, W. (1942) *Archeology and the Religion of Israel.* Baltimore.
Berger, P. & T. Luckmann (1967) *The Social Construction of Reality. A Treatise in the Sociology of Knowledge.* Harmondsworth.
Brown, G.G. (1957) Some problems of culture contact with illustrations from East Africa & Samoa. *Human Organization 16.*
Carless Hulin, L. (1982) The worshippers of Asiatic Gods of Egypt. *Papers for Discussion I,* 269–78.

Carless Hulin, L. (1988) The diffusion of religious symbols within complex societies, in *The Meaning of Things. Material Culture and Symbolic Expression* (ed. I. Hodder). *One World Archaeology 6*. London.
Catling, H.W. (1964) *Cypriote Bronzework in the Mycenaean World*. Oxford.
Catling, H.W. (1971) A Cypriot bronze statuette in the Bomford Collection, in *Alasia I* (C.F.A. Schaeffer) 15–32. Paris.
Catling, H.W. (1973) The Achaean settlement of Cyprus. *Acts 1973*, 34–9.
Collon, D. (1972) The smiting god. A study of a bronze in the Pomerance Collection in New York. *Levant 4*, 111–34.
Courtois, J-C (1971) Le sanctuaire du dieu au lingot d'Enkomi-Alasia, in *Alasia I*, (C.F.A. Schaeffer) 151–362.
Courtois, J-C (1973) Le sanctuaire du dieu au lingot d'Enkomi-Alasia (Chypre) et les dieux de culte contemporains en méditerranée Orientale. *CRAI*, 223–46.
Dalley, S. (1987) Near Eastern patron deities of mining and smelting in the Late Bronze Age and early Iron Ages. *RDAC*, 61–6.
Douglas, M. (1970) *Natural Symbols*. London.
Drennan, R.D. (1976) Religion and social evolution in formative Mesoamerica, in *The Early Mesoamerican Village* (ed. K.V. Flannery) 345–64. New York.
Drower, M.S. (1973) Syria c. 1550–1400 B.C. *CAH³* II.1, 417–525. Cambridge.
Dunnell, R.C. (1978) Style and function: a fundamental dichotomy. *Am Anth*, 192–202.
Durkheim, E. (1957) *The Elementary Forms of the Religious Life*. New York.
Eco, U. (1976) *A Theory of Semiotics*. Bloomington.
Frankfort, H. (1948) *Kingship and the Gods*. Chicago.
Friedrich, M.H. (1970) Design structure and social interaction: archaeological implications of an ethnographic analysis. *Am Ath 35*, 332–43.
Geertz, C. (1965) Religion as a cultural system, in *Anthropological Approaches to the Study of Religion* (ed. M. Banton). London.
Goff, B.L. (1963) *Symbols of Prehistoric Mesopotamia*. New Haven.
Gombrich, E.H. (1960) *Art and Illusion*. Oxford.
Goodenhough, E.R. (1954) *Jewish Symbols in the Greco-Roman Period*. (Bollingen Series 38) New York.
Hodder, I.R. (1982) *Symbols in Action*. Cambridge.
Karageorghis, J. (1977) *La Grande Déesse de Chypre et son Culte*. Lyon.
Karageorghis, V. (1973) Contributions to the religion of Cyprus in the 13th and 12th centuries B.C. *Acts 1973*, 105–9.
Karageorghis, V. (1982) *Cyprus from the Stone Age to the Romans*. London.
Knapp, A.B. (1986a) *Copper Production and Divine Protection: Archaeology, Ideology and Social Complexity on Bronze Age Cyprus. (SIMA Pocket-book 42)* Göteborg.
Knapp, A.B. (1986b) Production, exchange and socio-political complexity on Bronze Age Cyprus. *Oxf JA 5*, 35–60.
Knapp, A.B. (1988) Ideology, archaeology and polity. *Man 32*, 133–63.
Ladurie, E. Le Roy (1978) *Montaillou*. Paris.
Maier, F-G. (1986) Kinyras and Agapenor. *Acts 1986*, 311–18.
Masson, O. (1973) Remarques sur les cultes Chypriotes à l'époque du Bronze Récent. *Acts 1973*, 110–121.
Muhly, J.D. (1980) Bronze figurines and Near Eastern metalwork. *Isr Exp J 30*, 148–61.
Negbi, O. (1976) *Canaanite Gods in Metal: An Archaeological Study of Ancient Syro-Palestinian Figurines*. Tel Aviv.

Negbi, O. (1982) Evidence for early Phoenician communities on the east Mediterranean islands. *Levant 14*, 97–122.
Niebuhr, H.R. (1969) The social sources of denominationalism. *Sociology and Religion. A Book of Readings.* (eds. N. Birnbaum & G. Lenzer) 314–18.
Ortner, S.B. (1973) On key symbols. *Am Anth 75*, 1338–46.
Plog, S. (1978) Social interaction and stylistic similarity: a reanalysis, in *Archaeological Method and Theory I*, 144–82.
Pritchard, J.B. (1950) *Ancient Near Eastern Texts relating to the Old Testament.* Princeton.
Radcliffe-Brown, A.R. (1939) *Taboo (The Frazer Lecture).* Cambridge.
Schäfer, H. (1930) *Von ägyptischer Kunst.* Leipzig.
Schaeffer, C.F.A. (1952) *Enkomi-Alasia I.* Paris.
Schaeffer, C.F.A. (1953) Engomi. *ARDAC*, 15.
Schaeffer, C.F.A. (1965) An ingot god from Cyprus. *Antiquity 39*, 56–7.
Schaeffer, C.F.A. *et al.* (1971) *Alasia I.* Paris.
Seeden, H. (1981) *The Standing Armed Figurines in the Levant. (PBf I.1).* Munich.
Sjöberg, G. (1960) *The Preindustrial City. Past and Present.* New York.
Sperber, D. (1975) *Rethinking Symbolism.* Cambridge.
Talmon, Y. (1969) Pursuit of the millennium: the relation between religious and social change, in *Sociology and Religion. A Book of Readings* (eds. N. Birnbaum & G. Lenzer) 238–54.
Wright, G.R.H. (1985) *Ancient Building in South Syria and Palestine I.* Leiden.
Wobst, H.M. (1977) *Stylistic Behaviour and Information Exchange.* Michigan.

POSTER SUMMARY
17
Identification of Cypriot votive statues (Archaic through Hellenistic periods). A preliminary case study

Cecilia Beer
University of Stockholm

The vast amount of votive statuary in Cyprus presents problems of identification as to what category they belong: do they represent royalties, images of deities, members of a priesthood, common votaries or others? Insufficient epigraphic evidence, lack of literary sources and too many uncertain provenances/find contexts add to these difficulties.

One would have liked to know the complete diffusion pattern of the different types of statuettes (Heracles-Melqart, 'temple-boy', *kourotrophos* etc), their frequency, the combination of types and their numerical relation to one another at each site. For instance, was there ever a similar mixture of types of votives to a certain divinity, or is it an altogether arbitrary choice from the part of the votary? How limited are the functions of the deities and the purposes of the votive statuettes? Are they dependent on strictly local necessities or even private decision?

The poster display is part of a study that suggests and questions some approaches to the investigation of a series of sitting *kourotrophoi*, statuettes of limestone (Beer 1987, forthcoming). I have suggested elsewhere that there might be an intimate relationship between the 'temple-boys' and the *kourotrophoi*, at least in some cases. The conclusion has been reached through a comparative method of analogous attributes restricted to these two types of statuettes, their contemporaneity and their occurrence at the same sites. The *kourotrophoi* are chiefly attested from Golgoi (*ca* 85 specimens), Idalion (*ca* 55) and Chytroi (*ca* 25), which corresponds with a high frequency of temple boys. The sanctuaries are here related to cults of Aphrodite/Astarte or the Great Goddess of Cyprus and the association of fertility. Temple-boys also appear elsewhere in a masculine sphere, where *kourotrophoi* are absent, connected with the aspect of healing.

But who is the child (swaddled or more grown) in the woman's lap? Is it supposed to represent an ideal child or a real child in a determined situation? That the *kourotrophos* generally represents a goddess seems less likely.

LIST OF REFERENCES

Beer, C. (1987) Comparative votive religion: the evidence of children from Cyprus, Greece and Etruria, in *Gifts to the Gods. Proceedings of the Uppsala Symposium 1985 (Boreas 15)*, 21–9. Uppsala.

Beer, C. (forthcoming) Cultes chypriotes et éléments phéniciens? *2nd International Congress of Phoenician and Punic Studies*, Rome 9–14 November 1987. Rome.

PART FOUR
Artefact Evidence

18
Regionalism, cultural variation and the culture-area concept in Later Prehistoric Cypriot studies

Diane L. Bolger
University of Maryland

CARTOGRAPHY AND CULTURE

Glyn Daniel has stated that the prehistorian and the geographer meet in the map (1964, 141) and so it seems appropriate in a discussion of cultures and areas in prehistoric archaeology to begin with a geographical map—not a map of Cyprus, but a rather curious map of Europe drawn up in the mid-1950's by the Austrian geographer Karl Sinnhuber (Haggett 1972, 85). Sinnhuber's map summarizes the views of sixteen scholars concerning the regional divisions of 'Central Europe' and illustrates the difficulty of establishing a comprehensive regional framework for geographical studies. With the exception of Austria and western Czechoslovakia, which all sixteen managed to agree *do* lie in Central Europe, there is profound disagreement about which areas to include. Lack of consensus is particularly evident for the area between northern Italy, southern Sweden, the Netherlands, and the Ukraine. Extended globally, this frustrating state of affairs has led geographers to question the validity of regional analysis and has contributed to the general decline of regional approaches in geography over the last thirty years. But what of our own field? For it appears that archaeology has not yet sunk to such low levels of despair, and despite the current popularity of systemic approaches favouring wholes rather than parts, that regional analysis in archaeology is very much alive and well. Those of us working in Cyprus would appear to have even less cause for concern, since we can hardly dispute the borders of an island. Internal regional divisions can pose difficulties, however, and a variety of solutions have been proposed for Cyprus, with dividing lines based on geographical, geological, geomorphological, demographic or other criteria. To consider but three examples:

1. Gjerstad's analysis (1926, 17), the first comprehensive attempt at

regional analysis of the island. On the basis of eighty known sites he isolated six settlement groups;

2. Catling's analysis (1963, 134–5) which increased Gjerstad's regional count to eleven as the result of an additional 400 sites identified by the Cyprus Survey; and

3. Stanley Price's regional divisions (1979, 4 Fig 3) based on solid geology, since he judged it to be the least variable feature of the environment. He uses these as the basis for a discussion of prehistoric settlement patterns from 6500–3000 BC.

These three maps agree on one thing at least—that the Troodos and Kyrenia Mountains are the most salient topographical features of the island, and that they loosely define four major settlement regions (the North Coast, the Mesaoria, the south coast, and the West). Stanley Price's analysis, however, differs from the others in one important respect. Instead of deriving regions from the settlement patterns themselves, it distinguishes them environmentally, apart from the settlement patterns. This marks an important departure from earlier regional analysis in Cyprus, for it opens up the possibility of exploring the dynamic interrelationships between prehistoric cultures and their surroundings. The ultimate aims of regional analysis in archaeology lie beyond the plotting of sites and documentation of regional groups; and there is more to cultural cartography than drawing lines. At the very least we must attempt to explain and interpret them, mindful of what it is we are circumscribing, what theories or methods we are utilizing, and what degree of accuracy we can realistically hope to attain given the limited nature of the evidence. The ability to do this depends in part upon an understanding of the growth of the relationship between geography and archaeology over the last hundred years, and in particular upon our understanding of the ways in which archaeology has borrowed concepts of regionalism from geography and tailored them to its own purposes. Before turning to specific problems of regionalism and cultural variation in prehistoric Cyprus, then, I would like to trace the path of regional analysis from its nineteenth century roots to its twentieth-century infiltration of prehistoric studies in general and Cypriot archaeology in particular.

THE RISE OF HUMAN GEOGRAPHY

We begin in the Old World of the late 19th century, with the work of the German geographer Friedrich Ratzel, widely recognized as the founder of a branch of geography known today as 'human' or 'social' geography. Ratzel named it 'Anthropogeographie' and wrote a two-volume *opus* with that title (Ratzel 1975) in which he explored the role played by the environment in the origin and transmission of cultural traits. In theoretical terms, Ratzel was a diffusionist; methodologically he relied upon criteria of form and decoration of material objects to determine the degree of interrelation between cultures, a process he called 'Formengedanke' (de Waal Malefijt

1974) and one that is not unlike the 'mental template' concept in archaeology today. Through 'Anthropogeographie' Ratzel hoped to create a single, unified science of mankind encompassing history, geography and ethnology (Lebon 1963, 35–6). In this he did not succeed; but if we manage to overlook some of the more questionable aspects of his work (for example, his ideas about the amount of space appropriate to given cultures, or *Lebensraum* (Ratzel 1906), which were all too readily incorporated into Nazi ideology a generation later) Ratzel can be said in a positive sense to have laid the groundwork for regional and environmental approaches used in anthropology, archaeology and geography during much of the present century.

Ratzel characterized anthropogeography as a 'beschreibende Wissenschaft', a 'descriptive science' (Ratzel 1975), and this empirical bent was furthered by a younger colleague of his in Frankfurt, the anthropologist Leo Frobenius, and at about the same time by members of the German *Kulturkreis* School (chief among them museum curator Fritz Graebner and anthropologist Father Wilhelm Schmidt). Froebenius contributed little on the theoretical front to Ratzel's work, but he did improve upon its methodology by establishing what he called 'geographical statistics' or assemblages of cultural traits in different societies which he compared in order to hypothesize cultural migrations (de Waal Malefijt 1974). Meanwhile, a group of ultra-diffusionists known collectively as the Culture Circle *Kulturkreis* School were drawing upon masses of elaborate field data in the attempt to reconstruct the migratory routes of the four or five primordial culture groups ('Urkulture') from which they believed all subsequent cultures could be derived (de Waal Malefijt 1974). A critical weakness of these early attempts to reconcile cultures and their environments is the tacit assumption among them all (Ratzel and Frobenius included) that similarity of form among artefacts, regardless of their contexts, offers proof of an historical relationship between the cultures represented by the artefacts (de Waal Malefijt 1974). Secondly, these early approaches were descriptive rather than prescriptive, a problem we shall return to shortly with regard to the mapping of prehistoric culture-areas in Cyprus. First, however, we need to make a spatial leap across the Atlantic in order to witness the reception of Ratzel's theories and methods by anthropologists and archaeologists in the New World. For it is in the United States that the precepts of anthropogeography were fully transmitted into our own discipline.

THE DIFFUSION OF DIFFUSIONIST THOUGHT: ANTHROPOGEOGRAPHY DISCOVERS THE NEW WORLD

A pivotal figure in the transmission of Ratzel's ideas to America was the American geographer Ellen Churchill Semple, who studied with Ratzel in Leipzig, translated some of his works into English, and in 1906 delivered the first lecture on anthropogeography to an American audience (Buttmann 1977, 82). Unlike Ratzel, Semple was a strict environmental determinist, and it is therefore ironic that it was not among the determinists, but among their adversaries the possibilists that Ratzel's thinking most firmly took root. Whereas the determinists believed that environmental constraints dictate cultural developments, the possibilists viewed the role of the environment in culture as vaguely permissive or restrictive, encouraging some adaptive strategies, discouraging others, but causing none (de Waal Malefijt 1974). An early example is provided by the work of Yale anthropologist Clark Wissler (1926) in which American Indian populations were divided into eight groups on the basis of their varying subsistence patterns. He called the geographical units represented by these groups 'Food Areas' and drew up lists of the cultural traits belonging to each group, designating for each region a particular site or 'culture center' from which the various traits had spread. And so was born, full-blown out of the diffusionist heads of Ratzel and the *Kulturkreis* School, American culture-area theory. It was left to another American anthropologist, Alfred Kroeber, to play Frobenius to Wissler's Ratzel. Kroeber's research among American Indian tribes attempted to define and distinguish culture-areas more sharply by compiling elaborate trait lists made up of thousands of items—what we might call 'cultural statistics'. Kroeber's *magnum opus* on the subject, *Cultural and Natural Areas of Native North America*, soon came to be regarded as the definitive statement of the American culture-area approach. In it he mapped out seven 'Grand Areas', twenty-one 'Areas', and sixty-three 'Sub-Areas' for native cultures of North and Central America. Each area had a focal point or 'culture climax' where cultural attributes within the region were most frequently and intensely expressed. Boundaries between areas were drawn by connecting the points at which the influences of two or more foci met. The great probability of subjective bias in this process necessitated the prodigious trait lists just mentioned, and even then, Kroeber recommended that lines be drawn 'only when they must'. As for the role of the environment in the determination of culture-areas, Kroeber remarked:

> 'While it is true that cultures are rooted in nature and can therefore never be understood except with reference to that piece of nature in which they occur, they are no more produced by that nature than a plant is produced or caused by the soil in which it is rooted. The immediate causes of cultural phenomena are other cultural phenomena' (Kroeber 1939, 1).

Although these words were clearly intended to distinguish Kroeber's own approach from the determinist viewpoint, they unwittingly reveal something more interesting about his methods and the methods of American culture-area theory in general, namely the substitution of 'cultural determinism' for 'environmental determinism'. For in rejecting the crass environmental approach of the determinists, Kroeber in effect removed the environment from the process of cultural adaptation altogether. A brief example from his 1939 book illustrates the now-tangential role of the environment in Kroeber's view of the spatial organization of culture. In the text accompanying a map of seasonal levels of precipitation in the American southwest, two conclusions are reached about the culture inhabiting the region, the Pueblo Indians:

1. That where environmental conditions for maize growing fail, the limits of maize growing are reached, and

2. that the maize-dependent Pueblo remained limited to an area of sufficient precipitation during the growing season of the plant (Kroeber 1939, Chapter 13). If we follow these statements to their logical, or tautological, conclusion, it is the dependence of the Pueblo on maize that restricts them to an area in which maize can be grown successfully. The reasons for the Pueblo's dependence on maize, however, are not explored here. Is maize dependence, as Kroeber adumbrates, a cultural phenomenon? Or did environmental factors contribute to a subsistence strategy based primarily on maize cultivation? In the end, Kroeber's failure and the failure of the American culture-area theory in general to define the role of the environment in culture process led to the theory's decline in American anthropological and archaeological circles during the 1950's. It also contributed to the disenchantment among geographers with regional analysis referred to earlier. Finally, I would suggest that it helps explain the somewhat muddled state of regional affairs in Old World archaeology today: since the turn of the century, prehistoric studies in the Mediterranean and elsewhere have absorbed many of the essential ingredients of the culture-area approach—not, as a rule, consciously, but rather as a vague constellation of ideas that, never having been properly chewed and digested, have never been duly processed or eliminated.

THE CYPRUS CONNECTION

Unfortunately, time does not permit us to trace the path of scholarly thinking from the New World back to the Old, although for Cyprus a variety of possible trade routes can be reconstructed. One is published evidence of correspondence between Alfred Kroeber and J.L. Myres that documents one instance at least of direct exchange of these ideas (Kroeber 1939, 2). Another concerns the utility of the culture-area approach to the arrangement of artefacts in museum collections and handbooks. For Cyprus, its application is manifested to varying degrees in Myres' *Handbook of the Cesnola Collection*, Dikaios' revised editions of Myres' and Ohnefalsch-Richter's *Guide to the Cyprus Museum*, and Stewart and Trendall's *Handbook to the Nicholson Museum*. Finally, there is the indirect but nonetheless palpable evidence of settlement pattern studies such as those of Gjerstad and Catling. For the analytical process involved here, namely, plotting sites onto a map and partitioning the map into regions based on the configurations of those same sites, closely parallels the process followed by Kroeber in his Pueblo culture study. As with Kroeber, a kind of 'cultural determinism' is employed, the determining factor in this case being the inherent propensity of Cypriot populations to settle in particular areas, with the mediating role of the environment only sketchily defined. Where does this leave us *vis-à-vis* a regional analysis of the island? While it admittedly lies beyond the scope of this paper to solve the theoretical and methodological problems raised thus far, I would like to focus now on a specific culture and area of Cypriot prehistory, the Chalcolithic Erimi culture of the Paphos District. It is hoped in the process that many of the theoretical points stressed thus far will be illustrated more graphically, and that we shall have moved a little closer to an understanding of regional and cultural variation on the island during its later prehistoric phases.

ASPECTS OF THE SPATIAL ORGANIZATION OF CYPRIOT CULTURE BEFORE THE BRONZE AGE

Among the regions of Cyprus, the Paphos District is perhaps the easiest to define, due to the pronounced topographical barriers separating it from the rest of the island. The greatest barrier to overland communication is, of course, the Troodos Range, which forms most of the district's eastern border. To the north in Tillyria, outliers of Troodos extend to the coast, effectively severing the West from the Mesaoria; and to the south, limestone hills of the Koronia formation impede access to the east. A closer look at the map, however, shows that even within the Paphos District itself there is a distinct lack of geographical and topographical uniformity. The District can be divided into four parts: the narrow strip of terrace deposits along the west coast known as the Ktima lowlands; the hilly upland region (or Paphos Plateau) made up of limestone of the Koronia and Pakhna formations; the igneous Mamonia Complex forming the core of the Akamas Peninsula; and the Khrysokhou River valley in the northeast, including Polis and composed of terrace deposits and reworked fanglomerates (Bear 1963, chapter 2). What we want to explore now is whether we can treat the Paphos District as a cultural entity during the Chalcolithic period, or whether we can detect local variations which can be shown to correspond to the regional vicissitudes just outlined.

Two groups of Erimi culture sites are relevant to this discussion (Fig 18.1). The first has been the primary work for over a decade of the Lemba Archaeological Project. Under the direction of E.J. Peltenburg, the Project has focussed its activity upon the excavation of three sites in the Ktima Lowlands, Kissonerga-Mylouthkia, Lemba-Lakkous, and, more recently, Kissonerga-Mosphilia. From time to time over the years, some Project members have ventured into the hinterland to carry out surveys in other parts if the district (Sheen *in* Peltenburg 1981; Baird *in* Peltenburg 1984; and Baird 1985). One of the areas surveyed most intensively has been along the Stavros tis Psokas River and adjacent areas to the south. Here, along the hilly slopes above the Khrysokhou valley, a second group of Chalcolithic sites has been identified—including the sites of Evretou-Amakharos, Sarama-Katavlaka, Philousa-Koprikoes and Miliou-Rhodaeos; we can add also the sites of Meladhia and Tremithousa reported by Dikaios (1936, 75).

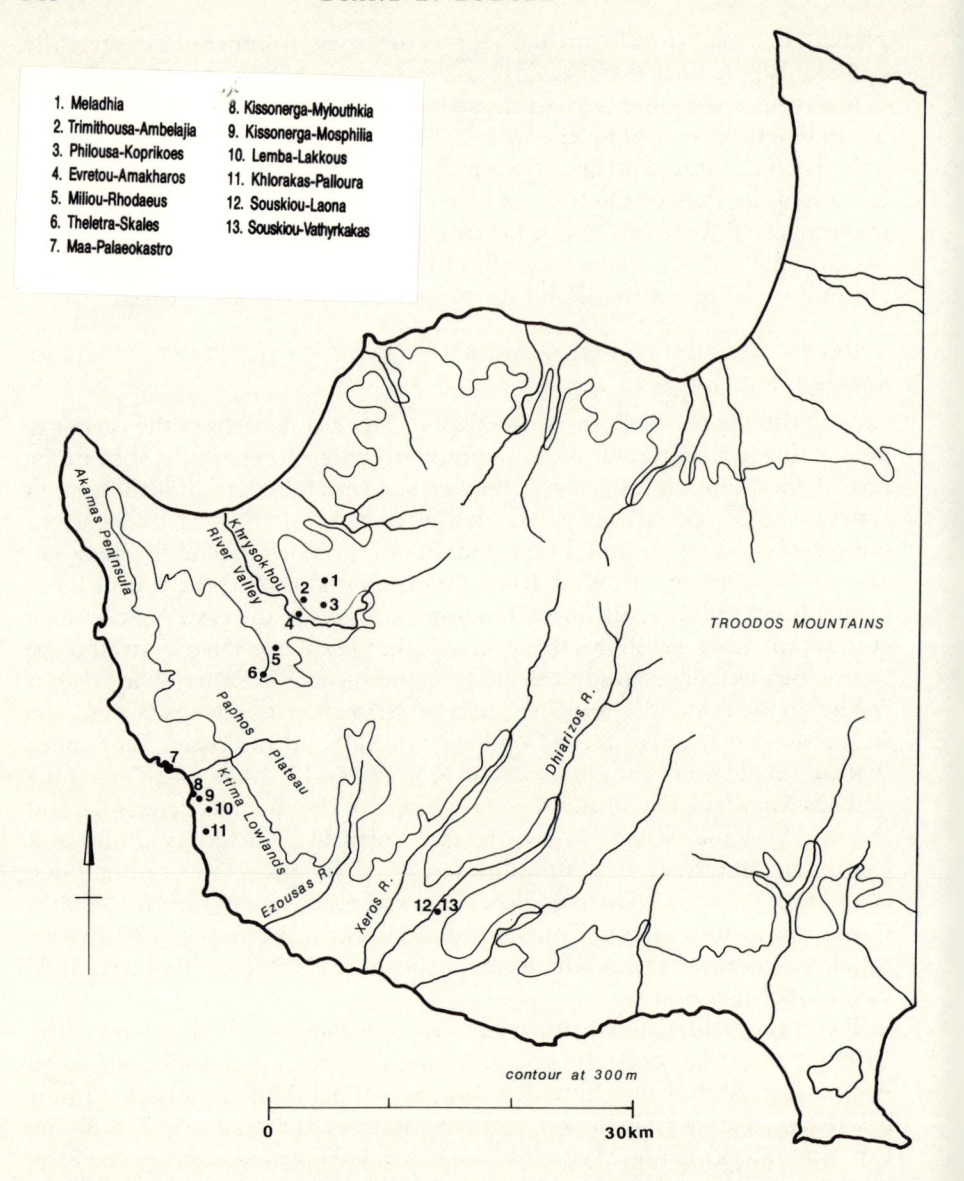

Figure 18.1 Map of western Cyprus showing major Erimi culture sites mentioned in the text

Seriation of well-defined and stratified ceramic types at the Lemba sites has made it possible to establish a ceramic profile for western Cyprus during the periods under discussion. Table 18.1 shows the main wares of the period: to the left in chronological order, from Late Neolithic to Early Bronze; and to the right spatially by the sites where they are represented. As the far right hand column indicates, Chalcolithic settlement is attested

Table 18.1. Western Cyprus—Ceramic Sequence—(Pre-Bronze Age)

	WARE	PERIOD	SITE(S)
I.	Combed	Late Neolithic	Peyia, Sarama, Anadhiou
	Red-on-White (Broad Line)		Kissongerga-Mosphilia
II.	Glossy Burnished	Early Chalcolithic	Kissonerga-Mylouthkia Miliou-Rhodaeus
III.	Red-on-White (Close Line)	Middle Chalcolithic	Lemba-Lakkous Kissonerga-Mosphilia Miliou-Rhodaeus
	Black Topped Ware		Stavros tis Psokas sites
IV.	Red-and-Black Stroke-Burnished	Late Chalcolithic	Lemba-Lakkous Kissonerga-Mosphilia Milious-Rhodaeus
	Coarse Painted Ware		Stavros tis Psokas sites
V.	Red Polished (Philia)		
	Black Slip-and-Combed	Early Bronze Age	Kissonerga-Mosphilia

in Ktima and Khrysokhou for all phases of the period; and within each area one site appears to have been longer-lived and more prosperous than its neighbours—Miliou-Rhodaeos in the Khrysokhou area, and Kissonerga-Mosphilia in Ktima. So far only Mosphila has yielded evidence of transition to the Bronze Age, however (Bolger *in* Peltenburg *et al* 1986, 37–9).

Among the sites in the Khrysokhou region, Miliou has yielded the most extensive ceramic evidence, so it is here that we might most profitably seek indications of local variation. In a preliminary study of the pottery from Miliou, Jennifer Stewart identified nine wares, including Glossy Burnished, Close-Line RW, RB/B, and Coarse Painted, suggesting occupation at the site during all phases of the Chalcolithic (Stewart *in* Peltenburg 1981, 42–6). Morphological attributes were found to correspond closely to those at Lemba, and although some differences were observed in fabric types, this is not surprising given the tendency of potters to exploit local clay sources. But Peltenburg has drawn attention to stylistic differences between the CLRW at Miliou and Lemba, in particular the relatively restricted range of motifs at Miliou and the inclusion there of elements, such as squared rim dashes, not attested at the Lemba sites (1981, 38). This 'Miliou RW style' has been recorded at other Khrysokhou sites as well and thus offers proof of a regional style distinct from the more elaborate style of the Lemba sites. At Lemba, meanwhile, the painted style exhibits stronger links with sites outside the Paphos District, notably with Erimi near Limassol. Indeed, almost all of the thirty motifs isolated on CLRW sherds from Erimi now in the Cyprus Museum are found singly and in similar combinations at Lemba and Mosphilia (Bolger 1987, 74); and although the calibre and complexity of RW pottery recently discovered at Mosphilia are paralleled only at Souskiou, the cultural affinities between these two sites can probably be attributed to their extraordinary wealth rather than to environmental circumstance.

Peltenburg has suggested that an association between the South and the West existed already during the Late Neolithic period, for ceramic evidence from Late Neolithic sites such as Peyia-Elia tou Vatani evinces close ties with Sotira-Teppes and its similar preference for Combed, rather than painted (RW) ware (1987, 53). The total picture emerging from the evidence to date, then, is one of gradual divergence of ceramic traits at Ktima and Khrysokhou during the Chalcolithic period. The initial unity implied by the close ceramic ties between these regions during the Early Chalcolithic was somehow displaced during the Middle Chalcolithic period when regional tendencies became much more pronounced. What factors may have contributed to this development? Although we may never be in a position to answer this question definitively, several possiblities should be considered which will hopefully be tested in future investigations.

One possible factor, distance, does not appear to have been decisive, since the Lemba sites are only 15 km from the Khrysokhou group but more than 50 km from Erimi where ceramic links are stronger. Nevertheless, it would be worthwhile to perform cluster analysis on CLRW motifs recorded at sites throughout the island in order to substantiate, or revise, this preliminary assumption. It is interesting that Frankel's study of motifs on Middle Cypriot White Painted pottery demonstrated greatest stylistic similarities among neighbouring sites, with a constant fall-off in similarity as distance between them increased (1974). While a similar pattern could perhaps be detected within localized groups of Erimi culture sites, this pattern does not appear to hold true at the inter-group or inter-regional level. One wonders whether these changing patterns might also reflect changes in the spatial organization of culture in Cyprus from the end of the Chalcolithic period onward.

If distance was not a factor, what was? The radically different sitings of the Lemba and Miliou groups, the former in coastal lowlands, the latter on hilly inland slopes, may have encouraged similarly diverse patterns of adaptation reflected by the divergence of the painted styles of these regions during the Middle Chalcolithic. A divergent pattern, once underway, may have been reinforced by topographical barriers to communication and interaction. One way in which this hypothesis might be tested would be through temper selection studies of Chalcolithic sherdage in both areas to determine spatial and temporal variations in the exploitation of raw materials used in the manufacture of clay bodies. Temper identification study of sherds from the Lemba sites, which is now underway, will provide valuable comparative evidence for studies in other areas as well; it is hoped that the results of these investigations can lend sustenance to the more abstract evidence of stylistic variation which *via* the 'mental template' concept is presumed to reflect similar differences in non-material aspects of culture.

An additional factor which may have contributed to local variation in culture during the period is the typical arrangement of sites into clusters, a settlement pattern which, as Hodder has shown for a number of modern traditional societies, reinforces interaction and exchange within groups and fosters the growth of local ethnic identities which can act as barriers to the dispersal of cultural traits (1978, 248–54). Here Hodder maintains that the phenomenon of local ethnicity does not preclude contact and interaction with outside areas, and that interaction is normally expressed in the diffusion of some traits, but not others (1978, 246–7). Consequently, we should not be troubled by the uniformity of morphological traits among the Lemba and Khrysokhou groups, when decorative elements exhibit marked variations. In order that we do not fall prey to cultural determinism, however, it should be stressed that the clustering of sites during the Chalcolithic period was not simply a cultural phenomenon, but part and parcel of a subsistence strategy that within these particular environments appears to have enjoyed a reasonable measure of success.

Preliminary study of pottery from Kissonerga-Mosphilia points to a breakdown of established ceramic traditions at the end of the Chalcolithic period, perhaps signalling the arrival of new ideas and techniques from abroad (Bolger 1986). The quantities of Red Polished (Philia) pottery from upper levels, moreover, suggest a shift of western cultural alliances from the south to the north as the Bronze Age approached. If this was indeed the case, then part of the change from the Chalcolithic to the Bronze Age in Cyprus would appear to have involved a reorganization of spatial relations among existing communities during the last phase of the Chalcolithic period—a reorganization that may have foreshadowed the change to a more unified, centralized society during the course of the Bronze Age. Evidence of site ranking during the Chalcolithic period corroborates this view. Miliou and Mosphilia, among the longest-lived sites in the west, were also among the wealthiest, and Building 3 at Mosphilia, with its vast array of stacked *pithoi,* testifies to the need for collection, storage, and perhaps redistribution at the end of the period. Finally, the discovery of a ritual deposit of figurines in and around a painted architectural vessel (*above 113–122*) may suggest the additional function of this site as a ceremonial or cult centre.

In conclusion, the ceramic evidence of Mosphilia and other Erimi culture sites of the West, argues that we carefully consider, or reconsider, our views on regionalism in Cyprus before the Bronze Age. Rather than envisage the Paphos District as a monolithic tract housing a culturally homogeneous population, we should direct our thinking along lines better suited to traditional, decentralized societies inhabiting terrains which, although not vast, exhibit significant environmental vicissitudes. Stanley Price (1979) has written that 'the extreme diversity of the natural relief in Cyprus has always encouraged a similarly diverse pattern of adaptation.' To this I would add the prospect that it will ultimately encourage a greater diversity of analytical approaches to the study of cultures and areas in prehistoric Cyprus as well.

LIST OF REFERENCES

Baird, D. (1984) Survey of the Drousha area of western Cyprus, in E.J. Peltenburg, Lemba Archaeological Project, Cyprus 1982: preliminary report. *Levant 16*, 63–5.

Baird, D. (1985) *An archive report for the Department of Antiquities Cyprus on the L.A.P. Survey in the Stavros tis Psokas River Valley.* unpublished.

Bear, L.M. (1963) *The Mineral Resources and Mining Industry of Cyprus.* Nicosia.

Bolger, D. (1986) Wares of the Late Chalcolithic/Early Bronze Age Transition, in E. Peltenburg et al, Excavations at Kissonerga-*Mosphilia* 1985. *RDAC*, 37–9.

Bolger, D. (1987) Is there a western Cyprus? A Chalcolithic perspective, in *Western Cyprus: Connections (SIMA 77)* (ed. D. Rupp) 69–78. Göteborg.

Buttmann, G. (1977) *Friedrich Ratzel.* Stuttgart.

Catling, H. (1962) Patterns of settlement in Bronze Age Cyprus. *Op Ath 4*, 129–69.

Chisholm, M. (1975) *Human Geography.* London.

Daniel, G. (1964) *The Idea of Prehistory.* London.

de Waal Malefijt, A. (1974) *Images of Man; A History of Anthropological Thought.* New York.

Dikaios, P. (1936) Excavations at Erimi 1933–35. *RDAC*, 1–75.

Frankel, D. (1974) *Middle Cypriot White Painted Pottery. (SIMA 42).* Göteborg.

Gjerstad, E. (1926) *Studies on Prehistoric Cyprus.* Uppsala.

Haggett, P. (1972) *Geography: A Modern Synthesis.* New York.

Hodder, I. (1978) *The Spatial Oranization of Culture.* London.

Koeber, A. (1939) *Cultural and Natural Areas of Native North America.* University of California, Los Angeles.

Lebon, J. (1963) *Introduction to Human Geography.* London.

Peltenburg, E.J. (1981) Lemba Archaeological Project, Cyprus 1979: preliminary report. *Levant 13*, 28–50.

Peltenburg, E.J. (1987) A Late Prehistoric Pottery Sequence for Western Cyprus, in *Western Cyprus: Connections (SIMA 77)*, (ed. D. Rupp) 53–68. Göteborg.

Ratzel, F. (1901) *Der Lebensraum.* Tübingen.

Sheen, A. (1981) Stavros tis Psokas 1979, in E. Peltenburg, Lemba Archaeological Project, Cyprus 1979: preliminary report. *Levant 13*, 39–42.

Stanley Price, N.P. (1979) *Early Prehistoric Settlement in Cyprus 6500–3000 B.C. (BAR Int Ser 65).* Oxford.

Stewart, J. (1981) A brief guide to the pottery wares of Miliou-*Rhodaeus*, in Peltenburg 1981, 42–6.

Wissler, C. (1926) *Relationship of Nature to Man in the Native North America.* New York.

19
The glyptics of Bronze Age Cyprus: 'through a glass darkly'

R.S. Merrillees with the collaboration of P.H. Merrillees
Canberra

The origins of a locally-made, distinctively Cypriot school of glyptic design in the Bronze Age remain, despite the volume of research conducted since the Second World War, to be credibly established. The problem lies not in the amount of material available for study but in the shortage of well stratified and otherwise reliably dated cylinder seals found in the island. The basic deficiency has been compounded by a tendency amongst scholars to differentiate between indigenous and imported styles less on the intrinsic technical and artistic merits of each piece in relationship to Cypriot traditions and resources than on the process of elimination, whereby what is not purportedly foreign is *ipso facto* local. As a result specialists in the island's prehistory have been ready to accept as Cypriot groups of cylinders whose attribution has been made on essentially stylistic criteria in a Near eastern cultural environment. It has, for example, been widely assumed that the secondary figures on the well known Old Babylonian cylinder seal from Nicosia-Ayia Paraskevi T.1884, 1 (Figs 19.1, 3), were added in Cyprus by an indigenous engraver (*cf* Merrillees 1986, 133—with references), but this view has now been challenged by the author in his commentary on the glyptics from the burial deposit (Merrillees 1986, 133–6). This conference provides a timely opportunity to take the argument another step further by attempting to define what should and should not be considered authentically Cypriot amongst the cylinders associated with the island's Bronze Age civilisation.

There is no dispute amongst the experts that the Old Babylonian cylinder seal from Nicosia-Ayia Paraskevi T.1884, 1 No.w, was recut at a later stage of its circulation in use and that to the field were added, uncomfortably and without relevance to the original scene, three figures, one of a bird, the other two of beings standing upright with two legs and an animal-shaped head (Merrillees 1986, 120–3, 127–9). What is much less certain is when,

Figure 19.1 Cyprus Museum N76. Old Babylonian cylinder seal. Nicosia-Ayios Paraskevi T. 1881.1.

Figure 19.2 Cyprus Museum N76. Original engraving.

where and by whom these secondary insertions were made into the scene. The attribution of the deposit to the second half of LC IA, *ca* 1600–1550 BC (Merrillees 1986, 138), gives a *terminus ante quem* for the re-engraving, but does not help pinpoint the period at which the seal was modified, since it could have happened any time after the cylinder was first produced in *ca*

Figure 19.3 Cyprus Museum N76. Secondary engraving.

1850–1800 BC (Collon *apud* Merrillees 1986, 128). Collon argues on stylistic and technical grounds that the recutting probably dates to *ca* 1750–1700 BC, upwards of a century and a half before its deposition (Merrillees 1986, 129). The cylinder itself must also have done a fair amount of travelling, for it was manufactured in Mesopotamia, probably reaching Cyprus via N. Syria, and had to make its way to the centre of the island before being laid to rest with the grave goods amongst which it was found. It would be idle to speculate on the identity of the individual(?) with whom it was interred, though the bulk of the funerary furnishings were typically Cypriot, but the exceptional nature of the foreign articles encountered in the deposit makes one think irresistably of the so-called 'Tomb of the Seafarer' at Karmi-Palealona, which belongs to MC I, *ca* 1900–1800 BC (*SCE* IV.1A, 205–391).

The real point at issue is whether the secondary figures on the Nicosia-Ayia Paraskevi cylinder seal were inserted by a Cypriot or non-Cypriot, possibly Syrian engraver. Leaving aside the resemblances between these depictions and the motifs representative of a North Syrian school identified by Collon (Merrillees 1986, 129), this study will attempt to do no more than compare the figures added to the cylinder with traditional Cypriot iconography and draw some tentative conclusions on the degree to which any relationship can be established. To begin with, we must recapitulate the specifics of each additional element for which the expert descriptions of Parvine Merrillees and Dominique Collon are available (Merrillees 1986, 120–3, 127–9).

The first creature (Fig 19.3) is a bull, or griffin-type monster with short horns, beaked snout and forked tongue. It is standing upright with forearms (legs) upraised, long tail hanging down, and evidently ithyphallic. Its feet are the hooves of an animal. The second figure (Fig 19.3) is more humanoid than mythical. It too is standing upright and has a caprid-shaped head with short horns and one ear, but its arms and legs appear to be more those of a human than a beast, and the impression it gives is a man wearing a kilt with an animal-headed mask. The bird (Fig 19.3) is schematically represented with one wing outstretched as though in flight, two legs hanging down and a fish-like tail. A double circle was also inserted into the field at the same time as the figures (Fig 19.3). There is nothing remotely like this composition in the whole of Cypriot art preceding the Late Bronze Age, and indeed nothing even vaguely similar, except in the most generic terms, to its individual elements. Not too much, however, should be read into the arrangement of the figures, as their placement was clearly dictated by the exigencies of space, and it is not sure whether they should iconographically be related to each other. There is, nevertheless, little doubting their contemporaneity and so they can at least be considered manifestations of the same magico-cultural milieu, wherever that lay.

The first thing to be said about the Cypriot cultural context is that representation in stone of the human or animal form in Bronze Age Cyprus is exceedingly rare. Apart from four limestone/alabaster, free-standing plank or slab figures, two without provenance, which have been assigned to the EC/MC periods and schematised to the point where they have lost nearly all their human attributes (Morris 1985, 137 Figs 176–7; 143 Figs 216–17), the only naturalistic stone sculpture found in Cyprus is the celebrated if scarcely concupiscent bas relief plank or slab figure of what is probably a male on the wall of a *dromos* of a MC I tomb in the cemetery at Karmi-Palealona on the north coast of the island (Merrillees 1980, 173 —with references). There are no graphic or pictorial representations of zoomorphic or anthropomorphic figures in stone attested from the Early and Middle Bronze Ages, and portrayals of these motifs on ceramic manufactures are scarce.

The only painted example is of a stylised human being standing upright on the front of a White Painted V askos of MC III date (Åström 1971, 10 Figs 3, 4, 10–11), and it bears no resemblance to the secondary figures on the Old Babylonian cylinder from Nicosia-Ayia Paraskevi T.1884, 1. Only two painted birds are recorded on all the pottery of the EC and MC periods, and both are so simple in design that no useful comparisons can be made (Åström 1971, 11 Fig 6 top row, second from right; 11–12 Fig 7). One occurred on a White Painted V sherd from Dhiorios-Aloupotrypes and can be dated also to MC III, while the other was encountered on an imported Syro-Cilician jug from a tomb also in Nicosia-Ayia Paraskevi belonging probably to MC I (Merrillees & Tubb 1979, 225 Fig 2, Pl 24.2; 223, 228).

The only possibly significant observation to be made is that neither bird had an outstretched wing like the depiction on the cylinder seal.

Portrayals of human- or animal-like figures incised on clay vessels are no less infrequent. The best known are the schematic designs on two Red Polished vases of EC I date, *ca* 23rd century BC, from Bellapais-Vounous (Merrillees 1980, 176—with references). They consist of compositions representing an extended animate form with trunk, ribs, legs and arms, together with horns or antlers in the place of heads, and were interpreted by J.R. Stewart as 'masked dancers', that is, humans wearing animal heads or even dressed entirely in animal costumes. Morris, however, has questioned this proposition and prefers to see the mouflon headed figure as having 'the shape of a ram seen from above... its four legs with cloven hooves suggest that it is more probably a plan view of the animal itself' (1985, 217). These motifs in any case stand apart from the general range of graphic designs used by the Cypriot potters and have no successors in the extant art of the rest of the EC and MC periods. More problematic from an analytical point of view are the so-called 'comb figures' whose rendition is also linear but association with the human form less easy to define. Morris has recently assembled the relevant data and carefully considered the nature of these curious depictions, which belong to both EC and MC times, and come to the conclusion that the artist was probably more inspired by the human than artefactual prototype (1985, 138–41). On the other hand plastic representations of humans and animals whether as low relief decoration on pottery containers, semi-detached projections or as free standing models, or in the shapes of vases themselves, are very common and amongst the most characteristic of the ceramic products of the Early and Middle Bronze Ages. Indeed their number, ingenuity and variety give a comprehensive idea of native Cypriot perceptions and styles, which makes it possible to draw culturally valid observations from a comparison of extraneous depictions with this body of representative material.

Sufficient work has been done on the salient features of these portrayals to enable the categories of subject matter to be adequately classified for the purpose of providing an artistic benchmark for this analysis. Studies by the writer (Merrillees 1980), Belgiorno (1984) and Morris (1985) show that the human form, however summarily or whimsically rendered, remained identifiably anthropomorphic and could not be mistaken for an animal or monster. Likewise animals and birds, whatever the peculiarities of their translation into relief or models through the medium of clay, retained essentially naturalistic features and postures, which enables them to be genetically typed (*cf* Morris 1985, 184–233). There are no parallels in Cypriot plastic or sculptural art for the monster and caprid-headed figure depicted on the Old Babylonian cylinder seal, and only the bird has (generic) equivalents in ceramic representations. Neither the erect penis on the monster nor the kilt on the 'masked' being conform to the canons of Cypriot stylistic expression, for there are few if any antecedents for this mode of portrayal, and it may be that they were originally of foreign derivation. This is not to say that tumescence and the Bronze Age precursor of the Vracha were unknown in the EC and MC periods—certain plank figurines may have been ithyphallic (Merrillees 1980, 174) and kilted figures appear on two local Bichrome wheel-made tankards of LC IB (after the deposition of the seal from Nicosia-Ayia Paraskevi) (Karageorghis 1979, 198–203)—but that they were not part of the regular repertory of Cypriot motifs and designs. Apart, then, from the putative representations of human beings wearing animal masks from Bellapais-Vounous (see above), there are no parallels for the caprid-headed figure on the seal from Nicosia-Ayia Paraskevi in Early and Middle Bronze Cyprus, and the glyptic monster is completely without precedent in the island's civilisation before 1500 BC.

On iconographic grounds, therefore, there is no evidence to support the argument that the secondary designs on the Old Babylonian cylinder were of Cypriot origin. Indeed all the available data militate against such an hypothesis. There is no tradition of seal-cutting in Cyprus prior to the mid-second millennium BC and almost no continuity of stone working from the Neolithic and Chalcolithic into the EC and MC periods, except in the production of implements or tools (Swiny 1986, 1–31). The cylinder from Nicosia-Ayia Paraskevi T.1884, 1 is the earliest so far securely dated from the island, which, because of its foreign origin, makes it extremely unlikely that the later additions to the engraving were inserted in Cyprus rather than Syria or some other point further east. Finally, there are the parallels for the secondary motifs which Collon has found in her North Syrian school of the mid-18th century BC, which suggest that the recutting of the seal took place before the object left the Asiatic mainland (Collon *apud* Merrillees 1986, 129; Collon 1987, Nos 206, 209, 210, 212; 52). But if the evidence lends no weight to the case for a Cypriot rendition of the secondary designs, it in no way detracts from the proposition that the kinds of figures which appeared on the Old Babylonian cylinder became typical of the island's glyptic repertory. Collon herself argued that the seal was recut 'probably in North Syria or Cyprus sometime after 1750 BC by a seal cutter who used and adapted North Syrian motifs' (Collon *apud* Merrillees 1986, 129), and the main characteristic of the Cypriot cylinders attributed by Porada to her Group I is 'their dependence upon Syrian glyptic' (Porada 1948, 182). Since this form of figural representation cannot be shown to have entered Cyprus by any other medium than glyptics, the conclusion seems inescapable that one at least of the styles that was adopted by Cypriot seal cutters originated in Syria and that the secondary engraving on the Old Babylonian cylinder from Nicosia-Ayia Paraskevi Tomb 1884, 1 was an early if not the first of the imported artistic connections from this source attested in the island.

LIST OF REFERENCES

Åström, P. (1971) Pictorial motifs in the Middle Cypriot Bronze Age, in *Alasia I* (C.F.A. Schaeffer) 7–14. Paris.

Belgiorno, M.R. (1984) Le statuette antropomorfe Cipriote dell 'Età del Bronzo. I Parte. Gli idoli del Bronzo Antico III—Bronzo Medio I. *SMEA* 25, 9–63.

Collon, D. (1987) *First Impressions - Cylinder Seals in the Ancient Near East*. London.

Karageorghis, V. (1979) Kypriaka IV. *RDAC*, 198–209.

Merrillees, R.S. (1980) Representation of the human form in prehistoric Cyprus. *Op Ath 13*, 171–84.

Merrillees, R.S. (1986) A 16th century BC tomb group from Central Cyprus with links both East and West. *Acts 1986*, 114–48.

Merrillees, R.S. & Tubb, J.N. (1979) A Syro-Cilician jug from Middle Bronze Age Cyprus. *RDAC*, 223-9.

Morris, D. (1985) *The Art of Ancient Cyprus*. Oxford.

Porada, E. (1948) The cylinder seals of the Late Cypriot Bronze Age. *AJA* 52, 178–98.

Swiny, S. (1986) *The Kent State University Expedition to Episkopi Phaneromeni Part 2 (SIMA 74.2)*. Nicosia.

20
Local Cypriot features in the ceramics of the Late Cypriot IIIA period

Barbara Kling
University of Pennsylvania, Philadelphia

This paper is about points of emphasis. It is concerned with the question of local Cypriot features in the ceramics of LC IIIA, and ceramic continuity from LC IIC to LC IIIA. It comprises a review of the highlights of scholarship related to this problem, and discussion of some questions and directions for further study that are suggested by current trends.

According to the system of relative chronology established in the early years of this century by Gjerstad and Sjöqvist, LC IIIA was characterized ceramically primarily by the replacement of typical LC IIC fine wares—Base Ring, White Slip, imported Mycenaean IIIB and other wares—with some new ones, Wheelmade Bucchero and what they called Submycenaean pottery (Gjerstad 1926, 280–5; Sjöqvist 1940, 126–31, 135).

For many details of LC IIIA ceramics, they observed continuity from the earlier period. Sjöqvist argued that the Wheelmade Bucchero ware of LC IIIA was simply a wheelmade development of the handmade variety that began much earlier in the Late Bronze Age (Fig 20.2 e, f) and that the ware in general was closely related to local Base Ring pottery (Sjöqvist 1940, 50–1, 84); and that the Plain White Wheelmade II ware of LC IIIA showed typological continuity from earlier plain wares (Sjöqvist 1940, 59). In addition, other wares characteristic of LC IIC were seen to die out in the course of LC IIIA, rather than disappear suddenly at its beginning (Sjöqvist 1940, 126). Submycenaean pottery was seen as a 'fusion of elements from both the Cypriote Plain Wheel-made ware I and Mycenaean pottery,' and, of the latter, this included types that were present in Cyprus during the immediately preceding, LC IIC period, the so-called Levanto-Helladic ware, especially a variety of bowl types (Sjöqvist 1940, 97).

Furumark, in a more detailed study of the Submycenaean or, as he called it, Decorated Late Cypriot III ware, spelled out some of these elements (1944). Shapes in this ware that were seen as simple continuations of earlier

Local Cypriot features in LC IIIA ceramics 161

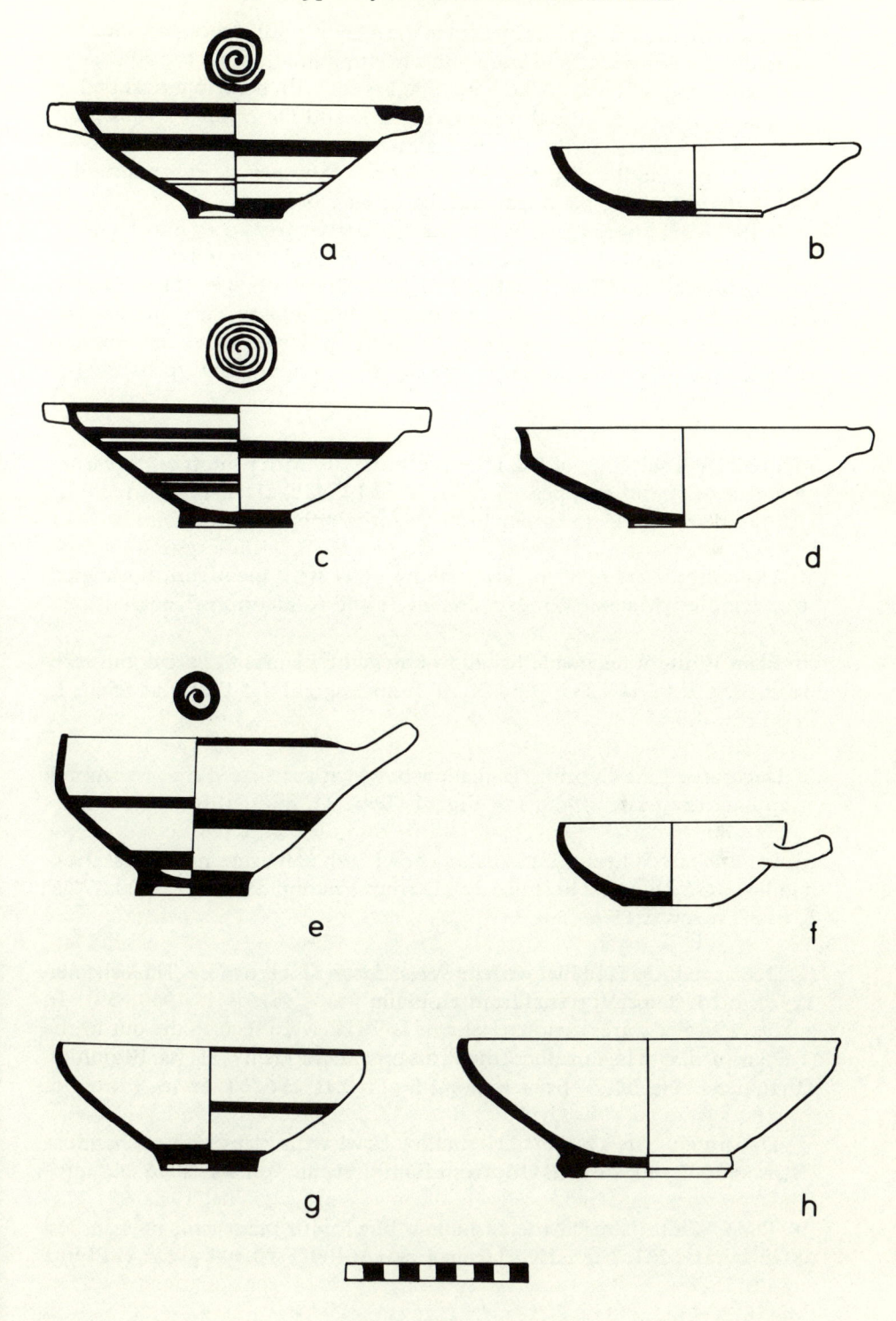

a

b

c

d

e

f

g

h

types, which had a long prior history in local Cypriot ceramics, included the jug with tubular spout, well known in earlier painted wares (Fig 20.2 a,b);[1] and many types of bowls. These included types with hemispherical bodies and plain, incurved, nicked or grooved rims and flat, rounded sunken or ring bases; without handles or with handles in the form of horizontal loops or wishbone handles (eg Fig 20.1 e,f,g,h).[2] Another type has straight, slightly flaring sides, plain rim and flat or ring base.[3]

Of the bowl shapes that were seen to derive from Levanto-Helladic pottery, most familiar are those with shallow conical or rounded bodies and two horizontal strap handles (Fig 20.1 a,c). Shallow bowls of this general type were popular in LC IIC contexts in fine quality, lustrous-painted Mycenaean pottery that was thought to be imported from the Aegean, although the type itself was seen to be especially popular in Cyprus and the

---

Figure 20.1 A selection of LC IIIA pottery types with prototypes in earlier ceramics. (Types that appear in LC IIIA or LC IIC-IIIA are shown on the left; their prototypes in earlier local ceramics appear on the right).

(a) Decorated Late Cypriot III shallow bowl with plain rim, horizontal strap handles (Maier 1985, 123, Fig 14, Type I, left) from Kouklia;

(b) Plain White Wheelmade I shallow bowl with plain rim, horizontal strap handle (*SCE* IV.1C, 235, Fig LX.10) from Enkomi Sw T 11.2.54 (*SCE* I, Pl 83 row 4:4);

(c) Decorated Late Cypriot III shallow bowl with carinated rim, horizontal strap handles (Maier 1985, 123 Fig 14, Type II, middle) from Kouklia;

(d) Plain White Wheelmade I shallow bowl with plain rim, horizontal strap handle (*SCE* IV.1C, 240, Fig LX.11) from Enkomi Sw T 18.1.100 (*SCE* I, Pl 88.1, row 1:11);

(e) Decorated LC III bowl with one raised horizontal handle (Maier 1985, 123, Fig 14, Type V, right) from Kouklia;

(f) Plain White Wheelmade I bowl with one raised horizontal handle (*SCE* IV.1C, 234, Fig LX.5) from Enkomi Sw T 3.10 (*SCE* I, Pl 76, row 6:3);

(g) Decorated Late Cypriot III shallow bowl with plain rim, no handles (Benson 1972, 80, Pl 44.B416) from Bamboula at Kourion T 16.34;

(h) Plain White Wheelmade I shallow bowl with plain rim, no handles (*SCE* IV.1C, 237, Fig LIX.5) from Enkomi Sw T 13.108 (*SCE* I, Pl 85, row 13:5).

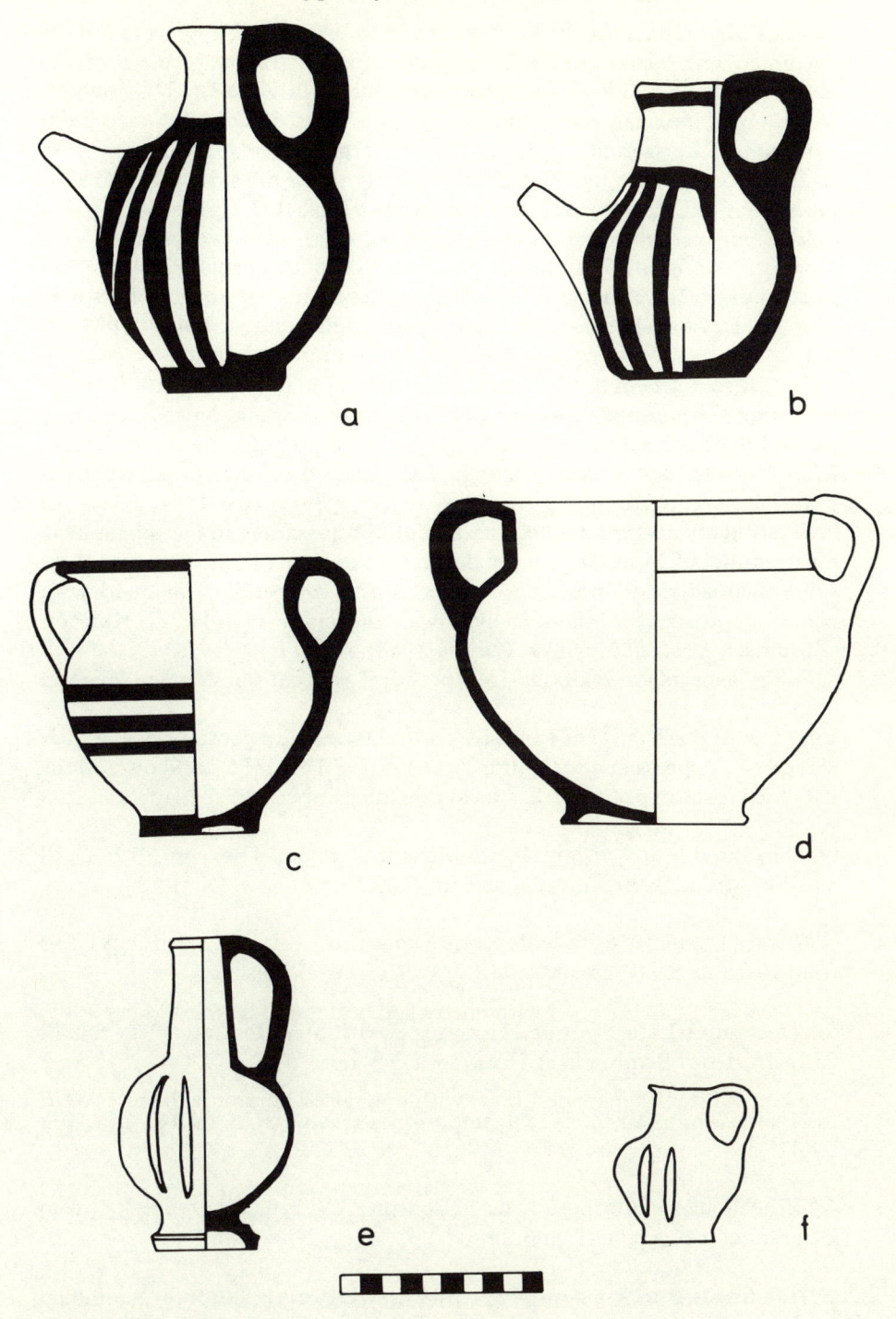

Figure 20.2 (See p 164)

Eastern Mediterranean (Furumark 1941, 636, FS 296). These were usually decorated with bands and sometimes additional abstract or pictorial Mycenaean motifs and added white paint. Also found in some LC IIC contexts were bowls similar in shape, but in a coarser fabric decorated in matt paint with simple horizontal bands which were regarded as local imitations of these imported examples. Furumark not only noted the similarity LC IIIA Decorated Late Cypriot III bowls showed to LC IIC Levanto-Mycenaean bowls, but also emphasized the affinity all of these bowls have to local Cypriot Plain White Wheelmade ware (Fig 20.1 b,d; Furumark 1944, 236). Stubbings, in fact, queried if these might have been the source of inspiration for 'Levanto-Helladic' shallow bowls in general (Stubbings 1951, 40 n 2).

For the majority of the new shapes that appeared in LC IIIA in this ware, including the amphoroid krater, jug with strainer spout, lentoid flask and stand, Furumark suggested that prototypes were to be found in the Levant. The skyphos, also a new shape in LC IIIA, was seen to derive from Mycenaean IIIC:1b pottery of the Aegean (Furumark 1944, 238). An interesting phenomenon noted was that of hybridization, in the appearance, for example, of Mycenaean style decoration on some local shapes, such as a low hemispherical bowl with raised wishbone handle decorated with panels of abstract designs, which was especially popular at Kourion (Furumark 1944, 239; cf also Catling 1964, 51 n 1).

Other aspects of material culture were seen to show some marked

---

Figure 20.2 A selection of LC IIIA pottery types with prototypes in earlier ceramics. (Types that appear in LC IIIA or LC IIC-IIIA are shown on the left; their prototypes in earlier local ceramics appear on the right).

(a) Decorated Late Cypriot III jug with tubular spout (Benson 1972, 87, Pl 56.B593) from Bamboula at Kourion T 40D.7;

(b) White Painted VI jug with tubular spout (*SCE* IV.1C, 61, Fig XLI.9) from Enkomi Sw T 13.100 (*SCE* I, Pl 75, row 10, last);

(c) Decorated Late Cypriot III amphoroid krater (Benson 1972, 86, Pl 55.B574) from Bamboula at Kourion T 3B.1;

(d) Plain White Wheelmade I amphoroid krater (*SCE* IV.1C, 242, Fig LXIII.3) from Enkomi Sw T 11.2.132 (*SCE* I, Pl 83, row 1:7);

(e) Wheelmade Bucchero jug (Benson 1972, 92, Pl 47.B694) from Bamboula at Kourion T 33B.28;

(f) Handmade Bucchero jug (Benson 1972, 74, Pl 18.B280) from Bamboula at Kourion T 19A.51.

changes at the LC IIC-LC IIIA transition. Shaft graves and military architecture appeared for which Sjöqvist saw parallels in Anatolia. The period in general coincided with a time of upheaval throughout the eastern Mediterranean. Despite the many elements of continuity in ceramics that he observed, Sjöqvist spoke of a 'radical change in the ceramic repertory' at this juncture, the primary foreign element of which he recognized as Mycenaean. He suggested, therefore, that the changes in Cyprus were the result of the arrival in the island of new population from the Aegean and Anatolia (Sjöqvist 1940, 186–90; 207–9).

This concept of change was emphasized by the application of a terminology to the painted ceramics of LC IIIA—Decorated Late Cypriot III—that distinguished it from the painted ceramics of LC IIC—Levanto-Helladic. As I have noted elsewhere, however, these differences were by no means clear, and were questioned by other scholars in discussions of pottery classification and chronology (Kling 1987). The historical interpretation, also, was not regarded as totally consistent with the picture presented by the pottery. Furumark's comments, based on his assessment of the Decorated Late Cypriot III ware, provide an example. Although he concurred with the idea of an invasion of Cyprus at this time, he commented that 'the pottery cannot be used as a means of proving an Anatolian or Achaean nationality of the invaders' (Furumark 1944, 263–4; *cf* also Daniel 1942, 292).

The emphasis on the concept of change at the LC IIC-IIIA transition was considerably strengthened with the excavations of Dikaios at Enkomi (*Enkomi*). Level IIB at the site, dated LC IIC by its typical ceramic repertoire, was separated from the subsequent level, IIIA, by a destruction, rebuilding with a new style of architecture that utilized ashlar masonry, and the covering up of tombs. The pottery types that Dikaios noted in Level IIIA were essentially the same as comprised Sjöqvist's LCIII A ceramic repertoire. Local LC IIC wares were present, but in small quantities compared to the previous level. LC IIIA Plain White Wheelmade II, Decorated Late Cypriot III and Wheelmade Bucchero made their appearance. There was, however, one major difference: this was the presence of large quantities of Mycenaean IIIC:1b style pottery. This material comprised the predominant decorated ware, as much as 90 per cent in some contexts (*Enkomi*, 457–9).

This Mycenaean IIIC:1b pottery was seen by Dikaios to be sharply differentiated from the Mycenaean IIIB pottery—including the locally produced shallow bowls, which Dikaios renamed Late Mycenaean IIIB, and Rude Style kraters—that was found in the earlier level, both in types and in the chronological phase represented, such that he suggested there was a gap, corresponding to the earliest IIIC phase in the Aegean (*Enkomi* 481). It was also regarded as quite distinct from other locally produced painted pottery of LC IIIA, Furumark's Decorated Late Cypriot III ware. All of these groups were referred to by separate terminologies, which emphasized their differences and the changes at the LC IIC-LC IIIA transition (Kling 1987).

Together with the other differences and changes that he saw between Levels IIB and IIIA at Enkomi, and parallels in the Aegean world that he cited for many aspects of LC IIIA material culture, Dikaios saw in LC IIIA the arrival of Mycenaean colonists and a totally new, Aegean culture at the site, following the collapse of major centres in the Argolid at the end of LH IIIB (*Enkomi*, 509–23). A similar stratigraphic sequence was observed at several other sites excavated subsequently, and Dikaios' view that LC IIIA marked a sharp break with the past and the arrival of Mycenaeans and Mycenaean culture in Cyprus predominated in the literature for several years (eg, Sinda: Furumark 1965; Kition: Karageorghis 1976, 58–9; Kouklia: Maier 1973; Dothan & Ben Tor 1983; *cf* also summaries of the period in Catling 1975, 207–8; Merrillees 1977, 42; *SCE* IV.1D, 776).

Recently, however, this view of LC IIIA as an overwhelmingly new, Aegean-based phenomenon, has begun to be challenged. Closer links for some features of the period have now been observed in the Levant than the Aegean and the earlier presence in Cyprus itself of some features—such as ashlar masonry—has been increasingly appreciated (Hult 1983). LC IIC-IIIA continuity was stressed by Karageorghis in his recent publication of the pre-Phoenician levels at Kition (*Kition* V.1 276); and LC IIIA culture is seen more and more as what Catling called a 'fusion of Cypriot, Aegean and Near eastern elements' (1980, 22). Recent developments in the study of the painted pottery of this period in Cyprus are moving in essentially the same direction.

One of these developments is the growing recognition that 'Mycenaean IIIC' pottery in Cyprus cannot be so readily separated from other pottery —in particular, what Dikaios would have called Late Mycenaean IIIB, Rude Style or Decorated Late Cypriot III ware—as he thought. There is an overlapping in shapes, motifs and fabric in pottery that has been classified by various scholars to one or other of these categories. This recognition has resulted in a fairly recent trend to treat all of the matt-painted, wheelmade pottery from the late phases of the Late Cypriot Bronze Age as essentially one ceramic group. This trend is reflected in the introduction of the term White Painted Wheelmade III by Paul Åström as an inclusive category for these groups that have previously been separated (*SCE* IV.1C, 276–89; *HST* 3, 92; Kling 1984).

One effect of this development has been the recognition of the continuity of some features of this particular type of pottery in contexts that have been dated to LC IIIA from the immediately preceding period, which seems indicated by the near identity of certain types, particularly of bowls, that occur in both LC IIC and LC IIIA. These similarities, in fact, are so striking that they have created problems in distinguishing the periods ceramically (Sherratt 1980, 197; Kling 1984; 1987; Maier 1985; Podzuweit 1987).

Another effect is the renewed appreciation of and interest in the fact that some features of this material were present in the island from much earlier phases of the Late Bronze Age, as Furumark pointed out long ago; and, as recently observed by Sherratt and Crouwel, some of those that came into the Cypriot ceramic repertoire from abroad apparently did so at different times (Sherratt & Crouwel 1987). The bell krater, for example, which is popular in LC IIIA contexts, was already locally produced in LC IIC for the Rude Style; and the amphoroid krater appeared in local Plain White Wheelmade ware during LC IIB (Fig 20.2 c,d; Sjöqvist 1940, 115). The possibility that new fashions in ceramics may have resulted from movements of goods as items of trade rather than movements of people has been put forward in some recent studies (Maier 1986; Sherratt & Crouwel 1987).

We may also note the increased appreciation of the existence in the painted pottery of LC IIIA of stylistic hybrids that combine local, Aegean and Near Eastern elements. Sometimes these take the form of shapes with an earlier history in Cyprus which are decorated in new ways that show foreign influence. This phenomenon was noted, for instance, by Karageorghis in his discussion of an elaborately decorated amphoroid krater from Kition, and is seen also in numerous bell kraters from Enkomi (Karageorghis 1977). Sometimes we can see new shapes decorated with a combination of new and local motifs—such as appear on a strainer jug from Kouklia decorated with LH IIIC style birds and local Cypriot Rude Style bulls (Kling forthcoming).

These pieces of internal evidence provided by the painted pottery in LC IIC and LC IIIA contexts in Cyprus itself thus seem to point to some continuity—perhaps even some fuzziness—at the LC IIC-IIIA transition, rather than an abrupt break with the past. A look at the evidence provided by some other wares can be seen to point in the same direction.

For example, although the emphasis in discussion of LC IIIA ceramics has been on pottery of Mycenaean style, it should be remembered that the other LC III wares were also present in Level IIIA at Enkomi—the Wheelmade Bucchero and Plain White Wheelmade II, for which Sjöqvist convincingly argued a continuity from the earlier local wares. There has been little or no discussion of material of these types from other LC IIIA sites, but what indications there are suggest that they are represented (Athienou: Dothan & Ben Tor 1983, 111–17; Sinda: Furumark 1965, 107; Kition: *Kition* V.2, 95).

Secondly, it may be noted that Base Ring and White Slip wares, the LC II pottery types par excellence, are also present in virtually all settlement contexts that have been dated LC IIIA (*SCE* IV.1D, 693–5; eg Kourion: Benson 1970; *HST* 3, 92–134; *HST* 4, 46–71; *HST* 5, 22–34; *HST* 7, 21–39; *HST* 8, 61–6, 73–6, 108–15; *Kition* V.2, 9–36; 93–152). The recent trend has been to regard them as intrusive survivals of an earlier phase of occupation, particularly at sites, like Enkomi, where a long history of occupation is well documented (eg *SCE* IV.1D, 700–1 chart). The evidence provided by some other sites, however, suggests some possible alternative interpretations. At Idalion, for example, the earliest occupation level excavated by the Swedish Cyprus Expedition contained Base Ring and White Slip wares as well as typical LC IIIA material, which could not be distinguished stratigraphically (*SCE* II, 618–24; Sjöqvist 1940, 132). At the very least, this would seem to suggest that no sharp break separated the use of these different kinds of pottery. Might it not also indicate that all of these wares were used—perhaps even manufactured, at least for a short period—at the same time? Whether we should say that such contexts span the LC IIC-IIIA transition, or show continuity of LC IIC features into LC IIIA, strikes me as a terminological problem that is less important than simply recognizing and appreciating that this continuity exists.

We are still a long way from understanding what happened in Cyprus at the end of the Late Bronze Age—what the LC IIC-IIIA transition represents, and what is the nature of LC IIIA culture. That the effects of foreign cultures were present is beyond doubt (for a possible foreign ceramic intrusion, *cf* Karageorghis 1986). The review presented here of the study of the pottery at this transition period suggests that an emphasis on change and these foreign influences in past studies of material culture may have somewhat obscured what elements of continuity do exist. It suggests that a greater attention to possible local inspiration may be a start to reaching a more balanced picture of this period in general.

NOTES

[1] Squat type: Sjöqvist 1940, 67 Fig 18; 73: painted Submycenaean jug Type 1a; Tall ovoid type: Gjerstad 1926, 223 Submycenaean jug 8; Sjöqvist 1940, 67 Fig 18; 73: Painted Submycenaean jug Type 1b. Furumark 1944, 234, 235, Fig 10; 236–7 Decorated Late Cypriot III Type H and *SCE* IV.1C, 286 White Painted Wheelmade III Type Xa include both varieties; *cf* eg White Painted II ware, *SCE* IV.1B, Fig IV.5–7; White Painted III-IV ware, *SCE* IV.1B, Fig X.11; White Painted VI ware, *SCE* IV.1C, Fig XLI.4, 8, 9).

[2] Gjerstad 1926, 222, Submycenaean Types 1, 6, 7, 8; Furumark 1944, 235, Decorated Late Cypriot III Types C8 and C9; *SCE* IV.1C, 276–85, White Painted Wheelmade III Types IA, IB, IC, ID, IE, IIIa; VIII.f; Karageorghis 1965, 174–6, Late Mycenaean IIIB Types A1, A2, A3, A4, A6; Benson 1972, 83–4, Decorated Late Cypriot III Types 4, 6; *cf* eg Plain White Wheelmade I ware: *SCE* IV.1C, Fig LIX, LX, LXI).

[3] Flat base: Furumark 1944, 233, Decorated Late Cypriot III Type D; Benson 1972, 85 Decorated Late Cypriot III type 7; *SCE* IV.1C, 280, White Painted Wheelmade III Type IFa; *cf* eg Plain White Wheelmade I ware, Sjöqvist 1940, 56, Fig 14.3a, 3b. Ring base: Furumark 1941, 620, Mycenaean Type FS 209; *SCE* IV.1C, 280, White Painted Wheelmade III Type IGa.

ACKNOWLEDGMENTS

Figures 1a, 1c, 1e are reproduced with permission of Dr F-G. Maier.

Figures 1b, 1d, 1f, 1h, 2b, 2d are reproduced with permission of Prof P. Åström. Figures 1g, 2a, 2c, 2e, 2f are reproduced with permission of University of Pennsylvania Press. All figures have been redrawn by B. Kling.

LIST OF REFERENCES

Anson, D. (1980a) The Rude Style Late Cypriot IIC-III pottery: an analytical typology. *Op Ath 13*, 1–18.
Anson, D. (1980b) Composition and provenance of Rude Style and related wares. *RDAC*, 109–27.
Benson, J.L. (1970) Bamboula at Kourion. The stratification of the settlement. *RDAC*, 25–74.
Benson J.L. (1972) *Bamboula at Kourion. The Necropolis and the Finds*. Philadelphia.
Catling, H.W. (1964) *Cypriot Bronzework in the Mycenaean World*. Oxford.
Catling, H.W. (1975) Cyprus in the Late Bronze age, in CAH^3 II. 2a, 188–216.
Catling, H.W. (1980) *Cyprus and the West 1600–1050 BC*. (Ian Sandars Memorial Lecture). Sheffield.
Daniel, J.F. (1942) Review of Sjöqvist 1940. *AJA 46*, 285–93.
Dothan, T. & A. Ben Tor (1983) *Excavations at Athienou, Cyprus, 1971–1972, (Qedem 16)*. Jerusalem.
Furumark, A. (1941) *The Mycenaean Pottery. Analysis and Classification*. Stockholm.
Furumark, A. (1944) The Mycenaean IIIC pottery and its relations to Cypriot fabrics. *Op Arch 3*, 232–65.
Furumark, A. (1965) The excavations at Sinda: some historical results. *Op Ath 6*, 99–116.
Gjerstad, E. (1926) *Studies on Prehistoric Cyprus*. Stockholm.
Hult, G. (1983) *Bronze Age Ashlar Masonry in the Eastern Mediterranean. Cyprus, Ugarit, and Neighbouring Regions. (SIMA 66)*. Göteborg.
Karageorghis, V. (1965) *Nouveaux Documents pour L'Étude du Bronze Récent à Chypre*. Paris.
Karageorghis, V. (1976) *View from the Bronze Age. Mycenaean and Phoenician Discoveries at Kition*. New York.
Karageorghis, V. (1986) "Barbarian" Ware in Cyprus. *Acts 1986* 246–64.
Kling, B. (1984) Mycenaean IIIC:1b pottery in Cyprus: principal characteristics and historical context, in *Cyprus at the close of the Late Bronze Age* (eds. V. Karageorghis & J.D. Muhly) 29–38. Nicosia.
Kling, B. (1987) Pottery classification and relative chronology of the LC IIC-LC IIIA periods, in *Western Cyprus: Connections* (ed. D. W. Rupp), *(SIMA 77)* 97–113. Göteborg.
Kling, B. forthcoming (1988) The strainer jug from Kouklia Tomb KATI: a stylistic hybrid. *RDAC*.
Maier, F-G. (1967) Excavations at Kouklia (Palaepaphos) Site A. Preliminary report on the seasons 1952–1955 and 1966. *RDAC*, 30–49.
Maier, F-G. (1973) Evidence for Mycenaean settlement at Old Paphos, in *Acts 1973*, 68–78.
Maier, F-G. (1985) A note on shallow bowls. *RDAC*, 122–5.
Maier, F-G. (1986) Kinyras and Agapenor. *Acts 1986*, 311–20.
Merrillees, R.S. (1977) The absolute chronology of the Bronze Age in Cyprus. *RDAC*, 33–50.
Podzuweit, C. (1987) Zypern am Übergang von Spätzyprisch IIC zu IIIA, in

Ägäis-Kolloquium. Schriften des deutschen Archäologen-Verbandes IX. Kolloquium zur Ägäischen Vorgeschichte. (ed. W. Schiering) 185–92. Mannheim.

Sherratt, E. S. (1980) Regional variation in the pottery of Late Helladic IIIB. *BSA* 75, 175–202.

Sherratt, E.S. (1981) *The Pottery of Late Helladic IIIC and its Significance.* Somerville College D Phil, Thesis.

Sherratt, E.S. (1982) Patterns of contact: manufacture and distribution of Mycenaean pottery, 1400 BC, in *Interaction and Acculturation in the Mediterranean. Second International Congress of Mediterranean Pre- and Protohistory.* (eds. J. Best & N. DeVries) 179–95. Amsterdam.

Sherratt, E.S. & J.H. Crouwel (1987) Mycenaean pottery from Cilicia in Oxford. *Oxf J A* 6, 325–52.

Sjöqvist, E. (1940) *Problems of the Late Cypriot Bronze Age.* Stockholm.

Stubbings, F.H. (1951) *Mycenaean Pottery from the Levant.* Cambridge.

21
Hunting scenes on Cypriot vases of the Geometric Period

M. C. Loulloupis
Department of Antiquities, Cyprus

The repertory of ancient Cypriot vase-painting is extremely rich in designs and pictorial compositions. Hunting scenes in the broad sense of the word occupy an important place in the sphere of pictorial compositions. Having first made their appearance in the Late Bronze Age in painting (Buchholz & Karageorghis 1973, 152, 157 Figs 1625, 1671; Vermeule & Karageorghis 1982, 81, 198, Fig IV.32), incision (Kenna 1967, 557, 569 Figs 11, 26), relief (Buchholz & Karageorghis 1973, 163 Figs 1747–9 and cylinder impressions (Buchholz & Karageorghis 1973, 161 Fig 1758), hunting scenes continued through the Geometric Period (Karageorghis & Des Gagniers 1974a, 31, 40) to reach their culmination in the Archaic Period in both the so-called 'restricted' or 'metope' decoration and the well-known 'Free-field' style (Karageorghis & Des Gagniers 1974a, 28–9, 32–45 etc). Such scenes continue in later periods (Dikaios 1961, 72 no 279e) until Mediaeval times (Bakirtzi-Papanikola 1986, 568–9). In the majority of these scenes, indeed almost without exception, the meaning of the representations is clear: they depict hunting scenes. However, there are certain representations where the meaning is not so obvious. This is why a number of interpretations have been proposed so far in various efforts to clarify the meaning of these scenes. Here we shall deal with three examples of these more obscure scenes.

The first example is a pictorial composition painted in two sections on the body of a loop-leg jar of Bichrome III ware, dating to the CG III Period (850–700 BC) of unknown origin, now in the Cyprus Museum, Nicosia (Inv no C.M.B 1988) (Karageorghis & Des Gagniers 1974b, 493). Scholars agree that either two similar scenes are depicted, or one scene in two sections. Interpretations proposed so far refer to (a) the composition as a whole, or (b) concentrate on certain elements of these compositions (Figs 21.1a, b, 2).

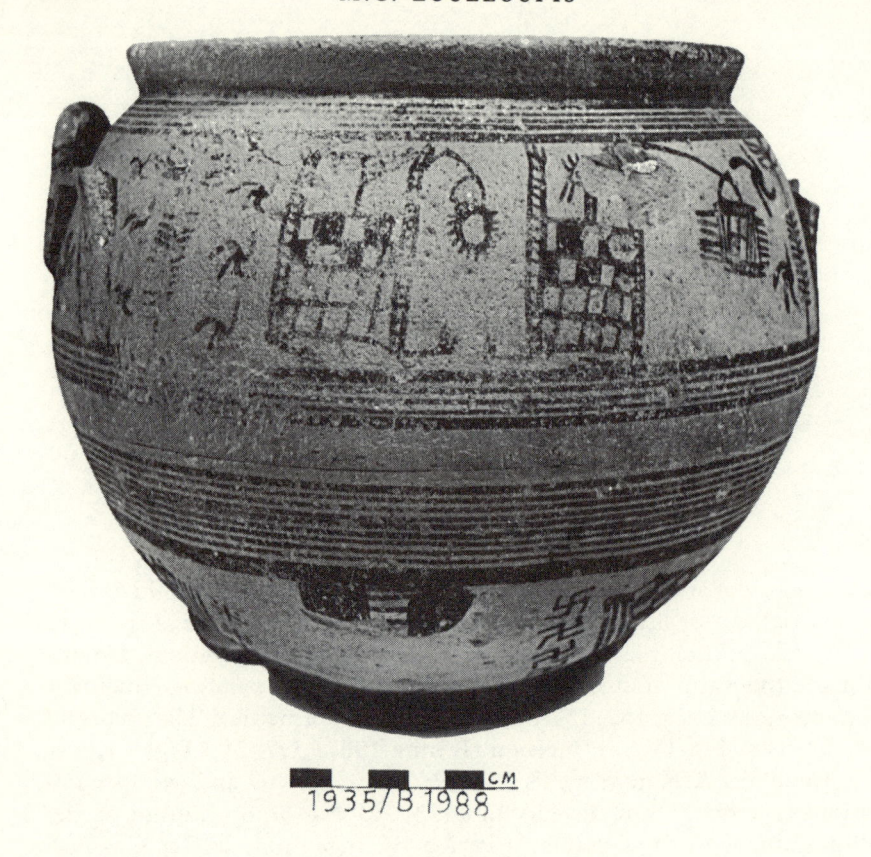

Figure 21.1a Bichrome III jar (Cyprus Museum).

In the first group (a) we have the proposal put forward by Professor Einar Gjerstad who saw in these representations 'a tripartite temple of the *liwan* type similar to that of the temple of Aphrodite at Paphos' (*SCE* IV.2, 62). To the same group belongs a proposal made in 1973 by Dr V. Karageorghis who saw in these scenes a 'representation of a temple', 'sacred architecture' or 'a temple of an oriental type which has as prototypes the temple of Aphrodite at Paphos or that of Astarte at Kition' (1973, 9, 10, 13). In 1974 however the same author modified his earlier view and suggested that the unknown vase-painter started painting a building which he later turned into human beings by adding hands and legs (Karageorghis & Des Gagniers 1974b, 81). This idea was apparently taken over by Professor John Boardman who, having expressed the view that no buildings of secular or sacred character are shown on the vase, also interpreted these representations as human beings. According to this point of view, the former oriental buildings can thus be transformed into 'princesses', 'graceless' though they may be, by the kind co-operation of a Good Fairy. Boardman would like to

Figure 21.1b Bichrome III jar (Cyprus Museum).

see in these representations two seated girls, very probably 'temple courtesans holding the tools of their profession', ie combs and wreaths (1976, 154). All the above views have been summarized by Dr J. Karageorghis in her excellent dissertation on the Great Goddess of Cyprus, in which she expresses her scepticism about them ('un temple'?) (1977, 170–1) and wisely considers these presentations as very controversial.

In the second group (b), the interpretation of certain elements of the same compositions, the following picture emerges. The element which lies between the two 'buildings' in the first picture and hangs from a hook in the second has been interpreted as a 'bundle of thin rods which will be used for sacred fire' (fire-wood) by Cesnola (1882, 249–50) and Ohnefalsch-Richter (1893, 104). The same design has been described by A. Pieridou, as 'a double-faced' or 'two-sided comb' (1967, 62–3), due to its similarity to ivory combs which have been discovered on the island. The same interpretation has been adopted by Chr. Morris (1983, 223). Professor H. -G. Buchholz discusses several possibilities: comb, lantern, musical

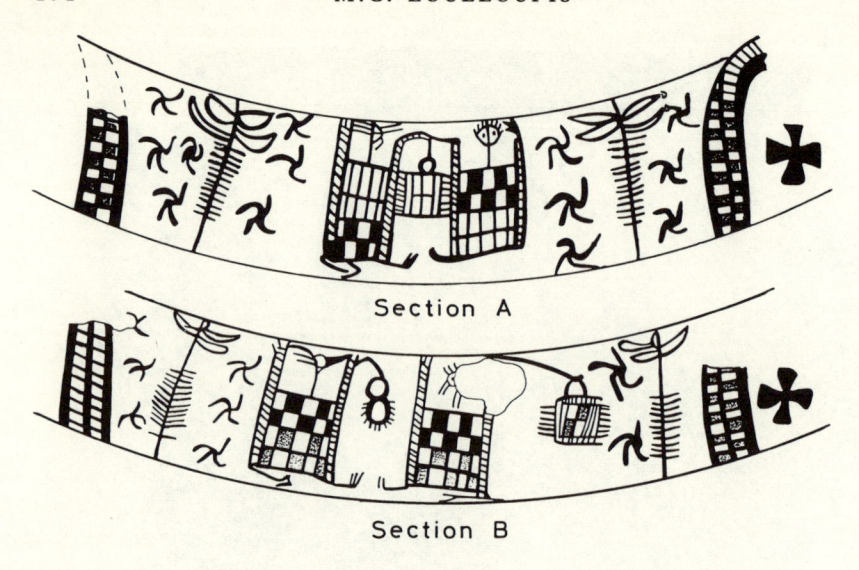

Figure 21.2 Decoration on jar of Fig 21.1a, b.

instrument (syrinx or shepherd's pipe, even xylophone) but he rather favours the idea of 'a utensil of ritual character' (representative or symbolic) (1968, 95–9). Finally the same element has been described as a window (Karageorghis & Des Gagniers 1974b, 493), porch, table or even an altar (Morris 1987, 221 n 17).

The element which is suspended from a hook from the first 'building' on the left of the second composition has been described as a crown ('couronne') (Karageorghis & Des Gagniers 1974b, 493) or wreath (Boardman 1976, 154). It can also be considered as a loop or noose.

Let us now turn to another approach to the meaning and significance of these representations. We shall make use of a later philological source as well as of an illumination. We shall use terms and phrases taken from a book entitled Ἀνωνύμου Παράφρασις εἰς τὰ Διονυσίου Ἰξευτικά ('Anonymi Paraphrasis in Dionysii Ixeutica') (Papathomopoulos 1976, henceforth DI). We shall also compare the vase-painting with a miniature of the 11th century A.D. from an illuminated manuscript now kept in the Library of the Greek Orthodox Patriarchate in Jerusalem, illustrating a speech by Saint Gregory of Nanziazos 'Λόγος εἰς τὴν Καινὴν Κυριακήν' (Speech/Sermon on New Sunday, ie the Easter Sunday) (Codex Taphou 14, f 33^v cf Cod. Marc. Gr. 479, f.2^v in Weitzmann 1959, 27, Pl XV Fig 33; Cod. Par. g.533 in Lazarev 1967, 191, Fig 250) (Fig 21.3).

The Mediaeval illumination depicts the following: On the left there is a young man pruning or trimming a tree. On the right hand side there is a 'Θηρευτής' or 'Θηρατὴς ἰξοεργός' (Liddell & Scott 1951, 799) (a bird-catcher, a fowler who uses lime-rods). The same person may also be called 'ἰξοβόλος'

Figure 21.3 Mediaeval manuscript illustration (Greek Orthodox Patriarchate, Jerusalem).

or 'ἰξευτής' (DI 27). He is also an 'ὀρνιθοθήρας', a bird-cather (Liddell & Scott 1951, 1254). Our bird-catcher (fowler) is represented seated in a hut ('καλύβη') (DI 35) made from branches of trees. In front of him there is a tree with leaves and lime-rods ('ἰξόβεργα') (Koukoules 1952, 398). The tree is flanked by two stands supporting two cages where there are two birds. One of them is inside a cage while the other stands on top of it, though it may be considered as being tied to the cage. These birds are called 'κράκται' (bawlers) or 'πλάνοι' (deceivers) (Koukoules 1952, 402) for the free-flying birds. In other words these two are the birds which by their singing attract or drive birds of the same species ('σύφυλος ὄρνις') (DI 28) near their cage, and thus trap them on the lime-rods. The latter are shown fixed on the little branches of the tree or are attached to pieces of reeds ('δόνακες ἰξοφόροι' or 'δόνακες ἰξοφορῆες') (Liddell & Scott 1951, 831). The art of the work performed by a man hidden in the hut is called 'ἰξεύειν' or 'ἰξευτική' (ibid), in other words the art of catching birds by means of glue-sticks, lime-rods or simply by liming.

Bearing in mind what we have learned from the illumination and coming back to the vase-painting we may now observe the following. On Section A there are two human beings hidden behind two huts ('καλύβη λανθάνοντες' or 'καλύβη κρυπτόμενοι') (DI 31, 35). The huts are fixed to the ground by pegs or rods and pieces of rope. At either side of both the compositions (on Sections A and B) there are trees with leaves (foliage) and lime-sticks. A cage supplied with lime-rods at either side hangs out of the right hut while a circular device, a figure-of-eight-shaped loop made of wood or metal ('χαλκοῦ ἁψίς') (DI 32–3) and also provided with lime-rods fixed on its lower circle, hangs out of the left hut.

On Section B we have the same trees, the same huts and a cage with lime-rods hanging between the huts. We may therefore suggest that the representations on the Cyprus Museum loop-legged jar are two hunting scenes, more precisely scenes where bird-catchers or fowlers, having set their lime-rods on trees and having hung up two cages and a loop furnished with lime-sticks are hiding themselves behind huts. They watch the free-flying birds and wait for them to be attracted by the singing of their bawlers and approach the cages and the loop, to sit on them and finally to be stuck and caught by the lime-rods.

The second representation which we shall now examine was discovered in a tomb at Kato Dheftera village, not far from Nicosia (Christou 1974, 177, 183–4, Fig 3, Pl 26.5). It is a shallow dish of Black-on-Red I (III) Ware dating to the CG III period (850–700 BC) (Fig 21.4). It also depicts a bird-catching scene as follows: a large bird, presumably a sea-bird, is approaching or rather hovering above two fish which are merely decoys, while below there stands a trap fixed on the ground in the shape of a rectangular hunting net ('λίνου πάγη', 'πηκτίς') (DI 28–9, 35) along with three cages supplied with lime-sticks. The bird, attracted and allured by the fish decoy, will unsuspectingly enter the trap, the net, which will immediately be pulled up to enclose the bird, or will fall upon the bird and decoy trapping them together. In the present representation the fowler tries to lure the bird by offering it food (the fish) ('τροφὴ δελεάζει τό πτηνόν') (DI 32), which is finally caught in the net trap, ('αἱρεῖται ὑπὸ τοῦ λίνου') (DI 33), which is then lifted up by the fowler ('το δίκτυον ἀναστήσας') (DI 35). Therefore we have here a bird-catching scene where the catching instrument is a 'λίνον' or 'δίκτυον', ie, a net. One may detect a wishful sense of teaching in this scene. The vase-painter shows to a future fowler a method by means of which he will be able to catch a large sea-bird ('ἐνάλιον ὄρνιν') (DI 34) such as a heron, flamingo or pelican by using a fish as a decoy and a net ('λίνον') which can be lifted up, or a trap ('πάγη') of rectangular form supplied with a deep net which will fall down or be turned over or up to cover and eventually catch the bird.

Our last representation comes from a White Painted I plate which was discovered in a tomb at 'Skales' cemetery close to Kouklia village, dating to the Early Geometric Period (1050–950 BC) (Karageorghis 1983, 120 no 104, Pl 87, Fig 112) (Fig 21.5).

It has been suggested that this scene portrays two male figures fighting against a two-headed snake or serpent. The first hunter attacks the neck of

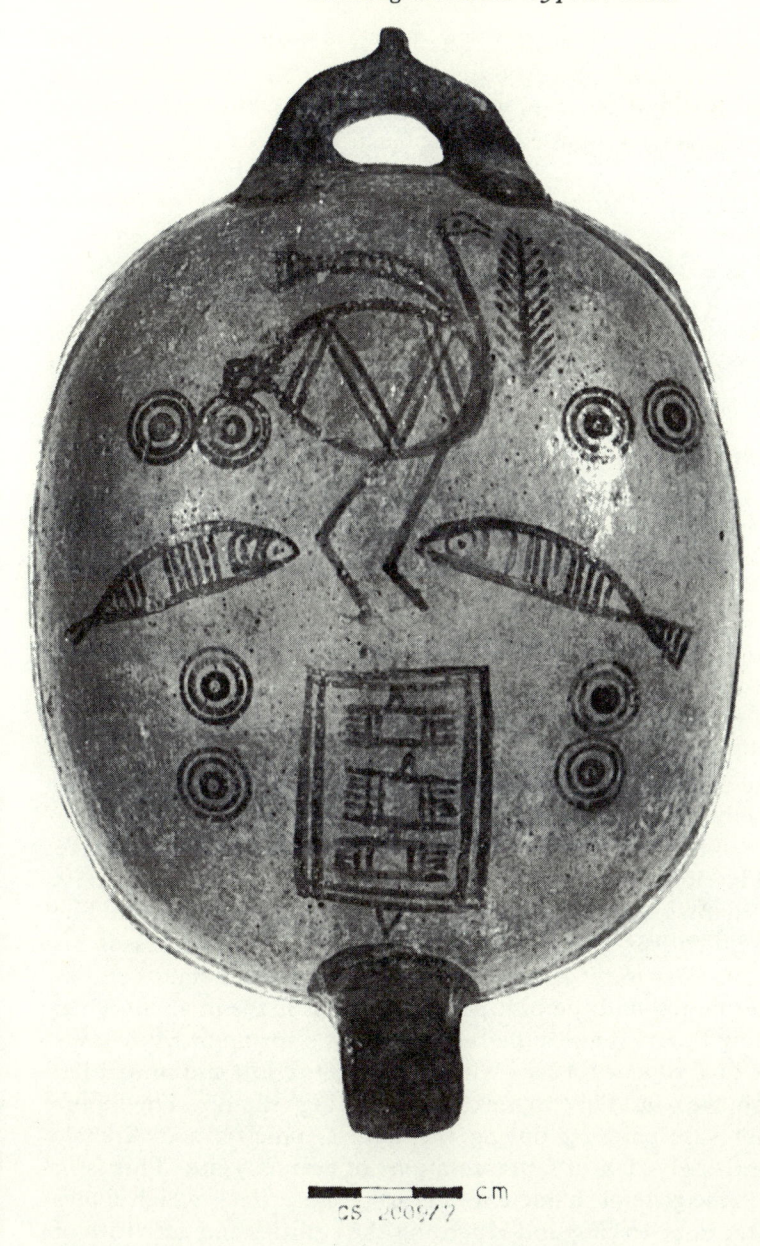

Figure 21.4 Black-on-Red I (III) dish from Kato Dheftera.

the serpent with bow and arrows, while the second hacks at the tail of the snake with a sword. Furthermore, it has been proposed that this representation may be the first attempt to show in painting the myth of Herakles and Iolaos slaying the Hydra at Lerna (Maier & Karageorghis 1986, 145; Karageorghis 1980, 128). Is that so? I rather doubt it for many reasons but

Figure 21.5 White Painted I plate from Kouklia-Skales.

mainly because this myth could not have been so well known and widespread as to have reached the Palaepaphos region in Cyprus at the beginning of the first millennium BC, more than three centuries before the birth of Homer and Hesiod. Greek mythology as we now know it, did not exist at that time. What we have here, therefore, is again a hunting scene. The painter wishes to convey the following message to the spectators of his work. It is much easier to hit and kill a large animal when it stands still as it offers a better target; and the best position for this is the moment when the animal, being thirsty, enjoys the fresh water of a spring or river. This is the moment to aim your arrows, when the target is still and immobile.

In conclusion, we would like to make the following remarks. The repertory of Cypriot vase-painting during the Late Geometric and Archaic Periods is surprisingly rich in representations of everyday life. This is in accordance with the general character of the art of these times, which shows a special interest in observing and recording the realities and activities of daily life. It was natural for the early vase-painter to be inspired by the works and toils of everyday life. His compositions become real genre paintings. Furthermore, the artist sometimes appears to give the impression that he is trying to present through his paintings his personal knowledge and in this way to teach, to pass his treasured experience to his fellow men. In this way certain vase-paintings of those period may be said to have served didactic purposes.

LIST OF REFERENCES

Bakirtzi-Papanikola, D. (1986) Γεράκια καί Γερακάρηδες σέ Κυπριακά Μεσαιωνικά ἐφυαλωμένα ἀγγεῖα. *Acts 1985*, B Mediaeval Section, 567–75.
Boardman, J. (1976) Iconographica Cypria. *RDAC*, 152–5.
Buchholz, H. -G. (1968) Die Östliche Herkunft eines Griechisch-Geometrischen Gefässdetails. *JdI 83*, 49–99.
Buchholz, H. -G. & Karageorghis V. (1973) *Prehistoric Greece and Cyprus*. London.
Cesnola, A. Palma di (1882) *Salaminia (Cyprus). The History, Treasures and Antiquities of Salamis in the Island of Cyprus*. London.
Christou, D. (1974) Pottery types from a new necropolis at Kato Dheftera. *RDAC*, 174–85.
Dikaios, P. (1961) *A Guide to the Cyprus Museum*. Nicosia.
Karageorghis, J. (1977) *La Grande Déesse de Chypre et son culte*. Lyon
Karageorghis, V. (1973) A Presentation of a temple on an 8th century B.C. Cypriote Vase. *R St Fen 1*, 1–13.
Karageorghis, V. (1980) Fouilles à l'Ancienne-Paphos de Chypre: les premiers colons grecs. *CRAI*, 122–36.
Karageorghis, V. (1983) *Palaepaphos-Skales, an Iron Age Cemetery in Cyprus. Ausgrabungen in Alt-Paphos auf Cypern III*. Konstanz.
Karageorghis, V. & Des Gagniers, J. (1974a) *La céramique chypriote de style figuré. Illustrations et descriptions des vases*. Roma.
Karageorghis, V. & Des Gagniers, J. (1974b) *La céramique chypriote de style figuré. Texte*. Roma.
Kenna, V. (1967) The seal use of Cyprus in the Bronze Age II. *BCH 91*, 552–77.
Koukoules, Ph. (1952) Βυζαντινῶν Βίος καί Πολιτισμός, V. Athens.
Lazarev, V. (1967) *Storia della Pittura Bizantina*. Torino.
Liddell, H. & Scott, R. (1951) *A Greek-English Lexicon*[9]. Oxford.
Maier, F. & Karageorghis, V. (1986) *Paphos, History and Archaeology*. Nicosia.
Morris, Chr. (1983) Combs on Cypriote Iron Age Pottery. *RDAC*, 219–24.
Ohnefalsch-Richter, M. (1893) *Kypros, The Bible and Homer*. London.
Papathomopoulos, M. (ed.) (1976) Ἀνωνύμου Παράφρασις εἰς τά. Ioannina.
Pieridou, A. (1967) Ὁ Ζωγραφικός Ρυθμός τῆς Πρωίμου Κυπρο γεωμετρικῆς Περιόδου. *Κυπ Spoud 51*, 53–64.
Vermeule, E. & Karageorghis, V. (1982) *Mycenaean Pictorial Vase Painting*. London.
Weitzmann, K. (1959) *Ancient Book Illumination*. Cambridge (Mass.).

22
Témoignage des documents figurés sur la société chypriote d'époque classique

Antoine Hermary
Centre National de la Recherche Scientifique, Paris

La rareté des sources littéraires et épigraphiques concernant Chypre aux Ve-IVe s.av.J-C rend particulièrement précieux le témoignage des documents figurés, essentiellement celui des sculptures en calcaire de la région de Golgoi et d'Idalion. Dans cet abondant ensemble, ce sont probablement les 'adorants' masculins qui apportent les informations les plus intéressantes sur la société chypriote classique.

Au sommet de cette société se trouvent une dizaine de petits dynastes qui, bien que vassaux du Grand Roi, excercent une souveraineté de fait sur leur territoire. Ils frappent des monnaies sans y faire graver leur portrait, si bien qu'aucun des noms connus par les textes littéraires et les inscriptions ne peut être associé avec certitude à des représentations conservées. Il y a cependant, dans un cas au moins, une forte présomption: si la belle tête coiffée de la couronne double égyptienne avec disque(?) ailé et uraeus trouvée dans la 'rampe des Perses' à Palaepaphos est bien, comme il est vraisemblable, celle d'un des rois-prêtres attestés par des inscriptions paphiennes du IVe s.,[1] il devrait s'agir d'Onasicharis, le roi qui semble avoir été au pouvoir juste avant le siège de 498 (Masson & Mitford 1986, 24–5). D'autres têtes sculptées de la fin de l'époque archaïque sont coiffées de cette même couronne, attestée encore, vers la fin du Ve s., par une tête du Louvre qui provient de Golgoi ou de sa région (Figs 22.1, 2; AM 2946, Ht 38cm: Masson & Caubet 1980, 150.41). Une autre coiffure royale, qui ne paraît pas être associée à une fonction religieuse, est mentionnée par Hérodote et peut être identifiée sur certaines sculptures: la 'mitra enroulée autour de la tête' qui coiffait les rois de Chypre enrôlés dans l'armée de Xerxès[2] correspond selon toute vraisemblance à l'épais bandeau, parfois retenu par une lanière appliquée sur le haut du crâne, attesté sur plusieurs sites de Chypre,[3] mais aussi à Arados et à Sidon;[4] une tête du Louvre trouvée à Golgoi en donne un très bel exemple pour le milieu du Ve s. (Figs 22. 3,

4; AM 2835, Ht 43 cm: Masson & Caubet 1980, 146.13, Pl 23.4). Ces coiffures royales ne sont plus représentées dans la sculpture du IVe s. Autour des rois et de leur famille gravitent des dignitaires religieux, militaires et civils dont on s'attend à trouver l'image dans les statues des sanctuaires ou sur les monuments funéraires: à côté de quelques types caractérisés, comme des musiciens (surtout des femmes) ou des scribes,[5] la grande masse des sculptures des sanctuaires est composée d'"adorants' tenant un animal, un rameau ou une boîte à encens, et celle des stèles funéraires de personnages au banquet (Dentzer 1982, 279–81 et 568–70, Figs 185–207). La symbolique religieuse, dont dépend aussi en grande partie l'image du banquet, tient donc une place prépondérante, alors que les représentations liées à la guerre et au sport, si importantes dans le monde grec, sont pratiquement inconnues.

Il y a d'autres enseignements à tirer de l'ensemble des 'adorants' des Ve-IVe s. découverts dans les sanctuaires de Golgoi et d'Idalion. Jusqu'à une date avancée dans le Ve s., les sculptures chypriotes restent soumises aux traditions de l'archaïsme et du 'style sévère' grecs: les très nombreuses têtes barbues couronnées qui sont conservées sont probablement celles de princes ou de dignitaires, mais elles forment des séries répétitives, écho hellénisé de l'image du Gand Roi ou de hauts personnages de l'empire achéménide. Une évolution importante se manifeste dans les dernières décennies du Ve s., quand les dynastes chypriotes et anatoliens introduisent à leur usage les nouvelles formes d'expression du visage humain mises au point par les artistes grecs: la parenté entre le profil du satrape Tissapherne sur ses monnaies les plus anciennes (Fig 22.5; Kraay & Hirmer 1966, Pl 184.621) et celui d'un 'adorant' de la collection Cesnola (Fig 22.6; Myres 1914, no 1408), encore proche des traditions archaïques, n'est sûrement pas fortuite, et un certain nombre d'autres têtes sont caractéristiques de cette période par l'association de traits archaïsants (sourire, coiffure) à une conception relativement réaliste du visage (Fig 22.7).[6]

En 411 Evagoras I prend le pouvoir à Salamine et établit aussitôt des relations privilégiées avec Athènes qui, dès 410 semble-t-il, lui accorde le droit de cité (*IG* I,[2] 113; Chavane & Yon 1978, no 247). En 405, après la défaite d'Aigos Potamoi, il accueille chez lui le stratège Conon 'avec qui il entretenait des liens d'amitiés' et les deux hommes se retrouvent alliés au roi de Perse pour vaincre les Lacédémoniens à Cnide, en 394: aussitôt après les Athéniens votent un nouveau décret en l'honneur du roi de Salamine et érigent sa statue sur l'Agora avec celle de Conon, près de Zeus Eleutherios (Lewis & Stroud 1979, 180–93, avec bibliographie). Alors que l'on a cru pouvoir identifier plusieurs copies de la tête du stratège athénien, jamais, à ma connaissance, on ne s'est interrogé sur la statue du roi chypriote: il ne me paraît pas impossible qu'une tête conservée au Musée des Thermes à Rome,[7] qui ressemblerait tout à fait à celles des stratèges de l'époque si elle n'était coiffée d'un bonnet oriental au lieu du casque corinthien, soit une copie de l'Evagoras de l'Agora (Figs 22.8, 9).

Figure 22.1 Paris, Louvre AM 2946 (photo du Musée).

Quoi qu'il en soit, le long règne du Salaminien (411–374) marque une étape évidemment importante pour le sujet qui nous occupe. On connaît le texte où l'orateur athénien Isocrate rapporte comment le roi, après avoir chassé un usurpateur phénicien, ouvre à la culture grecque son royaume

Figure 22.2 Paris, Louvre AM 2946 (photo du Musée).

Figure 22.3 Paris, Louvre AM 2835 (photo du Musée).

alors plongé dans la barbarie (Isocrate, *Evagoras* 47–50). Qu'en a-t-il été réellement? L'utilisation officielle de l'écriture alphabétique grecque à côté du syllabaire témoigne d'une évolution significative, mais demeure occasionnelle et ne semble donner lieu à aucune dédicace de type grec; les

Figure 22.4 Paris, Louvre AM 2835 (photo du Musée).

nouvelles monnaies au type d'Héraclès ont certainement été exécutées par des graveurs venus de Grèce, mais elles répondent sans doute à l'intention peu 'classique' de présenter le dynaste à la manière d'un nouvel Héraclès, comme le fait à la même époque le Lycien Arbinas. Des sculpteurs, des architectes ou des orfèvres grecs sont-ils venus travailler dans le royaume d'Evagoras? Les témoignages directs font presque entièrement défaut,[8] mais, pour ce qui est des arts plastiques, plusieurs belles têtes en calcaire découvertes dans de petits sanctuaires ruraux montrent que, vers le début du IVe s., l'influence du style grec classique était suffisamment forte pour que les sculpteurs locaux tournent définitivement le dos aux conventions archaïques: la tête 55 de Potamia (Fig 22.10; Karageorghis 1979, 295.55, Pl 35), à laquelle on peut associer, entre autres, la tête du Louvre AM 2760 (Fig 22.11; Masson & Caubet 1980, 150.33; Ht 32cm), sont caractéristiques de ce courant qui, en Lycie et à Sidon, s'exprime sur des reliefs funéraires

Figure 22.5 Monnai de Tissapherne (d'après Kraay & Hirmer).

plutôt que dans la sculpture en ronde bosse. Il est peu douteux qu'à Chypre cette nouvelle vague d'influence artistique grecque doit beaucoup à la personnalité et à la politique d'Evagoras.

On constate que des dédicaces phéniciennes ou bilingues sont les premières à évoquer précisément l'offrande de statues dans les sanctuaires: à

Figure 22.6 New York, MMA 74.51.2462 (photo A Hermary).

Figure 22.7 Paris, Louvre AM 2935 (photo du Musée).

Tamassos-Phrangissa, sous le règne de Milkyaton de Kition (vers 392–362), des personnages nommés Menahem et 'Abdsasôm consacrent chacun à Reshef-Apollon une statuette désignée en grec comme ἀνδρίας, terme qui ne suffit malheureusement pas à affirmer que ces représentations étaient des portraits miniatures.[9] Quelles qu'aient été leur langue et leur origine ethnique, les notables chypriotes du milieu du IVe s. sont incontestablement au courant de l'évolution de la plastique grecque, mais restent surtout sensibles à l'expression du visage: à Golgoi et à Idalion les commanditaires font confiance aux artistes locaux qui réalisent quelques beaux portraits au visage émacié et à la barbe courte, comme celui d'un 'adorant' de la collection Cesnola (Myres 1914, no 1406) ou une tête provenant du sanctuaire d'Apollon (Pryce 1931, no 176 Fig 110); quelques grandes têtes en terre cuite s'inscrivent dans la même tradition (ainsi Karageorghis 1985, no 237).

Le dernier stade de l'évolution avant la chute des royaumes chypriotes est marqué, vers 330–320, par une confrontation directe entre les artistes grecs venus travailler dans l'île et les sculpteurs locaux: il en résulte, apparemment, une baisse dans le nombre et la qualité des sculptures de grandes dimensions en calcaire et en terre cuite. Il est cependant caractéristique que, par opposition aux têtes grecques en marbre dont le style traduit l'idéalisme en vigueur dans les ateliers attiques, les artisans chypriotes continuent à suivre les recherches de réalisme menées par certains artistes grecs: citons en particulier une tête du Cyprus Museum (Fig 22.12)[10] où les atteintes de l'âge sont exprimées à peu près de la même façon que sur l'une des têtes en argile du pyré de Nikokréon, daté de 311–310 (Karageorghis 1973, 163 no 347 Pls O (coul.) et 209–10). Les seize personnages figurés autour du bûcher du dernier roi de Salamine constituent à Chypre un témoignage exceptionnel de ces groupes familiaux attestés, à une échelle gigantesque, au Mausolée d'Halicarnasse, un peu plus modestement, quoique dans des matériaux très coûteux, dans les statues chryséléphantines du Philippeion d'Olympie (dont on trouve sans doute un écho direct dans les appliques de la tombe de Vergina), ou encore dans les consécrations du Thessalien Daochos à Pharsale et à Delphes.

Il est vraisemblable que parmi les personnages en argile du pyré de Salamine figuraient quelques ancêtres déjà morts en plus des victimes du suicide collectif. Certaines des statues-portraits en calcaire ou en terre cuite que je viens d'évoquer ne seraient-elles pas, elles aussi, des images d'ancêtres ou de 'grands hommes' défunts?[11] Je me suis demandé si la présence de grosses boucles frontales en tire-bouchon, évidemment en contradiction avec la mode des coiffures au IVe s., ne serait pas une convention pour définir le personnage comme un défunt; cette hypothèse ne peut cependant pas être appuyée par des arguments vraiment déterminants, malgré une possible comparaison avec un relief d'un sarcophage lycien de la même époque, sur lequel un jeune homme à mèches frontales bouclées se présenterait devant les juges des Enfers (Borchhardt 1969–70, 189–90 Pls 34.1, 36.1). Il est curieux de constater qu'à Halicarnasse et à Priène, vers le milieu du IVe s., ce type de coiffure n'est attesté que sur des têtes féminines (Waywell 1978, 70–2 Pl 16; Blümel 1966, nos 104–5 Figs 138–41) alors qu'elle ne l'est, à Chypre, que chez les hommes, y compris sur des re-

Figure 22.8 Rome, Museo Nazionale Romano 130 (photo DAI Rome).

présentations d'Héraclès et de Baal-Hammon, à rapprocher des images archaïsantes de Dionysos et d'Hermès en Grèce. Il est probable, en définitive, que ces boucles à l'ancienne servent surtout à indiquer l'appartenance à une catégorie sociale supérieure, à une famille noble et vénérable, souvent en charge d'une fonction religieuse importante.[12]

Figure 22.9 Rome, Museo Nazionale Romano 130 (photo DAI Rome).

Résumons les principaux points abordés au cours de cette brève enquête:
—Malgré leur nombre important, les documents figurés tiennent une place moins prestigieuse dans la société chypriote classique que dans la Grèce des cités: pour les monuments funéraires comme pour les statues des sanctuaires ce sont les ressources locales en calcaire qui expliquent la

Figure 22.10 Nicosie, Cyprus Museum Potamia 55 (photo EFA).

Figure 22.11 Paris, Louvre AM 2760 (photo du Musée).

concentration de la documentation dans la région de Golgoi-Idalion, où s'étaient constitués dès l'époque archaïque des ateliers très actifs.

—Dans les zones où elle a été largement pratiquée, la sculpture de grande taille en pierre ou en terre cuite répond alors à des principes qui diffèrent

Figure 22.12 Nicosie, Cyprus Museum D 294 (photo du Musée).

à la fois de ceux des autres régions de la Méditerranée du sud-est, où la part des sculptures funéraires est largement supérieure à celle des statues votives, et de ceux de la Grèce propre où, à l'époque classique, les statues-portraits (quel que soit leur degré de réalisme) sont loin d'être d'usage courant.

—L'accentuation des contacts avec la Grèce, sous le règne d'Evagoras I, se traduit par une importante évolution stylistique qui n'implique cependant aucune rupture profonde avec la tradition locale: pendant une bonne partie du IVe s. les sculpteurs travaillant le calcaire ou la terre cuite ne sont guère concurrencés par les artistes grecs. La vraie rupture a lieu probablement à l'époque d'Alexandre.

Il en ressort l'image d'une société aristocratique, hiérarchisée et traditionnaliste, dont, cependant, les souverains ne cherchent pas à pérenniser leur renommée par des monuments de prestige, contrairement à leurs voisins de Lycie ou de Sidon. On est surtout frappé par le profond attachement à la religion dont témoignent les vestiges matériels et qui, au-delà des personnages les plus importants, concernait sans aucun doute toutes les classes de la société chypriote.

NOTES

[1] Voir l'étude de F.G. Maier au-dessus 00–00.
[2] Hérodote VII, 90. Sur le sens du mot mitra voir Tölle-Kastenbein 1977, 23–36.
[3] Pryce 1931, nos 77–8 Figs 47–8; Young & Young 1955, 200–7; le personnage central d'un groupe de Lefkoniko (Myres 1940–45, 62.114 Pl 12.6), une petite tête en calcaire d'Amathonte, inédite, et probablement un personnage de Kazaphani tenant un coutelas ou une épée courte (Karageorghis 1978, Pl 23.58).
[4] Mendel 1912, nos 96 et 98 (couvercles de sarcophages anthropoïdes); Dunand 1973, Pl 9 (tête fragmentaire en marbre du sanctuaire d'Echmoun à Sidon).
[5] Ainsi celui du Louvre AM 1148, Ht 33 cm.
[6] Louvre AM 2935, Ht. 25.5: Cassimatis 1982, 157 Pl 34.1. Je remercie Annie Caubet qui a mis à ma disposition les photos des sculptures du Louvre reproduites ici; j'étudierai plus en détail ces documents dans le catalogue des sculptures chypriotes du Louvre, en cours d'achèvement.
[7] Hafner 1956, 22–5 Figs 9–10, avec bibliographie, propose d'y reconnaître Xanthippos, père de Périclès, interprétation aussi peu satisfaisante que celle de Pfuhl ('Ulysse').
[8] La belle tête féminine en mabre du gymnase de Salamine est probablement postérieure au règne d'Evagoras, malgré Karageorghis 1964, 8–11, Pls 8–9.
[9] ICS, nos 215–16 (l'encastrement supérieur recevait une plinthe de statuette en pierre plutôt qu'en bronze). Bien que le mot 'andrias' désigne le plus souvent, à partir de la fin du Ve s., un personnage humain, J. Bousquet me signale une inscription de Delphes datée de 340 dans lequel le terme s'applique visiblement à une statue de dieu (Apollon sans doute); *Fouilles de Delphes* III 5, no 22 1.29–30. Le même mot est employé dans la bilingue du sanctuaire d'Apollon à Idalion (*ICS*, no 220); voir aussi les dédicaces phéniciennes *CIS* 90–1.
[10] Inv. D 294, Ht 33cm. Je remercie Vassos Karageorghis et Michaël Loulloupis qui m'ont procuré les photographies et m'ont autorisé à les publier.

[11] Rappelons qu'à Lédra un certain Archaios, qui ne semble pas appartenir à la famille royale, offre dans le sanctuaire d'Aphrodite, probablement après la mort du roi de Paphos, une statue de Nikoklès, 'fils de Timarchos, descendant de Kinyras': Mitford 1961, 136–8, Pl 51.

[12] Le cas des Kinyrades de Paphos, ou celui des descendants de Teucros à Salamine, est bien connu; ajoutons qu'une inscription d'Amathone de la fin du IVe s. désigne un certain Aristôn comme 'eupatride', c'est-à-dire comme 'un noble de l'aristocratie locale': *ICS*, no 196.

RÉFÉRENCES

Blümel, C. (1966) *Die klassisch griechischen Skulpturen der Staatlicher Museen zu Berlin*. Berlin.

Borchhardt, J. (1969–70) Ein Totengericht in Lykien. . . *Ist Mitt 19–20*, 187–222.

Cassimatis, H. (1982) A propos de couronnes sur les têtes masculines en calcaire de Chypre. *RDAC*, 156–63.

Chavanne, M-J. & Yon, M. (1978) *Salamine de Chypre X. Testimonia Salaminia I*. Paris.

Dentzer, J-M. (1982) *Le motif du banquet couché dans le Proche-Orient et le monde grec du VIIe au IVe s. av. J-C*. Paris.

Dunand, M. (1973) Le temple d'Echmoun à Sidon. Essai de chronologie. *BMusBeyr 26*, 7–25.

Hafner, G. (1956) Anakreon und Xanthippos. *JdI 71*, 1–28.

IG I^2 *Inscriptions Graecae*, editio minor (1924). Berolini.

Karageorghis, V. (1964) *Sculptures from Salamis* I. Nicosia.

Karageorghis, V. (1973) *Excavations in the Necropolis of Salamis* III. Nicosia.

Karageorghis, V. (1978) A 'Favissa' at Kazaphani. *RDAC*, 156–93.

Karageorghis, V. (1979) Material from a sanctuary at Potamia. *RDAC*, 289–315.

Karageorghis, V. (1985) *Ancient Cypriote Art in the Pierides Foundation Museum*. Larnaca.

Kraay, C.M. & Hirmer, M. (1966) *Greek Coins*. London.

Lewis, D.M. & Stroud, R.S. (1979) Athens honors King Evagoras of Salamis. *Hesperia 48*, 180–93.

Masson, O. & Caubet, A. (1980) À propos d'antiquités chypriotes entrées au Musée du Louvre de 1863 à 1866. *RDAC*, 136–51.

Masson, O. & Mitford, T.B. (1986) *Les inscriptions syllabiques de Kouklia-Paphos*. Konstanz.

Mendel, G. (1912) *Musée impériaux ottomans. Catalogue des sculptures grecques, romaines et byzantines 1*. Constantinople.

Mitford, T.B. (1961) Further contributions to the epigraphy of Cyprus. *AJA 65*, 93–151.

Myres, J.L. (1914) *Handbook of the Cesnola Collection of Antiquities from Cyprus*. New York.

Myres, J.L. (1940–45) Excavations in Cyprus, 1913. *BSA 41*, 54–68.

Pryce, F.N. (1931) *Catalogue of Sculpture in the Department of Greek and Roman Antiquities of the British Musuem. I.II. Cypriote and Etruscan*. London.

Tölle-Kastenbein, R. (1977) Zur Mitra in klassischer Zeit. *RA*, 23–36.

Waywell, G.B. (1978) *The Free-Standing Sculptures of the Mausoleum at Halicarnassus in the British Museum*. London.

Young, J.H. & Young, S.H. (1955) *Terracotta Figurines from Kourion in Cyprus*. Philadelphia.

POSTER SUMMARY
23
Selective use of clays within Red Polished ware

Jane A. Barlow
Cornell University, New York

A recent study of Red Polished pottery at the Middle Bronze Age site of Alambra suggests that an understanding of manufacturing techniques from the point of view of the ancient potters may help to clarify both relationships among sites and chronological development.

A combination of petrographic analysis and chemical analysis revealed the selective use of two fundamentally different clay types. Petrographic analysis of rock and mineral inclusions in 17 thin sections of Red Polished sherds taken from the lowest levels of the Alambra settlement showed that some vessels were made from a clay originating in a sedimentary soil, some from a clay originating in a volcanic or igneous soil and some from a mixture. Analysis of the chemical composition of another 24 specimens by scanning electron microprobe confirmed the petrographic results and suggested that a common hydrochloric acid field test could be used to enlarge the sample and gain a broad view of the use of two different types of clay. The field test, a drop of a 10 per cent solution of HCl on a fresh surface, was used on 434 well-stratified RP sherds that were identifiable by shape.

The results showed two distinct groups within Red Polished ware. Although both groups had similar slips made from clays of volcanic origin, the first group, Red Polished A, had a paste made from clay originating in sedimentary soils. The second, Red Polished B, had a paste made either from clays containing only volcanic inclusions or from clays containing both volcanic and sedimentary inclusions. Both RP B sub-groups were nearly identical in appearance, but the use of the calcareous sedimentary component correlated with specific vessel shapes. For example, 92 per cent of RP B jugs and juglets and 96 per cent of medium-size jars were made from a combination of the two clays, but 85 per cent of outwardly similar large bowls and nearly 100 per cent of cooking vessels were made from volcanic clay alone.

Technical characterization has helped to define Red Polished fabrics objectively and to sort the excavated pottery into groups that will facilitate comparison with other sites. In addition, the field test confirmed the routine exploitation of two different clay sources at a single site and raised questions about previous interpretations of regional origins based upon very small samples. For details of this study as well as further information on other Alambra wares and fabrics, see Barlow and Idziak, 'Selective use of clays at a Middle Bronze Age site in Cyprus. *Archaeometry,* forthcoming. A pilot study (Barlow, *AIA Abstracts,* 1987, 45) indicates that the patterns that appear in Alambra Red Polished ware are likely to be present at other contemporary sites.

Thanks are due to Dr. Vassos Karageorghis, Director of the Department of Antiquities, Cyprus for permission to perform tests and to export sherds. Support for the technical analyses has come from the Institute for Aegean Prehistory and the Townsend Fund of the Classics Department of Cornell University.

POSTER SUMMARY

24
Cypriot bronzework in the Levantine world: an attempt to situate the metal weapons of the Early and Middle Cypriot periods relative to the contemporary mainland material

Graham Philip
University of Edinburgh

Familiar EC weapon types, hooked-tang spearheads and small daggers, have good parallels in the mainland repertoire of the third millennium and should be seen as simple, local variants of widespread forms. As on the mainland, most weapons are from graves, presumably those of the 'elite'. The closest parallels come from the less-developed areas of the Levant, such as Palestine and the coast, rather than the urban centres of inland Syria. We should note in particular the rarity of axes from graves in the former areas, as in Cyprus, in contrast to their frequency in the latter. No doubt this reflects the relative capacities of the different metal industries, and the regions' differing levels of socio-economic development.

The Middle Bronze Age sees the advent of new mainland types—socketed spearheads, fenestrated and narrow-bladed axes and daggers with decorated blades—found throughout the Levant, forming a widely-understood system of prestige goods cutting across ceramic and linguistic boundaries, and probably connected with palace-dominated urban centres and their representations of eliteness. These are absent from the early MC repertoire where the existing forms continued in production, hence the development of distinct 'Cypriot' styles derived from third millennium types. The use of tin-bronze on Cyprus by this time indicates that the local industry was not isolated from the mainland industry, so the rejection of the new mainland forms must result from deliberate choice; these weapons had no 'meaning' in Cyprus at this time.

The later MC period sees the appearance of local versions of the new mainland types, socketed axes in particular, and warrior-burials with belts. It is only now that Cyprus adopts the new modes of expression, probably connected with wider socio-economic changes on the island at this time. Alongside this we see the appearance of MC pottery at many mainland sites, Cypriot-style daggers at Ras Shamra and Tell el-Yahudiyeh Ware in Cyprus, suggesting that the island is now part of the wider Levantine world, providing the vital lead-in to the much greater Cyprus-mainland contact of the Late Bronze Age.

POSTER SUMMARY
25
On the origin of the Black-on-Red Ware

F. De Cree
Belgium

Excavations in the Near East and Cyprus have revealed two kinds of Proto Black-on-Red Ware: 1) *Akhziv Ware* and 2) *Ashdod Ware*.

1) *Akhziv Ware* has a heavy red slip, dark red, brown or black concentric circles which lack preciseness, wavy crossed lines and hatched triangles. It is dated around 1025 ± 25 BC (Prausnitz 1972, 154) and has also been found at Khirbet Silm and Qrayé (Chapman 1972, 114).

2) *Ashdod Ware* has a heavier red slip decorated with black and white bands. It first appears at Ashdod no later than 990 BC (Dothan 1981, 10–11). It has also been found at Tell Masos (Aharoni, Fritz & Kempinski 1975, 108–9) and Khalde (Culican 1982, 58).

In Cyprus these wares have also been excavated at Kaloriziki (Benson 1973, 118) and Palaepaphos-Skales (Bikai 1983, 401). They can be dated to the LC III (Kaloriziki) (Benson 1978, 118)-CG I (Palaepaphos-Skales) (Bikai 1983, 405).

The Proto Black-on-Red, derived from the 11th century BC Red Slip, was exported to Cyprus where it developed independently from Phoenicia and Palestine into the Cypro-Phoenician Black-on-Red Ware.

LIST OF REFERENCES

Aharoni, Y., Fritz, V. & Kempinski, A. (1975) Excavations at Tell Masos (Khirbet el Mashash) 1974. *Tel Aviv J Inst A 2,* 97–124.
Benson, J.L. (1975) *The Necropolis of Kaloriziki. (SIMA 36).* Göteborg.
Bikai, P. (1983) The imports from the East, in V. Karageorghis *Palaepaphos-Skales. An Iron Age Cemetery in Cyprus. Ausgrabungen in Alt-paphos auf Cypern III.* 396–406. Konstanz.
Chapman, S. V. (1972) A catalogue of Iron Age pottery from the cemeteries of Khirbet Silm, Joya, Qrayé and Qasmieh of South Lebanon, *Berytus 21,* 55–194.
Culican, W. (1982) The repertoire of Phoenician pottery, in *Phönizier im Westen, Madrider Beiträge 8,* (ed. H.G. Niemayer). 45–78.
Dothan, M. (1981) *Ashdod IV. (Atiqot IX),* Jerusalem.
Prausnitz, M. W. (1972) Red-Polished and Black-on-Red Wares at Akhziv. Israel and Cyprus in Early-Middle Iron Age. *Acts of the first international congress of Cypriot studies,* A' 151–6. Nicosia.

PART FIVE
Trade and External Influence

26
Trade in the Late Cypriot Bronze Age

P. Åström
University of Gothenburg

It is useful to recall that we have an eye witness report of an Egyptian tradesman who was shipwrecked on the shores of the land of Alasia about 1075 BC. It seems that the report throws much light on the subject of trade and like most people—*pace* Merrillees—I regard the equation of Alasia with Cyprus as a working hypothesis. The report states that the inhabitants of the landing place charged against the Egyptian to kill him. He forced his way through the crowd where the princess of the town was. Her name was Hatuba. He saw her when she went from one house to another. He greeted her and asked the people around her: 'Isn't there one among you who can understand Egyptian words?' One of them said: 'I understand.' The Egyptian said to him that he had heard as far away as Thebes, the place where Amun is, that 'evil is done everywhere except in the land of Alasia. Or is evil committed here too?' The princess said: 'What is it that you talk about?' He said: 'As the sea raged and the winds blew me to your land —do you allow them to kill me? As I am an envoy of Amun, one should welcome me. And if they kill the crew of the ruler of Byblos, would not their lord find ten crews of yours and kill them?' She summoned the culprits, who were ready to break the laws of hospitality and arraigned them. Then she asked him to stay and rest. And there the text ends abruptly.

I have quoted from the report of Wenamun, which is regarded as an administrative, historical document (Goedicke 1975, 4, 5). As it is preserved in a copy, we may hope that the original will be found one day with more details about Wenamun's adventures in the land of Alasia.

After having left Byblos the ship Wenamun was sailing on was caught by unexpected strong winds, and driven to the eastern or southern coast of Cyprus (*cf* Denham 1964, 140). The town which Wenamun was brought to may have been Enkomi, Kition, Hala Sultan Tekke or one of the towns along the south coast. Inhabitants were apparently not used to foreign ships and foreigners, since they were so hostile to Wenamun and his crew. Or maybe they had some experience of pirates. It is, however, implied in Wenamun's text that Alasia sent its own ships to Byblos. He said that the lord of Byblos might retaliate against the crews from Alasia if any harm was done to the seamen from Byblos. On the whole one gets the impression of a somewhat isolated site with sparse contacts with the outer world. I cannot help but remember an incident in Anatolia in the early 1950's when I was exploring rock-cut tombs in remote archaeological places. At one time we were surrounded by suspicious villagers, who had rarely seen a foreigner, who did not speak foreign languages, and who by no means tried to kill us, but firmly escorted us to the police station where the situation was cleared up.

A point of interest in Wenamun's story is the fact that the town evidently was ruled by a woman of royal birth. We have some rare parallels for that in the ancient world, for instance in Egypt where Hatshepsut and Taousret are well known exceptions.

One should have liked to interview Wenamun about what he saw, how the public and private buildings and sanctuaries looked, how the town was organised, what the people were doing, how they were dressed, etc. He was sent on a mission to obtain a lumber contract 'for the great and august bark of Amun' in Thebes. He went from Thebes to Tanis and from there to Dor and Byblos. It is of interest to note what the Egyptians sent in exchange for the timber. I quote:

'of gold: 4 jars, 1 . . . vessel; of silver: 5 jars; clothing of byssus: 10 pieces; Upper Egyptian linen: 10 veils; smooth material: 500 doublets; 500 ox-hides; 500 ropes; lentils: 20 sacks; fish: 30 baskets.'

In addition Wenamun himself received, while he was in Byblos, 5 pieces of clothing of Upper Egyptian linen, 5 veils of Upper Egyptian linen, 1 sack of lentils and five baskets of fish (Goedicke 1975, 155).

This list contains many luxury goods, food and what may have been a culinary delicacy. One wonders what Wenamun was going to do with the veils? Were they meant to be used for exchange or to attract women? It may be mentioned in this context that Egyptian linen has been found at Tell es Sa'idiyeh adhering to bronze objects (information from Dr. J.N. Tubb). Regarding the other items Goedicke (1975, 97) pointed out in his commentary that today lentils from Esna are highly reputed all over Egypt and beyond and dried fish from the region of Bialah are considered a delicacy.

Lentils have, for instance, been identified by Helbaek from impressions in MC vases from my excavations at Kalopsidha (Åström 1966, 122–3). Lentils are basic food and this is an exception to Portugali's and Knapp's (1985, 65) statement that trade in the East Mediterranean 'was not a trade in ordinary goods for consumption, but rather one in metals, luxury goods, and surplus commodities,' They deal, however, with the 17th to the 14th centuries BC.

Regarding the fish, Wenamun's text may now be illustrated by a recent exciting find from Hala Sultan Tekke. Dr David S. Reese and Dr Mark Rose have been able to identify and have verified by other experts in London, that some of the fish bones from Hala Sultan Tekke are of the Nile perch, *Lates niloticus,* a large fish which must have come from the Nile river in Egypt (letter from Dr David S. Reese of 5th October 1987). This is so far the earliest evidence of fish trading in the Mediterranean, dating from the Late Bronze Age. It was imported in a dried state probably in baskets as in Wenamun's report. Karageorghis has found fish bones in shallow bowls in Tomb 79 at Salamis dating from *ca* 700 BC. They belong to a fresh water species, *Clarias,* which is restricted to South-east Asia, Africa and the Middle East. It was suggested that these fish were imported alive and not as smoked or dried meat (Greenwood & Howes *in* Karageorghis 1973, 117, 259–68; *cf* also Brewer forthcoming). This fish is able to breath atmospheric air and capable of living for several days out of water, so they could survive readily a passage from Egypt to Cyprus.

Continuing along the lines of Egyptian imports and restricting myself to Hala Sultan Tekke we have until now identified about 40 Egyptian or Egyptianizing objects at that site (Åström 1984; *cf* Peltenburg 1986). Since our host encouraged contributions on the theme of trade and its effects on local economies and social organization I shall try to see if the finds throw light on that problem.

Some glass and faience objects from Egypt were probably luxury items for cosmetics, perfume and the like. Other objects were no doubt used as amulets. Popular Egyptian magic connected with the scarab aimed at promoting fertility and protecting the children (Hölbl 1987). Carnelian so-called lotus shaped beads were used for adornment. Three Egyptian games —*senet, mehen* and *tchaou*—are represented at Hala Sultan Tekke, and I believe that they played a role in the daily life of the inhabitants along with the astragals. Otherwise the fairly small amount of Egyptian imports at the site suggests that Egyptian influence may not have been great.

I should like to consider for a moment a gold hoard from Hala Sultan Tekke and its implications (*HST* 8, 8–15; Goring 1983). It was found in a trial trench in 1978 and consisted of 24 objects: 15 of gold, 6 of stone, 2 of faience and 1 of bronze.

Some of the objects have Palestinian counterparts, particularly from Deir el Balah. For the pendants of gold wire coiled into antithetic spirals there are parallels at Ashur in the 13th century. The bezel of the gold ring is inscribed in Egyptian hieroglyphs with a female personal name, Nebuwy. This may have been the lady who owned the hoard or who gave it to a Cypriot lady. It may have belonged to a wandering salesman or it may have been part of the dowry of a lady who buried them in a pouch in the earth in times of danger about 1175 BC. During the war in 1974 in Cyprus, people even buried pound notes in the earth in the hope of being able to return soon to retrieve them.

Let us look at the chased figurines on the gold pendants. One shows a

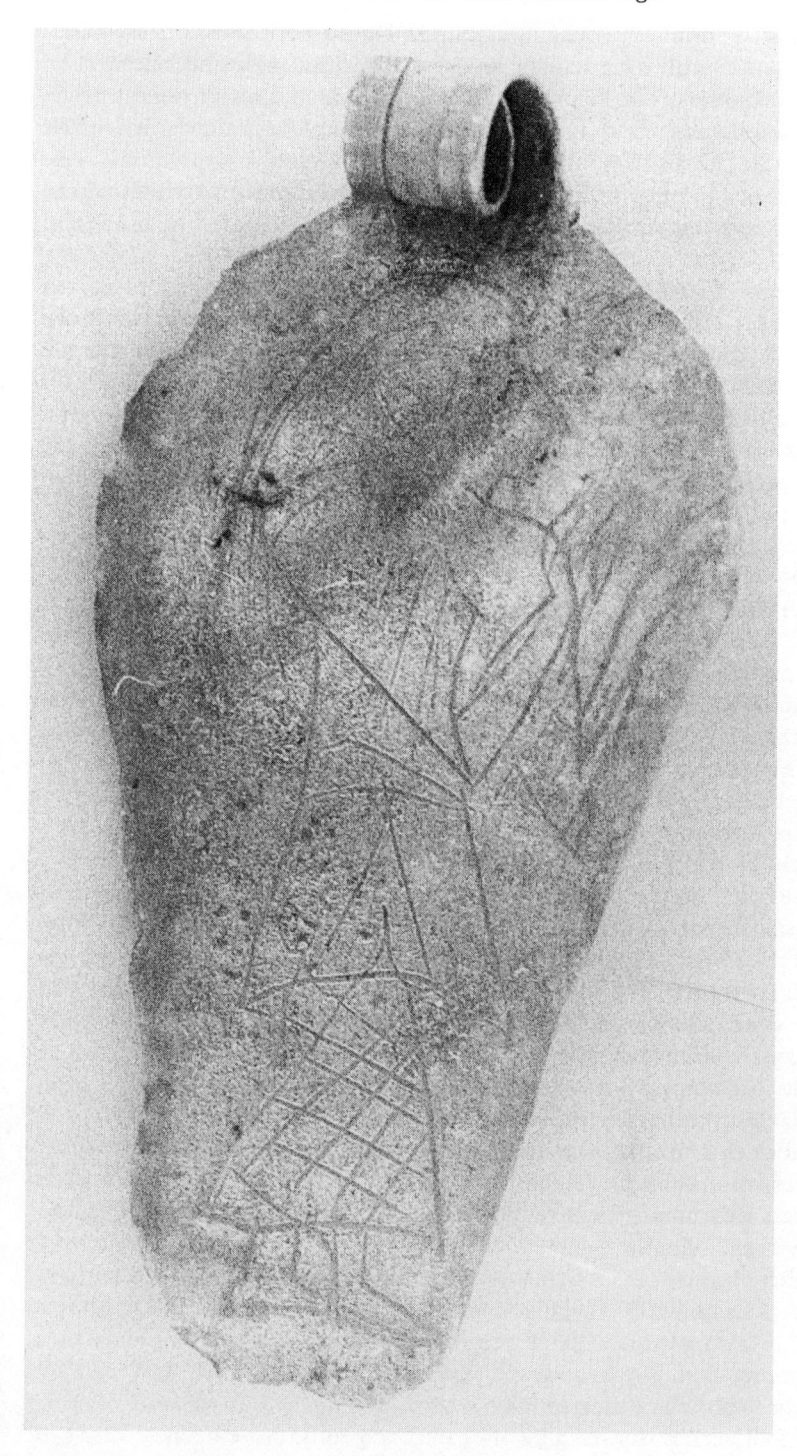

Figure 26.1 Gold pendant from Hala Sultan Tekke.

standing naked youth very much like an Archaic Greek statue, the other a standing woman with long hair or a wig in Egyptian style and a long robe girdled at the waist (Fig 26.1). The upper part is vertically hatched, the middle part is decorated with chevrons and curves. A belt may be indicated by two parallel, horizontal lines. The lower part is cross-hatched in a most suitable manner to be shown in this city: a Scottish tartan pattern like the pattern on the Minoan so called sacred knots (Gullberg & Åström 1970, 22).

She apparently wears an Egyptian wig (Vandier 1958, 481–92), but it is not easy to see which fashion she has followed. The girdled dress looks more Syrian than Egyptian (Fohrer 1964, Fig 2.4). We can recognize Minoan and Egyptian dress fashions and we know that Roman empresses dictated the fashions of their times, but where were the centres of fashions or the Paris of the Late Bronze Age in the East Mediterranean? I am sure that the ladies of those days obeyed the fashions of the seasons as today. Peltenburg (1977, 188) has observed that the straight hair tresses and the lengthy necklaces on Cypriot female bronze figurines betray influence from Babylonia.

We have heard that Egyptian linen and textiles were exported to Byblos and to Tell es Sa'idiyeh. Some of these may have had patterns like those on the gold pendant. I would suggest that import of textiles and clothes together with their patterns obviously had an effect on the people who acquired them and perhaps imitated them. We can suppose that garments worn by the woman on the pendant were also imported but not preserved among archaeological finds.

A simple formula would be to say that the more foreign imports there are at a site, the more foreign effects we may find there.

If we quantify the foreign imported pottery at Hala Sultan Tekke we find that they constitute a small proportion of the whole. When over 200,000 potsherds have been classified, the Mycenaean pottery—about 3,500 sherds —amounts to 1.7 per cent of the total. The Late Minoan fragments are 472 or 0.2 per cent. The Grey Minyan sherds from the area of Troy total 92, which is an insignificant number statistically. There are, however, more than 8,000 Canaanite jar fragments, which is 7.3 per cent of the total (Åström 1986). All in all the foreign influence was thus not great.

What does this mean? The so-called Canaanite jars came from Cilicia, Syria, Palestine and Egypt (Raban 1980). They presumably contained wine from these areas, small vases or perhaps various goodies as shown by the Kaş shipwreck. Maybe this had an influence on the local inhabitants. Minoan and Mycenaean stirrup jars probably held perfumed oil (Shelmerdine 1985, 25, 141–153). I do not know what the Grey Minyan vessels contained. I also assume that foreign pots were prestigious objects in a Cypriot home, each representing a kind of status symbol. I shall end by showing three objects which may be interpreted in various ways. A papyriform terminal with the cartouche of Horemhab could have been brought to

Cyprus by way of trade, by a diplomat or it may have been a souvenir or part of tomb robbery (Åström 1979; Peltenburg 1986; cf Pomerance 1973). It may have been used as a prestige object.

A fragment of a faience face pendant published by Peltenburg (1977) was found in a bathroom at Hala Sultan Tekke. Such objects appear in the Levant in temples and graves sometimes worn at the neck. The type is associated with Ishtar, Dr Peltenburg (1977, 188) suggests that if it 'was not simply an object of plunder from the mainland... it signifies the presence of Asiatic influence and cultic practices at Hala Sultan Tekke.' However, particularly since this fragment was probably not found in an original context, it is uncetain whether it had any religious effect outside its country of origin.

A silver bowl from Tekke had a Canaanite inscription. It has been translated and means either 'Bowl of' or 'Made by Aky son of Yiptahaddu'. There are parallels for it at Megiddo. Is it an import or locally made? Why was it found upside down in a wall? Several vessels of Canaanite type were found in the same room. Was it a status symbol or a valuable object owned by a Palestinian living in Hala Sultan Tekke?

With a limited number of texts at our disposal, taking Alasia to be Cyprus, it is difficult to penetrate through the mists that separate us from the past. What do the foreign objects preserved to our times mean? Those which are preserved are mainly luxury objects of gold, silver, faience, ivory or pottery containers for perfumed oil and cosmetics. It may be coincidence that the rich repertory of imported luxury material in Ayios Dhimitrios Tomb 11 belonged to women. Did women fancy exotic and expensive objects more than men? Luckily enough, to balance this picture we have the burial of a man in a shaft grave at Hala Sultan Tekke richly adorned with a necklace composed of beads of gold, lapis lazuli, faience and agate. He even had a pair of gold earrings. So foreign objects obviously had an effect on both men and women in Cypriot society. We can imagine that many luxurious items were imported along with ordinary items which are no longer preserved. Perhaps they were souvenirs brought by sailors who returned home after trips abroad or evidence of visits from itinerant tradesmen, smiths, artists, bards, musicians, diplomats or casual visitors. How deeply these remains affected the indigenous population can only be speculated upon.

LIST OF REFERENCES

Åström, P. (1966) *Excavations at Kalopsidha and Ayios Iakovos in Cyprus.* Lund.
Åström, P. (1979) A faience sceptre with a cartouche of Horemhab. *Studies Presented in Memory of Porphyrios Dikaios.* 46–8. Nicosia.
Åström, P. (1984) Aegyptiaca at Hala Sultan Tekke. *Op Ath 15,* 17–24.
Åström, P. (1986) Hala Sultan Tekke and its foreign relations. *Acts 1986,* 63–8.
Brewer, D.R. (forthcoming) *The Fishes of Ancient Egypt.* Warminster.

Denham, H.M. (1964) *The Eastern Mediterranean. A Sea-Guide to its Coasts and Islands.* London.
Goedicke. H. (1975) *The Report of Wenamun.* Baltimore and London.
Goring, E. S. (1983) *Late Cypriot Goldwork.* Dissertation. Bedford College. University of London. forthcoming in *SIMA*.
Gullberg, E. & Åström, P. (1970) *The Thread of Ariadne. (SIMA 21).* Göteborg.
Hölbl, G. (1987) Zur kulturellen Stellung der Aegyptiaca in der mykenischen und fruehgriechischen Welt. *Forschungen zur Aegaeischen Vorgeschichte. Das Ende der mykenischen Welt.* Akten des Internationalen Kollokviums 7–8 Juli 1984 in Köln. 123–42. Köln.
Karageorghis, V. (1973) *Excavations in the Necropolis of Salamis.* III. Nicosia.
Peltenburg, E.J. (1977) A faience from Hala Sultan Tekke and second millennium B.C. Western Asiatic pendants depicting females. *HST 3,* 177–200.
Peltenburg, E.J. (1986) Ramesside Egypt and Cyprus. *Acts 1986,* 149–72.
Pomerance, L. (1973) (printed 1980) The possible role of tomb robbers and viziers of the 18th Dynasty in confusing Minoan chronology. *Antichità cretesi. Studi in onore di D. Levi.* 1. 21–30. Catania.
Portugali, Y. & Knapp, A.B. (1985) Cyprus and the Aegean: a spatial analysis of interaction in the seventeenth to fourteenth centuries B.C., in *Prehistoric Production and Exchange. The Aegean and Eastern Mediterranean.* (eds. A. Knapp & T. Stech) (Monograph XXV Institute of Archaeology, University of California) 44–69. Los Angeles.
Raban, A. (1980) *The Commercial Jar in the Ancient Near East. Its Evidence For Interconnections Amongst the Biblical Lands.* Jerusalem.
Shelmerdsine, C.W. (1985) *The Perfume Industry of Mycenaean Pylos. (SIMA Pocket-book 34).* Göteborg.
Vandier, J. (1958) *Manuel d'archéologie egyptienne.* III. Paris.

27
Trade and local production in Late Cypriot faience

A. Caubet
Musée du Louvre, Paris

A. Kaczmarczyk
Tufts University, Medford

In our quest towards a better understanding of early Cypriot society from the point of view of highly skilled industry, we have been confronted many times with the irritating problem of faience finds from Cyprus: Were these imported or not, and if so, from where, Egypt, the Levant or the Aegean? Was there a local production of faience in Cyprus, and, if any, what was the date of its appearance? Were the raw materials imported and from where?

The present paper is a report about research dealing with these problems, in a joint programme of stylistic and chemical investigation of Near Eastern faience.[1] The method of investigation by X-Ray Fluorescence, pioneered by McKerrell and demonstrated by Kaczmarczyk and Hedges (1983) on a large series of faience from Egypt, allows us to determine the composition of the chromopherous oxides that colour the glaze. Thus, the presence of various impurities or combined elements in the oxides may point to the use of different ores, or different recipes. We are aware that ancient circulation of metal ores may confuse our investigation. However, the fast, non-destructive, X-Ray Fluorescence method used by Kaczmarczyk allows us to screen large series, in which technological traits may be perceived and group of manufacture may be distinguished.

Our investigation is progressing by stages: using the large series of faience from Egypt as a background, we began with the plentiful material from Ougarit now in the Louvre, then proceeded to Cyprus, then to other Syro-Palestinian sites (Jericho, Farah), to the middle Euphrates valley (Meskene and Mari) and Mesopotamia (mostly Tello), to end with the material from Susa; the last site spans the whole period of production between the 4th millennium and the Islamic period.

As had been explained in a preliminary report on Ougarit faience, black glaze is the most frequently used colour, after blue-green, in faience objects from the Levant. Many shades of blue-green were obtained from all sorts

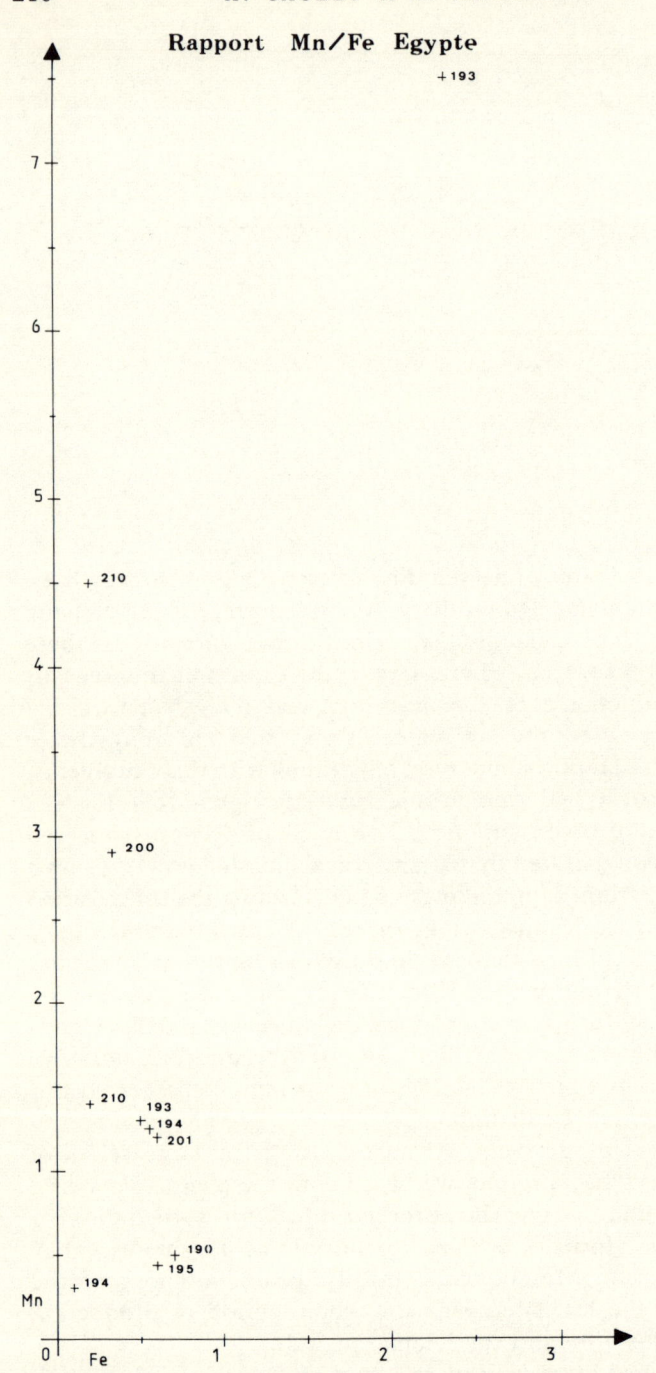

Figure 27.1 Percentage of manganese (Mn) and iron (Fe) in Late Bronze Age Egypt, according to Kaczmarczyk and Hedges 1983 (numbers are taken from the list of analyses C 39–41): percentage of Mn varies, while Fe remains well within the 1 per cent.

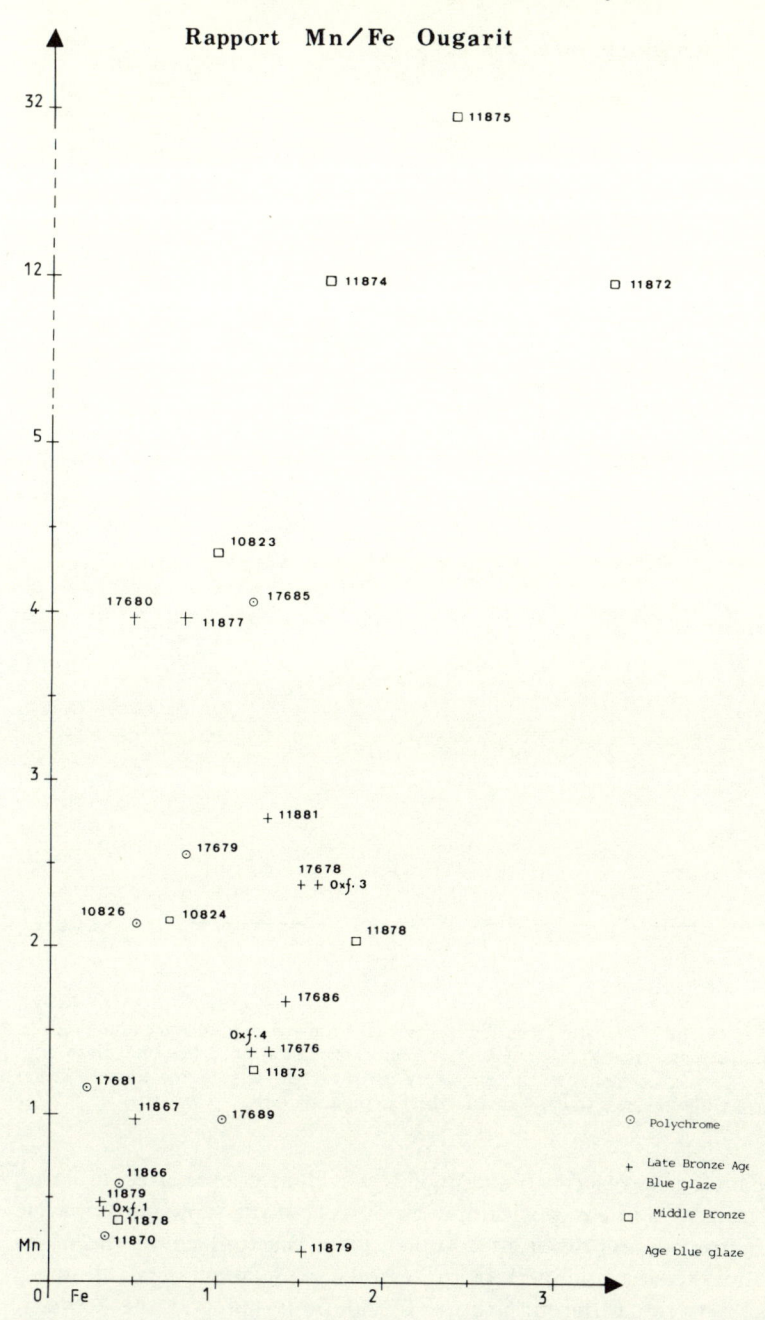

Figure 27.2 Percentage of Mn and Fe in Ougarit: square: Middle Bronze Age blue glaze and figurines cross: Late Bronze Age blue glaze dotted circle: polychrome and Levantine style Notice that appart from the figurines and MB objects with a completely different composition, the pattern of dispersion between cross (LB blue glaze) and circle (LB polychrome) is very similar, with amounts of Fe averaging 1 per cent to 1.5 per cent; however, a cluster of both blue glaze and polychrome faience stays within the 0.5 per cent Fe.

Rapport Mn/Fe Chypre

[Scatter plot with Mn on vertical axis (0 to 4) and Fe on horizontal axis (0 to 3), showing the following data points:
- ⊙ 17621 (at approx. Fe 0.8, Mn 2.8)
- + 17625 (at approx. Fe 0.7, Mn 2.3)
- + 17695 (at approx. Fe 0.6, Mn 2.0)
- ⊙ 17622 (at approx. Fe 1.7, Mn 1.9)
- ⊕ 17628 (at approx. Fe 0.7, Mn 1.7)
- ⊕ 17630 (at approx. Fe 0.5, Mn 1.6)
- + 17626 (at approx. Fe 0.4, Mn 1.3)
- ⊙ 17623 (at approx. Fe 0.6, Mn 1.1)
- ⊕ 17631 (at approx. Fe 0.4, Mn 1.0)
- + 17696 (at approx. Fe 0.7, Mn 0.8)

Legend:
⊙ Polychrome
+ Bronze Age Blue glaze
⊕ Iron Age Blue glaze]

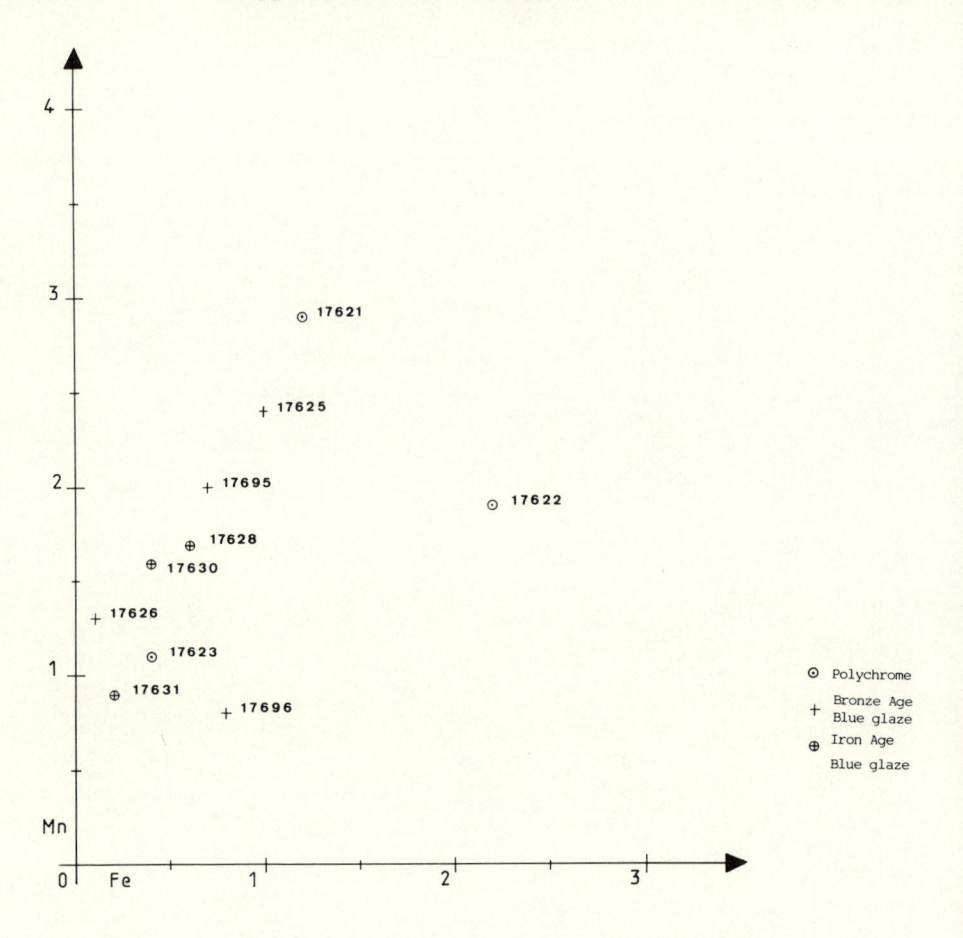

Figure 27.3 Percentage of Mn and Fe in Cyprus: cross: Bronze Age blue glaze dotted circle: Bronze Age polychrome crossed circle: Iron Age blue glaze The Bronze Age blue glaze stays within the Fe 1 per cent range as in contemporary Egypt, while polychrome shows a larger variety. Iron Age blue glaze also conforms to the Egyptian pattern.

of sources, such as re-used bronze objects as well as copper ores, creating very wide variations in composition; even objects of the same period, style and provenance possess different compositions. Black glaze on the other hand was universally obtained from ferrous manganese ores, allowing comparison between different groups found in Egypt and the Levant. X-Ray Fluorescence shows that Ougarit faience has a somewhat different Mn/Fe ratio than in contemporary Egypt, with a larger amount of iron in the oxides, suggesting the use of different manganese ores (Caubet & Kaczmarczyk 1987, 52).

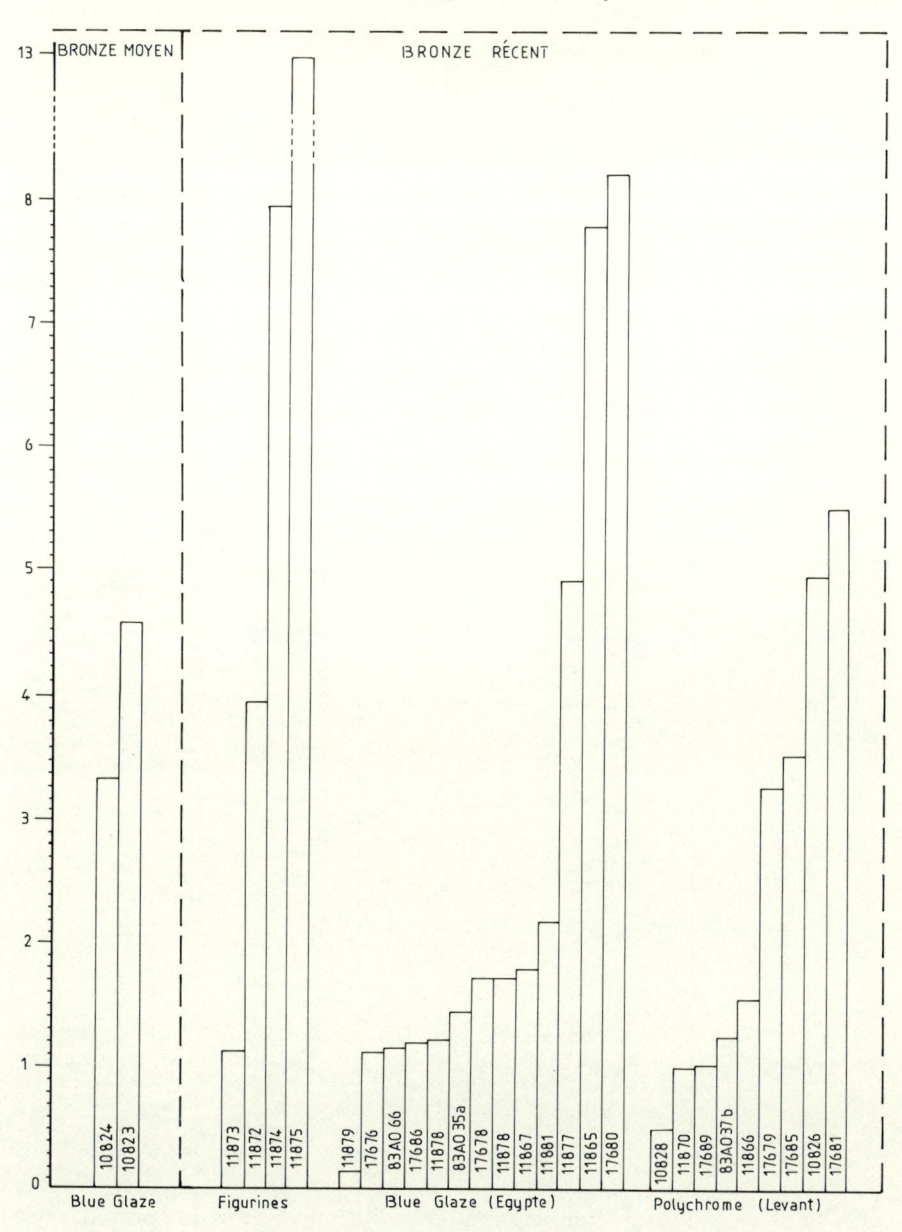

OUGARIT. Rapport Mn / Fe

Figure 27.4 Mn:Fe ratios pattern for Ougarit. Again, apart from the peaks of the figurines, the blue glaze pattern conforms with polychrome patterns at Ougarit. Perhaps the peaks, indicating a lower amount of Fe, already noticeable in Fig 27.2, indicate a different source of ore and perhaps Egyptian manufacture and importation.

CHYPRE. Rapport Mn/Fe

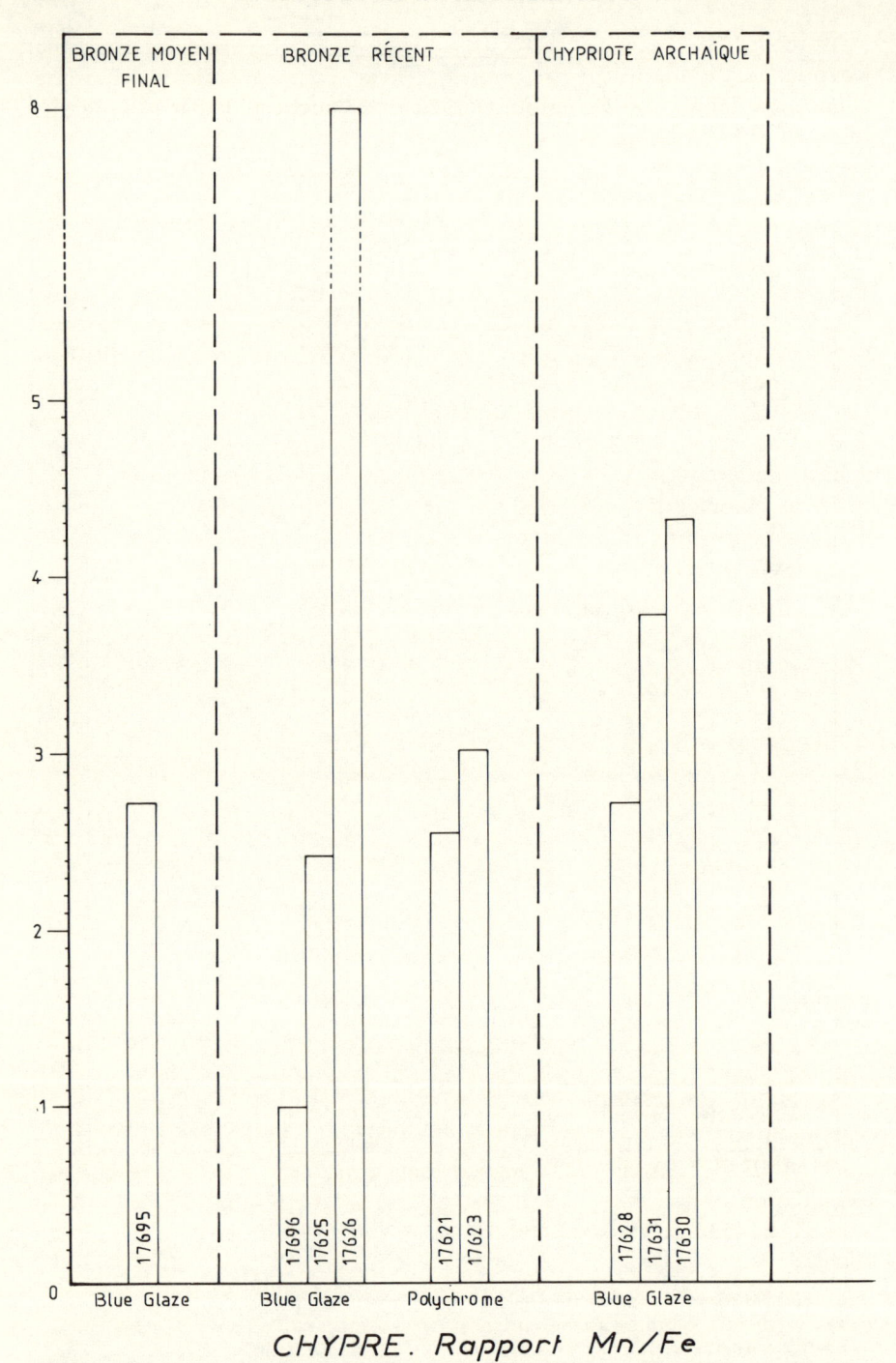

Figure 27.5 Mn:Fe ratios pattern for Cyprus. The graphics show a consistently higher ratio, indicating a lower Fe amount, as in contemporary Egypt. The peak in LB blue glaze (a fish bowl) almost certainly indicates an Egyptian manufacture.

Moreover, at Ougarit, the recipe seemed to be the same for both the Egyptian style monochrome and the Near Eastern style polychrome faience, as defined by Peltenburg (1972): this suggested that at Ougarit, some of the Egyptian style faience were of non-Egyptian origin, and probably local.

With these preliminary results in mind, it was tempting to question the Egyptian character of other Egyptianising faience from the Levant and Cyprus. Before we had the opportunity to procure X-Ray Fluorescence analyses for recently excavated Late Cypriot faience from Kition, we had suggested the possibility of local manufacture for some of the outstanding works found at this site (Caubet 1985, 61–73). Peltenburg has challenged these conclusions, specifically with regard to the Cypriot faience (1986, 173). We have since completed the analysis of the small Late Cypriot series in the Louvre: it shows that Cypriot faience presents a different situation than that at Ougarit (Figs 27.1–5): it will be no great surprise to find that, as far as composition of glazes is concerned, Cyprus stands somewhere between Egypt and the Orient! However, it will be necessary to gather more evidence from recent excavations to obtain a better picture for trade and local manufacture of these luxury goods in Cyprus.

NATURE OF THE CYPRIOT SAMPLE IN THE LOUVRE

Catalogue

1. AM 815 LRMF 17695 Middle Bronze Age juglet, acq. Malis (Kition ?)
2. AM 2106 LRMF 17696 LB black on blue stirrup jar, Enkomi Fr Tomb 5.
3. 85 AO 416 LRMF 17624 blue pedestal base, Enkomi Fr Tomb 13
4. 85 AO 417 LRMF 17623 beaked bowl, Enkomi Fr Tomb 5
5. AM 2111 LRMF 17622 polychrome garland pot, Enkomi Fr Tomb 5
6. AM 2107 LRMF 17621 blossom bowl Enkomi Fr Tomb 5
7. S 575 LRMF 17625 Ramesside oil jar, black on blue, Kition ?
8. AM 569 not analysed, relief black on blue jar, acq. Malis (Kition ?)
9. AM 836 LRMF 17626 fish bowl, black on blue, no prov.
10. N 3292 LRMF 17628 Nefertum, black on blue-green, Kition
11. AM 390 LRMF 17627 core formed glass, Kourion Tomb
12. AM 107 LRMF 17631 female carrying jar, black and blue, Kition
13. MNB 99 LRMF 17630 naked female in pudic attitude, black and blue, Kition
14. AM 1453 LRMF 17632 pilgrim flask variant D, green core and glaze, Nicosia
15. MNB 98 LRMF 17629 Bes and Beset, variant D blue-green core and glaze, Kition
16. AM 570 not analysed, seated flute player, variant D blue-green core and glaze, acq. Malis (Kition ?)

17. AM 1452 LRMF 17634 Tarsus amphora, clay with yellow and green glaze, acq. Malis, Kition.

Date

MB ?:	1
LB:	2, 3, 4, 5, 6, 7
Iron I:	8, 9
Iron II:	10, 12, 13, 14, 15, 16
Classic:	11
Hellenistic:	17

Provenance

Enkomi: 2, 3, 4, 5, 6: Late Bronze Age.
Larnaca/Kition: 7 (Kition ?), 8 (Kition ?), 10, 12, 13, 15, 16 (Kition ?): Iron Age; 17 : Hellenistic.
Kourion: 11.
Nicosia: 14.
No provenance: 1, 9.

Techniques

BA to IA I	: Blue glaze ("monochrome"): 1, 2, 3, 7, 9
	: Polychrome: 4, 5, 6
Iron Age II	: blue monochrome variant D: 8
	: blue glaze, style of the Nile Delta: 12, 13
	: Egyptian style blue glaze "monochrome": 10
Classical to Hellenistic:	core-formed glass: 11
	: glazed clay, Tarsus style: 17

NOTES

[1] Programme conducted by Alek Kaczmarczyk (Tufts University, Medford) and A.Caubet together with the Laboratoire de Recherche des Musées de France (LRMF:Jacques Ligot and Jean Lahanier), with the special collaboration of Ellen Hatcher at the Research Laboratory for Archaeology, University of Oxford for the atomic absorption analyses. For a preliminary report see Caubet & Kaczmarcyk 1987, 47–56.

LIST OF REFERENCES

Caubet, A. (1985) Matières vitreuses, in *Kition Bamboula III*, (Yon, M. & Caubet, A.) 61–73. Paris.
Caubet, A. & Kaczmarczyk, A. (1987) Bronze Age faience from Ras Shamra (Ugarit), in *Early Vitreous Materials* (eds. M. Bimson, & I. Freestone) *(BMOP 56)*, 47–56. London.
Kaczmarczyk, A. & Hedges, R. (1983) *Ancient Egyptian Faience*. Warminster.
Peltenburg, E. (1972) On the classification of faience vases from Late Bronze Age Cyprus. *Acts of the First International Congress of Cypriot Studies, A'* 129–36. Nicosia.
Peltenburg, E. (1986) Ramesside Egypt and Cyprus. *Acts 1986*, 149–79.

28
Late Bronze Age long distance trade in the Mediterranean: the role of the Cypriots

Lucia Vagnetti
Istituto per gli studi micenei ed egeo-anatolici, CNR, Rome

Fulvia Lo Schiavo
Soprintendenza archeologica per le province di Sassari e Nuoro

INTRODUCTORY REMARKS

The pattern of trade in the Eastern Mediterranean in the Late Bronze Age has been the subject of several studies in recent years and the involvement of Cyprus has been considered from various points of view, taking into account archaeological and written records. Recent surveys of the subject have repeatedly stressed the importance of Cyprus as a copper producing region. With few exceptions the identification of Cyprus wholly or in part with Alashiya is accepted (Baurain 1984; Muhly 1986; Knapp 1986). For the definition of such a role the evidence in the Near Eastern texts is of paramount importance.

If we turn our attention to the Aegean and the areas further west, the scantiness or total lack of written evidence obliges us to rely mainly on archaeology. With this severe limitation in mind, we are aware that our title sounds much too ambitious! Nevertheless, we believe that the increasing evidence for Cypriot material outside the Aegean may provide a contribution to the debate, if not definite answers. We are encouraged by the fact that a somewhat hazardous working hypothesis expressed many years ago about the possible Cypriot component in the Late Bronze Age trade in the Central Mediterranean (Vagnetti 1968) has received more confirmation than confutation from recent archaeological discoveries.

In the paper that follows, we shall present the new evidence in a chronological order that also corresponds to the two classes of finds involved: pottery and metalwork. The recently discovered material will be discussed with brief reference to what was already known and in connection with new evidence from other areas, with particular attention to the preliminary information about the Kaş (Ulu Burun) shipwreck, which sheds a good deal of light on the western finds as well as on many other questions (Bass 1986; 1987; Pulak 1988).

POTTERY (L. VAGNETTI)

Before tackling specifically this part of the investigation, it seems useful to recall briefly some fixed points concerning Cypriot materials in the Aegean.

G. Cadogan (1972), discussing his list of Cypriot imports in the Aegean, pointed out that their distribution in the LM/LH I-IIIA period was limited to Rhodes, Crete and a few other islands, while Attica, the Argolid and Crete again seemed to be the main destinations in LH/LM IIIC. He also stressed the limited amount of material of LH/LM IIIA:2-B date. H.W. Catling (1980), in his survey of Cyprus and the West, was able to add a few more pieces from Crete—*White Slip II* pottery from Chania and Kommos—and sherds of the same fabric from Tiryns, the first finds of this type in mainland Greece.

More recent research has greatly increased the number of Cypriot imports in Crete. Apart from a fragmentary *Red Polished III* amphora of the EC III period identified at Knossos (Catling & MacGillivray 1983), most of the new finds come from Kommos. According to a recent preliminary summary by Watrous (1985), Cypriot material appears in this important harbour town in southern Crete possibly as early as MM IB and certainly from MM III onwards. The peak of Cypriot imports, however, is in the LM IIIA period with a marked decrease in LM IIIB. More Cypriot material is now reported in LH IIIB:2 levels at Tiryns, where Klaus Kilian has identified *White Slip* and *White Shaved* sherds and terracotta wall brackets (1978, 452, Fig 7; 1988, 121, Figs 24–5; and forthcoming).

The most recent general survey by Portugali and Knapp (1985) is confined to the period between the 17th and the early 14th century BC, confirmed as the zenith of this type of evidence at least in Crete. The importance of this period for the Cyprus-Crete trade is indirectly confirmed by the finds at Marsa Matruch, an important harbour site on the Libyan coast. There, excavations were carried out on a small island inside the lagoon at the beginning of the century by O. Bates and more recently by D. White for the Univerity Museum of Philadelphia (White 1986). Several Cypriot sherds of *White Slip II, Base Ring, Red Lustrous* and *White Shaved* wares were found in the Late Bronze Age levels. They were mixed with a few objects of Levantine type (Canaanite jar and a lamp) and with a few sherds of Aegean origin among which a LM III closed vessel and a LH IIIA:1 cup decorated with *stipple pattern* have been recognized. They give a good hint for a chronology not later than the early 14th century BC. Other important evidence is provided by traces of local metallurgical activity (slags and crucibles) and by numerous ostrich egg fragments, perhaps representing one of the commodities provided by the Libyans in exchange for the Cypriot products.

All this activity, mirrored also in a number of Aegean finds in Cyprus and like them preceding the great increase there of the ubiquitous LH III pottery, seems to take place in the framework of an intensive exchange pattern between the Aegean and the Eastern Mediterranean that, in most cases, is strongly Cretan in character (Hägg & Marinatos 1984; *TMM*). At the same time, the emerging Mycenaean centres of mainland Greece become progressively more active in the Mediterranean trade network. In the early part of the Late Bronze Age they seem to direct their interest to the Central Mediterranean, leaving considerable archaeological traces on various sites, but mainly on the islands of the southern Tyrrhenian sea, namely the Lipari group and the islands in the Bay of Naples (Taylour 1958; Vagnetti 1982; *TMM* with ample bibliography). Mycenaean sherds have also been reported recently from the Guadalquivir valley in Spain (Martin de la Cruz 1987).

No Cypriot imports have been recognized in the western contexts of this period. For the later period the Cypriot pottery found at Thapsos in Sicily is already known: an imported *White Shaved* juglet and two *Base Ring* type juglets that are apparently not of Cypriot fabric. These items are associated with local Bronze Age material and with LH IIIA2 material (Voza 1973; Lo Schiavo, Macnamara & Vagnetti 1985). Dr Karageorghis has kindly pointed out to me that the Cypriot and Cypriot-type material found at Thapsos could easily belong to the 13th century. In the absence of detailed and complete publication of the Thapsos tomb—which incidentally contained several burials—we cannot say if the Cypriot material should be considered as contemporary or later than the Mycenaean pottery.

It should be noted that other finds from other parts of Sicily that have been regarded as Cypriot imports or imitations seem to be at home in the 13th century BC or even later. The 13th century also provides a suitable date for the few further sherds of Cypriot type found elsewhere in Italy (Lo Schiavo, Macnamara & Vagnetti 1985; Vagnetti 1986).[1] One very interesting piece comes from Eboli, an inland site located in southern Campania. There, under a settlement of the Hellenistic period, traces of Bronze Age occupation came to light. Sherds of 'Aegean-type' pottery have been published in preliminary reports (Schnapp-Gourbeillon 1982, 1986); one of them is decorated with a goat with elongated body filled with small chevrons (Fig 28.1c). Apart from the interesting appearance of a pictorial-style sherd in this rather remote site, I would like to stress that the best parallels for the style of the sherd are in the Cypriot *Rude* or *Pastoral style* of the LC II period. It is well known that this class of pottery has a specifically Cypriot distribution with the exception of a few examples found on the nearby Levantine coast, especially at Ugarit. To my knowledge no pottery of this class has been identified in the Aegean (Anson 1980; Vermeule & Karageorghis 1982, 59). The sherd from Eboli has not yet been analysed. We hope to include this and other sherds from the same site in the programme of physico-chemical analysis of Aegean-type pottery from Italy in progress—with interesting results—in the Fitch Laboratory at the British School at Athens under the direction of Dr R.E. Jones (Jones 1986; Jones & Day 1987; Vagnetti & Jones 1988).

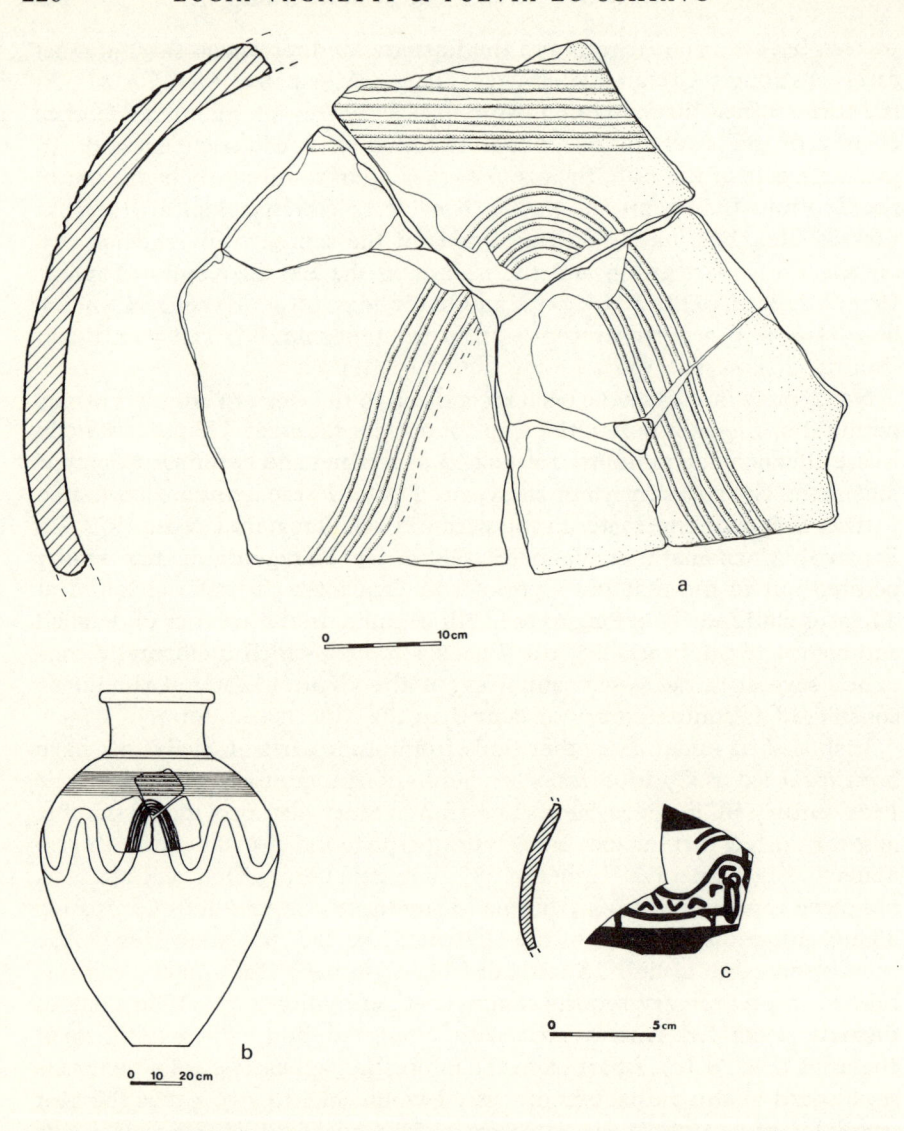

Figure 28.1 (a) and (b) Pithos from Nuraghe Antigori, Sarroch (Cagliari); (c) Pictorial style sherd from Montedoro di Eboli.

The area where archaeometric research on the Aegean type pottery has been more rewarding is undoubtedly Sardinia. Some Cypriot and Cypriot-like sherds have been identified among the exotic pottery found there. Two sherds with Cypriot affinities from Nuraghe Antigori are already known (Lo Schiavo, Macnamara, Vagnetti 1985; Vagnetti 1986). The original hypothesis that they could be ascribed to *Base Ring* fabric has not been confirmed by chemical analysis. The same analysis, however, seems to rule out an Aegean or local origin at least for one of the sherds (Jones & Day 1987).

More recently, three large sherds belonging to a *pithos* were found in room *p* of the same nuraghe. They were used as paving slabs, set upside down on a floor together with stones, in one of the deepest layers of the room. The decoration of horizontal and wavy bands immediately recalls *pithoi* of the LC II and early LC III period, known from many sites on the island and from Ugarit (Ferrarese Ceruti, Vagnetti & Lo Schiavo 1987) (Fig 28.1a-b). In this case, the chemical and petrographic analysis by Jones and Day (1987) gave a definite result: the composition of our *pithos* matches examples from the central-southern part of Cyprus (especially Maroni and Ayios Dhimitrios) and also seems very close to a similar *pithos* of Cypriot manufacture found at Kommos in Crete. The importance of this find is self-evident. Not only do we have the first archaeometric confirmation of a suspected Cypriot import in the Central Mediterranean: we also have a further link with Crete, which was certainly an important staging-point on the journey towards the west. LM IIIB pottery, on the other hand, is fairly common among the Aegean imports to Antigori, although it is not as abundant as the Mycenaean imports. It includes fine table ware from central and western Crete, and coarse containers and *pithos* sherds from central Crete (Ferrarese Ceruti, Vagnetti & Lo Schiavo 1987; Jones & Day 1987).

In order to understand better the significance of a Cypriot *pithos* in Sardinia we can use the evidence from the Kaş shipwreck, where *pithoi* have been found full of various goods such as glass beads or Cypriot pottery (Bass 1986, 279). It is most likely that the Cypriot *pithos* found at Antigori arrived there as a container of smaller objects. We cannot exclude that the numerous sherds of one or more LM III *pithoi* from the same site also had a similar function.

At this point we should also mention that V. Watrous has defined a number of sherds found at Kommos in LM IIIA-B layers as 'Italian imports' (1985). They include *wheelmade grey ware* and *brown impasto ware*. None of these has yet been published in detail. Elsewhere I have expressed my doubts about the labelling of the grey wheelmade ware as of Italian origin (Vagnetti 1985). When the impasto ware is published, we shall be able to evaluate the possible regional links that are concealed behind the too general 'Italian' label. At the moment, Sardinian affinities could be the most predictable.

Cylinder seals in the West

In the last few years, Sardinia has emerged as the major source of new and revolutionary information for the pattern of trade between the Eastern and the Central Mediterranean in the Bronze Age. To the evidence of pottery and metalwork one can now add a cylinder seal of olivine, in very bad condition, found in a Late Bronze Age 'Giants' tomb' at San Sperate near

Cagliari. G. Ugas has given a preliminary illustration and account of it suggesting a Near Eastern origin (1987). The piece is unfortunately very worn, and it is difficult to give a clear reading of the figures depicted and of their style; the object clearly needs a specialist's expertise that I am unable to offer. One can, however, wonder if a possible origin for the seal could be Cyprus, in view of the fact that cylinder seals were widely used in the local glyptic of the Late Bronze Age (*SCE* IV.1D, 623–74; Schaeffer 1983; Courtois & Lagarce 1986). The recent find of another seal from Sicily associated with Mycenaean and Cypriot pottery makes this working hypothesis more probable.[2]

An Italian sword in the Kaş shipwreck?

The Kaş shipwreck has already been cited in connection with some of the finds considered above. There is universal agreement on the extreme importance of this underwater excavation that has unexpectedly shed a completely new light on long distance trade in the Bronze Age. George Bass (1987) has already listed seven different provenances for the goods found in the cargo and it is likely that their number will grow as research continues. Here I would like to suggest a western provenance for one of the objects published in the last preliminary report. Its connection with Cyprus is only indirect and depends on the 'nationality' of the ship.

I refer to a sword with triangular hilt, three big rivets arranged in a triangular scheme and a lozenge-shaped section. Cemal Pulak (1988, 22–3, Fig 22) ingeniously explains its odd shape as a very fragmentary example of Sandars' type C I (Fig 28.2a). However, the lozenge-shaped section is not known in this Aegean type and one can find better parallels in Southern Italy and Sicily where the Thapsos-Pertosa type of sword, fairly common in the local Middle to Late Bronze Age, has several affinities with the find from Kaş (Bianco Peroni 1970, 23–6, Pls 5.38, 6.39–46; Bianco Peroni 1974; Cipolloni Sampò 1986, 16–18; D'Agata 1986) (Fig 28.2b).

The Thapsos-Pertosa sword, especially in its Sicilian variety, is supposed to derive from remote Aegean or Cypriot prototypes (Sandars 1961, 26–7; D'Agata 1986); it develops locally to an independent type with regional variations (Fig 28.2c). One of the elements of variation is the section of the blade that includes the most common lozenge shape (Bianco Peroni 1970, Pl 5.38) and examples with a distinct mid-rib (D'Agata 1986, Fig 2b). A short tang appears on many examples from Sicily. The section of the Kaş sword is lozenge-shaped with concave sides and is particularly close to some examples from Southern Italy (Bianco Peroni 1970, Pl 6.41), while its heavy rivets with conical ends also recall examples from Lipari (Bernabó Brea & Cavalier 1980, Pls 291–3).

If this parallel is acceptable, we require a satisfactory explanation for the presence of an Italian or Sicilian sword on a ship that is supposed to sail from East to West. It is not easy to believe that a sword of such dimensions was the personal property of a crew member. It is more possible that,

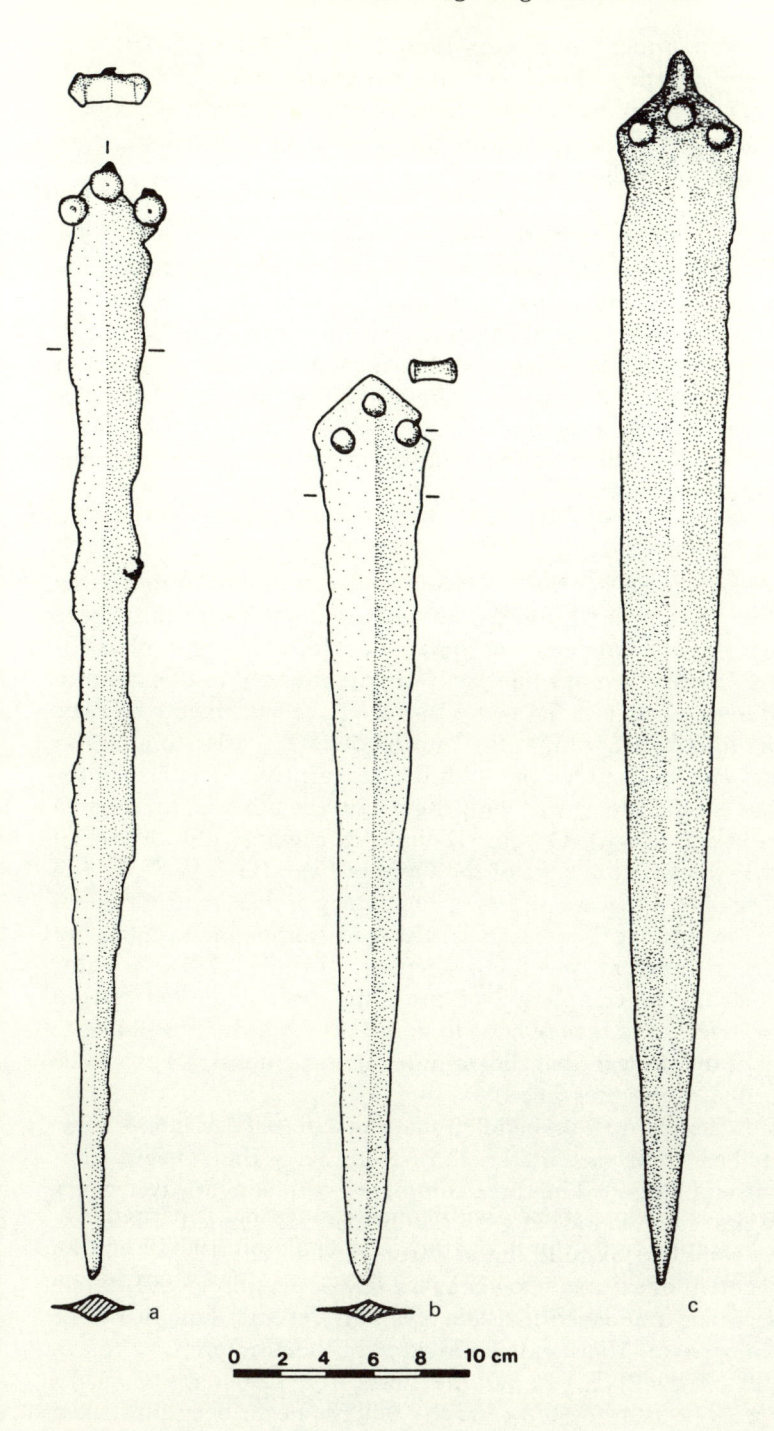

Figure 28.2 Daggers from (a) Ulu Burun (Kaş); (b) Venosa and (c) Matrensa.

together with a few amber beads (Bass 1986, 286 Fig 25), it was left over from a previous journey. Moreover, its extremely poor preservation suggests that it was scrap metal rather than a functional object. Whatever its status, the sword is perhaps the earliest object of Western manufacture found in the Eastern Mediterranean.

METALLURGY (F. LO SCHIAVO)

The main evidence for metallurgical links between Cyprus and Sardinia —double axes, smithing tools, mirrors, metal vessels and their attachments, bronze figurines—has become familiar to scholars in recent years. Although new discoveries have enlarged almost all these groups, it is not my purpose here to discuss again all the various categories that have already been examined (Lo Schiavo, Macnamara & Vagnetti 1985); the following treatment is limited to oxhide ingots and tripod-stands, with especial reference to recent and exciting finds.

Ox-hide ingots

Ox-hide ingots are the objects that currently have most to contribute to the definition of the relationship between the two islands. Most of them have been sampled for a wide ranging archaeometric project that covers physicochemical as well as lead isotope analyses.[3] Its preliminary results seem to suggest a difference between the composition of the bun ingots and the ox-hide ingots found in Sardinia; the bun ingots are similar to artefacts from the island and seem to fit well with the 'fingerprints' established for some Sardinian copper ore; the ox-hide ingots, on the other hand, seem to have more in common with Cyprus 'though, as a whole, the Sardinian ingots lie rather towards the edge of the Cypriot field' (Gale & Stos-Gale 1987, 156). For the evaluation of these preliminary archaeometric results, also bearing in mind that the validity of the lead isotope method has not attracted universal agreement among scientists (Muhly 1983), it seems preferable to await the completion of the other tests and their overall interpretation. Even so, it is now beyond doubt, as it was before and since the beginning of the project, that the ox-hide ingots demonstrate extensive Cypriot influence, if not presence.

Leaving aside the square four-handled shape of external derivation, a few ox-hide ingots bear impressed marks: those from Serra Ilixi, Ozieri, Capoterra, Sardara and Teti(?). The three complete ox-hide ingots from Serra Ilixi were the first to be found, in 1857 (Lo Schiavo & Vagnetti 1980, 384 n 9); another complete ox-hide ingot, discovered in the years 1940–45 under the pavement of a nuragic tower at the site of S. Antioco di Bisarcio (Ozieri, Sassari) and published in 1958, was only recently bought by the Museo Archeologico of Ozieri and placed on public exhibition (Lo Schiavo & Vagnetti 1980, 380 n 2) (Fig 28.3a); the 'horn' from Capoterra (Cagliari) is known since 1973 from the bibliography but has never been illustrated (Fig 28.3d); the twelve fragments from Sardara (Cagliari) were found in a

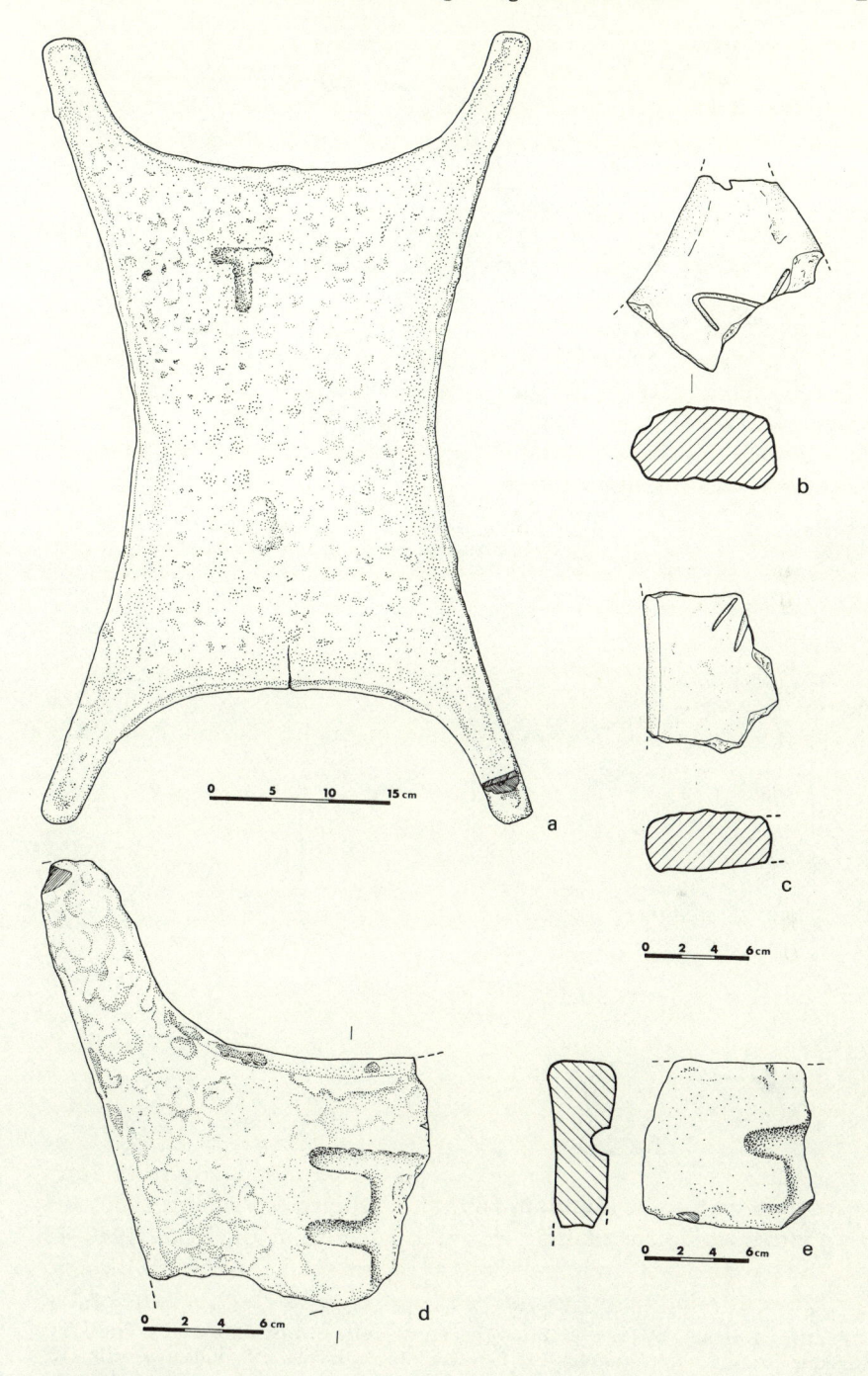

Figure 28.3 Ox-hide ingots bearing impresssed marks, from (a) Ozieri; (b) and (c) Sardara; (d) Capoterra and (e) Teti (?).

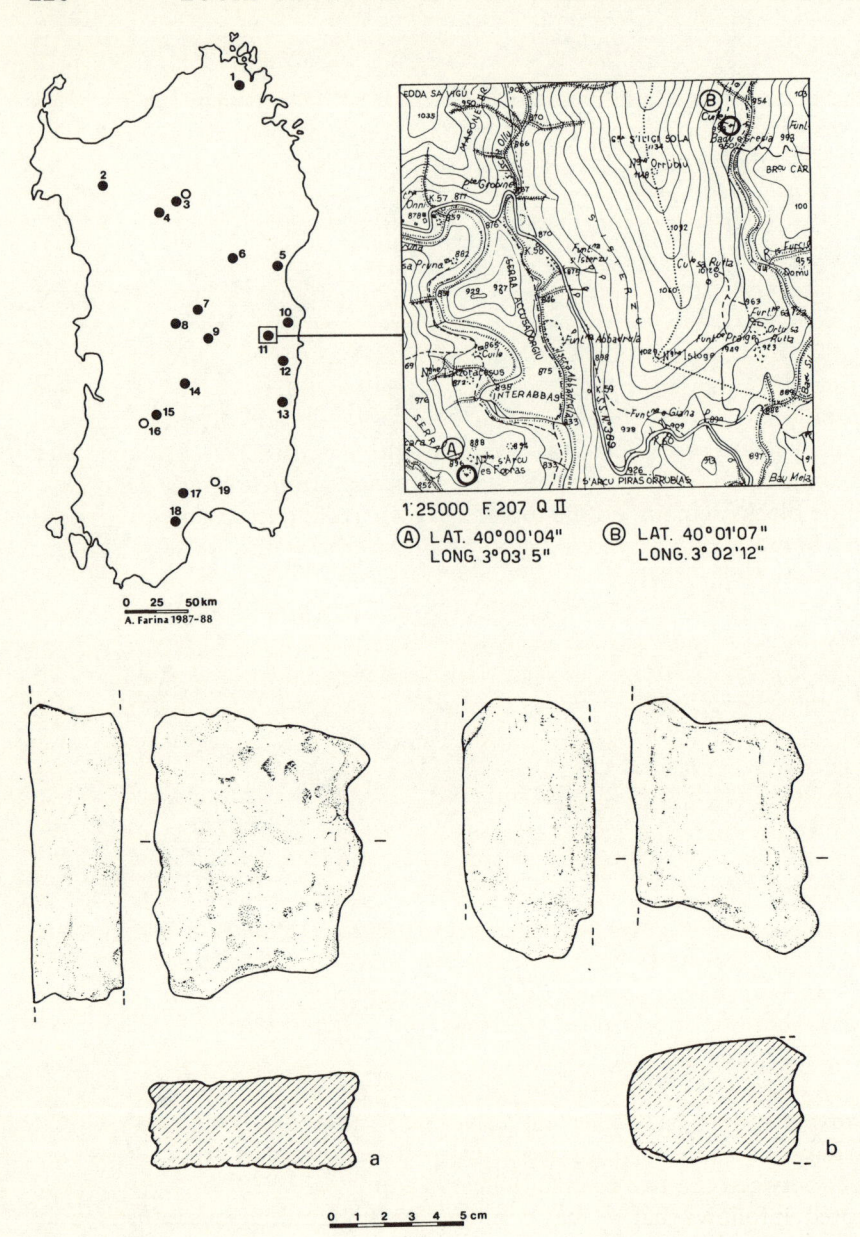

Figure 28.4 Distribution of the ox-hide ingots: (1) Arzachena; (2) Ossi; (3) Ozieri; (4) Ittireddu; (5) Dorgali; (6) Prov. Nuoro; (7) Teti; (8) Ortueri; (9) Belvi; (10) Triei; (11) Villagrande Strisàili; (12) Lanusei; (13) Tertenia; (14) Nuragus; (15) Villanovaforru; (16) Sardara; (17) Assemini; (18) Capoterra; (19) Soleminis. The solid circles indicate old finds; open circles indicate new finds. Below, a–b, two fragments of ox-hide ingots from S'Arcu 'e is Forras, Villagrande Strisàili (Nuoro).

hoard during the 1980–84 excavation of the nuragic village of S. Anastasia (Ugas & Usai 1987) (Fig 28.3b-c); the fragment from Teti(?) was identified in the deposits of Cagliari Museum (Fig 28.3e). More than twenty years ago, in his publication of the Cape Gelidonya shipwreck, George Bass collected all the marks impressed and incised on the ox-hide ingots and, while admitting that the signs cannot be identified, made comparisons with Linear A, Linear B and Cypro-Minoan (1967, 72–3).

The latest ox-hide ingots, bearing no marks, to have been found are the four fragments from Soleminis (Cagliari), a recently published surface find (Santoni 1987), and the two fragments, here illustrated, from S'Arcu 'e is Forras, a site that will be discussed later (Fig 28.4, below). From the same district of Villagrande Strisàili (prov. Nuoro) another twelve pieces have been collected from the Nuraghe Corte Acca (or Corte Macceddos), preserved in a private collection and bought by the State in 1987. The structure of the monument is in a very poor state of preservation, and only a few lines of stone blocks remain, on the top of a granite rock; presumably the twelve pieces found together were a hoard hidden in the wall.

Iron working and the lost-wax technique

Eastern Mediterranean seafaring is also responsible for the early introduction of iron to Sardinia, as is now demonstrated by the discovery of a fragment of worked iron in the undisturbed Bronze Age level 4 of the upper room of tower *c* in the Nuraghe Antigori. It was in close association with a wish-bone handle of Cypriot type and with some sherds of Aegean manufacture. This is the earliest evidence of iron in the western Mediterranean (Ferrarese Ceruti 1986, 185, Fig 4. 5; Lo Schiavo, Macnamara & Vagnetti 1985, 5 n 3, Fig 2.5; Ferrarese Ceruti, Lo Schiavo & Vagnetti 1987, 24).

The early introduction of iron working in Cyprus is well known, but there are apparently no economically viable sources of iron in the island, and a few alternative sources have been suggested, such as the large slag heaps resulting from copper smelting, the ochers, umbers and gossans ('several non-ore sources': Åström *et al* 1986, 28). Perhaps the search for iron, as distinct from the search for tin of which Sardinia is not certainly a primary source (iron ores are ubiquitous there), constitutes a better explanation for the Cypriot presence in the West than the exchange of copper between the two islands richest in copper ores. If this suggestion is accepted, it follows that we may contemplate the simultaneous introduction of the investment or lost-wax technique, known in the Aegean and in the Near East since Early Bronze Age I, and applied in Sardinia to the most extraordinary production of bronze figurines in antiquity (Ferrarese Ceruti, Lo Schiavo & Vagnetti 1987, 23–4).

Tripod-stands

A few fragments of two bronze Cypriot tripod-stands were found in the

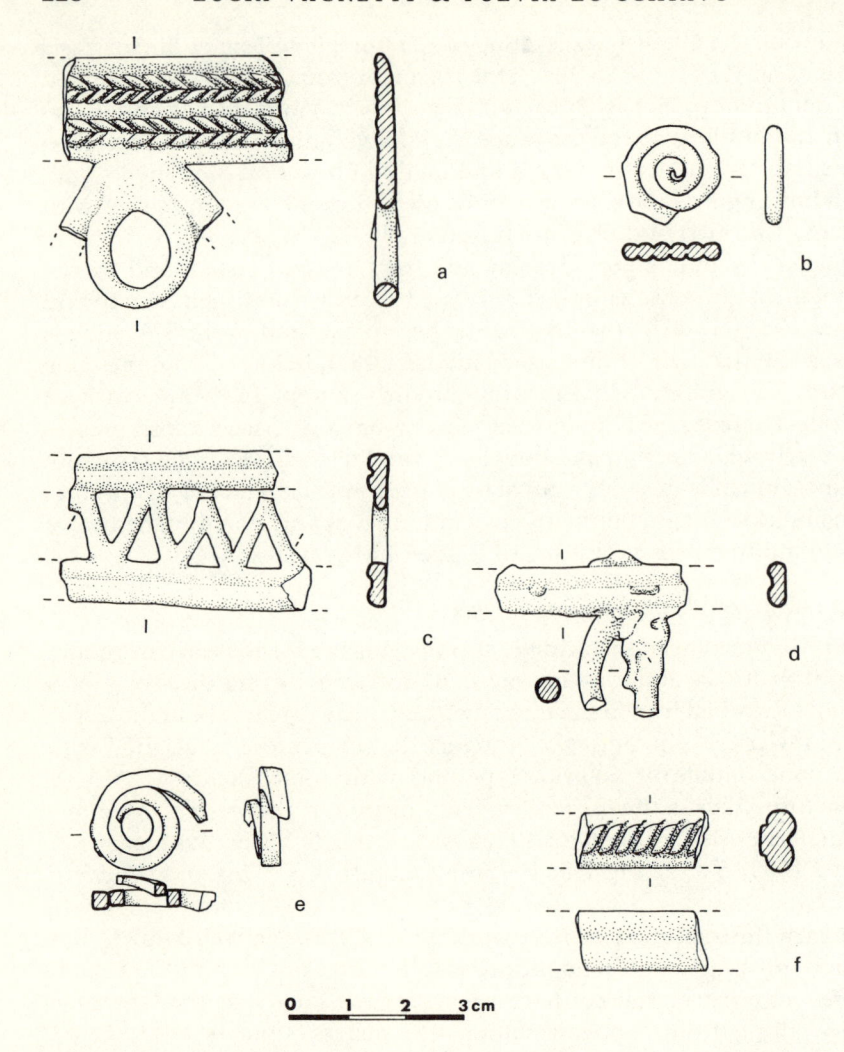

Figure 28.5 Fragments of tripod stands from S'Arcu 'e is Forras, Villagrande Strisáili (Nuoro).

preliminary rescue excavation of the nuragic site of S'Arcu 'e is Forras (Villagrande Strisáili, Nuoro). Since investigation of the site is still at an early stage, I cannot provide precise details of the context of this discovery, mentioned here by courtesy of Dr Maria Ausilia Fadda (see Appendix). The quantity of raw metal, slags and fragments of ingots (both planoconvex 'buns' and ox-hides) and of artefacts recovered on the site suggests the presence of a bronze workshop. In particular, the *'megaron'* temple has yielded a heap of raw metal, scraps, ingots and artefacts, including the items discussed below, all scattered around a large bronze cauldron, extensively patched in antiquity and now smashed. Many stones, found all around the

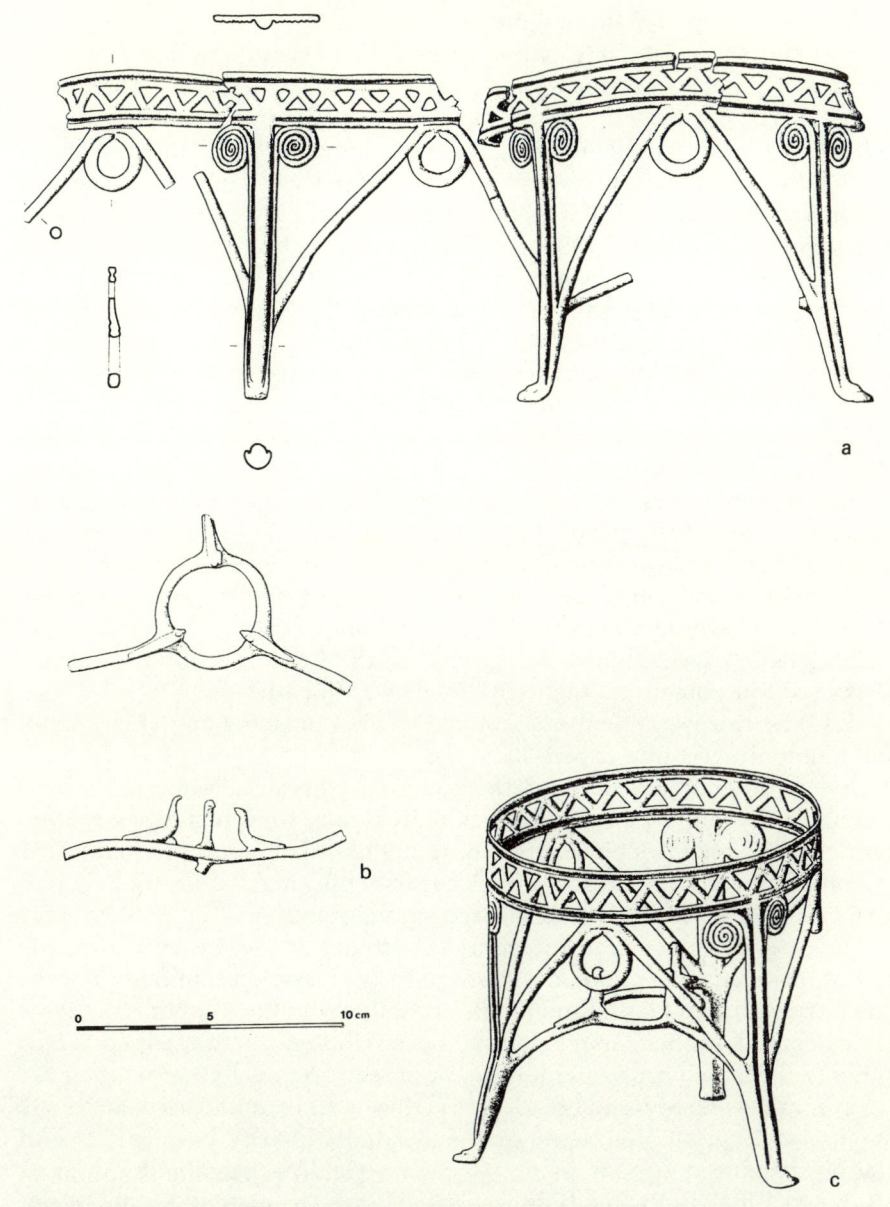

Figure 28.6 Tripod stand from Oristano, Private Collection.

temple, possess regular sets of holes with lead fillings for the insertion of votive bronzes, of which a number of fragments survive. The chronology of the monuments obviously cannot be defined after a preliminary campaign; the archaeological remains range, so far, from the Italian Late Bronze Age (12th-10th century) to the Early Iron Age (9th-8th century), but there are also indications of an earlier period.

The three tripod-stand fragments consist of:

I—a short piece of a ring, with an upper and lower double-bar connected by diagonal supports which form a zig-zag pattern (4.4; h.3.7; th.0.4 cm) (Fig 28.5a); its pattern and dimensions are almost identical with the Oristano tripod-stand (Fig 28.6), closely compared by Ellen Macnamara with two unprovenanced examples, one in Florence and one in Nicosia, and with many Group A Rod Tripods of both II and III types (Lo Schiavo, Macnamara & Vagnetti 1985, 36–40). The Samugheo ring looks comparable too, but since it only survives in a bad drawing, we do not know if it had single or double upper and lower bars (Lo Schiavo, Macnamara & Vagnetti 1985, 42 n 3, Fig 14.3).

II—The second fragment is again a piece of a ring, smooth on the inner side and divided on the outer face into seven well defined bars, among which the upper, central and lower bars are undecorated, while the second-third and fifth-sixth bars form two pairs, each decorated with opposed diagonal lines to form a very debased cable or herring-bone pattern; from the lower bar is set a pendant loop with the outer struts rising from each side of it (4; h.4.3; th.0.3 cm) (Fig 28.5c).

The shape and dimensions are again strikingly similar to the Oristano tripod-stand, while the pattern is closely comparable to the Piediluco—'Contigliano' fragments, and in general to the Episkopi tripod-stand (Lo Schiavo, Macnamara & Vagnetti 1985, 40–2, Fig 14.4–5).

III The third fragment is a volute (1.7; h.1.0; th.0.3 cm) (Fig 28.5b), undoubtedly part of a tripod-stand leg.

A few other fragments must be mentioned because, while not clearly referable to other tripod-stands, they show similar workmanship: a double-cable with pendant loop (3.3; h.2.6; th.0.3 cm) that can be related to the second fragment (Fig 28.5d), a thick bar with diagonal incision (2.2; h.1; th 0.6 cm) (Fig 28.5f), and a square-section volute (2; h.1.7; th.0.3 cm) (Fig 28.5e), clearly demonstrate metallurgical activity on the site. It is obviously likely that many more objects will be found as excavation continues. For the time being, two explanations are equally possible: either the three fragments described above should be attributed to two tripod-stands imported from Cyprus—used, re-used, broken and finally ending their life in a temple workshop and hoard; or else they were manufactured on the site by actual Cypriot bronze-workers. Indeed, we already have evidence of locally produced tripods in the Cypriot style (Macnamara, Ridgway & Ridgway 1984). Both possibilities speak volumes for a strong direct Cypriot presence and influence in Sardinia.[4]

The presence of two tripod-stands in one native sanctuary sheds new light not only on the relationship between the Cypriot bronzesmiths and sailors and the Nuragic people, but also on the structure of Nuragic society in the 12th century: two of the most characteristic prestige objects of the East Mediterranean island were brought and reproduced—as far as we can see in the present state of knowledge—not for a single chief but, directly or indirectly, for a votive destination. The same is true, a couple of centuries later, of the bronze figurines of Olmedo and of S. Cristina di Paulilatino, both found in a nuragic sacred well (Lo Schiavo, Macnamara & Vagnetti 1985, 55–6, Fig 16.2; 59–60). The fragments of these two tripod-stands double the number of this category in Sardinia, where the Oristano tripod-stand and the Samugheo ring have already been recognized. Adding to these also the Piediluco—'Contigliano' fragments on the Italian mainland, now widely accepted as coming from Cyprus, most probably via Sardinia,[5] the presence of specialised and highly refined prestige goods in the West combines with the local imitations to become impressive.

A few more words about the site. Though inland, it can be reached from the sea; the Tortolì Marsh and the harbour at Arbatax are about 30km due east. In the same district of Villagrande Strisàili, as already mentioned, twelve ox-hide ingot fragments have been found at Corte Acca (or Corte Macceddos) and two ox-hide ingots and two tripod-stand fragments at S'Arcu 'e is Forras. Other ox-hide ingot fragments have been found in the past at Perda 'e Floris, Lanusei district, about 15 km to the south-east (Lo Schiavo & Vagnetti 1980, 382 n 7), and in recent times at Bau Nuraxi, Triei district, about the same distance to the north-east (Lo Schiavo, Macnamara & Vagnetti 1985, 64 B). If these objects can be considered as imports, their point of entry into Sardinia could well be located between the Ogliastra islands and Bellavista Cape.[6]

CONCLUSIONS (L. VAGNETTI, F. LO SCHIAVO)

In summing up this paper, we would first like to stress that the two main categories of evidence examined—pottery and metalwork—also fall into two quite distinct chronological groups.

The few pottery imports are earlier. Some of them could go back to the 14th century BC, and in no case do they seem later than the 13th century BC.

The chronological setting of the bronze imports is more elusive, since —at least in Sardinia—they often come from long-lived contexts or are stray finds. However, with the exception of the ox-hide ingots, known in the Aegean and in Cyprus in earlier contexts, the majority of the metal imports and imitations found in Sardinia repeat types that are not earlier than the late 13th and the 12th century BC.

The pottery evidence, limited and scattered as it is, is perhaps not enough to suggest an independent Cypriot component in the more general framework of Aegean (especially Mycenaean) trade with the West; the only possible exception is the *pithos* from Antigori. It should also be borne in mind that recent discoveries at Tiryns have considerably enlarged the picture of Cypriot material arriving in the Argolid in the 13th-12th centuries BC (Kilian 1988 and forthcoming). The metallurgical evidence, however, speaks almost entirely in favour of a connection with Cyprus and, more specifically, between Cyprus and Sardinia.

The Kaş shipwreck, with the seven provenances recognized by Bass in the cargo's composition, to which one more could now be added, does not offer a definite answer to the identity of the carriers, although the presence on board of a great deal of Cypriot material cannot be overlooked. The imported pottery found at Antigori, though consisting of minute sherds, enables us to reconstruct a picture that in great part matches the pottery types found at Kaş, namely Mycenaean fine table ware, Mycenaean coarse containers, Cypriot-type pottery, *pithoi,* necklace beads (Bass 1986; 1987; Pulak 1988). The ivory head from Decimoputzu (Ferrarese Ceruti, Vagnetti & Lo Schiavo 1987) and the cylinder seal from San Sperate (Ugas 1987) accord well with this picture, showing that the kind of trade in which the Kaş find was involved could reach the Far West at least occasionally.

We must return to the question formulated for the original title of the second part of this paper, i.e. 'What were the Cypriots looking for in the West?' The answer depends in great part on a more complete knowledge of the nature of the ox-hide ingots; this will hopefully be obtained soon, when all the results of the archaeometric research are made available. If the ingots are imported from Cyprus, as suggested by a preliminary and partial set of lead isotope analyses recently published by the Gales (Gale & Stos-Gale 1987), one should find a satisfactory explanation for the import of copper to Sardinia—an island rich in copper ore, that developed a local metallurgy since the Chalcolithic period (Lo Schiavo 1986). Other commodities that Sardinia could have supplied directly or indirectly to the Eastern Mediterranean sea-farers are of course tin, as has already been suggested, and possibly iron (Muhly 1985; Ferrarese Ceruti, Vagnetti & Lo Schiavo 1987).

The search for strategic raw materials as a matter pertaining to the sphere of 'trade' seems especially valid for the 13th century BC. The later evidence for metallurgical connections, especially in the domain of prestige objects like tripod-stands, could be better explained in the framework of the troubled years that saw destruction and turbulence in the Aegean and the Near East.

> 'Were there any workshops, anywhere. . . that recovered the technical skills required to make Cypriot stands in order to supply a demand for new patrons who admired the originals and wanted copies made as faithfully as possible?
> Could artist/craftsmen survivors from the destruction of the Cypriot workshops have escaped to other areas to found new shops which continued to work in the old idioms for several generations longer? Of the two possibilities, the latter is perhaps more likely.' Catling 1984, 90).

Two years later, commenting on Vagnetti's paper at the Nicosia conference, Catling added that he

> 'visualized them [i.e. his 'hypothetical tripod workshop people'] as being extinguished but perhaps, in fact, they were not extinguished and they travelled for safety, not just west to the Aegean, but further

west still to Sardinia . . . Perhaps . . . the lineal descendants of the Enkomi workshops carried on their work in Sardinia.' (Catling 1986, 215).[7]

The hypothesis of some Cypriot bronze-workers reaching Sardinia as early as the 12th or beginning of the 11th century is not only likely; it is also the only suggestion that can explain such a large production of close imitations as well as freely inspired craftsmanship.

It needs to be stressed that we are not suggesting a migration or a colonization (and even less a 'precolonizing') pattern, but a restricted movement, mostly of craftsmen, towards a land already well known through traders' tales because of its abundance of metal ores. We persist in the belief that, in one way or another, there was a fund of knowledge common to Aegean and Mediterranean seafarers or, at least, to those who had travelled as far as Sicily and the Lipari islands.

Regarding Sardinia, which in the 8th-7th centuries is affected by a real and powerful colonizing phenomenon, the Late Bronze Age Cypriot elements do not admit more than one interpretation: none of them can be referred to the Phoenicians; all of them come from local nuragic settlements, mostly inland, without any association with Phoenician material; each bears a distinctive character connecting it, directly or indirectly, with Late Bronze Age Cyprus. Apparently, this is also what happened in the Aegean, on Crete, where a few workshops carried on Cypriot traditions in the Early Iron Age (Matthäus 1987, 1988).

As to the chronology, there are still strong reasons to believe in an early contact, supported by the presence of 14th and 13th century Aegean and Cypriot pottery imports, followed by later local evolution; it would otherwise be impossible to explain so many 12th century elements strikingly similar to the Cypriot originals.

APPENDIX

Villagrande Strisàili (Nuoro)—'megaron' temple at S'Arcu 'e is Forras

M. Ausilia Fadda
Soprintendenza archeologica per le province di Sassari e Nuoro

Following damage by unidentified clandestine operators, the Sassari Archaeological Superintendency conducted an excavation in the S'Arcu 'e is Forras locality, commune of Villagrande Strisàili (province of Nuoro, Sardinia). The ancient settlement there is situated on a hill near the Correboi pass, below the peak of Allue in Fogu (1300 m above sea level). The hill is flanked by tributaries of the Flumendosa to the west (Bacu Alleri) and to the east (Iscra Abbatrula).

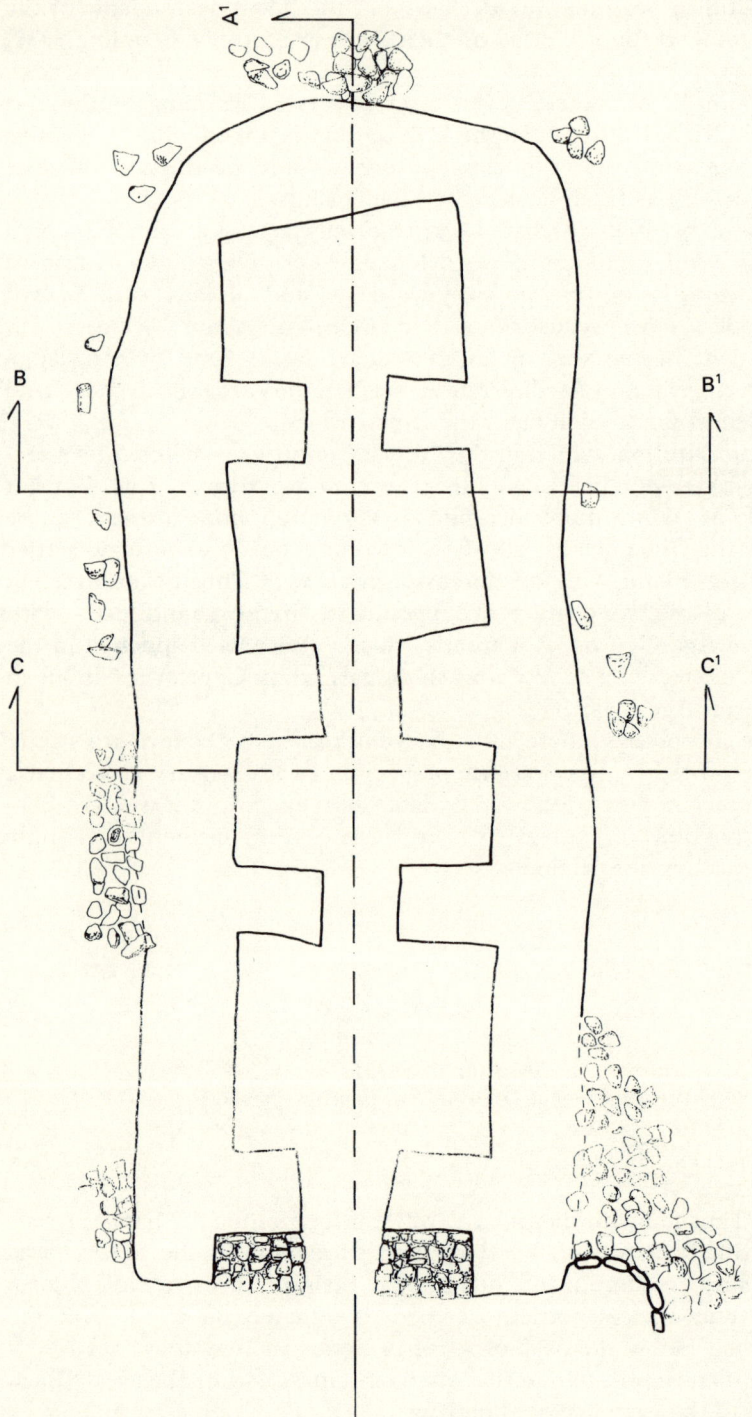

Figure 28.7 Plan of S'Arcu 'e is Forras, Villagrande Strisàili (Nuoro), 'megaron' temple.

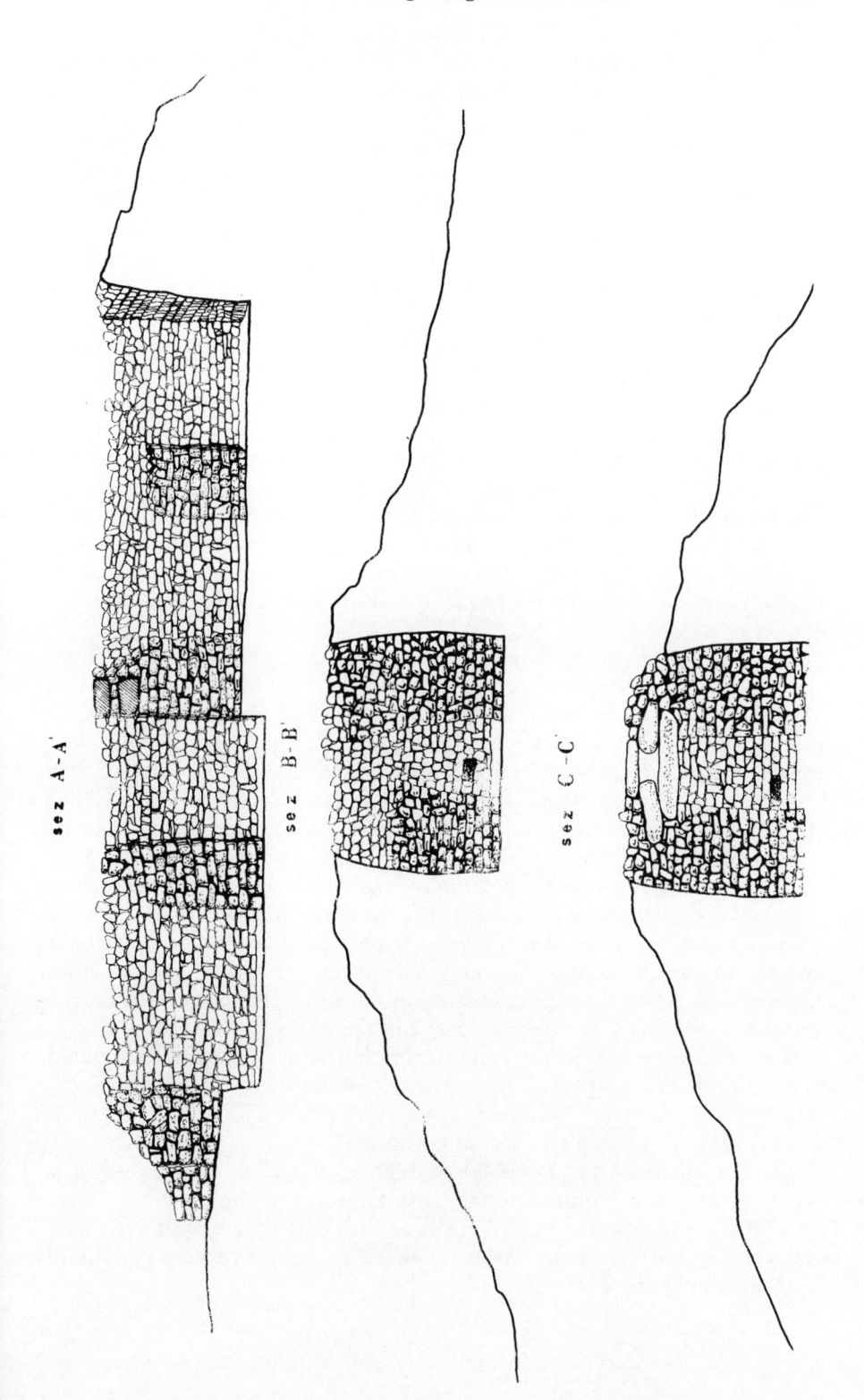

Figure 28.8 Sections through S'Arcu 'e is Forras, Villagrande Strisaili (Nuoro), 'megaron' temple.

The impressive site, of the Nuragic period, includes a complex nuraghe, trilobate in plan, built of medium sized stones, roughly worked and arranged in irregular courses. The remains of several huts, facing east, are visible halfway down the hill. At the top of the hill, the remains of a *'megaron'* temple[8] have been discovered, with massive walls of roughly worked stones (degraded granite; schist) of various sizes arranged in courses. The temple is rectangular, with an apse at one end. Its total external length is 17 m; the variations in the width of the structure, from a minimum of 5.5 m at the apsidal end to a maximum of 6.5 m elsewhere, are caused by the considerable irregularity in the thickness of the outer walls (minimum 1.10 m—maximum 1.50 m).

The groundplan is complex (Fig 28.7). Seven courses of squared stone facing are preserved at the front, composed of medium sized polygonal blocks more carefully worked at the sides of the entrance passage to the first of four rooms (A: 3.10 × 3.60 m). Here, a small open jar was found in the south corner; its concave base had been sunk into a thick floor of beaten clay with traces of burning. A fragment of a votive sword and part of an askoid jug with incised geometric decoration were found nearby. A short passage leads to room B (3.70 × 1.80/1.65 m), the smallest in the temple, which produced a few small sherds of much abraded impasto. Another fragment of a votive sword and a few bronze scraps were found in the passage to room C.

The entrance to room C is still covered by an architrave with a small relieving window above it (Fig 28.8, section C-C^1). The walls of this room (2.30/2.50 × 3.50 m) have a marked inner slope towards the roof. A number of schist slabs and other flat stones, clearly from the roof, were found in the earth that had been disturbed by the *clandestini*. Room C also yielded numerous sandstone slabs, some merely shaped and smoothed at the edges and others with round perforations. Among them was a massive T-shaped sandstone block with a large mastoid protuberance on the plain surface. Other sandstone blocks from the same room have a flat rectangular base and a number of holes in the upper part, which is narrower, disposed either in straight lines or in no precise pattern; some of the holes still contain traces of the lead blobs that once held votive bronzes in place. Other finds from room C: a broken sandstone basin, square in shape, with a small circular depression in the middle and carefully smoothed surfaces; numerous pottery fragments, mainly of globular vases and small carinated cups; and finally, among the fallen débris, pieces of sheet bronze, small fragments of pins, and the remains of casting jets left on bronze figurines as pins to fix them into position in cult places.

The fourth room, D (2.60/2.00 × 3.40 m; Fig 28.8, section B-B^1), is reached through an entrance passage that is ogival in section. Set well above ground in the back wall is a small niche, aligned with the axis of the passages that connect the four rooms A-D. Inside room D lay an enormous slab of granite, thin at one end.

Outside the building, a wall joined to the north side of the façade encloses a small semicircular area within which lay a stone parallelepiped (57 × 24 × 20 cm); of the six large holes on its upper face, one still contained the base of a votive sword.

The investigation of the temple has revealed two distinct phases in its construction. The long walls originally projected beyond the entrance; the angles thus formed were subsequently blocked with masonry to make a uniform façade. The temple is situated within a *temenos,* the edge of which runs parallel to that of the building. Abundant evidence of foundry activity associated with the temple was retrieved in its immediate vicinity. Many fragments of ingots, both of Aegean type and buns, were found in the nuraghe and in the huts, as were three flanged axes, a leech fibula, fragments of bronze figurines, one *bronzetto* of Orientalizing type (a crouching lion), along with fragments of lead and slag—some of them in a sheet bronze cauldron (rim diameter 40 cm), repaired in antiquity; and its round lid (diameter 47 cm) with two perforations, made of lead and weighing 11.7 kg.

The circumstances of this discovery have not as yet permitted the retrieval of the complete stratigraphy, since investigation was limited to the removal of the material disturbed by the *clandestini* and to selected soundings in the undisturbed areas. The pottery and bronzes so far found suggest a chronology for the monument in the Recent-Final Bronze Age range: *ca* 1300–900 BC.

NOTES

[1] A very recent discovery (November 1987), relevant to this discussion, has been presented by Dr Giuseppe Voza, Archaeological Superintendent of Eastern Sicily, at the International Conference of Sicilian Studies (Palermo, April 1988). In a tomb group found in the centre of Syracuse and on partial display in the new Archaeological Museum there, a *Base Ring* jug was found together with a LH IIIA2 angular alabastron and local pottery. A 'cylinder seal' is also reported from the same tomb. It is hoped that this exciting find will soon be published.

[2] A few lentoid Aegean seals allegedly found in Italy are known in the archaeological bibliography. Unfortunately, none of them comes from a known archaeological context (*TMM* 63–4).

[3] Attention was drawn to this class of object in 1980 (Lo Schiavo & Vagnetti 1980); a full catalogue was given of all the finds then known in Sardinia, together with a critical evaluation of the archaeological context and an up-to-date bibliography. A second enlarged edition of the 1980 catalogue is now in the press (Lo Schiavo, forthcoming). During the last seven years, ox-hide ingots have invariably been mentioned as an increasingly important category of evidence, thanks to new discoveries and to more precise news about the old discoveries (Lo Schiavo 1983; 1985a, b; 1986; Lo Schiavo, Macnamara & Vagnetti 1985). A major project was planned during the Naples Symposium on Archaeometry in April 1983: its aim is the rigorous analysis from all possible aspects of the copper ox-hide ingots of Sardinia, thus uniting the work of the Robert Maddin-Jim Muhly-Tamara Stech Wheeler team, which had already dealt extensively with Cypriot copper ox-

hide ingots and their trade in the Mediterranean (Muhly 1973; 1977; 1979; 1980; more recently 1985; 1986; Maddin & Muhly 1974; Muhly, Maddin & Wheeler 1977; 1980; Stech Wheeler, Maddin & Muhly 1975; Stech Wheeler, Muhly & Maddin 1979), with the thorough geological and archaeological survey by the Archaeological Superintendency in Sassari, and with the new and intriguing method of lead isotope analysis pioneered by Nöel Gale and Zofia Stos-Gale, already tried in the Cyclades and in the Laurion mines (Gale 1978; Gale and Stos-Gale 1981, 1982; more recently 1985; 1986). Later, John Merkel was added specifically for the elemental analyses (see Merkel 1986). This major work has developed widely, and now includes hundreds of analyses and the comparison of ox-hide ingots with other copper ingots (plano-convex or 'buns') and with nuragic artefacts, generally from hoards; it is scheduled for completion within the year 1988.

In spite of a few short preliminary overviews (Lo Schiavo, Maddin, Muhly & Stech 1985; Lo Schiavo, Stech, Maddin & Muhly 1987; Stech forthcoming) and some wider anticipations based on the lead isotope analyses (Gale & Stos-Gale 1987; 1988, forthcoming), the main problems are still open. Any tentative solution raises crucial new questions that cannot be left without a reasonable answer. If, for example, *all* the ox-hide ingots are accepted as imports, what can be said about their wide—indeed ubiquitous—distribution in Sardinia? The hypothesis that they were all carried to and round the island on one ship cannot be accepted. What is the rationale behind the distribution pattern? What is the date of the imported specimens, and of the circulation and use of the fragments? The sheer magnitude of questions like these makes it at least imprudent and at worst dangerous to draw conclusions before the reseach is finished and fully published; and the temptation should be avoided at all costs. For further bibliography on the ox-hide ingots see Lo Schiavo, Macnamara & Vagnetti 1985.

[4] It has been observed that these fragments could not originally have been part of a four-sided bronze stand. The open-work fragment no 1 should have belonged to the upper ring (see Episkopi ?-London 1920/12–2/I; Catling 1964, Pl 34), and the cable pattern fragment no 2 to the lower part of the stand (see Larnaca ?-Berlin 8947; Catling 1964 Pl 36a) where there are sometimes pendent loops. But besides the fact that a precise comparison is lacking, the tiny dimensions and the reduced section of the pieces do not correspond to the stout construction of a four-wheeled stand.

[5] A lively discussion has arisen about the Piediluco—'Contigliano' Cypriot tripod-stand: it is strongly asserted that the three groups of bronzes (Piediluco, 'Contigliano' and 'Terni') are three different hoards, because of the circumstances of the discoveries and also because of the different patinas, but everybody agrees about the possibility of the Cypriot tripod-stand being only one. Local scholars have tried to show that its provenance in Umbria is independent of Sardinia and as early as the late 13th-12th century. Renato Peroni accepts our suggestion (Lo Schiavo, Macnamara & Vagnetti 1985, 40–2) that the hoards were buried at the beginning of the 9th century; but it is likely that the tripod-stand fragments got mixed in the hoard as scrap metal, from a land—namely Sardinia—where they were formerly assembled, possibly in their original condition (Carancini, Massetti & Posi 1986, 83; Filippi 1986, 212 n 40; Pacciarelli 1986, 273, 282 n 23; Peroni 1986, 394, 420–1).

With reference to other possible examples of Cypriot bronze tripod-stands in the West, it may be recalled that 'two bronze fragments found just outside room A [of the *anaktoron*] at Pantalica could possibly have belonged to a tripod, perhaps akin to Cypriot types' (Bergonzi 1985, 361). While it is tempting to see some significance in the association of metallurgical activity with a monumental structure at both Pantalica (the *anaktoron*) in Sicily and at S'Arcu 'e is Forras (the *megaron*) in Sardinia, the considerable differences in the architecture and perhaps also in the function of the two buildings should not be forgotten.

[6] The site of 'Sulsi' was located in the area of the Tortoli Marsh, according to the *Antonine Itinerary* (Cecchini 1969, 109; Barreca 1967, 119–21; 1985, 82 n 62).

[7] In our work in the Rome School's Papers in 1985, we reached the same conclusions before knowing Dr Catling's views; it had been impossible for us to see his 1984 text before our publication. Likewise, Dr Catling expressed his views before he knew about the Sardinian material: such mutual support is very encouraging.

[8] In Sardinia, the term '*a megaron*' was first applied to the two small temples at Serra Orrios near Dorgali (prov. Nuoro) and later extended to all nuragic buildings with a rectangular ground plan. This is a most unusual feature in the nuragic world, where the majority of buildings, whether simple or complex, are round. About a dozen '*megara*' have so far been identified in the island (Santoni 1985, 197).

ACKNOWLEDGMENTS

We wish to express our gratitude to George Bass and Cemal Pulak, who kindly provided us with a drawing of the dagger from Kaş and allowed us to publish it here. We are also most grateful to Ellen Macnamara and to Maria Luisa Ferrarese Ceruti for their friendly support; to G. Dore, A. Fresi, A. Farina and G. Tendas for their excellent drawings; and to David Ridgway for his encouragement and practical help in the presentation of this paper and for his translation of the Appendix. Sources of illustrations: Soprintendenza Archeologica per le provincie di Sassari e Nuoro: A. Fresi (Fig 28.1a, b); A. Farina (Figs 28.3a, d, e; 28.4; 28.5); G. Dore (Fig 28.6); F. Tendas (Figs 28.7–8); Fig 28.1c: from Schnapp Gourbeillon 1986, Fig 7.2; Fig 28.2a: Netia Piercy, kindly provided by George Bass and Cemal Pulak (Pulak 1988, Fig 22); Fig 28.2b: Bianco Peroni 1970, Pl 6.41; Fig 28.2c: Orsi, *BPI 29* (1903) Pl 10.5; Fig 28.3b-c: Ugas & Usai 1987, Pl IV.2–3.

LIST OF ADDITIONAL ABBREVIATIONS

PGP French, E., Wardle, K. eds (1988) *Problems in Greek Prehistory. Papers presented at the Centenary Conference of the British School of Archaeology at Athens, Manchester April 1986*. Bristol.

QP I Carancini, G.L. ed. (1986) *Gli Insediamenti perilacustri dell 'Età del Bronzo e della Prima Età del Ferro: Il caso dell'antico Lacus Velinus*, Atti dell' Incontro di Acquasparta 1985, Quaderni di Protostoria I, Perugia.

SSA II Balmuth, M.S. ed (1986) *Sardinia in the Mediterranean, Studies in Sardinian Archaeology II*. Ann Arbor.

SSA III Balmuth, M.S. ed (1987) *Nuragic Sardinia and the Mycenaean World, Studies in Sardinian Archaeology III (BAR Int Ser 387)*. Oxford.

TMM Marazzi, M., Tusa, S. & Vagnetti, L. eds (1986) *Traffici micenei nel Mediterraneo. Problemi storici e documentazione archeologica, Atti del Convegno di Palermo, maggio e dicembre 1984*. Taranto.

LIST OF REFERENCES

Anson, D. (1980) The Rude Style Late Cypriot IIC-III pottery: an analytical typology. *Op Ath 13*, 1–18.
Åström, P. *et al* (1986) Iron artefacts from the Swedish excavations in Cyprus. *Op Ath 16*, 27–41.
Barreca, F. (1967) L'esplorazione topografica lungo la costa orientale della Sardegna. *Monte Sirai IV*, 103–26.
Barreca, F. (1985) L'archeologia fenicio-punica in Sardegna. *Boll Arte 31–2*, 56–95.
Bass, G.F. (1967) Cape Gelidonya: a Bronze Age shipwreck. *Trans Am Phil Soc 57, 8*. Philadelphia.
Bass, G.F. (1986) A Bronze Age shipwreck at Ulu Burun (Kaş): 1984 Campaign. *AJA 90*, 269–96.
Bass, G.F. (1987) Splendors of the Bronze Age. *National Geographic Magazine 172 (6)*, 693–732.
Baurain, C. (1984) *Chypre et la Méditerranée Orientale au Bronze Récent. Synthèse Historique*. Paris.
Bergonzi, G. (1985) Southern Italy and the Aegean during the Late Bronze Age: economic strategies and specialized craft products. *Papers in Italian Archaeology IV-3 (BAR Int Ser 245)*. 355–87.
Bernabó Brea, L. & Cavalier, M. (1980) *Meligunis-Lipára* IV. Palermo.
Bianco Peroni, V. (1970) Le spade nell' Italia continentale. *PBF IV, 1*, München.
Bianco Peroni, V. (1974) Altre spade nell' Italia continentale. *PBF XX, 1*, 1–26. München.
Cadogan, G. (1972) Cypriot objects in the Bronze Age Aegean and their importance. *Praktika I Diethn Kypr Syn*, 5–13. Nicosia.
Carancini, G.L., Massetti, S. & Posi, F. (1986) Gli insediamenti perilacustri di età protostorica individuati nell'alveo dell'antico Lacus Velinus: dati e considerazioni. *QP I*, 65–91.
Catling, H.W. (1964) *Cypriot Bronzework in the Mycenaean World*. Oxford.
Catling, H.W. (1980) *Cyprus and the West, 1600–1050 BC. (Ian Sanders Memorial Lecture)*. Sheffield.
Catling, H.W. (1984) Workshop and heirlooms: prehistoric bronze stands in the East Mediterranean. *RDAC*, 69–91.
Catling, H.W. (1986) Discussion following Vagnetti 1986, 215.
Catling, H.W. & MacGillivray, A. (1983) An Early Cypriot III Vase from the Palace at Knossos. *BSA 78*, 1–8.
Cecchini, S.M. (1969) *I ritrovamenti Fenici e Punici in Sardegna*. Rome.
Cipolloni Sampò, M. (1986) La tomba tre dell'Acropoli di Toppo Daguzzo (Potenza). Elementi per uno studio preliminare. *Ann A Stor Ant 8*, 1–40.
Courtois, J.C. & Lagarce, J.& E. (1986) *Enkomi et le Bronze Récent à Chypre*. Nicosia.
D'Agata, A.L. (1986) Considerazioni su alcune spade siciliane della media e tarda età del bronzo. *TMM*, 105–110.
Ferrarese Ceruti, M.L. (1986) I vani *c, p, q* del complesso nuragico di Antigori (Sarroch, Cagliari). *TMM*, 183-92.
Ferrarese Ceruti, M. L., Vagnetti, L. & Lo Schiavo, F. (1987) Minoici, Micenei e Ciprioti in Sardegna alla luce delle più recenti scoperte. *SSA III*, 7–37.
Filippi, G. (1986) La protostoria della conca velina attraverso evidenze archeologiche e tradizione mitica. *QP I*, 201–12.
Gale, N.H. (1978) Lead isotopes and Aegean metallurgy, in *Thera and the Aegean World, I*, 529–45.

Gale, N.H. & Stos-Gale, Z. (1981) Cycladic lead and silver metallurgy. *BSA* 76, 169–224.
Gale, N.H. & Stos-Gale, Z. (1982) Bronze Age copper sources in the Mediterranean: a new approach. *Science 216*, 11–19.
Gale, N.H. & Stos-Gale, Z. (1985) Lead isotopes and Alashiya. *RDAC*, 83-99.
Gale, N.H. & Stos-Gale, Z. (1986) Oxhide ingots in Crete and Cyprus and the Bronze Age metals trade. *BSA 81*, 81–100.
Gale, N.H. & Stos-Gale, Z. (1987) Oxhide ingots from Sardinia, Crete and Cyprus and the Bronze Age copper trade: new scientific evidence. *SSA III*, 135–78.
Gale, N.H. & Stos-Gale, Z. (1988) Recent evidence for a possible Bronze Age metal trade between Sardinia and the Aegean. *PGP*, 349–84.
Gale, N.H. & Stos-Gale, Z. (forthcoming) The copper ox-hide ingot trade in the Eastern Mediterranean c. 1500–1100—new scientific evidence, in *Proceedings of the Conference "Seaborne trade in metals and ingots"*. Oxford 1987.
Hägg, R. & Marinatos, N. eds (1984) *The Minoan Thalassocracy. Myth and Reality* (Athens 1982). Stockholm.
Jones, R.E. (1986) Chemical analysis of Aegean-type Late Bronze Age pottery found in Italy. *TMM*, 205–14.
Jones, R.E. & Day, P.M. (1987) Late Bronze Age Aegean and Cypriot-type pottery on Sardinia. Identification of imports and local imitations by physico-chemical analysis. *SSA III*, 257–69.
Kilian, K. (1978) Ausgrabungen in Tiryns 1976. *AA*, 449–98.
Kilian, K. (1988) Ausgrabungen in Tiryns 1982/3. *AA*, 105–51.
Kilian, K. (forthcoming) Quadro culturale della Grecia fra XVI e XIII secolo a.C., *La Sardegna nel Mediterraneo tra il Bronzo Medio e il Bronzo Recente (XVI-XIII sec. a. C)*, Conference held at Selargius-Cagliari, November 1987.
Knapp, A.B. (1986) Production, exchange and socio-political complexity on Bronze Age Cyprus. *Oxf J A 5*, 35–60.
Lo Schiavo, F. (1982) Copper metallurgy in Sardinia during the Late Bronze Age: new prospects on its Aegean connections. *EMC*, 271–82.
Lo Schiavo, F. (1983) Le componenti egea e cipriota nella metallurgia della Tarda Età del Bronzo in Italia. *Magna Grecia e Mondo Miceneo. (Atti XXII Conv. St. sulla Magna Grecia, Taranto 7–11 ott. 1982)*. 285–320.
Lo Schiavo, F. (1985a) *Nuragic Sardinia in its Mediterranean setting: recent advances*. (Univ. of Edinburgh, Dept. of Archaeology Occ. Paper No. 12).
Lo Schiavo, F. (1985b) La Sardegna nuragica e il mondo mediterraneo. *Sardegna Preistorica (exhibition catalogue)*, 255–84. Milan.
Lo Schiavo, F. (1986) Sardinian metallurgy: the archaeological background. *SSA II*, 231–50.
Lo Schiavo, F. (forthcoming) Early metallurgy in Sardinia: the copper oxhide ingots. *Int Symp on Old World Archaeometallurgy, 5th-7th Oct. 1987*. Heidelberg.
Lo Schiavo, F., Macnamara, E. & Vagnetti L. (1985) Late Cypriot imports to Italy and their influence on local bronzework. *BSR 53*, 1–71.
Lo Schiavo, F., Maddin, R., Muhly, J.D., Stech, T., (1985) Preliminary research on ancient metallurgy in Sardinia: 1984. *AJA 89*, 316–18.
Lo Schiavo, F., Stech, T., Maddin, R., Muhly, J.D. (1987) Nuragic metallurgy in Sardinia: second preliminary report. *SSA III*, 179–87.
Lo Schiavo, F. & Vagnetti, L. (1980) Micenei in Sardegna? *Rend Linc. (8th series) 25, fasc. 5–6*, 371–91.

Macnamara, E., Ridgway, D. & Ridgway, F.R. (1984) The Bronze Hoard from S. Maria in Paulis, Sardinia. *BMOP 45.* London.

Maddin, R. & Muhly, J.D. (1974) Some notes on the copper trade in the ancient Mid-East. *J of Metals,* 24–30.

Martin de la Cruz, J.C. (1987) Ceramicas micenicas en Andalucia? *R Arqueologia 8, fasc. 78,* 62–4.

Matthäus, H. (1987) Bronzene Stabdreifüsse in Cypern und Griechenland. Zur Kontinuität Ostmediterranen Metallhandwerks, in *Akten des intern. Kolloquium "Das Ende der Mykenischen Welt" (Köln 1984)* 93–121. Köln.

Matthäus, H. (1988) Heirloom or tradition—Bronze stands of the second and first millennium B.C. in Cyprus, Greece and Italy. *PGP,* 285–300.

Merkel, J.F. (1986) Ancient smelting and casting of copper for "ox-hide" ingots. *SSA II,* 251–64.

Muhly, J.D. (1973) Copper and tin—The distribution of mineral resources and the nature of the metals trade in the Bronze Age. *Trans Conn Acad Arts and Sciences 43,* 155–535.

Muhly, J.D. (1977) The copper oxhide ingots and the Bronze Age metal trade. *Iraq 39,* 73–83.

Muhly, J.D. (1979) Cypriot copper: some geological and metallurgical problems. *Acts 1979,* 87–100.

Muhly, J.D. (1980) The Bronze Age setting, in *The Coming of the Age of Iron.* (eds T.A. Wertime & J.D. Muhly) 25–67. New Haven.

Muhly, J.D. (1983) Lead isotope analysis and the Kingdom of Alashiya. *RDAC,* 210–18.

Muhly, J.D. (1985) Sources of tin and the beginnings of bronze metallurgy. *AJA 89,* 275–91.

Muhly, J.D. (1986) The rôle of Cyprus in the economy of the Eastern Mediterranean during the second millennium B.C. *Acts 1986,* 45–60.

Muhly, J.D., Maddin, R. & Wheeler, T.S. (1980) The oxhide ingots from Enkomi and Mathiati and Late Bronze Age copper smelting in Cyprus. *RDAC,* 88–99.

Muhly, J.D., Maddin, R.& Wheeler, T.S. (1977) The Cape Gelidonya shipwreck and the Bronze Age metal trade in the Eastern Mediterranean. *J Field A 4,* 353–62.

Pacciarelli, M. (1986) Considerazioni sugli insediamenti perilacustri dell' Italia Centrale. *QP I,* 269–99.

Peroni, R. (1986) Discussion. *QP I,* nos 85, 133.

Portugali, Y. & Knapp, A.B. (1985) Cyprus and the Aegean: a spatial analysis of interaction in the 17th-14th century B.C., in *Prehistoric Production and Exchange. The Aegean and Eastern Mediterranean.* (eds A.B. Knapp & T. Stech) 30–78. Los Angeles.

Pulak, C. (1988) The Bronze Age shipwreck at Ulu Burun, Turkey: 1985 Campaign. *AJA 92,* 1–37.

Sandars, N. (1961) The first Aegean swords and their ancestry. *AJA 65,* 17–29.

Santoni, V. (1985) I templi di età nuragica. *Sardegna Preistorica (exhibition catalogue),* 181–207. Milan.

Santoni, V. (1987) Le stazioni nuragiche all'aperto nell'entroterra del golfo di Cagliari. *Cultura del paesaggio e metodi del territorio.* 63–88. Cagliari.

Schaeffer, C. (1983) *Corpus des cylindres-sceaux de Ras Shamra-Ugarit et d'Enkomi-Alasia I.* Lyon.

Schnapp Gourbeillon, A. (1982) Montedoro di Eboli, *in* Vagnetti 1982, 160–63.

Schnapp Gourbeillon, A. (1986) Ceramica di tipo miceneo a Montedoro di

Eboli. *TMM*, 175–78.

Stech, T. (forthcoming) Nuragic metallurgy in Sardinia: third preliminary report. *Int Symp on Old World Archaeometallurgy*, 5th-7th Oct. 1987. Heidelberg.

Stech Wheeler, T., Muhly, J.D. & Maddin, R. (1979) Mediterranean trade in copper and tin in the Late Bronze Age. *Ann Ist It Num 26*, 139–52.

Stech Wheeler, T. Maddin, R. & Muhly, J.D. (1975) Ingots and the Bronze Age copper trade in the Mediterranean: a progress report. *Expedition 17–4*, 31–9.

Taylour, W.D. (1958) *Mycenaean Pottery in Italy and Adjacent Areas*. Cambridge.

Ugas, G. (1987) Un nuovo contributo per lo studio della tholos in Sardegna. La fortezza di Su Mulinu, Villanovafranca. *SSA III*, 77–132.

Ugas, G. & Usai, L. (1987) Nuovi scavi nel santuario nuragico di S. Anastasia di Sardara. *La Sardegna nel Mediterraneo tra il II e il I Millennio a.C. (Atti II Conv. Studi, Selargius-Cagliari, 27–30 Nov. 1986)*, 167–218.

Vagnetti, L. (1968) I bacili di bronzo di Caldare sono ciprioti? *SMEA 7*, 129–40.

Vagnetti, L. ed. (1982) *Magna Grecia e Mondo Miceneo. Nuovi Documenti (exhibition catalogue)*. Naples.

Vagnetti, L. (1985) Late Minoan III Crete and Italy: another view. *PP 220*, 29–33.

Vagnetti, L. (1986) Cypriot elements beyond the Aegean in the Bronze Age. *Acts 1986*, 202–14.

Vagnetti, L. & Jones, R.E. (1988) Towards the identification of local Mycenaean pottery in Italy. *PGP*, 335–48.

Vermeule, E. & Karageorghis, V. (1982) *Mycenaean Pictorial Vase Painting*. Cambridge, (Mass).

Voza, G. (1973) Thapsos. *Archaeologia della Sicilia Sud-orientale*. Naples.

Watrous, V.L. (1985) Late Bronze Age Kommos: imported pottery as evidence for foreign contact, *in* A great Minoan triangle in Southcentral Crete: Kommos, Haghia Triada, Phaistos. *Scripta Mediterranea 6*, 7–11.

White, D. (1986) 1985 excavations on Bates' Island, Marsa Matruch. *JARCE 22*, 51–84.

29
Cypern und Sardinien im frühen 1. Jahrtausend v.Chr.

Hartmut Matthäus
Archäologisches Institut der Universität Heidelberg

Unser Bild der kulturellen Beziehungen zwischen den beiden Kupferinseln des Altertums, zwischen Sardinien und Cypern, während des späten 2. Jahrtausends v. Chr. hat in den letzten Jahren eine ausserordentliche Bereicherung erfahren.[1] Mannigfache neue Feldforschungen und eine Aufarbeitung der älteren Museumsbestände auf Sardinien offenbaren überaus enge Verbindungen nicht nur nach Cypern, sondern darüber hinaus in den gesamten östlichen Mittelmeerraum—von der Ägäis bis an die syrisch-palästinensische Küste. Art und Charakter ostmediterraner Importe auf Sardinien lassen sich nun ebenso definieren wie lokale Nachahmungen bzw. Adaptionen und kulturelle Wechselwirkungen. Zeichnen sich die archäologischen Fakten inzwischen deutlich ab und können wir auch einen ersten Versuch der chronologischen Eingrenzung dieses Beziehungsnetzes unternehmen, so dürfte die kulturgeschichtliche Interpretation, die Frage nach Motiven und historischem Hintergrund derart auffälliger Fernkontakte die archäologische Forschung noch auf absehbare Zukunft beschäftigen. Die letzte zusammenfassende Behandlung des einschlägigen Materials, die als Grundlage für alle weiteren Überlegungen dienen muss, haben F. Lo Schiavo, E. Macnamara und L. Vagnetti gegeben (1985; vgl. auch an neuerer Literatur ferner: Lilliu 1982, 118–19; Lo Schiavo 1982, 271–82; 1983; 1985a; 1985b; Vagnetti 1986; Marazzi, Tusa & Vagnetti 1986; Ferrarese Ceruti, Vagnetti & Lo Schiavo 1987; Smith 1987).

Spätmykenische Importkeramik (Ferrarese Ceruti 1979; Lo Schiavo & Vagnetti 1980; Ferrarese Ceruti 1981; Vagnetti 1981, 165–87; Ferrarese Ceruti 1985), zu der sich auch einige Beispiele cyprischer Herkunft gesellen (Lo Schiavo, Macnamara & Vagnetti 1985, 4–9; Ferrarese Ceruti, Vagnetti & Lo Schiavo 1987) häuft sich nach den jüngsten Entdeckungen geradezu auf Sardinien. Eine noch deutlichere Sprache jedoch sprechen die Metallfunde auf der Insel: Kupferbarren ostmediterranen Typs, z.T. mit Schriftfunde auf der Insel: Kupferbarren ostmediterranen Typs, z.T. mit Schriftzeichen, die gleichfalls in den östlichen Mittelmeerraum weisen (ausser den zitierten Arbeiten von F. Lo Schiavo vgl. Buchholz 1980, 143–5, 149–50; Schriftzeichen: Lo Schiavo 1985a, 257 Figs 3–5), Werkzeuge zur Metallverarbeitung wie Holzkohleschaufeln, Schmiedezangen und Treibhämmer, aber auch andere Geräte wie Doppeläxte, kreuzschneidige Äxte und Schaufeln, welche allesamt Gegenstücke in Cypern finden, illustrieren intensivste Kontakte (dazu vgl. bes. die zitierten Arbeiten von F. Lo Schiavo).

Das Material wirft zugleich Fragen auf, die kontrovers diskutiert werden: Haben wir die Barrenfunde etwa als Anzeichen des Importes ostmediterranen Rohmaterials nach Sardinien zu deuten? Dies würde voraussetzen, dass die sardischen Erzvorkommen im späten 2. Jahrtausend v. Chr. noch nicht oder nur in geringem Umfange abgebaut worden seien. Oder besitzt nicht doch nach wie vor die alte Hypothese mehr Wahrscheinlichkeit, dass Sardinien gerade aufgrund seiner Rohmetallschätze für den östlichen Mittelmeerraum in dieser Zeit Bedeutung gewann, dass hier Kupfererz nach Techniken, die sich dort—vor allem auf Cypern—entwickelt hatten, abgebaut und verhüttet wurde, vielleicht unter Mitwirkung von Bergbauspezialisten und Metallarbeitern aus dem Osten. Die Schriftzeichen der Barren wie die Werkzeuge, welche ostmediterrane Prototypen spiegeln, erführen so eine plausible Erklärung. Der Autor kann nicht verhehlen, dass er manch neuem 'revolutionierendem' und eilfertigem Interpretationsversuch von naturwissenschaftlicher Seite, durchweg auf quantitativ geringem Material basierend, mit äusserstem Misstrauen gegenübersteht.

Ein—bislang vereinzeltes—Prunkobjekt, ein cyprischer Stabdreifuss, der, obgleich ohne genaue Provenienzangabe, doch sicher auf Sardinien zutage kam und sich jetzt in einer Privatsammlung in Oristano befindet (Lo Schiavo 1983, 309–14; Lo Schiavo, Macnamara & Vagnetti 1985, 35–51; Bisi 1986, 343–4; Lo Schiavo 1985a, 258; allgemein zum Typus: Catling 1964, 190–223; 1984, 69–91; Matthäus 1985, 299–334; 1988) bezeugt, dass die Verbindungen zum Osten über den rein technologischen Austausch, über Import oder Export von Rohmaterial hinausgingen: Derartige wertvolle Objekte gehörten mit Sicherheit zum Ausstattungsluxus wohlhabender, den sozialen Durchschnitt überragender Bevölkerungsschichten, einer Aristokratie, wenn man diesen terminus *faute de mieux* benutzen will, die sich offenbar zumindest gelegentlich mit Luxusgütern östlicher Herkunft umgab. Dass wir mit mehr als nur sporadischen Importen gerade von cyprischen Stabdreifüssen auf Sardinien zu rechnen haben, wird aus der Tatsache offenkundig, dass sardische Bronzegiesser des frühen 1. Jahrtausends v. Chr. diese Form weitertradiert haben: Funde aus S. Maria in Paulis (Macnamara, Ridgway & Ridgway 1984) und der Grotte Pirosu-Su Benatzu, Santadi (Lilliu 1973; Barreca 1981, 391, Fig 415; Lilliu 1982, 156, Fig 181; Niemeyer 1984, Taf 2.5; Ugas 1985, 223, Fig 16; Barreca 1986, 21,

Fig 6) belegen in dieser Hinsicht eigenwillige und erfolgreiche Formexperimente.

Wie entwickelten sich die sardisch-cyprischen Kulturbeziehungen während des 1. Jahrtausends v. Chr. weiter? Klar hebt sich ein östlicher Formenhorizont auf Sardinien seit dem späten 8. und 7. Jahrhundert v. Chr. ab, der mit der beginnenden phönikischen Westexpansion und der daraus resultierenden phönikischen Besiedlung der Insel einhergeht (vgl. dazu u.a. Pesce 1961; Cecchini 1969; Barreca 1981; 1985; 1986; Niemeyer 1982; 1984; Bartoloni 1983; Acquaro 1984; Ugas & Zucca 1985; Bisi 1986; 1987; Hölbl 1986; Moscati 1986; Aubet 1987). Von einigen Fundmaterialien, die mit diesem die Geschichte des westlichen Mittelmeerraumes wandelnden und neu gestaltenden Prozess verknüpft sind, soll noch die Rede sein. Wie aber sah es in der vorhergehenden Phase, d.h. dem 10., 9. und frühen 8. Jh. v. Chr. aus?

Besonders wichtige Einblicke scheinen mir die jüngsten Grabungen in Sardara—Sant'Anastasia (Prov. Cagliari) zu vermitteln, die in der Umgebung des schon von A. Taramelli entdeckten nuraghenzeitlichen *tempio a pozzo* zur Freilegung verschiedener Rundbauten führten (vorläufig: Ugas & Usai 1987), unter denen sich das Gebäude Nr. 5 ('Sala del Consiglio') durch das reiche Fundmaterial heraushob. Die Erbauung der Anlage geht anscheinend in den Beginn des 1. Jahrtausends v. Chr. zurück, ihre Auflassung erfolgte vermütlich gegen Ende des 8. Jahrhunderts v. Chr.

Der Rundbau (Dm. 5,40 m) wird durch zwei Nischen im Norden (Nische 1) und Süden (Nische 2) charakterisiert; im NW ist an die Aussenmauer eine *ca* 40 cm hohe und 60 cm breite Bank angebaut. Eine ähnliche Bank war nach der Beschreibung der Ausgräber am nordöstlichen Mauerabschnitt einst vorhanden ('Un seggio analogo è da supporsi dall'altra parte della nicchia 1'). In diesem Bereich fand sich 'scavata nel banco roccioso naturale' eine 'fossa rettangolare' (Tiefe 0.70 m, Länge 1,15 m, Breite 60 cm), die einen Bronzehort—die kleineren Bronzen lagen in einem Tongefäss—enthielt, welcher auch drei bronzene Gefässe umfasste, die Importe aus dem östlichen Mittelmeergebiet sind bzw. sardische Nachahmungen solcher Prototypen. Die Ausgräber haben die Gefässe in das späte 8. Jahrhundert v. Chr., die Zeit der Auflassung des Gebäudes, datiert.

Für den kritischen Beobachter erhebt sich schon hier die Frage, wie sich der Schacht für die Niederlegung der Bronzen relativchronologisch zu den Benutzungsphasen des Gebäudes verhält, insbesondere, falls die Annahme einer ursprünglichen Bankkonstruktion über dem Schacht bzw. anstelle des Schachtes zutreffen sollte. Wurde der Schacht tatsächlich erst gegen Ende der Benutzungsphase unter Zerstörung der Bank in diesem Mauerabschnitt angelegt oder gehörte er von Anfang an zur Baukonzeption, d.h. wurde er bei Errichtung des Rundbaus eingetieft und die u.U. darübergebaute Bank erst später entfernt oder zerstört? Diese Frage, die für die stratigraphische und damit chronologische Beurteilung des Depots von entscheidender Bedeutung ist, lässt sich leider nicht beantworten, solange keine abschliessende Publikation mit genauer Dokumentation der Schichtenverhältnisse vorliegt. Da auch die Beifunde der Gefässe—Dolche, eine bronzene Schmiedezange, Bleibarren—noch der Auswertung durch die zuständigen Spezialisten bedürfen (m. E. aber durchaus ein frühes Datum zulassen), hilft zunächst nur die Analyse der drei Bronzegefässe selbst weiter. Methodisch ist gerade bei der Untersuchung kostbarer Metallgefässe—nicht zuletzt wertvollen Importgutes—stets angebracht, zwischen Fundkontext, d.h. der Zeit der Niederlegung, und Entstehungszeit zu trennen, da derartige Gegenstände durchaus über längere Zeitperioden benutzt und vererbt werden können.

Bei dem ersten der drei, bei der Niederlegung ineinandergestapelten Gefässe (Ugas & Usai 1987, Pl X) handelt es sich um eine sehr grosse (H. 25 cm; Randdm. 37 cm) halbkugelige Schale, die über den Rand emporgeschwungene, von Lotusblüten bekrönte Henkel trägt (Ugas 1985, 224, Fig 19; Ugas 1986, Pl VII oben). Ein Mittelsteg verbindet die runden Henkelattachen, so dass die Form einer liegenden Acht ensteht; dünne Bronzestäbe verknüpfen Henkelbahn und oberen Attaschenrand. Derartige lotusgeschmückte Schalen, deren Format erheblichen Schwankungen unterliegen kann, zählen zu den beliebtesten Formen der früheisenzeitlichen cyprischen Toreutik (Matthäus 1985, 124–7). Die cyprischen Parallelen, z.B. aus Kouklia-Skales (Karageorghis 1983, Pls 89.32, 90; 115.32; 116.90; vgl. auch ebd. Pls 60.1; 88.1) oder Amathus (Matthäus 1985, Taf 20. 347–8; vgl. auch die Beispiele unbekannter Provenienz: Taf 20.350; 21.351), kommen typologisch dem Beispiel aus Sardara - Sant'Anastasia so nahe, dass man an echten Import glauben möchte. Die wenigen sicher datierten cyprischen Exemplare gehören der Periode CG I und II, d.h. den frühen 1. Jahrtausend v. Chr. (*ca* 1050–850 v.Chr.) an, obgleich Exporte solcher bronzener Schalen ausserhalb Cyperns ein längeres Nachleben des Typs möglich scheinen lassen. Bronzeschalen mit Lotushenkel erfreuten sich in Vorderen Orient, besonders auch in Griechenland, sowie vereinzelt im westlichen Mittelmeerraum (z.B. in Satricum in einem Grab des 8. Jahrhunderts v. Chr.) grosser Beliebtheit (Matthäus 1985, 126–7 mit Literatur).

Das zweite Gefäss aus Sardara - Sant'Anastasia gehört dem gleichen Typus an (Ugas 1986, Tav VII Mitte, VIIA oben), ist aber wesentlich flacher (H. *ca* 10 cm; Dm. *ca* 40 cm). Es trägt im Inneren eine eingepunzte Dekoration aus Kreisen und Dreiecken, für die es in Cypern keine Parallele gibt, so dass sich die Frage erhebt, ob dieses Stück u. U. in enger Nachahmung eines östlichen Vorbildes in Sardinien selbst entstand oder ob vielleicht nur ein einheimischer Handwerker einem importierten Gefäss zusätzlich Punzdekor hinzugefügt hat—es lässt sich allerdings nicht leugnen, dass auch auf Sardinien sich kaum gute Entsprechungen zu dieser Art des Ornamentes nachweisen lassen.

Die beiden gut erhaltenen Schale helfen, einige Fragmente besser einzuordnen, die teilweise schon früher als Zeugnisse cyprisch-sardischer

Beziehungen angesprochen wurden. F. Lo Schiavo hat bereits auf eine verwandte, leider fragmentierte achtförmige Henkelattasche aus der Siedlung von Serra Orrios (Prov. Nuoro) hingewiesen, die einem ähnlichen Typus angehört (Lo Schiavo 1980, 147, Tav 41.6; Lo Schiavo, Macnamara & Vagnetti 1985, 33, no 4, Fig 13.9–10).

Noch weiter führen zwei bislang in unserem Zusammenhang nur wenig beachtete Gefässhenkel aus dem umfangreichen Bronzedepot von Monte Sa Idda (Taramelli 1921; 1984, 371–424), einem Hort, der vielfach pauschal in das 8. Jahrhundert v. Chr. datiert wird, obgleich sich zeigen lässt, dass wenigstens ein Teil der Bronzen mit einiger Sicherheit an den Beginn des 1. Jahrhunderts v. Chr. zurückweist (Lo Schiavo 1985a, 261–4). Die Henkel (Taramelli 1921, 62–3, Figs 88–9; Lilliu 1966, 466–7, no 358; Lo Schiavo 1981a, 326, Figs 368–9; Taramelli 1984, 401–2, Figs 88–9) spiegeln die gleiche Grundform cyprischer Herkunft—achtförmige Attasche, hochgeschwungener Henkel ohne Lotusbekrönung, jedoch in einem Fall sogar mit der typischen Schrägstrebe zwischen Henkelbahn und oberem Attaschenrand,—während ihr teils gravierter, teils reliefierter, teils rundplastischer Dekor (Fischgräten, Spiralverzierung, Vogelfigürchen) einheimischen Stil verrät. Sie repräsentieren also sardische Nachahmungen cyprischer Vorbilder. Diese Beispiele dürften belegen, dass wir auf Sardinien doch wohl mit einem quantitativ umfangreicheren Import cyprischen Formengutes zu rechnen haben, als das bis jetzt eher spärliche Fundgut erkennen lässt, denn gerade lokale Nachahmungen setzen aller Wahrscheinlichkeit nach mehr als nur sporadischen Austausch voraus.[2] Zugleich deuten die Lotusschalen aus Sardara wie die Henkel vom Monte Sa Idda auf Kulturbeziehungen schon im frühen 1. Jahrtausend v. Chr., d.h. vor Beginn der phönikischen Kolonisation Sardiniens.

Diese letzere Annahme scheint das dritte Gefäss aus Sardara-Sant'Anastasia (Ugas 1986, Tav VII A unten; Ugas & Usai 1987, Tav X b) durchaus zu stützen. Es ist eine flache rundbodige Situla (H. *ca* 14 cm, Dm. *ca* 36 cm), auf deren Rand kleeblattförmige spiralverzierte Attaschen sitzen, deren über die Gefässmündung emporragende, parallel zum Gefässrand gestellte Ösen zum Einhängen eines beweglichen Bügelhenkels dienten. Umfangreiche Reparaturen (genietete Flickbleche) im Gefässboden deuten auf längere Benutzung. Dies ist von Interesse, da die nächsten typologischen Entsprechungen und offenkundigen Vorbilder spätbronzezeitliche Situlen (d.h. des späten 2. Jahrtausends v. Chr.) aus Ras Shamra-Ugarit (vor 1200 v. Chr; Matthäus 1982, 192–3, Abb 6; 1985, 225, Taf 131.3), Enkomi und Kouklia (beide wohl 13. oder 12. Jahrhundert v. Chr.; Matthäus 1985, 222–5) sind, wie Gefässform, Attaschentyp und -dekor sowie auch die Henkelkonstruktion deutlich machen. In Sardinien ist dieses Gefäss, sollte es ein Importstück sein, über längere Zeit verwendet worden; sollte sich um eine einheimische Nachahmung handeln, wurde die Form weitertradiert. Die wenigen Parallelen im östlichen Mittelmeerraum lassen in diesem Punkt keine endgültige Entscheidung zu. In jedem Falle scheint der Befund auf einen Kontakt zu deuten, der zeitlich vor der phönikischen Kolonisation Sardiniens lag.

Auch diese Situla steht auf der Insel Sardinien nicht isoliert, wie zwar nicht verwandte Gefässformen, wohl aber zwei Varianten spiralverzierter Henkelattaschen belegen: zum einen begegnet an flachen Becken eine kleeblattförmige Abart mit einer Henkelöse, welche im Gegensatz zu jener der Situla von Sardara im rechten Winkel zur Attasche vorspringt. Ein Becken dieser Gattung kommt aus der Grotta Su Benticheddu, Oliena (Prov. Nuoro); ein Attaschenfragment fand sich in der Siedlung von Sa Sedda e Sos Carros, Oliena (Prov. Nuoro). Eine Parallele im Hort von S. Francesco, Bologna ergibt das 8. Jahrhundert v. Chr. als *terminus ante quem* (Lo Schiavo 1976, 71, 78, no 464, Pls 20.464, 21.464; 1978a, 90, no 1 Pl 28.2; 1981a, 325, Figs 364, 366; 1981b, Pl 61 d, e; 1985a, 258, Figs 28–9, 32; Lo Schiavo, Macnamara & Vagnetti 1985, 33–5). Eine unmittelbare Vorform in Megiddo wurde von den Ausgräbern der Schicht VII, d.h., auch wenn man die schwankende absolute Datierung der Schichten diese Platzes berücksichtigt, sicher der Zeit noch vor 1000 v. Chr. zugewiesen (Loud 1948, Pl 188.10). Dieses Fragment kommt den sardischen Denkmälern noch näher als die Attaschen der zitierten Situlen aus Ugarit und Cypern und mag zugleich andeuten, dass im östlichen Mittelmeerraum im späten 2. Jahrtausend v. Chr. Metallarbeitern mit verschiedenartigen Formen solcher spiralverzierten Kleeblattattaschen experimentierten.

Daneben begegnen in Sardinien (Cala Gonone, Dorgali) wie in Bologna, San Francesco an Kesseln Henkelattaschen, die aus waagerecht gereihten Spiralschnecken zusammengesetzt sind. Hierfür wiesen bereits F. Lo Schiavo, E. Macnamara und L. Vagnetti (1985, 33–5; vgl. ferner Guido 1963, Pl 58; Lo Schiavo 1985a, 258, Figs 30–1) Parallelen aus Hama (frühes 1. Jahrtausend v. Chr.; Fugmann 1958, 212, Fig 268. 6C84) und Byblos (undatiert; Dunand 1954, 353, no 10290, Fig 387) nach.

Die Besonderheit und Eigenart des hier diskutierten Formenhorizontes wird noch deutlicher, stellt man ihm andere, seit langem in ihrem östlichen Ursprung erkannte Denkmälergruppen gegenüber, die sich sowohl zeitlich wie auch von ihrer Verbreitung her deutlich abheben. Gemeint sind solche Formen, die um 700 v. Chr. im Zuge der phönikischen Expansion auf Sardinien erscheinen, wobei auch hier cyprische Werkstätten keine unbeträchtliche Rolle spielten—das phönikische Element auf Cypern war in dieser Phase ja durchaus kulturbestimmend.

An den Beginn sei eine nur schlecht erhaltene halbkugelige Bronzeschale aus dem Nuraghen Su Igante, Uri (Prov. Sassari) gestellt (Contu 1962, 298; Nicosia *in* Colonna 1978, 592, Pl 98.c, d; Nicosia 1980, 208, Nrs 37–8; 1981, 443, Fig 471). Sie trägt auf dem Rand zwei silberne Attaschen mit reliefierten Palmetten, welche aus antithetischen nach aussen gerichteten Voluten hervorwachsen, an die ein schon antik in Höhe der Gefässmündung sehr grob abgeschnittener senkrechter Henkel ansetzte.

Material (Silber auf einem bronzenen Gefäss!) und Form des Palmetten-

Voluten-Dekors entsprechen sehr genau den Henkelabschlüssen der wohlbekannten sog. phönikischen Metallkannen der orientalisierenden Periode (Grau-Zimmermann 1978; Matthäus 1985, 238-44): Ihre Verbreitung reicht von Cypern im Osten über Mittel- und Unteritalien bis in die von der phönikischen Kolonisation berührte Zone der Iberischen Halbinsel. Zeitlich konzentrieren sie sich auf das 7. Jahrhundert v. Chr.; Vorläufer im 8. Jahrhundert sind wahrscheinlich, das gleiche gilt für ein Nachleben in das 6. Jahrhundert.

Das merkwürdige Fundstück aus Su Igante, Uri, das anzeigt, dass Sardinien in diesen Importstrom aus dem Osten einbezogen war, lässt sich als Schöpfung eines einheimischen Metallarbeiters erklären, der zwei silberne Henkelattaschen von vermutlich unbrauchbar gewordenen phönikischen Kannen sekundär als Schmuck auf einer Bronzeschale andrachte—ein recht barbarisches Pasticcio.

Dass gerade Kannen mit Palmettenattaschen oder verwandte Produkte cypro-phönikischer Toreutik auch sonst in Sardinien im 7. Jahrhundert v. Chr. geschätzt wurden, lässt sich im übrigen auch an einem bronzenen Askos aus Buddusò (Prov. Sassari) ablesen (Nicosia 1980, 205, Abb 135a, b; *in* Colonna 1978, 587-8, Pl 98 a, b; 1981, 494, Fig 473; Lilliu 1982, 142, Fig 157; Ugas 1986, 41-2, Tav 2.2): Den Bandhenkel dieses Gefässes einheimischer Form—es gibt Parallelen aus Ton (Lilliu 1982, 145, Fig 160; Ugas 1986, 41-2, Tav 2.1)—ziert die Nachahmung eines gleichartigen Palmettenabschlusses.

Zeitlich wie kulturell dem gleichen Kontext cypro-phönikischen Einflusses darf man ein weiteres Importstück, eine Fibel mit dreieckigem, reich profiliertem Bügel, den oben ein Knopf bekrönt, zuweisen. Dieser Typus, in Sardinien durch ein Exemplar aus der Nuraghensiedlung Su Nuraxi, Barumini repräsentiert (Lo Schiavo 1978b, 42-4, Fig 6.3; 1981a, 329 unten rechts; 1985a, 279, Fig 59 unten rechts; Buchholz 1986, 225, Abb 3a), hat einen eindeutigen Verbreitungsschwerpunkt auf Cypern (dort in Grabzusammenhängen des 7. und 6. Jahrhunderts v. Chr.), streut nach Osten an die syrisch-palästinensische Küste und lässt sich nach Westen über den griechischen Raum, Sizilien und Südfrankreich bis hin nach Spanien verfolgen, wobei sich vielerorts lokale Derivatformen ausbildeten (Cunisset-Carnot, Mohen & Nicolardot 1971; Buchholz 1986). H.-G. Buchholz, der diesen Typ jüngst noch einmal untersucht hat, wies schon darauf hin, dass die Verbreitung sich im grossen und ganzen mit der phönikischen Westbewegung decke (Buchholz 1986, 242, 244).

Schliesslich gehören in den gleichen Horizont die bekannten bronzenen 'Kandelaber' mit Blattüberfall, die in vier Exemplaren auf Sardinien vertreten sind (Tore 1986): zu dem bekannten und häufig abgebildeten Stück aus San Vero Milis (Pesce 1961, 95, Fig 88; Cecchini 1969, 88; Barreca 1981, 391, Fig 416; Lilliu 1982, 154, Fig 178; Taramelli 1983, 42, 245, Fig 117; Barreca 1985, 319, Fig 5; 1986, 147, Fig 106; Moscati 1986, 189, Fig 18; Tore 1986, Tav 22) kommen Beispiele aus S. Vittoria di Serri (Taramelli 1911, 42; 1914, 424, Fig 117; Cecchini 1969, 90–1; Tore 1986, Tav 23), Tadasuni-Oristano (Tore 1986, Tav 24) und Bithia (unveröffentlicht; Tore 1986, 68 m. Anm. 19). Verbreitungsschwerpunkt solcher Kandelaber ist die Insel Cypern, sie begegnen jedoch auch weiter im Osten, z.B. in Sidon und lassen sich über Griechenland (z.B. Samos, Athen, Olympia), Etrurien, Malta bis hin nach Spanien verfolgen. Die datierbaren Beispiele weisen wiederum in die orientalisierende Periode (Jantzen 1972, 43–6; Almagro Gorbea 1974; Raubitschek 1978).

Versuchen wir, aus der Zusammenschau der hier kurz diskutierten Denkmäler eine Summe zu ziehen, so wird deutlich, dass Sardinien aufgrund seiner zentralen Lage im westlichen Mittelmeer wie aufgrund seiner Bodenschätze seit dem 2. Jahrtausend v. Chr. die seefahrenden Völker des Ostens angezogen hat. Die Verbindungen hin zur Ägäis und nach Cypern gewannen gegen Ende der späten Bronzezeit eine ungeheure Intensität.

Schwerpunktmässig kristallisiert sich während des 8. und vor allem während des 7. Jahrhunderts v. Chr. ein Kontakthorizont heraus, der mit grosse Gewissheit in Zusammenhang mit der phönikischen Westkolonisation steht: Formen wie die phönikischen Metallkannen, Fibeln mit dreieckigem, reich profiliertem Bügel und bronzene Kandelaber zeigen eine ähnliche, immer wiederkehrende Streuung im Mittelmeergebiet: Syrien-Palästina, eine Konzentration auf Cypern, Ägäis, Italien und umliegende Inseln, Spanien. Dass sich dieses geographische Bild mit der phönikischen Kolonisationstätigkeit deckt, bedarf kaum der Betonung—allein Nordafrika stellt im Augenblick noch einen weissen Fleck auf der Landkarte dar.

Wenn wir die angesprochenen Materialgattungen im Vorhergehenden als cypro-phönikisch definiert haben, so deshalb, weil die Ausbildung dieser Typen sich offenbar im stark phönikisch geprägten Kulturmilieu Cyperns vollzog bzw. Formen östlicher Herkunft von cyprischen Ateliers übernommen wurden. Es sollte allerdings betont werden, dass wir noch ganz am Anfang einer regionalen Aufgliederung des Materials stehen, einfach deshalb, weil das geniun phönikische Metallhandwerk des asiatischen Festlandes immer noch kaum bekannt ist. In jedem Fall hatte Cypern an dem Güterstrom, der um 700 v. Chr. nach Westen floss, einen Anteil. Neben den Metallarbeiten erreichte bald auch phönikische Keramik Sardinien, wobei im Augenblick, soweit ich sehe, die Scheidung phönikischen und späteren punischen Materials noch Schwierigkeiten bereitet (Bartoloni 1983; auch Ugas & Zucca 1985), und es kommt wohl schon zu dieser Zeit zu einer regelrechten Kolonisationstätigkeit, von der ja auch phönikische Inschriften zeugen.

Sind dies Beobachtungen, die aus der Literatur vertraute Ergebnisse noch einmal bestätigen, so scheint mir ein zweiter Punkt, der sich nun im Fundmaterial ansatzweise greifen lässt, um so wichtiger. Wir warfen eingangs die Frage nach kulturellen Kontakten zwischen Sardinien und Cypern während des frühen 1. Jahrtausends v. Chr. (d.h. des 10. bis frühen

8. Jahrhunderts) auf. Diese Frage lässt sich beim jetzigen Stand der Denkmälerkenntnis offenbar positiv beantworten. Die Neufunde aus Sardara-Sant'Anastasia, die zum Teil in sehr alter Tradition stehen, aber auch die einheimischen Nachschöpfungen cyprischer Formen bereits im Depot von Monte Sa Idda und sardische Spiegelungen anderer Vorbilder ostmediterraner Toreutik eröffnen die Möglichkeit, einen älteren Importhorizont abzutrennen, der noch vor der Periode der phönikischen Kolonisation gelegen hat und der wohl kontinuierlich an die intensiven cyprisch-sardischen Beziehungen während des späten 2. Jahrtausends v. Chr. anschliesst. An der Existenz solcher vorphönikischen Kontakte scheint aufgrund der beschriebenen Denkmälergruppen kaum noch Zweifel ein möglich. Die Frage nach der historischen Grundlage derartiger Beziehungen im frühen 1. Jahrtausend v. Chr. wird sich dagegen erst mit Hilfe weiterer Neufunde klären lassen—der Boden Sardiniens ist, wie die letzten Jahre gezeigt haben, für Überraschungen gut.

ANMERKUNGEN

[1] Der Autor hat die angenehme Pflicht, E. Schalk, Heidelberg zu danken, die bei der Erstellung der kürzeren englischen Version, welche in Edinburgh vorgetragen wurde, hilfreich zur Seite stand. Der Text in seiner jetzigen Form wäre nicht ohne den tatkräftigen Beistand von F. Lo Schiavo, zustandegekommen, die mit ihrer unübertroffenen Kenntnis des sardischen Fundmaterials manche Frage klären und mit Hinweisen auf schwer zugängliche Literatur manche Lücke schliessen half. Ihr gilt mein besonders herzlicher Dank.

[2] Hingewiesen sei in diesem Zusammenhang auf ein meist übersehenes, da unscheinbares Fundstück aus dem Depot von Monte Sa Idda: Eine—an den Enden beschädigte—schmale Bronzeleiste mit zwei Ringösen (Taramelli 1921, 63, Fig 90; 1984, 402, Fig 90). Es ist die fragmentierte Attasche einer Schale; die Ösen dienten zum Einhängen eines beweglichen ring- oder omegaförmigen Henkels. Derartige Leistenattaschen mit Schwinghenkeln zählen seit dem späten 2. Jahrtausend im Nahen Osten zu den beliebtesten Handhaben von Schalen; sie werden auch in der cyprisch-phönikischen Toreutik noch tradiert (Matthäus 1985, 128–33). Man dürfte das Beispiel von Monte Sa Idda daher gleichfalls als Zeichen ostmediterranen Kultureinflusses deuten. Dazu passt, dass den unten diskutierten Kesselattaschen mit waagerecht gereihtem Spiraldekor (etwa Cala Gonone) eine ähnliche Henkelkonstruktion zugrunde liegt. Erwähnt sei noch, dass sich ein Henkel ohne Fundkontext und Provenienz im Museum von Nuoro vielleicht einem ähnlichen Typ zuordnen lässt, ohne dass man angesichts der Langlebigkeit solch einfacher Form eine zu enge Eingrenzung versuchen könnte. Der Henkel (Boninu 1978, 176, no 52, Fig 63.2) ist bisher in hellenistisch-römische Zeit datiert worden.

LITERATUR

Acquaro, E. (1984) *Arte e cultura punica in Sardegna*. Sassari.
Almagro Gorbea, M. (1974) Dos thymiateria chipriotas procedentes dela Peninsula Ibérica. *Miscelánea Arqueológica* (XXV anniversario de los cursos

internacionales de prehistoria y arqueología en Ampurias (1947–1971) I), 41–55. Barcelona.
Aubet, M.E. (1987) *Tiro y las colonias fenicias de occidente*. Barcelona.
Barreca, F. (1981) La Sardegna e i Fenici, *in* Pugliese Carratelli 1981, 351–417.
Barreca, F. (1985) Sardegna nuragica e mondo fenicio-punico. *Civiltà nuragica*, 308–28. Mailand.
Barreca, F. (1986) *La civiltà fenicio-punica in Sardegna*. Sassari.
Bartoloni, P. (1983) *Studi sulla ceramica fenicia e punica di Sardegna*. Rom.
Bisi, A.M. (1986) Le rôle de Chypre dans la civilisation phénicienne d'occident. *Acts 1986*, 341–50.
Bisi, A.M. (1987) Bronzi vicino orientali in Sardegna. Importazioni ed influssi, in *Studies in Sardinian Archaeology III. Nuragic Sardinia and the Mycenaean World. (BAR Int Ser 387)* (Hrsg. Balmuth, M.S.) 7–37. Oxford.
Boninu, A. (1978) Collezione Biblioteca Comunale "Sebastiano Satta" di Nuoro. Materiali di età ellenistica e romana, in *Sardegna centro-orientale dal neolitico alla fine del mondo antico*, 171–82. Sassari.
Buchholz, H-G. (1980) Metallurgie, in *Kunst und Kultur Sardiniens vom Neolithikum bis zum Ende der Nuraghenzeit*. 142–55. Karlsruhe.
Buchholz, H-G. (1986) Ein kyprischer Fibeltypus und seine auswärtige Verbreitung. *Acts 1986*, 223–44.
Catling, H.W. (1964) *Cypriot Bronzework in the Mycenaean World*. Oxford.
Catling, H.W. (1984) Workshop and heirlooms: prehistoric bronze stands in the East Mediterranean. *RDAC*, 69–91.
Cecchini, S.M. (1969) *I ritrovamenti fenici e punici in Sardegna*. Rom.
Colonna, G. (1978) Scavi e scoperte. *St Etr 46*, 539–93.
Contu, E. (1962) Sardegna. *Riv Sc Pr 17*, 296–300.
Cunisset-Carnot, P., Mohen, J.P. & Nicolardot, J-P. (1971) Une fibule 'chypriote' trouvée en Côte d'Or. *B Pr Hist Fr 68*, 602–9.
Dunand, M. (1954) *Fouilles de Byblos* II. Paris.
Ferrarese Ceruti, M.L. (1979) Ceramica micenea in Sardegna. *Riv Sc Pr 34*, 243–53.
Ferrarese Ceruti, M.L. (1981) Documenti micenei nella Sardegna meridionale, *in* Pugliese Caratelli 1981, 605–12.
Ferrarese Ceruti, M.L. (1985) La Sardegna e il mondo miceneo. *Civiltà nuragica*, 245–54. Mailand.
Ferrarese Ceruti, M.L., Vagnetti, L. & Lo Schiavo, F. (1987) Minoici, Micenei e Ciprioti in Sardegna alla luce delle più recenti scoperte, in *Studies in Sardinian Archaeology III. Nuragic Sardinia and the Mycenaean World. (BAR Int Ser 387)* (Hrsg. Balmuth, M.S.) 7–37. Oxford.
Fugmann, E. (1958) *L'architecture des périodes préhellénistiques. Hama. II.1* (Fouilles et recherches de la Fondation Carlsberg 1931–138). Kopenhagen.
Grau-Zimmermann, B. (1978) Phönikische Metallkannen in den orientalisierenden Horizonten des Mittelmeerraumes. *MM 19*, 161–218.
Guido, M. (1963) *Sardinia*. London.
Hölbl, G. (1986) *Ägyptisches Kulturgut im phönikischen und punischen Sardinien*. Leiden.
Jantzen, U. (1972) *Ägyptische und orientalische Bronzen aus dem Heraion von Samos. (Samos VIII)* Bonn.
Karageorghis, V. (1983) *Palaepaphos-Skales. An Iron Age Cemetery in Cyprus. Ausgrabungen in Alt-Paphos auf Cypern III*. Konstanz.
Lilliu, G. (1966) *Sculture della Sardegna nuragica*. Verona.
Lilliu, G. (1973) Tripode bronzeo di tradizione cipriota dalla Grotta Pirosu-

Su Benatzu di Santadi (Cagliari), in *Estudios dedicados al Profesor Dr. Luis Pericot*, 283–37. Barcelona.
Lilliu, G. (1982) *La civiltà nuragica*. Sassari.
Lo Schiavo, F. (1976) Fonderia nuragica in loc. "Sa Sedda 'e Sos Carros" (Oliena, Nuoro), in *Nuove testimonianze archeologiche della Sardegna centrosettentrionale*. 69–78. Sassari.
Lo Schiavo, F. (1978a) Bronzi della Grotta 'Su Benticheddu', Oliena, in *Sardegna centro-orientale del neolitico alla fine del mondo antico*. 89–91. Sassari.
Lo Schiavo, F. (1978b) Le fibule della Sardegna. *St Etr 46*, 25–46.
Lo Schiavo, F. (1980) Il villaggio nuragico di Serra Orrios: I bronzi, in *Dorgali - Documenti archeologici*. 145–54. Sassari.
Lo Schiavo, F. (1981a) Economia e società nell 'etá dei nuraghi, *in* Pugliese Carratelli 1981, 255–347.
Lo Schiavo, F. (1981b) Osservazioni sul problema dei rapporti fra Sardegna ed Etruria in età nuragica, in *L'Etruria mineraria* (Atti del XII convegno di studi etruschi e italici, Firenze - Populonia - Piombino 1979) 299–314. Florenz.
Lo Schiavo, F. (1982) Copper metallurgy in Sardinia during the Late Bronze Age: New prospects on its Aegean connections. *EMC*, 271–82.
Lo Schiavo, F. (1983) Le componenti egea e cipriota nella metallurgia della tarda età del bronzo in Italia, in *"Magna Grecia e mondo miceneo"* (Atti del XXI convegno di studi sulla Magna Grecia, Taranto) 285–320. Neapol.
Lo Schiavo, F. (1985a) La Sardegna nuragica e il mondo mediterraneo. *Civiltà nuragica*, 255–84. Mailand.
Lo Schiavo, F. (1985b) *Nuragic Sardinia in its Mediterranean Setting: Some Recent Advances. (University of Edinburgh, Dept. of Archaeology occasional paper No. 12)*. Edinburgh.
Lo Schiavo, F., Macnamara, E. & Vagnetti, L. (1985) Late Cypriot imports to Italy and their influence on local bronzework. *BSR 53*, 1–71.
Lo Schiavo, F. & Vagnetti, L. (1980) Micenei in Sardegna? *Rend Linc (ser. 8) 25, fasc.5–6*, 371–91.
Loud, G. (1948) *Megiddo II (OIP 62)*. Chicago.
Macnamara, E., Ridgway, D. and Ridgway, F.R. (1984) *The Bronze Hoard from S. Maria in Paulis, Sardinia. (BMOP 45)* London.
Marazzi, M., Tusa, S. & Vagnetti, L., Hrsg. (1986) *Traffici micenei nel Mediterraneo. Problemi storici e documentazione archeologica* (Atti del convegno di Palermo). Tarent.
Matthäus, H. (1982) Die zyprische Metallindustrie in der ausgehenden Bronzezeit: Einheimische, ägäische und nahöstliche Elemente. *EMC*, 185–99.
Matthäus, H. (1985) *Metallgefässe und Gefässuntersätze der Bronzezeit, der geometrischen und archaischen Periode auf Cypern. (PBF II.8)*. München.
Matthäus, H. (1988) Heirloom or tradition? Bronze stands of the second and first millennium B.C. in Cyprus, Greece and Italy, in *Problems in Greek Prehistory* (Papers presented at the Centenary Conference of the British School of Archaeology at Athens) (Hrsg. E.B. French & K.A. Wardle) 285–300. Bristol.
Moscati, S. (1986) *L'arte della Sardegna punica*. Mailand.
Nicosia, F. (1980) Etruskische Zeugnisse und Einflüsse, in *Kunst und Kultur Sardiniens vom Neolithikum bis zum Ende der Nuraghenzeit*. 200–11. Karlsruhe.
Nicosia, F. (1981) La Sardegna nel mondo classico, *in* Pugliese Carratelli 1981, 421–76.

Niemeyer, H.G., Hrsg. (1982) *Phönizier im Westen* (Beiträge des internationalen Symposiums über 'Die phönizische Expansion im westlichen Mittelmeerraum'). Mainz.
Niemeyer, H.G. (1984) Die Phönizier und die Mittelmeerwelt im Zeitalter Homers. *Jb Z Mus Mainz 31*, 3-94.
Pesce, G. (1961) *Sardegna punica*. Cagliari.
Pugliese Carratelli, G. Hrsg. (1981) *Ichnussa. La Sardegna dalle origini all'età classica*. Mailand.
Raubitschek, I.K. (1978) Cypriot bronze lampstands in the Cesnola Collection of the Stanford University Museum of Art, in *Proceedings of the Xth International Congress of Classical Archaeology*. 699–707. Ankara.
Smith, T.R. (1987) *Mycenaean Trade and Interaction in the West Central Mediterranean (BAR Int Ser 371)* Oxford.
Taramelli, A. (1911) Serri. *N Sc* 1911, 291–312.
Taramelli, A. (1914) Il tempio nuragico ed i monumenti primitivi di S. Vittoria di Serri (Cagliari). *Mon Ant 23*, 313–440.
Taramelli, A. (1921) Il ripostiglio dei bronzi nuragici di Monte Sa Idda di Decimoputzu (Cagliari). *Mon Ant 27*, 5–108.
Taramelli, A. (1983) *Scavi e scoperte 1903–1921, II*. Sassari.
Taramelli, A. (1984) *Scavi e scoperte 1903–1921. III*. Sassari.
Tore, G. (1986) Intorno un 'torciere' bronzeo di tipo cipriota da San Vero Milis (s'Uraki)-Oristano, in *Società e cultura in Sardegna nei periodi orientalizzante ed arcaico. Rapporti fra Sardgna, Fenici, Etruschi e Greci* (Atti del 1° convegno di studi "Un millennio di relazioni fra la Sardegna e i paesi del Mediterraneo") 65–76. Cagliari.
Ugas, G. (1985) Il mondo religioso nuragico. *Civiltà nuragica*, 209–25. Mailand.
Ugas, G. (1986) La produzione materiale nuragica. Note sull'apporto etrusco e greco, in *Società e cultura in Sardegna nei periodo orientalizzante ed arcaico. Rapporti fra Sardegna, Fenici, Etruschi e Greci* (Atti del 1° convegno di studi "Un millennio di relazioni fra la Sardegna e i paesi del Mediterraneo") 41–53. Cagliari.
Ugas, G. & Usai, L. (1987) Nuovi scavi nel santuario nuragico di S. Anastasia di Sardara, in *La Sardegna nel Mediterraneo tra il secondo e il primo millennio a.C.* (Atti del II convegno di studi "Un millennio di relazioni fra la Sardegna e i paesi del Mediterraneo") 167–218. Cagliari.
Ugas, G. & Zucca, R. (1985) *Il commercio arcaico in Sardegna. Importazioni etrusche e greche (620–480 a.C.)*. Cagliari (o.J., ca 1985)
Vagnetti, L., Hrsg. (1981) *Magna Grecia e mondo miceneo*. Tarent.
Vagnetti, L. (1986) Cypriot elements beyond the Aegean in the Bronze Age. *Acts 1986*, 201–14.

30
Le rayonnement des terres cuites chypriotes au Levant aux premiers siècles de l'âge du Fer

Anna Maria Bisi
University of Urbino

Les travaux récents de F. Vandenabeele (1985a, b; 1986) ont fourni les premiers essais de synthèse sur les apports phéniciens à la coroplastie chypriote du premier âge du Fer. D'autre part, ils s'inscrivent dans les dernières mises au point que sur les influences chypriotes dans tous les domaines de la civilisation phénicienne de l'Ouest viennent de paraître, dues à S. Moscati (1974, 49–58; 1982, 87–9) et à moi-même (Bisi 1966; 1985a; 1986).

En revanche, on n'a jamais essayé, pour autant que je sache, de démêler l'action constante que le très riche répertoire de terres cuites de l'île exerce sur la coroplastie des régions environnantes du Levant, la Phénicie et la Palestine en tout premier lieu, où il se greffe sur un noyau de traditions techniques et figuratives 'cananéennes', remontant à l'âge du Bronze, et surtout au Bronze Récent (Bisi 1988).

La raison de cette absence d'études est peut-être à rechercher dans le caractère très dispersé de cette production phénico-palestinienne du Fer II (EI II A-C, 1000–586 av. J-C),[1] qui n'a connu, à peu d'exceptions près (eg Chéhab 1951–4; Pritchard 1975, 34–7; Fig 46), aucune approche d'ensemble. L'ouvrage remarquable de E. Stern (1982), ainsi que le titre le montre bien, se borne à l'analyse du matériel de l'âge perse; il est représenté par plusieurs dépôts votifs, de Tell es-Safi à Tell Sippor à Makmish, où les terres cuites empruntées à des modèles chypriotes archaïques et sub-archaïques se rangent à côté de quelques pièces en calcaire dont la provenance chypriote avait été reconnue depuis la publication par F.J. Bliss d'un aperçu de la *favissa* de Tell es-Safi au début du siècle (Stern 1982, 158, 271 n 31). Dans cette perspective, E. Stern (1975, Pls XIX-XX; 1982, 158–76) et G. Schmidt (1968) ont abordé plus récemment l'étude des importations chypriotes de la région de Gaza et de l'Héraion de Samos; grâce enfin à la contribution de L. Wriedt Sørensen (1978; Sørensen & Lund, voir ci-dessous 294–6), les lignes de rayonnement et la chronologie des statuettes en pierre et des figurines en terre cuite chypriotes retrouvées dans la Grèce de l'Est ont été suffisamment clarifiées.

Le but de cet exposé c'est d'esquisser une première approche au problème de la coroplastie chypriote en Phénicie et en Palestine avant la domination perse; je me bornerai à la fourchette chronologique entre le VIIIe et le VIIe siècle avant notre ère, qui est représentée à Chypre par le fin du CG III et par le CA I (750–600 av. J-C). C'est en effet l'époque qui voit les échanges les plus poussés dans le domaine artistique entre l'île et la côte syro-palestinienne (Karageorghis 1977, 149–64, 178), bien que l'introduction de quelque variante iconographique de la Grande Déesse de Chypre, inspirée à l'imagerie syro-palestinienne, remonte à deux ou trois siècles auparavant (CG I) (Karageorghis 1977, 154–6, 159, 163).

Malheureusement, pour ce qui a trait aux terres cuites de cette époque, l'évidence archéologique est maigre sur le versant levantin, les trouvailles importantes d'Akhziv demeurant pur la plupart inédites.[2] L'exposition phénicienne de Bruxelles en 1986 (Gubel 1986, 111–27) et celle qui se déroule en ces mois à Venise (Bisi 1988) ont fait connaître des pièces remarquables; à côté des joueses de tympanon d'Amathonte, dont on va parler par la suite (Bisi 1988, 330 Fig à droite), il y a une déesse enceinte de Sidon (Gubel 1986, 115.39) et une femme nue soutenant ses seins provenant, ainsi qu'un dieu barbu assis à la couronne *atéf*, des anciens pillages des nécropoles d'Akhziv (Gubel 1986, 113.36, 115.40). Les deux types se retrouvent à Makmish à l'âge perse.[3] D'autres terres cuites, un peu plus récentes que celles que je viens de mentionner, qui remontent au VIIIe siècle, ressentent fortement des modèles chypriotes: il s'agit alors d'une tête féminine à la coiffure en tresses serrée sur le front par un mince ruban (Gubel 1986, 117.42), provenant de Phénicie, d'une figurine d'Astarté tirée d'un moule profond, caractérisée par une coiffe à franges rapportées et par de multiples bijoux, provenant de Amrit[4] et à ranger parmi les nombreuses importations chypriotes mises au jour dans ce site phénicien. Elles datent pour la plupart de l'âge perse (Stern 1982, 270–1 nn 1, 31), mais la présentation à l'exposition bruxelloise d'un cavalier casqué monté sur un cheval au harnais très élaboré, provenant de Byblos et daté des années 700–550 av J-C (Gubel 1986, 116.41; Bisi 1988, 133 Fig), ouvre à nouveau le problème des influences chypriotes sur la coroplastie phénicienne avant l'arrivée des Perses. En fait, la quadrige de Amrit au Louvre, reprise récemment par Crouwel (1985, 204 n 6; 1987, Pls 38.2a-b; Cassimatis 1986, Pl 38.2–3, 5) daterait du VIIe-VIe siècle, ainsi que ses correspondants chypriotes de Ayia Irini, de Méniko, de Ovgoros (Crouwel 1987, Pls 37–8.1a-b, 3); d'après ce même auteur, les quadriges à quatre personnages, représentés à Amrit aussi, seraient à considérer un petit groupe homogène, 'presumably of 7th century date' (Crouwel 1987, 104 n 24), emprunté au schéma connu par les bas-reliefs assyriens du VIIIe-VIIe siècle et à relater à la période de la mainmise assyrienne sur Chypre (709–669 environ) (Crouwel 1987, 112, 115). A l'Assyrie renvoie aussi le détail de l'anneau derrière la caisse, auquel était accroché un bouclier à ombon façonné en moufle de lion, qui apparaît aussi sur le char de Amrit; une variante, sur un autre quadrige en terre cuite du Louvre, provenant de Chypre, est représentée par une tête de sanglier (Cassimatis 1986, 181, Pl 38.5, No MNB 103).

A mon avis, le quadrige d'Amrit au Louvre, de même que la porteuse d'offrande au costume chypriote et à la riche parure de bijoux, répandue dans l'île durant le CA II,[15] mais dont l'origine semble remonter au VIIIe siècle, parallèlement à l'introduction de l'imagerie syro-palestinienne à Chypre et à la technique proche-orientale du moulage, comme Mme J. Karageorghis vient de montrer (1977, 206–8), s'avèrent des importations chypriotes à Amrit. La diffusion du même type de porteuse d'offrande parmi les *ex-votos* des dépôts de l'Héraion de Samos avant le milieu du VIe siècle (Wriedt Sørensen 1978, 115–18), oblige encore une fois à réviser la chronologie des pièces phéniciennes. Le costume chypriote des figurines en terre cuite de Arsos (première moitié du VIe siècle) et de Achna (fin du VIe) (J. Karageorghis 1977, 210–14), est documenté en effet déjà au CA I, dans quelques vases de la variété Bicrome IV (J. Karageorghis 1977, 186–91).

Il y a six ans, en publiant une terre cuite de Amrit, le dieu à cornes de bélier assis sur un siège à haut dossier dont les accoudoirs sont flanqués par deux béliers, provenant de l'ancienne collection Péretié et aujourd'hui au Louvre, j'avais proposé d'y voir une importation chypriote (1982, 189–96, Pl 47). Elle se rapproche en effet, à la fois pour l'iconographie et le traitement stylistique, d'une série de groupes en argile, dont le plus célèbre provient du sanctuaire rural de Méniko, consacré, d'après V. Karageorghis, au dieu phénicien Baʿal Hammon (Bisi 1982, 182 avec refs, Pl 46.1, 2). Un autre exemplaire de dieu à cornes de bélier, très fragmentaire, a été mis au jour dans les déblais archaïques du rempart de Salamine (Monloup 1984, 143–4. 564, Pl 28); il s'agit d'une statuette modelée plein ainsi que l'autre, bien conservée, de Ayios Dhimitrianos à Kythréa (Bisi 1982, 192–3, Pl 48.1).

L'iconographie du dieu à cornes de bélier, qui connaît au cours du Chypro-Archaïque trois variantes (Bisi 1985b), relève de l'assimilation du Baʿal Hammon phénicien au dieu égyptien Amon Ra (Zeus Ammon), facilitée par l'homophonie et par quelque trait pareil de leur personnalité. Je n'aborderai pas ici le problème du syncrétisme Baʿal Hammon/Zeus Ammon, qui semble issu du milieu chypriote à travers l'oasis de Siwa et Cyrène, grâce aux relations amicales que le roi de Salamine Evelthon (560–525 av. J-C) entretenait avec la colonie théréenne (Bisi 1985b, 310–12), car à ce sujet ont été consacrées des études récentes par V. Karageorghis (1977, 35–6, 44–5), E. Lipinski (1986, 307–32) et moi-même (Bisi 1982; 1985b).

J'aimerais plutôt souligner, pour ne pas déborder du thème qui nous concerne, que ces *mischbilder* chypriotes ont leur pendant dans une statuette en pierre de dieu barbu assis sur un trône dont les accoudoirs sont soutenus par deux béliers, provenant du sanctuaire de l'âge perse de Makmish (Stern 1982, 164, Fig 278). Le Prof. Avigad, auteur du rapport préliminaire des fouilles exécutées dans ce site sud-palestinien en 1958, avait déjà remarqué les analogies que plusieurs figurines en terre cuite et statuettes en pierre de Makmish présentaient avec les produits du style Chypro-grec sub-archaïque du Ve siècle—voir par exemple la figurine en argile d'un jeune homme nu tenant une coupe dans la main gauche (Avigad 1960, 93–4, Pl 12A) - Héraklès ? -, qui évoque de près l'Apollon de Mersinaki (*SCE* III, Pl 111.712; Borda 1946–7, 103–4, 144, Fig 9). E. Stern, qui a publié le premier le dieu aux béliers,[6] vient de nous donner un aperçu exhaustif des statuettes en pierre et des figurines en terre cuite de style chypriote mises au jour dans les sites palestiniens de l'époque perse (1982, 158–76); elles prouvent à suffisance le rayonnement des ateliers de l'île au Levant, en faisant pendant aux trouvailles provenant de Amrit, dont nous possédons maintenant une synthèse remarquable (Dunand & Saliby 1985).

Pour démêler la question du lieu de manufacture des statuettes et des terres cuites chypriotes retrouvées au Levant et dans l'Egée, il faudra sans doute attendre la publication des sept cent pièces de Rhodes, qui demeurent pour la plupart inédites (Wriedt Sørensen 1978, 119), avant de confirmer le rôle joué par l'île à côté des ateliers chypriotes.[7] Pour le moment, je me bornerai à remarquer que la distinction faite par Stern entre un groupe 'oriental' et un groupe 'occidental' de statuettes et figurines en argile provenant des niveaux de l'âge perse de plusieurs sites palestiniens (1982, 165–82), s'avère un peu schématique, surtout si l'on n'attribue pas aux Phéniciens, eux-seuls, l'introduction des types étrangers en Palestine. A la lumière de l'évidence archéologique fournie par une autre catégorie de documents, celle des amphores à anses de panier, dont le rayonnement d'un focus chypriote paraît assuré[8] et qui remonte à la fin du CG III,[9] on a supposé, d'après les trouvailles de ces amphores à Tell Keisan, un commerce de l'huile entre Chypre et la Palestine au cours du $VIII^e/VII^e$ siècle avant notre ère (Salles 1980, 137, 302–3:E. Puech). A ces relations d'ordre économique on pourrait ramener la présence de quelques terres cuites chypriotes du même âge au Levant, sans nier, bien entendu, l'existence de rapports consolidés entre les villes-état phéniciennes et leurs colonies de Chypre.

En tout cas, si nous revenons à l'horizon chronologique envisagé, nous trouvons d'autres témoignages de ces rapports parmi les terres cuites phéniciennes et palestiniennes du VIIIe et du VIIe siècle.

La joueuse de tympanon provenant d'une tombe de Shiqmona, près de Haïfa (*EAEHL,* 1103, Fig; Karageorghis 1987, 18, Figs 2, 3), a le corps tourné tandis que les lourdes tresses, les bras et l'instrument de musique appuyé à la poitrine sont faits de boudins d'argile rapportés. La datation proposée par J. Elgavish (*EAEHL,* 1103)—fin du IXe début du VIIIe siècle

—paraît un peu haute, face à la chronologie donnée aux termes de comparaison les plus proches: une figurine de Tyr de la fin du VIIIe siècle (Gubel 1983, 32, 48, Fig 7), une autre de l'Héraion de Samos, datée par Schmidt vers 670 av. J-C (1968, 84. T1799, Pl 91), et surtout deux tympanistres provenant des tombes chypro-archaïques de Amathonte, qui viennent d'être publiées par Karageorghis (1987, 17–18, Fig 1, Pl 2). Elles diffèrent l'une de l'autre uniquement pour la technique: l'exemplaire T.289/4 étant modelé plein, le T.276/253 présentant le visage moulé et le corps en cloche fait au tour.

E. Gubel voit dans la figurine de Shiqmona une importation tyrienne (1983, 32), bien que la coiffe en tresses nouées, sans boucles, soit repandue dans la coroplastie chypriote de l'âge du Fer, comme souligne à juste titre V. Karageorghis (1987, 17 n 14). Il faut d'autre part rappeler que toutes les terres cuites importées de Samos semblent venir de Chypre[10] et qu'une école amathousienne, de laquelle sont issues beaucoup de joueuses de tympanon, est florissante au cours du CA II (Karageorghis 1987, 18–19, Pls 2–7).

Certes, la situation des influences réciproques de l'art phénicien à Chypre et des traditions de l'île au Levant, n'est pas aisée à démêler, tant les types —et sans doute les idéologies aussi, cachées sous les types plastiques—sont strictement imbriqués. Faut-il souscrire alors à l'opinion de V. Karageorghis (1987, 17 n 16):

'...the very difficult problem of the origin and character of the 'Phoenician' art of Cyprus ... still awaits solution. For the time being we believe there is no reason why we should consider all or even any object, particularly terracottas of a "Phoenician" type, as imports.'

Tout porte en effet à croire que les ateliers de Chypre, à la suite de l'introduction de quelques composantes de l'imagerie proche-orientale, telle que la déesse nue syrienne, dès la fin du XIe siècle,[11] aient développé aux siècles suivants des types iconographiques à eux-mêmes, où les emprunts étrangers se mêlent aux traditions enracinées dans le milieu local.

Cela dit, on peut donner encore quelques exemples, choisis parmi les pièces publiées, de l'influence de la coroplastie chypriote en Phénicie et en Palestine dans la période envisagée ici.

Un masque d'homme avec barbe et moustaches peints en noir et à la coiffe à rainures verticales, provenant d'une tombe de Akhziv du Fer II (Culican 1975–6, 55 Fig 10), s'avère très proche, ainsi que deux autres masques d'un type un peu différent, caractérisé par un disque d'argile rapporté sur le front, provenant de Khaldé et de Palestine (Culican 1975–6, 55, Fig 11, 57, Fig 17), des masques chypro-archaïques de Kourion et d'autres sites Chypriotes (Stern 1976, 112–14, Pl 9 c; voir aussi Caubet & Courtois 1975, 45 Pl 6.1, 2), qui ont leurs antécédents dans les exemplaires d'Enkomi, datés du XIIe siècle (Lagarce & Lagarce 1973).

Et encore: une tête en terre cuite provenant avec toute vraisemblance de Arsos, a été trouvée à Tell Dan, dans la Palestine du nord, aux pentes de l'Hermon, dans un contexte apparemment daté du VIIIe siècle (*EAEHL,* 315, Fig). D'autres têtes féminines, qui ressentent de près le style chypriote archaïque, ont été mises au jour dans un autre site palestinien de la région de Gaza, Tell esh-Shari'a, où elles semblent dater du VIIIe siècle (*EAEHL,* 1069, Fig).

Une allure chypriote se dégage de quelques terres cuites du *Shrine 1* de Sarepta, dont le Prof. Pritchard a mis en évidence les liens architecturaux avec le temple d'Astarté à Kition, troisième phase (600–450 av. J-C) (1975, 19–20), surtout dans les cas de la porteuse d'offrande au corps en cloche et aux lourdes tresses épanouies (1975, 23, Fig 41.1) et du trône soutenu par un couple de sphinx très égyptisants (1975, 25–6, Fig 42.3).

Si le jugement d'une influence chypriote à Sarepta doit être retenu avec prudence, face à la documentation très maigre de la coroplastie proprement phénicienne du VIIIe-VIIe siècle, il est désormais assuré que les porteuses d'offrande au costume chypriote, issues des ateliers d'Arsos et d'autres endroits de l'île, sont bien documentées dans le Héraion de Samos avant le milieu du VIe siècle. Cette chronologie, qui ressort de la fine analyse de L. Wriedt Sørensen (1978, 115–18), s'applique aussi au petit lot d'importations chypriotes du sanctuaire du port à Chios et à la terre cuite de Arsos retrouvée dans une tombe de Camiros à Rhodes, datée vers 600 av. J-C (Wriedt Sørensen 1978, 113–14; Schmidt 1968, 94). A la fin du VIIe siècle semblent remonter même les pièces en pierre et en terre cuite chypriotes du sanctuaire d'Apollon à Naucratis, de Vrulià et des dépôts votifs du temple d'Athana Lindia à Rhodes; pour ce qui touche aux pièces rhodiennes, elles ne sont en aucun cas postérieures aux années 570 et 550 av. J-C (Wriedt Sørensen 1978, 114–15, 118).

Il faut donc admettre que des terres cuites issues des ateliers chypriotes du CA I (700–600 av. J-C) aient été exportées à la fois en Phénicie et en Palestine et dans les îles de l'Asie Mineure, c'est à dire quelques décennies avant la mainmise de la Perse sur Chypre, pour laquelle je me rallie à la date proposée jadis par Hill et Gjerstad (*SCE* IV.2, 471–3), le 545 av. J-C, immédiatement après la prise de Sardis, au lieu du 525, conquête de l'Egypte par Cambyse.

Au Levant, ces apports chypriotes se greffent sur le vieux fond de la coroplastie 'cananéenne' qui garde ses types principaux, modelés ou tournés (masques rituels, *pillar-women,* etc), tout au long du Fer II.

A propos des masques phéniciens et palestiniens du premier âge du Fer, on a déjà souligné leur présence à Enkomi à la fin du Bronze Récent. Or, un cas tout à fait pareil de continuité et d'imbrication entre héritage syro-palestinien et apports individuels chypriotes, se dègage de l'étude poussée que A. Caubet et M. Yon viennent de consacrer aux appliques murales (*wall-brackets*) (1974), repandues au Proche-Orient et à Chypre depuis le XIVe jusqu'au VIIIe siècle avant notre ère. Deux sont les résultats les plus remarquables auxquels aboutit leur recherche: d'une part, les appliques du CG I-III s'avèrent les héritiers directes du type représenté à Mégiddo au niveau VII, n'ayant aucune relation avec celles du LC IIA-III (Caubet & Yon 1974, 125, Fig 3d); d'autre part, elles manifestent, bien qu'empruntées à un type levantin du Bronze Récent, un caractère tout à fait local au cours de leur développement à l'âge du Fer, en ressentant dans les motifs du décor des traditions coroplastiques indigènes.[12]

Je voudrais conclure très brièvement cette esquisse, qui a une valeur tout à fait liminaire, en proposant une méthode d'approche plutôt que prétendre d'avoir épuisé le sujet.

J'ai laissé de côté tous les problèmes ayant trait à l'aspect socio-économique et commercial que l'on aperçoit au fond de ce réseau d'échanges entre les ateliers chypriotes du premier âge du Fer et les centres de l'Egée et du Levant qui reçoivent leurs produits. Il s'agit en effet d'un argument touché jadis par plusieurs savants, sans aboutir à des conclusions assurées, face à la documentation très maigre et dispersée sur le versant levantin. Si l'évidence archéologique demeure encore mal connue, il me semble toutefois qu'il ne soit plus nécessaire de souscrire à le thèse de E. Gjerstad (*SCE* IV.2, 463, 470), qui envisageait une implantation chypriote à Amrit pour expliquer la vague de statuettes en pierre et en terre cuite importées de l'île dans ce site de la côte phénicienne. C'est vrai qu'elle atteint toute catégorie artisanale, même celle, bien enracinée en Phénicie, des sarcophages anthropoïdes,[13] mais les trouvailles pareilles de Samos, de Rhodes, de Naukratis, et, plus loin encore du foyer chypriote, le long de la côte palestinienne jusqu'aux alentours de Gaza (Stern 1975), montrent à la fois la complexité et la généralisation d'un phénomène qui remonte au Bronze Récent et qui demeure ininterrompu au cours de l'âge du Fer.

En fait, contrairement à ce qu'on pensait jadis, c'est un même courant de relations dans le domaine artistique et culturel qui jalonne la route des échanges commerciaux de Chypre avec le Levant, depuis la grande époque du royaume d'Alashiya[14] et qui entraîne des emprunts dans la technique, la typologie et l'iconographie, surtout lorsque cette dernière cache une symbologie polyvalente (la déesse ou prêtresse nue, vue de face, le porteur ou la porteuse d'offrandes, le dieu trônant, etc).

Dans mon étude sur le Baʿal Hammon de Amrit, j'avais déjà souligné (1982, 195) que cette terre cuite était à considérer le témoignage d'une 'action de retour' exercée par les coroplastes chypriotes sur les ateliers phéniciens, face à l'absence du schéma du dieu à cornes de bélier dans l'imagerie phénicienne d'Orient et d'Occident (Bisi 1982, 190–1 n 16). En tout cas, il faut dorénavant refuser l'idée que l'exportation des terres cuites et des statuettes en calcaire chypriotes soit un phénomène limité à l'âge perse, lorsque Chypre, la Phénicie et la Palestine sont rassemblées sous Darius Ier, dans la Ve satrapie de l'empire achéménide (Hérodote III, 91).

Le réseau des relations entre Chypre et le Levant, qui est l'aboutissement de la *koiné* culturelle amarnienne, se poursuit, en dépit des troubles apportés par les Peuples de la Mer durant le XIe et le Xe siècle, comme montrent la 'forte impulsion orientale qui se fait sentir à Chypre, au début de la période géométrique . . . surtout à l'Est de l'île' (Caubet & Yon 1974, 128–9) et le nouvel essor de l'activité métallurgique, bien documentée à Palaepaphos-Skalès et ailleurs (Karageorghis 1982; 1983). L'arrivée des Phéniciens, entre le Xe et le IXe siècle avant notre ère, ne fait qu'enrichir un répertoire figuré et technique déjà bien développé et entamé d'apports proche-orientaux, en introduisant le moule et en multipliant les iconographies de dieux et des porteurs d'offrandes pour ce qui a trait à la coroplastie. Au même temps, la Phénicie et la Palestine, qui jouent de la même ambiance culturelle, marquée par l'héritage 'cananéen' du Bronze (en dépit de la coupure idéologique imposée par les prophètes d'Israël), font accueil aux produits issus des ateliers chypriotes et en donnent des imitations locales; parmi elles se rangent peut-être quelques masques de Akhziv et les joueuses de tympanon de Tyr et de Shiqmona (voir ci-dessus, p 260).

En conclusion, l'union des trois régions dans la Ve satrapie ne fait qu'accentuer un processus qui remonte bien avant dans les temps et qui demeure assez peu exploité pour les premiers siècles de l'âge du Fer: d'ores et déjà on peut néanmoins en suivre le développement à travers les rares importations chypriotes de terres cuites de Byblos, de Tell Dan, de Amrit, qui sont les devancières du rayonnement au Levant de la petite plastique chypriote de l'époque perse.

NOTES

[1] On adopte ici le schéma chronologique de *EAEHL*.
[2] Quelques-unes des terres cuites de Akhziv sont discutées par Culican, 1975–76; Stern 1976. Voir aussi le catalogue dans Gubel 1986.
[3] Avigad 1960, 93, Pl 10A, 11 A-B; voir aussi quelques exemplaires de Kharayeb tout à fait pareils dans Chéhab 1951–4, 84, Pl 7.2, 4–6 (datés 'aux environs de la conquête d'Alexandre' *ibid,* 155).
[4] Gubel 1986, 119, 48. Pour le rayonnement de ce type et d'autres moules de Arsos représentant la porteuse d'offrande nue ou vêtue et s'échelonnant entre la fin du VIIe et le début du VIe siècle, voir Schmidt 1968, Pls 49–53, 59, 70–81.
[5] Voir par exemple, à côté des exemplaires de Arsos cités par Schmidt 1968, 22, Karageorghis, J. 1977, Pl 34 c-d.
[6] Dans le rapport de Avigad (1960) on ne trouve aucune mention de cette pièce, pour laquelle je renvoie à Stern (1982) 164, Fig 278.
[7] Wriedt Sørensen 1978, 120: l'existence d'ateliers locaux entre la fin du VIIe et le cours du VIe siècle est prouvée par exemple à Naukratis, où les sculptures de style chypriote sont tirées de l'alabastre et du grès qui font entièrement défaut dans l'île.
[8] Stern 1982, 110–12, où l'auteur penche au contraire pour une origine rhodienne de la *basket-handle jar*. Le rayonnement à partir d'un focus chypriote est proposé par Salles 1980, 136–41, Pls 23–4.
[9] Salles 1980, 140–1 (il s'agit de la tombe 79 de Salamine).
[10] Sauf peut-être le T.497, Pl 29 ('ohne Fundgabe') dans Schmidt 1968, pour lequel je ne connais aucun parallèle chypriote: le turban ou la tiare arrondie et le voile (ou les cheveux?) qui l'entourent semblent refléter des modèles de la coroplastie mésopotamienne.

[11] Karageorghis, J. 1977, 154–5: il s'agit des plaques en or de Lapithos, s'échelonnant entre la fin du XIe et le début du Xe siècle av. J-C.

[12] Caubet & Yon 1974, 128–9: on peut mentionner à ce propos la tête de taureu, dont le symbolisme 'reconduit au milieu chpyriote depuis le Bronze Ancien'.

[13] Voir par exemple la tête du sarcophage en terre cuite provenant de Amrit et datée du Ve siècle, qui ressent de la coroplastie chypriote archaïque: Gubel 1986, 94. 11.

[14] On renvoie au tableau frappant de ces commerces et de ce milieu de l'Est méditerranéen esquissé dans les ouvrages récents de Knapp 1985, 1986.

RÉFÉRENCES

Avigad, N. (1960) Excavations at Makmish 1958. Preliminary report. *Isr Expl J 10*, 90–6.

Bisi, A.M. (1966) *Kypriakà. Contributi allo studio della componente cipriota della civiltà punica.* Roma.

Bisi, A.M. (1982) Su una terracotta di tipo cipriota da ʿAmrît. *R St Fen 10*, 189–196.

Bisi, A.M. (1985a) Les influences de l'art chypriote dans le milieu phénicien d'Occident. *Acts 1985*, 221–8.

Bisi, A.M. (1985b) Origine e diffusione del culto cirenaico di Zeus Ammon, dans *Cyrenaica in Antiquity (BAR Int Ser 236)* (eds. G. Barker, J. Lloyd & J. Reynolds) 307–17. Oxford.

Bisi, A.M. (1986) Le rôle de Chypre dans la civilisation phénicienne d'Occident: état de la question et essai de synthèse. *Acts 1986*, 341–50.

Bisi, A.M. (1988) Le terrecotte figurate. *Catalogue de l'exposition "I Fenici - Venezia, Palazzo Grassi"*, 328–32. Milan.

Borda, M. (1946–7) "Kyprios Charaktér". Aspetti della scultura araica cipriota. *Rend Pont Acc 22*, 87–154.

Cassimatis, H. (1986) Terres cuites chypriotes à Dublin. *RDAC*, 173–82.

Caubet, A. & Courtois, J. (1975) Masques chypriotes en terre cuite du XIIe s.av. J-C. *RDAC*, 43-9.

Caubet, A. & Yon, M. (1974) Deux appliques murales chypro-géométriques au Louvre. *RDAC*, 112–31.

Chéhab, M.H. (1951–4) Les terres cuites de Kharayeb. *B Mus Beyr 10 et 11*.

Crouwel, J.H. (1985) Carts in Iron Age Cyprus. *RDAC*, 203–21.

Crouwel, J.H. (1987) Chariots in Iron Age Cyprus. *RDAC*, 101–18.

Culican, W. (1975–6) Some Phoenician masks and other terracottas. *Berytus 24*, 47–87.

Dunand, M. & Saliby, N. (1985) *Le temple d'Amrit dans la Pérée d'Aradus.* Paris.

EAEHL Avi-Yonah, M. & Stern E. (1975–1978) *Encyclopedia of Archaeological Excavations in the Holy Land.* I-IV. Oxford.

Gubel, E. (1983) Art in Tyre during the First and Second Iron Age. A preliminary survey. *St Phoen 1. Sauvons Tyr*, 23–52. Leuven.

Gubel, E. ed (1986) *Les Phéniciens et le monde méditerranéen.* Bruxelles.

Karageorghis, J. (1977) *La grande déesse de Chypre et son culte à travers l'iconographie, de l'époque néolithique au V;4ème s.a. C.* Lyon-Paris.

Karageorghis, V. (1977) *Two Cypriote Sanctuaries of the End of the Cypro-Archaic Period.* Rome.

Karageorghis, V. (1982) Metallurgy in Cyprus during the 11th century B.C. *EMC*, 297–302. Nicosia.
Karageorghis, V. (1983) *Palaepaphos-Skales. An Iron Age Cemetery in Cyprus.* Konstanz.
Karageorghis, V. (1987) La nécropole d'Amathonte. Tombes 113–37. III. 1. The Terracottas. *Études Chypriotes 9*. Nicosia.
Knapp, A.B. (1985) Alashiya, Caphtor/Keftiu, and Eastern Mediterranean trade. *J Field A 12*, 231–50.
Knapp, A.B. (1986) Production, exchange and socio-political complexity in Bronze Age Cyprus. *Oxf J A 5*, 35–60.
Lagarce, E. & Lagarce, J. (1973) A propos du masque A.71.1 d'Enkomi. *Syria 50*, 349–54.
Lipiński, E. (1986) Zeus Ammon et Baal-Hammon. *St Phoen 4. Religio Phoenicia*. 307–32. Namur.
Monloup, T. (1984) Les figurines de terre cuite de tradition archaïque. *Salamine de Chypre XII*. Paris.
Moscati, S. (1974) *Problematica della civiltà fenicia*. Roma.
Moscati, S. (1982) *L'enigma dei Fenici*. Milano.
Pritchard, J.B. (1975) *Sarepta. A Preliminary Report on the Iron Age*. Philadelphia.
Salles, J.F. (1980) dans Salles, J.F., Briend, J. & Humbert, J.B. *Tell Keisan (1971–1976). Une cité phénicienne en Galilée*. 136–41. Paris.
Schmidt, G. (1968) Kyprische Bildwerke aus dem Heraion von Samos. *Samos VII*. Bonn.
Stern, E. (1975) A group of Cypriot limestone sculptures from the Gaza region. *Levant 7*, 104–7.
Stern, E. (1976) Phoenician masks and pendants. *PEQ 108*, 109–18.
Stern, E. (1982) *Material Culture in the Land of the Bible in the Persian Period*. Warminster. (éd. Hebraïque 1973. Jerusalem).
Vandenabeele, F. (1985a) L'influence phénicienne sur la coroplasthie chypriote. *St Phoen 3. Phoenicia and its neighbours*, 203–11. Leuven.
Vandenabeele, F. (1985b) Les terres cuites chypriotes à lampe. *Acts 1985*, 301–6.
Vandenabeele, F, (1986) Phoenician influence on the Cypro-Archaic terracotta production and Cypriot influence abroad. *Acts 1986*, 351–8.
Wriedt Sørensen, L. (1978) Early Archaic limestone statuettes in Cypriote style. A review. *RDAC*, 111–21.

31
Has Phoenician influence modified Cypriot terracotta production?

Frieda Vandenabeele
Vrije Universiteit, Brussels

In the 9th century BC the Phoenicians founded their first colony on the south coast of Cyprus at Kition. Probably at the same period or a little later they introduced the use of the mould for terracotta figurine production, known in the Near East from the third millennium BC. This new technique was used from the Archaic period onwards for entire figurines, plain or hollow, or, more often, only for the face.

Together with this new technique the Phoenicians brought in new types of terracottas. There is the 'dea gravida', the representation of a pregnant woman, a Phoenician type *par excellence*. But except for some examples from Amathus, it remains confined to the Kition area, whether imported or locally made. More numerous and more widespread are the representations of nude female figurines pressing the breasts with both hands, the so-called Astarte type. They are found in many parts of Cyprus, at Kition, Tamassos, Salamis, Amathus, and other sites, both in tombs and sanctuaries. The type is certainly of Near Eastern origin and its introduction to Cyprus corresponds to the period when the Phoenician rulers extended their influence, both political and cultural, over other towns of Cyprus (Vandenabeele 1986b, 351–3, Pl 30.1–3). The iconography of the tambourine-holders is specifically of Mesopotamian origin. Their introduction coincides, as for the representations of Astarte, with the heyday of the Phoenician penetration on the island (Karageorghis 1987, 22). Three representations of Baal further illustrate the Phoenician influence: the statuette from the sanctuary of Meniko, one from Chytroi and one from Salamis found in the debris of the Archaic rampart. Female figurines bearing a lamp on their head, mostly from the locality of Kamelargá at Kition, as well as a male statuette from Ayia Anna tou Psephala in the Larnaka district illustrate another Phoenician feature. The same is true for the two sphinx thrones from the sanctuary of Ayia Irini and perhaps for some 'scènes de genre' such as the three bathing scenes or some figurines illustrating the process of bread-making (Vandenabeele 1986b, 353–6, Pls 30.4, 5; 31.1, 4).

While this evidence demonstrates that there can be no doubt about Phoenician influence on the Cypriot terracotta production of the Archaic Period, the majority of the terracottas, nonetheless, reflect a local character.

Most of them are small-sized. Technically they can be divided into five groups: entirely hand-made, hand-made with the face made in a mould; hand- and wheel-made; hand- and wheel-made, with the face made in a mould; and mould-made. Naturally, it is impossible to give here a full catalogue of all the Cypriot groups of terracottas of the Archaic Period, particularly as there is perhaps no other country in the Mediterranean which has produced so many examples. I shall thus limit myself to some relevant types.[1]

HAND-MADE TERRACOTTAS

The group of hand-made terracottas comprises chariots—*bigae* and *quadrigae*—carrying two persons, found in large numbers in the rural sanctuaries of Ayia Irini and of Apollo Hylates at Kourion (*SCE* II Pls 234, 235; Gjerstad 1963, Fig 11–15; Young & Halstead Young 1955, Pls 21.1172, 1189, 1159; 22.1214; 25.1427, 1373, 1410); horses with or without a rider (Monloup nd 96–102, Figs 2–4, 7–13[2]); animals (for example: *SCE* II Pls 227–8; Karageorghis 1987, Pls 30–1; Monloup 1984, Pls 1–9, 17–21); dancers (for example: Gjerstad 1963, 14–15, Fig 16; Karageorghis 1977a, Fig 6, Pl 2.4–8); goddesses with uplifted arms (eg J. Karageorghis 1977, Pls 20 e, 21 a-c, 22c, 23a, Karageorghis 1977a *passim*); bread-making scenes (Vandenabeele 1986a, 39–43),[3] and so on. The figurines are made in the snowman technique. They can be decorated with black and purple paint, like the vases of the same period. Their look is typically Cypriot and—as the terracotta-studies progress—more and more local work-shops begin to emerge, for example at Amathus and Kourion (see above).

HAND-MADE FIGURINES WITH THE FACE MADE IN A MOULD

The group of handmade figurines with the face in a mould comprises representations of childbirth (Karageorghis 1981, 154–5 no 120); standing figurines with two children attached to the body (Karageorghis 1981, Fig 120 left) and standing plank-shaped figurines with a child in their left arm (Walters 1903, A 132, Pl).[4] There is no foreign influence in the rendering of the face. Most of them were found in a cave at *Empros Temenon* near Lapithos (Vandenabeele forthcoming). The cave was perhaps dedicated to Eileithyia as at Tsoutsourou on the south coast of Crete, but until now no traces of a cult belonging to this deity have been found in Cyprus. It is possible that the universal cult of Aphrodite had assimilated, and thereby obscured, any traces of the cult of the goddess protecting childbirth, known in the Aegean from the Late Bronze Age onwards (Bennett 1980, 397–8). Other examples of this category are *bigae* and *quadrigae* (Gjerstad 1963,

Figs 9–10; Young & Halstead Young 1955, Pls 26–7) again found in the rural sanctuary of Ayia Irini and in the sanctuary of Apollo Hylates at Kourion. In most cases the moulding of the face is typically Cypriot, but equally there are affinities with Syro-Palestinian sculpture as for example in a chariot group of Ovgoros (Karageorghis 1977b, 186 no 3).

HAND- AND WHEEL-MADE FIGURINES

The group of hand- and wheel-made figurines consists of offering-bearers;[5] goddesses with uplifted arms (J. Karageorghis 1977, Pl 24 c-d; Karageorghis 1977a, Pls 4.3, 4; 5.15); women bearing a vase on their head (for example J. Karageorghis 1977, Pl 24 b; Karageorghis 1977a, Pl 6.6; *Chronique 1978*, Fig 58; 1979, Fig 43), and other types. Some of them—including warriors, musicians, goddesses with uplifted arms and figurines bearing a vase on their head—have movable legs attached to the body by strings (Vandenabeele 1973, 47–57[6]). The head, the upperpart of the body, the arms in various positions and the object or the weapons they carry are hand-made, but the body is turned on the wheel. They are usually in White Painted and Bichrome techniques. Their distribution pattern is not quite clear as many of them remain unpublished or of unknown provenance, but they are surely Cypriot.

Hand- and wheel-made figurines, with the face made in a mould

To the group of hand- and wheel-made terracottas with the face made in a mould belong the enormous class of tambourine-players and of offering-bearers with a beast or a chalice in their arms or hands (for example: *SCE* II Pl 232.92, 880). As with the last group, the body is turned on the wheel, while the arms, the tambourine and the offerings are hand-made; but the face of the head which is inserted into the body by a cone is made in a mould. They mostly belong to the White Painted or the Bichrome technique. The rendering of the face sometimes recalls Egyptian or Near Eastern prototypes, but they are of local manufacture.

Entirely mould-made figurines

Finally, the entirely mould-made terracottas consist of reliefs and figurines in the round. To the first group belong, among others, some reliefs representing a *kourotrophos* (Vandenabeele forthcoming), some draped female figurines from Amathus (Karageorghis 1987, Figs 25–8, Pls 37.196–7; 38–9.202–4) and from other sites. More numerous are the examples moulded in the round as representations of dressed women from the sanctuary of Artemis at Achna (Ohnefalsch-Richter 1893, Pls 11, 12; Walters 1903, 7–12, Pl 1), the clothed women with a hand on the belly from Arsos (Sophocleous 1985, Pl 25.3) or the *kourotrophoi* from Lapithos (*Kition* II Pl 33.3; Walters 1903, 23–4, Pl 3:A 134). The front of all these terracottas is made in a mould. Most have some traces of paint. Some groups are entirely Cypriot, others—as the *kourotrophoi*—have a head of Egyptian type with receding forehead and ears placed high.

Apart from the enormous Archaic production of small-sized terracottas, there is an important number of *life-size* figures mostly from the sanctuary of Ayia Irini (*SCE* II Pls 189–228), but also known from the 'favissa' of Kazaphani (Karageorghis 1978a, 189–90) and from the deposit of Patriki (Karageorghis 1971, 27–36, Pls 13–16). Yet, as far as I know, the Phoenicians ignored the concept of 'grandeur nature', so we shall not consider this aspect of the Cypriot clay sculpture.

CONCLUSIONS

From the foregoing it is clear that Phoenician influence on Cypriot terracotta production was very limited, as it was on other arts and crafts such as architecture or pottery. The rule of the Phoenicians from the 9th century until the disappearance of the independent kingdoms of Cyprus in 312 BC was more a political and economic one. Cypriot culture never became dependent on that of her eastern neighbour, except at the Phoenician colony of Kition and perhaps to some extent at Amathus and Tamassos, where the Phoenician rulers extended their power.

The bulk of the terracottas in the CA I and II periods is, as shown above, of local character. Moreover, with more publication of sites, the existence of a great number of local workshops becomes more and more evident or as Young & Halstead Young wrote already in 1955:

'There is no such thing as a typical 'Cypriote' figurine ... Yet not only are the distances between Marion, Amathus, Kition and Karpasia more than comparable with those of Greece proper, but the political distinction of the ten kingdoms of Cyprus, unlike the Greek city-states, was magnified by total differences in custom...' and 'Furthermore, clay, unlike bronze or stone, is usually procured locally and differs from place to place...' (Young & Halstead Young 1955, 1, 2).

But, for clay procured locally, perhaps George Bass is nearer to the truth when commenting on a Filipino vessel sailing from Savannah to Algeciras in Spain loaded with tons of clay, he writes 'I never believed it possible that Cyprus would have imported clay from the Argolid. Maybe I'm wrong!' (Bass 1988).

Returning to the local workshops it seems clear, for instance, that if I compare the hand-made CA horse and rider from the tombs of Amathus (Karageorghis 1987, Pls 19–26) with those from the Archaic Precinct of the temple of Apollo Hylates at Kourion (Young & Halstead Young 1955, Pls 19, 20) which are roughly of the same date, I can establish that they are all in frontal pose with the arms stretched forward to touch the horse's mane and that the details are either added as separate pieces or painted. But here the resemblances between the two groups end. At Amathus the legs and the necks of the horses are very short. Tails adhere at the backside. The rider sometimes wears a conical cap, but this is never sharply-pointed. More often he wears a turban. The nose is pronounced as on most of the terracottas of Amathus. Finally, the rider is thick-set. At Kourion, on the contrary, the legs of the horses are more slender. Tails are always detached from the backside. The conical cap is sharply-pointed and the rider is always very tall.

Another example which illustrates the existence of different workshops is shown by the childbirth groups of three women and a baby. The figures are always placed on a roughly shaped plate. One female figurine supports the woman giving birth to a child, the other, staying in front, is receiving the baby—a separately made terracotta—out of the belly. The terracottas are hand-made except for the face, for which two types of mould have been used. So in the present state of our knowledge two different workshops can be recognized. The first produced terracottas with faces of very good quality, the forehead surmounted by curls and a 'bandeau', the eyes, nose and mouth delicately modelled. It was probably situated in the region of Lapithos as the figurines are said to come from a cave at *Empros Temenon* in its vicinity and it was also responsible for the production of plank-shaped *kourotrophoi*. The second one is only represented by two examples which are clearly more crudely modelled and moulded. They resemble each other, but the faces, much obliterated, are not necessarily made in the same mould. One was found in the sanctuary at Lapithos, the other is said to come from Idalion. The workshop can, as yet, not be located, but the clay of the one from Lapithos is very different from that of the first group (Vandenabeele forthcoming).

The existence of many production centres is beyond doubt but, as the study of the Cypriot workshops is beyond the scope of this lecture, I shall confine myself to these two examples.

NOTES

[1] If no relevant study has been published, I shall refer to some characteristic examples.
[2] To this can be added a series of terracottas from the recently excavated tombs at Amathus (Karageorghis 1987, Pls 19–26).
[3] To this can be added: Decaudin 1987, Pl 63.140; Pottier 1909, Pl.1.no 24.
[4] Only one is published. Others are preserved in the collections of the Musée du Louvre (AM 1586) and in the Cyprus Museum (C 308, C309 & C310).
[5] Mostly published.
[6] To this can be added many other examples, published and unpublished, notably: Breitenstein 1941, Pl.2.7, 8; Karageorghis 1987, Pl 7.30; *Chronique 1972*, Fig 18).

LIST OF REFERENCES

Bass, G. F. (1988) *Nestor*, 2179.
Bennett, C.G. (1980) *The Cults of the Ancient Greek Cypriotes*. Ann Arbor.
Breitenstein, N. (1941) *A Catalogue of the Terracottas. Cypriote, Greek, Etrusco-Italian and Roman*. Copenhagen.
Decaudin, A.J. (1987) *Les antiquités chypriotes dans les collections publiques françaises*. Nicosia.
Gjerstad, E. (1963) Supplementary notes on finds from Ayia Irini in Cyprus.

Medelhavs Mus B 3, 3–40.
Karageorghis, J. (1977) *La Grande Déesse de Chypre et son Culte.* Lyon.
Karageorghis, V. (1971) A deposit of Archaic terracotta figures from Patriki, Cyprus. *RDAC,* 27–36.
Karageorghis, V. (1977a) *The Goddess with Uplifted Arms in Cyprus (Scripta Minora ... Lundensis).* Lund.
Karageorghis, V. (1977b) *Two Cypriote Sanctuaries of the end of the Cypro-Archaic Period.* Nicosia.
Karageorghis, V. (1978a) A "Favissa" at Kazaphani. *RDAC,* 156–92.
Karageorghis, V. (1981) *Ancient Cyprus. 7000 Years of Art and Archaeology.*
Karageorghis, V. (1987) *Études Chypriotes IX: La nécropole d'Amathonte. Tombes 113–367.* Nicosia.
Monloup, Th. (1984) *Salamine de Chypre XII: Les figurines de terre cuite de tradition archaïque.* Paris.
Monloup, Th. (nd) Le cheval à Chypre d'après les figurines de terre cuite, *Chypre. La vie quotidienne de l'Antiquité à nos jours.* Paris.
Ohnefalsch Richter, M. (1893) *Kypros. Die Bibel und Homer.* Berlin.
Pottier, E. (1909) *Diphilos et les Modeleurs de Terre Cuites.* Paris.
Sophocleous, S. (1985) *Atlas des Représentations Chypro-Archaïques des Divinités.* Göteborg.
Vandenabeele, F. (1973) Quelques terres cuites chypriotes aux jambes articulées. *BCH 97,* 47–57.
Vandenabeele, F. (1986a) Bread in the Cypriote terracotta production of the Archaic period. *Medelhavs Mus B 21,* 39–43.
Vandenabeele, F. (1986b) Phoenician influence on the Cypro-Archaic terracotta production and Cypriot influence abroad. *Acts 1986,* 351–60.
Vandenabeele, F. (forthcoming) Kourotrophoi in the Cypriote terracotta production from the Early Bronze Age to the Late Archaic period. *RDAC.*
Walters, H. B. (1903) *Catalogue of the Terracottas in the Department of Greek and Roman Antiquities of the British Museum.* London.
Young, J.H. & Halstead Young, S. (1955) *Terracotta Figurines from Kourion in Cyprus.* Philadelphia.

32
Cypriot mosaics: local traditions and external influences

D. Michaelides
Department of Antiquities, Cyprus

Ladies and gentlemen, I will, quite unashamedly, bring these discussions on early Cyprus right up to early Byzantine times—times that for most of you are decidely modern. I feel, however, that the pattern of many of the commercial and cultural trends already established during the earlier periods continued within a similar framework and without a fundamental change right up to the arrival of the Arabs in Cyprus around the middle of the 7th century AD.

The mosaics of Cyprus are particularly well suited for illustrating this point, because Cyprus was one of the main centres of mosaic production, especially during the Roman and the early Christian periods (Michaelides 1987a, 1987b; Daszewski & Michaelides 1988; also Balty, J. 1981). Because of its small size, however, and, above all, because of its geographical position, Cyprus produced mosaics which, in spite of their own distinct character, always reflect the major artistic currents emanating from the surrounding areas. These, after all, included Asia Minor with Cilicia (Budde 1969; 1972; 1987) on the north, Egypt and Alexandria (Daszewski 1985a) on the south, island Greece (Pelekanides & Atzaka 1974) on the west, and, last but not least, the Syro-Palestinian coast with such centres as Antioch and Apamea[1] on the east—all areas famous for their mosaic production that, to a greater or lesser extent, played their role in the moulding of the Cypriot mosaic workshops.

The aim of this paper is not to give an account of mosaic art in Cyprus, but to concentrate on a few examples made during some of the crucial periods of the island's history, and through them try and define the artistic, cultural and commercial climate in Cyprus.

There can be little doubt that the first mosaics in Cyprus, like the panel of Scylla from Nea Paphos (Fig 32.1), made of pebbles and attributed to the late 4th/ early 3rd century BC (Nicolaou 1984, 219–25, Figs 6–8; Salzmann

Figure 32.1 Nea Paphos. Scylla mosaic (Department of Antiquities, Cyprus).

1982, 126, Suppl 3, Pl 64.1; Michaelides 1987a, 10, Pl I), were made by foreign artists. There can, moreover, be no doubt that the artists came from the Greek world. These early mosaics, in fact, belong to the full flowering of the process of bringing Cyprus more fully into the Hellenistic world —a process that had already started in the previous century, both through Greek commercial expansionism to the East (especially after the so-called Peace of Kallias of 488 BC which gave Athens the right to carry on trade in the Near Eastern harbours) (*SCE* IV.2, 484–9) and through the activities of enlightened rulers like Evagoras I of Salamis and his successors, who invited Greek men of letters, artists and musicians to come to Cyprus, and who introduced on an official basis the Greek alphabet (*SCE* IV.2, 501–5). Speaking of the alphabet, it is interesting to observe that some of the earliest alphabetic or digraphic inscriptions on the island were not written on local limestone, but on marble slabs or blocks imported from Greece.[2] Ready-made statues were also imported during this same period as shown by several funerary stelae from Marion (Megaw 1979) and a recently discovered statue of a lion from Nea Paphos (Maier, Karageorghis *et al* 1984, 236, Fig 215). Greek art gradually established itself in other fields too, as shown by the fresco decoration of some of the tombs excavated in Nea Paphos.[3] It is then in the light of this commercial and cultural expansion of Greece towards the East—a process that was only completed with the advent of Alexander the Great and later the Ptolemies—that we have to interpret the panel of Scylla, the earliest known mosaic in Cyprus, which, in fact, finds its closest parallels in floors from Piraeus (Fig 32.2) and Eretria

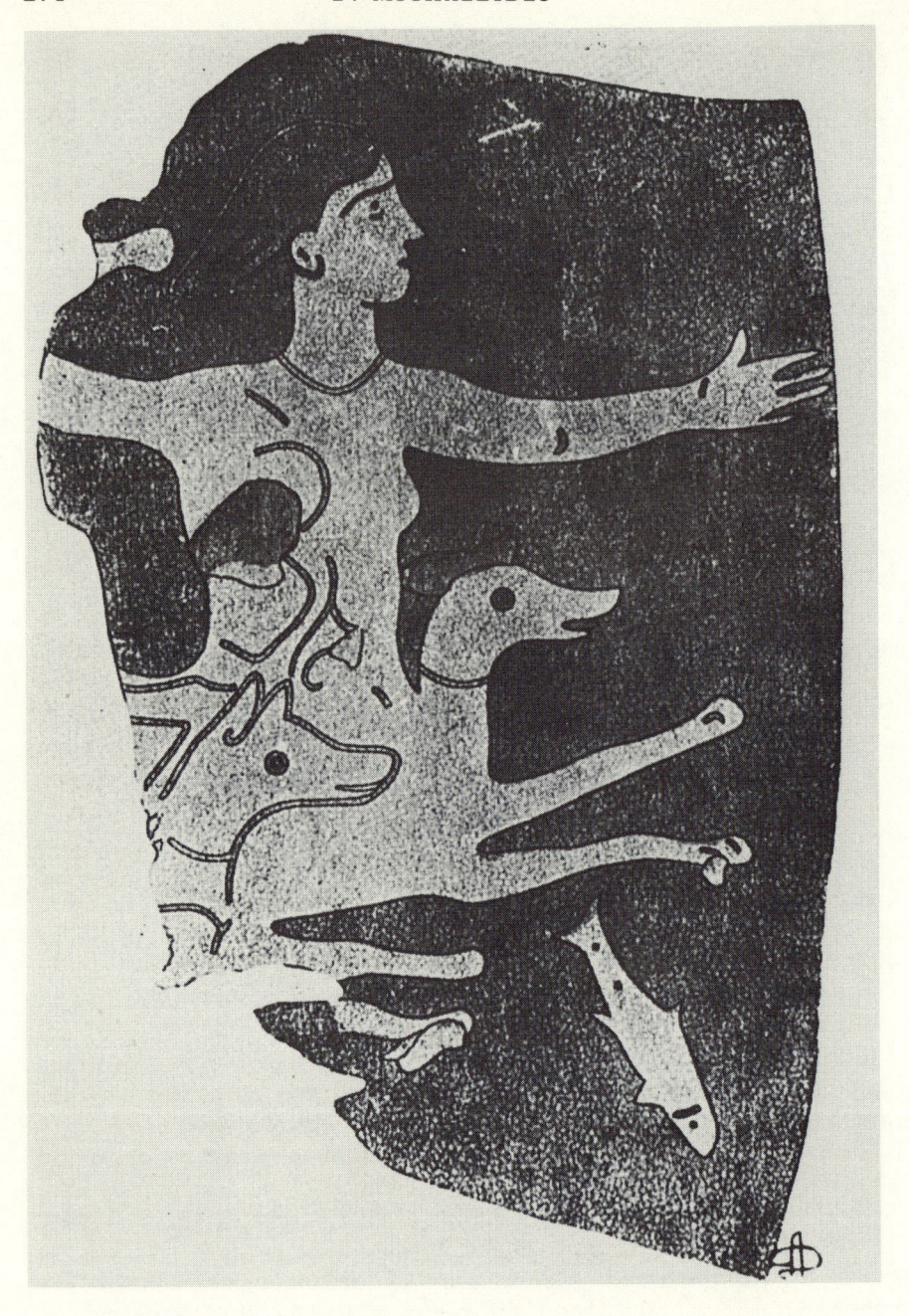

Figure 32.2 Piraeus. Scylla mosaic (*from* Salzmann 1982, Pl 25.2).

Figure 32.3 Nea Paphos, House of Dionysos: Narcissus (Department of Antiquities, Cyprus).

(see Salzmann 1982, 92, no 41, Pls 49.3, 50.2, 102.3; 109, no 108, Pl 25.2, respectively). A glance at Salzmann's distribution map of pebble mosaics (1982, Map 1), shows quite clearly that Cyprus and Sinope, with the only exception of the later and certainly surprising examples at Ai Khanoum in Afghanistan, are the easternmost outposts of this essentially Greek form of art. It shows, moreover, that no true pebble mosaics have yet been found in Egypt, and that the art was completely unknown in the Syro-Palestinian world which in earlier times had such close links with Cyprus, and which later on would be the main influence on Cypriot mosaic production.

From this first appearance of mosaics, we will now jump to the late 2nd/

Figure 32.4 Antioch, House of Narcissus: Narcissus (*from* Levi 1947, Pl X b).

early 3rd century AD, when the art was firmly established on the island. This is a period of great prosperity in Cyprus and mosaic decoration was *de rigeur* in every affluent household. By this time, the old technique, employing natural, uncut pebbles, had long since been abandoned, and mosaics were made with specially cut tesserae of stone, marble, glass and other materials. Mosaic decoration was used in all parts of the Roman world and it followed a more or less universal vocabulary. Even so, the styles and traditions of the large centres of mosaic production (and their spheres of influence) can be easily distinguished. The discoveries of the last 25 years in Cyprus, especially at Nea Paphos, have shown beyond doubt that the demand for mosaic decoration was large enough to warrant the formation of local workshops. It has not yet been established what the formative influences on these workshops were. It is certain, however, that their closest affiliations were no more with Greece but with the Syro-Palestinian coast —which, because of its geographic proximity, was always in close contact with Cyprus. It must be emphasized, however, that these strong East Mediterranean affiliations did not at any time bar ideas and influences coming from other parts of the ancient world.

We will now examine some of the similarities between the Cypriot and the East Mediterranean workshops. One thing that immediately puts the figured decoration from these different centres in the same artistic and cultural ambience, is their predilection for mythological subjects which leave practically no room for genre scenes and scenes from daily life, so dear to workshops in other parts of the ancient world, North Africa in particular. The choice of specific myths also shows the same cultural background, as I hope the following selection will show. In Nea Paphos, in the House of Dionysos (Michaelides 1987a, 14–15, Pl II), there is a representation of Narcissus gazing at his reflection, and in Antioch there are four mosaics with the same scene, one in the House of Narcissus (Levi 1947, Pl X.6), one in the House of the Red Pavement (Levi 1947, Pl XIV.6), one in the House of the Buffet Supper (Levi 1947, Pl XXIIIc) and one in the House of Menander (Levi 1947, Pl XLVa). In Cyprus, the Rape of Ganymede is depicted in the House of Dionysos in Nea Paphos (Michaelides 1987a, 18, col Pl XXI), and in the Building of the Achilles Mosaic at Kourion (Kondoleon 1982, 101, Fig 76), and the myth is again found depicted in the House of the Buffet Supper in Antioch (Levi 1947, Pl XXIV). The House of Dionysos at Nea Paphos has a panel depicting Pyramos and Thisbe (Michaelides 1987a, 19, Pl VII), and the two heroes are also depicted (as river-gods) in the House of the Porticoes at Seleucia (Antioch) (Levi 1947, Pl XVIIIc, d).[4] In the same house in Nea Paphos there is a rendering of the myth of Apollo and Daphne (Michaelides 1987a, 21, Pl IX), a myth that is also found represented in the House of Menander in Antioch (Levi 1947, Pl XLVII.6). And, so as not to restrict the comparisons to Antioch only, I should mention that Phaedra and Hippolytos are represented not only in the House of Dionysos in Nea Paphos (Michaelides 1987a, 17, Pl XXI) and

Figure 32.5. Nea Paphos. Bust of Summer (D. Michaelides).

Figure 32.6 Antioch, House of the Porticoes: Bust of Nicostratos (*from* Levi 1947, Pl XIX d).

the House of the Red Pavement in Antioch (Levi 1947, Pl XIb) but also at Sheikh Zoueda in the Sinai (Clédat 1915, Pl III) and on a pavement found during the excavations under the Church of the Virgin at Madaba in Jordan (Buschhausen 1986). I should also mention that the only other known representations of Akme, the nymph in the Icarios mosaic from the House of Dionysos in Nea Paphos (Michaelides 1987a, 20, Pl VIII), are found on a mosaic from Byblos (Chéhab 1975, 371–2, Pl CLXXVII.2) and another from Baalbek in Lebanon (Moreno 1984). Moreover, stretching the chronological limits (of the Cypriot examples) to include the 4th century, we find even more affinities in the choice of rarely represented subjects, such as the Birth of Dionysos, found in the House of Aion in Nea Paphos (Daszewski 1985b 35–8, Pls 16–19)[5] and in Bath D of Antioch (Levi 1947, Pl LXVb); and, even more so, the myth of Cassiopeia known in ancient

Figure 32.7 Antioch, House of Dionysos and Ariadne: Perseus and Andromeda (*from* Levi 1947, Pl XXIX c).

Figure 32.8 Nea Paphos, House of Dionysos: Phaedra and Hippolytos (Department of Antiquities, Cyprus).

mosaic art from three examples only, one in the House of Aion at Nea Paphos (Daszewski 1985b, 29–33, Pls 7–11; and Daszewski 1986), one from Palmyra (Stern 1977) and one from Apamea (Balty, J. Ch. 1981b).

Apart from these thematic similarities, however, there are also stylistic parallels between the mosaics of Cyprus and the other East Mediterranean workshops. For example, the already mentioned panel of Narcissus (Fig 32.3) from Nea Paphos (Michaelides 1987a, 14–15, Pl II) is almost identical with the one from the House of Narcissus (Fig 32.4), at Antioch (Levi 1947, Pl Xb). The laurel wreath around the bust of Summer (Fig 32.5) in a recently recomposed fragment in Nea Paphos (Michaelides 1986a), finds its closest parallels in the wreath around the bust of athletes (Fig 32.6) in the Portico of Nicostratos in the House of the Porticoes at Seleucia (Antioch) (Levi 1947, Pl XIXb, d). The stylistic similarities in the rendering of figures is also clearly discernible when we compare the figure of Perseus in the scene with Andromeda in the mosaic from the House of Dionysos and Ariadne (Fig 32.7) at Antioch (Levi 1947, Pl XXIXc) with that of Hippolytos in the scene with Phaedra (Fig 32.8) from the House of Dionysos in Paphos (Michaelides 1987a, 17, Pl XXI).

As we shall see presently, these links with the Syro-Palestinian coast became even stronger in the early Christian period. Before we examine them, however, let us look at some other sources of influence during this mid-Roman period. Such influences occur usually in isolated examples and do not on the whole leave a permanent mark on the vocabulary or style of the local workshops. In fact, more often than not, by the time these foreign

Figure 32.9 Nea Paphos, House of Dionysos: Detail of Hunting scene (Department of Antiquities, Cyprus).

Figure 32.10 Volubilis. Detail of Hunting mosaic (D. Michaelides).

ideas reached Cyprus (presumably through copy-books) and were recreated by the local artists, they had become thoroughly Cypriot in their general character.

The Hunting Scenes in the House of Dionysos at Nea Paphos (Michaelides 1987a, 18–19, Pl VII), for example, are stylistically identical to the rest of the mosaic decoration of the house. Iconographically, however, such scenes, depicting tigers, lions, leopards, etc (animals that were probably unknown to most Cypriots), betray their North African origin. Admittedly, such scenes found their way to most parts of the Roman world. They did, however, remain a predominantly North African/ West European speciality. One detail of the Paphos example will, I hope, illustrate the point I want to make. It shows a leopard walking away from the decapitated body of an onager, holding the bleeding head of her victim between her jaws (Nicolaou 1968, Pl XXXVIII; Maier, Karageorghis *et al* 1984, Fig 231 (Fig 32.9). This is a detail that, as far as I know, is not found anywhere east of Cyprus, while in the West it is rather common. In North Africa, where such scenes presumably originated, we find it in several versions on a floor at Volubilis in Morocco,[6] with the scene reduced to its essentials (there is no decapitated body) and with combinations of different animals for hunter and victim in each panel (Fig 32.10). Almost as surprising as the occurrence of the scene in Paphos is the one in the baths of Philippi in Greece (Waywell 1979, Pl 50, Fig 38 (Fig 32.11) which is iconographically the closest to Paphos since it shows the decapitated body of the onager. The leopard,

Figure 32.11 Philippi, Baths: Tiger and Onager (*from* Weywell 1979, Pl 50, Fig 38).

however, has been replaced by a tiger. Further west the scene is found at Orbe in Switzerland (Gonzenbach 1961 178–9, Pls 54–5; 1974, Fig 8) (Fig 32.12), where a lion holds a stag's head, and it reached even the then remote shores of England where we find an example, again with a lion holding a stag's head, at Verulamium (Neal 1981, Pl 75) (Fig 32.13).

Another floor in the House of Dionysos in Nea Paphos, this time geometric, betrays its almost certain western origins. It consists of 16 small panels, each containing a different geometric design (Eliades 1984, 51, Fig.). The designs themselves belong to the standard decorative repertory of mosaic art, and do not present anything unusual. What is unusual is the way in which they are used all together, each in a separate small compartment, giving the floor the appearance of a page from a sample book. Mosaics decorated in this fashion, known as 'mosaïques à décor multiple', are not found elsewhwere in Cyprus, and are, in fact, very rare except in western Europe where they characterize the mosaics of France and Switzerland.[7]

Before we abandon the subject of western influences, mention must also be made of the gladiatorial mosaics of Kourion (Michaelides 1987a, 22–4, Pl X; col ills in *Guide to Kourion* 1987, Figs 14–16). Although it is now generally accepted that gladiatorial shows were a lot more popular in the Greek East than it had been assumed in the past,[8] there is no doubt that their representation in mosaic art is practically unknown in the East, while, on the contrary, it is common in the West. In fact, the only other gladiatorial mosaics that I know of in the Greek world are the two examples from the island of Cos (Asemakopoulou-Atzaka 1973, 234, no 29, and 232, no 25), which, by the way (and surely not by coincidence) frame a composition of Orpheus and the Beasts that has iconographic similarities with the Orpheus mosaic in the house of the same name in Nea Paphos (Michaelides 1986b).

It is clear, however, that in spite of these flirtations with the western iconographic world, Cypriot mosaic art was firmly rooted in the East Mediterranean, and had its closest links with such centres as Antioch and Apamea. These links were to become even closer in the early Christian period, and they were further enhanced by political and religious factors. In AD 293, with the division of the Empire into East and West under Diocletian, Cyprus, together with SE Asia Minor, Syria and Palestine, went to the Diocese of the East. Thus the island was no more governed by its own Proconsul but by a *consularis* functioning under the Praetorian Prefect of the Orient who was based at Antioch in Syria. Even though further changes followed, the subordination of Cyprus to Antioch was to continue for another two centuries: first, under the Vicar of the Orient, and after AD 331, under the Count of the Orient, always based in Antioch. In the religious domain there were many controversies and a hostility that came about especially after the Church of Antioch claimed supremacy over that of Cyprus. In spite of this, however, the art of the two Churches is often practically identical.

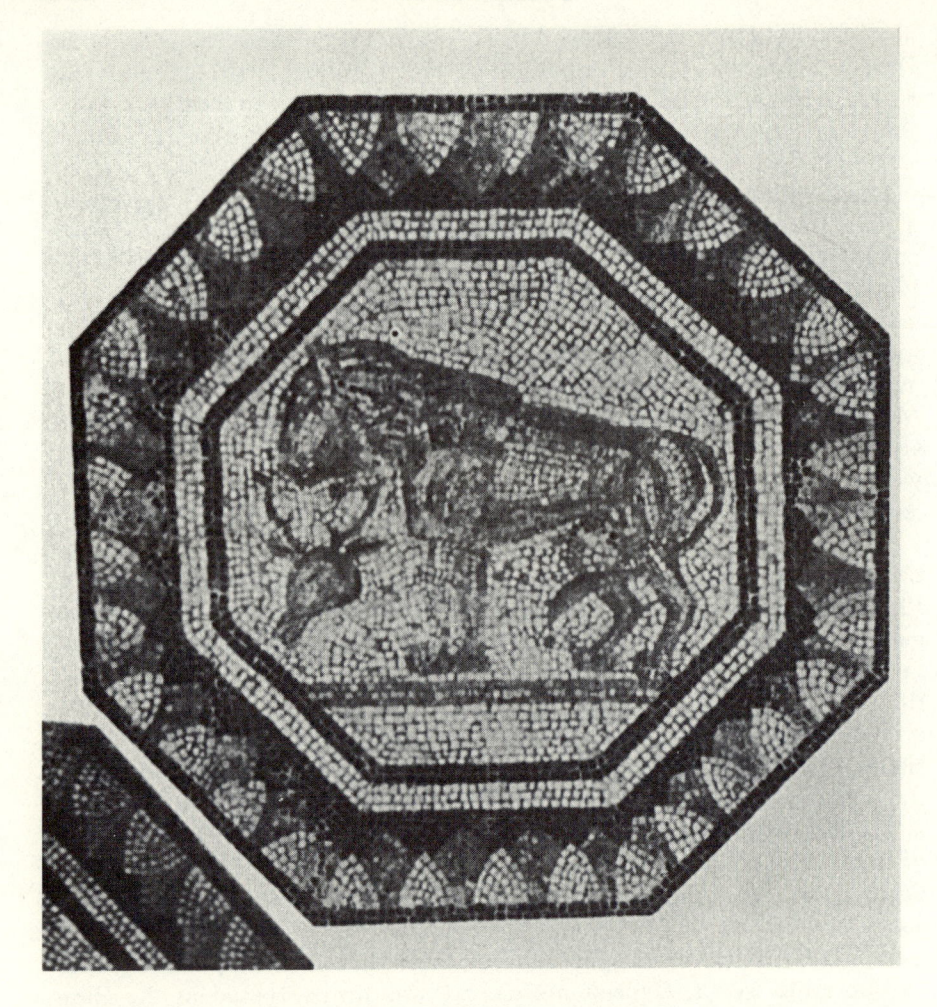

Figure 32.12 Orbe. Lion mosaic (*from* Gozenbach 1974, Fig 8).

The local schools continued to be very active on the island, but their products now belonged to an early Christian artistic *koiné*, and are often almost indistinguishable from mosaics found along the East Mediterranean coast. The early-expressed iconoclastic tendencies of the Christian religion meant that early Christian art was essentially uniconic, and although figured decoration was occasionally employed, its character remained always very restricted. Here too, the East Mediterranean workshops followed a common tradition. Suffice to mention the 6th century example on the atrium of basislica A at Ayios Yeoryios of Peyia depicting four rampant animals (Fig 32.14), a wild boar, a bear, a lion and a humped ox or zebu (Megaw 1976, 15, Pl XI.26; Michaelides 1987a, 48, PL XXXIV), and compare it to the nearly contemporary mosaic of Leontios at Awza'i in

Figure 32.13 Verulamium. Lion mosaic (*from* Neal 1981, Pl 75)

Lebanon (Chéhab 1958 & 1959, 127-8, Pl LXXXVII) (Fig 32.15), where, in an admittedly different geometric framework, there are four very similar animals, a zebu, a lion a boar and a rabbit.

Such similarities can be illustrated even better when we examine certain geometric patterns which first appeared during this period, were used for about two centuries and then went out of fashion. One of these is the so-called scalloped square, of which there are three examples in Cyprus: one in the Basilica of Chrysopolitissa in Nea Paphos (Daszewski & Michaelides 1988, 135, Fig 59), one from the Complex of Eustolios at Kourion (Daszewski & Michaelides 1988, 135, Fig 46) (Fig 32.16), and an almost identical one from the Basilica of Ayia Trias near Yialousa (Megaw 1976, 53, Fig 18; Pelekanides & Atzaka 1974, 148-9, Pl 135; Daszewski & Michaelides 1988, 135, Fig 30) (Fig 32.17). This is a pattern used exclusively by East Mediterranean workshops. There are numerous renderings throughout the region (Daszewski & Michaelides 1988, 135-8 and n 107) amongst which the following are particularly close to the Cypriot examples: the Magdouh mosaic from Antioch (Levi 1947, Pl CXXXVIIa, b), the one from the Church of St Menas at Rihāb in Jordan (Piccirillo 1981, 76, Pl 18), one from the church of the Herodium in the Occupied West Bank (Ovadiah 1987, 70, Pl LXXXII) and the one at 'Agur (Fig 32.18) in Israel (Ovadiah 1987, 11, Pl I). I must again emphasize, however, that the pattern is absent from any other region, Greece included, except for one isolated example in the Basilica of St Anastasia at Arkasa on Carpathos (Pelekanides & Atzaka

286   D. MICHAELIDES

Figure 32.14 Ayios Yeoryios, Peyia. Basilica A: Atrium mosaic (Department of Antiquities, Cyprus).

Figure 32.15 Awza'i. Mosaic of Leontios (*from* Chéhab 1958–9, Pl 87).

Figure 32.16 Kourion, Complex of Eustolios: Geometric mosaic (D. Michaelides).

Figure 32.17 Yialousa, Basilica of Ayia Trias: Nave mosaic (Department of Antiquities, Cyprus).

Figure 32.18 'Agur. Geometric mosaic (*from* Ovadiah 1987, Pl I).

1974, 55–61, Pl 18), a fact that is not without significance since Carpathos is one of the southernmost islands of the Dodecanese.

Another group of patterns characteristic of this period and of these workshops is the one created by the continuous interlacing of cables, which owe their effect to the relentless repetition of one and the same motif over a large area. Two examples will, I think, suffice to show the closeness of the Cypriot and the Antiochene workshops. The Cypriot one comes from Basilica A at Ayios Yeoryios of Peyia (Daszewski & Michaelides 1988, 140, Fig 64) (Fig 32.19), and the almost identical Antiochene one comes from the House of the Phoenix (Levi 1947, Pl CXXXV) (Fig 32.20).

The 6th century, however, saw some major changes in Cypriot mosaic art, and in the cultural equilibrium of the East Mediterranean as a whole. Antioch, for example, one of the main centres and sources of influence, was destroyed by earthquakes and then sacked by Chorsoes. It was, however, Justinian and his provincial reorganization that brought about the biggest changes. In AD 535 the governor of Cyprus ceased to function under the Count of the Orient in Antioch, and became directly responsible to the central government in Constantinople (Hill 1949, 257–8). This administrative reorientation also brought about an artistic and commercial reorientation. Cypriot art suddenly broke with the East Mediterranean tradition, and turned to follow the mainstream art of the new metropolis, Constantinople. In the big building programme of this period, we find for the first time on the island Proconnesian marble playing a major role in architectural decoration, in the form of columns and capitals, as well as church furniture

Figure 32.19 Ayios Yeoryios, Peyia. Basilica A, Baptistery: Geometric mosaic (D. Michaelides).

Figure 32.20 Antioch, House of the phoenix: Geometric mosaic (*from* Levi 1947, Pl CXXXV).

(more often than not imported ready-made from Constantinople) as exemplified by the decoration of the three Basilicas at Ayios Yeoryios of Peyia (Megaw 1974, 71–2, Figs 16, 18). Proconnesian and other marbles were also used for floor decoration. Here it was employed either in large slabs, to be enjoyed for the beauty of the marble itself, as in the Bapistery of the Basilica of Ayios Epiphanios at Salamis-Constantia (Megaw 1976, 6, Pl V.4; Michaelides 1987a, 54, Pl XXXIX), or in wonderfully complex compositions of *opus sectile*, as in the examples from the Baths adjoining the Basilica of Campanopetra, also at Salamis-Constantia (Michaelides 1987a, 52–3, Pl XXXVIII), and the floors of the Basilica of Ayios Philon at ancient Carpasia (Megaw 1976, 5–6, Fig 3; du Plat Taylor & Megaw 1981 Pls XXXVII-XXXVIII, XLIII-XLIV).

What best reflects the change towards Constantinople, however, are the three apse mosaics surviving until recently on the island. All three decorated the apses of early Christian basilicas that were incorporated into later churches. Two of these, the one at Panayia Kanakaria at Lythrankomi (Megaw & Hawkins 1977; Megaw 1985, 173-98; Michaelides 1987a, 54–5, Pls XXV, XL) and the one at Panayia Kyra at Livadhia (Megaw & Hawkins 1976; Megaw 1985, 173-98; Michaelides 1987a, 56, Pl XLI), were destroyed (except for a few fragments of the former) after the Turkish invasion of 1974. The third one, at Panayia Angeloktistos at Kiti near Larnaca, is the only one to survive more or less intact (Megaw 1985, 173-98; Michaelides 1987a, 55–6, col Pls XXVI, Pl XLI). It depicts the Virgin *Hodegetria* with Christ and the Archangels, and it is executed in the full metropolitan style. It also represents the last but splendid flowering of Cypriot mosaic art that came to an end with the Arab invasions of the mid 7th century AD which plunged the island into the Dark Ages.

NOTES

[1] For Antioch, see Levi 1947. For Apamea see Balty, J.Ch. 1981a with previous biliography. See also Balty, J. 1986. For Syrian mosaics in general, see Balty, J. 1977. For mosaics from other regions of the Eastern Mediterranean, see Chéhab 1958, 1959 for Lebanon, Avi-Yonah 1933-5 for Palestine and Ovadiah 1987 for Israel.

[2] Like, for example, the 4th century BC statue base found in the Temple of Demeter and Kore at Kourion and now in the British Musuem (Dept. of Greek and Roman Antiquities, inv no 96.2–1), for which see Mitford 1971, 62–4, n 26; and Nicolaou 1971, 16, Pl XIVb.

[3] Like, for example, Tomb 1 at the locality *Ammoi*. See Nicolaou 1966, 600, Fig 28.

[4] Pyramos is also depicted, without Thisbe, in a mosaic in the House of Cilicia at Antioch (Levi 1947, Pl IX.6).

[5] For different views see Deckers 1986.

[6] The floor is as far a I know unpublished.

[7] On mosaics of this type, see Gonzenbach 1961, *passim;* and Stern 1965.

[8] For the earlier theories, see Chapot 1924, *s.v.* 'Gladiateur'; Lafaye 1877; and Friedländer 1920, 105–6. Most of the evidence for gladiatorial shows in the Greek East is collected in Robert 1940, and Robert 1946, 1948, 1950 and 1951.

LIST OF REFERENCES

Asemakopoulou-Atzaka, P. (1973) 'Κατάλογος Πωμαϊυῶν Ψυφιδωίων Δαπέδων μέ Ανθρώπινες Μορφές στὸν 'Ελλυνικὸ ὧρο', *Hellenika* 26, 216–54. '

Avi-Yonah, M. (1933–5) Mosaic pavements in Palestine. *QDAP* 2, 136–81; *3*, 26–73; *4*, 187–93.

Balty, J. (1977) *Mosaïques Antiques de Syrie*. Brussels.

Balty, J. (1981) La mosaïque antique au Proche-Orient. I, Des origines à la Tetrarchie, in *Aufstieg und Niedergang der römischen Welt*, II, 12, 2. Berlin.

Balty, J. (1986) *Mosaïques d'Apamée (Musées Royaux d'Art et d'Histoire, Guide du Visiteur)*. Brussels.

Balty, J. Ch. (1981a) *Guide d'Apamée*. Brussels.

Balty, J. Ch. (1981b) Une version orientale méconnue du mythe de Cassiopée, in *Mythologie gréco-romaine. Mythologies péripheriques*, Paris 17 mai 1979 (Colloques Internationaux du Centre National de la Recherche Scientifique no 593) (eds. L. Kahil & Ch. Auge) 95–106. Paris.

Budde, L. (1969 & 1972) *Antike Mosaiken in Kilikien*, I & II *(Beiträge zur Kunst des christlichen Ostens*, 5 & 6). Recklinghausen.

Budde, L. (1987) *St. Pantaleon von Aphrodisias in Kilikien (Bieträge zur Kunst des christlichen Ostens*, 9). Recklinghausen.

Buschhausen, H. (1986) La sala dell' Ippolito, presso la Chiesa della Vergine Maria, in *I Mosaici della Giordania. Catalogo della Mostra.* (M. Piccirillo) 117–27. Rome.

Chapot, V. (1924) *Dictionnaire d'Archaeologie chrétienne.* Paris.

Chéhab, M. (1958 & 1959) Mosaïques du Liban. *B Mus Beyr* 14 & 15.

Chéhab, M. (1975) Mosaïques inédites du Liban, in *La Mosaïque Gréco-Romaine. IIe Colloque International pour l'Étude de la Mosaïque Antique*, Vienne 30 Août-4 Septembre 1971. 371–6. Paris.

Clédat, J. (1915) Fouilles à Cheikh Zouêde. *ASAE 15*, 15–17.

Daszewski, W.A. (1985a) *Corpus of Mosaics from Egypt*, I *(Aegyptiaca Treverensia, 3)*. Mainz am Rhein.

Daszewski, W.A. (1985b) *Dionysos der Erlöser (Trierer Beiträge zur Altertumskunde*, 2). Mainz am Rhein.

Daszewski, W.A. (1986) Cassiopeia in Paphos, a Levantine going West. *Acts 1986*, 454–71.

Daszewski, W.A. & Michaelides, D. (1988) *Mosaic Floors in Cyprus (Biblioteca di Felix Ravenna, 3)*. Ravenna.

Deckers, J.G. (1986) Dionysos der Erlöser? *Röm Q Schr 81*, 145–72.

du Plat Taylor, J. & Megaw, A.H.S. (1981) Excavations at Ayios Philon, the ancient Carpasia, part II. *RDAC*, 209–56.

Eliades, G. (1984) *The House of Dionysos*. Paphos.

Friedländer, L. (1920) *Darstellungen aus der Sittengeshichte Roms, II*. (10th ed). Leipzig.

Gonzenbach, V. von (1961) *Römische Mosaiken der Schweiz*. Basel.

Gonzenbach, V. von (1974) *Les mosaïques romaines d'Orbe (Guides Archéologiques de la Suisse, 5)*.

Guide to Kourion (1987) The Bank of Cyprus Cultural Foundation in collaboration with the Department of Antiquities. Nicosia.

Hill, G. (1940) *A History of Cyprus, I*. Cambridge.

Kondoleon, C. (1982) The mosaics - Areas I and II, in *An Archaeological Guide to the Ancient Kourion Area and the Akrotiri Peninsula*. (ed. H. Wylde Swiny) 98–105. Nicosia.

Lafaye, G. (1877) Gladiator, in *Dictionnaire des Antiquités grecques et romaines*, vol. 5. (C. Daremberg & E. Saglio) 1563-99. Paris.

Levi, D. (1947) *Antioch Mosaic Pavements*. Princeton.

Maier, F-G. Karageorghis, V. *et al* (1984) *Paphos. History and Archaeology*. Nicosia.
Megaw, A.H.S. (1974) Byzantine architecture and decoration in Cyprus: metropolitan or provincial? *DOP 28*, 59–88.
Megaw, A.H.S. (1976) Interior decoration in Early Christian Cyprus, in *Rapports et Co-Rapports. XVe Congrès International d'Études Byzantines*. Athens.
Megaw, A.H.S. (1979) The head and feet fragments and another stele from Marion, in *Studies presented in memory of P. Dikaios*. 139–54. Nicosia.
Megaw, A.H.S. (1985) Mosaici parietali Paleobizantini di Cipro, in *XXXII° Corso di Cultura sull'arte Ravennate e Bizantina, "Cipro e il Mediterraneo Orientale,"* Ravenna 23–3 Marzo 1985, 173-98. Ravenna.
Megaw, A.H.S. & Hawkins, E.J.W. (1976) A fragmentary mosaic of the orant Virgin in Cyprus, in *Actes XIVe Congrès International d'Études Byzantines* Bucharest 1971 III 363–66. Bucharest.
Megaw, A.H.S. & Hawkins, E.J.W. (1977) *The Church of Panagia Kanakaria at Lythrankomi in Cyprus, its mosaics and frescoes*. Dumbarton Oaks.
Michaelides, D. (1986a) A season mosaic from Nea Paphos. *RDAC*, 212–21.
Michaelides, D. (1986b) A new Orpheus mosaic in Cyprus. *Acts 1986*, 473–89.
Michaelides, D. (1987a) *Cypriot Mosaics (Picture Book no 7)*. Nicosia.
Michaelides, D. (1987b) A catalogue of the Hellenistic, Roman and Early Christian Mosaics of Cyprus with representations of human figures. *RDAC*, 239–52.
Mitford, T.B. (1971) *The Inscriptions of Kourion*. Philadelphia.
Moreno, P. (1984) Kairós, Akmé e Cháris da una pittura di Apelle, in *Dialoghi di Archeologia*, n 2, 115–18.
Neal, D.S. (1981) *Roman Mosaics in Britain* (Britannia Monograph Series no 1). London.
Nicolaou, I. (1971) *Cypriot Inscribed Stones (Picture Book no 6)*. Nicosia.
Nicolaou, K. (1966) The topography of Nea Paphos, in *Mélanges offerts à K. Michalowski*, 561–601. Warsaw.
Nicolaou, K. (1968) *Ancient Monuments of Cyprus (Picture Book no 4)*. Nicosia.
Nicolaou, K. (1984) Three new mosaics at Paphos, Cyprus, in *III° Colloquio Internazionale sul Mosaico Antico*, Ravenna 6–10 settembre 1980, 219–25. Ravenna.
Ovadiah, R. & A. (1987) *Hellenistic, Roman and Early Byzantine Mosaic pavements in Israel (Biblioteca Archaeologica 6)*. Rome.
Pelekanides, S. & Atzaka, P. (1974) Σύνταγμα τῶν Παλαιοχριστιανικῦν Ψυφιδωτῶν Δαπέδων τῆς Ἑλλάδος Ι, Νυσιώτικυ Ἑλλὰς (= Βυζαντινὰ Μνυμεία, 1). Salonica.
Piccirillo, M. (1981) *Chiese e Mosaici della Giordania Settentrionale (Studium Biblicum Franciscanum, Collectio Minor no 30)*. Jerusalem.
Robert, L. (1940) *Les gladiateurs dans l'Orient Grec*. Paris.
Robert, L. (1946, 1948, 1950, & 1951) Monuments des gladiateurs dans l'Orient Grec. *Hellenika 3, 5, 7 & 8*.
Salzmann, D. (1982) Untersuchungen zu den antiken Kieselmosaiken. *A Forsch 10*. Berlin.
Stern, H. (1965) Ateliers de mosaïstes rhodaniens d'époque galloromaine, in *La Mosaïque Gréco-romaine*. Colloque International, Paris 29 Août - 3 Septembre 1963, 233–43. Paris.
Stern, H. (1977) *Les mosaïques des Maisons d'Achille et de Cassiopée à Palmyre (Institut Francais d'Archéologie de Beyrouth 201)*. Paris.
Waywell, S.E. (1979) Roman mosaics in Greece. *AJA 83*, 293–31.

POSTER SUMMARY

33
A comparative analysis of the Late Cypriot pottery from North Sinai and Egypt and its implications for the study of patterns of trade in the Late Bronze Age

Celia Bergoffen
New York University

Did Late Cypriot pottery arrive in Egypt from its province in southern Canaan, via the North Sinai 'landbridge', an area under its direct control during most of the New Kingdom?

Poster 1: map showing the location of the 23 New Kingdom sites in North Sinai (about 300 LC sherds) and major Late Bronze Age centres in South Canaan (over 1100 LC sherds). The analysis of the LC material from Egypt is based on Merrillees' study (1968).

Poster 2: quantitative and proportional distribution of wares and forms in the three areas, histogram, pie charts, tables.

1. *Monochrome, White Shaved* wares: Egypt: not represented; North Sinai, South Canaan: well attested.

2. *White Slip II:* Egypt: rare; North Sinai, South Canaan: present in about equal proportions. *White Painted VI:* Egypt: rare; North Sinai, South Canaan: better represented, proportional distribution in North Sinai closer to South Canaan than to Egypt.

3. *Base Ring:* Egypt: juglets, about 76 per cent of BR assemblage; jugs, bowls, very rare or not attested; collection remains proportionately virtually unchanged from BR I to II, sharp quantitative decrease of BR II; North Sinai, South Canaan: typologically far more diversified collections. Most common BR I forms: North Sinai—jug, South Canaan—bowl, distribution of forms more even in BR II, marked decrease in South Canaan of BR II over I, in inverse proportion to the decrease in Egypt.

The analysis demonstrates that LC pottery in North Sinai derived from South Canaan. The typological and proportional distribution of BR vessels underscores the absence of overt links between the Egyptian collection on the one hand, and that of either of the other two regions. The assemblage from North Sinai in no way reflects the distribution in Egypt and was not affected by the reduced supplies of BR II wares there. Imported wares may have been sent along with routine consignments of supplies furnished by Egypt's province in southern Canaan to the Egyptian establishments in North Sinai.

REFERENCE

Merrillees, R. (1968) *The Cypriote Bronze Age Pottery found in Egypt (SIMA 18)*. Lund.

POSTER SUMMARY

34
Cypriot finds in Greece and Greek finds in Cyprus *ca* 950–500 BC.

Lone Wreidt Sørensen & John Lund
National Museum of Denmark, Copenhagen

Since the publication of Gjerstad's survey in *SCE* IV.2 new material has been brought to light making it interesting to re-study the exchange of artefacts between Cyprus and Greece. This contribution concentrates on ceramic finds and Cypriot figurines. It is intended as a step towards a more comprehensive study of the interconnections between Greece and Cyprus (*cf* the approach taken by Portugali & Knapp 1985).

The connection between Cyprus and Greece was re-established about 900 BC (Karageorghis 1982) as witnessed by Greek pottery—mainly Euboean and Attic *bowls*, reaching Cyprus (Sørensen 1988), and Cypriot pottery reaching Greece, especially small unguent *flasks*. Cypriot pottery of type II has been found in Euboea and Rhodes, and pottery of type III occurs here and in Crete and Cos as well. Cypriot pottery of type IV has been unearthed at these places as well as at Thera, Delos and Aegina (Coldstream 1969, 1979, 1982, 1984 and 1985).

Presumably both Euboeans and Phoenicians were involved in the intercommunication, but the trade in unguents to the Dodecanese and Crete is believed to have been in the hands of the Phoenicians on Cyprus (Coldstream 1985, 57). However, since little CG II pottery has been found in the western Mediterranean (Shefton 1982, 339 n 3) it may be concluded that Crete was the final destination for ships carrying these Cypriot vases and not merely a station en route to the Phoenician colonies in the west.

The Euboean/Cypriot connection ended about 700 BC, perhaps as a consequence of the Lelantine war. The submission of Phoenicia and Cyprus to Assyria may have contributed to the discontinuity, but this should hardly be overrated, since Assyria did not interfere heavily with the Cypriot kingdoms (Garelli 1983; Elayi 1983). At any rate the amount of Greek pottery imports in Cyprus decreased dramatically after *ca* 700 BC, and the Cypriot imports in Greece also declined (Boardman 1979).

The larger part of the Cypriot ceramic finds in Crete as well as Cos is constituted by Black-on-Red vessels, which predate *ca* 700 BC, whereas the majority of the finds from Rhodes belongs to type IV and comprises White Painted and Bichrome pottery. The situation in Cos thus resembles that of Crete rather than Rhodes and the occurrence in both Crete and Cos of a class of ware decorated with circles imitating Cypriot pottery (Coldstream 1984, 126) supports the hypothesis of a link between the two islands. The lack of finds of Cypriot figurines on Cos is perhaps a further indication that the Cypriot connection with Cos came to an end before such figurines made their appearance in the Greek world.

The character of the relationship appears to have changed when the import of Greek pottery in Cyprus was resumed in the second half of the 7th century. The vessels, again predominantly *bowls,* were at first mainly of East Greek origin, but from the middle of the 6th century onward almost all are of Attic manufacture. Whereas these imports peaked in the beginning of the 6th century it is curious that the import of Cypriot pottery in Greece declined after *ca* 600 BC, perhaps indicating that Greek merchants were by now the driving force in the relationship.

At the same time, however, Cypriot limestone and terracotta figurines were imported in Greece. They functioned primarily as votives in sanctuaries in Rhodes, Samos and Naucratis, a further sign that the character of the relationship had changed. The picture is not uniform, however, since Cypriot pottery has not been found at Samos, whereas such pottery as well as figurines occur in settlements and tombs in Rhodes. The society was apparently more cosmopolitan in Rhodes with resident Phoenicians having set up local workshops (Coldstream 1969; Bisi 1987).

The Cypriot figurines found in Greece correspond especially with finds from the south-eastern part of Cyprus, and an increase in the import of Greek pottery at Salamis at the very time when Cypriot figurines were dedicated in the Greek sanctuaries, support the idea that this part of Cyprus was a focal point for the inter-relationship (Schmidt 1968). Surprisingly, however, the supposed Eteo-Cypriot centre of Amathus received Greek pottery at a much more stable rate until the end of the 6th century, suggesting that the pattern of external communication was not uniform for the entire island but varied from one coastal kingdom to the other.

ADDENDUM

Since this paper went to press a number of important relevant studies by various authors have been published. *Acts 1986* and M. Andreose (ed.) *The Phoenicians* Milan 1988.

LIST OF REFERENCES

Boardman, J. (1979) Crete and Cyprus in the seventh century BC. *Acts 1979,* 264–8.
Bisi, A.M. (1987) Ateliers Phéniciens dans le monde égéen. *St Phen 5,* 225–37.
Coldstream, J.N. (1969) The Phoenicians of Ialysos. *BICS 16,* 2–8.
Coldstream, J.N. (1979) Some Cypriote traits in Cretan pottery, ca. 950–700 B.C. *Acts 1979,* 257–63.
Coldstream, J.N. (1982) Greeks and Phoenicians in the Aegean, in *Phönizier im Westen,* (ed H. G. Niemeyer) *Madrider Beiträge 8,* 261–72.
Coldstream, J.N. (1984) Cypriaca and Cretocypriaca from the north cemetery of Knossos. *RDAC,* 122–37.
Coldstream, J.N. (1985) Archaeology in Cyprus 1960–1985: The Geometric and Archaic periods, in *Archaeology in Cyprus 1960–1985* (ed. V. Karageorghis), 47–59. Nicosia.

Elayi, J. (1983) Les Cités Phéniciennes et l'Empire Assyrien à l'Epoque d'Assurbanipal. *R Assyr 77*, 45–58.

Garelli, P. (1983) Remarques sur les Rapports entre l'Assyrie et Cités Pheniciennes, in *Atti del I Congresso Internazionale di Studi Fenicie e Punici Roma, 5–10 Novembre 1979*, 61–6. Rome.

Karageorghis, V. (1982) *Cyprus from the Stone Age to the Romans*. London.

Portugali, Y. & Knapp, A.B. (1985) Cyprus and the Aegean: A spatial analysis of interaction in the 17th-14th centuries BC, in *Prehistoric Production and Exchange, The Aegean and Eastern Mediterranean, (Monograph 15)* Institute of Archaeology, University of California, 44–78. Los Angeles.

Schmidt, G. (1968) *Samos VIII. Kyprische Bildwerke aus dem Heraion von Samos*. Bonn.

Shefton, B.B. (1982) Greeks and Greek imports in the south of the Iberian peninsula, in *Phönizier im Westen*, (ed H.G. Niemeyer) *Madriger Beiträge 8*, 337–70.

Sørensen, L. (1988) Greek pottery in Cyprus, *Acta Hyperborea 1*, forthcoming.

PART SIX
The Emergence of Social Complexity

35
The organisation of the copper industry in Late Bronze Age Cyprus

J.D. Muhly
University of Pennsylvania

With the publication of *Kition* V, by V. Karageorghis and M. Demas, in 1986, the study of the Late Bronze Age in Cyprus saw the completion of 15 years of incredibly intense research and publication, covering all aspects of the period. The year 1971 was devoted to Enkomi, with the appearance of *Alasia I* and the final volumes of Dikaios' monumental publication of his own work at that site. It would be impossible to enumerate everything that appeared in the following 15 years, but special mention must be made of three more *Alasia* volumes, of the eight volumes devoted to work at Hala Sultan Tekke, and of the publication of renewed excavations at Pyla-Kokkinokremos. The imminent appearance of the final report on Maa-Palaeokastro, again by Karageorghis and Demas, will, in a very real sense, complete the series.

This work had given us a totally new picture of Cyprus in the 13th and 12th centuries BC. Years that used to be perceived in terms of invasion and destruction, of marauding Sea Peoples and Achaean colonists, are now seen as some of the most creative and expansive decades in Cypriot prehistory. Fundamental to the wealth and importance of Cyprus in this period was the island's copper industry, an industry that underwent an unprecedented expansion during the 13th century BC, the LC IIC period.

We now also realise that developments in Cyprus after *ca* 1200 BC were very different from those in the Greek mainland. There was a 'Dark Age' in Greece, especially during the years *ca* 1100–900 BC (even though that age does seem to be getting brighter with every passing excavation season); in contrast, Cyprus seems to have flourished during those years (Karageorghis 1988, 2–3), to the extent that Cypriot developments actually began to influence cultural changes in Greece rather than *vice versa* (Iakovou 1988, 11). The state of the copper industry during those centuries cannot be determined with any certainty for lack of evidence, since our knowledge of the period is based entirely upon cemetery evidence,[1] but the very wealth of the graves in those cemeteries indicates a high level of prosperity, one presumably still based, at least partially, upon the exploitation of the islands rich mineral resources.

The state of affairs in Cyprus prior to *ca* 1300 BC is also imperfectly understood, even now. We know little of any LC I or LC II site save Enkomi, and our knowledge of the Cypriot copper industry during the years *ca* 1600–1300 BC comes almost entirely from Dikaios' excavations at Enkomi, with very limited evidence for the MC III/LC I transition from Kalopsidha (Watkins 1966) (for Toumba tou Skourou see below).

It is entirely possible that Enkomi actually controlled the copper industry of the entire island by virtue of its status as the capital of the kingdom of Alashiya. I would even venture to suggest that the city was probably called Alashiya; the name served both as designation of the capital and of the kingdom, exactly as at nearby Ugarit.[2]

I am currently working in the Cyprus Museum on all the metallurgical materials excavated by Dikaios at Enkomi. I have gone through roughly one-tenth of all the trays from Enkomi, having studied some 600 trays out of the *ca* 6000 stored in the Cyprus Museum. From these I have catalogued some 400 fragments of tuyères or blow pipes. I know of no other Bronze Age site in the Mediterranean that has produced more than half-a-dozen such objects. It is clear that there were significant industrial operations at Enkomi or in its vicinity. Single deposits of tuyères have produced as many as 43 examples. Most of these are fragments of straight tuyères, having a bore of *ca* 2.0 cm. In general they appear not to be as massive as those from the site of Apliki-Karamallos, to be discussed below, but there are exceptions.

In addition to the straight tuyères there are several examples of the bent or elbow variety, also known as an angular tuyère, and at least one example of the so-called D-shaped tuyère, a type hitherto known only from Apliki. It is particularly significant that one of the elbow or bent tuyères (that from tray 2295D) comes from a deposit below Floor IX (Area III, Room 101, Level IA), indicating that the type was in use right from the beginning of the history of Enkomi. This tuyère comes, in fact, from a deposit regarded by Dikaios as representing '. . . the earliest evidence of copper smelting in the Fortress' (*Enkomi*, 18).

In other words the entire complex of copper smelting technology seems to have been in place right from the initial period of occupation at Enkomi. Regarding its antecedents we have no evidence whatsoever. The industry seems to appear full-blown at Enkomi, at the beginning of LC IA and, in terms of tuyères (and perhaps even of slag), seems to continue unchanged down to the end of LC IIC. At that time, according to Dikaios, the copper workshops were sealed by new floors, following the destruction of the level IIB building, and the entire metal industry was '. . . probably transferred to another part of the town, away from the Fortification Wall' (*Enkomi*, 87).

Enkomi does not represent the beginning of copper working on Cyprus. As demonstrated chiefly by the organizer of this Conference, E.J. Peltenburg, copper artefacts appear in Cyprus as early as *ca* 3500 BC (1982). The MC I date for copper mining at Ambelikou-Aletri established by Robert Merrillees, on the basis of ceramics found in the ancient mine shafts (1984), can now be supported by two radiocarbon determinations made on charcoal from the site of Ambelikou:

Lu-1694 3660 ± 55 BP

Lu-1726 3630 ± 55 BP

These dates, calibrated by Ingrid Olsson to 2044–1929 BC (1987, 33), are in perfect agreement with the accepted chronology for the beginning of the MC period.

More recently, our computer work on the PIXE analyses of EC and MC artefacts from Lapithos, published by Judy Weinstein Balthazar (1986), indicates that these objects were probably made of the same copper that was used in the copper ox-hide ingots found at Mathiati and Skouriotissa, dating to *ca* 1200 BC. As those ingots were made of Cypriot copper (Gale & Stos-Gale 1986; Stos-Gale, Gale & Zwicker 1986), it is reasonable to suggest that Cypriot copper deposits were already being exploited at least as early as the Early Cypriot period. But for copper production we have only very limited evidence, again from MC I Ambelikou-Aletri (Zwicker *et al* 1981; Zwicker 1982; Merrillees 1984, 7–11); there is no way of making a connection between this isolated evidence and the beginnings of copper production at Enkomi during the LCIA period.

The rapid development of the copper industry at Enkomi has not been sufficiently appreciated. Dikaios emphasized the importance of the industry during his Level IB, equivalent to LC IB or *ca* 1550–1450 BC (*Enkomi*, 22–4, 502, 505); this has been amply documented by my study of the tuyères. Of the 226 tuyère fragments photographed (by Stuart Swiny) in 1986 over half (146) came from Level IB. This is the period of Egyptian references to the land of Asy/Asija, when Tuthmosis III recorded the receipt of several different types of copper from Asy/Asija (Lalouette 1979, 341). There is still much discussion about the identification (Merrillees 1987), but I would now regard references to the land of Asy/Asija as equivalent to references to the land of Alashiya (Muhly 1987; *contra* Helck 1985).

Dikaios saw Enkomi as a major copper-producing site involved in the primary smelting of copper ore, an activity that took place in a series of workshops located chiefly in the western part of the large building that made up his Area III. This building, which began life as a Fortress, had a history of copper working that Dikaios thought went back to the end of the MC period. Enkomi, however, is better seen as a LC site, but one of those rare Cypriot sites with real stratigraphy, with ten successive phases or floors, divided by Dikaios into at least six different levels.

For Dikaios, his Area III building had both residential and industrial functions; the industrial operations were located in the western wing for 'topographical reason, namely that smoke and heat could be carried away from the residential part by the sea breeze' (*Enkomi*, 44). During his Level IIB (LC IIC), he argued, the Area III building was taken over by Mycenaean industrialists who expanded the copper smelting to such an extent that a great slag heap or dump accumulated in the open area to the northwest of the building (*Enkomi*, 61–2, 65, 510). For Dikaios, then

'. . . the great impetus in the copper production, was due to the presence of Mycenaean industrialists who settled at Enkomi and built a residence with some suggestion to Mycenaean palace architecture' (*Enkomi*, 512; also *Enkomi* 66).

It is here that we must confront one of the most significant changes, since the days of Porphyrios Dikaios, in our conception of Cyprus during the years *ca* 1300–1100 BC. Virtually no archaeologist today would accept the presence of a Mycenaean industrialist at Enkomi. More importantly, no one would explain the growth of the Cypriot industry in such terms. Today we can see that, in the 13th century BC, copper production was going on not just at Enkomi but all over the island.

The 13th century in Cyprus was a time of great urban expansion with new settlements springing up all across the island, especially along the southern coast, from Pyla-Kokkinokremos to Maa-Palaeokastro (Negbi 1986). All of these settlements were concerned with metal working and copper production. An industry that, prior to *ca* 1300 BC seems to have been confined to the region of Enkomi, was now in operation over much of the southern part of the island. Even that localization could turn out to be misleading. It must be remembered that our appreciation of the significance of the copper industry, has come about largely since 1974, when archaeological work was restricted to the southern half of the island.

Sites such as Apliki-Karamallos, and even the sanctuary at Myrtou-Pighades, should remind us that a similar industrial expansion was underway in the north as well. Excavations at Toumba tou Skourou, hopefully soon to appear in print, indicate that some sort of industrial activity was underway in the Morphou area already in the LC IA period, contemporary with the beginnings of copper metallurgy at Enkomi (Vermeule & Wolsky 1978; Catling 1980). Toumba tou Skourou is often described as strictly a ceramic production centre, but we have analyzed at least one piece of primary copper smelting slag from the site (Stech 1982, 108).

On the basis of presently available evidence, copper production was underway in some fashion at the following LC IIC sites:
1. Enkomi (Muhly, Maddin & Wheeler 1980; Tylecote 1982)
2. Athienou (Dothan & Ben-Tor 1983, 139–40; Muhly 1985, 33)

3. Pyla-Kokkinokremos (Karageorghis & Demas 1984, 12)
4. Kition (Stech, Maddin & Muhly 1985; Zwicker 1985; Tylecote 1985)
5. Hala Sultan Tekke (Åström 1982; Bachmann 1982)
6. Maroni-Vournes (Cadogan 1986)
7. Kalavassos-Ayios Dhimitrios (South Todd 1985, 119–20)
8. Kourion-Bamboula (Benson 1972, 135–8)
9. Alassa-Pano Mandilaris (Hadjisavvas 1986)
10. Maa-Palaeokastro (Demas 1984, 151–2)
11. Apliki-Karamallos (Taylor 1952; Stech 1982, 107–8)
12. Myrtou-Pigadhes (Catling 1957; Matthäus & Schumacher-Matthäus 1986, 171)

It is easy to list the sites involved in metallurgical operations. It is much more difficult to define the exact nature of the activities carried out at any one of these sites. All concerned scholars seem to agree on one central point: it makes little sense to us that, in the Late Bronze Age, metal-workers would have carried out the primary smelting of copper sulphide ores within the confines of a large urban area. But did the LBA metal-workers themselves see things in quite the same way? To put the question another way, why is it that examples of primary copper slag keep turning up at such urban centres?

It is hard to imagine anyone taking the trouble to transport this slag to an urban area. Yet analytical work has confirmed the presence of primary smelting slags at Hala Sultan Tekke (Bachmann 1982, 145–8), Enkomi (Zwicker, Grembler & Rollig 1977, 309–10), Kition and Toumba tou Skourou (Stech 1982, 108–9). It is often stated that the copper industry at the major urban centres, especially those along the south coast of the island, involved the secondary resmelting (or 'refining') of the large chunks of impure copper that were shipped to them from primary production centres, located at or near the mining sites themselves (Stech 1982, 111–12; Stech, Maddin & Muhly 1985, 398–9).

There is much to be said for such a reconstruction. The characteristic furnace conglomerate, the form in which impure copper was shipped from the primary smelting centres, has now been identified at many of the 13th century settlement sites in Cyprus. It was first recognized by Tylecote at Kition, in the form of what he called 'skull-shaped plano-convex blocks of slag' (Tylecote 1971, 53; 1985); this identification was confirmed by analytical work on similar examples from Athienou (Maddin, Muhly & Wheeler 1983, 134, 136–8) and from Kition (Stech, Maddin & Muhly 1985, 397–9). I have now found such conglomerate chunks amongst the metallurgical materials from Enkomi, Kalavassos-Ayios Dhimitrios, Maroni-Vournes and Myrtou-Pigadhes (unpublished).

The widespread distribution of this distinctive smelting product certainly indicates the existence of a common method of copper production, spread over much of the island of Cyprus. What of the possibility of a corresponding political framework? If the city of Enkomi/Alashiya dominated the copper industry prior to *ca* 1300 BC, what sort of political organisation, if any, was in place during the centuries *ca* 1300–1000 BC? If the seven (mentioned in inscriptions of the 8th century BC Assyrian king Sargon II) or ten (Esarhaddon) kingdoms of Archaic Cyprus are to be projected back into the Late Bronze Age, it is doubtful that their genesis goes back any earlier than the 13th century BC. Did that century witness the creation of a series of regional copper industries sharing a common technology, but controlled by separate administrations imposed by a newly emergent royal bureaucracy? Such a framework would provide for separate copper producing areas, each under the control of a separate administrative centre.

If that is to be the case, then the years *ca* 1300–1000 BC should also mark the decline (and eventual disappearance) of the kingdom of Alashiya. The name would have lived on, for some period of time, as the name of a city, perhaps even a more glorified city-state; this political entity can only have been located at Enkomi. As Merrillees has recently argued at some length (1987, 67–8), the Egyptian Tale of Wenamun refers to just such a city (*dmi*) of Alashiya; this can now be seen as a last reference to the city of Enkomi at the end of LC IIIB, just prior to the founding of the kingdom of Salamis (in the second half of the 11th century BC). I would see the formation of the Cypriot kingdoms as a movement going from West to East, with the earliest kingdom being located at Paphos (Maier 1983; 1987) and one of the latest being that at Salamis (but still considerably earlier than the date advocated by D.W. Rupp 1987; 1988).

It is quite possible, as argued at the Conference by G. Cadogan and A. South (see above 00–00 and below 00–00) that these regional production centres were first set up by the central kingdom of Alashiya (ruled from Enkomi) during the course of the 13th century BC. With the decline of central authority, during the years *ca* 1250–1150 BC, these regional centres were quick to take the opportunity to claim autonomy and to set out on a path of development that led to the formation of the various Iron Age kingdoms.

At each of these urban industrial areas, often located in the northwestern part of the site (as at Enkomi and Kition), the conglomerate chunks were further 'smelted' in small furnaces—the best examples of which come from Kition (Stech, Maddin & Muhly 1985, 388–91)—forming a pool of copper at the bottom of the chunk and prills of copper within the lower, outer portions. Copper recovery in the extractive metallurgy of 13th century Cyprus thus came about largely through the crushing of slag in order to remove the prills trapped therein; the accumulated prills were eventually melted down to form a copper ingot (Maddin, Muhly & Wheeler 1983, 137–8; Stech, Maddin & Muhly 1985, 399).

This is the copper smelting technology advocated by Steinberg and Koucky for LBA Cyprus, in their major study of ancient Cypriot copper smelting slags published in 1974. They saw copper smelting as taking place in small furnaces lined with refractory clay and fired using a natural draft, with a small 'bowl'-shaped pit dug in the bottom of the furnace to receive the prill-laden conglomerate chunks. Such activities, in their opinion, took place first at inland sites, such as Tamassos and Idalion, and were later transferred to the scene of the mines themselves. The copper-enriched slags were then transferred to the coastal cities for 'resmelting' and then for remelting of the accumulated prills to fabricate bronze objects and to transship copper (1974, 176–7; Stech 1982, 106). The problem is that this reconstruction does not account for the presence of primary smelting slags at several LBA urban centres, often in association with the conglomerate chunks (Stech, Maddin & Muhly 1985, 397–400; also unpublished material, especially from Enkomi).

The crushing of slag in order to extract prills is an old fashioned method of copper extraction, one that probably goes back at least as early as the Chalcolithic period, and one that was in the process of being replaced, in the latter part of the LBA, by a far more efficient smelting technology that achieved a separation of metal from slag, producing an ingot of copper that formed in the bottom of the furnace, and a slag that was tapped off into a pit dug next to the furnace. The early use of this technology is best documented at early Iron Age (12th century BC) Timna, in the southern Negev, in the tapped slag rings (weighing ca 15–25 kg) from Layer I at Site No. 2 (Bamberger et al 1986, 3 and Table 2). It must be pointed out, however, that even at Timna it has been argued that 'none of the furnace bottoms found in the Timna furnaces could have produced a bun-shaped ingot or an ingot of a smaller shape' (Rothenburg 1985, 133), suggesting that there is no necessary connection between tapped slags and ingot formation. Clearly we must, in the future, study not only slags but also furnace design and furnace construction.

There is good indication that tap slags were already being produced at 13th century BC Timna, as evidenced by the fragmentary tapped slag plates from Layer II of Site No. 2 and Layers II and III at Site No. 30, although there is still some ambiguity regarding the dating of these installations.[3] But was this technology being used in 13th century BC Cyprus?

The researches of U. Zwicker have concluded that there were no tapped slags at Enkomi (Zwicker, Grembler & Rollig 1977, 310), the best candidate for a primary smelting site amongst all the urban centres of LBA Cyprus (Zwicker, Rollig & Schwarz 1972, 35–6; Muhly, Maddin & Wheeler 1980, 90). This seems to be the case at other urban centres as well. Zwicker and his colleagues suggested the use of a small furnace similar to those used in New Kingdom Egypt, about 30 cm in diameter without a tapping hole but making use of tuyères and bellows for a forced draft of air (Zwicker, Grembler & Rollig 1977, 310).

This would account for the presence of the numerous tuyère fragments and the two pot bellows from Enkomi. The physical form of the suggested furnace is also not unlike the installations found by Dikaios in the copper workshops that he excavated (*Enkomi*, 22 (Room 103), 23 (Room 105), 39 (Room 77) and 58 (Rooms 8 and 77). The existence of the tuyères is crucial. The study of the material remains excavated at Timna concluded that:

'The main technological differences between the Chalcolithic and later periods are the use of larger and thermally better insulated furnaces as well as the use of forced air supplied by pot bellows through tuyères. The technological break-through from copper and slag separation in solid state, which involved many difficulties, to liquid separation, resulted probably from improvement of the thermal conditions during the process' (Bamberger et al 1986, 1167).

But, at Enkomi, such tuyères go back to the very beginning of occupation, in LC IA. What are we to conclude from what seems to be an unbroken history of industrial activity, extending over more than 400 years, with continuous evidence for the presence of tuyères in significant numbers from every level at the site, down to the end of LC IIIA?

We cannot answer this question at the present time. The slags from Enkomi should hold the key, but the problem with virtually all slag analyses published to date is that they have been based upon surface finds, upon unstratified material collected during visits to the site. What is now needed, what is absolutely essential in order to understand the development of copper smelting technology at a site such as Enkomi, is a careful study of stratified slags coming from all the major periods of smelting activity at the site.

The material for such a study exists in the Enkomi trays stored in the Cyprus Museum, but no one has yet attempted to undertake such an analytical programme. Steinberg and Koucky carried out a very laudable programme of slag analysis 15 years ago (1974), but their work was based almost entirely upon unstratified surface finds. Stratified slag examples do exist; they exist in some quantity and it is time that we took advantage of the opportunities presented to us.

The problem is that we are not yet accustomed to thinking of slag as an archaeological material, as something that can have a date, something that should have a date and an archaeological context. A similar attitude was prevalent in Assyriology with regard to clay tablets. Slags have been seen as self-contained entities, the evidence they contained being physically locked up within the slag block itself. Likewise tablets were seen as self-contained entities. As a written document the tablet carried it's own internal historical and chronological background and had no need for an archaeological context.

We have now learned that careful attention to find spot and context can reveal hitherto lost evidence relating to ancient libraries, archival practices and ancient attitudes regarding genre and classification. Our understanding of the uses and importance of writing has been greatly enhanced by the careful excavation of tablet archives and the close co-operation between archaelogists and Assyriologists. I am sure that there is equal profit to be gained through the close co-operation between archaeologist and archaeometallurgist (Veenhof 1986).

There is one site that has produced a large quantity of copper smelting slag in good archaeological contexts, slag that is now being studied by H.-G. Bachmann, one of the foremost scholars in the field. This is the site of Apliki-Karamallos in the Morphou area, just four miles south of the village of Lefka (on the right bank of the Marathasa river), in the copper-mining belt of the foothills of the Troodos. Excavated in a very preliminary way, in two brief campaigns during 1938 and 1939, by Joan du Plat Taylor, then Assistant Curator of the Cyprus Museum, Apliki remains the best candidate we have for a true copper production centre, a primary smelting site established to mine and smelt the rich copper deposits in the surrounding hills, especially those on the North Hill of Apliki.

Apliki-Karamallos was a Late Bronze Age miners' village; in the 1930's the land was still owned by the Cyprus Mines Corporation, from which Miss Taylor received much of the funding that made possible her excavations. The site had actually been discovered by modern miners, working for the CMC, during the course of their prospecting operations. Fortunately they alerted the Cyprus Museum and, at least in this one case, an important archaeological and metallurgical site was saved for future study.

Apliki is famous for its hand-made burnished pottery, christened 'Apliki Ware' by Miss Taylor. In our forthcoming final publication of the excavations at Apliki the pottery is being dealt with by Dr. Barbara Kling. What is important here is the evidence, from pottery and stratigraphy, for uninterrupted occupation and industrial activity at Apliki, from LC IIC into LC IIIA. The destruction level seen at some Cypriot sites at the end of LC IIC is not present at Apliki, where copper production seems to have continued into the early 12th century BC.

In her preliminary report on Apliki, published in the *Antiquaries Journal* for 1952, Joan du Plat Taylor refers to the presence of black, so-called Roman slags (in contrast to red slags not present at Apliki but thought to be earlier and identified as Phoenician) found in the rooms of a LBA house (Taylor 1952, 152–3). This is what first brought me to Apliki, although we now realise that the colour of Cypriot slags has nothing to do with their date, the difference being due simply to the degree of oxidation present in the iron compounds found in all the slags.

What Miss Taylor found in the rooms of her House A at Apliki, the only structure fully excavated at a site described as extending all over the neck of the hill between two spurs, were large quantities of a black ropy slag present in all eight rooms of the house. These are massive blocks of slag, weighing as much as 14 kg. What sets Apliki apart is the quantity of slag from the site. Apliki has massive blocks of slag, not the usual small bits present at almost every LBA site in Cyprus. In her preliminary report Miss Taylor refers to the recovery of '. . . almost a sackfull of slag' from the northwest corner of Room 7 in House A (1952, 142) (Fig 35.1).

Figure 35.1 Massive block of copper smelting slag from Apliki, House A, Room 7. Inventory No. AK 33a. GPL 36.0 cm; GPW 27.0 cm; GPTh 5.0 cm. Weight 14 kg roughly triangular in shape; has ropy surface only on top. Bottom surface of slag block gives appearance of having been formed in some sort of mould (? in slag pit). Photograph by S. Swiny.

I was able to locate this very item in the storerooms of the Cyprus Museum: a large gunnysack full of massive pieces of black, ropy slag. The size of these slag blocks leaves no doubt that extensive mining and smelting operations were carried out at Apliki during the 13th and 12th centuries BC. This would also be in keeping with the massive size of the tuyères from the site, quite unlike the much smaller examples known from Enkomi (Fig 35.2).

Black ropey slag of the type known from Apliki has traditionally been known in Cyprus as Roman slag. Indeed Miss Taylor believed that much of the ancient mining evidence preserved at Apliki was of Roman date. In her first report on Apliki, published in the *Illustrated London News* for 24 February 1940, she refers to the '. . . number of Roman galleries and shafts found, and also a slag-heap near the foot of the hill' (Taylor 1940). Surviving photographs show the ancient galleries, with well-preserved timber supports still in position. The galleries were cut into the side of the hill and

Figure 35.2 Two fragmentary tuyéres from Apliki. Top is example of bent or elbow tuyére Inventory No. AK IV 4 84. GPL 24.5 cm; GPW 9.0 cm; diameter of bore *ca* 4.0 cm. From House A, Room 1 (*Ant J 32*, 136, 161). Bottom is example of straight tuyére Inventory No. AK 14a. GPL 26.5 cm; GPW 8.5 cm; diameter of bore *ca*. 4.0 cm. From House A, Room 2 (*Ant J 32*, 138). Photograph by S. Swiny.

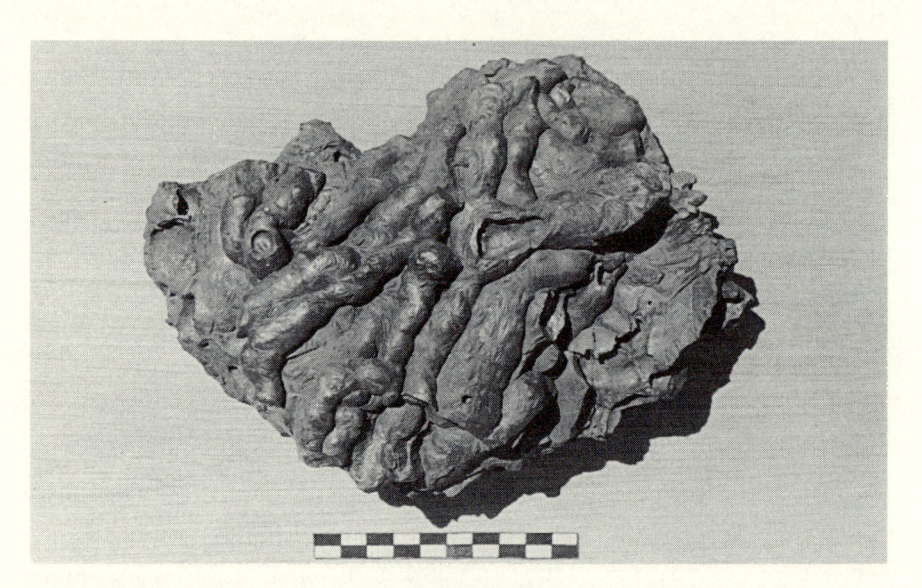

Figure 35.3 Example of 'Roman' (Skouriotissa-type) copper smelting slag from Apliki. From slag heap at foot of hill. GPL 21.0 cm; 14.0 cm; GPTh 4–5 cm. Weight 3.5 kg. Photograph by S. Swiny.

seemed to have been constructed to permit the ancient miners to walk in almost upright.

It was this very state of preservation that convinced everyone at the time that such work could not be earlier than Roman times, a logical conclusion when considered in association with the great quantity of 'Roman' slag all over the surrounding area. Yet nothing Roman is included in the preliminary report on Apliki and no Roman finds are included with the Apliki material in the Cyprus Museum. Thanks to the efforts of Dr. Karageorghis I had an opportunity to meet with Mr. Paraskevas of Dhali on 6 June 1986, the man who, as a lad of eighteen, had served as a foreman for the Apliki excavations. Mr. Paraskevas assured me that nothing Roman was found at the site, even though he still believed that the mining and smelting operations at Apliki were basically of Roman date. In particular he thought that the great slag heap at the foot of the hill was of Roman date, and Taylor does refer to Roman material from this location (1952, 150). The slag heap also produced a different type of slag, quite unlike that known from House A and clearly of Roman type, to judge from the one example preserved in the Cyprus Museum (Fig 35.3).

With the knowledge we now possess, of mining operations going back into the fifth millennium BC, we need have no difficuly in seeing Apliki as a LBA mining and smelting site. Why should the slags be of Roman date when they were found on the floors of rooms filled with Mycenaean and Cypriot pottery of the 13th and 12th centuries BC? Some of the metallurgical finds from Apliki can be duplicated at Enkomi and there is nothing from the site that need be out of place in a LBA context. The D-shaped and elbow tuyères are known from Enkomi and the latter now have a most interesting parallel from early XIX Dynasty Egypt, found at Qantir in excavations conducted by the Pelizaeus-Museum in Hildesheim (Pusch 1987, 5, Fig 3).

But why copper smelting slag in such a domestic context, in the rooms of what must be seen as a private house? Smelting activity certainly was not being carried out in the rooms of House A, rooms that had been cut out of the rocky hillside and surrounding an open courtyard. We have to assume that, for whatever reason, the slag was being stored in the houses of the miners' village. Taylor says that

> 'Traces of beds for heap roasting have been found in the neighbourhood, and the slag heaps contained many remnants of discarded furnaces' but that 'No indications of this work could be observed in the immediate neighbourhood of the village. . .' (1952, 152).

No record of any of these discarded furnaces seems to have been kept, but Steinberg and Koucky do publish a photograph of what could be one such furnace (1974, 151, Fig 109). In her 1940 report Taylor states that

> 'To search for the actual remains of furnaces and foundries on the site would require expensive and costly excavation, which was not within the scope of the expedition' (1940).

I can only hope that, at some future date, the opportunity to do so will present itself once again.

Cyprus at the end of the second millennium presents us with a series of regional metallurgical centres, each under the control of a local ruler but showing a common production technology. Such regionalism seems to be a response to the breakdown of central authority in the post-Amarna period, a time when Cyprus was doing its best to stay out of the superpower showdown when the armies of Egypt and the Hittites met at the battle of Qadesh in the 5th year of Ramesses II. This very regionalism could be seen as one of the reasons why Cyprus did not experience a total economic collapse at the end of the LBA, resulting in a so-called Dark Age. The palace-dominated, economy known from the Aegean (Chadwick 1987) and Syria (Margueron 1987), never developed in Cyprus and this seems to be a critical factor in explaining the island's prosperity during the years *ca* 1200–1000 BC.

Liverani has recently suggested that

> '... the particular concentration in the Palace of all the elements of organization, transformation, exchange, etc—a concentration which seems to reach its maximum in the Late Bronze Age—has the effect of transforming the physical collapse of the Palace into a general disaster for the entire kingdom' (Liverani 1987, 69).

In escaping such disaster, by virtue of its regionalized economic and political structure, Cyprus was able to move quickly into the new world of iron metallurgy and Iron Age regionalism.

NOTES

[1] For Cypriot copper production in the early Iron Age (CG and CA periods) see W. Fasnacht (1983) and P. Rabar (1987). Rabar believes that, in the Polis region, copper production *began* only in the Iron Age, that period marking the first exploitation of the ore deposits in the Limmi mining area. This thesis is argued in greater detail in Rabar's unpublished Ph.D. Dissertation (1984).

[2] The question of Alashiya as city and as country is discussed in great detail by R. Merrillees (1987, 38–43; 67–74, summarizing earlier work by scholars such as M. Astour, O. Carruba and G. Buccellati. Merrillees protests that

> 'In the space of one article, never mind over a given range of studies, the ancient toponym can be called a kingdom, country, land, state, city, town, landing place, mountain, or a synonym of any of these, without regard to their definable meaning in the ancient Near Eastern context' (1987, 67).

Merrillees wants to hold modern scholars to what he seems to visualize as the absolute consistency of ancient scribes. Unfortunately, as well known to all Assyriologists, ancient scribes were no more consistent than their modern counterparts tend to be. Nor can we be sure that we understand all the conventions of ancient scribal practises. Are we to read KUR URU *A-la-ši-ya* or KUR^{URU} *A-la-ši-ya*? That is, are we to read URU as a determinative or is it a fully grammatical part of the sentence? So we translate 'the land of the city of Alashiya' or 'the land of the (city) Alashiya'? And what is the exact geo-physical difference between the two expressions, if any?

By the mid-second millennium BC the words 'KUR URU/^{URU} XXX' had become a frozen expression often used in ambiguous or misleading ways by contemporary scribes. It is doubtful whether the presence/absence of either the KUR ('land') or the URU ('city') signs in roughly contemporary writings of the toponym Alashiya reveals anything regarding the geopolitical status of that land.

We can state, with reasonable certainty, that the writing^{URU} *A-la-ši-ya* need not be taken as a reference only to the *city* of Alashiya. When the Hittite scribe wanted to make sure that his readers realized that he was referring only to the *city* of Carchemish—in a description of the siege of that city by Šuppiluliuma I—he wrote URU *Kar-ga-mi-iš-ša-an* URU-*an* (KBo V 6, III. 27), to be translated something like 'Carchemish, as a City.' This is a clear indication that the mere use of the URU sign was seen as being ambiguous, that references just to URU Carchemish are probably to be taken as designating more than just the city, and that the toponym Carchemish designated both a city and a land or kingdom. The same must hold true for the toponym Alashiya.

[3] The problem concerns the dating of the relevant installations at Timna. The dates given here are those used in Bamberger *et al* 1986. The published radiocarbon dates, however, do not support this chronology, as I have argued elsewhere (J.D. Muhly, 'Timna and King Solomon,' *Bi Or* 41 (1984) 275–92). Indeed a recently excavated sample taken from lumps of unburned charcoal found at the bottom of a well preserved rock-cut furnace (with one clay tuyère found *in situ*) from Site 2, thought to date to the 12th century BC, gave a date of 1210 ± 100 BP (BM - 2242), suggesting use in the Early Islamic period (Rothenberg 1985, 128).

This problem has now been discussed by B. Rothenberg, the excavator of Timna, in the *Institute for Archaeo-Metallurgical Studies Newsletter* No. 9 (December 1986), 7. He argues that new radiocarbon determinations, made at the British Museum and the National Physical Research Laboratory in Pretoria, support the Late Bronze Age (Ramesside) dating for Site 2 at Timna but also indicate an unexpected period of smelting activity in the Early Islamic period, even at the site of Beer Ora, hitherto regarded only as a Roman period smelting site.

This unanticipated emergence of a major period of smelting activity in the Early Islamic period, producing the same type of ring-shaped tap slag once thought to be characteristic of the Late Bronze Age, raises disturbing questions regarding the archaeological work at Timna and the dating of excavated remains. Rothenberg claims (*Institute for Archaeo-Metallurgical Studies Newsletter* No. 10/11 (June/December 1987), 14–15) that the unauthorized publication of radiocarbon dates from Timna, made from samples collected without the knowledge of the excavator, has caused 'a great deal of misleading and futile arguments.' I know of no other archaeological site where this problem has arisen; it would seem to be a further indication of the lack of control over the archaeological work at Timna. On early Islamic smelting activity at Timna see also B. Rothenberg, 'Early Islamic Copper Smelting—and worship—at Beer Ora, Southern Arabah (Israel),' *Institute for Archaeo-Metallurgical Studies Newsletter* No. 12 (June 1988), 1–4.

LIST OF REFERENCES

Åström, P. (1982) The bronzes of Hala Sultan Tekke. *EMC* 177–83.
Bachmann, H.-G. (1982) Copper smelting slags from Cyprus: Review and classification of analytical data. *EMC,* 143–52
Balthazar, J. W. (1986) New compositional and metallographic analyses of copper-base objects from Lapithos, Vrysi tou Barba. *MASCA Journal 4,* 60–9.
Bamberger, M., P. Wincierz, H.-G. Bachmann & B. Rothenberg (1986) Ancient smelting of oxide copper ore. *Metall 40,* 1166–74.
Benson, J. L. (1972) *Bamboula at Kourion. The Necropolis and the Finds.* Philadelphia.
Cadogan, G. (1986) Maroni II. *RDAC,* 40–4.
Catling, H. W. (1957) The metal objects and coins, in *Myrtou-Pigadhes. A Late Bronze Age Sanctuary in Cyprus,* (Taylor, J. du Plat) 86–91. Oxford.
Catling, H. W. (1980) *Cyprus and the West 1600–1050 BC.* (Ian Sanders Memorial Lecture) Sheffield.
Chadwick, J. (1987) L'économie palatiale dans la Grèce mycénienne, in *Le système palatial en Orient, en Grèce et à Rome* (ed. E. Levy) Leiden (Univ. des Sciences Humaines de Strasbourg. Travaux du centre de recherche sur le Proche-Orient et la Grèce antiques, 9) 283-90.
Demas, M. V. (1984) *Pyla-Kokkinokremos and Maa-Palaeokastro: Two Fortified Settlements of the end of the 13th Century B.C. in Cyprus.* Unpub. Ph.D. Dissertation, Univ. of Cincinnati (University Microfilms International, No. 8420868).
Dothan, T. and A. Ben-Tor (1983) *Excavations at Athienou, Cyprus. 1971–1972. (Qedem* 16) Jerusalem.
Fasnacht, W. (1983) Copper Processing at Ayia Varvara-*Almyras. RDAC,* 89–91.
Gale, N. H. & Z. A. Stos-Gale (1986) Oxhide copper ingots in Crete and Cyprus and the Bronze Age metals trade. *BSA 81,* 81–100.
Hadjisavvas, S. (1986) Alassa. A new Late Cypriote site. *RDAC,* 62–7.
Helck, W. (1983) Asija. *ZÄS 100,* 29–36.
Iakovou, M. (1988) *The Pictorial Pottery of Eleventh Century B.C. Cyprus. (SIMA 78)* Göteborg.
Karageorghis, V (1988) The Greek language in Cyprus: The archaeological background, in *The History of the Greek Language in Cyprus,* (J. Karageorghis & O. Masson) 1–8. Nicosia.
Karageorghis, V & M. Demas (1984) *Pyla-Kokkinokremos. A Late 13th-Century B.C. Fortified Settlement in Cyprus.* Nicosia.
Lalouette, C. (1979) Le "Firmament de cuivre". Contribution à l'étude du mot bἰ з . *BIFAO 79,* 333–53.
Liverani, M. (1987) The collapse of the Near Eastern regional system at the end of the Bronze Age: the case of Syria, in *Centre and periphery in the Ancient World,* (eds. M. Rowlands, M. Larsen & K. Kristiansen) 66–73. Cambridge.
Maddin. R., J. D. Muhly & T. S. Wheeler. (1983) Metal working, *in* T. Dothan and A. Ben-Tor (1983). 132–8.
Maier, F. G. (1987) *Paphos in the History of Cyprus.* Nicosia.
Margueron, J. (1987) Les palais syriens à l'âge du bronze, in *Le système palatial en orient, en Grèce et à Rome,* (ed. E. Levy) Leiden (Univ. des Sciences Humaines de Strasbourg. Travaux du centre de recherche sur le Proche-Orient et la Grèce antiques, 9) 127–58.
Matthäus, H. & G. Schumacher-Matthäus. (1986) Zyprische Hortfunde. Kult und Metal-handwerke in der späten Bronzezeit, in *Gedenkschrift für Gero*

von Merhart: *Zum 100 Geburtstag*. Marburg (Marburger Studien zur Vor- und Frühgeschichte, Bd. 7) 129–91.

Merrillees, R. S. (1984) Ambelikou-*Aletri:* A Preliminary Report. *RDAC,* 1–13.

Merrillees, R. S. (1987) *Alashia Revisited.* (Cahiers de la Revue Biblique, 22). Paris.

Muhly, J. D. (1985) The Late Bronze Age in Cyprus: A 25 year retrospect, in *Archaeology in Cyprus 1960–1985,* (ed. V. Karageorghis) 20–46, Nicosia.

Muhly, J. D. (1987) Alashiya in the context of Cypriot archaeology and the world of the Amarna Letters. Paper delivered at International Symposium to Commemorate the Centennial Anniversary of the Discovery of Tell El Amarna (Chicago, 1–3 February 1987). To be published in proceedings of the Symposium.

Muhly, J. D., R. Maddin & T. S. Wheeler. (1980) The oxhide ingots from Enkomi and Mathiati and Late Bronze Age copper smelting in Cyprus. *RDAC,* 84–99.

Negbi, O. (1986) The climax of urban development in Bronze Age Cyprus. *RDAC,* 97–121.

Olsson, I. U. (1987) Carbon-14 dating and interpretation of the validity of some dates from the Bronze Age in the Aegean, in *High, Middle or Low? Acts of an International Colloquium on Absolute Chronology Held at the University of Gothenburg, 20th-22nd August 1987.* Part 2, (ed. P. Åström) 4–38. (SIMA Pocket-book 57). Göteborg.

Peltenburg, E.J. (1982) Early Copperwork in Cyprus and the Exploitation of Picrolite: Evidence from the Lemba Archaeological Project. *EMC,* 41–62.

Pusch, E.B. (1987) Recent work at Northern Piramesse. Results of the excavation of the Pelizaeus-Museum Hildesheim at Qantir. To appear in Proceedings of the Symposium on *Ramsses the Great* (Memphis, Tenn., Spring 1987).

Rabar, P. (1984) *The Organization and Development of Early Copper Metallurgy in the Polis Region, Western Cyprus.* Unpub. Ph.D. Dissertation, Penn State Univ. (University Microfilms International No. 8419658).

Rabar, P. (1987) Early copper production in the Polis Region, Western Cyprus. *J Field A 14,* 297–312.

Rothenberg, B. (1985) Copper smelting furnaces in the Arabah, Israel: the archaeological evidence, in *Furnaces and Smelting Technology in Antiquity,* (eds. P. T. Craddock & M. J. Hughes) (BMOP 48) 123–50. London.

Rupp, D. W. (1985) Prolegomena to a Study of Stratification and Social Organization in Iron Age Cyprus, in *Status, Structure and Stratification: Current Archaeological Reconstructions,* (eds. M. Thompson, M. T. Garcia & J. F. Keene) 119–31. Calgary.

Rupp, D. W. (1987) *Vive le roi.* The emergence of the state in Iron Age Cyprus, in *Western Cyprus: Connections. An Archaeological Symposium* (ed. D. W. Rupp) (*SIMA* 77) 147–68. Göteborg.

South Todd, A. (1987) The Late Bronze Age in the Vasilikos Valley. *Acts 1985,* 113–24.

Stech, T. (1982) Urban metallurgy in Late Bronze Age Cyprus. *EMC,* 105–16, Nicosia.

Stech, T., R. Maddin & J. D. Muhly. (1985) Copper production at Kition in the Late Bronze Age, *Kition* V Part I, 388–402.

Steinberg, A. & F. Koucky. (1974) Preliminary metallurgical research on the ancient Cypriot copper industry, in *American Expedition to Idalion, Cyprus, First preliminary Report: Seasons of 1971 and 1972,* (eds. L. E. Stager, A.

Walker & G. Ernest Wright) Cambridge, Mass (Supplement to *BASOR* No. 18) 149–78.

Stos-Gale, Z. A., N. H. Gale & U. Zwicker. (1986) The copper trade in the South-East Mediterranean region. Preliminary scientific evidence. *RDAC,* 122–44.

Taylor, J. du Plat (1940) Mines where the Mycenaeans got their copper discovered in Cyprus. *ILN 196,* 251.

Taylor, J. du Plat (1952) A Late Bronze Age settlement at Apliki, Cyprus. *Ant J 32,* 133–67.

Tylecote, R. F. (1971) Observations on Cypriot copper smelting. *RDAC,* 53–8.

Tylecote, R. F. (1982) The Late Bronze Age copper and Bronze metallurgy at Enkomi and Kition. *EMC,* 81–103, Nicosia.

Tylecote, R. F. (1985) Copper working at Kition. *Kition* V Part I, 430.

Veenhof, K. R. (1986) Cuneiform archives. An introduction, in *Cuneiform Archives and Libraries,* (ed. K. R. Veenhof) (30^e Rencontre Assyriologique Internationale) 1–36, Istanbul.

Vermeule, E. & F. Wolsky. (1978) New Aegean relations with Cyprus: the Minoan and Mycenaean pottery from Toumba tou Skourou, Morphou. *Proc Amer Phil Soc 122,* 294–317.

Watkins, T. (1966) Metal finds, in *Excavations at Kalopsidha and Ayios Iakovos in Cyprus.* (P. Åström) (*SIMA* 2) 113–15, Lund.

Zwicker, U. (1982) Bronze Age metallurgy at Ambelikou-Aletri and arsenical copper in a crucible from Episkopi-Phaneromeni. *EMC,* 63–8. Nicosia.

Zwicker, U. (1985) Investigations of samples from the metallurgical workshops at Kition, *Kition* V Part I, 403–29.

Zwicker, U., G. Constantinou, H. -G Buchholz & V. Karageorghis (1981) Investigations on ore, flux and crucible slag from prehistoric coppersmelting at Ambelikou, Cyprus. *Revue d'Archeometrie, Supplement III* (X Int. Archaeometry Symposium, Paris, 26–29 March 1980) 331–40.

Zwicker, U., E. Grembler & H. Rollig (1977) Investigations on copper-slags from Cyprus (Second Report). *RDAC,* 309–16.

Zwicker, U., H. Rollig & U. Schwarz (1972) Investigations on Prehistoric and Early Historic copper-slag from Cyprus. *RDAC,* 34–45.

36
From copper to kingship: aspects of Bronze Age society viewed from the Vasilikos Valley

Alison K. South
Maroni, Cyprus

INTRODUCTION

After more than ten years of archaeological survey[1] and excavation in the Vasilikos Valley (Fig 1.1) it is possible to offer some tentative suggestions concerning the development of society in this region of the central south coast of Cyprus. This paper aims to give a brief overall survey of the evidence for the Bronze Age, taking up the story from the discussion of the aims of the Vasilikos Valley Project and of the earlier periods by Todd (see above 2–13). In contrast to the presumably entirely pastoral/agricultural economies of earlier times, a major new factor is the possible exploitation of the Kalavasos copper sources which may have contributed to the accelerating development of complex society which will be seen in this period.

EARLY BRONZE AGE

Recognition of Early Bronze Age material in the south coast region has proved notoriously difficult (eg Herscher 1980) although the situation is gradually improving and will be further clarified by the publication of recent work, notably Swiny's excavations at Sotira-Kaminoudhia (see above 14–31). The Vasilikos Valley survey has located half a dozen sites with small quantities of ceramics which probably date to the Late Chalcolithic and/or Early Bronze Age, but a better understanding of this material, preferably by excavation of a site, will be necessary before a worthwhile assessment of this period can be attempted.

MIDDLE BRONZE AGE

Far more sites are known for the Middle Bronze Age (Todd 1988 lists 39 and more are being discovered by current survey), showing a notable increase in population from earlier periods. They include large (up to 6–10 ha) settlements such as Kalavasos-Laroumena and Mitsingites, located just north and south of Kalavasos Village at a strategic narrowing of the valley on the route to the mining area. Many other sites of various types and sizes are located on the low ridges and slopes of the valley sides from 1.75 km north of the coast to the vicinity of the mining area. No settlement sites have yet been excavated, and it is difficult as yet to assess the chronological development of the settlement pattern within the Middle Bronze Age.

A major resource for understanding the development of Middle Bronze Age society is a large cemetery in Kalavasos village, of which more than 60 tombs have been excavated by the Department of Antiquities and the Vasilikos Valley Project at various times from the 1940s to 1987.[2] Although many of these tombs have been partially looted or damaged by modern construction many were either intact or contained considerable quantities of material, and altogether they provide one of the largest available samples of evidence for material culture and tomb types of this period.

The cemetery comprises chamber tombs of the usual Cypriot type, dating to all phases of the MC period (Todd 1986, 183–4). A rich repertoire of ceramics belongs mainly to types common in the south coastal region (with Red Polished ware predominating and a lack of White Painted), but includes some imports from more distant northern and eastern parts of the island (*ibid* 151, 154–9). Most of the tombs contained at least a few bronze artefacts of well-known Cypriot types, with greater quantities in a few cases (*ibid* 159–65). The overall amount of metal is quite large, especially considering that many tombs were looted. Numerous faience beads and a few stone and bone objects were also found. Human skeletal remains were not well preserved, but they do provide some information about the population (*ibid* 168–79).

No clear evidence for the existence of ranked society has yet been observed in this cemetery, with the possible exception of considerably greater amounts of bronze in some tombs. The 23 tombs excavated in 1987 included many well preserved examples with skeletal remains in relatively good condition, and the completion of studies now in progress may be expected to reveal further information concerning the population and its burial customs. It is hoped that by seriation and comparisons with material from other sites the chronological development of the ceramics can be clearly defined. This should lead not only to a better understanding of the history of this important cemetery, but also to greatly improved precision in dating the numerous sites known from survey.

It is suggested that the evident prosperity and large population enjoyed by the region during the Middle Bronze Age was related to exploitation of the copper sources of the Kalavasos mining area. Although actual evidence of mining has not yet been discovered in this region, surface finds of a crucible fragment and slag of probable early date at Laroumena just north of Kalavasos hint that information on Middle Bronze Age metallurgy might be forthcoming from future excavation of such a site. It is known that mining was carried out in another region of the island at this time (Merrillees 1984), and it is likely that the inhabitants of the Vasilikos Valley also exploited this technology. Although the first historical references to probable export of Cypriot copper occur at this period (Muhly 1986, 52), and international trade is demonstrated by imported items found at sites in other regions, nothing from outside Cyprus has yet been found in the Vasilikos Valley which appears to have thrived solely on local and inter-regional trade.

It is hoped that when the survey and studies of the extensive evidence are complete it will be possible to assess whether the Middle Bronze Age in the Vasilikos Valley demonstrates any increase in settlement size and social complexity as might be expected in a time of burgeoning international trade and prior to the development of urban centres in the Late Bronze Age.

LATE BRONZE AGE

The settlement pattern in the Late Bronze Age is overwhelmingly dominated by the excavated LC IIC settlement of Kalavasos-Ayios Dhimitrios, but field survey together with emergency excavation of tombs at Kalavasos Village, Mangia and Ayios Dhimitrios provide some evidence on which to base an assessment of developments in the earlier part of the period.

The large Middle Bronze Age settlement and cemetery of Mitsingites, on a low ridge just south of Kalavasos, appears to have continued in use into the beginning of the Late Bronze Age, and LC I material has also been found at Khorapheri/Vounaritashi in a secluded tributary valley west of the Vasilikos, and at predominantly Chalcolithic Ayious. LC IA is represented by two tombs in Kalavasos Village, and Tomb 4 at Ayios Dhimitrios may have been first used in LC IB.

The meagre nature of the evidence for this period, even after completion of extensive survey, might suggest a reduction in population possibly linked to the disturbed conditions believed to have affected many areas of the island at this time (eg Karageorghis 1982, 61–2). Herscher (1984, 25–7) noted a surprising lack of similarity in the ceramics of the Kalavasos and Maroni areas in LC IA, contrasting with the situation in both earlier and later periods. On the other hand, the tombs in Kalavasos Village revealed the first imports to the region, all from the east. Tomb 51 included an early example of a Canaanite jar and a bronze dagger of Near Eastern type (Pearlman 1985), while Tomb 2 contained a pilgrim flask with bichrome decoration of at least foreign inspiration (Merrillees 1985). Possibly these few strands of evidence could all be incorporated in a scenario of readjustment of regional relationships at a time of competition for control of the increasingly international copper trade, but with strong elements of continuity in the use of at least some Middle Bronze Age settlements and cemeteries.

The LC IIA and IIB periods are clearly known only from several tombs at Kalavasos Village, Ayios Dhimitrios and Mangia, representing continuation of long-term cemetery use in Kalavasos and probably new use of the latter two areas. Two LC IIA:1 tombs (10 and 22; Todd 1986, 196–7, 203–4) in Kalavasos Village contained a variety of local ceramics[3] with only one import (a Mycenaean IIIA:1 pithoid jar), two tombs at Mangia ca 750 m east of Ayios Dhimitrios were in use by this period (McClellan, Russell & Todd 1988) and further LC II tombs occur at both cemeteries.

Several tombs at Ayios Dhimitrios (South, Russell & Schuster 1988, Ch. VI) were in use in LC IIA, and the two with the best preserved evidence reveal striking differences in wealth and quantity of imports. Tomb 4 contained 79 objects, consisting mostly of a wide variety of White Slip II and Base Ring I and II vessels, three stone spindle-whorls of a common type and a cylinder seal in a crude local style; no imported artefacts were present. Although the tomb had been looted, the ceramic vessels had been carefully piled on one side of the chamber, and the total absence of even any small imported items such as sherds, beads, seals and ivory fragments, which are often found on the floors of looted tombs is regarded as significant. The looters would presumably have removed most bronze objects, if any were present, but again the lack of even any small fragments is suggestive. The tomb users had access to an abundant supply of ceramics perhaps from nearby production centres, but could not command any further luxuries.

A very different picture is revealed by Tomb 11,[4] one of the richest known from the Cypriot Bronze Age (see also Goring, above (95–105)). The largest tomb known at the site (max length 4.20 m), it is the only one provided with a rock-cut bench on each side of the chamber. It was used, probably during a fairly short span of time in LC IIA:2, for the burials of three young women (all *ca* 17–24 years old), a young child and three infants. They were provided with grave goods including much gold (a total of 432 grams) and silver jewellery, together with various ivory, bone, glass, faience, bronze, amber, alabaster and other stone objects. About 45 ceramic vessels included seven fine Mycenaean examples, an unusually high number of Red Lustrous spindle bottles and flasks[5] and a few Base Ring and White Slip vessels. A stone stamp seal and two gold signet rings with Cypro-Minoan inscriptions were included. The majority of the objects are of an unusual or luxury nature, either imported artefacts (eg Mycenaean ceramics and gold beads, Egyptian glass vessels) or at least made from imported materials, and many of them were supplied in sets of similar or identical items.

Tomb 11, which was unlooted and not seriously disturbed by flooding or collapse, provides much evidence on burial customs, and the limitation of its use to women of a certain age group suggests selective burial procedures. However, its potential as evidence will only be fully realised if it can in future be compared with other contemporary tombs in the same cemetery. In terms of the overall structure of society, it shows that by LC IIA some members of society, young and female, had access to very considerable wealth displayed in the form of gold jewellery and other luxury and imported objects, and were literate or at least bore signet rings probably with names or titles. No other tombs in the area, and very few elsewhere (notably at Enkomi) are as wealthy.

The great wealth of the users of Tomb 11 could easily be accounted for by the hypothesis that they belonged to an elite who controlled large scale copper production and were involved in international trade. Since no settlements or mines of this period have yet been excavated in the Vasilikos Valley this is necessarily difficult to prove. Tomb 11 contained only two bronze objects, a large dagger and a shapeless lump which may have derived from metallurgical activity.

Similarly elite contemporary tombs existed at least at Enkomi (eg Tomb 2, described by Schaeffer, 1952, 111–36) where metallurgical activity was already substantial (see Muhly, above (298–314)). But if wealthy elites existed at several sites, were there various independent centres all exporting copper; or can we identify any larger centre which could have been the abode of a King of Alashia who was able to organise copper production on a large scale and sufficiently important to address the King of Egypt as 'my brother' (*cf* Knapp 1986b, 41)?

The settlement pattern in the Vasilikos Valley in LC II is dominated by the large urban centre at Ayios Dhimitrios, but several other, mostly small sites are known from survey including one on the coast at Tokhni-Lakkia, small probably agricultural settlements at Ayiasmata and Arkhangelos/ Malouteri east and northwest of Kalavasos, and small scatters of sherds in various other locations. Construction work has revealed the existence of a settlement underlying the north part of Kalavasos Village, and another at Mangia on the plateau on the east side of the valley opposite Ayios Dhimitrios. Some of these cannot be more accurately dated than 'LC II', but most probably belong to the later part of this period.

Ayios Dhimitrios[6] is a settlement covering about 11.5 ha, located on low-lying gently sloping terraces about 200 m west of the Vasilikos River, 3.5 km north of the coast. The situation is poor from the defensive point of view, but excellent for trade and communications: it is at a crossroads of the route linking the eastern to the southern and western regions of the island, and the route from the coast to the hinterland and the Kalavasos mining area.

Various parts of the site have been excavated (about 5 per cent of the total area), and substantial stone buildings all with the same orientation have been found in all of them. Most of the excavated architecture is clearly dated to LC IIC only, but some buildings in the western part are less securely dated and may have been occupied at a slightly earlier period—if so, however, their common orientation with the rest would show continuity in town planning. It seems very probable that somewhere in the near vicinity there existed a settlement of LC IIA-IIB, which would have used the several tombs of this period found within the LC IIC settlement area. The identical orientation of Tomb 11 with the adjacent Building X, together with the fact that the tomb was respected by the LC IIC builders, also suggest continuity of spatial planning and social hierarchy. However, no earlier settlement has yet been found by survey or excavation, and it can only be speculated that one may exist in part of the Ayios Dhimitrios area not yet excavated. The LC IIC town may be a new foundation, or at least represents a major expansion of earlier settlement.

The LC IIC town plan (see South 1984c, 12–16; 1987, Map 2) shows a high degree of organisation. Several fairly large (*ca* 100–350 m^2) multi-roomed buildings front onto at least one long straight street about 3.80 m wide which leads north towards a much larger public building (Building X) at the northeast edge of the site. No clear evidence for a defensive wall has yet been found. The majority of the buildings had well constructed stone walls (without ashlar masonry), probably with mud brick superstructures and perhaps upper storeys. They appear to have been the residences of fairly prosperous 'middle class' members of society, judging from their size and finds including numerous bronze objects, small amounts of imported ceramics, a few seals, etc. The quantity of imports (mostly Mycenaean and 'Canaanite' ceramics and a few Minoan sherds) is fairly small considering the possible involvement of the settlement in international copper trade and its proximity to the coast, and leads us to suspect that the main centre of organisation of the trade may have lain elsewhere.

Metallurgical activities were among those carried out in the settlement. A few pieces of slag have been found in all the excavated areas, with greater concentrations in certain places. The quantities are not enormous (approximately 135 kg altogether) but major smelting areas may have been located closer to the mines, and/or in areas outside the centre of the settlement.

The best evidence for metalworking is in Building IX which appears to have been a coppersmith's residence and workshop. One room contained many crucible or furnace lining fragments in an ashy deposit near a small hearth or furnace, while the adjacent room held numerous bronze tools and pieces of scrap, presumably awaiting repair or remelting. Oxhide ingot fragments, a bronze bowl filled with yellow ochre, an unusual bronze cylinder seal and a haematite weight were also found in this building. This evidence is interpreted as representing small-scale, private enterprise. A larger building revealed a set of 14 haematite and bronze weights in the form of various animals and a human negroid head (Courtois 1983), presumably used for trading in some valuable commodity; they were found in the same room as one of the finest Mycenaean vessels recovered from the settlement.

By far the largest building at the site, and the only one with ashlar masonry, is Building X (Fig 36.1). The main part of the building is square (*ca* 30.5 × 30.5 m) with a tripartite plan around a central square courtyard; peripheral areas on the north and east appear to have been associated with the central building. It is massively constructed with foundations up to 2 m thick, and probably had an upper storey accessible via a staircase near the main entrance. Ashlar blocks up to 3.20 m long, many with drafted margins, were used mainly on the exterior faces of the building; they were of calcareous sandstone brought from the Tokhni quarry area about 4 km away.

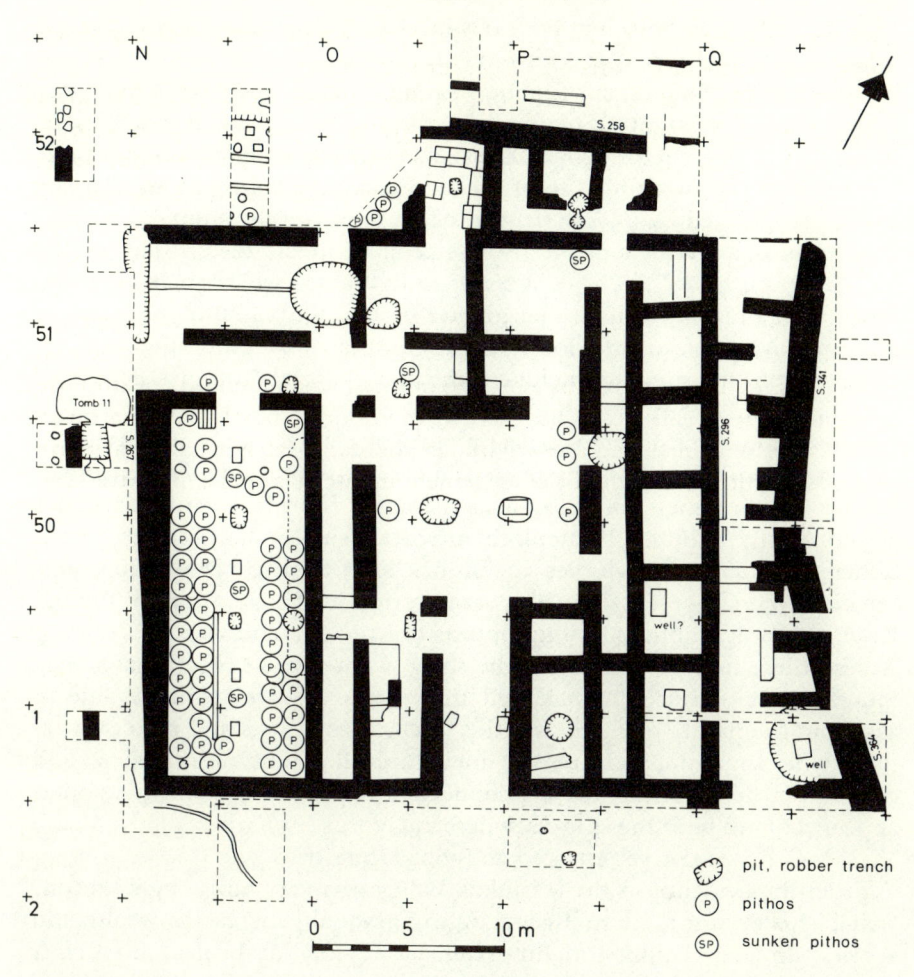

Figure 36.1 Plan of Building X at Kalavasos-Ayios Dhimitrios after completion of the 1987 excavations.

Although it is difficult to understand the function of some of the rooms within Building X, it is clear that storage was a major preoccupation. The largest architectural unit, a hall *ca* 19.5 × 7.25 m in extent with six monolithic stone pillars to support the ceiling, was devoted entirely to storage with most of the space occupied by double rows of large *pithoi*. At least 47 *pithoi* stood on the floor, and six more were sunk in pits below floor level. Their total capacity is estimated at about 33,500 litres, and their sizes may have been standardized judging from the volumes calculated from available profiles. The nature of the contents of the *pithoi* is so far unknown, but may perhaps be determined by analyses now in progress.

Building X also revealed the best evidence of literacy (known elsewhere in the settlement mostly from single signs on pot handles or weights). Five small clay cylinders with Cypro-Minoan inscriptions of multiple lines are a major addition to the known corpus of long inscriptions (Masson 1983;

1986) from Bronze Age Cyprus. A few inscribed stone *pithos* lids and single signs on other objects also occurred.

No evidence of a religious function for Building X has come to light, nor is there any significant amount of metallurgical material. It seems most likely that it was the residence of elite members of society who had some control over the economic life of the community. Their high standard of living is suggested by a large deposit of ceramic vessels, animal, bird and fish bones and seeds found in a well-like shaft in the eastern part of the building (South 1988). The ceramics, mostly 'tableware' of small cups and bowls with a few jugs, show a far greater percentage (about 60 per cent) of imported Mycenaean and local imitations than any other deposits recovered from the site, and include some fine pictorial examples decorated with birds and dolphins.

Ayios Dhimitrios provides a clear picture of a large, highly organised LC IIC settlement which was involved in metallurgy, presumably controlling the products of the nearby Kalavasos mines. It had at least one major administrative building, particularly important since it has previously been difficult to identify examples in Bronze Age Cyprus. More questions remain to be answered about the organisation of the community: further large, probably public buildings appear to exist east and west of Building X, and there may be another to the south where ashlar blocks have been found on the surface. It is hoped that future research will be able to ascertain the nature of these, whether a sanctuary exists and if so of what type, whether any larger areas of metallurgical activity are present, and especially whether there was any connection of metallurgy with religion as appears to have been the case elsewhere in Cyprus (eg Knapp 1986a; *Kition* V, 253–4) but is not yet attested at Ayios Dhimitrios.

From the evidence in the Vasilikos Valley it is very tempting to reconstruct a history for the Late Bronze Age of gradually increasing wealth and social complexity culminating in extremely wealthy local rulers in LC IIA (Tomb 11), followed by a takeover by a larger, well organised and bureaucratic state (Building X and efficient town planning) under which fewer luxuries and imports reached the inhabitants of the area. It may be possible to make a good case for the probable development of a unified state in Cyprus in LC IIC, based on evidence such as new or expanded settlements and similarities in town planning, ashlar masonry, and public buildings at many sites. A good candidate for the capital of such a state would be Kition with its very great area and long-lived major religious centre. But the apparent sudden flowering of LC IIC may be an illusion, for there is far too little evidence yet available, either from the Vasilikos Valley or anywhere else, for the nature of settlements in the earlier phases of the Late Bronze Age.

Bronze Age activity in the Vasilikos Valley came to an end with the abandonment of Ayios Dhimitrios at about 1200 BC. Most of the town appears to have been peacefully yet thoroughly deserted, but a fire in Building X at or shortly after the abandonment may be connected with the more widespread destructions at some other sites. The reason for the abandonment is not apparent from the local evidence, but the absence of any material datable to LC III anywhere in the area, despite the presence of important copper sources, shows that very drastic changes must have taken place.

CONCLUSION

The archaeological record in the Vasilikos Valley shows a clear picture of increasing settlement size and social complexity through the Bronze Age, apparently linked to exploitation of the local copper sources. The plentiful evidence available for the Middle Bronze Age will, when study of recently excavated material is complete, allow for a detailed understanding of the development of a south coastal region during this formative period. The Late Bronze Age evidence contributes much which is relevant to major issues concerning the development of Cypriot society. It is hoped that excavation at Ayios Dhimitrios and eventually other sites will continue for several years, with the objective of solving outstanding problems and filling the gaps in the story.

NOTES

[1] The field survey, entailing intensive examination of E-W transects 100 m wide at intervals of 500 m, has been completed from the coast to the mining area (but excludes a military zone which includes much of the mining area). The results are being prepared for publication in two volumes in the *Vasilikos Valley Project* series. New information continues to come to light during extension of the survey area to the north, and as a result of chance discoveries.

[2] See Karageorghis 1940–48 for tombs excavated by the Department of Antiquities in the 1940s, and Todd 1986 for tombs excavated by the Vasilikos Valley Project in 1978 and a summary of previously excavated tombs. A forthcoming volume in the *Vasilikos Valley Project* series will provide full information concerning the tombs excavated in 1987.

[3] A foreign origin for Red Lustrous Ware, which occurred in these tombs, is regarded as not proven.

[4] Tomb 11 will be published as a volume in the *Vasilikos Valley Project* series. Brief preliminary reports were published in South 1984b and *Chronique* 1985, 928–32.

[5] See note[3].

[6] Ayios Dhimitrios has been excavated by the Vasilikos Valley Project in 1979–84 and 1987; preliminary reports have been published in South 1980; 1982; 1983; 1984a; 1984b and 1988 and short summaries in South 1984c; 1985; 1987 and South & Todd 1985. Four volumes of final reports are in preparation of which the first to appear is South, Russell & Schuster 1988.

LIST OF REFERENCES

Courtois, J-C. (1983) Le trésor de poids de Kalavasos-Ayios Dhimitrios 1982. *RDAC*, 117–30.

Herscher, E. (1980) Southern Cyprus and the disappearing Early Bronze Age. *RDAC*, 17–21.

Herscher, E. (1984) The Pottery of Maroni and regionalism in Late Bronze Age Cyprus, in *Cyprus at the Close of the Late Bronze Age* (eds. V. Karageorghis & J.D. Muhly) 23–8. Nicosia..

Karageorghis, V. (1940–48) Finds from Early Cypriote cemeteries. *RDAC*, 115–52.

Karageorghis, V. (1982) *Cyprus from the Stone Age to the Romans*. London.

Knapp, A.B. (1986a) *Copper Production and Divine Protection: Archaeology, Ideology and Social Complexity on Bronze Age Cyprus. (SIMA Pocket-book 42)* Göteborg.

Knapp, A.B. (1986b) Production, Exchange, and Socio-political Complexity on Bronze Age Cyprus. *Oxf J A* 5, 35–60.

McClellan, M.C., Russell, P.J. & Todd, I.A. (1988) Kalavasos-Mangia: Rescue Excavations at a Late Bronze Age Cemetery. *RDAC* forthcoming.

Masson, E. (1983) Premiers documents Chypro-Minoens du site Kalavasos-Ayios Dhimitrios. *RDAC*, 131–41.

Masson, E. (1986) Les écritures chypro-minoennes: reflet fidèle du brassage des civilisations pendant le Bronze Récent. *Acts 1986*, 180–200.

Merrillees, R.S. (1984) Ambelikou-Aletri: A preliminary report. *RDAC*, 1–13.

Merrillees, R.S. (1985) A Late Cypriote Bronze Age tomb and its Asiatic connections, in *Papers in Honour of Olga Tufnell* (ed. J.N. Tubb) 114–35. London.

Muhly, J.D. (1986) The role of Cyprus in the economy of the Eastern Mediterranean during the second millennium BC. *Acts 1986*, 45–62.

Pearlman, D. (1985) Kalavasos Village Tomb 51: Tomb of an Unknown Soldier. *RDAC*, 164–79.

Schaeffer, C.F.A. (1952) *Enkomi-Alasia. Nouvelles Missions en Chypre 1946–1950*. Paris.

South, A.K. (1980) Kalavasos-Ayios Dhimitrios 1979: a Summary Report. *RDAC*, 22–53.

South, A.K. (1982) Kalavasos-Ayios Dhimitrios 1980–81. *RDAC*, 60–8.

South, A.K. (1983) Kalavasos-Ayios Dhimitrios 1982. *RDAC*, 92–116.

South, A.K. (1984a) Kalavasos-Ayios Dhimitrios 1983. *RDAC*, 14–41.

South, A.K. (1984b) Riches of Late Bronze Age Cyprus. *ASOR Newsletter* 36.2, 3–5.

South, A.K. (1984c) Kalavasos-Ayios Dhimitrios and the Late Bronze Age of Cyprus, in *Cyprus at the Close of the Late Bronze Age* (eds. V. Karageorghis & J.D. Muhly) 11–18. Nicosia.

South, A.K. (1985) The Late Bronze Age in the Vasilikos Valley. *Acts 1985*, 113–24.

South, A.K. (1987) Contacts and contrasts in Late Bronze Age Cyprus: the Vasilikos Valley and the West, in *Western Cyprus: Connections*, (ed. D.W. Rupp) *(SIMA 77)* 83-91. Göteborg.

South, A.K. (1988) Kalavasos-Ayios Dhimitrios 1987: an important ceramic group from Building X. *RDAC* forthcoming.

South, A.K., Russell, P. & Schuster, P. (1988) *Vasilikos Valley Project 3: Kalavasos-Ayios Dhimitrios II. Ceramics, Objects, Tombs, Specialist Studies. (SIMA 71.30)*. Göteborg.

South, A.K. & Todd, I.A. (1985) In Quest of Cypriote Copper Traders: Excavations at Kalavasos-Ayios Dhimitrios. *Archaeology* 38, 40–7.

Todd, I.A. (1986) *Vasilikos Valley Project I: The Bronze Age Cemetery in Kalavasos Village. (SIMA 71.1)* Göteborg.

Todd, I.A. (1988) The Middle Bronze Age in the Kalavasos Area. *RDAC* forthcoming.

37
Status symbols in Cyprus in the eleventh century BC

J.N. Coldstream
University College, London

The last two decades have seen impressive advances in our knowledge of the eleventh century BC, a pivotal period in Cypriot history; a century which saw the transition from the Bronze Age to the Iron Age, and the foundation of the historic Cypriot kingdoms. Only twenty years ago Karageorghis (1967, 1–2), publishing the LC IIIB tomb at Palaepaphos-Xerolimni, could still remark that the eleventh century was 'not yet adequately documented by archaeological discoveries.' In fact, no tomb of that period had yet received proper publication. Today, over twenty tombs of the early eleventh century have been fully published, with at least twenty-two burials. These, when added to the known finds of the later eleventh century—forty-eight published tombs of CG IA with at least seventy-six burials—should allow at least some preliminary observations and conjectures about the various orders of Cypriot society during the earliest years of the historic kingdoms. Table 37.1 presents a consolidated list of published eleventh-century tombs, dated according to the view of the excavators in their site reports. More recent research on pottery classification (eg Iacovou 1984) may present a good case for lowering the relative dates of some tombs; even so, an extension of their chronological range some way down into the tenth century will not impair the general thoughts put forward in this paper concerning the social structure of Cyprus at the outset of the Iron Age.

In search of the highest stratum of society we should first consider the Skales cemetery in the remote south-eastern quarter of Paphos (Karageorghis 1983). Skales was not the only wealthy Paphian cemetery of this period; indeed, rich offerings are also reported from the eastern burial ground of Hassan Agha (Karageorghis & Iacovou 1982) where no records were kept of the tomb contexts. Nevertheless, the richest Skales tombs have been singled out as belonging to a Mycenaean aristocracy. Both words

Table 37.1. Register of eleventh century tombs in Cyprus

SITE locality	Abbreviation	PUBLICATION	LC IIIB Tombs, burials	CG IA Tombs, burials
PALAEPAPHOS				
Xerolimni	PX	Karageorghis 1967	(PX)	
Skales	P	Karageorghis 1983		(43), 44, 49$^{1-3}$ (CGIA&B), (50, 51), 58, 61, 67,$^{1-2}$ 68, 76$^{1-3}$, 78$^{1-2}$ 84, 85$^{1-3}$, 88 , 89$^{1-5}$, 91$^{1-3}$, 92
KOURION				
Bamboula	KB	Benson 1972	(8,27), 30, 33^3	19^{*1,2}, 20^1,
Kaloriziki	K	MacFadden 1954	25, 26^1	21, 26^2, 33, 34$^{1-2}$, 35,
		Benson 1973	40$^{(1)}$, 2	36, 39, 41^{12}
AMATHUS	A	*SCE* II		22^1
KITION				
Turabi Tekke	KirTT	Myres 1910		(TT)
IDALION				
Av. Georgios	I	Karageorghis 1965	(I)	

Status symbols in the eleventh century BC

Site			Reference	Tombs
GASTRIA	Alaas	GA	Karageorghis 1975a	11, 12*, 14, 15, 16, 17$^{1-2}$, 18*, 19
CHYTROI	Kythrea	C	Nicolaou 1965	$^{1-3}$4(CGIA&B)
LAPITHOS	Kastros	L	SCE I	406$^{1-3}$, 407* 410*, 414* 417$^{1-3}$, 420$^{1-5}$, 422$^{1-2}$,
	Ay. Anastasia		Pieridou 1966 Gjerstad 1944	(503)^1
	Plakes Prostemenos		SCE I Pieridou 1965	(502)^1 (503)^2 603 P74$^{1-2}$
AYIA IRINI	Kharangas	AI	Rocchetti 1976	1^2, 3^1, 6^1
MARION	Sikarka-Kokkinia	M	SCE II	65, 68, (70)

* - robbed tomb
( ) - excavation data lacking

require reflection and even definition in the unusual circumstances of the eleventh century. The chamber tombs themselves are indeed Mycenaean in form, approached by long and narrow *dromoi* leading to carefully squared chambers. In Greece such tombs had been constructed during the Mycenaean *koiné* of the thirteenth century and, less carefully, in the twelfth—but certainly no longer in the Greek Protogeometric period with which the earliest Skales tombs are contemporary. Tombs of this type are as yet unknown in Cyprus before the eleventh century, when their first appearance seems to coincide with the foundation of new settlements destined to become the historic Greek Cypriot kingdoms. These tombs are also aristocratic, in the context of eleventh-century Cyprus, in that they entail a greater command of labour than do the indigenous Cypriot form of chamber tomb with a much shorter *dromos*. In this sense the most aristocratic tombs of all are Skales 49 and 58 whose unusually spacious chambers, with a floor area of at least twelve square metres, are among the largest anywhere in Cyprus (Table 37.2). It is no surprise that they also contain an outstandingly rich assemblage of offerings, with many symbols of high status.

One reliable index of wealth is an accumulation of bronze vessels. Out of a published total of fifty-one for the eleventh century, twenty-one are from these same two tombs. Fairly commonplace are the small hemispherical bowls, found singly or in pairs in several tombs at Lapithos, Alaas, Kition and Amathus, but in sets of at least six in Skales 49 and 58. Larger bronze vessels, truer indicators of high status, are confined to these two tombs (Karageorghis 1983, Pls 60–3, Figs 115–16) and to Kaloriziki 39 and 40 (McFadden 1954; Benson 1973, 48–50). Skales has produced four shallow cauldrons including some with lotus or goat attachments; also a tripod

Table 37.2. Eleventh century tombs in Cyprus: tomb floor sizes (For site abbreviations see Table 37.1)

m^2	LC IIIB	CG IA
over 12	K 41	P 49, 58
10–12	none	none
8–10	none	none
6–8	K 26	L 417, 420; KB 11; K 34; P 44, 76, 89
5–6	none	L 406, P 74; KB 33; K 10, 40; P 50, 67; M 68; C 4
4–5	GA 11	S 1; L 603; K 33, 35, 36 P 85, 91; M 65
3–4	GA 15, 16, 19	L 422; K20; P 61, 78; A 22; M 70
2–3	K 25 GA 13, 14, 17	P 84, 88
1–2	GA 12, 18	K 21; P 92 AI 1, 3, 6

cauldron of Aegean type. Rod tripods occur in Skales 49 and Kaloriziki 39 and 40; the last tomb is also the source of two fragmentary amphoroid kraters. We do not know how many of these bronze vessels were actually made in Cyprus, and some may well be antiques. The tripod cauldron, with Mycenaean antecedents, was certainly known in the Aegean during the late eleventh century, since small clay copies occur in an Early Protogeometric grave in the Athenian Kerameikos cemetery (Kraiker & Kübler 1939, 147 Pls 63–4). Even so, a case has been argued for a bronze shortage at this time in the Aegean (Snodgrass 1971, 237–9). If this was so, the Skales cauldron is the more likely to have been made in Cyprus where there can have been no lack of bronze, and the Attic potters could have copied the type from imported vessels made by their kinsmen recently settled in Cyprus. But it is the rod tripods which deserve special consideration here as objects of prestige. Made in Cyprus no later then the early twelfth century, they were to enjoy a wide circulation both in space and in time: to Crete in the tenth and ninth centuries, to Athens in the eighth, and to Thera even as late as the seventh (Catling 1964, 190–223; 1984). Changing hands many times, these tripods may sometimes answer to the gifts exchanged in Homeric and other early poetry, when the poet mentions tripods and cauldrons as separate articles in the same line.[1]

Military equipment is reserved for an élite of only twelve tombs. The weapons number nineteen in all, thirteen of which are from Skales including the only four swords and daggers, all in iron. More plentiful are the spearheads, four in iron, nine still in bronze. Items of unusual distinction are the trunnion axe from Skales 76, the scale armour from Alaas 12, and the shield fittings from the plundered male burial of Kaloriziki 40; but the military display is never ostentatious, since no male burial is known to contain more than one weapon.

The gold jewellery has a rather wider distribution, occurring in nineteen tombs, five of which[2] contain skeletal evidence of association with female burials; no jewellery is certainly associated with male burials. Earrings, singly or in pairs, are the most commonplace form, found in all but two of the tombs; they follow either the oriental leech type, or carry single 'mulberries' of not very skilfully granulated drops.[3] An exceptionally wide variety is offered by four of the richest tombs, Skales 67, Lapithos 417 and 420, and Salamis French tomb 1, including repoussé rosettes of Aegean character, and two types which look towards the Near East: circular pendants with filigree border, and sets of identical rectangular plaques with figured relief decoration, suitable for a coronet or tiara.[4];14;4 An alternative source of sophistication lies in the Cypriot past. The two gold rings from the Salamis tomb, elaborated with cloisonné enamelling, recall the set from Palaepaphos Evreti 8, in a technique forgotten after the early twelfth century; it is seen also in that gigantic jewel, the head of the sceptre from Kaloriziki 40, most spectacular of all status symbols in eleventh-century Cyprus, and already an antique in its tomb context.

Indeed, antiques are not all uncommon in rich eleventh-century tombs, in compensation for the general decline in all fine arts requiring high technical skill. To the jewellery and rod tripods already mentioned, we must add the ivory roundels from Kaloriziki, several seals and scarabs—notably the scarab set in gold from Salamis 1, the massive stone bath from Skales 89, the large stone scarab from the same tomb bearing an Egyptian text of the time of Amenophis III, and, oldest of all, the bronze amphoroid krater from Kaloriziki 40 with pairs of Minoan genii in relief on the handles, dating from the era of the second Cretan palaces; here I am convinced by the reasoning of Baurain and Darcque (1983, 52 n 213; 1985), who argue for a sixteenth-century date. Burials of only moderate wealth may even contain antique pots, such as the Myc IIIA:2 jar from Alaas 15, and the Base Ring bowl in Kaloriziki 34.

Other ceramic offerings which might pass for luxury come from the Orient. Approximately one burial in three contains one or more Levantine unguent vessels, flasks or bottles in Bichrome or Red Slip. Evidently, such mundane luxuries were quite widely enjoyed; whatever the delectable contents may have been, they and their Cypriot imitations gradually replaced the stirrup-jars of Mycenaean type during the course of the eleventh century (among the published tombs, twenty-eight stirrup-jars occur in LC IIIB contexts, but only eleven in CG IA tombs which contain a far higher aggregate of pottery). The exceptionally rich tombs, however, contain large concentrations of imported Levantine flasks, and sometimes a large oriental container, the amphora of Canaanite type; symptomatic of the uppermost social stratum are the accumulation of eastern flasks, eight in Skales 58, five in Salamis 1, and also the four Canaanite amphorae in Skales 49.

The eastern vessels were imported for their contents; but for excellence in the more usual fine pottery shapes, as containers of food, drink and other comforts in the next world, there was no need to look either to the east or to the past. Thanks to recent discoveries, the eleventh century is coming to be recognized as one of the great periods of Cypriot pottery. On a largely Mycenaean repertoire of fine painted shapes, the local potters improvised with adventurous ingenuity especially in the creation of ritual vessels and of a highly original figure style. The most elaborate vessels, both ritual and figured, are concentrated mainly in the richest tombs. Within a wealthy family, ritual at a burial ceremony—presumably libation,—was served by the fairly frequent bird and animal askoi. More exceptional, and more aristocratic, are the sprinkler vessels with human faces from Skales 49 and 78, and the anthropoid vessel from Salamis 1; also the trick vases in Skales 58 and in a tomb in the Turabi Tekke cemetery of Kition, in the form of a Mycenaean kylix but with a frog mouth and a bull spout. As for the figured pots, perhaps less than one per cent of the total corpus, at least one occurs in the richest tombs, Skales 49 and 58 and Salamis 1; but at least ten other tombs contain them too. Among the figured motifs the only obvious subject suggesting high status is the warrior; one thinks especially of the warrior on an unprovenanced pyxis, apparently wearing a figure-of-eight shield (Karageorghis & Des Gagniers 1974, 4). There is also the military musician on the kalathos from the Xerolimni tomb (Karageorghis 1967, Pl 1) who, in a Paphian context, would seem to have more to do with Kinyras than with Agapenor. In particular, one misses any reference to the chariot team, and to other motifs characteristic of the aristocratic Mycenaean amphoroid kraters, which had once been so popular as exports to Cyprus. Although the shape was copiously reproduced in the local eleventh-century repertoire, it never carries figured decoration at this time; Skales 58.10, which bears a solitary quadruped (horse?) on the neck, is considered 'a late CG I type' (Karageorghis 1983, 122) and therefore later than the period considered here. In general, the favourite figured motifs of the eleventh century—birds, goats, horned quadrupeds and palm trees—do not in themselves suggest high status. Perhaps a more positive indication of wealth, though not an essential one,[5] may be seen in the vast quantity of pots in some tombs: for example, over a hundred and seventy vessels in Salamis 1, and well over a hundred in Skales 43, 44, 49, 50, 58, 67, 76 and 89. Here let us note in passing that we do not find these vast accumulations of pottery in the rich burials of Mycenaean Greece, but there is plenty of precedent for them well back in the Cypriot Bronze Age.

Finally, we come to that rarest of all status symbols, the tomb offering with an inscribed personal name. As such, the bronze spit in Skales 49 inscribed with the Arcadian genitive of the name Opheltas is apparently unique; unique not only in the eleventh-century Cyprus, but in any Cypriot burials before Archaic times. The next named tomb offering, if L.P. di Cesnola's account is correct, would be the silver bowl bearing a seventh-century syllabic inscription giving the name of its original owner, Akestor king of Paphos, and also the name of a later owner, Timukretes (Mitford 1963). Returning to the *obelos* in Skales 49, one reflects how strange it is that this personal inscription should occur in a tomb context at a time when any writing is so rare; perhaps that very rarity enhances the social standing of the incumbent with whom the spit was found, whether or not his name was Opheltas. We must not, of course, lose sight of the other two bronze spits in Skales 49, which also bear syllabic signs; but these cannot with confidence be attributed to any particular syllabary, either Cypro-Minoan or Cypro-Greek (Masson E. & O. 1983, 411–15 Fig 88.17, 18). There is, however, another inscribed object from Skales, definitely in Cypro-Minoan: a hemispherical bronze bowl with five syllabic signs, ending with the arrow sign which, in earlier Cypro-Monoan inscriptions—for example, on the clay balls—suggests an inflexion of a personal name (Masson 1971a; 1971b). Although the bowl was found in a surface level, there arises the likelihood that the incumbents in the Skales cemetery were not all of Aegean origin, but included an indigenous element. Indeed, not all the tombs are of Mycenaean type; 50 and 61 have the very short *dromos* characteristic of Cyprus, while 68 is a pit grave.

The Skales inscriptions prompt some enquiry into the distribution of wealth between tombs of indigenous and Aegean type. Four excavated sites have produced exclusively indigenous tombs: Kourion-Bamboula and Ayia Irini, three tombs each; Lapithos-Plakes 603, and the first burial of Amathus 22. None contains any weapon, any gold; any metal is very rare, the maximum number of pots is fifteen in Lapithos 603, and there are no oriental imports. Richer than the overall average is the solitary Turabi Tekke tomb at Kition, presumably pre-Phoenician, and containing bronze spits, an iron spear, a pair of bronze bowls, and some simple gold jewellery; but we must leave it out of this discussion since we do not know its form. Otherwise, positive symbols of wealth and high status come exclusively from cemeteries of predominantly Mycenaean type. How that wealth may have been acquired, we cannot say—whether by inheritance, by intermarriage with the indigenous population, by commerce, by gift exchange, or by plunder; thus, for precious grave goods from a bygone age, the neutral term 'antique' is preferable to 'heirloom'.

In reality, the number of cemeteries with eleventh-century tombs wholly of Mycenaean type is limited to two only: Lapithos-Kastros and Marion, with four and three tombs respectively. The Marion tombs are sparsely furnished; far richer are the offerings in Lapithos-Kastros, including plenty of gold jewellery and vast numbers of pots. Peculiar to Lapithos at this time is the most barbaric of status symbols: in three out of the four Kastros tombs, skeletons found without offerings just inside the chamber entrance are thought to have been slaves sacrificed to serve their masters in the next world (*SCE* I, 236, 244–5; Hood 1973, 40–1). At Lapithos, perhaps, relations between the two communities may have been less cordial than elsewhere, an impression also given by the apparent segregation of the two ethnic groups into separate cemeteries, Kastros and Plakes. This theory, however, rests on rather slender foundations, since Plakes boasts a total of three tombs, of which only one goes back into the eleventh century.

Be that as it may, the other three cemeteries where the Aegean element predominates—Alaas, Skales and Kaloriziki—all show some evidence of coexistence within the eleventh century. All contain some tombs constructed in the Cypriot tradition, not obviously poorer than chamber tombs of Aegean type in the same cemeteries, and much more generously furnished than burials in wholly indigenous cemeteries. Thus the female burial in Alaas 16, a pit cave with a vertical shaft, enjoys a pair of gold earrings, bronze dress ornaments, an ivory disc and, among a fine assembly of eighteen pots, a choice Proto-Bichrome pyxis including a lotus flower among its rich ornament. Skales, in addition to the Cypro-Minoan inscribed bronze bowl, contains three tombs of indigenous character, as we have already seen. Likewise, at Kaloriziki, three of the published tombs seem more Cypriot than Mycenaean in form: 36, a double tomb connected by a common *dromos;* 39, with a short pit-shaped *dromos;* and the much-discussed 40, a spacious rectangular shaft without any sign of a *dromos,* and quite consistent with Late Cypriot Bronze Age tradition (*SCE* IV.1C, 51 Fig 27.10). The tomb contained a female and probably also a male cremation, both housed in antique bronze amphoroid kraters. Those who wish to see, in the goods looted in 1903, an Achaean prince with his enamelled sceptre and his bronze-lined targe, either suppose that a long *dromos* may have been entirely eroded away (Benson 1973, 49), or argue that the unusual rite of cremation is alien to Cyprus (McFadden 1954, 134). In the Aegean, however, cremation had nowhere become the general rule as early as the first half of the eleventh century (Melas 1984), the date of the tomb; furthermore, other eleventh-century cremations in Cyprus, besides several in the Skales tombs, include one in a wholly indigenous cemetery, Bamboula 30, and another in Kaloriziki 39, a tomb of Cypriot type. In default of any convincing argument to the contrary, it would seem that the chief incumbent in tomb 40 was an indigenous Cypriot prince, who chose to ally himself with the new settlers from the Aegean. If so, this tomb will contain by far the richest Eteocypriot burials of the eleventh century.

With this distinguished exception, then, it appears that the wealth of Cyprus had largely passed into the hands of the Aegean immigrants: that is, if tomb goods are a true reflection of life style. On that assumption, if we take into consideration all the various kinds of status symbol reviewed here, the eleventh-century burials of Cyprus can be tentatively assigned their

Table 37.3. Eleventh century tombs in Cyprus: the social scale (For site abbreviations see Table 37.1)

	LC IIIB	CG IA
Outstandingly rich; highest social stratum	K $\underline{40^{1-2}}$	P 49^{1-3}, 58, 76, 89 S 1 L 417^1
Richer than average	K 25, 26^1	P 43, 44, $\underline{50}$, 67, 91, K 33, 34, $\overline{39}$ L 406^{1-3}, 417^2, 420^{1-2}, L 502, P 74^{1-2} KitTT
Moderate wealth	PX GA 15, $\underline{16}$ GA 17, $\overline{19}$	P 51, $\underline{61}$, 78, 84, 85 K 19, $\overline{21}$, 26^2, 35, $\underline{36}$ L 420^3, 422^1 M 68^1 A 22^1 C 4
Poorly furnished	$\underline{\text{KB 8, 27}}$ $\underline{\text{KB 30, }33^3}$ K 41^1 GA 11, 13, 14	P $\underline{68}$, 88, 92 K $\overline{20^1}$, 41^2 L 603 $\overline{\text{AI }1^2}$, 3^1, 6^1 M 65, 70
Without offerings slaves (?)		L 417^3, 420^{4-5}, 422^2

Indigenous tombs underlined; robbed tombs and chance finds omitted.

place in a social scale (Table 37.3), with marked differences in wealth and status. In that scale, all but the very lowest stratum would have been thought extremely fortunate and enviable by those Aegean people who stayed behind in the bleak world of Submycenaean Greece and Subminoan Crete where, among the grave offerings, pots are confined to single figures, and any form of metal is an unusual luxury.

NOTES

[1] eg Hesiod fr. 200.5 (Merkelbach & West); *Homeric Hymn IV*, 61. See Bruns 1970, 37–9.
[2] Skales 88, Alaas 15 & 16, Lapithos 417[1] & 420.[1]
[3] Skales 43, 67, 79, 85, 87; Goring 1983. Also Lapithos 420, 422, *SCE* I Pl 155.9, 11.
[4] Lapithos 417[1], Skales 67[1] & 76; Karageorghis 1975b; Goring 1983.
[5] For example, Kaloriziki 40, surpassingly rich in metal offerings, contained only nine pots.

LIST OF REFERENCES

Baurain, C. & Darcque, P. (1983) Un triton en pierre à Malia. *BCH 107*, 3–73.
Baurain, C. & Darcque, P. (1985) Chypre et l'Égée: Nouvelles perspectives sur "L'amphora aux génies" du Cyprus Museum. *Acts 1985*, 171–4.
Benson, J.L. (1972) *Bamboula at Kourion, the Necropolis and the Finds*. Philadelphia.
Benson, J.L. (1973) *The Necropolis of Kaloriziki. (SIMA 36)*. Göteborg.
Bruns, G. (1970) *Archaeologica Homerica* II Q. *Küchenwesen und Mahlzeiten*. Göttingen.
Catling, H.W. (1964) *Cypriot Bronzework in the Mycenaean World*. Oxford.
Catling, H.W. (1984) Workshop and heirloom. Prehistoric bronze stands in the East Mediterranean. *RDAC*, 69–91.
Gjerstad, E. (1944) The initial date of the Cypriote Iron Age. *Op Rom 3*, 73–106.
Goring, E. (1983) Techniques of the Palaepaphos-*Skales* jewellery, *in* Karageorghis 1983, 418–22.
Hood, M.S.F. (1973) Mycenaean settlement in Cyprus and the coming of the Greeks. *Acts 1973*, 40–50.
Iacovou, M. (1984) *The Eleventh Century Pictorial Pottery of Cyprus*. University of Cincinnati, Ph D thesis, unpublished.
Karageorghis, V. (1965) *Nouveaux Documents pour l'Étude du Bronze Récent à Chypre. (École Française d'Athènes Études Chypriotes III)*. Paris.
Karageorghis, V. (1967) An early XIth century BC tomb from Palaepaphos. *RDAC*, 1–24.
Karageorghis, V. (1975a) *Alaas, a Protogeometric Necropolis in Cyprus*. Nicosia.
Karageorghis, V. (1975b) A gold ornament with a representation of an "Astarte". *R St Fen 3*, 31–5.
Karageorghis, V. (1983) *Palaepaphos-Skales, an Iron Age Cemetery in Cyprus. Ausgrabungen in Alt-Paphos auf Cypern III*. Konstanz.
Karageorghis, V. & Des Gagniers, J. (1974) *La Céramique Chypriote de Style Figuré*. Rome.
Karageorghis, V. & Iacovou, M. (1982) Cypro-Geometric material from Palaepaphos. *RDAC*, 123–37.

Kraiker, W. & Kübler, K. (1939) *Kerameikos. Ergebnisse der Ausgrabungen I. Die Nekropolen des 12 bis 10 Jahrhunderts.* Berlin.
McFadden, G. (1954) A Late Cypriot III tomb from Kourion. *AJA 58,* 131–42.
Masson, E. (1971a) *Studies in the Cypro-Minoan Scripts. (SIMA 13.1).* Göteborg.
Masson, E. (1971b) Rouleau inscrit chypro-minoen trouvé à Enkomi en 1967, in *Alasia* I (ed. C. F-A Schaeffer) 457–78. Paris.
Masson, E. & O. (1983) Les objets inscrits de Palaepaphos-Skales *in* Karageorghis 1983, 411–15.
Melas, E. (1984) The origins of Aegean cremation. *Anthropologika 5,* 21–36.
Mitford, T.B. (1963) Akestor, king of Paphos. *Bulletin of the Institute of Classical Studies 10,* 27–9.
Myres, J.L. (1910) A tomb of the Early Iron Age from Kition in Cyprus containing bronze examples of the "Sigynna" or Cypriote javelin, *Liverpool Annals of Archaeology & Anthropology 3,* 107–17.
Nicolaou, K. (1965) Γεωμετρικοι ταφοι κυθραιας *RDAC,* 30–73.
Pieridou, A. (1965) An early Cypro-Geometric tomb at Lapithos. *RDAC,* 74–111.
Pieridou, A. (1966) A tomb-group from Lapithos 'Ayia Anastasia'. *RDAC,* 1–12.
Rocchetti, L. (1976) Tombe geometriche presso Aghia Irini, in località Kharangas. *Studi Ciprioti e Rapporti di Scavo* II, 131–63.
Snodgrass, A.M. (1971) *The Dark Age of Greece.* Edinburgh.
Yon, M. (1971) *Salamine de Chypre* II, *la Tombe T.1.* Paris.

38
Puttin' on the Ritz: manifestations of high status in Iron Age Cyprus

David W. Rupp
Brock University

BACKGROUND

Wearing a well-tailored day coat, pants with stripes and a cut-away coat and carrying a walking stick or an umbrella as one strolls down the avenue to the Ritz, looking like an English chappie, are not universal and constant symbols of wealth and high status in all societies. When a member of the elite in the Cypriot Iron Age desired to put on the Ritz' in order to communicate his or her superordinate social position *vis-à-vis* other members of the society he or she did so in a variety of ways through norms of behaviour and patterns of consumption. In order to project this image properly and with total effect in a given social setting he or she would first have to know many things, namely, the geographical location, the chronological date and the specific social context.

In the last twenty years archaeologists increasingly have investigated the structure and characteristics of complex societies throughout the world and the processes that contributed to their emergence. Central to this research is the construction of ancient social systems. Such research has also appeared in the work carried out in Cyprus in the context of Prehistoric and Bronze Age studies, as a number of papers at this Conference attest. Scholars such as Bernard Knapp (1986) and Priscilla Keswani (1988) have examined systematically the evidence for social organization in the LC period.

The Iron Age is a crucial epoch for the development of social complexity on Cyprus. Of importance is the question of when and how the historically documented hereditary regional monarchies or states appeared. Was it in the eighth century (*cf* Rupp 1987) or earlier, in the LC period (*cf* Snodgrass 1988)? There are a number of ways to tackle this contentious problem. One approach is to scrutinize the material evidence for social complexity between 1050 and 475 BC. One could infer the level of social complexity from variability in the spatial and chronological patterning of the archaeological evidence. One of the material correlates of an agrarian society with a complex social structure is a consistent pattern of unequal distribution of valuable goods or commodities. This reflects status differentiation and hereditary ranking.

PART I

1. The symbols of status and their manipulation by elites

The social structure of a society is an ideal model of the relative ranking of individuals within it (Morris 1987, 39). Susan Pollock argues (1983, 14–15) that in a culture social positions are assigned different levels of *prestige* or *status* to symbolically express the value of each category and its interrelationships with the other categories. In many senses, in a pre-capitalist agrarian society, status or prestige is the medium by which the message of the exact character of the expected social relations between individuals is sent (Parker-Pearson 1984, 69–71; Bradley 1985, 31). Frequently the expression of status or prestige is manifested in a non-material form. In complex societies with permanent social positions, however, concrete material expressions of prestige gain a degree of ascendancy over non-material forms (Pollock 1983, 15).

Colin Renfrew has noted that it is a 'human inclination to give social and symbolic significance to material goods' (1972, 497). The central concept in a definition of goods or commodities is that of *value*. Pollock (1983, 11) would agree with Renfrew that in a given social context value is a property that is assigned arbitrarily to an object by an individual or by a group with the explicit implication of ranking among a given set of objects (1986, 158). It is important to note here that objects considered to have 'prestige value' in a society need not have potential usefulness ('use value'), require a significant labour input ('labour value') in their creation or depend upon the interaction of supply and demand ('exchange value') (Renfrew 1986, 158; Schneider 1974, 43–84). This is because an elite in a society can establish arbitrarily, by premeditated envaluation and use, what their value and prestige are in that society (Renfrew 1986, 148). The expression of prestige occurs in sets or suites of symbols, rather than individually. In short, there is redundancy for effect.

Another approach to the problem of establishing value is Mary Douglas and Baron Isherwood's (1979, 114–127) characterization of value by the frequency of consumption ('periodicity') and by the relative level or esteem of the social context. In short, necessities (lower esteem, high frequency events) are the opposites of luxuries (higher esteem, low frequency events) (Douglas and Isherwood 1979, 116). In this way, the symbolic meaning of an object is arbitrarily assigned by the members of the society through the social context and frequency of its use in that society.

Closely related to this point is Arjun Appadurai's opinion (1986, 36) that one consider luxury goods not as the opposites of necessities but as objects employed within a society in a rhetorical and social fashion. He sees them as a special register of consumption for those individuals who dominate the society politically rather than as a separate artefact class. This register is recognizable by the attributes mentioned above as well as in other ways. First, luxury goods have the capacity to transmit very complex social messages. Second, in order to consume or use them properly one must possess specialized prior knowledge. And finally, their use and consumption are closely linked to 'body, person, and personality' (Appadurai 1986, 38). In short, individuals send and receive social messages through their patterns of consumption.

Access to the sets of symbols which are the physical manifestations of prestige or 'excellence' (Clarke 1986) must be restricted to a particular social segment or position in a culture if they are to keep their meaning (Pollock 1983, 16–43). There are three, fundamental strategies to limit access to the goods or commodities that symbolize prestige. First, ideological and/or political sanctions are invoked. These include sumptuary laws, the control of local, specialist craft production or the regulation of long distance exchange networks. By these means, either alone or in combination, the distribution and redistribution of prestige goods are severely restricted. Second, prestige goods are made too costly for all but a small segment of society to produce or to acquire. Different strategies produce this situation. One uses either raw materials in limited supply locally or those only available via the long distance exchange networks. Excessive levels of skill and/or decorative elaboration can be required in the production of these goods. The size and/or relative abundance of the object in question is another possible strategy. Typically, one increases the cost of production of an object by using more than one of these mechanisms. Third, the deliberate disposal or destruction of wealth by its placement in contexts such as graves or votive deposits where there was no intention of later retrieval. These actions remove permanently prestige items from circulation among the living thereby reducing the supply of high status goods available to those individuals with aspirations of higher social status. Furthermore, the donor of the gift earns prestige in the process. Many scholars view this strategy as a major method for the preservation of the exclusivity of top-ranked or high status gifts (Bradley 1985, 31–2; Morris 1986, 9). These observations reinforce the view there must be a direct relationship between any observed differential distribution patterns of commodities in a society and the underlying social structure of that society (Miller 1982, 97).

2. The ever changing manifestations of high status in a society

Despite apparent stability, change is a constant feature of these sets of symbols for prestige. As a direct consequence of these changes their meaning and value alter with time. Change in the types of objects that symbolize prestige can occur suddenly when the established social and political order is upset by internal stasis or by external events or conquest. Normally, however, change is gradual and continuous. Such change is caused by the mechanisms of emulation, largesse and innovation argues Pollock (1986, 20–2, 272–3).

In emulation, individuals imitate the behaviour and patterns of consumption of their equals or betters in order to demonstrate that they have wealth and, hence, prestige. Their aspirations of upward social mobility motivates this 'conspicuous consumption' and 'conspicuous waste' (Veblen 1934 [1918]). This would be a constant feature of ranked and stratified societies. As this mechanism involves imitation, there is no actual exchange of goods. The result is that the copy always is somehow different from the original in some combination of the raw materials used, the form and size, the level of craftsmanship exhibited or the understanding of the decorative elements, style and/or iconography that are present. There is also an inherent time lag between the creation of the archetype and its use by the elite group and the emulation by a wider circle of the non-elite.

In largesse or gift exchange superiors give prestige goods to subordinates in order to reward them for services rendered or to inspire them to greater achievements. These exchanges can also take place among elite group members or to visitors as a form of diplomacy. The donors are seeking to symbolically reinforce and/or increase their dominant position vis-à-vis the recipient and to promote the established value system (Clarke 1986, 2). At the same time their action 'sets up obligations for a reciprocal gesture of comparable dimensions in the future' (Renfrew 1986, 161). Until these obligations are fulfilled the recipient is in debt to the donor and is thus at a definite social disadvantage. These transfers of goods usually occur at a specific time and involve only limited quantities and varieties of prestige goods. Rites of passage and formalized competitions typically provide socially acceptable situations for the exchange of ordinally ranked prestige goods (Morris 1986, 8). As a consequence of such an exchange the context of the object involved changes and, therefore, its meaning and value (Pollock 1986, 21–2).

By the mechanisms of emulation and largesse/gift exchange prestige goods and their imitations are disseminated in a society from the higher ranked individuals to some, but not all, of the lower ranked ones. In order for the 'movers and shakers' in a society to maintain their control and dominance over their inferiors they must create constantly new symbols of prestige. This would create a premium in a culture on novelty and innovation, as Pollock believes (1986, 22–3), following Daniel Miller (1982). The innovations may ensue through the use of new raw materials, standard materials in a different context, changes in form, size or stylistic attributes or the number of goods required. Thus, one can not predict *a priori* what will be envalued by the elite of a culture as its symbols of excellence.

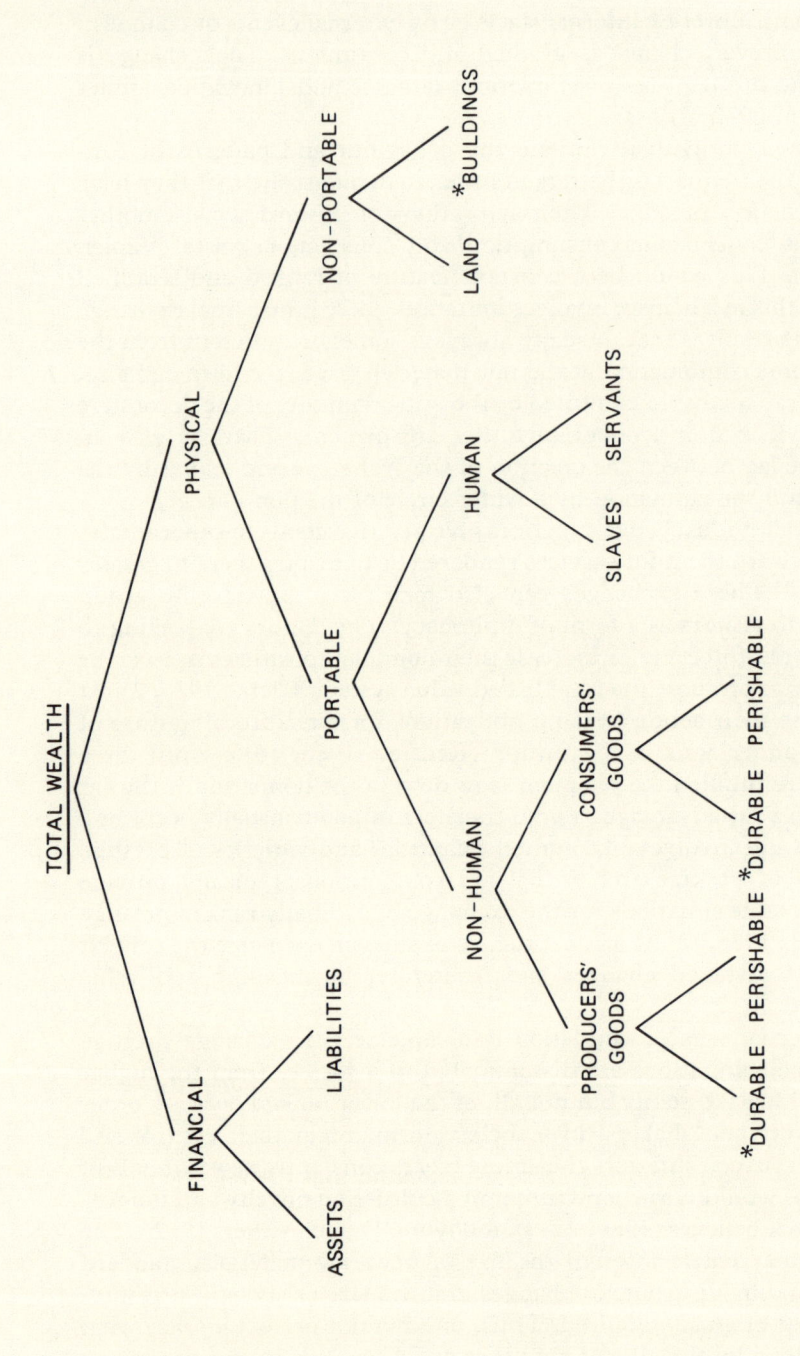

NOTE: * — Possible to document in the archaeological record.

Figure 38.1 General classification of wealth of a household (Modified from Smith 1987, Fig 1 and Table 1, *after* Jones 1980).

3. Constructing social structure through the material correlates of status and wealth

Social structure is revealed, in part, in the archaeological record through the differential distribution of specific classes of artefacts considered as having significant value. This patterning is the result of their use and manipulation by the elite of a society for symbolic purposes. These artefacts and their archaeological context constitute the physical manifestations of the wealth of an individual or household (Schneider 1974, 256). The household, located in a dwelling or compound, is the basic unit of production and consumption in agrarian societies. Alice Jones' (1980) classification of the total wealth of a household (Fig 38. 1), based on her exhaustive study of the American colonies immediately prior to their revolution, is an adequate and useful system for categorizing the various components that make up household wealth in a pre-industrial, agrarian society. Only a small portion of a household's total wealth, however, is susceptible to preservation in the archaeological record.

One can analyze the material correlates of individual and/or family status and prestige in a society by physical wealth as seen in residential architecture, the material possessions of a household and/or the burial assemblages of members of the household (Smith 1987, 288). Each approach has advantages and disadvantages for the archaeologist. Cross-cultural ethnographic, sociological and historical studies demonstrate clearly that the number and type of household possessions correlate strongly with total household wealth (Fig 38.1) (Smith 1987, 307–8). Jones (1980) proved that portable non-human physical wealth is an entirely adequate measure of total wealth patterns in a society. In this manner the total wealth of a household (Fig 38.2) and, hence, its relative rank in the society can be estimated from its possessions. Michael Smith sums up the data relating to household wealth by asserting that, in general, the most consistent and strongest indicators of wealth in agrarian societies are clothing and serving wares followed by furniture and non-utilitarian or personal luxury items (1987, 318). He goes on to argue that food and beverage serving and consumption wares are the most important predictors for accessing household wealth. Following Douglas & Isherwood (1979, 74–6) Smith sees the use of this functional class of artefacts in various public gatherings in the house marking rites of passage, cooperative work parties, banquets, etc. (or 'public consumption rituals') in a symbolic fashion. These artefacts as emblems of privilege communicate to the outsiders at these social gatherings the relative wealth and status of the household.

4. Problems and possibilities in the use of the mortuary record for documenting status and wealth

Many scholars believe that the detailed study of burial assemblages can indicate patterns of rank and social structure in a society. Studies based on this opinion operate, however, with the *caveat* that there are qualifying

FUNCTIONAL CATEGORY	SYSTEMIC CONTEXT			ARCHAEOLOGICAL CONTEXT[a]
	WITHIN ELITE	ELITE VS. COMMONERS	WITHIN COMMONERS	
I. FURNITURE	**	**	**	**
II. CLOTHING	**	**	**	*
III. TOOLS AND HOUSEHOLD EQUIPMENT	*	*		
IV. FOOD/BEVERAGE PREPARATION AND STORAGE WARES	*	*	*	**
V. FOOD/BEVERAGE SERVING AND CONSUMPTION WARES	**	**	**	**
VI. RELIGIOUS/FUNERARY ITEMS	*	**	**	**
VII. WEAPONS AND ARMOUR	**	**	**	**
VIII. TRANSPORTATION	**	**	**	**
IX. UTILITARIAN (PERSONAL) LUXURIES	**	**	**	*
X. NON-UTILITARIAN (PERSONAL) LUXURIES	**	**	*	*

KEY: ** = CONSISTENTLY USEFUL CATEGORY; * = POTENTIALLY USEFUL IN SOME CASES
a = ARCHAEOLOGICAL USEFULNESS BASED ON A COMBINATION OF PRESERVATION FACTORS AND THE EFFECTS OF VARIOUS CULTURAL TRANSFORMATION PROCESSES SUCH AS REUSE, CURATION AND SCAVENGING
MODIFIED AFTER M.E. SMITH, JOURNAL OF ANTHROPOLOGICAL ARCHAEOLOGY 6 (1987), TABLE 5.

Figure 38.2 Summary assessment of the usefulness of non-human, portable wealth indicators.

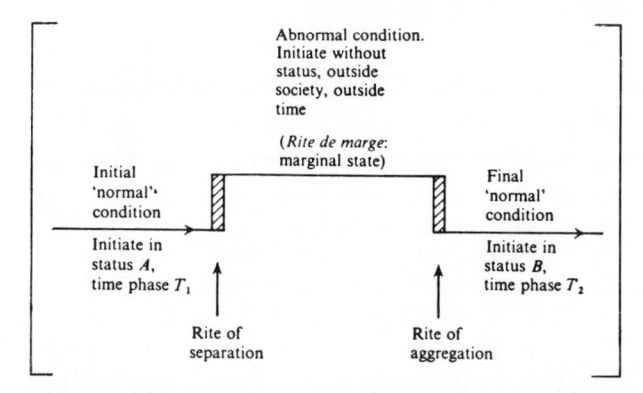

```
                    Abnormal condition.
                    Initiate without
                    status, outside
                    society, outside
                    time

                    (Rite de marge:
                    marginal state)
  Initial                                        Final
  'normal'                                       'normal'
  condition                                      condition

  Initiate in                                    Initiate in
  status A,           ↑              ↑           status B,
  time phase T₁                                  time phase T₂

                  Rite of         Rite of
                  separation      aggregation
```

Figure 38.3 The tripartite structure of the rite of passage (*from* Leach 1976, Fig 7).

factors which may affect significantly the mortuary record. In this regard, Ian Morris has provided a useful, intelligent and wide-ranging over view of types of information relating to a society which are obtainable from an analysis of the burial assemblages of the deceased individuals from that society. He rightly asserts that the burial itself is only one aspect of a funeral and that a funeral is only a part of the social circumstances which surround death (1987, 29). Morris believes that the funeral was one of the rites of passage in an individual's existence. This rite has a tripartite structure (Fig 38.3) during which the corpse is disposed of and the deceased is separated from the world of the living. The funerary ritual must re-integrate the mourners with the rest of society. The social position of the deceased and of the mourners determines the scale and the rites required to achieve this end. In the face of social disorder precipitated by a death, the funeral ceremony accomplishes the reaffirmation of the ideal norms of the social roles of the survivors and the dead (Morris 1987, 31).

When an archaeologist excavates a burial he or she does not excavate by any means the complete funerary ceremony. The different social personalities of the dead produce the differences in the material remains among the burials. According to Lewis Binford (1971, 17) the survivors give symbolic recognition in a funeral to the social persona of the deceased. This is a composite of the various social identities that a person had in life. The picture sketched from the preserved material evidence of the various social personae in a cemetery is not an isomorph of the social organization that they once were a part of. This is because 'in death people often become what they have not been in life' (Hodder 1982, 146). Therefore, Morris concludes

> 'in burial archaeology we study not a social system but rather a ritual expression of social structure, which is constituted largely in terms of roles'

and social personalities (1986, 40, 42). In other words, we observe in the archaeological record the way members of a community wished to see themselves not necessarily the way that they behaved (Morris 1986, 42).

PART II

1. The potential and the reality of the study of status and social structure in Iron Age Cyprus

If one desired to correlate the different forms of physical wealth preserved in the archaeological record with the social standing of the individuals and households that once owned them, the preferred approaches are to study the material possessions of a household or the residential architecture. As shown above burial assemblages are considered laden with problems, uncertainties and unknowns. Even data on potential status markers found in the most meticulously excavated cemeteries are open to opposing interpretations. It is ironic, then, that the present archaeological record for Iron Age Cyprus cannot sustain a rigorous scrutiny of the material possessions or the residential architecture of a household. The bias towards mortuary remains, religious sanctuaries and shrines, artistic production and iconography is a tradition well-rooted in the history of Cypriot archaeology and scholarship. The systematic excavation of the CG and CA levels of the residential and secular quarters of the Iron Age kingdom centres has not been a prominent research objective until recently. The work of Franz Maier in the Evreti area at Palaepaphos (Maier & von Wartburg 1985a, 113–18; 1985b, 152–5), of Pamela Gaber in the lower city at Idalion (pers comm) and that of William Childs at Marion (pers comm) represent the vanguard of such investigations in Cyprus.

The only substantial data that we have to study status and social structure in this period are the myriad burial assemblages that have been carefully excavated throughout the island in the last fifty years or so. These burials form a sizable, if imperfect, data base with which to suggest the indicators of status and wealth and to construct in a preliminary fashion the social structure of Iron Age Cypriot society. This is possible because in death, the final rite of passage for an individual, the idealized structure of a society is ritually reaffirmed by various means for both the deceased and the survivors.

2. Previous research

Five years ago I began a pilot study of sixty published Iron Age burial assemblages from Cyprus in order to obtain evidence relating to the probable level of social organization and stratification that existed between approximately 1050 and 475 BC (Rupp 1985). On the basis of my simple descriptive analyses, I suggested (Rupp 1985, 128 and Table 3) that the presence of certain artefact material classes (Fig 38. 4) in the burial assemblages, the degree of diversity in the artefact material classes, the location, type and size of the interment facilities and the elaborateness of the funerary rituals were strong indicators of high status in the society.

More recently other scholars have proposed additional markers of high status in Cypriot society in the Iron Age. For the eleventh century J.N.

1. TERRACOTTA
    Vessels
    Lamps
    *Sculpture
    Other
2. CERAMIC
    Non-decorated Cypriote wares
    Decorated Cypriote wares: simple
    **Decorated Cypriote wares: elaborate
    **Decorated Cypriote wares: tin encrusted
    *Imported wares
3. STONE
    *Vessels
    **Sculpture
    Jewelry
    Tools
    Other
4. OTHER
    Seashells
    *Glass paste: beads
    *Glass paste: scarabs
    Bone
    Other
5. FAIENCE
    *Vessels
    *Sculptures + relief plaques
    *Jewelry
    **Scarabs
    Other
6. IVORY
    **Vessels
    **Sculptures
    **Weapons (decoration)
    *Jewelry
    **Horse trappings (decoration)
    *Other
7. IRON
    Tools
    *Weapons
    Utensils
    **Horse trappings
    **Vehicle hardware
    Other
8. BRONZE
    *Vessels and lamps
    *Weapons
    **Armour
    *Sculpture
    Tools
    *Jewelry
    **Horse trappings
    **Vehicle hardware
9. SILVER
    **Vessels
    **Jewellery
    **Utensils
    **Other
10. GOLD
    **Vessels
    **Jewelry
    **Horse trappings (with leather)
    **Other
11. FURNITURE
    *Wood only
    **With ivory plaque decoration
    **With ivory, glass paste, gold, silver decoration
    **With silver decoration
    *Other

Key: * = possible markers of higher rank/status;   ** = probable markers of highest rank/status.

Figure 38.4 Artefact material class used to analyse Cypriot Iron Age burial assemblages (*from* Rupp 1985, Table 3).

Coldstream (325–355) associates an array of traits in the Palaepaphos-Skales burial assemblages with the symbols of high status. They include, 1) the accumulation of bronze vessels (especially large ones); 2) bronze and iron rod tripods; 3) military paraphernalia; 4) gold jewellery; 5) ivory artefacts; 6) seals and scarabs; 7) artefacts inscribed with a personal name; 8) vast quantities of ceramic vessels; 9) elaborately decorated vessels (especially with a depiction of a warrior); 10) ritual vessels; 11) imported ceramic vessels; and 12) Mycenaean vessels as heirlooms. Previously, he formulated (1986, 327) a general rule for the ninth and eighth centuries, based on his exhaustive study of Greek Geometric period ceramic exports to Cyprus, that eastern imports accompany any concentration of Greek pottery in a Cypriot tomb. He viewed both imported ceramic wares as indicators of prosperity and high status in Early Iron Age Cyprus. In the course of arguing a different but related point Anthony Snodgrass (1988,

16–17) postulates that bronze sceptres were part of the regalia of individuals who may have possessed kingship. Cecilia Beer (1984, 261–3) has suggested that silver and bronze *oinochoai*, the so-called 'Cypro-Phoenician bowls', bronze *thymiateria* and lamp stands, bronze horse trappings and carved ivory plaques for furniture embellishment represent *objets de prestige*.

A sample set of fifteen iron objects from excavations by the Swedish Cyprus Expedition at Idalion, Lapithos and Amathus (Åström et al 1986) and another set of fifteen from Karageorghis' excavations at Palaepaphos-Skales (Stech et al 1985) were subjected to instrumental analysis by an international team. The goals of these metallurgical analyses were to determine the nature of the Cypriot iron industry that produced them and 'to see how [this industry] fits into the economic and cultural life of the Early Iron Age' (Stech et al 1985). In order to determine the relative value of iron they analyzed a selected sample set of burial assemblages from Lapithos, Amathus and Palaepaphos-Skales. The selected burials that contained most of the iron objects came from the cemeteries under consideration. The results of their tabulations of the occurrence of iron with copper/bronze, silver and gold in this sample showed that iron usually occurred in a rich tomb, frequently in association with gold (Åström et al 1986).

3. Case Study

I have continued my exploratory study of the patterning of the burial assemblages in Iron Age Cyprus by creating a data base with 299 burials that date between 1050 and 475 BC. The burials are from cemeteries scattered across the island (Fig 38.5). Only 172 of these burials, or 57.5 per cent, are single interments that are either intact or have suffered only a limited degree of disturbance. The remainder are either multiple interments and/or have signs of significant disturbance. I first classified the grave goods found with the burials according to thirteen material classes (ie terracotta, ceramic, glass, etc) and then by artefact type (ie weapon, jewellery, vessel, etc) (Fig 38.6A). Afterwards, this data base was reorganized according to ten functional classes that were derived from those established by Jones (1980) and Smith (1987) (Figs 38.2 and 38.6B) as well as additional ones generated from the Cypriot data themselves.

In order to analyze the data I have created some groupings which overlap the standard chronological subperiods. This was necessary because of the uncertainty of dating some of the burial assemblages with multiple interments to a specific subperiod. I will not discuss the sample for the CG III/CA I grouping due to its small size. I have not included these burials with the preceding CG III or the succeeding CA I groupings because I believe that doing this would tend to mask the patterns of distribution in one or the other grouping. Even though the slightly larger CA I/II and II grouping also suffers from this deficiency I have included it in the discussions. The data collected for the burials in each grouping will be explored for significant patterning in the variety of the grave goods present and the

High status in the Iron Age 347

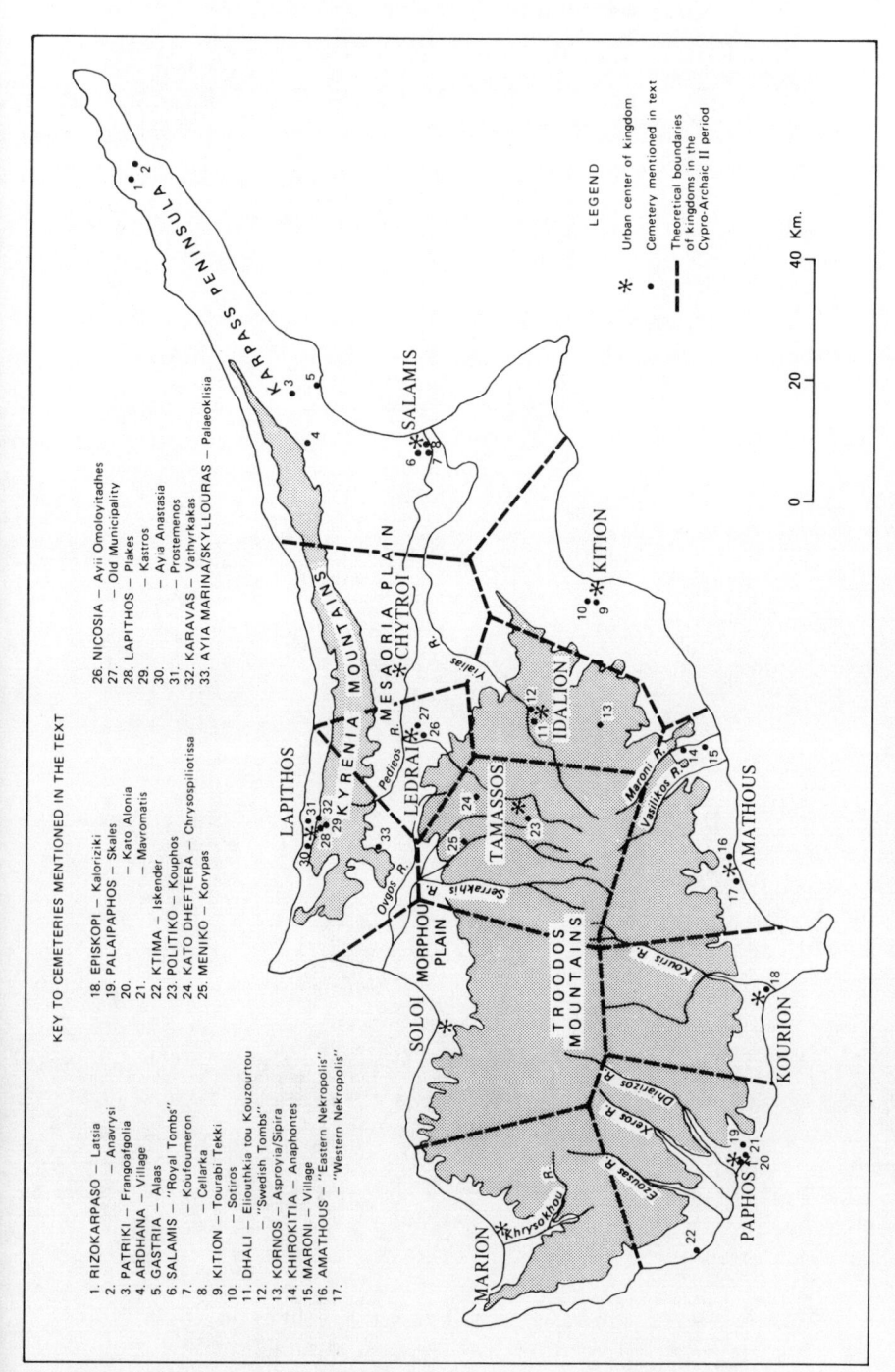

Figure 38.5 Map of Iron Age Cyprus showing location of cemeteries, urban centres and kingdoms mentioned in the text.

KEY TO CEMETERIES MENTIONED IN THE TEXT

1. RIZOKARPASO – Latsia
2. – Anavrysi
3. PATRIKI – Frangoatgolia
4. ARDHANA – Village
5. GASTRIA – Alaas
6. SALAMIS – "Royal Tombs"
7. – Koufoumeron
8. – Cellarka
9. KITION – Tourabi Tekki
10. – Sotiros
11. DHALI – Eliouthkia tou Kouzourtou
12. – "Swedish Tombs"
13. KORNOS – Asproyia/Sipira
14. KHIROKITIA – Anaphontes
15. MARONI – Village
16. AMATHOUS – "Eastern Nekropolis"
17. – "Western Nekropolis"
18. EPISKOPI – Kaloriziki
19. PALAIPAPHOS – Skales
20. – Kato Alonia
21. – Mavromatis
22. KTIMA – Iskender
23. POLITIKO – Kouphos
24. KATO DHEFTERA – Chrysospiliotissa
25. MENIKO – Korypas
26. NICOSIA – Ayii Omoloyitadhes
27. – Old Municipality
28. LAPITHOS – Plakes
29. – Kastros
30. – Ayia Anastasia
31. – Prostemenos
32. KARAVAS – Vathyrkakas
33. AYIA MARINA/SKYLLOURAS – Palaeoklisia

LEGEND

* Urban center of kingdom
• Cemetery mentioned in text
– – – Theoretical boundaries of kingdoms in the Cypro-Archaic II period

A

```
PAGE 1                    IRON AGE CYPRIOTE BURIAL ASSEMBLAGE ENTRY FORM

VILLAGE:Salamis                        LOCALITY: Cellarka
   PROBABLE IRON AGE KINGDOM: 01  CYPRUS SURVEY/MUSEUM NUMBER:
       TOMB NUMBER:005  PIT/GRAVE NUMBER:    IS THE TOMB AREA DEFINED? T
TOMB/PIT INFORMATION: TOMB TYPE:03  TOMB CONDITION:2  TOTAL NUMBER OF BURIALS: 2
    TOMB MARKER? F  TOMB/PIT DIMENSIONS: WIDTH/DIAM  2.0  LENGTH  1.5  HEIGHT  1.0
    IF MORE THAN 1 BURIAL, CAN INDIVIDUAL BURIAL ASSEMBLAGES BE DISTINGUISHED? F
BURIAL INFORMATION: BURIAL NUMBER     01 2     BURIAL LOCATION      00
                    BURIAL TYPE          1     BURIAL CONDITION      3
                    BURIAL ORIENTATION         SEX 0           AGE   0
                    BURIAL RITUALS       3     CHRONOLOGICAL PERIOD 14
                    INHUMATION TREATMENT 0     ARTIFACT TOTAL    5

         ARTIFACT CLASSES    TERRACOTTA: PRESENT/ABSENT T
                                TC1: VESSELS                               0
                                TC2: LAMPS                                 1
                                TC3: SCULPTURE                             0
                                TC5: SPINDLEWHORL/LOOM WEIGHT              0
                                TC6: JEWELLERY                             0
                                TC7: RELIGIOUS OBJECTS                     0
                                TC8: TOYS                                  0
PAGE 2              POTTERY:    PRESENT/ABSENT T
                                CERAMICS1:  PLAIN CYPRIOTE                 1
                                CERAMICS2:  SIMPLE DECORATION CYPRIOTE     0
                                CERAMICS3:  ELAB (VEGETAL ONLY) DECO CYPRIOTE  0
                                CERAMICS4:  ELAB (WITH SCENES) DECO CYPRIOTE   0
                                CERAMICS5:  IMPORTED GREEK                 0
                                CERAMICS6:  IMPORTED PHOENICIAN            0
                                CERAMICS8:  CYPRIOTE IMITATION OF AN IMPORT 0
                                CERAMICS9:  ZOO /ANTHROPOMORPHIC VESSELS   0
                                CERAMICS10: RELIGIOUS OBJECTS              0
                                CERAMICS11: TIN ENCRUSTED VESSELS          0
                    STONE:      PRESENT/ABSENT T
                                STONE1:  TOOLS                             0
                                STONE2:  JEWELLERY                         0
                                STONE3:  SCARABS/SEALS                     1
                                STONE4:  VESSELS                           0
                                STONE5:  SCULPTURE                         0
                                STONE7:  SPINDLEWHORL                      0
                                STONE8:  RELIGIOUS OBJECTS                 0
                                STONE9:  VESSEL STAND                      0
                                STONE10: GAMING STONE or BATH TUB          0
```

B

```
PAGE 1                    IRON AGE CYPRIOTE BURIAL ASSEMBLAGE ENTRY FORM

VILLAGE:Salamis                        LOCALITY: Cellarka
   PROBABLE IRON AGE KINGDOM:01
TOMB/PIT INFORMATION:  TOMB NUMBER: 005  PIT/GRAVE NUMBER:
   TOMB TYPE:03  TOMB CONDITION:2
   IF MORE THAN 1 BURIAL, CAN INDIVIDUAL BURIAL ASSEMBLAGES BE DISTINGUISHED? F
BURIAL INFORMATION: BURIAL NUMBER:01 2   BURIAL CONDITION:3
                    SEX:0  AGE:0  CHRONOLOGICAL PERIOD:14  ARTIFACT TOTAL:  5

FUNCTIONAL ANALYSIS OF GRAVE GOODS:
-----------------------------------
   1.  FURNITURE>>                              Subtotal 1:   0
          Furniture decoration: BON7    0
             IVO3   0  IVO4    0  IVO5   0  IVO6   0  BRO8   0  SIL5   0  GOL5   0

   2.  CLOTHING>>                               Subtotal 2:   0
          Clothing attachments:       BON1    0  IVO11   0
          Clothing decoration(?):     GOL1    0

   3.  TOOLS AND HOUSEHOLD EQUIPMENT>>          Subtotal 3:   1
          Tools:       BON6   0  STO1  0  BRO2   0  IRO1   0
          Weaving/sewing:      BON3   0  TC5   0  STO7   0  FAI6   0  GOL10   0
          Utensils:    BON5   0  BRO1  0  IRO2   0  SIL1   0
          Lamps:       TC2    1  BRO5  0

   4.  FOOD/BEVERAGE PREPARATION AND STORAGE>>  Subtotal 4:   1
          Cypriote plain wares:   TC1    0  CER1   1

   5.  FOOD/BEVERAGE SERVING AND COMSUMPTION>>  Subtotal 5:   1
          Cypriote decorated wares:   CER2   0  CER3   0  CER4   0
          Imported wares/imitations:  CER5   0  CER6   0  CER8   0
          Metalic: BRO4   1  SIL3   0  GOL6   0
          Imitation of silver vessel: CER11   0
          Vessel stand: STO9   0

   6.  RELIGIOUS/FUNERARY ITEMS>>               Subtotal 6:   0
          Sculpture:   TC3    0  STO5   0  FAI4   0  FAI5   0  IVO7   0  BRO10   0
          Astragali:   BON4   0
          Ceremonial equipment TC7   0  STO8   0  CER10   0
          Zoo-/anthropomorphic vessels:  CER9   0
          Funerary use:   SH2   0  GOL9   0
```

Figure 38.6 First two computer screens or pages of the forms created with dBASE III + data base management software which were used to record information concerning individual Iron Age Cypriot burials and artefact material classes (A) and the artefact functional classes (B) that were found as grave goods.

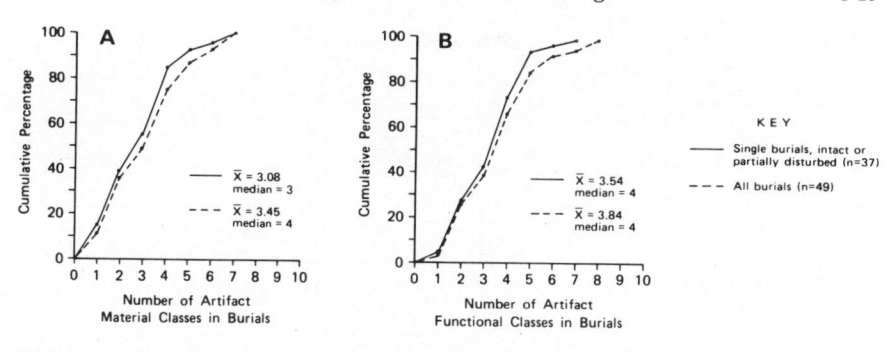

Figure 38.7 Cumulative curve graphs for Cypro-Geometric I burial assemblages.

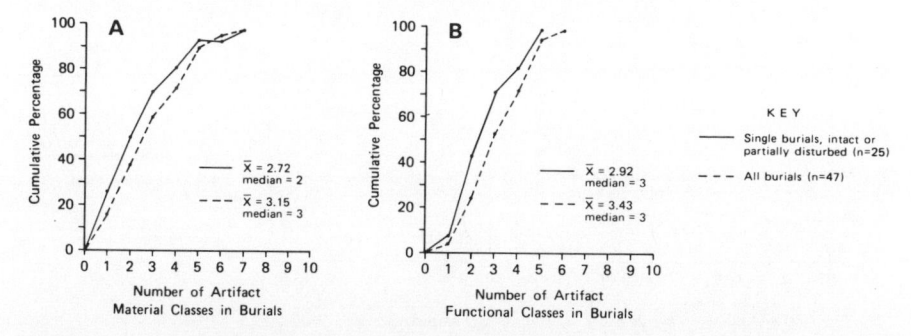

Figure 38.8 Cumulative curve graphs for Cypro-Geometric I/II, II and II/III.

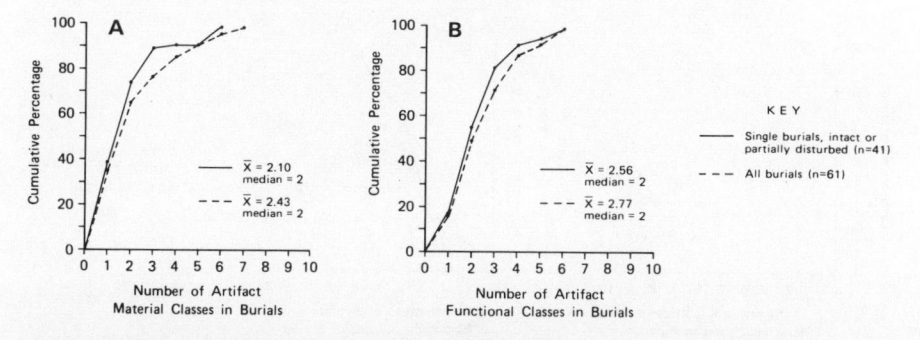

Figure 38.9 Cumulative curve graphs for Cypro-Geometric III.

presence/absence of metal using the exploratory data analysis approach (Shennan 1988, 22–47). The intent of these preliminary observations is to identify trends in the distribution of single variables relating to the use of symbols of high status. This will be accomplished by summarizing the data visually by frequency distributions and numerically by measures of central tendency. When one looks at the entire sample the essential trends seen in the selected samples are usually present. I will also comment on the probable relationship of these trends to the levels of social complexity in Iron Age Cyprus. In my initial study I suggested that a high degree of

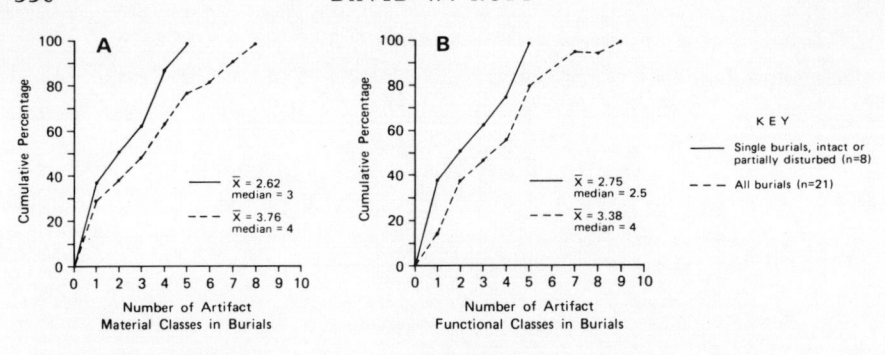

Figure 38.10 Cumulative curve graphs for Cypro-Geometric III/Cypro-Archaic I burials.

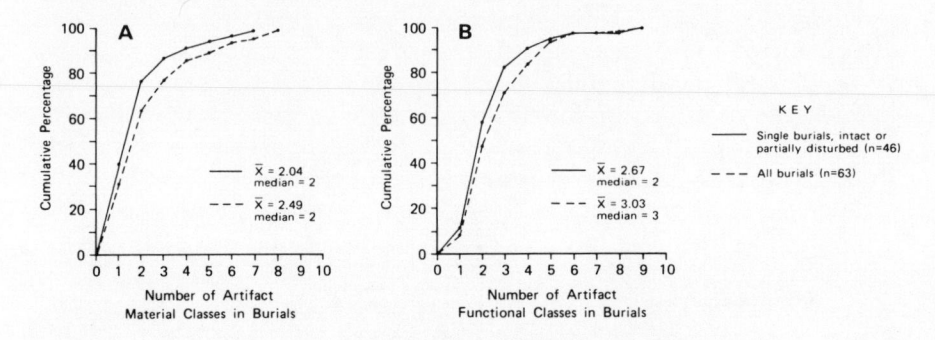

Figure 38.11 Cumulative curve graphs for Cypro-Archaic I burials.

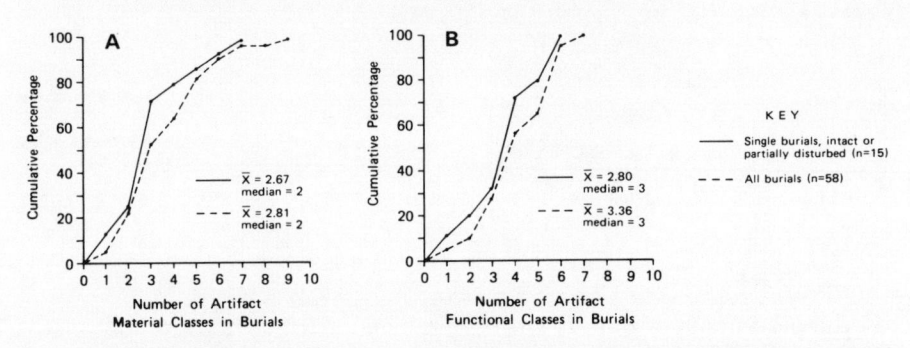

Figure 38.12 Cumulative curve graphs for Cypro-Archaic I/II and II burials.

diversity or variety in the artefact material classes present in a burial assemblage should indicate relative wealth and, hence, relative status. The data from my expanded study summarized by cumulative frequency distribution curves (Figs 38.7–12) supports this original conclusion.

The shape of the cumulative frequency curves for both the artefact material classes and the functional classes for the CG I and the CG I/II, II and II/III groupings (Figs 38.7–8) is essentially the same. That is, the average for the material classes is 2 plus and for the functional classes between 2 and 3. Eighty per cent of each sample has almost 4 material classes and 4 ± functional classes. While these first two groupings reveal the greatest 'sharing' of the wealth of the entire set, in the second grouping one can see a slight regression from this tendency. For the CG III grouping (Fig 38.9) there is a significant decrease in the number of classes present in 50 per cent and 80 per cent of the sample in both the material and the functional classes. At the same time the top 20 per cent has much more diversity than before. These distribution patterns repeat in the CA I grouping (Fig. 38.11) where there is heightened disparity between the upper 20 per cent and the lower 80 per cent of the sample. The distribution of wealth appears most restricted in this grouping. Another change, a slight reversal of this trend of restriction, shows up in the CA I/II and II grouping (Fig 38.12). Here the number of material and functional classes present increase for 50 per cent and 80 per cent of the sample and the upper 20 per cent for the functional classes has markedly less diversity.

The patterns of the arithmetic mean and the average for the groupings (Figs 38.7–12) for both artefact material and functional classes also mirror these trends. They steadily decrease in value from the first grouping through the CA I grouping after which there is a slight increase in the last grouping. Commencing in the later part of the CG III period the lowest half of the sample has as grave goods only two artefact material classes (typically ceramic and terracotta objects) and two to three artefact functional classes (typically food/beverage serving and consumption wares, food/beverage preparation and storage wares and non-utilitarian, personal 'luxury' items).

Most archaeologists (*cf* Matthäus above (244–255)) consider metal artefacts as having high value in agrarian societies and, therefore, that their distribution and associations with other artefacts display observable restrictions. The data from this study will be examined now to test this hypothesis. The largest percentage of burials with one or more types of metal artefacts present (Fig 38.13) is in the CG I grouping. The single burials which are either intact or only partially disturbed in this grouping are also the only examples which can have four metal types in them. In each subsequent grouping through the CA I grouping there is a decrease both in the percentage of burials with some metal artefacts present and in the percentage of burials with three different types of metal present. By the CA I grouping only 26.1 per cent have metal and only 4.4 per cent of these have three metal types. Starting with the CG III grouping there is a parallel decline in the percentage of burials with two metal types present. Metal, thus, became less frequent in the burials over time and when it did occur, only a small fraction of the burials have more than one metal type. There was a slight reversal of these trends in the final grouping. The observed distribution patterns for diversity of artefact material and functional classes repeat with metal types.

In those burials with at least one metal type present (Fig 38.14) bronze

CHRONOLOGICAL PERIOD	n =	% WITHOUT METAL	% WITH 1 METAL	% WITH 2 METALS	% WITH 3 METALS	% WITH 4 METALS
C–G I	37*	24.3	35.1	27.0	10.8	2.7
	49**	22.4	28.6	26.5	20.4	2.0
C–G I/II,II and II/III	25*	36.0	32.0	24.0	8.0	0.0
	47**	25.5	34.0	28.6	8.5	2.0
C–G III	41*	58.5	26.8	9.8	4.9	0.0
	61**	57.4	23.0	14.8	4.9	0.0
C–G III / C–A I	8*	37.5	25.0	12.5	25.0	0.0
	21**	28.6	19.0	23.8	19.0	9.5
C–A I	46*	73.9	15.2	6.5	4.4	0.0
	63**	61.9	14.3	19.0	4.8	0.0
C–A I/II and II	15*	53.3	26.7	13.3	6.7	0.0
	58**	46.6	24.1	19.0	8.6	1.7

Key: * = Single burial, intact or partially disturbed
     ** = All burials

Figure 38.13 Percentage of burial assemblages without metal artefacts and with one or more types of metal.

is the principal metal used for artefacts. Although in the CG I grouping bronze is almost universal, it decreases in frequency with the passage of time. In the early groupings iron and gold occur in similar frequencies. Subsequently, iron artefacts soon rise in frequency while those of gold decrease. Iron even overtakes bronze as the most frequently occurring metal in the CA I grouping. We should realize here that ancient scavenging and/or modern looting may have combined to significantly distort this picture. The oscillating but uniformly low frequency of silver lends support to the thesis that it had a high value, possibly higher than gold, as it was the case in the Assyrian sphere of influence (Frankenstein 1978). Lead appears infrequently and then only in crude jewellery. Bronze artefacts by themselves appear to have been only weak indicators of wealth in a burial. Stronger indicators were the display of two groups of metal artefact classes. High degrees of artefact material and functional class diversity in a burial have very strong correlations with the presence of three or four metal types.

4. Discussion

The identification in the archaeological record of the markers of high status in a society is not a straight forward, simple process. Since these symbols of prestige occur in sets, have specific patterns of use in carefully defined social contexts and change with the passage of time one cannot automatically equate an artefact made of a 'valuable' material with high status. The same is true for a particular functional type, a certain artistic style or iconography and/or an object that appears to have had a high labour input. The designation of an artefact as a marker of high status requires knowledge of its geographical findspot, its archaeological and architectural context, the associated artefact assemblage, the manner and purpose of deposition and its date. In addition, one must know the spatial and chronological patterning of the artefact type to substantiate its association with high status. All too often these minimum information requirements are ambiguous or totally lacking.

With these *caveats* in mind I can suggest a tentative construction of the physical manifestations of high status in Iron Age Cyprus based on the preliminary analysis of the selected burial assemblages and the observations of other scholars. First, the grave offerings display a high degree of diversity in the artefact material classes and the artefact functional classes. Second, bronze, iron, silver and/or gold are used in the fabrication of artefacts. Third, significant quantities of vessels intended for the serving and consumption of food and drink on formal occasions are present. These vessels are frequently made of metal or faience, or are Greek ceramic imports or Cypriot ceramic wares with elaborate figural and/or vegetal decoration. Fourth, bronze *thymiateria* and lamp stands are found. Fifth, 'luxury' objects of a utilitarian nature such as scarabs and seals, Phoenician/Levantine vessels for perfumed unguents, personal grooming utensils and scales and weights for weighing are encountered. Sixth, weapons and

CHRONOLOGICAL PERIOD	n =	% WITH LEAD	% WITH BRONZE	% WITH IRON	% WITH SILVER	% WITH GOLD
C–G I	29*	0.0	89.7	41.4	3.4	41.4
	38**	0.0	94.7	44.7	5.3	50.0
C–G I/II,II and II/III	16*	6.2	87.5	37.5	0.0	31.1
	35**	2.5	91.4	42.9	5.7	28.6
C–G III	17*	0.0	82.4	41.2	0.0	23.5
	26**	0.0	88.5	42.3	3.9	26.9
C–G III / C–A I	4*	0.0	75.0	100.0	0.0	50.0
	15**	6.7	80.0	66.7	26.7	46.7
C–A I	12*	0.0	50.0	75.0	8.3	25.0
	24**	0.0	66.7	87.5	4.2	16.7
C–A I/II and II	6*	0.0	83.3	50.0	33.3	0.0
	31**	3.2	77.4	48.4	25.8	12.9

Key: * = Single burial, intact or partially disturbed
** = All burials

Figure 38.14 Percentage of different metals in the burial assemblages which possess metal artefacts.

armour are associated with, presumably, male burials. Seventh, jewellery made of metal, ivory, amber, faience and/or semi-precious stones occurs. Eighth, there is evidence for slaughtered horses and other equids with decorated bronze trappings, often with a chariot, cart and/or hearse. Ninth, one finds faint traces of ceremonial furniture such as thrones, chairs, stools or beds decorated with carved, inlaid and gilded ivory plaques or covered with silver strips. Tenth, clothing and headdresses embellished with gold appliqués and/or ivory attachments are in evidence. Eleventh, bronze and iron rod tripods are present in the earlier burials. Twelfth, artefacts that have a personal name inscribed or painted on them. Thirteenth, bronze sceptres. It is important to note here that the geographical location of the interment facility, its plan, size, materials and manner of construction, the presence of carved or painted decoration of the exterior facade and/or the interior walls and ceilings and the nature and the extent of the funerary rituals are also very strong indicators of wealth and status and, therefore, the deceased's position in society.

The grave goods, the interment facility and its location, type and elaborateness as well as the energy and wealth expended on the funeral ceremony communicated to the survivors multiple and overlapping symbolic messages of the social persona of the deceased (*cf* Rupp 1988). Furthermore, for the elite the suites of high status indicators evolved and changed with the passage of time as they sought to retain their dominant position over those below them who sought to emulate and to join them or, even worse, to replace them at the apex of the social hierarchy. The strategies of the superordinates and of the subordinates to achieve their antithetical social goals can be documented in the spatial and chronological patterning of the physical manifestations of high status and of their imitations.

Smith's thesis (1987, 318) that the strongest predictors of household wealth and, hence, status are food and beverage serving and consumption wares is, on the surface, not supported by the data in this study. Such artefacts are present at a minimum in 97 per cent of the burials and frequently in all of the burials of a particular grouping. Further, food and beverage preparation and storage wares are present in 50 per cent to 81 per cent of the burials. For Iron Age Cypriot burials other variables related to this class of functional artefacts indicate more distinctly the relative status of the deceased. These include quantity and the presence of one or more of the following artefact types, imported Greek ceramics (*cf* Sørensen 1988), Cypriot imitations of Greek vessels, elaborately decorated Cypriot ceramics, Cypriot ceramics with pictorial compositions and metallic vessels and serving utensils. If one re-analyzed the burial assemblage data with these burials in mind, it is probable that food and beverage serving and consumption wares would provide an important predictor of high status. Other less sensitive predictors would corroborate these assessments.

We have observed that the percentages of metallic artefacts present or absent in the burials are not constant. Coldstream's (above 325–335) metallic high status indicators for the eleventh century are noticeably different from those for the eighth century burials let alone those from the sixth century. This evidence clearly supports the contention that innovation and change are a central feature of the sets of symbols of prestige that an elite uses to denote their superior status within the society.

Emulation occurs in the Cypriot burial assemblage data. The appearance of small quantities of Cypriot imitations of Greek drinking and serving vessels starting in the early eighth century is an excellent example. Their limited number and pattern of distribution, mostly outside the later kingdom centres, suggests that they were attempts by a few individuals with higher social aspirations to imitate the behaviour of their betters living in the major centres. The appearance of Black-on-Red ware in CG III may well represent another effort on a larger scale to emulate those in the elite who possessed genuine Levantine pots.

The process of gift giving or largesse in order to establish and/or maintain a superior/inferior social relationship may explain the large number and distinctive distribution pattern of Greek Geometric *skyphoi* (as well as *kotylai* and plates to a much lesser extent) in the tombs of the Western Necropolis at Amathus (Coldstream 1986; 1987; *Chronique* 1987, 695–722). Although 'dinner sets' of Greek Geometric pottery imports are present in a few tombs at Amathus, most of the Greek Geometric *skyphoi* occur alone or in pairs in the burial assemblages (Sørensen 1988). These drinking vessels may represent gifts from superordinate individuals to subordinates in the elite. Their use would have been in public consumption rituals. If this interpretation accurately explains the distribution pattern then those individuals who possessed 'dinner sets' probably were associated at Amathus with the procurement and internal distribution of the imported Greek ceramics.

No man is an island and neither is Cyprus. The cultural processes (above) inferred from the Iron Age mortuary data are not unique ones but recurring ones common in prehistoric and historic agrarian societies throughout the world. The analyses of the burial assemblages in this study have demonstrated that Iron Age Cypriots envalued, as symbols of prestige or excellence, certain locally made commodities as well as imported ones and scarce raw materials. Conscious attempts appear to have been made to limit the circulation of these high status goods, in part, by their deliberate disposal or destruction in mortuary contexts. This was especially true of those few burials that had large quantities of these commodities. Complex social messages were transmitted by these value-laden grave goods and their probable manner of use. The presence in significant quantities of unusual vessels and other objects intended for public consumption rituals and/or display testify to the demand by the elite for visible emblems of privilege. The noteworthy architectural treatment of some of the interment facilities combined with the evidence for more elaborate funerary rituals

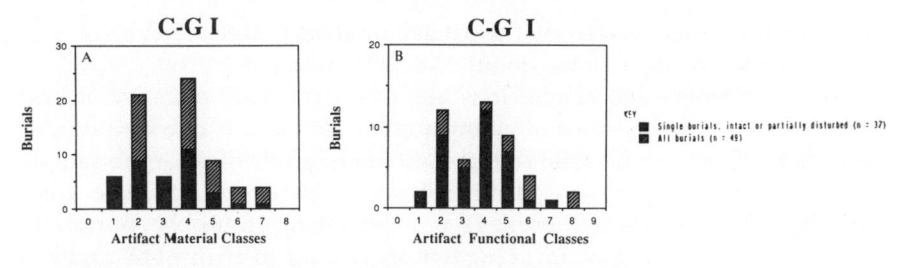

Figure 38.15 Bar graph for Cypro-Geometric I burial assemblages.

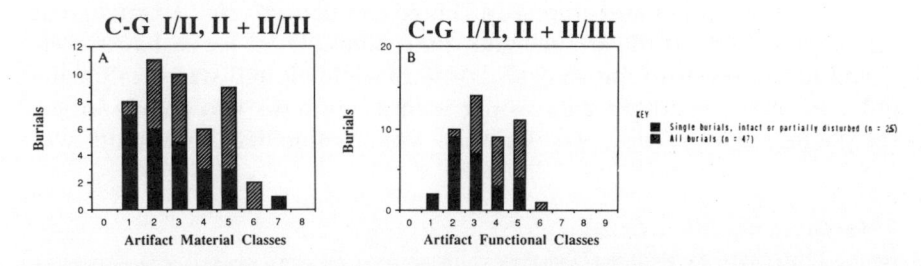

Figure 38.16 Bar graph for Cypro-Geometric I/II, II and II/III burial assemblages.

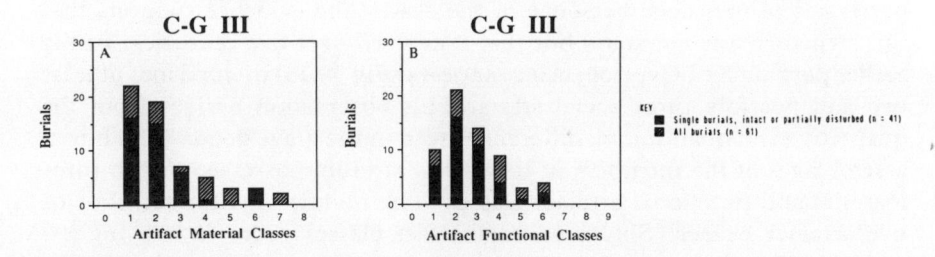

Figure 38.17 Bar graph for Cypro-Geometric III burial assemblages.

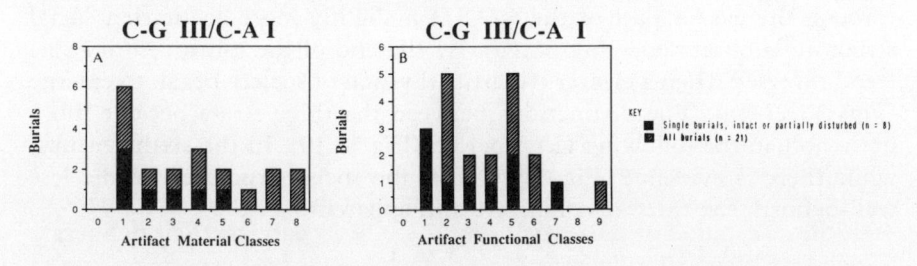

Figure 38.18 Bar graph for Cypro-Geometric III/Cypro-Archaic I burial assemblages.

performed at them (*cf* Rupp 1988; Karageorghis 1987, 695–722), reinforced these balatant symbolic messages of societal status and power for both the deceased and his/her survivors. The presence of small quantities of genuine prestige goods in many burials suggests that largesse or gift exchange was practiced by the elite. Cypriot imitations of some of the imported artefacts, in particular of Greek drinking vessels, point to a segment of the population that sought to emulate actively the behaviour and life style of its betters by the acquisition of high status goods and/or their copies.

These inferences and conclusions are, of course, only tentative at best and are subject to revision and augmentation. To do this one would need to test the hypotheses by conducting a systematic study of as large a sample as possible of reasonably undisturbed single burials which date from twelfth through sixth centuries. It is essential to group the burials in subsets based on their probable kingdom association to attempt to establish if spatial patterning of the types mentioned above did in fact exist within a particular kingdom and among the kingdoms collectively. A concurrent osteological study would add the vital dimensions of sex, age and nutritional and health levels to the analyses. A more sophisticated statistical manipulation of the resulting data would identify patterns and trends in the sample in a more accurate fashion than was possible here (*cf* Sabloff *et al* 1987).

5. Conclusions

What can be said of the idealized social structure of Iron Age Cyprus that was expressed ritually in the burial assemblages through the tangible portrayals of the social personae of the dead? The evidence suggests that this structure was not static but that it evolved over five centuries. In the earlier part of CG I Cypriot society appears (Fig 38.15) divided into at least two and possibly three social strata. This observation derives from the qualitative and quantitative differences seen in the grave goods. The burial assemblages of the members of the lowest stratum possessed one to three material and functional artefact classes. The middle stratum had four or five artefact classes. Six or seven artefact classes occur in the highest stratum. The divisions between these strata do not seem to have been sharply drawn. Toward the end of this period and probably continuing through the earlier part of the CG III a slightly more egalitarian social structure is observable (Fig 38.16). By the end of the ninth century this trend reversed when a clearer tripartite division of society began to emerge (Figs 38.17–18). The distinctions between the three strata became more noticeable in the following CA I period (Fig 38.19). In the sixth century, while there is evidence (Fig 38.20) that the social structure became less well-defined, the three divisions are still apparent.

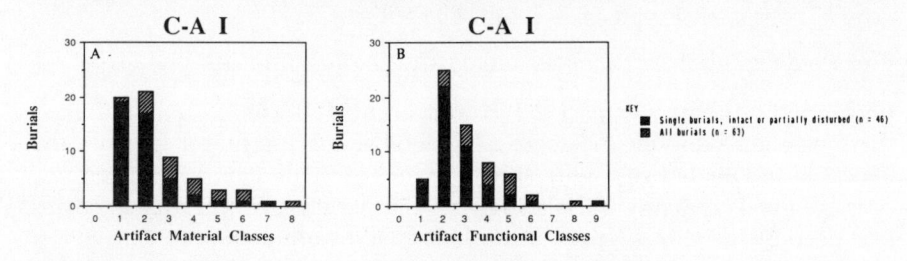

Figure 38.19 Bar graph for Cypro-Archaic I burial assemblages.

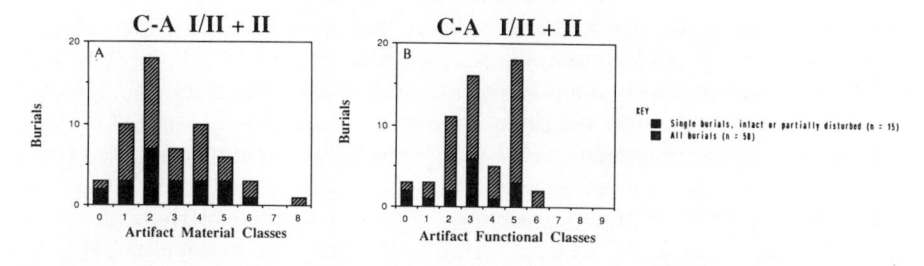

Figure 38.20 Bar graph for Cypro-Archaic I/II and II burial assemblages.

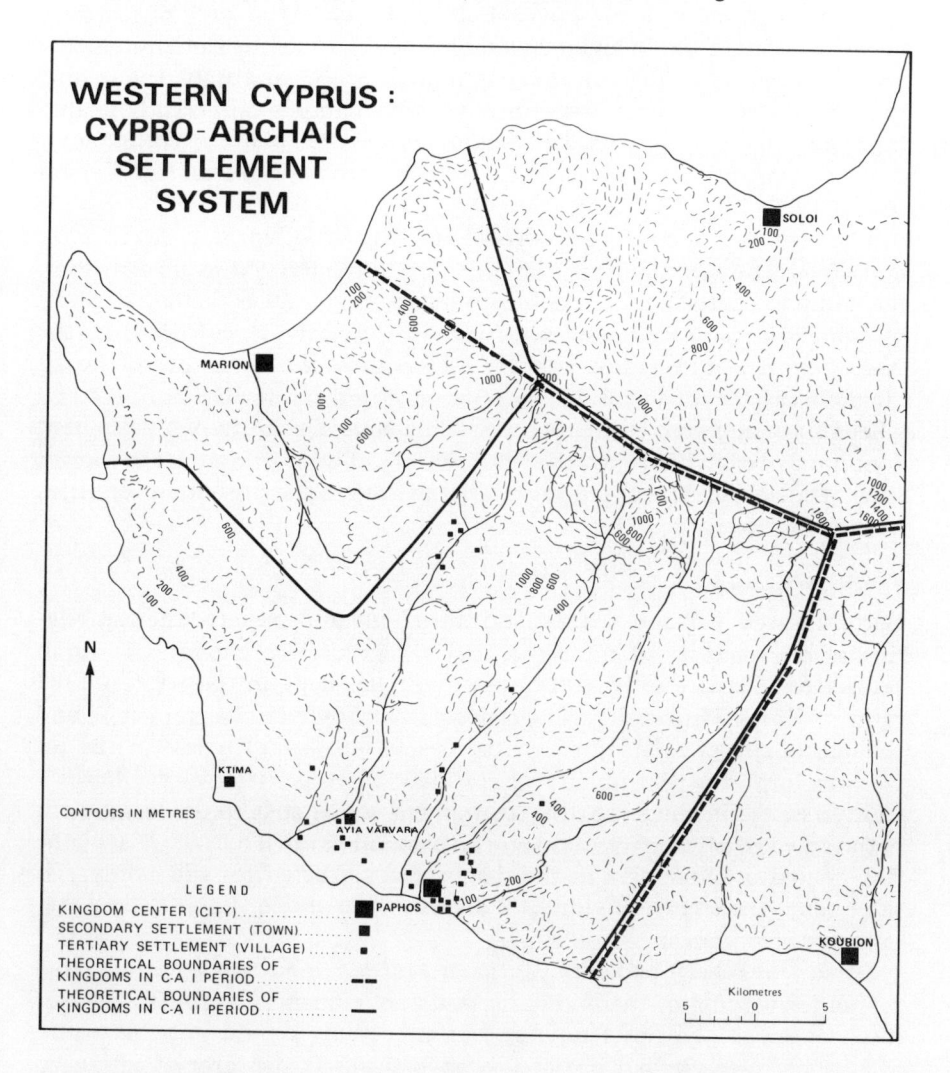

Figure 38.21 Settlement system of western Cyprus in the Cypro-Archaic period (modified *after* Rupp 1987, Map 2).

The members of the highest stratum who occupied the apex of the hierarchy and controlled the society, were what one could call the 'governing elite'. This phrase denotes here those individuals whose burial assemblages display the greatest variety of material and functional artefact classes as well as a disproportionate access to scarce resources and services. These individuals tended to reside almost exclusively in the urban kingdom centres (Fig 38.21). Other individuals who belonged to a slightly larger middle stratum, or what one could label as the 'non-governing elite', appear to have lived in both the kingdom centres and in the secondary settlements or towns in the hinterland. This subdivision is inferred from the existence of burial assemblages which show only limited access to scarce resources and services. The bulk of the population, the denizens of the lowest stratum, or 'commoners', lived in both of these types of settlements and, especially, in the tertiary small, 'satellite' villages that made up the majority of the settlements in the hierarchical settlement system of Iron Age Cyprus (Rupp 1987, 149–151; Rupp *et al* 1986; Rupp *et al* 1984).

The characteristics of the mortuary evidence in Cyprus between 1050 and 475 BC for status differentiation and for the idealized social structure, including its spatial and chronological patterning, implies that a state form of political organization emerged (or more correctly, re-emerged) on the island by the mid-eighth century. This took the form of territorial kingdoms each with a stratified society comprised of a small elite headed by a hereditary monarch at the top of the citizenry. This form of government continued to evolve through the sixth century. This is in contrast to a lower level of socio-political organization that existed in the preceding centuries of the Iron Age.

ACKNOWLEDGMENTS

Bernice Cardy, Roxanne Guttin and Ruth Turnbull executed the compilation of the majority of the burial assemblage data as part of a research project for Classics 4P05, Problems in Archaeology in the winter, 1987 term at Brock University. Their perceptive observations, diligence and thoughtfulness greatly improved the design and completeness of the recording form and the quality of the data entered. Afterwards, Bernice Cardy assisted in checking the accuracy and consistency in the assignment of the grave goods to artefact categories in the individual burials. Marilynne Box helped to enter data in the database constructed for this study. To these four persistent individuals I dedicate this article. Loris Gasparotto executed the figures.

Discussions that I had with Margaret Morden in Nicosia have increased my understanding of the numerous and subtle nuances of this topic. Her dissertation on Cypriot Iron Age burial customs should put this entire avenue of research in Cypriot archaeology on firmer ground. Bernard Knapp's encyclopaedic knowledge of current archaeological literature made me aware of a number of crucial lines of inquiry pertinent to this study. His astute, thoughtful comments and those of Sarah Stewart and Pamela Gaber have improved the clarity, organization and readablity of the article. All shortcomings and errors remaining are mine.

LIST OF REFERENCES

Appadurai, A. (1986) Introduction: commodities and the politics of value, in *The Social Life of Things. Commodities in Cultural Prospective* (ed. A. Appadurai), 3–63. Cambridge.

Åström, P. et al (1986) Iron Artifacts from Swedish Excavations in Cyprus. *Op Ath 16*, 27–41.

Beer, C. (1984) Quelques aspects des contacts de chypre aux VIIIe et VIIe siécles avant notre ere. *Int J for Social & Economic Hist Ant 3*, 253–76.

Binford, L. (1971) Mortuary practices: their study and potential, in *Approaches to the Social Dimensions of Mortuary Practices* (ed. J.A. Brown) 6–29. *(Memoirs of the Society for American Archaeology 25)*. Washington.

Bradley, R. (1984) *The Social Foundations of Prehistoric Britain: Themes and Variations in the Archaeology of Power*. London.

Bradley, R. (1985) *Consumption, Change and the Archaeological Record. The Archaeology of Monuments and the Archaeology of Deliberate Deposits*. (University of Edinburgh, Department of Archaeology Occasional Paper 13). Edinburgh.

Clarke, G. (1986) *Symbols of Excellence. Precious Materials as Expressions of Status*. Cambridge.

Coldstream, J.N. (1986) Kition and Amathus: some reflections on their westward links during the Early Iron Age. *Acts 1986*, 321–9.

Coldstream, J.N. (1987) The Greek Geometric and Archaic imports, in *La nécropole d'Amathone: Tombes 113–367, II. Ceramiques non-chypriotes*, (eds. V. Karageorghis, O. Picard & Chr. Tytgat) 26–31. Nicosia.

Douglas, M. & Isherwood, B. (1979) *The World of Goods: Toward an Anthropology of Consumption*. New York.

Frankenstein, S. (1978) The Phoenicians in the Far West: a function of Neo-Assyrian imperialism, in *Power and Propoganda: A Symposium on Ancient Empires* (ed. M.T. Larsen), *(Mesopotamia 7)*. Copenhagen.

Hodder, I. (1982) *The Present Past: An Introduction to Anthropology for Archaeologists*. London.

Jones, A.H. (1980) *Wealth of a Nation to be: The American Colonies on the Eve of the Revolution*. New York.

Keswani, P.S. (1988) Dimensions of a social hierarchy on Late Bronze Age Cyprus: An analysis of the mortuary data from Enkomi. *AJA 92*, 245.

Knapp, A.B. (1986) *Copper Production and Divine Protection: Archaeology, Ideology and Social Complexity on Bronze Age Cyprus. (SIMA Pocket-Book 42)*. Göteborg.

Leach, E. (1976) *Culture and Communication: The Logic by which Symbols are Connected*. Cambridge.

Maier, F.G. & von Wartburg, M-L. (1985a) Reconstructing history from the earth, c.2800 B.C.–1600 A.D.: Excavating at Palaepaphos, 1966–1984, in *Archaeology in Cyprus 1960–1985* (ed. V. Karageorghis), 142–72. Nicosia.

Maier, F.G. & von Wartburg, M-L. (1985b) Excavations at Kouklia (Palaepaphos). Thirteenth preliminary report: seasons 1983 and 1984. *RDAC*, 100–21.

Miller, D. (1982) Structures and strategies: an aspect of the relationship between social hierarchy and cultural change, in *Symbolic and Structural Anthropology* (ed. I. Hodder) 88–98. Cambridge.

Morris, I. (1986) Gift and community in Archaic Greece. *Man 21*, 1–17.

Morris, I. (1987) *Burial and Ancient Society. The Rise of the Greek City-state.* Cambridge.

Parker-Pearson, M. (1984) Economic and ideological change: cyclic growth in the pre-state societies of Jutland, in *Ideology, Power and Prehistory* (eds. D. Miller & C. Tilley), 69–92. Cambridge.

Pollock, S.M. (1983) *The Symbolism of Prestige: An Archaeological Example from the Royal Cemetery at Ur.* Ph.D. Ann Arbor.

Renfrew, C. (1972) *The Emergence of Civilisation: The Cyclades and the Aegean in the Third Millennium BC.* London.

Renfrew, C. (1986) Varna and the emergence of wealth in prehistoric Europe, in Appadurai (1986) 141–68.

Rupp, D.W. (1985) Prolegomena to a study of stratification and social organization in Iron Age Cyprus, in *Status, Structure and Stratification. Current Anthropological Reconstructions. Proceedings of the Sixteenth Annual Conference* (eds. M. Thompson, M.T. Garcia, & F.J. Kense), 119–31. Calgary.

Rupp, D.W. (1987) "Vive le roi": The emergence of the state in Iron Age Cyprus, in *Western Cyprus: Connections. An Archaeological Symposium held at Brock University, St. Catharines, Ontario, Canada, March 21–22, 1986* (ed. D.W. Rupp), *(SIMA 77)* 147–68. Göteborg.

Rupp, D.W. (1988) The 'Royal Tombs' at Salamis (Cyprus): ideological messages of power and authority. *J Medit Arch 1* 111–39.

Rupp, D.W. *et al* (1984) Canadian Palaipaphos (Cyprus) Survey Project: second preliminary report, 1980–1982. *J Field A 4*, 133–54.

Rupp, D.W. *et al* (1986) Canadian Palaipaphos (Cyprus) Survey Project: third preliminary report, 1983–1985. *Acta Arch 57*, 27–45.

Sabloff, J.A. *et al* (1987) Understanding the archaeological record. *Antiquity 61*, 203-9.

Schneider, H.K. (1974) *Economic Man. The Anthropology of Economics.* New York.

Shennan, S. (1988) *Quantifying Archaeology.* Edinburgh.

Smith, M.A. (1987) Household possessions and wealth in agrarian states: implications for archaeology. *J Anthrop Arch 6*, 297–335.

Snodgrass, A. (1988) *Cyprus and Early Greek History.* Cultural Foundation of the Bank of Cyprus, Nicosia.

Sørensen, L. Wriedt (1988) Greek pottery found in Cyprus. *Acta Hyperborea 1*, (in press).

Stech, T. *et al* (1985) The analysis of iron artifacts from Palaepaphos-Skales. *RDAC*, 192–202.

Veblen, T. (1934) *The Theory of the Leisure Class. An Economic Study of Institutions.* New York.

39
Sur l'administration de Kition a l'époque classique

M. Yon
Université de Lyon

Depuis une vingtaine d'anneés, les fouilles régulières aussi bien que les découvertes consécutives au développement urbain de Larnaca ont multiplié de façon extraordinaire la documentation qui concerne l'histoire du royaume phénicien de Kition (Figs 39.1–2). Les documents que l'on connaissait déjà, en particulier les quelques allusions des textes classiques et les inscriptions phéniciennes découvertes au XIXe s.,[1] en reçoivent un éclairage nouveau qui a rendu nécessaire de réexaminer l'ensemble dans une perspective historique nouvelle.[2] Je voudrais aujourd'hui m'attacher plus particulièrement à ce que l'on sait de l'organisation du royaume et de son fonctionnement administratif, pour la période que l'on connaît maintenant le mieux: l'époque classique des Ve et IVe s.

Je souhaite en particulier exploiter les informations que fournissent les inscriptions de cette période, phéniciennes pour la plupart, que l'on a trouvées à Kition même, mais aussi à Idalion, possession du roi de Kition à partir de 450, et à Tamassos, qui fut également pendant quelques années, au milieu du IVe s., une possession kitienne; on peut alors tenter de les mettre en relation avec ce qu'indiquent les autres sources d'informations, notamment les résultats de l'archéologie à travers lesquels apparaissent les résultats pratiques de la gestion du royaume. Naturellement je ne prétends pas faire une relecture des textes en phénicien, et je me référerai aux travaux récemment publiés par mes collègues sémitisants, ainsi qu'aux informations qu'ils m'ont aimablement fournies en répondant à mes questions. Je rappellerai en particulier d'une part l'étude de M. Sznycer sur les noms de métier (1985), d'autre part les travaux de J. Teixidor sur l'administration en Phénicie (1979; 1980). Quant aux textes phéniciens eux-mêmes, je renvoie d'abord au *CIS* paru en 1881;[3] ces inscriptions ont été reprises en 1977 par M.G. Guzzo Amadasi et V. Karageorghis (*Kition* III), qui y ont naturellement ajouté les textes trouvées depuis la parution du *CIS* (notam-

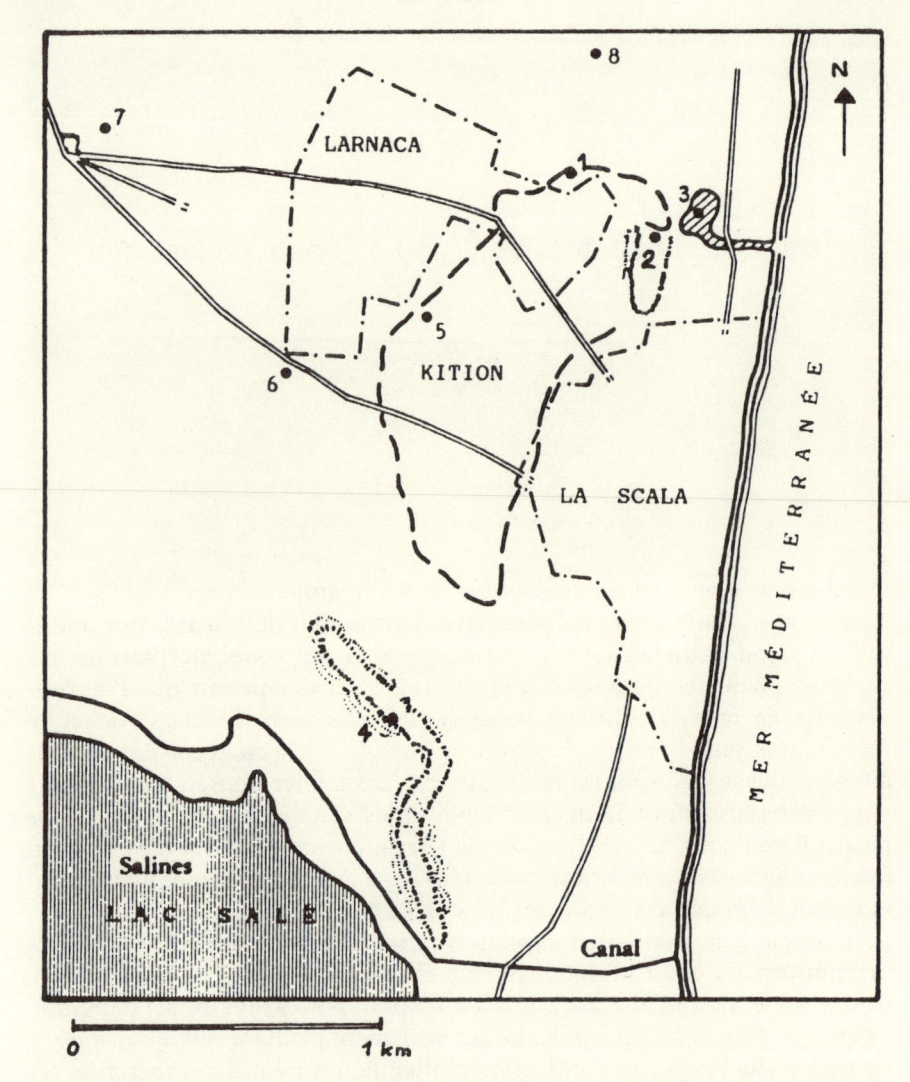

Figure 39.1 Le site de Kition à Larnaca (D'après le relevé d'A. Dozon, dans *CIS* I, 1881, 7).

1 – Kathari
2 – Bamboula
3 – Port fermé
4 – "Artémis Paralia"
5 – Kamelarga
6 – Tourabi
7 – Aghios Giorghios
8 – Aghios Prodromos

ment dans la fouille de Kathari). En 1977, un lot de grand intérêt a été découvert dans la nécropole d'Aghios Giorghios (Hadjisavvas *et al* 1984). Pour les inscriptions bilingues de Tamassos, découvertes en 1885 (après la parution du *CIS*), je renvoie à la publication des inscriptions syllabiques par O. Masson en 1960 (*ICS* Nos 215–16).

Figure 39.2 Partie nord-est de Kition à Larnaca: au premier plan Bamboula; au fond Kathari (Photo Mission Française de Kition-Bamboula 1985).

L'ORGANISATION POLITIQUE: FONCTION ROYALE

La première interrogation en ce qui concerne le fonctionnement d'une société, c'est son organisation politique. La fonction suprême est exercée par le roi: *Mlk (milk)* en phénicien, au témoignage de nombreuses inscriptions et des monnaies, équivalent du grec βασιλεύς, comme on le constate par exemple sur une inscription bilingue (grec syllabique et phénicien) trouvée sur une base de statue dans le temple d'Apollon à Idalion (Fig 39.3), et datée de la 4e année du régne de Milkyatôn, roi de Kition et Idalion (*ICS* no 220 = *CIS* I, 89), ou dans les récits des historiens grecs (Diodore et Douris sont les seuls à citer le nom du roi, de façon approximative du reste). Le monnayage, daté selon des critères stylistiques, nous fait connaître des noms royaux, et les inscriptions y ajoutent des dates, des filiations, des titulatures. On a pu établir la succession suivante aux Ve et IVe s. (*BM Cat. Coins* XXX-XLII):

Baalmilk I (après 480-milieu Ve s. ?)
Ozibaal (milieu Ve s.)
Baalmilk II (environ 425-fin Ve s. ?)
Baalrôm (vers 400)
Milkyatôn (début IVe s.-362)
Pumayyatôn (362–312)

Je n'entrerai pas ici dans le détail, puisque j'ai déjà eu l'occasion de le faire.[4] Je rappellerai seulement que les relations entre certains de ces personnages royaux connus par leur monnayage nous est précisée par des inscriptions. Ce qu'il est important de noter c'est que la royauté est héréditaire. Les inscriptions de Baalmilk II[5] le donnent comme fils de son

Figure 39.3 Dédicace bilingue (phénicien/grec/chypriote syllabique) d'Idalion, début IVᵉ s. (Photo British Museum).

prédécesseur Ozibaal, et petit-fils du premier Baalmilk; de la même manière au IVe s., Pumayyatôn ne manque pas une occasion de redire qu'il est fils de son prédécesseur Milkyatôn.[6]

La situation est moins claire vers 400, puisque Milkyatôn est fils d'un Baalrôm, qui n'est pas roi. Mais tout porte à croire que ce personnage appartient également à la famille royale, ce qui m'amène à évoquer le statut des proches du roi. La même inscription bilingue d'Idalion citée plus haut mentionne un certain Baalrôm: il porte dans le texte grec le titre de Ϝαναξ, rendu en phénicien par ʾdn (adôn), ce qu'on peut traduire par 'Seigneur', ou 'Prince'. Par chance, la signification de ce titre dans la hiérarchie sociale de Chypre nous est expliquée sans ambiguïté par Isocrate, à propos de Salamine, où 'les fils et les filles' d'Evagoras portaient, comme le voulait leur naissance, les titres de Ϝαναξ et Ϝανάσσα (Évagoras IX, 72). Ce Baalrôm appartient donc bien, de toute évidence, à la famille proche du roi Milkyatôn, et il porte le même nom que le père de ce dernier. On connaît d'autre part l'existence d'un autre Baalrôm, connu par son monnayage comme roi vers 400 et donc prédécesseur de Milkyatôn: on obtient ainsi un réseau familial serré qui détient le pouvoir royal. De nombreuses inscriptions du IVe. s.—telles les dédicaces à Ešmoun-Melqart trouvées à Batsalos (Lac Salé)—nomment Milkyatôn, et de nombreux textes portent la date de son année de règne; leur quantité montre bien la place centrale qu'ont prise au début du IVe s. le pouvoir royal et la personne du roi.

Il est alors temps de se demander comment se manifeste dans la ville cette puissance royale. A vrai dire, on ne connaît pas les bâtements royaux: aucun

Figure 39.4 Kition-Bamboula: Sanctuaire archaïque, recouvert fin Ve s. par la cour du sanctuaire classique; à gauche, collecteur, le long du bâtiment classique (Photo Mission Française de Kition-Bamboula 1984).

palais n'a encore été mis au jour (ni même localisé). Pourtant, à en juger par l'exploration archéologique (en particulier dans le quartier urbain de Bamboula que je prendrai comme exemple), la ville porte la marque de l'activité de ses rois des Ve et IVe s.

Il semble que c'est sous le règne de Baalmilk II (dernier quart Ve s.?) que le sanctuaire de Bamboula (Fig 39.4) a subi sa plus profonde transformation, avec la réorganisation complète du sanctuaire.[7] Le sanctuaire archaïque se présentait jusqu'au Ve s. comme un ensemble de petites constructions, au nord de la rue qui menait au port, et à quelque distance du rempart du VIe s. qui le protégeait vers le sud. Désormais, tous les bâtiments anciens sont abattus, et recouverts par une très grande cour sacrée, qui recouvre également la rue elle-même; et de nouveaux bâtiments de culte sont alors construits au sud (appuyés sur les fondations du rempart disparu) pour accueillir les activités du sanctuaire: on a, semble-t-il, l'évocation de ces travaux dans l'inscription des comptes du temple d'Astarté, avec la mention des sommes données aux 'bâtisseurs qui ont bâti le temple d'Astarté de Kition' (*CIS* I, 86 A, 1. 4). Dans ce bâtiment se déroulent aussi tous les rites de l'eau et sans doute les banquets.[8] Le sanctuaire se trouve alors immédiatement au voisinage du port et des hangars qui abritaient les trières au Ve s., et la partie supérieure des bateaux devait apparaître au-dessus du mur qui soutenait au nord la terrasse du sanctuaire.

Figure 39.5 Dédicace phénicienne de Kiti, 320 a.C. (Photo Cyprus Museum).

Aucun document ne nous indique explicitement quelle est la part de la volonté royale (Baalmilk II) dans ces entreprises du Ve s. Pourtant la décision de modifier l'espace public en absorbant la rue menant de la ville au port sous la cour du sanctuaire, et la destruction du rempart archaïque utilisé seulement comme fondation du bâtiment de culte, supposent une autorité qui détient aussi bien le pouvoir civil que la mainmise sur le sanctuaire qu'elle peut réorganiser à sa guise: on est tenté d'y voir la main royale, d'autant plus que le culte de Melqart, qui est comme à Tyr le protecteur de la dynastie royale (il figure sur les monnaies), paraît alors prédominant à Bamboula.[9]

Cette manifestation de l'autorité royale toute puissante est encore plus sensible au IVe s., avec Milkyatôn, lorsque vers 375, sont entrepris de grands travaux urbains qui font passer les égouts de la ville à travers le *temenos* du même sanctuaire. Les recoupements avec les quelques témoignages littéraires montrent Milkyatôn comme l'un des deux plus puissants rois de Chypre, dont la politique d'expansion et les ambitions politiques et territoriales se sont toujours heurtées à celles de son voisin Evagoras, roi de Salamine, l'un allié aux Perses, l'autre soutenu par Athènes. Tout paraît montrer que le pouvoir royal s'est développé au cours de l'époque classique, atteignant son *akmé* avec Milkyatôn, et retombant peu à peu dans la dernière partie du règne de son successeur.[10] La longue durée de son règne (au moins 30 ans) et celle de son fils Pumayyaton (Fig 39.5) (plus de 50 ans) sont remarquables dans un monde où l'espérance de vie était extrêmement courte,[11] et où les intrigues de palais se terminaient parfois dans des scandales sanglants: cette belle longévité suppose un pouvoir fort et un efficace système de protection des personnes royales.[12]

LES FONCTIONS ADMINISTRATIVES

Je ne parlerai que des titres désignant de véritables 'fonctions', et non des 'metiers' (pour les termes de métiers, au demeurant très intéressants également, on se reportera à M. Sznycer). On ne possède malheureusement aucun texte de quelque longueur qui expliciterait pour nous les responsabilités des grands personnages de l'état, comme on en connaît alors par exemple en pays grec (longs décrets, textes de lois etc). La plus longue mention que l'on puisse exploiter c'est le double texte *CIS* I, 86, qui donne les comptes du temple d'Astarté au début du IVe s., et énumère des salaires; pour le reste on dispose essentiellement des titres que les familles des défunts ont jugé utile (ou glorieux ?) de graver sur les stèles funéraires de la même époque; on a retrouvé également quelques dédicaces.

Très rare est le *špṭ (shouphet)*, le 'suffète' bien connu à Carthage; on en connaît à Kition un seul exemple sur une inscription funéraire du IVe s., celle de la 'fille d'Abdeshmoun, le suffète' (*CIS* I, 47: *Kition* III, B 31, dans l'église St-Antoine, à Kellia près de Larnaca). A vrai dire, si le terme évoque une haute fonction administrative en pays punique (où il n'y avait pas de roi), on ne sait pas très bien ce qu'il recouvre en Phénicie d'Orient, où le terme est très peu attesté. Selon J. Teixidor, on n'en connaît que trois exemples en Orient, dont celui de Kition (un autre du IIIe s. à Tyr, un au Pirée); il y voit un équivalent de 'juge', que l'on peut rapprocher du *špt (shophet)* des textes bibliques, au sens de 'chef du peuple': ce terme est du reste traduit en grec dans la *Septante (Juges)* I par: *kritès*, et dans Josèphe, *Contre Apion*, I, 156–7 par: *dikastès*. Leurs pouvoirs dans le monde phénicien oriental auraient été assez restreints. J. Teixidor (1979, 17) les rapproche, à juste titre, des *laokrites* de l'administration ptolémaïque, chargés de l'organisation judiciaire.

On a également un seul exemple de *Skn (souken)*, qui désigne un personnage extérieur au royaume: le *skn* de Tyr, dans l'inscription d'un sarcophage du IVe s., typiquement kitien. O. Masson et M. Sznycer traduisent par 'ministre de Tyr' (1972, 69–75). Le terme est peut-être à prendre au sens d' 'ambassadeur', d''envoyé' du roi de Tyr (?) Il est certain qu'à cette époque Kition avait acquis son indépendance totale à l'égard de la métropole: il ne peut donc s'agir d'un gouverneur, d'un 'haut-commissaire', qui représenterait un pouvoir suzerain auquel serait soumis le roi de Kition.

Mais le terme qui apparaît le plus fréquemment est celui de *Rb (rab, cf* textes bibliques *Rabbi*), que les éditeurs modernes traduisent en géneral par 'chef' (ce n'est pas très satisfaisant en français). Dans de nombreux cas, le mot suivi d'un complément de détermination paraît désigner, et depuis longtemps, une fonction d'administration civile de premier plan: on en trouve déjà l'exemple au Bronze Récent à Ougarit. Ainsi, dans les archives du Palais-Royal, une lettre sur des questions de navigation et de commerce, est écrite au roi d'Ougarit par le *Rab mihadu*, ce que l'on traduit pas 'maire du port'.[13] Employé seul, sur une stèle d'Oum el-Ammed (Phénicie) au IIIe s., le terme désigne sans doute le 'premier magistrat' de la ville: J. Teixidor (1979) y voit l'équivalent du grec *archonte*.

Les inscriptions phéniciennes d'époque classique à Kition nous en donnent plusieurs exemples:

—*Rb sprm (rab soupherim)*: 'chef des scribes'. Cette fonction apparaît à Kition dans les comptes du temple d'Astarté au début du IVe s., où le personnage reçoit une indemnité: '. . . Pour *Abdešmoun* chef des scribes, il a été envoyé ce jour-ci 3 QR et 3 QP . . .'. Il apparaît aussi sur une base de statue trouvée en 1972 à Kiti (Fig 39.5), datée de l'an 42 de Pumayyatôn (320/319), où le titre est celui de l'arrière grand-père du dédicant: '. . . ʿbdʾ (Abdou), fils de *Klky (Kilikay)*, fils de ʿbdʾ (Abdou), fils de *Šmr (Shamor)* chef des scribes. . .' (*Kition* III, A 30). On le trouve enfin sur la stèle funéraire du IVe s. citée plus haut, trouvée à Aghios Giorghios en 1979, où il qualifie également l'arrière-grand-père du défunt: '. . . *Mouttoun-ʿAštart, fils de ʿAzar-Yahou, fils de Mouttoun*, fils de *Šillem* chef des scribes'.[14]

Les mentions qu'on en a à Kition sont donc datées du Ve s. et du début du IVe s., mais la fonction est ancienne en pays syro-phénicien; on a déjà un 'chef des scribes' à Ougarit.[15] La comparaison avec les témoignages bibliques laisse voir qu'il s'agit d'une fonction importante, et qu'il devait exister un corps officiel de ces personnages groupés en collège. Le fait qu'un chef des scribes soit mentionné dans les comptes du temple d'Astarté n'implique pas qu'il y ait un corps de scribes spécial propre au sanctuaire: l'indemnité de ce personnage lui est *'envoyée'*, comme à quelqu'un d'extérieur au temple, sans doute le magistrat civil.

—*Rb Srsrm (rab sarsourim)*: 'chef des agents commerciaux', selon M.G. Guzzo Amadasi, 'chef des courtiers de la cour' selon M. Sznycer. Ce titre apparaît sur une stèle funéraire du IVe s., trouvée à Tourabi et conservée au British Museum;[16] la mention en est tout à fait remarquable. En effet, le titre est accolé au nom du signataire, mais il l'est également à celui de son père défunt et à ceux de ses ascendants jusqu'à six générations: . . .' *ʾrš (Arish)*, chef des a. c., pour son père *Prsy (Parsay)* chef des a. c., fils de *ʾrš (Arish)* chef des a.c., fils de *Mnhm (Menahem)* chef des a.c., fils de *Mšl (Mashol)* chef des a.c., fils de *Prsy (Parsay)* chef des a. c . . .' (*Kition* III, B 45). Cette accumulation nous mène en remontant le temps jusque vers 475 a.C.; il est notable que le premier à porter ce titre s'appelle *Parsay*: 'le Perse', à l'époque précisément où s'établit à Kition la dynastie de Baalmilk I, soutenue par les Perses. Plutôt qu'un véritable étranger venu d'Iran et installé à Chypre, j'y verrai volontiers un Phénicien de Kition, nommé ainsi pour avoir eu des fonctions à la cour du Grand Roi (ainsi dans un village grec aujourd'hui, *o Americanos* désigne celui qui a travaillé longtemps à Chicago!). Mais ce qui nous importe surtout ici, c'est le caractère héréditaire de cette fonction. Quelle qu'en soit la réalité pratique, il est évident qu'une fonction ainsi liée au commerce devait être une situation profitable. On ne saurait mieux exprimer la mainmise d'une famille sur le contrôle des activités du négoce, attestée ainsi pendant environ un siècle et demi, à l'époque de la plus grande puissance économique et commerciale du royaume.[17] Il s'agit donc là d'une famille riche et puissante de Kition.

—*Rb hz ʿnm (rab houzeenim)*: 'chef des inspecteurs des sources'. La fonction est signalée précisément sur la même inscription funéraire que les précédentes: les agents commerciaux constituaient la lignée paternelle du dédicant, celui-ci appartient à son ascendance maternelle: 'pour sa mère *Šmzbl* fille de *Bʿlrm (Baalrom)*, fils de *Mlktyn (Milkyatôn)*, fils de ʿ*zr*

(Azor) chef des 'inspecteurs des sources': on remonte là encore au moins au milieu du Ve s. L'importance de la fonction est attestée par la mention que l'on en fait encore au IVe s. Mais cette mention n'apparaît pas déraisonnable lorsque l'on mesure combien l'approvisionnement en eau potable est une donnée fondamentale pour la survie de la cité; on sait que Kition est particulièrement peu favorisée sous ce rapport: il n'y a pas de sources dans la ville, et le sous-sol est imprégné d'une nappe phréatique saumâtre qui remonte dès que l'on creuse (surtout après les pluies d'hiver), et dans laquelle donnent les puits. Je ne m'arrêterai pas aux conséquences néfastes sur la santé publique (épidémies, malaria), ni aux solutions architecturales décidées par le roi Milkyatôn pour drainer cette eau souterraine par la construction d'un réseau d'égout:[18] en l'occurrence ce qui nous intéresse, c'est l'approvisionnement en eau (la mention des 'sources' ici doit se comprendre comme les 'ressources'): l'eau potable devait venir de la région au sud de Kiti, ou des collines du nord-ouest, et bien qu'il n'en reste rien aujourd'hui, il est probable que certaines des canalisations mentionnées dans Larnaca par des voyageurs du XIXe s. ont été établies à l'époque classique. Elles représentent des travaux publics considérables, et des investissements qui ont pu donner lieu à des marchés fructueux.

Quoi qu'il en soit, le haut fonctionnaire qui en était responsable, ou en tirait les bénéfices, était un personnage important de l'État. Il est d'autant plus intéressant d'en revenir à cette famille qui a exercé de hautes fonctions: il n'est pas indifférent que le grand-père s'appelle *Baalrôm*. A vrai dire ce nom n'est pas exceptionnel à Kition: on connaît par exemple un *Baalrôm* fils d'*Eshmoun-Adon* (et toute son ascendance) sur une stèle de type très grec trouvée en 1979 à Aghios Giorghios (Hadjisavvas *et al* 1984, 101, 104–5 stèle II); mais pour en revenir à la stèle précédente, ce ne peut être par hasard que ce *Baalrôm* du IVe s. est fils d'un *Milkyatôn*. La présence dans cette lignée des noms dynastiques des rois contemporains laisse supposer qu'ils sont très proches, voire parents de la famille royale.

—Le même terme de *rab* apparaît encore sous la forme de *Rb.rš (rab horesh)*: 'chef artisan', 'maître artisan', sur l'épitaphe d'une 'Téora, femme de Milkyatôn, maître artisan'.[19] Mais il ne s'agit peut-être pas ici d'une charge ou d'une fonction publique. A la différence des titres précédents, le titre n'est pas accompagné d'un complément pluriel, supposant un collège, un corps de fonctionnaire sous l'autorité d'un 'chef': le 'chef artisan' a une prééminence à lui tout seul, mais il n'exerce pas une autorité. La mention de son activité sur le monument funéraire suppose que cette profession devait être de type plutôt industriel. On soulignera du reste que le personnage porte un nom royal: '*Milkyatôn*'. Il s'agit probablement d'une famille de l'entourage royal plutôt que d'un modeste artisan; mais ce n'est pas à proprement parler un 'fonctionnaire' du royaume.

Les attestations que l'on a de ce terme de *rab* en font un des titres les plus fréquents à Kition, et selon les cas, il s'applique aux activités les plus diverses, mais on a vu qu'il désigne généralement de hautes fonctions dans le royaume. On attachera du reste une grande importance à la manière dont ce titre est intégré dans les formules funéraires: on a vu en effet que ce titre n'est pas nécessairement celui du défunt bénéficiaire de l'inscription, mais qu'il peut être celui de son père, son grand-père, voire son arrière-grand-père et au delà. Il est bien évident que ces titres désignent des fonctions de première importance, puisque leur prestige rejaillit sur les descendants cent ou cent cinquante ans plus tard.

Dans certains cas, le titre est porté de la même manière par plusieurs générations (six, dans le cas des agents commerciaux !): situation de monopole, fonction rentable (la mainmise sur tout le commerce du royaume) qu'une famille se transmet de père en fils pendant au moins un siècle et demi.

Tels sont les plus clairs des titres qui se rapportent au fonctionnement du royaume. J'ai volontairement laissé de côté les termes désignant des activités qui relèvent simplement des 'métiers' ('fabricant de chariot', 'fabricant de coupes', 'homme des salines' etc), ainsi que la fonction un peu mystérieuse, attestée dans trois inscriptions (*Kition* III 24, A 9; B 40; F1), et qu'on propose de traduire par 'interprète des trônes': s'il s'agit de l'interprète du roi, son activité relève du personnel du palais, non d'une fonction de l'État.

FONCTIONS RELIGIEUSES

Dans une société où les croyances et les cultes tiennent un aussi grand rôle, les fonctions religieuses doivent être considérées comme des fonctions de première importance. Or si l'architecture, l'iconographie, l'épigraphie attestent de la place primordiale que tiennent les dieux, on ne dispose en revanche que de peu d'indications sur le personnel qui leur était consacré, malgré quelques mentions. Ainsi, sur une stèle récemment trouvée à Aghios Georghios (Hadjisavvas *et al* 1984, 10, 108, 110 stèle V), la bénéficiaire *Gerat-Milk* est 'fille du *šrt (shuret)*' que A. Dupont-Sommer propose à titre d'hypothèse de traduire par 'Officiant', 'ministre du culte'; mais on n'en sait pas beaucoup plus.

On en revient toujours au plus important texte, celui des comptes du temple d'Astarté trouvé à Bamboula:[14] il y est question des bénéficiaires des rémunérations, qui se répartissent en catégories très différentes. Un premier ensemble regroupe tout un personnel intérieur de portiers, de chantres, de serviteurs, de sacrificateurs, de barbiers, de prostituées, de boulangers. . ., attachés au déroulement des activités du temple. Quelques autres personnages cités sont au contraire des personnages extérieurs au sanctuaire, mais qui émargent au budget pour des raisons diverses: le 'chef des scribes' déjà cité (et qui est un fonctionnaire royal); les 'architectes' qui ont construit le temple d'Astarté (face A, 1.4), et les artisans qui ont fait les piliers dans le temple de Mikal (face A 1.13) (et qui mènent peut-être des entreprises privées). Ni les uns ni les autres ne sont donc de véritables 'fonctionnaires religieux'.

Les seules mentions qui paraissent pouvoir être ainsi considérées sont d'une part les 'magistrats de la néoménie' (cités face A 1.3, et face B 1.3), que les éditeurs depuis M. Sznycer et O. Masson comprennent comme exerçant une fonction liée au temple;[20] l'autre est le personnage dit b^c *lym* (*baal mym*), 'maître de l'eau', dont on sait qu'il n'est pas un magistrat civil, puisque le texte le précise: 'dans l'entourage de la divinité' (face B 1.4). J'ai déjà eu l'occasion de montrer les liens qui existent entre cette fonction du sanctuaire et les aménagements très particuliers qui ont été mis au jour à Bamboula (1982). Je n'y reviens pas ici; ce qui importe en l'occurrence, c'est qu'il s'agit d'une fonction sacrée limitée au déroulement des cérémonies du culte, et non à l'administration du sanctuaire. Comme on l'a déjà pressenti plus haut, en évoquant les constructions et les transformations urbaines qui n'ont pas épargné le sanctuaire, il apparaît que les décisions concernant les biens sacrés appartiennent non au personnel du temple, mais au pouvoir royal: le roi, qui est le protégé du dieu Melqart, est par voie de conséquence maître des biens du sanctuaire.

CONCLUSION

Il est bien difficile d'analyser vraiment le fonctionnenment du royaume, puisqu'on ne possède aucun texte officiel, aucun décret, aucune loi. Pourtant, le recensement que l'on vient de faire apporte tout de même quelques lumières sur les réalités administratives de la Kition classique. Le hasard des inscriptions retrouvées a permis notamment de mettre en évidence la place occupée par quelques familles, en nombre apparemment restreint; elles détiennent le monopole de situations sans doute fructueuses, comme les fonctions de 'courtiers royaux', ou la mainmise sur les 'ressources en eau'. L'onomastique montre également que ces familles sont alliées à la famille royale: le pouvoir, sans doute politique autant qu'économique, se concentre dans les mains de l'entourage du roi. Comme les royaumes phéniciens de la côte levantine, et vraisemblablement les autres royaumes chypriotes, le royaume de Kition est une théocratie, dans laquelle la protection du dieu (ici Melqart) assure à la personne du roi un statut quasi divin. A titre de comparaison, le soin avec lequel Evagoras de Salamine (contemporain de Milkyatôn) a cherché constamment à démontrer sa filiation divine, remontant à Zeus par l'intermédiaire du légendaire Teucros, montre à l'évidence la manière orientale dont on percevait à Chypre le pouvoir royal.

Il semble au reste que l'époque classique a vu croître ce pouvoir, fondé sur le principe dynastique, voire le népotisme. A Kition, le témoignage de l'archéologie, avec les ambitieux programmes de constructions urbaines, confirme ce développement à la fois politique et économique; il atteint son plus haut point dans le 1er quart du IVe s. sous le règne de Milkyatôn. Ainsi par exemple, le projet qu'il a su imposer de créer un réseau de collecteurs pour assainir la ville, et la mise en oeuvre du programme, nécessitent non seulement des techniciens qualifiés (dans les sciences de l'hydraulique et de l'urbanisme), mais aussi l'existence d'une organisation administrative capable de coordonner les travaux, puis d'en assurer la gestion et le bon fonctionnement: c'est ce qui se produit pendant plus de 60 ans, jusqu'à ce que la conquête ptolémaïque réduise à néant deux siècles de bonne administration. Mais il est probable que l'administration des Ptolémées a su mettre à profit l'héritage des princes phéniciens de Kition, comme celui des autres princes orientaux qui ont servi de modèles au princes hellénistiques.

NOTES

[1] Publiées dans le *CIS* en 1981, reprises par M.Guzzo-Amadasi et V. Karageorghis en 1972 dans *Kition* III. L'édition des textes littéraires classiques et celle du *corpus* épigraphique grec et latin sont en préparation (à paraître dans la série *Kition-Bamboula*, publiée par la Mission française).

[2] Voir les études d'ensemble sur l'histoire de Kition à l'époque archaïque (Yon 1987) et à l'époque classique (Yon sous presse). *Cf* également mes notices dans le *Dictionnaire de la civilisation phénicienne* (Liège à paraître), à la rubrique 'Kition', et aux noms des différents rois.

[3] *CIS* I, 1881, no 5, 10–88 (Kition), 89–94 (Idalion), repris dans *KAI;* certains textes ont été réexaminés dans Masson & Sznycer 1972.

[4] *Cf* Yon sous presse, avec références et bibliographie.

[5] Honeyman 1939, no 3 (trouvée à Idalion), et 7 (sans provenance connue).

[6] Par exemple *CIS* I, 10 (*Kition* III, A 2) ou 11 (*Kition* III, A 1).

[7] Voir nos rapports de fouille annuels dans *Chronique* 1977. *Cf* présentation d'ensemble des résultats: Yon 1985.

[8] Sur le bâtiment, voir Salles 1983; pour les rites de l'eau: Yon 1982.

[9] Représenté sous les traits d'un Héraklès (figurines de calcaire du *bothros* de Bamboula, trouvées par E. Gjerstad: *SCE* III; *cf* Yon 1986).

[10] Voir notices 'Milkyatôn' et 'Pumayyatôn', dans *Dict Civil Phén*

[11] *Cf* base de Kiti (voir n 14), datée de 'la 42e année du règne de Pumayyatôn'. A titre d'exemple, les squelettes de la nécropole classique de Kition que nous avons fait analyser en 1986 (Yon & Callot 1987) sont ceux d'un homme de 35–40 ans, et d'une femme de 37–42 ans; selon M. Domurad (1987), la moyenne établie pour le C-G donne 35,8 ans pour les hommes, 30,3 ans pour les femmes.

[12] Sur les intrigues de Palais et les morts violentes voir le dossier réuni pour Evagoras et Nicoclès de Salamine: M.Yon, dans *Salamine* X 1, 129–31 (Theopompe fr. 114 (126), in Athénée XII, 41; Aelien, *Variae Historiae*, VII, 2; Anaximène de Milet, dans Athénée XII, 531, d-e). Voir aussi *ibid*, 112, le texte de Cléarchos de Soli (Athénée VI, 255–6) sur le système d'espionnage intérieur pour le compte du roi—une sorte de 'police secrète'—organisé dans tous les royaumes de Chypre sur le modèle de celui de Salamine.

[13] Daté par la mention du pharaon Aménophis III; *PRU* V, 8; *cf* Lipinski 1977; *SDB*, 1303.

[14] Comptes du temple, trouvés en 1879 à Bamboula (British Museum 125.080): *CIS* I, 86 A 1.14 (*Kition* III, C 1, 105–6); *cf* édition Sznycer & Masson 1972, 21–68. Base de Kiti (Cyprus Museum 1972-X/11-1: *Kition* III, A 3, 45 (*BCH* 98, 1973, 610). Stèle d'Aghios Giorghios (Musée de Larnaca CS 2251/40): Hadjisavvas *et al* 1984, A.G. I, 101, 103–4.

[15] RS 6.174 (fouilles 934): *CTA*, 132–3, no 49.

[16] Trouvée en 1894 par J. Myres (British Museum 125.082): *Kition* III, B 45, 96–100, avec bibliographie antérieure. *Cf* Sznycer 1985, 82.

[17] Pour la prospérité du royaume aux Ve et IVe s., voir Yon sous presse.

[18] Pour ces constructions, voir Callot & Salles 1981; Salles 1983. Sur les conditions hydrologiques particulières à Kition et les conséquences: Yon *Colloque Athènes* 1988 (à paraître).

[19] Monument vu par R. Pococke au XVIIIe s., perdu depuis: *CIS* I, 64 I *Kition* III, B 9.

[20] 1972, 33–5 (contre les éditeurs précédents qui comprenaient 'les dieux de la néoménie').

RÉFÉRENCES

BMCat. Coins G.Hill (1904) *British Museum Catalogue of Coins, Cyprus.* London.

Callot, O. & Salles, J-F. (1981) Un collecteur à Kition (Chypre). *L'homme et l'eau* I, 49–68. Lyon.

CIS (1881) *Corpus Inscriptionum Semiticarum*, I. Paris.

CTA Herdner, A. (1963) *Corpus des Textes cunéiformes alphabétiques de Ras Shamra, campagnes I à IX, 1929 à 1939.* Paris.

Domurad, M. (1987) Annexe à Yon & Callot (1987) 168–9.

Hadjisavvas, S. et al (1984) Cinq stèles funéraires découvertes sur le site d'Ayios Georghios, à Larnaca-Kition, en 1979. *RDAC*, 101–16.

Honeyman, A. (1939) The Phoenician inscriptions of the Cyprus Museum. *Iraq 6*, 103–10.

ICS Masson, O. (1960) *Inscriptions chypriotes syllabiques.* Paris.

KAI Donner, H. & Röllig, W. (1966–1969) Kanaanäische und Aramäische Inschriften. 2e Wiesbaden.

Lipinski, E. (1977) An Ugaritic letter to Amenophis III. *Iraq 39*, 213–17.

Masson, O. & Sznycer, M. (1972) *Recherches sur les Phéniciens à Chypre.* Genève-Paris.

PRU Virolleaud Ch. (1965) *Palais Royal d'Ugarit* V. Paris.

Salamine X 1 Chavane, M-J. & Yon, M. (1978) *Salamine de Chypre* X, *Testimonia* 1. Paris.

Salles, J-F. (1983) *Kition-Bamboula* II, *Les égouts de la ville classique.* Paris.

SDB Liverani, M. (1979) Ras Shamra Ugarit, II. Histoire. *Supplément au Dictionnaire de la Bible*, 1295–1348. Paris.

Sznycer, M. (1985) Les noms de métier et de fonction... Colloque 'Chypre, la vie quotidienne de l'antiquité à nos jours', 79–86. Paris.

Teixidor, J. (1979) Les fonctions de Rab et de suffète en Phénicie. *Semitica* 29, 9–17.

Teixidor, J. (1980) L'assemblée législative en Phénicie d'après les inscriptions. *Syria 57*, 453–64.

Yon, M. (1982) Le maître de l'eau. *Archéologie au Levant, Recueil R. Saidah*, 251–63. Lyon.

Yon, M. (1985) Mission archéologique de Kition-Bamboula 1976–1984. *Archaeology in Cyprus 1960–1985*, (ed V. Karageorghis) 202–18. Nicosia.

Yon, M. (1986) A propos de l'Héraklès de Chypre. *Colloque 'Iconographie classique et Identités régionales' 1983*, 287–97. Paris.

Yon, M. (1987) Le royaume de Kition, époque archaïque. *St Phoen 5*, 357–74.

Yon, M. (sous presse) Le royaume de Kition, époque classique. *St Phoen 9*.

Yon, M. (à paraître) Eau profane et eau sacrée à Chypre. *Colloque Athènes 1988*.

Yon, M. & Callot, O. (1987) Nouvelles découvertes dans la nécropole ouest de Kition (Aghios Giorghios, époque classique). *RDAC*, 149–66.

40
Priest Kings in Cyprus

Franz Georg Maier
University of Zürich

Kingship is one of these general concepts which are open to very diverse interpretations. In a previous paper it has been pointed out, with good reason, how difficult it is to relate the general to the particular in archaeology. The Late Bronze Age is a case in point: what we presume to know about Cypriot kingdoms in that period still very much belongs to the realm of speculation, if not of factoids. We are on somewhat firmer ground during the Archaic and Classical periods, when the kings of Cyprus maintained their royal status under various foreign overlords. The basic structure of all these kingdoms, whether they were ruled by Greek or Phoenician dynasties, was very similar: a hereditary autocratic monarchy. The political system of Paphos, however, differed in resting on a form of sacral kingship. Her kings were at once temporal and spiritual rulers: 'King of Paphos and Priest of the Wanassa (the Ruling Lady)' they style themselves in their inscriptions, indicating that the political powers of the king were combined with the cult functions of the High Priest of Aphrodite (designed by her traditional Paphian cult name).

In his 'Politics' Aristotle discusses kingship as a purely political institution, defining it as the rule of one single person. Oriental kingship he judges invariably to be a form of tyranny, completely disregarding its theocratic aspects—although at his time Alexander had brought the Greeks into close contact with various forms of sacral kingship in the Oriental world.[1] To Greek eyes theocratic rule may have appeared as one of the time-honoured methods to win and keep power. Yet to the Oriental mind kingship as a purely secular institution would have seemed trivial if not incomprehensible. Human society formed part of the cosmic order, and thus the theocratic character of rule remained a basic conception of the Ancient Near East, although the nature of kingship was defined in different ways in Egypt and Mesopotamia (Frankfort 1948, 3–12, 231). To avoid misunderstandings it would seem best to define at the outset what we mean by 'Priest King' and differentiate it from other forms of rule. Theocracy in the proper sense of the word designates secular rule by priests acting as substitutes for a god. In divine kingship—the fundamental concept of the Egyptian monarchy—the rulers are not mortals, but gods. Divine kingship is not always easy to distinguish, however, from two other forms of rule: kingship ordained by gods (as represented by the Assyrian king Shamsi-Adad I styling himself: 'the appointee of Enlil'), and royal rule by consent of the gods (as typified by Assurbanipal declaring: 'Assur and Sin have pronounced my name for rulership since time immemorial'). Finally, in sacral kingship a secular ruler also fulfils priestly functions, it being considered one of his duties to maintain harmonious relations between human society and the supernatural powers.[2] Let us now discuss the literary and archaeological evidence relating to priest kings as a form of sacral kingship in Cyprus.

PRIEST KINGS AT PAPHOS

Unambiguous contemporary evidence for priest kings is represented at Paphos by a number of Syllabic inscriptions (eight altogether) of kings of the 4th century BC. They definitely attest that the two functions of king and high priest were combined, but there their factual information ends.[3] The existence of sacral kingship at Paphos is also confirmed by a body of literary tradition—the earliest author being Pindar, the most extensive Tacitus.[4] As the central figure appears the legendary king Cinyras, said to have founded the Paphian sanctuary and to have combined already the functions of king and priest of Aphrodite.[5] The kings of the Cinyrad dynasty retained the priestly office, as the Pindar scholia (in *Pyth*.II 15) and Hesychius (s.v. Κινυράδαι) testify. Tacitus actually relates that the 'Cinyradai' originally shared the sacred functions with the 'Tamiradai', but that an agreement was reached which gave the priesthood to the Cinyrads only (*hist*.II 3; Hesychius s.v. Ταμιράδαι). According to Diodorus (XX 49, 1) the Paphian kings remained high priests of Aphrodite until they were finally dethroned by Ptolemy I.

Yet despite the literary and epigraphical evidence our information about the powers and duties of the Paphian kings as priests is exceedingly scarce. One function only is definitely recorded: they acted as haruspices, giving oracles from the entrails of animals (Tacitus, *hist*. II 3). A further interesting scrap of tradition may be added: according to some Christian authors, the Cinyrad family was buried within the precincts of the Sanctuary of Aphrodite.[6]

PRIEST KINGS IN CYPRUS?

Was this idea of sacral kingship peculiar to Paphos, or did it apply to other Cypriot monarchies of the period as well? Neither the ancient authors nor inscriptions or monuments reveal any trace of such an institution else-

Figure 40.1 Late Archaic limestone head from Palaepaphos, KA 730 (Courtesy Merseyside County Museums, Liverpool).

Figure 40.2 Frontal view of Fig. 40.1.

where. Thus far there is no proof that kings of other dynasties in the island acted as high priests.[7] The combination of secular and religious powers at Paphos must indeed be regarded as unique. It may have originated from the special role of the Paphian Sanctuary of Aphrodite.

The unique position of the Paphian kings in Cyprus naturally raises the question of antecedents: was the conception of king and priest in Paphos autochthonous or was it modelled on foreign traditions? The written sources give no clue except a general 'Oriental connection' symbolised by the figure of Cinyras. Greek influences can hardly be assumed. Mycenaean kingship seems to have embraced certain priestly functions, but Agapenor —the traditional Greek founder-hero of the Paphian Sanctuary—never appears as priest.[18] More specific clues to Oriental traditions living on at Paphos may, however, be found in the archaeological heritage: of special importance in this respect are the regalia of the Paphian kings.

THE EVIDENCE OF MONUMENTS

Our most valuable evidence consists of the Late Archaic head of a 'priest king' and of the fragment of a 'royal throne' from Palaepaphos[9] (Figs 40.1–3). But can we be certain that this slightly over life-size head, as a work of art without doubt one of the most remarkable creations of Archaic sculpture from the island, represents a priest king? A brief survey of Cypriot votary sculpture with distinctive headdresses enables us to distinguish two main groups. The larger group is formed of statues wearing pointed caps either plain or patterned; their peak is sometimes replaced by an ornamental knob. Such votive statues occur on many sites, at Palaepaphos as well as at Golgoi, Idalion, Tamassos, Lefkoniko, or Kazaphani; they are especially numerous at Ayia Irini.[10] A similar type of cap is worn

Figure 40.3 Limestone throne fragment from Palaepaphos, RRKM 144 (Courtesy Cyprus Museum).

Figure 40.4 Late Archaic limestone head from Palaepaphos, KA 614 (Courtesy Cyprus Museum).

Figure 40.5 Late Archaic limestone statue from Palaepaphos, KA 248.

by priests in Assyria,[11] but the parallel should not be pressed as such caps may also form the headdress of kings and gods. In Cyprus the pointed cap seems to be used by both priests and lay worshippers. Only a certain number of completely preserved votary statues are definitely to be described, according to their attributes, as priests.[12]

A second, smaller group of statues wear several forms of headdress which may be classified as royal or princely. First, there is the diadem ornamented with rosettes as represented at Palaepaphos and some other sites[13] (Fig 40.4). The best parallels again come from Assyria where this particular headdress usually designates crown princes or high-ranking officials, although the diadem may sometimes also be worn by the king himself. Developed into a low crown, the diadem with rosettes is adapted by the Persian Great Kings.[14]

The second type of headdress is a plain double crown, represented thus far at Palaepaphos, Kazaphani and Aloa[15] (Fig 40.5). This double crown is without any doubt an imitation of the Egyptian royal headdress combining the Red Crown of Lower Egypt and the White Crown of Upper Egypt, as depicted in countless statues and reliefs from the Middle Kingdom to the Ptolemaic period.[16] In Cyprus, the Egyptian model is slightly modified: the White Crown is lower and thus appears more convex, the Red Crown is cut lower in front.[17]

Another type of double crown is far more elaborate than the one just described. This peculiar headdress seems thus far to be confined to Palaepaphos and Golgoi.[18] The elaborate double crown worn by the priest king from Palaepaphos differs in several respects from the plain version. The crown of Upper Egypt is decorated with a kind of scale pattern—a feature which also occurs on one of the three Golgoi statues, but never in Egypt.[19] The front of the crown of Lower Egypt is ornamented with a winged Uraeus. Generally, a representation of the sacred Uraeus snake forms an emblema of the royal crown of Egypt since the Middle Kingdom; so it does on one of the statues from Golgoi.[20] But the winged Uraeus in the crown of the Kouklia head is thus far unique. Winged Uraei do not appear on Egyptian crowns, although they are quite common on pectorals, royal monuments or religious representations.[21]

The throne from Palaepaphos, on the other hand, shows another winged emblema: a winged solar disc of usual, but fairly elaborate pattern.[22] Winged sun discs also appear on 5th century coins of the kingdom of Paphos, on the Urartian helmet from Kouklia-Mavromatis, or on the Melqart stele found in the Persian siege ramp.[23]

For the Paphian kings the difference between winged solar disc and Uraeus was possibly not very important: both were traditional and powerful symbols of royalty. Wadjet, the cobra of Lower Egypt represented by the Uraeus snake, was believed to be immanent in the Red Crown. The winged sun disc manifested the power of the sky-god Horus, which the king was believed to embody.[24] Such conceptions were not confined to Egypt. In Mesopotamia the ruler was often compared with the sun as the symbol of order and justice, although he always remained a mortal prince (Frankfort 1948, 307–9). Hittite kings were addressed as 'My Sun'; Assyrian and Phoenician kings used winged solar discs as symbols of power.[25]

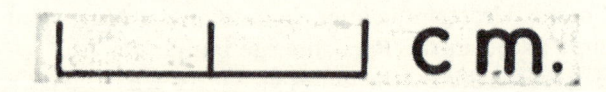

Figure 40.6 Head of bronze statuette in the Cyprus Museum, without provenance (Courtesy Cyprus Museum).

The elaborate double crown is manifestly of Egyptian inspiration and thus was adapted most likely before the beginning of Achaemenid rule, even if the surviving statues date from the end of the 6th century BC. One trait in the representation of the Paphian 'priest-king' is, however, definitely foreign to the Pharaonic regalia: the very elaborate, carefully executed beard. The Egyptian king is often depicted clean-shaven; if his quality as a god is stressed, a narrow artificial beard is added. The type of beard worn

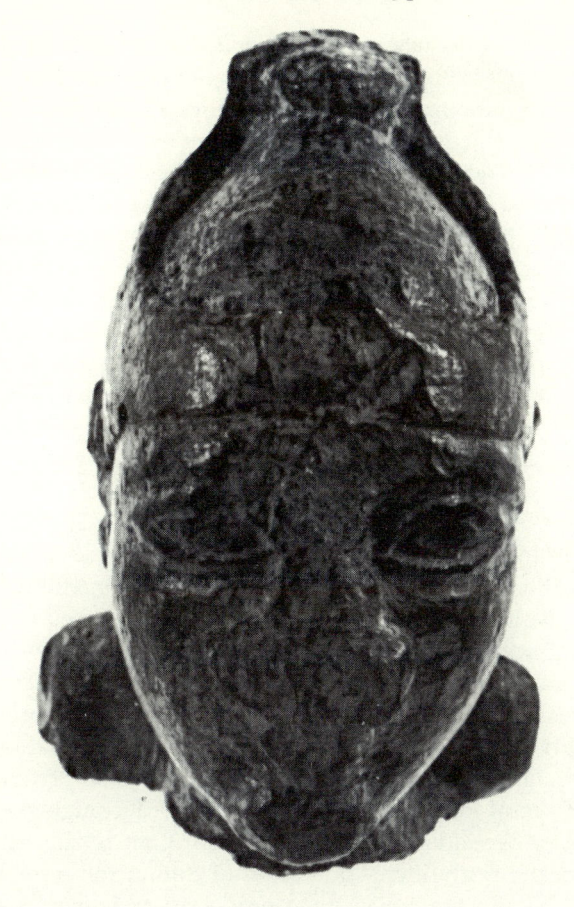

Figure 40.7 Frontal view of Fig. 40.6.

by the 'priest-king', however, evidently derives from Assyrian and Achaemenid prototypes. In contrast to Egypt, the kings of these empires always wear long and elaborate beards, as do many of their officials.[26]

To sum up: if we combine all these observations, there seems no doubt that the double crown formed part of the royal insignia in Cyprus. The Kouklia head therefore does represent one of the Paphian priest kings at the end of the 6th century BC. This statement begs a number of questions which can be asked, but can hardly be conclusively answered. Was the plain double crown the 'normal' royal headdress, so to speak, while the elaborate crown was worn for special functions only? Did Herodotus refer to this peculiar type of headgear when he recorded that at Salamis the Cypriot kings wore a 'mitra' (VII 90)? Did the ceremonial beard of the Paphian king —a type of beard customary with representations of priests, but as a rule not to be found on 'princely' statues[27]—constitute an element of royal dress connected with the office of high priest?[28] There is, furthermore, the temptation to reconstruct the complete formal dress of Cypriot kings at the end of the Archaic period from the monuments: elaborate double crown, triple pectoral over short-sleeved plain tunic, skirt decorated with Uraeus snakes—a definitely Egyptian-looking attire peculiar to this group of statues, and in complete contrast to the long robes of priests and votaries.[29] It could then be argued that informal dress consisted of plain double crown, tunic and skirt, while princes used to wear rosette diadems and 'Cypriot belts' decorated with rosettes.[30] Yet, considering our present state of evidence, this would constitute far too speculative an exercise.

CYPRIOT PRIEST KINGS IN CONTEXT

Strong Egyptian influence, combined with Assyrian and Achaemenid inspirations, possibly conveyed through a Phoenician medium:[31] this may seem a diffuse result of our researches. Yet there is no need to feel uneasy about it. It graphically represents the sequence and the crosscurrents of foreign contacts and influences to which the island was subjected from the late 8th to the early 5th century BC—impacts no doubt enforced through Assyrian, Egyptian and Achaemenid rule. This very situation makes it difficult to formulate a conclusive answer to our problem: from where did the tradition of sacral kingship at Paphos derive? Through the centuries, forms of divine or sacral kingship were ever-present in the Ancient Near East. Already in the Early Dynastic period of Sumer the *ensi* (ruler) could act as a priest. Hittite kings were not only leaders in war and supreme judges, but also chief priests of the realm who personally directed the great religious festivals and answered oracles.[32] The priestly functions of the Egyptian pharaoh are as copiously attested as are those of the Assyrian kings, who *inter alia* were charged with interpreting the will of the gods. The Persian Great Kings were believed to be of divine descent and fulfilled priestly duties.[33] Kings of Byblos and Sidon, the closest mainland neighbours of the Cypriot rulers, styled themselves 'kings and priests' down to the 4th century BC.[34]

Inspiration thus could have come from very different quarters. Yet the regalia of the Paphian rulers seem to demonstrate that their conception of sacral kingship was based primarily on Egyptian and Assyrian models. They never entertained the idea of being divine kings, but the other aspects of their rule as kings *and* priests are prefigured in the traditional forms of Oriental kingship. If the Κύπριος χαρακτήρ here reasserted itself at all, it did so in the peculiar form into which these traditions were blended at Paphos.

NOTES

[1] Aristotle, *Pol.* III 9–10, 5 (also I 1, 2. III 5, 2–4); specifically on Oriental monarchy: *Pol.* III 9, 3–4. He notes, without, however, drawing conclusions, that 'heroic monarchs' had some control over sacrifices (*Pol.* III 9, 7–8).

[2] See generally for these diverse forms: Labat 1939; Frankfort 1948; Hooke 1958; James 1959, 63–70; Posener 1966. Assurbanipal: Langdon 1923, 43; Šamši-Adad: Labat 1939, 17–18.

[3] *ICS* 6.7.90–91 (Nikokles); 4 (Timarchos); 16 (Timocharis); 17 (Echetimos); possibly also 5 (unidentified). Details of the chronology of these kings are still unsolved, but they all definitely belong to the 4th century.

[4] Pindar *Pyth.* II 15–16; Tacitus, *hist.* II 2–4; see also Firmicus Maternus, *de errore prof. rel.* 10.

[5] His legendary attributes comprise not only musical prowess and immense wealth (referred to eg by Pindar, *Nem.* VIII 17–18), but also various important inventions including the use of bronze and the making of tiles: Plinius, *n.h.* VII 56. The Cinyras legend cannot be considered seriously as proof for the existence of sacral kingship in Late Bronze Age Cyprus. It has to be noted that the Homeric tradition designates Cinyras simply as a secular ruler; Pindar is the first author to refer to the priestly office.

[6] Clemens Alex., *Protrept.* III 40; Arnobius, *adv. gentes* 5.

[7] See for instance the inscriptions of kings of Kition and Idalion, Donner & Röllig 1966–69, nos 32, 33, 38 (also all of 4th century date).

[8] Pausanias VIII 5.2 In this context it should also be noted that the dynasty retained the name of Cinyrads.

[9] Priest kings head: KA 730, published first by Iliffe & Mitford 1952, 61, no 7; see also Wilson 1974, 140; illustrated in Maier & Karageorghis 1984, 189, Fig 175. Throne: *Chronique* 1969, 225–6 with Fig 73.

[10] See for instance the Cesnola Collection: *Atlas* I, Pls 39–41, 49, 51, 53, 59, 61; Myres 1914, nos 1257, 1456–7. Kition: *SCE* III Pls 5, 6, 10, 11, 21, 26; Vouni: *SCE* III Pls 59, 63, 66. Kazaphani: Karageorghis 1978 Pls 17–20, 29, 31, 34, 39, 40; Potamia: Karageorghis 1979, Pls 40–1. The examples could be multiplied, especially from Ayia Irini. Some aspects of these votaries are discussed by Markoe 1987.

[11] See *RLA* I 205, VI 208; Hrouda 1965, 45 with Pl 7. Myres 1914, 195–6 discusses these Cypriot caps, referring to Hittite helmets but finding 'no precise parallel outside Cyprus'. Similar caps worn by kings: King Barrekab, Zincirli 8th century BC (Bittel 1976, Fig 305); King Nabonid, 556–539 BC (Orthmann 1975, 251) Here, as in the following notes, I shall not attempt an exhaustive documentation of relevant Oriental and/or Egyptian monuments, but rather illustrate my point by a limited number of pertinent references.

[12] Eg the statues *Atlas* I, Pls 45, 47–8, 50; Myres 1914 nos 1002, 1004, 1352–4, and especially no 1351 with the Syllabic inscription *ICS* 262 'τς παPίας'.

[13] Palaepaphos: KA 614, see Maier & Karageorghis 1984, 189 Fig 174. Cesnola Collection: *Atlas* I, Pls 19, 25, 48, 52, 67, 81, 86; Myres 1914, nos 1040–7, 1251–2, 1254–6. Michaelides Collection: *Chronique* 1968, 455, Fig 35, 456, Fig 36. Cyprus Collection Stockholm: *SCE* III Pl 206. Kazaphani: Karageorghis 1978, Pls 22.9; 36.25, 35, 42. Potamia: Karageorghis 1979, Pl 38.143. Collection E. Piot: Perrot & Chipiez 1885, 537, Fig 363.

[14] *RLA* I 202, VI 198, 208, 210; Hrouda 1965, 44 and Pl 6. Worn by Assurbanipal himself while out hunting: Parrot 1961, Fig 63; Frankfort 1970, Fig 211. The Persian king Dareios I: Ghirshman 1964, Fig 284. See also von Gall 1975.

[15] Palaepaphos: KA 248, see Maier & Karageorghis 1984, 185 Fig 172. The helmet may have had a painted decoration (as observed on several pieces of the Palaepaphos sculpture)—a possibility not definitely to be excluded. The small limestone head (*Chronique* 1975, 846, Fig 10) of unknown provenance represents the plain rather than the elaborate type. The terracotta head from Kazaphani (Karageorghis 1978, Pl 41.15) also seems to wear a double crown. All these representations are beardless. The limestone head from Aloa, published by Markoe (1987, 124, and Pl 42. 2–3), shows, however, an elaborate beard similar to the 'priest king' from Palaepaphos.

[16] Two wooden statues of Sesostris I show the two crowns separate: Vandersleyen 1975, Fig 154 and Pl 13. Double crowns: *ibid* Figs 86, 223, 229; Leclant 1980, Fig 346; 1981, Fig 77. As headdress of gods eg Leclant 1981, Fig 221. See generally Abu Bakr 1937.

[17] The two bronze statuettes from Ayia Irini, Inv. 1479 and 2758 (see *SCE* III, Pl 240.6–7) show the Egyptian Atef crown, as already does the seated statuette of a god from Ugarit: *Land des Baal* 1982 no 120 (14th/13th century). It does not seem advisable to consider small statuettes and figurines as decisive evidence for royal dress: the artist may have copied some Egyptian motif which took his fancy (see also Perrot & Chipiez 1885, 534). Thus the ivory sphinx from Salamis (Karageorghis 1969, Pl 5), wearing the Egyptian double crown with an Uraeus, can hardly be related to the regalia of the kings of Salamis; the identical motif appears, for instance, on an alabaster stele from Arados (6th-5th century BC), a terracotta plaquette from Ibiza (6th century), or an ivory plaquette from Nimrud (8th century BC; see *Phoenicians* 1988, 300, 347, 407). Life-size statues and coins, on the other hand, were bound to represent the correct regalia.

[18] Palaepaphos: KA 730, see above n 9; Golgoi (from the Cesnola Collection): *Atlas* I, Pls 33.212; 42.279 (= Myres 1914, no 1266); Pl 43.280 (= Myres 1914, no 1363). Without provenance: limestone heads de Ridder 1908, 67–8 nos 21–2; head of bronze statuette Dikaios 1961, Pl 25.1 (Figs 40.6, 7).

[19] *Atlas* I, Pl 43.280 (possibly). The crowns *Atlas* I, Pls 33.212 and 42. 279 are decorated with a rosette and lotus flower motifs. A decorated helmet, although not with proper scales, Leclant 1981, Fig 135 (29th Dynasty, *ca* 390 BC); a similar pattern of impressed circles on the helmet of terracotta heads from Salamis *SCE* IV.2, Pl 9, and from Potamia, Karageorghis 1978, Pl 39.109. The closest parallel seems to be, in a way, the vegetation god on a 12th century BC (?) relief from Assur: Parrot 1961, Fig 9.

[20] *Atlas* I, Pl 43.280. The small bronze head from the Cyprus Museum (see above n 17) shows (Uraeus?) snakes at the front of the Red Crown, the head from the Collection Clerq (above n 16) a winged solar disc. Egyptian royal crowns: Vandersleyen 1975, Figs 86, 175, 223, 229, Pl 17; Leclant 1980, Figs 134, 346; Leclant 1981, Figs 77, 125, 229; *Tutanchamun 1981*, 20, 34, 48, 70, 72, 83 etc. Yet the Uraeus also occurs frequently on the headdresses of gods such as Re, Horus and Seth.

[21] See eg Vandersleyen 1975, Figs 56 (Pyramidion of Amenhemet III), 105 (Horus-Tempel Edfu), 428 (Stele of prince Taktidamani); Leclant 1981, Figs 99, 103 (Stelai).

[22] See above n 9. A fairly close parallel is represented by the limestone slab from Chytroi, *Chronique 1970*, 342, Fig 12. Solar disc surmounting a stele at Golgoi: *ICS* 260; further: *Atlas* I, Pl 7.

[23] Coins: Masson 1982, 12–13; 'Urartian' helmet: Maier & Karageorghis 1984, Fig 162; Melqart-Stele KA 2144: Maier 1985, Pl 10.6.

[24] Frankfort 1948, 38–9, 57, 107–9, 131, 354; Bonnet 1971, 395, 845–6.

[25] Late Hittite: Bittel 1976, Fig 306. Assyrian: Orthmann 1975, Fig 232. Phoenicia: Jidejian 1968, Fig 104; *Phoenicians* 1988, 305.

[26] Assyria: Orthmann 1975, Figs 197, 212–3, 216, 221, 232. Pl 18; Parrot 1961, Figs 14, 39, 63–4, 76, 183; Persia: Ghirshman 1964, Figs 215, 226, 255, 284. Also on Late Hittite monuments: Bittel 1976, Figs 305, 327–8. An elaborate ceremonial beard is already worn by Puzur-Ishtar of Mari, see Barrelet 1974, 110 no F 128 with Fig 2 and Pl 5. For a detailed analysis of such beards see Markoe 1987.

[27] The other persons wearing plain or elaborate double crowns (above nn 15, 18) show with one exception (the Aloa head) either no beard at all or a close cropped beard; the same variety is found with the wearers of rosette diadems.

[28] The hypothesis seems plausible, but it would force us to assume that the head from Golgoi shown by A. Hermary (above 180–196) and the head from Aloa (above n 15) represent Paphian kings whose statues were erected outside Paphos, for reasons unknown to us.

[29] The statues in question are the three from Golgoi, see above n 12. Their skirts are decorated with Uraei, most elaborate *Atlas* I, Pl 42.279: the belt of the skirt shows a solar disc, above the Uraei appears a Medusa head and an Osiris eye. For the special type of skirt see Wilson 1974, 140. The differences of the pectorals seem to be of no consequence; a fragment from another statue with triple pectoral from Potamia: *Chronique 1968*, 454, Fig 34.

[30] Combination of both rosette diadem and belt: *Chronique 1968*, 455, Fig 35; *Atlas* I, Pls 25, 54; Myres 1914, nos 1040–7. No 1256 wears a belt tied with knotted strings. Several fragments of statues with rosette belt were found at Palaepaphos, such as KA 3 or KA 785.

[31] In Phoenicia symbols and dress elements of Egyptian gods and kings were adapted at an early time and used until the 4th century BC, see eg above n 15, or Parrot, Chébab & Moscati 1977, Figs 7, 29, 122; *Land des Baal* 1982, nos 120, 122; Jidejian 1968, 96 and Fig 104. The last-named stele of Yehawmilk (4th century BC) possibly also reproduces elements of Persian royal dress: Galling 1937, 47. Egyptian and Assyrian traits in the Golgoi statues were observed already by Perrot & Chipiez 1885, 530.

[32] Sumer: Frankfort 1948, 22–43. Kramer 1974, 174; Hooke 1958, 25–6. Hittites: Hooke 1958, 105–6; Cornelius 1974, 325.

[33] Egypt: Frankfort 1948, chapter 6; Assur: *ibid* 252–8, 265–6; Larsen 1974, 296, 299; Persia: Widengren 1959, 242–57.

[34] See Donner & Röllig 1966–69, nos 13 (late 6th century BC) and 11 (*ca* 350 BC). The royal inscriptions nos 1, 4–7, 9–10, 14–16, on the other hand, do not mention priesthood.

LIST OF REFERENCES

Atlas. L.P. di Cesnola (1885) *A Descriptive Atlas of the Cesnola Collection of Cypriote Antiquities in the Metropolitan Museum of Art, New York, I*. Boston.
Abu Bakr, (1937) *Untersuchungen über die altägyptischen Kronen*. Berlin.
Barrelet, M-Th. (1974) La "figure du roi", *in* Garelli 1974, 27–138.
Bittel, K. (1976) *Die Hethiter*. München.
Bonnet, H. (1971) *Reallexikon der ägyptischen Religionsgeschichte;*^{2}. Berlin.
Cesnola, L. Palma di (1879) *Cypern*. Jena.
Cornelius, F. (1974) Das hethitische Königtum, *in* Garelli 1974, 323–6.
Dikaios, P. (1961) *A Guide to the Cyprus Museum.*^{3} Nicosia.

Donner, H. & Röllig, W. 1966–69 *Kanaanäische und aramäische Inschriften I-III*.² Berlin.
Frankfort, H. (1970) *The Art and Architecture of the Ancient Orient.*⁴ Harmondsworth.
Frankfort, H. (1948) *Kingship and the Gods.* Chicago.
Gall, H. von (1975) Die grossköniglische Kopfbedeckung bei den Achämeniden, in *Proceedings of the IIIrd Annual Symposium on Archaeological Research in Iran 1974,* 219–225. Teheran.
Galling, K. (1937) Syrien in der Politik der Achämeniden. *Der Alte Orient 36,* Heft 3/4. Leipzig.
Garelli, P. ed (1974) *Le Palais et la Royauté. XIXᵉ Rencontre assyriologique internationale.* Paris.
Ghirshman, R. (1964) *Iran. Protoiranier, Meder, Achämeniden.* München.
Hooke, S.H. ed (1958) *Myth, Ritual and Kingship.* Oxford.
Hrouda, B. (1965) *Die Kulturgeschichte des assyrischen Flachreliefs.* Bonn.
Iliffe, J.H. & Mitford, T.B. (1952) Excavations at Aphrodite's Sanctuary of Paphos (1951). *Liverpool Bulletin 2,* 29–66.
James, E.D. (1959) The sacred kingship and the priesthood, in *Sacral Kingship,* 63–70.
Jidejian, N. (1968) *Byblos Through the Ages.* Beyrouth.
Karageorghis, V. (1969) *Salamis in Cyprus. Homeric, Hellenistic and Roman.* London.
Karageorghis, V. (1978) A "Favissa" at Kazaphani. *RDAC,* 156–96.
Karageorghis, V. (1979) Material from a sanctuary at Potamia. *RDAC,* 289–315.
Kramer, S.N. (1974) Kingship in Sumer and Akkad; the ideal king, *in* Garelli 1974, 163–76.
Labat, R. (1939) *Le caractére réligieuse de la royauté assyro-babylonienne.* Paris.
Land des Baal (1982) *Syrien—Forum der Völker und Kulturen.* Mainz.
Langdon, S.H. ed (1923) *Oxford Editions of Cuneiform Texts, I.* Oxford.
Larsen, M.T. (1974) The city and its king, *in* Garelli 1974, 285–300.
Leclant, J. (1980) *Aegypten. Zweiter Band: Das Grossreich.* München.
Leclant, J. (1981) *Aegypten. Dritter Band: Spätzeit und Hellenismus.* München.
Maier, F.G. (1985) *Alt-Paphos auf Cypern.* Mainz.
Maier, F.G. & Karageorghis, V. (1984) *Paphos.* Nicosia.
Markoe, G. (1987) A bearded head with conical cap from Lefkoniko: an examination of a Cypro-Archaic votary. *RDAC,* 119–25.
Masson, O. (1982) Notes de numismatique chypriote, III-V. *Rev Num 24,* 7–16.
Myres, J.L. (1914) *Handbook of the Cesnola Collection of Antiquities from Cyprus.* New York.
Orthmann, W. (1975) *Der Alte Orient.* Berlin.
Parrot, A. (1961) *Assur.* München.
Parrot, A., Chébab, M.H. & Moscati, S. (1977) *Die Phönizer.* München.
Perrot, G. & Chipiez, Ch. (1885) *Histoire de l'art dans l'Antiquité III: Phénicie-Cypre.* Paris.
Phoenicians. S. Moscati, ed (1988) *The Phoenicians.* Milan.
Posener, G. (1960) *De la divinité du Pharaon.* Paris.
de Ridder, A. (1908) *Collection Clerq V.* Paris.
RLA. Ebeling, E. & Meissner, B. *Reallexikon der Assyriologie.* Berlin-Leipzig.
Sacral Kingship 1959. *The Sacral Kingship. Studies in the History of Religions* (Supplement to *Numen*) IV. Leiden.
Tutanchamun 1981. Tutanchamun. Mainz.

Vandersleyen, C. (1987) *Das Alte Aegypten*. Berlin.
Widengren, G. (1959) The sacred kingship and the priesthood in *Sacral Kingship*, 242–57.
Wilson, V. (1974) The Kouklia Sanctuary. *RDAC*, 139–46.

Envoi

David Ridgway

Department of Archaeology, University of Edinburgh

I have been asked to contribute some concluding remarks from the outsider's point of view. As a refugee from Magna Graecia and Etruria, I will not presume either to summarize or to comment on all that I have just learnt about early society in Cyprus. Let me rather begin by admitting that your papers, discussions and posters have impressed me as consistently more exciting than those to which I am accustomed in the Italian peninsula. Why should this be? To a certain extent, of course, the grass is always greener in the next field. But after three extraordinarily informative days in your company, I am convinced that there is another and more substantial explanation: and I should like to take this opportunity of sharing it with you.

We all know that no excavation is complete until it is properly published. In Cyprus, the Director of the Department of Antiquities has turned this adage into a law that must be obeyed, and he has inspired obedience by his own magnificent example. The contrast with Italy is striking. There, lip-service apart, the definitive publication of excavations is not encouraged by the authorities to any extent that I have been able to detect in the last twenty-two years. More or less brilliant syntheses; hastily compiled and elusive exhibition catalogues; accounts of single categories (or even artefacts) divorced from their contexts; polemical interpretations, crystallizing into dogma, of selected evidence that is otherwise inaccessible: increasingly, such ephemera are all that we have to remind us of the major Italian sites, old and new. It is only exceptionally that a key peninsular toponym is also the title of a monograph that has been not only announced but also published and distributed in the normal way. You will, I think, be aware that Swedish scholars are in the van of such publishing activity as Italy receives at this level. Their *San Giovenale*, *Luni sul Mignone* and *Acquarossa* fascicules, along with your *Kition V*, *Palaepaphos-Skales*,

Khirokitia, Lemba I and many others have recently joined *Troy, Corinth* and *Hallstatt* in our libraries; the manuscripts of *Pithekoussai I* and *Pyrgi II* have been blocked since 1979 in an official pipeline that still, as I reported six years ago, 'shows no signs of bursting' (Ridgway 1982, 64). I hope you know how lucky you are to have so much banausic information about each other's sites, and I am not surprised that your discussions here have been livelier and more constructive than anything I have heard in recent years at conferences in Tuscany and Taranto.

Before you are overcome with pride in the virtuous behaviour implacably required of you by Dr Karageorghis, let me recall that no conference is complete until its proceedings are available. I trust that in this respect Cyprus will not copy Etruria, where the *Atti* of the May 1985 *Secondo Congresso Internazionale Etrusco* reached proof stage in April 1987 and currently show no signs of passing it. When these words appear in print, the world will know whether you have assisted your editor and publishers, in whom I have every confidence, to emulate or even surpass the achievements of your colleagues in Sardinia, whence the proceedings of not one but two impressive conferences (Balmuth 1987; Lilliu, Ugas & Lai 1987) reached me within a year of their occurrence in late 1986—to enhance my appreciation of at least two papers I have heard here. But then, Late Bronze Age metallurgy is not the only field in which Sardinia is more advanced than the adjacent peninsula. And the fact that Sardinia has been mentioned frequently and for good reason in a conference about Cyprus brings me to another point that I think is worth making at this stage.

There has always been something that is singularly attractive about the archaeology of islands. In the period so charmingly evoked for us now by Elizabeth Goring (1988, 1–41), I suspect that many of our predecessors selected Cyprus, Crete, Sicily and Sardinia for prolonged attention in the vain hope that physical delimitation by water had reduced problems and prospects to manageable dimensions. Nearer our own time, an equally ill-founded preference for closed systems promoted archaeology briefly to the status of a seemingly unimpeachable technique for establishing universal laws about human behaviour—in spite of the fact that residence in closed systems did not allow ancient peoples to travel, to exchange ideas, to look at each other's arts and crafts, or indeed to do any of the things that make human beings human. One anguished statement from this period even contrived to rebuke Gordon Childe for having correctly perceived the decisive role of Mycenaean influence and trade in the development of the Italian Bronze Age: 'This view, although undoubtedly 'diffusionist', is supported by the evidence *now available*' (Renfrew & Whitehouse 1974, 359; my italics).

Happily, we no longer have to confine our research interests to phantoms 'who do not live, but just cower in ecological niches, get caught in catchment areas, and are entangled in redistributive systems' (Piggott 1985,146). Perversely enough, my own view is that there is in fact a grain of truth in those words as a description of most societies, ancient and modern: but nowhere are they ever likely to constitute the whole truth. I have found much to support this conviction in your conference, where I have seen cultural, social and political change depending on both internal and external factors. Better still, I have heard you freely assessing the respective proportions in which those factors are present according to the specific merits of each case. Cyprus, like—and in the Late Bronze Age, *with*—Sardinia, has reminded archaeologists everywhere that the reconstruction of early trading patterns is fundamental to the understanding of early society.

Shortly to conclude. I have observed your progress over the last few days with what I can only describe as envy for the quantity, quality and variety of the archaeological evidence you have at your disposal. Envy, too, is what I feel for your good fortune in another way: I mean the Department of Antiquities, and Dr Karageorghis' wise administration through it of all these good things for Cyprus and for science. For the first and I suspect the last time in my life, I know that I can speak for both the City and the University of Edinburgh and thank you for coming so far to share your good fortune with us. Thank you, too, for leaving us a tangible souvenir of your visit to the Royal Museum of Scotland: *Aphrodite's Island* (Goring 1988, 43-93), which joins two other exhibitions currently open to the archaeologically minded citizens of Edinburgh and their guests, *Gold of the Pharaohs* (Coutts 1988) and *Piecing together the past* (Watkins 1987). Egypt and the Diamond Jubilee of our University Department have brought us from winter to what passes locally for spring; Cyprus will do much to alleviate the coming rigours of the Scottish summer.

Again on behalf of Edinburgh, and finally, I would like to thank those local heroes who caused you to come here by convincing the sponsoring institutions that their great generosity would not be misplaced. As an interested bystander, I can confirm that neither the conference nor the exhibition was achieved by the unaided force of gravity. Two other natural forces have been at work on your behalf for a long time. They are known to us all as Eddie and Elizabeth, and Edinburgh will long be grateful for their and your part in this memorable event. So, I am sure, will Aphrodite Herself: into Whose care I commend those of you who are leaving us now for the British Museum, which is in the heart of the biggest Cypriot city in the world.

LIST OF REFERENCES

Balmuth, M. S. ed (1987) *Nuragic Sardinia and the Mycenaean world. Studies in Sardinian Archaeology III* [= proceedings of the colloquium held at the American Academy in Rome, September 1986] *(BAR Int Ser 387)*. Oxford.

Coutts, H. ed (1988) *Gold of the Pharaohs: Catalogue of the exhibition of Treasures from Tanis*. Edinburgh.

Goring, E. (1988) *A Mischievous Pastime: Digging in Cyprus in the nineteenth* century (with a catalogue of the exhibition 'Aphrodite's Island: art and archaeology of ancient Cyprus'). Edinburgh.

Lilliu, G., Ugas, G. & Lai, G. eds (1987) *La Sardegna nel Mediterraneo tra il secondo e il primo millennio a.C. Atti del II Convegno di studi . . . Selargius-Cagliari, novembre 1986*. Cagliari.

Piggott, S. (1985) Review of *Prehistoric Europe* (T. Champion, C. Gamble, S. Shennan & A. Whittle). *Antiquity 59*, 145–6.

Renfrew, C. & Whitehouse, R. (1974) The Copper Age of peninsular Italy and the Aegean. *BSA 69*, 343-90.

Ridgway, D. (1982) Archaeology in South Italy, 1977–81. *A Rep London 1981–82*, 63–83.

Watkins, T. F. (1987) *From the Pieces of the Past: an introduction to archaeology*. Edinburgh.

Index

Note: Numbers in italics refer to maps and illustrations.

Achaean colonisation, 53, 57, 134, 136–7, 165–6, 298, 328–33
Achna, 258
Aeschylus, ix
after-life, Bronze Age belief, 24, 97–8, 103
Aghios Giorghios, 364, 370, 371, 372
agriculture
    Bronze Age, 22–3, 24, 39–40, 41, 43–51
    Neolithic, 60, 72
'Agur, geometric mosaics, *288*
Akhziv
    ware, 200, 257, 260, 263
Akrotiri-Aetokremnos, 12
Alaas, necropolis, 55–6, 106, 329, 332–3
Alambra-Mouttes, 14, 17, *19*, 20, 63, 197–8
Alasia/Alashiya, as Cyprus, 202–3, 207, 217, 299, 300, 303, 310n.
Alassa-Pano Mandilaris
    copper industry, 302
    Late Cypriot Bronze Age, 32–41, *33, 34, 35*
Amathonte, 257, 260
Amathus, 247, 267, 268, 295, 332, 346, 356
Ambelikou-Aletri, 14, *21*, 21, 28, 300
Amrit, 257, 258, 259, 262, 263
amulets, 90, 108, 204
analysis
    chemical, 197
    cluster, 150
    petrographic, 197
    'presence', 60
    regional, 142, 143–4, 146, 147
Anatolia, as source of settlers, 68
ancestor cult, 110, 116
Angel, J.L., 67, 74
animals, Bronze Age portrayal, 156–7
anthropogeography, 143–6
Antioch, supremacy over Cyprus, 284–8
Antioch mosaics
    geometric panel, *289*
    Narcissus panel, *276*, 277, 280
    Nicostratos panel, *278*, 280
    Perseus and Andromeda panel, *279*, 280
Aphrodite cult, 123–4, 140, 267, 376–7, 380
Apliki ware, 306
Apliki-Karamallos, 54, 299, 301, 306–9
Appadurai, Arjun, 337–8
Arados, 180
Archaic period
    portrayal of hunting, 171
    terracotta production, 266–70
architecture

Aceramic Neolithic, 4, 12, 112
    Bronze Age, *19*, 20–1, 26, 46–51, 63, 64, 165
    Byzantine, 288
    Chalcolithic, 9, 12, 62, 84–5
    Late Bronze Age, 35–9, 53, 319
    military, 165
Aristotle, on kingship, 376
Arsos, 258, 261
Ashdod ware, 200
Astarte figurines, 266
Åström, Paul, 166, 202–7
Athana Lindia, 261
Athienou, 54, 301–2
Avigad, N., 259
Awka'i, mosaic of Leontios, *285*, 286
Ayia Anna tou Psephala, 266
Ayia Irini sanctuary, 257, 266–9, 332
Ayios Dhimitrianos, 258
Ayios Epiktitos-Vrysi, 9, 11, 91, 110–11, *111, 112*, 113
Ayios Epiphanios basilica, mosaics, 290
Ayios Philon mosaics, 290
Ayios Yeorios, mosaics, *285*, 286, 288, *289*, 290
Ayious, *see* Kalavasos–Ayious

Baal figurines, 266
Bachmann, H.-G., 306
Baird, Douglas, 9
Balthazar, Judy Weinstein, 300
Bamberger, M. *et al.*, 305
Bambouler, 365, 366, 367, 368, 372, 373
Barlow, Jane A., 197–8;
    & P. Idziak, 197
Base Ring wares, 37, 53, 160, 167–8, 218, 219, 220, 293, 318
Bass, George, 222, 227, 232, 269
Bates, O., 218
Batsalos, 366
Baurain, C. & Darcque, P., 330
Beckman, G., 117
Beer, Cecilia, 140, 346
Belgiorno, M.R., 157
Bellapais-Vounous, 24, 26, 157, 158
Benson, J.L., 56
Bergoffen, Celia, 293
Bergonzi, G., 239n.
Bichrome III ware, 171–6, *172, 173*, 268, 294, 330
Binford, Lewis, 343
birth rituals, 117–20

Index

Bisi, Anna Maria, 256–64
Bithia, 251
Black Slip-and-Combed ware, *149*
Black Topped ware, *149*
Black-on-Red ware, 176, *177*, 200, 294, 356
Bliss, F.J., 256
Boardman, John, 172–3
Bolger, Diane L., 142–51
Bomford figurine, 127, *128*, 130–3, 137
bones, wormian, 68–9
bones, animal, in burials, 77–8, 84, 101, 103
Bradley, Richard, 100
Braudel, F., x
British Kouklia Expedition, 82–3, 88
Bronze Age
　Early, sites, 14–16, *15*, 18
　transition period, 325–34
Bronze Age, Late
　copper industry, 298–311
　evidence, 53–4
　see also ceramics; society
Brunner–Traut, E., 121
Bucchero ware
　Handmade, 160, *163*
　Wheelmade, 160, *163*, 165, 167
Buchholz, H.-G., 173–4, 250
Buddysò, 250
Buikstra, 100–1
bull, and ritual, 37–8, 41, 123
burials
　Aceramic Neolithic, 6–7, 66, 69, 71–80
　Bronze Age, 24, *25*, 25–8, 316
　Chalcolithic, 82–93
　chamber tombs, 328
　communal, 39, 101–2
　evidence from, 67–8, 95–8, 106, 316
　evidence of Mycenaean influence, 328–33
　as evidence of status, 341–3, 344–60
　Late Bronze Age, 35, 39–40, 41, 50, 52–3, 54–6, 95–104, 165
　metal in, 26–7, 325–32, 351–3
　orientation, 73–4, *75*, 77
　primary/secondary, 6, 100–2
　ritual, 116–17, 120
　shaft graves, 84, 165, 207
　see also cremation; pit burials; *dromoi*; *stomia*
Byblos, 80, 249, 257, as origin of settlers, 68–9, 80
Byzantine art, 272, 288–90

Cadogan, Gerald, 43–51, 218, 303
Cala Golone, 249
Camiros, 261
Çatal Hüyük, compared with Tenta, 4, 6–7, 68, 110, 116
Catling, H.W., 16, 123, 127, 131, 143, 146, 166, 218, 232–3

Caubet, A., 209–16
　& Yon, M., 261
Cauvin, J., 80
ceramics
　Bronze Age, 18, 20, 48, 53–5, 57, 197–8, 199
　Chalcolithic, 148–51, 315
　as evidence of trade, 218–24, 231–2
　Late Bronze Age, 293; continuity and change, 160–8
　Late Neolithic, 150
cereals, 23, 60–1
Cesnola, A. Palma di, 173, 331
　collection, 190
Chapman, R. & Randsborg, K., 104n.
chariots, terracotta, 267–8
charms, figurines as, 108, 120
childbirth, representations of, 267, 270
Childe, Gordon, 393
Childs, William, 344
Chios, 261
Christian era, mosaics, 286
Christou, D., 82–93
chronology
　Aceramic Neolithic, 8
　Late Bronze Age (LC IIIA), 160, 165, 218, 233
　Middle Bronze Age, 197–8
Chytroi, 140
Clark, D.V., Cowie, T. & Foxon, A., 95
clays
　for pottery, 53, 86–8, 149–50, 197–8
　for terracottas, 269–70
Close–Line RW ware, 149–50
Coarse ware, 20, 86
　painted, *149*, 149
Coldstream, J.N., 325–34, 344–5, 356
Colledge, S., 60–1
Collon, D., 155, 158
Combed ware, 88, *149*, 150
copper
　Bronze Age working, 18, 24, 28, 39, 40–1, 46–50, 217, 232, 315
　early industry, 300
　in faience glaze, 212
　Late Bronze Age industry, 298–311
　Middle Bronze Age, 316–17
　in ornaments, *92*, 92
　and religion, 133
　smelting technology, 28, 39–40, 302–6, 309–10, 320
　and social organisation, 318–19
correlation model, 64
Cos, Cypriot links with, 294–5
Courtois, J.-C., 103
cradleboards, use of, 67–8, 69
Cree F.de, 200
cremation, 333
Crete, Cypriot contact with, 218, 221

Crouwel, J.H., 257
crown, double, 383–6
cruciforms, picrolite, 82–4, 88–90, *89*, *91*, 122–3
cults, domestic, 36–9, 110–11
culture, evidence from, 66–7
culture-areas, 144, 145–6
currency, convertible, 103–4
cylinder seals
   as evidence of trade, 221–2, 232, 237n., 318
   Old Babylonian, 153–8, *154*, *155*
Cypriots, earliest, origins, 66–70
Cypro-Geometric period, 54, 106
Cypro-Mycenaean wares, 53, 54–5, 57
Cyprus Department of Antiquities, vii, 84, 85, 92

Daniel, Glyn, 142
Decorated Late Cypriot III (Submycenaean) ware, 53, 54, 160–7, *161*, *163*, 221
deities
   foreign, 130, 133–4
   portrayal, *see* Bomford figure; Ingot god
   syncretic, 134–7
Demas, M., 298
determinism
   cultural, 145–7, 151
   environmental, 144–5
Dhali-Kafkallia, 14, 17, 21
Dhikomo, 17
differentiation, social, 50–1, 62, 112–13, 135–6
differentiation, social
   Aceramic Neolithic, 4
   Bronze Age, 25, 27–8, 41
   Iron Age, 344–60
   Late Bronze Age, 316, 325–34
diffusionism, 144–6, 393
Dikaios, P., 71, 74, 75, 78, 88, 92, 146, 147, 165–6, 298–301, 304
Diodorus, 377
Domurad, Melodie, 66–70
Douglas, M., 136
Douglas, Mary & Isherwood, Baron, 337, 341
dromoi, 26–7, 39–40, 54, 56, 328, 331–3
Dupont-Sommer, A., 372
Dunnell, R.C., 137n.
Durkheim, E., 108

East Mediterranean, influence on mosaic art, 277–88
Eboli, Cypriot trade with, 219, *220*
Egypt
   Bronze Age trade with, 203–6, 300
   Late Cypriot pottery, 293

Eileithyia, figurines of, 267
Elgavish, J., 259
elites, 336–43
   Bronze Age, 28, 41, 111, 133, 135–6, 199, 319, 322, 325–34
   Iron Age, 344–60
Empros Temenon, 267, 270
Enkomi, viii, 41, 49, 54–5, 134, 248, 260, 261
   and copper industry, 298–305, 307, 309, 319
   evidence of transition, 165–6, 167
envaluation, 337, 356
Episkopi-Bamboula, 36, 40, 56
Episkopi-Phaneromeni, 14, 16–17, 21, *22*, 23
Erimi Culture
   sites, 147–51, *148*
   ware, 16, 87–8, 148–9
   see also Kissonerga–Mosphilia; Kissonerga–Mylouthkia; Lemba–Lakkous; Paphos
Erimi-Pamboules, 11, 16, 85, 90
Evagoras I of Salamis, 190, 195, 273, 366, 368
Evans, A., 109
Evans-Pritchard, E., 120
Evretou-Amakharos, 147

Fadda, F. Ausilia, 228, 233–7
faience, Bronze Age, 204, 207, 209–16, 316
family structure, Bronze Age, 21, 41
Fasnacht, W., 310n.
fertility rituals, 90, 119–20, 122, 123–4, 135, 140
figurines
   Bronze Age, 24, 36, 37, *38*, 41, 127, *128*
   bull, 37–8, *38*, 41
   Chalcolithic, 88, 90, 113, 113–22, *118*, *119*, 151
   as evidence for religion, 108–22
   Geometric period, 293–4
   life-size, 268–9
   Neolithic, 6, 78–80, 110–13
   Phoenician influence on, 266–70
   see also Bomford figurine; Ingot god
fish, trade in, 203–4
Flannery, K.V., 72
food
   control of production, 49–50
   as grave deposits, 102–3
   prehistoric plants, 60–1
foundation offerings, 117
Frankel, D., 16, 17–18, 150
Frobenius, Leo, 144, 145
Furumark, A., 55, 160–5, 167

Gaber, Pamela, 344

Gale, Nöel & Stos-Gale, Zofia, 224, 232, 238n.
games, 26, 204
gaming stones, 18
gender, and difference in burial customs, 72–5, 76
genre scenes, 23–4, 26, 108–9, 266–7
geography, and settlement patterns, 142–6, 151
geometric mosaics, *288*
Geometric period
   trade, 294–5
   vase-painting, 171–8
Geometric pottery, Greek, 356
Gjerstad, E., 19, 20, 52, 142–3, 146, 160, 172, 262, 294
   & Hill, 261
Glossy Burnished ware, 149
glyptics, Bronze Age, 153–8, 222
Goedicke, H., 203
Goff, B.L., 131
gold, 40, 204–6, *205*
Golgoi, 140, 180, 185, 190, 193
Goodenough, E.R., 131
Goring, Elizabeth, 95–104, 393
Graebner, Fritz, 144
grave goods
   bronze, 328–9, 353
   Bronze Age, 26–8
   Chalcolithic, 85
   as evidence, 97–8
   Iron Age, 346–53, 354–6, 358–60
   Late Bronze Age, 40, 41, 56, 97, 102–3, 318, 328–32
   metal, 26–7, 351–3, *352*, 355–6
   Neolithic, 7, 75
Greece
   Cypriot influence, 299
   influence on art, 273–7, 355–7
   trade with Cyprus, 273, 294–5, 355
Grey Minyan ware, 206
grey ware, wheelmade, 221
Grotta Su Benticheddu, 249
Grotte Pirosu-Su Benatzu, 245
Gubel, E., 260
Guzzo Amadasi, M.G., 363, 370

Hadjisavvas, S., 32–41
Hala Sultan Tekke, 41, 49, 54, 204–7, 298
   copper industry, 302
Halicarnasse, 193
Hama, 249
Hatcher, Ellen, 216n.
Hawkes, Christopher, ix
Helbaek, Hans, 203
Hermary, Antoine, 180–96, 389n.
Herodotus, ix, 57, 180, 385–6
Herscher, E., 317
Hesychius, 377

Hill & Gjerstad, E., 261
Hodder, I.R., 137n., 151, 343
Hulin, Linda Carless, 127–37
humans, Bronze Age portrayal, 156–8
hunting scenes
   mosaics, *281*, 281–3, *282*, *283*, *284*
   vase-paintings, 171–8

Iacovou, Maria, 52–7
Idalion, 140, 168, 180, 185, 190, 193, 270, 344, 346, 363, 365, 366
Idaean cave seal, *120*, 120
impasto ware, 221
Ingot god, 117, 127–34, *129*, 137
ingots
   bun, 28, 224, 228, 237, 304
   miniature, 41
   ox-hide, 38, 47, 224–7, *225*, *226*, 228, 231, 232, 237, 300, 320
iron
   industry, 227, 346
   trade in, 232
   use in faience, 212
Iron Age, Early, 256–64, 303
   evidence, 54, 56–7, 106
Isocrates, ix, 190, 366

jewellery
   Chalcolithic, 88–91
   Late Bronze Age, 102–4, 318, 329, 332, 345

Jones, A.H., 346
Jones, Alice, 341
Jones, R.E., 219
Jones, R.E. & Day, P.M., 221
Jones, W.H.S., 68

Kaczmarczyk, A., 209–16
Kaczmarczyk, A. & Hedges, R., 209
Kalavasos Village, tombs, 2, 27, 317–18, 319
Kalavasos-Ayious, Chalcolithic site, 9–11, *10*, 12
Kalavasos-Kokkinoyia/Pamboules, 9
Kalavassos-Ayios Dhimitrios, viii, 41, 48–9, 52, 113, 319
   Building X, 43, 320–3, *321*
   copper industry, 302, 317, 319–20, 322–3
   Tomb 11, 96, 98–104, *99*, 207, 318–19
Kalavassos-Tenta, Aceramic Neolithic site, 2–8, *5*, 71, 78, 109–10
Kalohorio-Khalandrikas, 14
Kalopsidha, *19*, 20–1, 25, 63, 203, 299
Kaloriziki, 56, 200, 328–30, 332–3
Karageorghis, J., 109, 110, 127, 173, 258
Karageorghis, V., 166, 167, 172, 196, 198, 204, 219, 258, 260, 298, 309, 323n., 325, 331, 346, 363, 393–4

Karmi-Palealona, 155, 156
Kaş shipwreck, 217, 221, 222–4, 232
Kathari, 364, 365
Kazaphani, favissa, 269
Keswani, Priscilla, 104n., 336
Khirokitia, Aceramic Neolithic settlement, 4–6, 7, 66–70, 71–80, 91, 110
Kilian, Klaus, 218
kingdoms, Cypriot, xi, 303, 325, 336, 360, 376
kingship, sacral, 41, 376–89
Kissonerga-Mosphilia, 12, 16, 18, 60, 62, *111*, 113–22, *118*, 149–51
  building model, *114*, 114–16, 117, 123
Kissonerga-Mylouthkia, 11, 12, 60
Kiti, 369, 370
Kition, 49, 53–4, 56, 121, 166–7, 215, 261, 263, 269, 332, 363–374
  Classical administration, 363–74
  copper industry, 302, 303
  Phoenician colony, 266
Kling, Barbara, 160–9, 306
Knapp, A.B., 28, 133, 137, 336
Kotchati model, 24, 123
Kouklia, 123, 167, 176, 248
Kouklia-Skales, 247
Kourion, 56, 117, 260, 267–70
  Achilles Mosaic, 277
  geometric mosaics, 286, *287*
  gladiatorial mosaics, 284
Kourion-Bamboula
  copper industry, 302
  tombs, 332, 333
kourotrophoi, 140, 268, 270
Krini, 17
Kroeber, Alfred, 145–6
Kulturkreis School, 144, 145

labour, division of, Late Bronze Age, 41, 51
Lang, A., 109
language, Greek, 57
Lapithos, copper industry, 300, 346
Lapithos-Kastros, tombs, 332
Lapithos-Plakes, 332
Lapithos-Vrysi tou Barba, 17, 26, 27–8, 270
Late Minoan ware, 206
Le Brun, A., 7, 71–80
Le Mort, F., 72
Lemba Archaeological Project, 147–51
Lemba-Lakkous, 11, 12, 18, 60, 62, 63, 85, 109, *111*, 149–50
  Building 1, 122–4
Levant
  as source of settlers, 68, 133–7, 166
  trade with, 256–64, 330
Levanto-Helladic ware

LC, III 218–19
LC IIC, 160, 162–5
Libya, Cypriot trade with, 218
Lipinski, E., 258
literacy, Late Bronze Age, 40, 41, 47, 57, 318, 321–2
Liverani, M., 310
Lo Schiavo, Fulvia, 217–39, 245, 248
Lo Schiavo, F., Macnamara, E. & L. Vagnetti, 244, 249
location, factors in, 5–6, 16–17, 146–7, 319
Lorenz, K., 110
lost-wax technique, 227
Loulloupis, M.C., 171–8
Lycie, 190, 195

Maa-Palaeokastro, viii, 36, 54, 298, 301
  copper industry, 301–2
McKerrell, H., 209
Macnamara, Ellen, 230
Maddin, Professor, 47
magic, evidence for, 108, 120, 204
Maier, F.G., 84, 344, 376–89
mainland, comparison with
  Aceramic Neolithic, 4–5, 7–8, 109
  Bronze Age, 199
  Chalcolithic, 11, 113, 116–17
mainland contact
  Aceramic Neolithic, 4, 8, 12, 80
  Late Bronze Age, 53, 165–6, 199
Makmish, 256, 257, 259
Malinowski, B., 120
manganese ores, in faience, 212
Mari-Mesovouni, Aceramic Neolithic site, 2, 5, 6, 78
Marinatos, N., 110
Marion, tombs, 273, 332, 344
Maroni-Vournes, 43–51, *44*, 52, 80
  Ashlar Building, 43–9, *45*
  copper industry, 46, 49, 302
  West Building, 47
Marsa Matruch, Cypriot finds, 218
Masson, O., 108, 137, 364
  & Mitford, T.B., 180
  & Sznycer, M., 369, 372–3
Matthäus, Hartmut, 244–52
'Megaron' temple, Nuoro, 228, 233–7, *234*, *235*
Megiddo, 249, 262
Meladhia, 147
Mellaart, J., 116
Meniko sanctuary, 257, 258, 266
Merkel, John, 238n.
Merrillees, R.S., ix, 108, 202, 300, 303, 310n.
Merrillees, R.S. & Merrillees, P.H., 153–8, 293
Mersinaki, 259

metallurgy, Late Bronze Age, 39, 40, 41, 46–9, 53, 224–32, 298–311
metopism, 68–9
Meyza, Henryk, 106
Michaelides, D., 272–90
migrations, cultural, 144
Miliou RW ware, 149
Miliou-Rhodaeos, 147, 149–51
Miller, Daniel, 339
Mitford, T.B. & Masson, O., 180
Mitsingites, Bronze Age cemetery, 317
Monochrome ware, 293
Monte Sa Idda, 248, 252n.
Morris, Chr., 173
Morris, D., 24, 108–9, 122, 157
Morris, Ian, 343
mosaics, 272–90
  geometric panels, 286–8, *287*, *288*
Moscati, S., 256
mould, use of, 266–8, 270
Muhly, J.D., 47, 133, 137, 298–311
Mureybet, 80
Mycenae
  and copper industry, 301
  settlers from, 133–7, 166, 325–8, 332
Mycenaean ware, 40, 322
  IIIB, 160, 162, 165–6
  IIIC, 53, 164, 165–6
Myers, J.L., 387n.
Myers, J.L. & Ohnefalsch-Richter, M., 146
Myrtou-Pighades, 32, 47, 49, 301
  copper industry, 301–2
mythology, portrayed in mosaics, 277–80

Natoufien, 80
Naucratis, 261, 262
Nea Paphos mosaics
  Birth of Dionysos panel, 279
  bust of Summer, *278*, 280
  Cassiopeia panel, 279–80
  geometric panels, 283–4, 286
  hunting scenes, *281*, 281–2
  Icarios panel, 279
  Narcissus panel, *275*, 280
  Phaedra and Hippolytos panel, *280*, 280
  Rape of Ganymede panel, 277
  Scylla panel, 272–3, *273*
necklaces
  Bronze Age, 207
  Chalcolithic, 82, 85, 88–9, *89*
Negbi, O., 52, 131
New Archaeology, 95
Nicosia-Ayia Paraskevi, Old Babylonian seal, 153–8
Niebuhr, H.R., 136
Nitovikla, 17

offering-bearers, figurines, 268
Ohnefalsch-Richter, M., 173
Olsson, Ingrid, 300
Orbe, hunting scenes mosaics, *283*, 283
Oristano, 245
O'Shea, J., 27, 95–6, 104n.
Ougarit, 369, 370; see also Ras Shamra *and* Ugarit
Ovgoros, 257
Oxford Bowl, 24

Pader, E.-J., 96–7
painting
  ceramic, Bronze Age, 23–4
  Cypro-Geometric vase-painting, 171–8
  wall, Neolithic, 6, 71, 78, 109–10
Palaepaphos, 41, 53–4, 56, 180, 200, 263, 325, 344, 346, 380, 383
Palaepaphos Survey Project, 17
Paliotaverna site, 32–4, 41
Panayia Angeloktistos mosaics, 290
Panayia Kanakaria mosaics, 290
Panayia Kyra mosaics, 290
Paphos
  as cultural entity, 147–51
  sacral kingship, 376, 377–80, 384–6
  see also Erimi Culture; Kissonerga-Mosphilia; Kissonerga-Mylouthkia; Lemba-Lakkous
Paraskevas, Mr, 309
Patriki, 269
paving, Late Bronze Age, 36, 221
Peltenburg, Edgar, ix–xi, 11, 12, 92, 108–24, 147, 149–50, 206–7, 215, 300
pendants
  Bronze Age, 204–6, *205*, 207, 329
  Chalcolithic, 82–5, 88–90, *90*, *91*, 114, 122
Peyia–Elia tou Vatani, 150
phalli, 90–1, *92*, 110, 112
Philia Culture, 14, 16, 18, *149*, 151
Philia-Drakos A, 11, 113
Philip, Graham, 199
Philippi, hunting scenes mosaics, *282*, 282–3
Philousa-Koprikoes, 147
Phoenicians
  influence on Cypriot terracotta production, 266–70
  role of, viii, 233
Pieridou, A., 173
Piggott, S., 393
Pindar, 277
Piraeus, Scylla mosaic, 273–6, *274*
pit burials, 6–7, 71–2, 80, 332
pit-dwellings, 9
Plain White ware, 38, 86

Wheelmade, 37, 160, *161*, *163*, 164, 165, 167
plough, elbow, 24
politics
  Iron Age, 360
  Late Bronze Age, 57, 302–3, 310
Pollock, Susan, 337, 339
population
  Bronze Age, 16, 18, 123, 315–17
  changes, ix–x, 12, 52, 165–7
  earliest, 66–70
  as heterogeneous, 7
  shifts, 53–6, 123, 130
Porada, E., 158
Portugali, Y. & Knapp, A.B., 203, 218, 294
possibilism, 144–5
Potamia, 190
pottery, *see* ceramics, *and individual wares*
Pritchard, J.B., 261
Proto-White Painted ware, 52, 54–6, 57
Pulak, Cemal, 222
Pyla-Kokkinokremos, 298, 301

Rabar, P., 310n.
Ras Shamra, 199, 248
  as origin of settlers, 68–9
Ratzel, Friedrich, 143–5
RB/B ware, 149
Red on Black ware, 18, *149*
Red Lustrous ware, 40, 84, 86–7, 102, 218, 318
Red Polished wares, 14, 18, 88, 123, *149*, 151, 157, 218, 316
  composition, 197–8
Red Slip ware, 330
Red-on-White ware, 82, 84, 85–8, *86*, *87*, 116, *149*
Reese, David S., 204
regalia, Paphian kings, ix, *378–9*, 380–6, *381*, *382*, *384–5*
regionalism, 18, 142–51, 303, 309–10, 317
religion
  Aceramic Neolithic, 6, 109–10
  Bronze Age, 20–1, 24, 123–4
  Chalcolithic, 90–1, 112–23
  Late Bronze Age, 36–9, 41, 133–4
  and metallurgy, 322
  pre-Bronze Age, 108–9
Renfrew, C., 109, 111, 121, 337, 339
Renfrew, C. & Whitehouse, R., 393
Reshef-Apollon, 190
Ridgway, David, 392–5
rites of passage, 339, *343*, 343, 344
ritual, and religion, 109–10, 112–17, 120–3, 151
Rose, Mark, 204
Rude Style ware, 165–6, 167, 219

Rupp, David W., 336–60
Rutkowski, B., 108, 122

sacrifice, evidence of, 77–8, 84–5
Salamine, 189, 193, 258, 366, 368, 373
Salamis, 55, 56
Salzmann, D., 276
sanctuaries
  Archaic period, 267–8
  Chalcolithic, 121
  Late Bronze Age, 32–4, *36*, 36–7, 41, 55
Sarama-Katavlaka, 147
S'Arcu é is Forras, 227, 228, 233–7, *234*, *235*
Sarepta, 261
San Francesco, 249
San Vero Milis, 250
Sardara-Sant'Anastasia, 246–9, 252
Sardinia, Cypriot trade with, 220–1, 224–33, 244–53, 394
Sa Sedda e Sos Carros, 249
S. Maria in Paulis, 245
S. Vittoria di Serri, 251
Satricum, 247
Schaar, Kenneth W., 63
Schmidt, G., 256, 260
Schmidt, Fr Wilhelm, 144
script, Cypro-Syllabic, 57
sculpture, stone, Bronze Age, 156
Semple, Ellen Churchill, 144–5
Serra Orrios, 248
Shaffer, Kathryn M., 64
Sherratt, E.S. & Crouwel, J.H., 167
Shiqmona, 259, 260, 263
shrines
  Chalcolithic, 121–2, 151
  Late Bronze Age, 37–8, 47, 110
Sicily, Cypriot trade with, 219
Sidon, 180, 190, 195, 251, 257
Sinda, 54
Sinnhuber, Karl, 142
Sjöberg, G., 134
Sjöqvist, E., 160, 165, 167
Skales, cemetery, 176, 325–33, 346
skeletal material, as evidence, 66–70
skull, deformation, 7, 67–9, 74
slags, copper, 37, 39–40, 299, 301–6, *307*, *308*, 320
Smith, M.A., 341, 346, 355
Snodgrass, A., 53, 345–6
society
  Aceramic Neolithic period, 4–5, 7–8, 12
  Bronze Age, 14–29, 52–7, 98–104, 151, 315–23; transition period, 325–34
  Ceramic Neolithic, 9
  Early Chalcolithic, 9–11, 12–13, 151
  Iron Age, 57, 325, 344–60

Middle Bronze Age, 315–16
Sørensen, Lone Wreidt & Lund, John, 294
Sotira-Kaminoudhia, 14, 18–20, *19*, 21, 23, 63, 69, *111*, 112–13, 315
Sotira-Teppes, 9, 11, 18, 150
Souskiou-Vathyrkakas, Chalcolithic cemetery, 62, 82–93, 149
South, Alison, 2, 98, 303, 315–23
sphinx, throne figurines, 266
Stanley Price, N., 112, 143, 181
statuary, votive, 140, 380–3
status symbols, 97, 337–41
   Bronze Age, 27–8, 206–7, 328–34
   Iron Age, 344, 349–60
Stech, T. *et al.*, 346
Steinberg, A. & Koucky, F., 303–4, 305, 309
Stern, E., 256, 259
Stewart, J. & Trendall,, 146
Stewart, James, 14, 18, 157
Stewart, Jennifer, 149
stomia, 39, 84
stone goods, Aceramic Neolithic, 8, 75
stones, in burials, 7, 74–7, *76*
Stubbings, F.H., 164
style, and interpretation of objects, 130–3, 149, 153, 155, 157–8
Su Igante, 249–50
Su Nuraxi, 250
Swedish Cyprus Expedition, 168, 346
Swiny, Stuart, 8, 12, 14–29, 300, 315
syncretism, 131, 134–7
Sznycer, M., 363, 368, 370
   & Masson, O., 369, 372–3

Tacitus, 277
Tadasuni-Oristano, 251
Talmon, Y., 136
Tamassos-Phrangissa, 190, 363, 364
tambourine-holder figurines, 266, 268
Taramelli, A., 246
Taylor, Joan du Plat, 306–7, 309
Teixidor, J., 363, 364
Tell Dan, 261, 263
Tell el-Yahudiyeh ware, 199
Tel esh-Shar'a, 261
Tel es-Safi, 256
Tel Keisan, 259
temper selection studies, 150
temple-boys, 140
temples, 123, 172
terracotta
   Early Iron Age, 256–64
   hand-made, 267–9
   Phoenician influence, 266–70
   trade with Greece, 295
   wheelmade, 268–9
tholoi, 110

Thomas, Gordon D., 62
Timna, copper industry, 304–5
tin, trade in, 232
Todd, Ian A., 2–13, 98, 110, 113, 315, 316n.
Toumba tou Skourou, 48, 301–2
Tourabi, 370
trade, Bronze Age, 25, 49–50, 202–7, 316–17, 394; Late, long distance, 217–37
   and ceramics, 167, 293, 294–5
   luxury goods, 202–7, 209–15, 318, 330
   in metals, 18, 26–8, 41, 227–33, 317, 319–20
Tremithousa, 147
tripod-stands, as evidence of trade, 227–31, *228*, *229*, 232, 329, 345, 355
triton shell, 120, 121
Tubb, J.N., 203
tunnels, 9, 113
tuyères (blow pipes), 299, 300, 304–5, 307, *308*, 309
Tylecote, R.F., 302
Tylor, E., 109
typology, Iron Age, 106
Tyr, 260, 263, 368, 369

Ugarit, 249
Ugas, G., 222
urbanism
   Late Bronze Age, 25, 48–50, 54, 301–4, 317, 319–20
   and religion, 108, 122

Vagnetti, L., 109, 217–39
Vandenabeele, Frieda, 256, 266–70
Vasilia-Evriman, 26
Vasilikos Valley Project, 2–13, 98, 315–16
Verulamium, hunting scenes mosaics, 283, *284*
Volubilis, hunting scenes, *281*, 282
Vounous Bowl, 24, 108, *115*, 123
Voza, Guiseppe, 237n.
Vrulià, 261

Warren, P., 109
Watkins, T., 113
Watrous, V.L., 218, 221
wealth, burial evidence, 97–8, 103, 299, 318–19, 328–34, 341–3, 344–53, 355–60
weapons, Bronze Age, 199, 222–4, *223*, 329
weight standards, 103–4
Wenamun, report of, 202–4, 303
West, influence on art, 283–5
White, D., 218
White Painted ware, 14, 17–18, 56, 150, 156, *163*, 176–8, *178*, 293, 294, 316
   Wheelmade, 38, 56, 166, 268
White Shaved ware, 218–19, 293
White Slip ware, 53, 102, 160, 167–8, 218,

293, 318
Wissler, Clark, 145
women, Bronze Age, 24
Wriedt Sørenson, L. 256, 261

Yialousa basilica, geometric mosaics, *287*, 288

Yon, M., 363–75
 & Caubet, A., 261
Young, J.H. & Halstead Young, S., 269

Zwicker, U., 304